JAPANESE KANJI POWER

A WORKBOOK FOR MASTERING JAPANESE CHARACTERS

by
JOHN MILLEN

TUTTLE Publishing

Tokyo | Rutland, Vermont | Singapore

ACKNOWLEDGMENTS

I would like to take this opportunity to thank the following people for their valued assistance: Ms. Sayuri Kawada, whose encouragement and advice relating to the text proved to be invaluable; Ms. Hana Shimada for her illustrations and the members of the foreign language department of Seikei High School for numerous consultations. Finally, allow me to express my gratitude to the editorial staff of Tuttle Publishing for their help in the development of this work.

Published by Tuttle Publishing, an imprint of Periplus Editions (HK) Ltd.

www.tuttlepublishing.com

Copyright © 2010 by Periplus Editions (HK) Ltd.

Library of Congress Control Number: 2009934812
ISBN 978-4-8053-0859-2

Distributed by

North America, Latin America & Europe
Tuttle Publishing
364 Innovation Drive, North Clarendon,
VT 05759-9436 U.S.A.
Tel: 1 (802) 773-8930; Fax: 1 (802) 773-6993
info@tuttlepublishing.com; www.tuttlepublishing.com

Japan
Tuttle Publishing
Yaekari Building, 3rd Floor 5-4-12 Osaki
Shinagawa-ku Tokyo 141 0032
Tel: (81) 3 5437-0171; Fax: (81) 3 5437-0755
sales@tuttle.co.jp; www.tuttle.co.jp

Asia Pacific
Berkeley Books Pte. Ltd.
61 Tai Seng Avenue #02-12, Singapore 534167
Tel: (65) 6280-1330; Fax: (65) 6280-6290
inquiries@periplus.com.sg; www.periplus.com

Revised and updated edition
16 15 14 13   10 9 8 7 6 5 4 3   1312CP
Printed in Singapore

TUTTLE PUBLISHING® is a registered trademark of Tuttle Publishing, a division of Periplus Editions (HK) Ltd.

The Tuttle Story: "Books to Span the East and West"

Many people are surprised to learn that the world's largest publisher of books on Asia had its humble beginnings in the tiny American state of Vermont. The company's founder, Charles E. Tuttle, belonged to a New England family steeped in publishing.

Immediately after WW II, Tuttle served in Tokyo under General Douglas MacArthur and was tasked with reviving the Japanese publishing industry. He later founded the Charles E. Tuttle Publishing Company, which thrives today as one of the world's leading independent publishers.

Though a westerner, Tuttle was hugely instrumental in bringing a knowledge of Japan and Asia to a world hungry for information about the East. By the time of his death in 1993, Tuttle had published over 6,000 books on Asian culture, history and art—a legacy honored by the Japanese emperor with the "Order of the Sacred Treasure," the highest tribute Japan can bestow upon a non-Japanese.

With a backlist of 1,500 titles, Tuttle Publishing is more active today than at any time in its past—inspired by Charles Tuttle's core mission to publish fine books to span the East and West and provide a greater understanding of each.

Contents

Introduction

About this book

This book is designed for students of the Japanese language interested in developing their reading and writing proficiency. Over the years, the popularity of studying Japanese has grown steadily and, at the same time, the number of textbooks and other resources available has also increased. Due to the continued interest in materials to assist learners with the written language, I decided, in consultation with the editors at Tuttle Publishing, that the original *Kanji Power* would benefit from a complete revision. As a result, this new version of the book is greatly expanded from the original and will, it is hoped, prove to be easier to use and more accessible to beginning students of the language.

The Scope of the Text

There are certain key aspects of the original text that have been preserved in this revision. The number of target characters, though, has been nearly doubled to 464 *kanji*. This incorporates all the characters included in the first two grades of the *kyōiku kanji*, being the 240 characters studied in Grades 1 and 2 of Japanese elementary school.

Many readers may wish to use this book to help prepare for the Japanese Language Proficiency Test (JLPT). For this reason, the book covers all the characters you will need to know for the new Level N5 (103 characters) and Level N4 (an additional 181 *kanji*) tests, as well as many of those required for Levels N2 and N3. Note that the JLPT switched from 4 to 5 levels in 2010. New levels N4 and N5 were formerly Levels 3 and 4 and merely underwent a name change. The new level N3 exam was introduced at the same time.

In addition, you may wish to use this book to help prepare for the Advanced Placement (AP) Japanese Language and Culture Examination, or as a supplemental resource for university-level Japanese courses. This book includes all 410 *kanji* recommended for study for the AP Japanese test. Moreover, since the AP Japanese *kanji* were selected based on the frequency of their inclusion in the leading 1st- and 2nd-year Japanese textbooks used by colleges and universities, learning the AP *kanji* will also be highly relevant to those studying the language in such courses.

In fact, given that the 464 *kanji* introduced herein are the most important and commonly seen *kanji* that you will find in everyday reading materials, mastering these *kanji* will take you a long way towards fluency in reading and writing Japanese.

The Layout of the Text

The book has been divided into three sections or 'parts'. Each part has then been sub-divided into a number of sets, with 12 target kanji for each set.

PART ONE	Sets 1–9	108 characters
PART TWO	Sets 10–25	192 characters
PART THREE	Sets 26–39	164 characters

The table located on the inside covers is provided to allow quick access to specific characters.

An important aspect of the presentation of characters herein is that, within each part of the book, the characters appear in order of ascending number of strokes. Characters with the same number of strokes appear according to their *on-yomi*, or Chinese reading, and are arranged according to the Japanese a-i-u-e-o order.

My choice to present characters in this order, of course, has certain short-comings. It does not allow for a thematic approach to the acquisition of *kanji*. However, it is my belief that a systematic approach to learning characters, where the *kanji* become steadily more complex, is somewhat kinder to the uninitiated student of the Japanese language.

As was the case with the original version of ***Japanese Kanji Power***, a set of exercises has been included after every three sets of characters, with a review following, to consolidate the *kanji* covered in a cumulative way. In order to simplify the process of acquiring new *kanji*, the reviews have generally been restricted to characters covered up until that particular point. Answers to the exercises and reviews are provided at the back of the book.

An **ON-KUN** reading index has been added at the back of the book to allow students quick access to particular character readings found herein.

Presentation of the Characters

The figure below shows a typical entry from the book. The circled numbers refer to the numbered explanations provided below the figure.

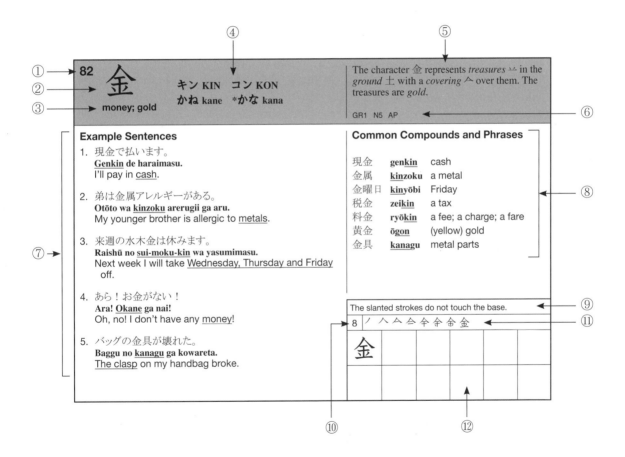

① The Character Reference Number

The characters are numbered 1 to 464 throughout the book.

② The Target Character

The character being presented is written in bold brush type.

③ **The Meaning of the Character in English**

A limited number of common meanings are provided to assist with memorization.

④ **The Readings of the Character**

Most *kanji* have more than one reading. Firstly, the *on-yomi*, or Chinese reading(s), is shown in *katakana* script, followed by the *kun-yomi*, or Japanese reading(s), written in *hiragana* script. The *jōyō kanji* readings, as designated by the Japanese Ministry of Education, have been made as comprehensive as possible, space permitting. Romanized readings are provided as well—**ON** readings being **capitalized**, with **kun** readings being set in **lower case**. Note that the portion of the reading given after the dot (in *hiragana*) and inside the brackets (in Romanized script) constitutes the portion of the Japanese reading referred to as *okurigana*. Irregular, unusual or rare readings are indicated by an asterisk in the Japanese script.

⑤ **Background Information About the Target Character**

This may include details about the etymology of the character or a suggestion to aid memorization. Certainly, when it comes to the question of the derivation of characters, there is much speculation. For students interested in furthering their understanding of *kanji* origins, Kenneth G.. Henshall's comprehensive work, *A Guide to Remembering Japanese Characters* (Tuttle Publishing, 1998), is highly recommended and, indeed, has been of great assistance to me in compiling this text.

⑥ ***Kanji* List Reference Numbers**

Four references are used—**GR 1**, for example, refers to a first grade character in the *Kyōiku Kanji* List, the 1,006 commonly used characters recommended by the Japanese Ministry of Education. **N5**, on the other hand, represents a character in the list of *kanji* designated for study for Level N5 of the new Japanese Language Proficiency Test (103 *kanji*). **AP** indicates that the character appears in the list of *kanji* recommended for study for the Advanced Placement Japanese Language and Culture Test. Finally, **JK** indicates that the character is found in the *Jōyō Kanji* List, a prescribed list of some 2,000 *kanji* used in everyday language situations.

⑦ **Example Sentences**

A number of example sentences are provided to illustrate the various uses of the target character in context. Wherever possible, the various readings of a *kanji*, both *on-yomi* and *kun-yomi*, are introduced in the order in which the readings are given. This method of presentation has been adopted to help simplify the process of *kanji* acquisition. Each example sentence is written in Japanese script, Romanized letters (*rōmaji*) and accompanied by an English translation. In each example sentence, the word or phrase employing the target *kanji* is underlined in both *rōmaji* and English to help you identify it and focus on its usage. The example sentences frequently employ conversational-style Japanese.

⑧ **Common Compounds and Phrases**

A set of seven common compound words or phrases, each containing the target *kanji*, is presented here. Japanese and *rōmaji* scripts and English equivalents are provided. Often, to reinforce familiarization, a *kanji* compound from a sample sentence will reappear in the 'Common Compounds and Phrases' list. Note also that an item marked with an asterisk represents an unusual or irregular reading. The *rōmaji* reading for the target *kanji* is underlined in each example.

⑨ **Writing Hint**

This section gives a brief suggestion about the writing of the character—this may take the form of advice on how to write particular strokes or the order of the strokes. Occasionally, similar characters that can be easily confused with the target *kanji* are presented.

⑩ **Number of Strokes**

This figure represents the total number of strokes or stroke count of the target character.

⑪ **Stroke-order Diagram**

A stroke-by-stroke schematic is presented as a guide to writing the target *kanji*.

⑫ **Writing Practice Grid**

A grid is included here to facilitate the practice of writing each new character. I strongly encourage you to use this space for this purpose.

Use of Romanization

You will note that the Hebon style is used throughout the textbook for romanization. In this style, the *hiragana* ん is written as **n** or **n'** and long vowel sounds appear with a macron, such as **ō**. While the use of *rōmaji* certainly makes language acquisition easier in the earlier stages of study, in the long term it can prove to be a hindrance. I encourage you to master the two Japanese syllabararies, *hiragana* and *katakana*, as quickly as possible.

Using This Book

Students of the language are often daunted by the study of *kanji* characters. However, once *hiragana* and *katakana* have been mastered, it is surprising how rapidly one can become absorbed in the challenges of learning *kanji*. A certain degree of patience and discipline is required in order to establish a regular routine of practicing, revising and thinking of innovative ways to memorize the characters.

Japanese Kanji Power has been devised to allow you to develop your own study habits. Once the 12 characters in a particular set have been covered, I recommend that you work through the quizzes, testing yourself and revising when you make mistakes. To assist you with your self-study, a series of ***Japanese Kanji Power*** cards and workbooks is planned to accompany this book. These will offer additional opportunities for reading and consolidation of the characters targeted herein.

In the meantime, I trust that this book will provide you with sufficient material to pursue your study of the Japanese language and to develop '*Kanji Power*'!

Rules for Writing Kanji

There are a number of fundamental rules that need to be observed when writing *kanji*.

1. Write from left to right.

kawa (river)

shū (a state)

2. Write from top to bottom.

san (three)

kō (craft)

3. Horizontal strokes are usually written <u>before</u> vertical strokes, even when the vertical line is curved.

jū (ten)

nana (seven)

4. Write the center stroke <u>first</u>, followed by the left and right strokes.

chiisai (small)

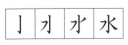

mizu (water)

5. Write the outside strokes, except for the bottom one, <u>before</u> the center portion.

| 丨 | 冂 | 月 | 日 |

hi (sun)

| 丨 | 冂 | 冂 | 冂 | 冈 | 国 | 国 | 国 |

kuni (country)

6. Write a left-hand sweeping stroke <u>before</u> a right-hand one.

| 丿 | 八 |

hachi (eight)

| 丿 | 八 | 分 | 父 |

chichi (father)

7. A vertical stroke which pierces the center is written <u>last</u>.

| 丨 | 冂 | 口 | 中 |

naka (middle)

| 一 | 厂 | 冂 | 冃 | 百 | 亘 | 車 |

kuruma (vehicle)

8. A horizontal stroke which pierces the center is written <u>last</u>.

| 𡿨 | 女 | 女 |

onna (woman)

| 乛 | 了 | 子 |

ko (child)

9. Write a short left sweeping stroke <u>before</u> a horizontal stroke.

| 丿 | 𠂇 | 才 | 右 | 右 |

migi (right)

| 丿 | 𠂇 | 才 | 右 | 有 | 有 |

aru (to be)

10. Write a long left sweeping stroke after a horizontal stroke.

| 一 | 𠂇 | 𠂇 | 左 | 左 |

hidari (left)

| 一 | 𠂇 | 方 | 友 |

tomo (friend)

Please note that there are some exceptions to these rules. For example:

3.
| 一 | 丁 | 王 | 王 |

ō (king)

| 丨 | 冂 | 冂 | 用 | 田 |

ta (rice field)

5.
| 一 | 丁 | 又 | 区 |

ku (ward)

| 一 | 丆 | 匚 | 㠯 | 歼 | 矢 | 医 |

i (doctor)

8.
| 一 | 十 | 卅 | 卋 | 世 |

yo (world)

Learning to write a Chinese character with the correct stroke order, giving attention to the appropriate size and balance of the character, will assist you in memorization and when looking up the *kanji* in a *kanji* dictionary or index. Of course, knowing either the **kun** or **on** reading of the character is a great benefit as well. I encourage you to write *kanji* using the correct stroke order and to practice counting the number of strokes in any new character being studied.

Origin of Kanji

There are a number of classifications of Chinese characters that describe the way they were formed.

1. *Kanji* which derive from pictures, or pictographs. These characters were originally pictures of concrete objects which were simplified over time.

Examples:

	KANJI	ON-YOMI	KUN-YOMI	MEANING
	日	NICHI / JITSU	hi	day; sun
	月	GETSU / GATSU	tsuki	moon; month
	木	MOKU / BOKU	ki	tree; wood
	山	SAN	yama	mountain
	川	SEN	kawa	river
	田	DEN	ta	rice field
	口	KŌ / KU	kuchi	mouth
	火	KA	hi	fire
	子	SHI	ko	child
	石	SEKI	ishi	stone

2. *Kanji* which derive from signs. These characters are made up of points and lines and are used to express abstract concepts, such as 'above', 'below' and 'in'.

Examples:

	KANJI	ON-YOMI	KUN-YOMI	MEANING
☺ ➡ 上	上	JŌ	ue	above; top
☺ ➡ 丁	下	KA / GE	shita	below; down
✚ ➡ 中	中	CHŪ	naka	middle; inside
大 ➡ 大	大	DAI / TAI	ō(kii)	big
本 ➡ 本	本	HON	moto	book; origin

3. *Kanji* which are made up of a combination of meanings (ideographic characters). These characters are made by combining other simple characters to create a new meaning.

Examples:

	KANJI	ON-YOMI	KUN-YOMI	MEANING
イ（人）man ＋ 木 tree	休	KYŪ	yasu(mu)	to rest
女 woman ＋ 子 child	好	KŌ	su(ku)	to like, favorable
日 sun ＋ 月 moon	明	MEI / MYŌ	aka(rui)	light; bright
田 rice paddy ＋ 力 strength	男	DAN / NAN	otoko	man; male

4. *Kanji* which are a combination of ideographic and phonetic elements. The majority of *kanji* fall into this category. The important characteristic of these *kanji* is that one component of the new character represents the meaning of the entire character (often the right-hand or upper part), while the other represents the pronunciation.

Examples

	KANJI	ON-YOMI	KUN-YOMI	MEANING
氵 water (水) + 先 previous [SEN]	洗	SEN	ara(u)	to wash
日 sun + 青 blue; green [SEI]	晴	SEI	ha(reru)	fine weather

Kanji Radicals

Most *kanji* are made up of two or more elements and these elements can be combined in different ways. These common components are called radicals, or *bushu* in Japanese, and are useful in that they are used to classify *kanji* in dictionaries. Any given *kanji* will have one radical with a basic meaning. There are over 200 radicals and they are positioned within *kanji* in the following ways:

1. **HEN** (on the left) This category is the most common.

Examples:

	KANJI	ON-YOMI	KUN-YOMI	MEANING
kuchi-hen (口 mouth)	味	MI	aji	taste
tsuchi-hen (土 earth)	地	CHI / JI		earth; land
onna-hen (女 woman)	姉	SHI	ane	elder sister
hi-hen / nichi-hen (日 sun)	時	JI	toki	time; hour
ito-hen (糸 thread)	紙	SHI	kami	paper
kuruma-hen (車 vehicle)	軽	KEI	karu(i)	light (in weight)
nin-ben (亻 man, from 人)	体	TAI	karada	body
san-zui (氵 water, from 水)	海	KAI	umi	sea; ocean
te-hen (扌 hand, from 手)	持	JI	mo(tsu)	to hold
kozato-hen (阝 hill; mound)	階	KAI		floor; rank; step

2. **TSUKURI** (one the right)

Examples:

	KANJI	ON-YOMI	KUN-YOMI	MEANING
chikara (力 power; strength)	動	**DŌ**	**ugo(ku)**	to move
rittō (刂 sword)	別	**BETSU**	**waka(reru)**	another; to separate
ono-zukuri (斤 axe)	新	**SHIN**	**atara(shii)**	new

3. **KANMURI / KASHIRA** (on the top)

Examples:

	KANJI	ON-YOMI	KUN-YOMI	MEANING
take-kanmuri (竹 bamboo)	算	**SAN**		to calculate
ame-kanmuri (雨 rain)	電	**DEN**		electricity
u-kanmuri (宀 from *katakana* ウ)	家	**KA / KE**	**ie**	house
kusa-kanmuri (艹 grass, from 草)	茶	**CHA / SA**		tea; light brown
ami-gashira (罒 net)	買	**BAI**	**ka(u)**	to buy

4. **ASHI** (at the bottom)

Examples:

	KANJI	ON-YOMI	KUN-YOMI	MEANING
kokoro (心 heart)	思	**SHI**	**omo(u)**	to think
shita-gi (ki-hen) (木 tree)	楽	**GAKU / RAKU**	**tano(shii)**	music; fun
hito-ashi (from 儿 human legs)	見	**KEN**	**mi(ru)**	to look; see; watch
yottsu-ten (rekka / renga) (灬 four dots from 火 fire)	熱	**NETSU**	**atsu(i)**	heat; hot

5. **TARE** (at the upper left)

Examples:

	KANJI	ON-YOMI	KUN-YOMI	MEANING
ma-dare (广 from 麻 linen; flax)	店	**TEN**	**mise**	store, shop
yamai-dare (疒 from 病 illness)	病	**BYŌ**	**yamai**	illness

6. **NYŌ** (at the bottom left)

Examples:

	KANJI	ON-YOMI	KUN-YOMI	MEANING
sōnyō (走 to run)	起	**KI**	**o(kiru)**	to get up; to occur
shinnyū / shinnyō (辶 from 進 to proceed)	道	**DŌ**	**michi**	road; way

7. **KAMAE** (an enclosure)

Examples:

	KANJI	ON-YOMI	KUN-YOMI	MEANING
mon-gamae (門 gate)	聞	**BUN / MON**	**ki(ku)**	to listen, hear
gyō-gamae (行 to go)	術	**JUTSU**	**sube**	tactics; practical art

Example:

	KANJI	ON-YOMI	KUN-YOMI	MEANING
kuni-gamae (囗 from 国 country)	回	**KAI**	**mawa(ru)**	to spin; times

1

一

one; first

イチ ICHI　イツ ITSU
ひと hito　ひと・つ hito(tsu)

The character 一, a single line, indicates the number *one*.

GR1　N5　AP

Example Sentences

1. コピーを一枚とって。
   Kopii o ichimai totte.
   Make <u>one copy</u> of this!

2. 彼はいつも電車の一番前に乗る。
   Kare wa itsumo densha no ichiban mae ni noru.
   He always rides in <u>the very front</u> of the train.

3. 私は一週間に二回外食する。
   Watashi wa isshūkan ni nikai gaishoku suru.
   I eat out <u>twice a week</u>.

4. 一休みしましょう。
   Hitoyasumi shimashō.
   Let's take <u>a break</u>.

5. みかんを一つもらいました。
   Mikan o hitotsu moraimashita.
   I was given <u>a (one)</u> mandarin.

Common Compounds and Phrases

一枚	**ichimai**	one (sheet, slice)
一番	**ichiban**	the first; the most
一週間	**isshūkan**	one week
一休み	**hitoyasumi**	a rest, a break
*一日	**tsuitachi;**	the first day of the
	ichinichi	month; one day
*一人	**hitori**	one person

Begin the stroke boldly, and end the stroke firmly.

1 一

一

2

九

nine

キュウ KYŪ　ク KU
ここの・つ kokono(tsu)
ここの kokono

The character 九 depicted a bent elbow, an ancient way of indicating the number *nine*.

GR1　N5　AP

Example Sentences

1. 鉛筆が九本そこにあります。
   Enpitsu ga kyūhon soko ni arimasu.
   There are <u>nine</u> pencils there.

2. 彼は九死に一生をえた。
   Kare wa kyūshi ni isshō o eta.
   He <u>narrowly escaped death</u>.

3. 東京まで九時間かかった。
   Tōkyō made kujikan kakatta.
   It took me <u>nine hours</u> to get to Tokyo.

4. 袋にあめが九つ入っていた。
   Fukuro ni ame ga kokonotsu haitte ita.
   There were <u>nine pieces</u> of candy in the paper bag.

5. 九日から授業が始まる。
   Kokonoka kara jugyō ga hajimaru.
   Classes begin on <u>the ninth of the month</u>.

Common Compounds and Phrases

九本	**kyūhon**	nine (long, thin cylindrical objects)
九ヶ月	**kyūkagetsu**	nine months
九時間	**kujikan**	nine hours
九月	**kugatsu**	September
九九	**kuku**	multiplication (times) table
九日	**kokonoka**	nine days; the ninth day of the month

End the second stroke with a hook.

2 ノ 九

九

3 七 seven

シチ SHICHI
なな nana　なな・つ nana(tsu)
*なの nano

The character 七, represented an ancient way of signaling *seven*, using the hands. Think of this character as a combination of five fingers and two.
GR1 N5 AP

Example Sentences

1. 七月七日は七夕です。
   Shichigatsu nanoka wa tanabata desu.
   July 7 is the *Tanabata* Festival.

2. この本は七千円しました。
   Kono hon wa nanasen-en shimashita.
   This book cost seven thousand yen.

3. 七つ目の駅で降りてください。
   Nanatsume no eki de orite kudasai.
   Please get off at the seventh station.

4. 一週間は七日です。
   Isshūkan wa nanoka desu.
   There are seven days in a week.

5. あの歌手は七色の声をもっている。
   Ano kashu wa nanairo no koe o motte iru.
   That singer can use many different voices.

Common Compounds and Phrases

七月	**shichigatsu**	July
七時	**shichiji**	seven o'clock
七五三	**shichigosan**	festival (November 15) for children aged 3, 5 and 7
七千	**nanasen**	seven thousand
七つ目	**nanatsume**	the seventh (one)
*七日	**nanoka**	seven days; the seventh day of the month
*七夕	**Tanabata**	the *Tanabata* (Star) Festival

End the second stroke with a hook.

2　一 七

七

4 十 ten

ジュウ JŪ　ジッ JI'
とお tō　と to

In the character 十, 一 represents *east-west*, while | represents *north-south*; thus, 十 signifies *all directions*. The idea of complete and the association of the number *ten* derived from this meaning.
GR1 N5 AP

Example Sentences

1. 十月の祭日はいつですか。
   Jūgatsu no saijitsu wa itsu desu ka.
   When is the public holiday in October?

2. 準備体操を十分にして下さい。
   Junbi taisō o jūbun ni shite kudasai.
   Don't rush through your warm up.

3. 駅まで歩いて十分です。
   Eki made aruite juppun (jippun) desu.
   It's a ten-minute walk to the station.

4. 今年の春休みは十日間でした。
   Kotoshi no haru-yasumi wa tōkakan deshita.
   My spring vacation this year was ten days long.

5. 食べ物の好みは十人十色。
   Tabemono no konomi wa jūnin toiro.
   When it comes to food, there are so many people, and so many tastes.

Common Compounds and Phrases

十月	**jūgatsu**	October
十分	**jūbun**	enough; plenty of
十分	**juppun, jippun**	ten minutes
十人	**jūnin**	ten people
十分の一	**jūbun no ichi**	one-tenth
十五夜	**jūgoya**	a night with a full moon
十日	**tōka**	ten days; the tenth day of the month

The lower part of the second stroke is longer.

2　一 十

十

5 人
man; people

ジン JIN　ニン NIN
ひと hito

The character 人 represents a side view of a *person*.

GR1　N5　AP

Example Sentences

1. 妻はドイツ人です。
   Tsuma wa Doitsujin desu.
   My wife is <u>German</u>.

2. ご家族は何人ですか。
   Gokazoku wa <u>nannin</u> desu ka.
   <u>How many people</u> are there in your family?

3. ここは人が多い。
   Koko wa <u>hito</u> ga ōi.
   There are many <u>people</u> here.

4. 人のせいにしないで。
   <u>Hito no sei</u> ni shinai de.
   Don't <u>blame</u> it on <u>somebody else</u>!

5. このレストランはとても人気がある。
   Kono resutoran wa totemo <u>ninki</u> ga aru.
   This restaurant is very <u>popular</u>.

Common Compounds and Phrases

ドイツ人	**Doitsu<u>jin</u>**	a German; the Germans
日本人	**Nihon<u>jin</u>**	a Japanese person; the Japanese
何人	**nan-<u>nin</u>**	How many people?
人気	**<u>nin</u>ki**	popularity
*一人	**hitori**	one person; alone
*大人	**otona**	adult
*仲人	**nakōdo**	a go-between, matchmaker

Keep the two strokes aligned and don't mistake 人 for 入.

2	ノ 人				
人					

6 二
two

ニ NI
ふた futa
ふた・つ futa(tsu)

Two lines are used to indicate the number *two*.

GR1　N5　AP

Example Sentences

1. 明日の午後二時に会いましょう。
   Ashita no gogo niji ni aimashō.
   Let's meet at <u>2:00 P.M.</u> tomorrow.

2. 二月に二人目の子供が生まれる。
   Nigatsu ni <u>futarime no</u> kodomo ga umareru.
   My <u>second</u> child will be born in February.

3. 日本語検定の二級に受かった。
   Nihongo kentei no <u>nikyū</u> ni ukatta.
   I passed <u>the second level</u> of the Japanese language examination.

4. 二度と同じ失敗を繰り返すな。
   <u>Nido</u> to onaji shippai o kurikaesu na.
   Don't make the same mistake <u>again</u> (a second time)!

5. むこうに山が二つ見えます。
   Mukō ni yama ga <u>futatsu</u> miemasu.
   You can see <u>two</u> mountains over there.

Common Compounds and Phrases

二時	**<u>ni</u>ji**	two o'clock
二級	**<u>ni</u>kyū**	second level (degree, class)
二度	**<u>ni</u>do**	twice; two degrees
*二日	**futsuka**	the second day of the month; two days
*二十日	**hatsuka**	the twentieth day of the month; twenty days
*二人	**futari**	two persons; two people
*二十歳	**hatachi**	twenty years of age

The second stroke is longer than the first stroke.

2	一 二				
二					

7

入

to enter,
to put in

ニュウ NYŪ
い・る i(ru)　はい・る hai(ru)
いれ・る ire(ru)

The character 入 represents the *entrance* of a house.

GR1　N5　AP

Example Sentences

1. 手術のため入院した。
   Shujutsu no tame <u>nyūin shita</u>.
   I <u>checked into the hospital</u> to have an operation.

2. 収入が増えた。
   <u>Shūnyū</u> ga fueta.
   My <u>total income</u> has increased.

3. 今日の映画は気に入りましたか。
   Kyō no eiga wa <u>ki ni irimashita ka</u>.
   <u>Did you like</u> the movie, today?

4. 私は毎晩ふろに入る。
   Watashi wa maiban <u>furo ni hairu</u>.
   I <u>take a bath</u> every evening.

5. ポケットに手を入れないで下さい。
   Poketto ni <u>te o irenai de</u> kudasai.
   <u>Don't put your hands</u> in your pockets!

Common Compounds and Phrases

入院	**nyūin**	admission to a hospital
収入	**shūnyū**	income; earnings
記入	**kinyū**	an entry (in a ledger)
入国	**nyūkoku**	immigration
輸入	**yunyū**	import(s)
入学	**nyūgaku**	admission into a school
入り口	**iriguchi**	an entrance; an outset

Keep the two strokes aligned and make the second stroke longer.

2	ノ	入			
入					

8

八

eight

ハチ HACHI　ハツ HATSU
や ya　や・つ ya(tsu)
やっ・つ yat(tsu)　*よう yō

The character 八 represents something that can be easily divided in two, ie. the number *eight*.

GR1　N5　AP

Example Sentences

1. 日本に来て八年になる。
   Nihon ni kite <u>hachinen</u> ni naru.
   It has been <u>eight years</u> since I came to Japan.

2. これは八百年前の寺です。
   Kore wa <u>happyakunen</u>-mae no tera desu.
   This temple dates from <u>eight hundred years</u> ago.

3. 今日帰りに八百屋で買い物をしよう。
   Kyō kaeri ni <u>yaoya</u> de kaimono o shiyō.
   I'll shop at <u>the vegetable store</u> on the way home, today.

4. 彼はおにぎりを八つも食べた。
   Kare wa onigiri o <u>yattsu</u> mo tabeta.
   He ate as many as <u>eight</u> rice balls!

5. 八日は彼女の誕生日だ。
   <u>Yōka</u> wa kanojo no tanjōbi da.
   Her birthday is on <u>the eighth</u>.

Common Compounds and Phrases

八年	**hachinen**	eight years
八月	**hachigatsu**	August
八時	**hachiji**	eight o'clock
八百	**happyaku**	eight hundred
七転び	**nanakorobi**	bouncing back after
八起き	**yaoki**	being knocked down
*八日	**yōka**	the eighth day of the month; eight days
*八百屋	**yaoya**	a vegetable store; a greengrocer's

Leave a space between the strokes.

2	ノ	八			
八					

9 下

カ KA　ゲ GE
した shita　しも shimo
さ・がる sa(garu)
くだ・る kuda(ru)
お・りる o(riru)

low; below;
to go down

The character 下 represents something below a horizontal line; ie., something *underneath*.

GR1　N5　AP

Example Sentences

1. 下線を引いて下さい。
   Kasen o hiite kudasai.
   <u>Underline</u> (that word)!

2. 七月下旬に夏休みを取る予定です。
   Shichigatsu gejun ni natsuyasumi o toru yotei desu.
   I'm planning to take my summer holidays at <u>the end of July</u>.

3. テーブルの下で猫が眠っていた。
   Tēburu no shita de neko ga nemutte ita.
   A cat was asleep <u>under</u> the table.

4. パソコンが値下がりしている。
   Pasokon ga nesagari shite iru.
   The prices of personal computers <u>are dropping</u>.

5. 友達とカヌーで川を下るつもりです。
   Tomodachi to kanū de kawa o kudaru tsumori desu.
   I'm planning to <u>go</u> canoeing <u>downriver</u> with a friend.

Common Compounds and Phrases

下線	**kasen**	an underline; underlining
地下	**chika**	underground
下旬	**gejun**	the last third of the month
靴下	**kutsushita**	socks; hosiery
川下	**kawashimo**	downriver
下さい	**kudasai**	please
*下手な	**heta na**	unskillful; poor at

End the third stroke firmly.

3　一 丁 下

下

---

10 口

コウ KŌ　ク KU
くち kuchi

mouth

The character 口 represents the shape of a *mouth*.

GR1　N5　AP

Example Sentences

1. 都市に人口が集中する。
   Toshi ni jinkō ga shūchū suru.
   <u>The population</u> is concentrated in the cities.

2. 非常口はあそこです。
   Hijōguchi wa asoko desu.
   <u>Emergency exits</u> are located over there.

3. 試合に負けて口惜しかった。
   Shiai ni makete kuyashikatta.
   I <u>felt frustrated</u> after losing the match.

4. 口に虫が入った。
   Kuchi ni mushi ga haitta.
   A bug flew into <u>my mouth</u>.

5. 彼女は早口で話す。
   Kanojo wa hayakuchi de hanasu.
   She's <u>a fast talker</u>.

Common Compounds and Phrases

人口	**jinkō**	a population
口座	**kōza**	a bank account
非常口	**hijōguchi**	an emergency exit
改札口	**kaisatsuguchi**	a ticket gate
出口	**deguchi**	an exit
窓口	**madoguchi**	a window; a counter
早口	**hayakuchi**	rapid talking

Note the stroke order.

3　丨 冂 口

口

11 三 three

サン SAN
み mi　み・つ mi(tsu)
みっ・つ mit(tsu)

The character 三, three horizontal lines, represents the number *three*.

GR1 N5 AP

Example Sentences

1. 三月三日はひな祭りです。
   Sangatsu mikka wa hinamatsuri desu.
   <u>March 3</u> is the Dolls' Festival.

2. 彼女はノートに三角を描いた。
   Kanojo wa nōto ni sankaku o kaita.
   She drew a <u>triangle</u> in her notebook.

3. 昨夜の三日月はきれいでした。
   Yūbe no mikazuki wa kirei deshita.
   <u>The new moon</u> was beautiful last night.

4. いとこに三つ子が生まれた。
   Itoko ni mitsugo ga umareta.
   My cousin gave birth to <u>triplets</u>.

5. 三つ質問があります。
   Mittsu shitsumon ga arimasu.
   I have <u>three</u> questions.

Common Compounds and Phrases

三月	**sangatsu**	March
三ヶ月	**sankagetsu**	three months
三角	**sankaku**	a triangle; triangularity
三日	**mikka**	three days; the third day of the month
三日月	**mikazuki**	the new (crescent) moon
三つ子	**mitsugo**	triplets; a three-year-old child
*三味線	**shamisen**	shamisen

The spacing is equal and the middle stroke is the shortest.

3 　一　二　三

三

---

12 山 mountain

サン SAN
やま yama

The character 山 represents the shape of a *mountain* with three peaks.

GR1 N5 AP

Example Sentences

1. お正月は富士山に登る。
   Oshōgatsu wa Fujisan ni noboru.
   I'm going to climb <u>Mount Fuji</u> at New Year.

2. 父は鉱山の技師でした。
   Chichi wa kōzan no gishi deshita.
   My father was a <u>mining</u> engineer.

3. 今年の夏休みは山で過ごした。
   Kotoshi no natsuyasumi wa yama de sugoshita.
   I spent this summer vacation in <u>the mountains</u>.

4. じゃがいもを一山百円で買った。
   Jagaimo o hitoyama hyaku-en de katta.
   I paid a hundred yen for <u>a pile</u> of potatoes.

5. 百年ぶりに火山が爆発した。
   Hyaku-nen buri ni kazan ga bakuhatsu shita.
   <u>The volcano</u> erupted after an interval of 100 years.

Common Compounds and Phrases

富士山	**Fujisan**	Mount Fuji
山脈	**sanmyaku**	a mountain range
鉱山	**kōzan**	a mine
火山	**kazan**	a volcano
下山	**gezan**	climbing down a mountain
一山	**hitoyama**	a pile; a heap; a mountain
山本	**Yamamoto**	Yamamoto (a name)

Space evenly between the vertical strokes.

3 　｜　凵　山

山

EXERCISE 1 (1 – 12)

A. Give the readings for the following kanji using hiragana or rōmaji.

1. 山 _____
2. 口 _____
3. 八 _____
4. 人 _____
5. 三 _____
6. 九 _____
7. 下 _____
8. 七 _____
9. 二 _____
10. 十 _____

7. 三十八 _____
8. 九十二 _____
9. 下 _____
10. 一人 _____

B. Give the English meanings of the following words.

1. 二十一 _____
2. 八人 _____
3. 山 _____
4. 七十九 _____
5. 口 _____
6. 九九 _____

C. Write the readings for the following kanji in hiragana.

1. 一つ (one thing) _____
2. 下さい (please) _____
3. 九つ (nine things) _____
4. 入れる (to put in) _____
5. 下がる (to come down; to drop) _____
6. 九人 (nine people) _____
7. 三つ (three things) _____
8. 入り口 (an entrance) _____
9. 七つ (seven things) _____
10. 人口 (population) _____

13	子	シ SHI　*ス SU こ ko	The character 子 represents a *baby* with a large head and both arms extended.
	child; baby		GR1　N5　AP

Example Sentences

1. 女子用トイレは二階です。
   Joshi-yō toire wa nikai desu.
   The <u>women's</u> toilet is on the second floor.

2. 様子を見ましょう。
   Yōsu o mimashō.
   Let's <u>wait and see</u>!

3. 子供が二人います。
   Kodomo ga futari imasu.
   I have two <u>children</u>.

4. もうすぐ子会社を作る。
   Mō sugu kogaisha o tsukuru.
   They are going to establish <u>a subsidiary company</u> soon.

5. 私たち親子は良く似ていると言われます。
   Watashitachi oyako wa yoku nite iru to iwaremasu.
   People say that <u>my father and I</u> look alike.

Common Compounds and Phrases

女子	**joshi**	a girl; a woman; a lady
男子	**dan<u>shi</u>**	a boy; a man; a son
様子	**yōsu**	a situation; a state; 　an appearance
親子	**oya<u>ko</u>**	father and son; mother 　and daughter
花子	**Hana<u>ko</u>**	Hanako (a name)
子供	**<u>ko</u>domo**	a child; a son; a daughter
子会社	**<u>ko</u>gaisha**	a subsidiary; an affiliate

The second stroke ends with a hook.						
3	フ 了 子					
子						

14 女

ジョ JO　ニョ NYO
*ニョウ NYŌ

woman

おんな onna　め me

The character 女 represents a *woman* with arms and legs bent in a gentle posture.

GR1 N5 AP

Example Sentences

1. その人は女性ですか、男性ですか。
   Sono hito wa josei desu ka, dansei desu ka.
   Is that person a man or a woman?

2. 長女は九歳です。
   Chōjo wa kyūsai desu.
   My eldest daughter is nine years old.

3. 壁に天女の絵があった。
   Kabe ni tennyo no e ga atta.
   There was a drawing of a celestial nymph on the wall.

4. 店の外で女の人が待っている。
   Mise no soto de onna no hito ga matte iru.
   A woman is waiting outside the store.

5. すべての権利は男女平等であるべきです。
   Subete no kenri wa danjo byōdō de aru beki desu.
   All rights should be gender-equal.

Common Compounds and Phrases

女性	**josei**	a woman; femininity
長女	**chōjo**	one's eldest daughter
彼女	**kanojo**	she; her
男女	**danjo**	men and women
天女	**tennyo**	a celestial nymph
女の人	**onna no hito**	a woman; a female
女神	**megami**	a goddess

Give the character a pentagon-like shape.

3　く 女 女

女

---

15 小

ショウ SHŌ

ちい・さい chii(sai)

small, little

こ ko　お o

The character 小 represents a large object being chipped away at, leaving *small* pieces.

GR1 N5 AP

Example Sentences

1. あの子は近くの小学校に通っている。
   Ano ko wa chikaku no shōgakkō ni kayotte iru.
   That child attends a nearby elementary school.

2. もっと小さいものがほしい。
   Motto chiisai mono ga hoshii.
   I'd like a smaller one.

3. 小型車は、人気がある。
   Kogatasha wa, ninki ga aru.
   Small cars are popular.

4. みんなで小高い丘に登った。
   Minna de kodakai oka ni nobotta.
   We all climbed the low hill.

5. 新幹線は小田原に止まりますか。
   Shinkansen wa Odawara ni tomarimasu ka.
   Does the Shinkansen stop at Odawara?

Common Compounds and Phrases

小学校	**shōgakkō**	an elementary (primary) school
小型	**kogata**	a small size; miniature
小高い	**kodakai**	slightly elevated
小切手	**kogitte**	a check (bank)
小山	**Koyama, Oyama**	Koyama / Oyama (a name)
*小豆	**azuki**	an adzuki bean
*小雨	**kosame**	light rain; drizzle

End the first stroke with a hook.

3　亅 小 小

小

16 上

above; top; to rise; to climb

ジョウ JŌ *ショウ SHŌ
うえ ue うわ uwa かみ kami
あ・がる a(garu) あ・げる a(geru)
のぼ・る nobo(ru)

GR1 N5 AP

The character 上 was originally written 二, indicating the area *above* a line. The vertical line was added later.

Example Sentences

1. 上等なカシミアのコートを買った。
   Jōtō na kashimia no kōto o katta.
   I bought a <u>high-quality</u> cashmere coat.

2. その机の上にレポートを置いてください。
   Sono tsukue no ue ni repōto o oite kudasai.
   Please place the report <u>on</u> that desk.

3. 上着を着たらどうですか。
   Uwagi o kitara dō desu ka.
   Why don't you put on a <u>jacket</u>?

4. 川上さんを知っていますか。
   Kawakami-san o shitte imasu ka.
   Do you know Mr. (Ms.) <u>Kawakami</u>?

5. 急いで階段を上がった。
   Isoide kaidan o agatta.
   He <u>hurried up</u> the stairs.

Common Compounds and Phrases

上等	**jōtō**	first-class; superior
向上	**kōjō**	improvement
上着	**uwagi**	a coat; a jacket; a blouse
川上	**kawakami**	Kawakami (a name); upriver
値上げ	**neage**	a price hike
売り上げ	**uriage**	sale
*上手	**jōzu**	skillful, good at

The vertical stroke does not cross the bottom stroke.

3 丨 卜 上

上

17 千

thousand

セン SEN
ち chi

GR1 N5 AP

The character 千 is made up of the characters for 亻 *person* and 一 *one*, which together represent *thousands* of people in a crowd.

Example Sentences

1. その会社の社員数は、約千人です。
   Sono kaisha no shain'sū wa yaku sennin desu.
   There are about <u>one thousand</u> employees in that company.

2. 税込み三千九十円です。
   Zeikomi sanzen kyūjūen desu.
   It is <u>¥3,090</u>, including tax.

3. 妹は子供に千秋という名前をつけた。
   Imōto wa kodomo ni Chiaki to iu namae o tsuketa.
   My sister called her child <u>Chiaki</u>.

4. 慰霊碑に千羽づるを捧げた。
   Ireihi ni senbazuru o sasageta.
   <u>The 1,000 paper cranes</u> were dedicated to the cenotaph.

5. 一万円を千円札にくずしてもらえますか。
   Ichiman-en o sen'en-satsu ni kuzushite moraemasu ka.
   Could you change 10,000 yen into <u>1,000 yen notes</u> for me?

Common Compounds and Phrases

千人	**sennin**	one thousand people
三千	**sanzen**	three thousand
一千万	**issen-man**	ten million
千円札	**sen'en-satsu**	a ¥1,000 note
千羽づる	**senbazuru**	1,000 folded paper cranes
千秋	**Chiaki**	Chiaki (a name)
千代田区	**Chiyoda-ku**	Chiyoda Ward

The first stroke tapers down from right to left.

3 ノ 二 千

千

18 川

セン SEN
かわ kawa

river

GR1 N5 AP

The character 川 represents *flowing water*.

Example Sentences

1. ただいま、河川工事を行なっております。
   Tadaima, <u>kasen</u> kōji o okonatte orimasu.
   <u>River</u> conservation work is in progress.

2. 川上は流れが速い。
   <u>Kawakami</u> wa nagare ga hayai.
   The current is swift <u>upstream</u>.

3. 信濃川は日本で一番長い川です。
   <u>Shinanogawa</u> wa Nihon de ichiban nagai <u>kawa</u> desu.
   The <u>Shinano River</u> is Japan's longest <u>river</u>.

4. 先週、川原でバーベキューをした。
   Senshū, <u>kawara</u> de bābekyū o shita.
   Last week, we had a barbecue on <u>a dry river bed</u>.

5. 友達と川岸まで泳いだ。
   Tomodachi to <u>kawagishi</u> made oyoida.
   I swam to <u>the riverbank</u> with my friend.

Common Compounds and Phrases

河川	**kasen**	a river
四川	**Shisen**	Sichuan (a place)
川原	**kawara**	a dry riverbed
川崎	**Kawasaki**	Kawasaki (a name / place)
小川	**ogawa**	a creek; Ogawa (a name)
川魚	**kawauo**	a river fish
川岸	**kawagishi**	a riverside, a riverbank

The first stroke tapers off, and the 2nd stroke is the shortest.

3 丿 川 川

川

---

19 大

ダイ DAI　タイ TAI
おお ō　おお・きい ō(kii)
おお・いに ō(i ni)

great; big; large

GR1 N5 AP

The character 大 depicts a person standing with arms outstretched, suggesting the concept of *big*.

Example Sentences

1. それは大問題になった。
   Sore wa <u>daimondai</u> ni natta.
   It became <u>a grave concern</u>.

2. 彼は大金を持っている。
   Kare wa <u>taikin</u> o motte iru.
   He has <u>a large sum of money</u>.

3. 大雨になりそうだ。
   <u>Ōame</u> ni narisō da.
   It looks like we're in for some <u>heavy showers</u>.

4. 東京は巨大な都市だ。
   Tōkyō wa <u>kyodai na</u> toshi da.
   Tokyo is a <u>huge</u> city.

5. いつか大きな地震が起こるだろう。
   Itsu ka <u>ōki na</u> jishin ga okoru darō.
   A <u>large</u> earthquake will strike some day.

Common Compounds and Phrases

大問題	**daimondai**	a big issue; a real problem
大学	**daigaku**	college; university
大金	**taikin**	a lot of money
大切	**taisetsu**	important; precious
大雨	**ōame**	heavy rain
大型	**ōgata**	a large size
*大人	**otona**	an adult

The second and third strokes taper off.

3 一 ナ 大

大

20 土

ド DO　ト TO
つち tsuchi

earth; soil;
land

The character 土 represents a seedling emerging from a mound of *earth*.

GR1　N5　AP

Example Sentences

1. 昔は船で本土へ渡った。
   Mukashi wa fune de hondo e watatta.
   We used to go to the mainland by ship.

2. 土日は仕事が休みです。
   Donichi wa shigoto ga yasumi desu.
   We have Saturdays and Sundays off.

3. そのうち、東京に土地を買いたい。
   Sono uchi, Tōkyō ni tochi o kaitai.
   I'd like to buy some land in Tokyo some day.

4. 球根を土に埋めた。
   Kyūkon o tsuchi ni umeta.
   The bulb was buried under the soil.

5. 裏庭で土器を発見した。
   Uraniwa de doki o hakken shita.
   I found some old earthenware in the backyard.

Common Compounds and Phrases

本土	**hondo**	the mainland
土日	**donichi**	the weekend; Saturday(s) and Sunday(s)
土器	**doki**	earthenware
土手	**dote**	a bank, embankment
領土	**ryōdo**	territory
土地	**tochi**	land; property
*土産	**miyage**	a souvenir; a present

The third stroke is longer than the first.

3　一　十　土

土

21 万

マン MAN　バン BAN
*よろず yorozu

ten thousand;
all sorts of

The character 万 derived from a pictograph of a scorpion pronounced *man* in Chinese. From phonetic borrowing and perhaps because scorpions were very numerous, the character became associated with *ten thousand*.

GR1　N5　AP

Example Sentences

1. サイクロンで十万人以上の死者が出た。
   Saikuron de jūman-nin ijō no shisha ga deta.
   The cyclone caused more than one hundred thousand deaths.

2. 昨日、一万円下ろしたばかりだ。
   Kinō, ichiman-en oroshita bakari da.
   I just withdrew ten thousand yen yesterday.

3. 万が一にもそんなことはないと思うよ。
   Man' ga ichi ni mo sonna koto wa nai to omou yo.
   There isn't a chance in a million that would ever happen.

4. 万国博覧会を一度見てみたい。
   Bankoku hakurankai o ichido mite mitai.
   I'd like to see an international exposition just once.

5. 防災に万全の備えをする。
   Bōsai ni banzen no sonae o suru.
   We will be fully prepared for disaster prevention.

Common Compounds and Phrases

十万人	**jūman-nin**	one hundred thousand people
一万円	**ichiman-en**	ten thousand yen
万が一	**man'ga ichi**	an unlikely event; by any chance
万年筆	**mannenhitsu**	a fountain pen
万歳	**banzai**	Hurrah!
万全の	**banzen no**	perfect; flawless; sure
万国 博覧会	**bankoku hakurankai**	a world's fair

The second stroke ends with a hook.

3　一　フ　万

万

22 円

エン EN
まる maru　まる・い maru(i)

yen; circle; round

Originally 圓, this character consisted of 囗 an *enclosure* and 員 representing a *round vessel*. From this came the meaning of a *round enclosure*.

GR1　N5　AP

Example Sentences

1. コンパスで円を描いた。
   Kompasu de en o kaita.
   I drew a circle with a compass.

2. 百九十円の地下鉄の切符を買いなさい。
   Hyaku kyūjū-en no chikatetsu no kippu o kainasai.
   Buy a ¥190 subway ticket.

3. 円高が長く続いた。
   Endaka ga nagaku tsuzuita.
   The value of the yen was high for a long time.

4. 関東一円に大雨が降るでしょう。
   Kantō ichien ni ōame ga furu deshō.
   Heavy rains are expected throughout the Kanto area.

5. 夫婦円満の秘訣はなんですか。
   Fūfu enman no hiketsu wa nan desu ka.
   What is the secret of harmony for married couples?

Common Compounds and Phrases

九十円	**kyūjū-en**	ninety yen
円高	**endaka**	a strong yen (rate)
円盤	**enban**	a disc
円満	**enman**	perfection; harmony
円心	**enshin**	the center of a circle
楕円	**daen**	an ellipse; an oval
円周率	**enshūritsu**	pi; a circle ratio

End the first stroke firmly and the second stroke with a hook.

4　丨　冂　冂　円

円

23 王

オウ Ō

king

The three horizontal lines symbolize *heaven*, *earth* and *man*, and the vertical line represents the person who connects them; namely a *king*.

GR 1　N2

Example Sentences

1. 国王は王子のときイギリスに留学した。
   Kokuō wa ōji no toki Igirisu ni ryūgaku shita.
   The king went to Britain to study when he was a prince.

2. エジソンは発明王といわれている。
   Ejison wa hatsumeiō to iwarete iru.
   Edison is said to be the 'King of Inventors.'

3. 王手！
   Ōte!
   Check! *(in Japanese chess)*

4. イギリス王室は最も古い王族のひとつです。
   Igirisu ōshitsu wa mottomo furui ōzoku no hitotsu desu.
   The British royal family is one of the oldest royal families.

5. 新しい国王が即位しました。
   Atarashii kokuō ga sokui shimashita.
   A new king ascended the throne.

Common Compounds and Phrases

国王	**kokuō**	a king; a monarch
王様	**ōsama**	a king; His Majesty
王子	**ōji**	a prince
王女	**ōjo**	a princess
女王	**joō**	a queen
王族	**ōzoku**	a royal family; royalty
王座	**ōza**	a throne

Use the same spacing between the first, third and fourth strokes. The last stroke is the longest.

4　一　丁　干　王

王

24 火 fire

カ KA
ひ hi *ほ ho

GR1 N5 AP

The character 火 represents a *blazing flame*.

Example Sentences

1. 火事を発見して通報した。
   Kaji o hakken shite tsūhō shita.
   He discovered <u>a fire</u> and reported it.

2. 来週の月火は連休だ。
   Raishū no getsu-ka wa renkyū da.
   Next <u>Monday and Tuesday</u> are consecutive holidays.

3. 火を貸してもらえますか。
   Hi o kashite moraemasu ka.
   May I have <u>a light</u>, please?

4. 最終ランナーが、聖火台に点火した。
   Saishū rannā ga, seikadai ni tenka shita.
   The last runner <u>ignited</u> the Olympic cauldron.

5. 花火を見に行きましょう。
   Hanabi o mi ni ikimashō.
   Let's go to see <u>the fireworks</u>.

Common Compounds and Phrases

火事	**kaji**	a fire
火災	**kasai**	a fire; a blaze
火力	**karyoku**	heat; firepower
点火	**tenka**	ignition; lighting
防火	**bōka**	fire prevention; fireproof
火花	**hibana**	a spark
花火	**hanabi**	fireworks

The third and fourth strokes taper off.

4 丶 ヽ ソ 火

火

EXERCISE 2 (13 – 24)

A. Give the readings for the following kanji using hiragana or rōmaji.

1. 女 _____
2. 川 _____
3. 千 _____
4. 上 _____
5. 万 _____
6. 火 _____
7. 円 _____
8. 土 _____
9. 小さな _____
10. 大きい _____

B. Write in kanji and kana.

1. adult _____
2. 8,000 _____
3. to raise _____
4. ¥3,073 _____
5. twenty million _____
6. a girl _____

7. to go up _____
8. Ms. Yamaguchi _____
9. nine thousand people _____
10. 7,020 _____

C. Fill in the kanji according to the meanings provided.

1. じょし (a woman; a female) _____
2. おおきくない (isn't big) _____ きくない
3. おがわ (a creek / Ogawa, a name) _____
4. はっせんえん (¥8,000) _____
5. かざん (a volcano) _____
6. さんまんにん (30,000 people) _____
7. おんなのひと (a woman) _____ の _____
8. せんえん (¥1,000) _____
9. じょおう (a queen) _____
10. かわかみさん (Mr. Kawakami) _____ さん

25 月

ゲツ GETSU　ガツ GATSU
つき tsuki

moon; month

The character 月 represents the *crescent moon*.

GR1　N5　AP

Example Sentences

1. 今夜は満月だ。
   Konya wa <u>mangetsu</u> da.
   There is <u>a full moon</u> tonight.

2. 三ヶ月禁煙した。
   <u>Sankagetsu</u> kin'en shita.
   I quit smoking for <u>three months</u>.

3. 燃えるごみは月・水に出してください。
   Moeru gomi wa <u>ges-sui</u> ni dashite kudasai.
   Please put out burnable trash on <u>Mondays and Wednesdays</u>.

4. 日本では学校は四月に始まります。
   Nihon de wa gakkō wa <u>Shigatsu</u> ni hajimarimasu.
   In Japan, school begins in <u>April</u>.

5. 月が雲に隠れている。
   <u>Tsuki</u> ga kumo ni kakurete iru.
   <u>The moon</u> is hidden behind the clouds.

Common Compounds and Phrases

満月	**mangetsu**	a full moon
三ヶ月	**sankagetsu**	three months
先月	**sengetsu**	last month
十一月	**jūichigatsu**	November
一月	**ichigatsu**	January
一月	**hitotsuki**	one month
正月	**shōgatsu**	New Year's

Use the same spacing between the 3rd and 4th strokes. End the second stroke with a hook.

4　丿　丿　月　月

月

---

26 五

ゴ GO
いつ itsu　いつ・つ itsu(tsu)

five

In the character 五 the upper horizontal stroke signifies *ten* and the lower one *one*; the middle line represents the half-way point, *five*.

GR1　N5　AP

Example Sentences

1. 五月五日は子供の日です。
   <u>Gogatsu itsuka</u> wa Kodomo no Hi desu.
   <u>May 5th</u> is Children's Day.

2. 可能性は五分五分だ。
   Kanōsei wa <u>gobu gobu</u> da.
   There's <u>a fifty-fifty</u> chance.

3. 五百五十円になります。
   <u>Gohyaku gojū-en</u> ni narimasu.
   That comes to <u>¥550</u>.

4. オリンピックの五りんマークのTシャツを買った。
   Orinpikku no <u>gorin</u> māku no T-shatsu o katta.
   I bought a t-shirt with the <u>(five-ring)</u> Olympic emblem on it.

5. 五つ星のホテルに泊まった。
   <u>Itsutsu-boshi</u> no hoteru ni tomatta.
   I stayed in <u>a five-star</u> hotel!

Common Compounds and Phrases

五月	**gogatsu**	May
五日	**itsuka**	the fifth of the month; five days
五つ星	**itsutsu-boshi**	five-star
五感	**gokan**	the five senses
五十音	**gojūon**	the Japanese syllabary
*五月晴れ	**satsukibare**	fine weather during the May rainy season

Use the same spacing between the horizontal strokes and make the last stroke longer than those above it.

4　一　丅　五　五

五

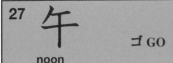

27 午 ゴ GO

noon

The character 午 originated from a pictograph of a *wooden pestle*. It came to have the meaning of *noon*, the middle of the day, perhaps because a pestle hits the middle of a mortar.
GR2 N5 AP

Example Sentences

1. 午前中にこの仕事をやっておいて下さい。
   Gozenchū ni kono shigoto o yatte oite kudasai.
   Please attend to this business <u>this morning</u>.

2. 午後なら行けます。
   Gogo nara ikemasu.
   I'll be able to go <u>in the afternoon</u>.

3. 子午線は北極と南極を結ぶ線です。
   Shigosen wa hokkyoku to nankyoku o musubu sen desu.
   <u>A meridian</u> is a line that links the North and South Poles.

4. 端午の節句にこいのぼりを飾りました。
   Tango no sekku ni koinobori o kazarimashita.
   I raised a carp streamer on <u>Tango no sekku</u>.

5. 列車は正午に出発します。
   Ressha wa shōgo ni shuppatsu shimasu.
   The train departs at <u>noon</u>.

Common Compounds and Phrases

午前	**gozen**	morning; A.M.
午前中	**gozenchū**	during the morning
午後	**gogo**	afternoon; P.M.
正午	**shōgo**	noon
子午線	**shigosen**	the meridian (line)
端午の節句	**Tango no sekku**	Children's Day (May 5th)

The third stroke is longer than the one above. Don't confuse 午 with 牛.

4 ノ 𠂉 𠂉 午

午

28 今 キン KIN コン KON いま ima

now; this; present

The character 今 depicts something being covered to prevent its escape. The meaning of *now* and *immediately* perhaps came from covering it *quickly*.
GR2 N5 AP

Example Sentences

1. 今週の予定を立てよう。
   Konshū no yotei o tateyō.
   Let's organize <u>this week</u>'s schedule.

2. ただ今、電話中です。
   Tadaima, denwachū desu.
   He is on the phone <u>at the moment</u>.

3. 今朝は寒い。
   Kesa wa samui.
   It is cold <u>this morning</u>.

4. ただいま(今)。
   Tadaima.
   I'm home!

5. 今度、いっしょに旅行に行きませんか。
   Kondo, issho ni ryokō ni ikimasen ka.
   Would you like to go on a trip with me <u>sometime</u>?

Common Compounds and Phrases

今週	**konshū**	this week
今月	**kongetsu**	this month
*今日	**kyō; konnichi**	today; now
今度	**kondo**	the recent; next time
今夜	**konya**	this evening; tonight
今頃	**imagoro**	about now; nowadays
*今朝	**kesa**	this morning

The first two strokes taper off.

4 ノ 人 𠆢 今

今

29 手

hand

シュ SHU
て te　*た ta

The character 手 derived from the shape of a *hand* with its five fingers extended.

GR1　N5　AP

Example Sentences

1. 彼に会ったとき握手した。
   Kare ni atta toki akushu shita.
   I <u>shook hands</u> with him when we met.

2. 別の手段を考えるべきだ。
   Betsu no shudan o kangaeru beki da.
   We should think of <u>a different method</u>.

3. やっとほしい本を手に入れた。
   Yatto hoshii hon o te ni ireta.
   I finally <u>got hold of</u> a book I had wanted.

4. あなたの手料理が食べたい。
   Anata no teryōri ga tabetai.
   I'd like to try some of your <u>home cooking</u>.

5. 彼は下手な日本語で話していた。
   Kare wa heta na Nihongo de hanashite ita.
   He spoke in <u>broken</u> Japanese.

Common Compounds and Phrases

握手	**akushu**	shaking hands
手段	**shudan**	a means; a way; a step
運転手	**untenshu**	a driver
手に入れる	**te ni ireru**	to get; to come by
手料理	**teryōri**	a home-made dish
手伝う	**tetsudau**	to help, assist
*下手な	**heta na**	poor, unskilled

The first stroke sweeps from right to left. Use equal spacing between the horizontal strokes.

4　一 二 三 手

手

30 少

little; few

ショウ SHŌ
すく・ない suku(nai)
すこ・し suko(shi)

The character 少 combines *small* 小 with an added stroke representing a *sword*. Thus it is a small object being made even *smaller*.

GR2　N5　AP

Example Sentences

1. 少々お待ち下さい。
   Shō shō omachi kudasai.
   Please wait <u>a moment</u>.

2. 少年少女向きの本を書いています。
   Shōnen shōjo-muki no hon o kaite imasu.
   I am writing a book aimed at <u>young boys and girls</u>.

3. これは幼少の頃の写真です。
   Kore wa yōshō no koro no shashin desu.
   This is a photograph of me <u>as a child</u>.

4. 昔、ここは客が少ない喫茶店だった。
   Mukashi, koko wa kyaku ga sukunai kissaten datta.
   This used to be a coffee shop with <u>few</u> customers.

5. 頭が少し痛い。
   Atama ga sukoshi itai.
   I have a <u>slight</u> headache.

Common Compounds and Phrases

少々	**shōshō**	a little; a short time
少なめ	**sukuname**	a smaller quantity
少女	**shōjo**	a young girl
減少	**genshō**	a decrease; a reduction
最少	**saishō**	the fewest; the youngest
多少	**tashō**	more or less; rather
青少年	**seishōnen**	young people

End the central stroke with a hook and end the third stroke firmly.

4　丨 亅 小 少

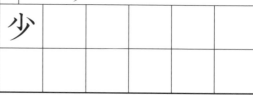

少

31 水

スイ SUI
みず mizu

water

The character 水 represents the *current* and *ripples* of a river.

GR1 N5 AP

Example Sentences

1. 水道代を払わなければならない。
   Suidōdai o harawanakereba naranai.
   I have to pay the water bill.

2. 水銀電池を使う必要がない。
   Suigin denchi o tsukau hitsuyō ga nai.
   We don't need to use mercury batteries.

3. 月・水・金は茶道を習っている。
   Ges-sui-kin wa sadō o naratte iru.
   I study the tea ceremony on Mondays, Wednesdays and Fridays.

4. 冷たい水が飲みたい。
   Tsumetai mizu ga nomitai.
   I want to drink some cold water.

5. 水平線に夕日が沈むのを見た。
   Suiheisen ni yūhi ga shizumu no o mita.
   I watched the sun set over the horizon.

Common Compounds and Phrases

水道	**suidō**	a water supply
水銀	**suigin**	mercury; Hg
水曜日	**suiyōbi**	Wednesday
水泳	**suiei**	swimming
水平	**suihei**	horizontal
水上スキー	**suijō skii**	water skiing
水玉	**mizutama**	a drop; a dewdrop; a dot pattern

The first stroke ends with a hook. Note the stroke order.

4 亅 ⺉ 才 水

水

32 中

チュウ CHŪ *ジュウ JŪ
なか naka

middle, inside

The character 中 represents an arrow penetrating the *center* of an object.

GR1 N5 AP

Example Sentences

1. 家は街の中心から少しはなれている。
   Ie wa machi no chūshin kara sukoshi hanarete iru.
   My house is a short distance from the center of town.

2. 彼は電話中です。
   Kare wa denwa-chū desu.
   He is on the phone.

3. 私立の中学校に通っている。
   Shiritsu no chūgakkō ni kayotte iru.
   I attend a private junior high school.

4. 体中が痛い。
   Karada-jū ga itai.
   I ache all over.

5. 冷蔵庫の中にビールが入っている。
   Reizōko no naka ni biiru ga haitte iru.
   There's beer in the refrigerator.

Common Compounds and Phrases

中心	**chūshin**	the center; the middle
電話中	**denwa-chū**	on the phone
中学校	**chūgakkō**	a junior high school; a middle school
途中	**tochū**	on the way; en route
中指	**nakayubi**	the middle finger
*体中	**karada-jū**	all over (one's body)
*一日中	**ichinichi-jū**	all day (long)

The last stroke bisects 口 in the character.

4 丨 冂 口 中

中

33 天

heaven

テン TEN
あめ ame *あま ama

The character 天 combines the characters 一 and 大. 大 represents a *person* while 一 suggests that which is above a person, namely *heaven*.
GR1 N5 AP

Example Sentences

1. 今日はいい天気ですね。
   Kyō wa ii <u>tenki</u> desu ne.
   The <u>weather</u>'s beautiful today, isn't it?

2. この部屋は天井が低い。
   Kono heya wa <u>tenjō</u> ga hikui.
   <u>The ceiling</u> in this room is low.

3. この石けんには天然香料が入っている。
   Kono sekken ni wa <u>tennen</u> kōryō ga haitte iru.
   This soap is <u>naturally</u> scented.

4. ぼくは天才じゃないよ。
   Boku wa <u>tensai</u> ja nai yo.
   I'm no <u>genius</u>!

5. 今夜、天の川の写真を撮ってみよう。
   Konya, <u>amanogawa</u> no shashin o totte miyō.
   I'm going to take some photos of <u>the Milky Way</u> tonight.

Common Compounds and Phrases

天気	**tenki**	the weather; fine weather
天井	**tenjō**	the ceiling; the roof
天然	**tennen**	nature; natural
天文台	**tenmondai**	an observatory
天国	**tengoku**	Heaven
天野	**Amano**	Amano (a name)
天の川	**amanogawa**	the Milky Way

The third stroke does not protrude, and the third and fourth strokes taper off.

4 | 一 二 チ 天

天

---

34 日

day, sun

ニチ NICHI ジツ JITSU
ひ hi か ka

The character 日 represents the shape of the *sun*.

GR1 N5 AP

Example Sentences

1. 日常会話には困りません。
   <u>Nichijō</u> kaiwa ni wa komarimasen.
   I have no problems with <u>day-to-day</u> conversation.

2. 彼女は映画の宣伝のため来日する。
   Kanojo wa eiga no senden no tame <u>rainichi</u> suru.
   She will <u>visit Japan</u> to promote her movie.

3. 先日はありがとうございました。
   <u>Senjitsu</u> wa arigatō gozaimashita.
   Thank you for (your help) <u>the other day</u>.

4. 今日は楽しかった。
   <u>Kyō</u> wa tanoshikatta.
   <u>Today</u> was fun.

5. 締め切りまであと三日しかない。
   Shimekiri made ato <u>mikka</u> shika nai.
   There are only <u>three days</u> until the deadline.

Common Compounds and Phrases

日常	**nichijō**	daily; every day
日本	**Nihon / Nippon**	Japan
日曜日	**Nichiyōbi**	Sunday
日記	**nikki**	a diary; a journal
先日	**senjitsu**	the other day; a few days ago
日付	**hizuke**	a date; dating
*昨日	**kinō / sakujitsu**	yesterday

Use equal spacing.

4 | 丨 冂 冂 日

日

35 父

フ FU
ちち chichi

a father

The character 父 derived from a pictograph of a hand gripping a stone axe, which represented someone with power, namely, a *father*.

GR2 N5 AP

Example Sentences

1. 祖父は九十歳です。
   Sofu wa kyūjussai desu.
   <u>My grandfather</u> is ninety years old.

2. 父は若い頃テニスの選手だった。
   Chichi wa wakai koro tenisu no senshu datta.
   In his younger days, <u>my father</u> was a tennis player.

3. お父さん、このふた開けて。
   Otōsan, kono futa akete.
   <u>Dad</u>, open this lid, will you?

4. こちらは叔父です。
   Kochira wa oji desu.
   This is <u>my uncle</u>.

5. 父の日のプレゼントは何がいいかな。
   Chichi no Hi no purezento wa nani ga ii ka na.
   I wonder what (present) I should get my father for <u>Father's Day</u>?

Common Compounds and Phrases

祖父	**sofu**	a grandfather
父母	**fubo**	mother and father
父兄	**fukei**	parents; guardians
神父	**shinpu**	a priest; a father
父の日	**Chichi no Hi**	Father's Day
*叔父	**oji**	an uncle
*お父さん	**otōsan**	a father; Father

The third and fourth strokes taper off.

4 | ′ ハ グ 父

父

36 分

ブン BUN フン FUN
ブ BU
わ・ける wa(keru)
わ・かる wa(karu)

portion; minute; rate; to divide; to understand

The character 分 combines 八 to *cut in two* and 刀 *sword* to give the meaning of *divide*.

GR2 N5 AP

Example Sentences

1. 今日は気分がいいなあ。
   Kyō wa kibun ga ii nā.
   I <u>feel fine</u> today!

2. 何か身分証明を持っていますか。
   Nani ka mibun shōmei o motte imasu ka.
   Do you have any <u>ID</u> on you?

3. 七時四十五分に予約がある。
   Shichi-ji yonjūgo-fun ni yoyaku ga aru.
   I have an appointment for <u>7:45</u>.

4. ケーキをみんなに分けた。
   Kēki o minna ni waketa.
   We <u>divided</u> the cake for everyone.

5. 今の話が分かりましたか。
   Ima no hanashi ga wakarimashita ka.
   <u>Did you understand</u> what was said just now?

Common Compounds and Phrases

気分	**kibun**	a feeling; a mood
身分	**mibun**	one's social position; circumstances
部分	**bubun**	a part
自分	**jibun**	oneself; one's own
十分	**jūbun**	enough
十分	**jippun, juppun**	ten minutes
3分の2	**sanbun no ni**	two-thirds
草分け	**kusawake**	a pioneer; a settler

Don't confuse 分 with 今. Leave a space between the first two strokes, and end the third stroke with a hook.

4 | ′ ハ 分 分

分

EXERCISE 3 (25 – 36)

A. Give the readings for the following.

1. 水 _____
2. 五十分 _____
3. 月 _____
4. 父の日 _____
5. 七ヶ月 _____
6. 少し _____
7. 五つ _____
8. 手の中 _____
9. 五日 _____
10. 今日 _____

B. Give the English meanings for the following.

1. ただ今。 _____
2. 水上スキー _____
3. お父さん _____
4. 分かりません。 _____
5. 五人 _____
6. 手に入れる _____
7. 水よう日 _____

8. 五千円 _____
9. 少ない _____
10. 十一月 _____

C. Write the following in kanji and kana.

1. to divide; to split _____
2. a young girl _____
3. three days; the third of the month _____
4. two-thirds _____
5. fifteen days; the fifteenth of the month _____
6. all day long _____
7. now _____
8. big hands _____
9. this month _____
10. one (a certain) day _____

REVIEW 1 (1 – 36)

A. Give the English meanings.

1. 下山 _____
2. 一月 _____
3. 今月 _____
4. 三日月 _____
5. 人口 _____
6. 手 _____
7. 九十円 _____
8. 女王 _____
9. 山 _____
10. 入り口 _____

B. Add the appropriate kanji.

1. ちいさい _____ さい
2. おんなのこ _____ の _____
3. じゅうがつ _____ _____
4. つち _____
5. てにいれる _____ に _____ れる
6. こんげつ _____ _____
7. ついたち _____ _____

8. いま _____
9. さがる _____ がる
10. すくない _____ ない

C. Write in hiragana or rōmaji.

1. 今日 _____
2. 二日 _____
3. 一日中 _____
4. 水 _____
5. 川下 _____
6. 王子 _____
7. 十月 _____
8. 女子 _____
9. 五分五分 _____
10. 火山 _____

D. Write in kanji and kana.

1. March 2nd _____
2. three months _____
3. Father's Day _____
4. fifty minutes _____
5. a young girl _____
6. to divide, split _____
7. two-thirds _____
8. three (things) _____
9. May 5th _____
10. water skiing _____

11. 八千二十円 _____
12. 川口さんに上げた。_____
13. まるい月 _____
14. お父さん _____
15. 少し大きい _____
16. 一つ少ない _____
17. 三月二十八日 _____
18. 川田さんと山下さん _____
19. 九千円 _____
20. 少し下さい。_____

E. Practice reading the following.

1. 大きな川 _____
2. 手の中 _____
3. 三上さんの子 _____
4. 川上さんと田口さん _____
5. 小さな女の子 _____
6. 土田という人 _____
7. 「今日は」 _____
8. 五月三日 _____
9. 水を下さい _____
10. 女子二人 _____

F. Match the following with their readings.

1. 三十円　（　）
2. 下手　（　）
3. 中川さん　（　）
4. 天の川　（　）
5. 水の中　（　）
6. 一日中　（　）
7. 九日　（　）
8. 今日　（　）
9. 上手　（　）
10. 八日　（　）

a. mizu no naka
b. kokonoka
c. kyō
d. jōzu
e. amanogawa
f. sanjūen
g. yōka
h. heta
i. ichinichijū
j. Nakagawa san

37　木

tree; wood

ボク BOKU　モク MOKU
き ki　*こ ko

The character 木 represents the trunk, branches and roots of a *tree*.

GR1　N5　AP

Example Sentences

1. 今朝から土木工事が始まった。
   Kesa kara doboku kōji ga hajimatta.
   The engineering works started this morning.

2. たくさんの木材を輸入している。
   Takusan no mokuzai o yunyū shite iru.
   They import lots of timber.

3. 燃えないごみの日は火・木です。
   Moenai gomi no hi wa ka-moku desu.
   Tuesdays and Thursdays are the days for nonburnable trash.

4. 桜の木の下でお花見をしよう。
   Sakura no ki no shita de ohanami o shiyō.
   Let's enjoy the blossoms beneath the cherry trees.

5. 植木に水をやるのを忘れないで！
   Ueki ni mizu o yaru no o wasurenai de!
   Don't forget to water the plants!

Common Compounds and Phrases

土木	**doboku**	engineering (public) works
木材	**mokuzai**	timber; wood
木曜日	**mokuyōbi**	Thursday
木造	**mokuzō**	(made of) wood
植木	**ueki**	a garden / potted plant
並木	**namiki**	a line of trees; roadside trees
*木の葉	**konoha**	leaves of a tree

The third and fourth strokes taper off.

4　一　十　オ　木

木

38 友 friend

ユウ YŪ
とも tomo

The character 友 depicts *two hands*, a symbol of *friendship*.

GR2 N5 AP

Example Sentences

1. 今、私には親友がいない。
   Ima, watashi ni wa shinyū ga inai.
   I don't have any <u>close friends</u> now.

2. 日本とその国は友好条約を結んだ。
   Nippon to sono kuni wa yūkō jōyaku o musunda.
   Japan has concluded <u>a treaty of friendship</u> with that country.

3. 友達が京都に住んでいます。
   Tomodachi ga Kyōto ni sunde imasu.
   <u>A friend of mine</u> lives in Kyoto.

4. 今晩、友人と約束があります。
   Konban, yūjin to yakusoku ga arimasu.
   I have an appointment with <u>a friend</u> tonight.

5. 悪友の言う事には耳を貸すな。
   Akuyū no iu koto ni wa mimi o kasu na.
   Don't pay any heed to what <u>bad company</u> may say.

Common Compounds and Phrases

親友	**shin'yū**	a close friend
友人	**yūjin**	a friend
友好	**yūkō**	friendship
友情	**yūjō**	friendship; fellowship
悪友	**akuyū**	bad company / companions
友達	**tomodachi**	a friend; a companion
メル友	**merutomo**	an e-pal; a cyberpal

The second stroke protrudes.

4 一 ナ 方 友

友

---

39 六 six

ロク ROKU
む mu　む・つ mu(tsu)
むっ・つ mut(tsu)　*むい mui

Although the origins of the character 六 are not clear, it now consists of 亠 *roof* and 八 *eight*.

GR1 N5 AP

Example Sentences

1. 六月六日の六時に来て下さい。
   Rokugatsu muika no rokuji ni kite kudasai.
   Please come at <u>6:00</u> on <u>June 6</u>.

2. 雪の結晶は六角形です。
   Yuki no kesshō wa rokkakukei desu.
   A snow crystal is <u>hexagonal</u>.

3. 木にリンゴが六つなりました。
   Ki ni ringo ga muttsu narimashita.
   There are <u>six</u> apples on the tree.

4. 日本で六ヶ月ホームステイをしました。
   Nihon de rokkagetsu hōmusutei o shimashita.
   I had a homestay for <u>six months</u> in Japan.

5. 来年、息子は小学六年生になります。
   Rainen, musuko wa shōgaku rokunensei ni narimasu.
   My son will become <u>a sixth grader</u> in elementary school next year.

Common Compounds and Phrases

六月	**rokugatsu**	June
六ヶ月	**rokkagetsu**	six months
六角形	**rokkakukei**	a hexagon
六年生	**rokunensei**	a sixth grader
第六感	**dairokkan**	a sixth sense
六本木	**Roppongi**	(a place)
*六日	**muika**	six days; the sixth day of the month

Give the character a pentagon-like shape and keep the last two strokes aligned.

4 ' 亠 六 六

六

40　右

right

ウ U　**ユウ** YŪ
みぎ migi

The character 右 combines ナ *right hand* and 口 *mouth*. In the past, people preferred to use their *right hand* for feeding.

GR1　N5　AP

Example Sentences

1. 右翼の車が家の前を通った。
   Uyoku no kuruma ga ie no mae o tōtta.
   A <u>right-wing party</u>'s truck passed my house.

2. 左右の確認をしなさい。
   Sayū no kakunin o shinasai.
   Make sure you look <u>both ways</u>.

3. 右手をけがした。
   Migite o kega shita.
   I hurt <u>my right hand</u>.

4. 字のうまさで彼の右に出る者はいない。
   Ji no umasa de kare no <u>migi ni deru mono wa inai</u>.
   When it comes to handwriting skill, he is <u>second to none</u>.

5. 彼は社長の右腕だ。
   Kare wa shachō no <u>migiude</u> da.
   He is the company president's <u>right-hand man</u>.

Common Compounds and Phrases

右翼	**uyoku**	the right wing, faction
右折	**usetsu**	a right turn
右派	**uha**	a right-wing faction
左右	**sayū**	left and right
右手	**migite**	the right hand; the right
右腕	**migiude**	the right arm; one's right hand
右利き	**migi-kiki**	right-handed

Don't confuse 右 with 石. Give equal spacing between the horizontal lines.

5 ノ ナ オ 右 右

右

41　外

external; other;
to remove

ガイ GAI　**ゲ** GE
そと soto　**ほか** hoka
はず・す hazu(su)

The character 外 shows a moon 夕 and a *turtle shell* ト, two objects that suggest *outside* and *external*.

GR2　N5　AP

Example Sentences

1. 外国へ行ったことがありません。
   Gaikoku e itta koto ga arimasen.
   I've never been <u>abroad</u>.

2. 人を外見だけで判断してはいけない。
   Hito o <u>gaiken</u> dake de handan shite wa ikenai.
   You shouldn't judge people just by their <u>appearance</u>.

3. 外科医に相談するべきだ。
   Gekai ni sōdan suru beki da.
   You should consult <u>a surgeon</u>.

4. 家の外に洗濯物を干した。
   Ie no soto ni sentakumono o hoshita.
   I hung the washing <u>outside</u> the house to dry.

5. ただ今、席を外しております。
   Tadaima, <u>seki o hazushite</u> orimasu.
   He <u>isn't at his desk</u> at the moment.

Common Compounds and Phrases

外国	**gaikoku**	a foreign country; abroad
外見	**gaiken**	an outward appearance
外出	**gaishutsu**	to go out
海外	**kaigai**	abroad; overseas
意外	**igai**	unexpected; surprising
外科医	**gekai**	a surgeon
仲間外れ	**nakama-hazure**	ostracism; exclusion

The second stroke tapers off.

5 ノ ク タ タ 外

外

42

ギョク GYOKU

たま tama

jewelry; ball

The character 玉 depicts *jewels* and a *thread* that strings them together.

GR1 N2

Example Sentences

1. 博物館に宝玉のコレクションがある。
   Hakubutsukan ni hōgyoku no korekushon ga aru.
   There is <u>a gem collection</u> at the museum.

2. 水玉模様のワンピースを買った。
   Mizutama moyō no wanpiisu o katta.
   I bought a one-piece dress with a <u>polka-dot</u> pattern.

3. 百円玉がポケットの中にあった。
   Hyakuen-dama ga poketto no naka ni atta.
   There was <u>a ¥100 coin</u> in my pocket.

4. この作品は珠玉の短編だ。
   Kono sakuhin wa shugyoku no tanpen da.
   This short story is <u>a literary gem</u>.

5. 古代エジプトでは、玉座を巡って暗殺が行われた。
   Kodai Ejiputo de wa gyokuza o megutte ansatsu ga okona-wareta.
   In ancient Egypt there were frequent assassinations to seize <u>the throne</u>.

Common Compounds and Phrases

宝玉	**hōgyoku**	a precious stone; a gem
珠玉	**shugyoku**	a gem; a jewel
玉座	**gyokuza**	the throne
水玉	**mizutama**	a drop of water; a dewdrop
玉乗り	**tamanori**	balancing on a ball
百円玉	**hyakuen-dama**	a ¥100 coin
あめ玉	**amedama**	a round, hard candy

Make the fourth stroke the longest.

5 　一 丁 王 王 玉

玉

43

コ KO

ふる・い furu(i)

ふる・す furu(su)

old; to wear out

The character 古 derived from a pictograph of a human skull, an object that represents something *old*.

GR2 N5 AP

Example Sentences

1. 古典を読んだことがない。
   Koten o yonda koto ga nai.
   I've never read <u>the classics</u>.

2. 大学で考古学を専攻している。
   Daigaku de kōkogaku o senkō shite iru.
   I'm majoring in <u>archaeology</u> at college.

3. 古着を誰かにあげたい。
   Furugi o dare ka ni agetai.
   I'd like to give <u>my old clothes</u> to someone.

4. 昨日、神田の古本屋に行った。
   Kinō, Kanda no furuhon-ya ni itta.
   I went to <u>a used bookstore</u> in Kanda yesterday.

5. 姉のお古のスーツケースを借りた。
   Ane no ofuru no sūtsukēsu o karita.
   I borrowed my sister's <u>well-worn</u> suitcase.

Common Compounds and Phrases

古典	**koten**	an old book; the classics
中古	**chūko**	secondhand (goods); the Middle Ages
考古学	**kōkogaku**	archaeology
古本屋	**furuhon-ya**	a secondhand bookseller
古着	**furugi**	secondhand clothing; old clothes
お古	**ofuru**	well-worn; much used

The first stroke is longer than the ones below it.

5 　一 十 十 古 古

古

44 左

サ SA
ひだり hidari

left

The character 左 combines ナ *left* hand and 工 *work*, and originally meant to help someone at work.

GR1 N5 AP

Example Sentences

1. 次の角を左折してください。
   Tsugi no kado o <u>sasetsu</u> shite kudasai.
   Please <u>turn left</u> at the next corner.

2. 選挙で左派が勝った。
   Senkyo de <u>saha</u> ga katta.
   <u>The leftists</u> won the election.

3. 左利きですか。
   <u>Hidari-kiki</u> desu ka.
   Are you <u>left-handed</u>?

4. 日本では、車は左側を走る。
   Nihon de wa, kuruma wa <u>hidarigawa</u> o hashiru.
   In Japan, cars drive on <u>the left</u>.

5. このあたりは、右も左も分かりません。
   Kono atari wa, migi mo <u>hidari</u> mo wakarimasen.
   I don't know my <u>left</u> from my right around here.

Common Compounds and Phrases

左折	**sasetsu**	a left-hand turn
左派	**saha**	the left wing; the leftists
左利き	**hidari-kiki**	a left-hander
左側	**hidari-gawa**	the left side; port
左手	**hidari-te**	the left hand
左向き	**hidari-muki**	facing left
右左	**migi-hidari**	left and right

Don't mistake 右 for 左 and be careful with the stroke order.

5　一 ナ 左 左 左

左

---

45 四

シ SHI
よ yo　よ・つ yo(tsu)
よっ・つ yot(tsu)　よん yon

four

The character 四 originally depicted breath coming out of a mouth. Some believe that the meaning *four* came from breath spreading out in *four directions*.

GR1 N5 AP

Example Sentences

1. 日本の四季は美しい。
   Nihon no <u>shiki</u> wa utsukushii.
   <u>The seasons</u> in Japan are beautiful.

2. 四方八方手を尽くして、人を探した。
   <u>Shihō happō</u> te o tsukushite, hito o sagashita.
   <u>No stone was left unturned</u> as they searched for the person.

3. 四人で旅行したらどうですか。
   <u>Yonin</u> de ryokō shitara dō desu ka.
   Why don't you travel <u>in a group of four</u>?

4. 昨夜、あの四つ角で事故を起こした。
   Sakuya, ano <u>yotsukado</u> de jiko o okoshita.
   I had an accident at those <u>crossroads</u> last night.

5. この四つの中から選ぶのは大変だ。
   Kono <u>yottsu</u> no naka kara erabu no wa taihen da.
   It's hard to choose from among these <u>four</u>.

Common Compounds and Phrases

四季	**shiki**	the four seasons
四方八方	**shihō happō**	from every direction
四月	**shigatsu**	April
四捨五入	**shisha gonyū**	rounding to the nearest whole number
四人	**yonin**	four people
四つ角	**yotsukado**	crossroads
四回	**yonkai**	four times

The third stroke does not touch the first stroke, and the fourth stroke bends.

5　丨 冂 冃 四 四

四

46 出

シュツ SHUTSU *スイ SUI
で・る de(ru) だ・す da(su)

to go out; to
take out; to send

The character 出 depicts a foot stepping over a line, to suggest the idea of go *out*, *emerge*.

GR1 N5 AP

Example Sentences

1. あの自動車は輸出用ですか。
   Ano jidōsha wa yushutsu-yō desu ka.
   Are those cars for export?

2. 月曜日会議に出席する。
   Getsuyōbi kaigi ni shusseki suru.
   I will attend a conference on Monday.

3. 去年、新しい辞書を出版しました。
   Kyonen, atarashii jisho o shuppan shimashita.
   They published a new dictionary last year.

4. 七時に家を出た。
   Shichiji ni ie o deta.
   I left the house at 7:00.

5. いつ手紙を出すつもりですか。
   Itsu tegami o dasu tsumori desu ka.
   When do you plan to mail the letter?

Common Compounds and Phrases

輸出	**yushutsu**	export
提出	**teishutsu**	submission; presentation
出席	**shusseki**	attendance; presence
出版	**shuppan**	publication
出張	**shutchō**	a business trip
出前	**demae**	home delivery (from a restaurant)
日の出	**hinode**	sunrise

The first stroke does not protrude.

5 ｜ 屮 屮 出 出

出

---

47 生

セイ SEI ショウ SHŌ
う・む u(mu) い・きる i(kiru)
お・う o(u) は・える ha(eru)
なま nama き ki

birth; life; to
grow; raw

The character 生 derived from a pictograph of a *growing* plant.

GR1 N5 AP

Example Sentences

1. うちの子供は中学生です。
   Uchi no kodomo wa chūgakusei desu.
   My child is a junior high school student.

2. お誕生日おめでとう！
   Otanjōbi omedetō!
   Happy birthday!

3. きのう女の子が生まれました。
   Kinō onna no ko ga umaremashita.
   A baby girl was born yesterday.

4. 祖母は九十歳まで生きた。
   Sobo wa kyūjussai made ikita.
   My grandmother lived until she was 90.

5. ジャズの生演奏を聴きにいった。
   Jazu no nama-ensō o kiki ni itta.
   I went to listen to a live jazz performance.

Common Compounds and Phrases

中学生	**chūgakusei**	a junior high school student
生徒	**seito**	a student; a pupil
生年月日	**seinen gappi**	date of birth
誕生日	**tanjōbi**	one's birthday
生け花	**ikebana**	flower arrangement; *ikebana*
生ビール	**nama-biiru**	draft beer
*芝生	**shibafu**	a lawn

Make the last stroke the longest.

5 ノ ヒ 屮 牛 生

生

48 石

stone

セキ SEKI　*シャク SHAKU
*コク KOKU

いし ishi

The character 石 depicts a *rock* at the bottom of a cliff.

GR1　N5　AP

Example Sentences

1. 石油を輸入することを止めた。
   Sekiyu o yunyū suru koto o yameta.
   They stopped importing <u>petroleum</u>.

2. 金沢は百万石の城下町でした。
   Kanazawa wa hyakuman-goku no jōkamachi deshita.
   Kanazawa was a castle town that produced <u>one million *koku*</u>† of rice.

3. 大きな石につまづいた。
   Ōki na ishi ni tsumazuita.
   I tripped on a large <u>stone</u>.

4. 父は石頭で本当に困る。
   Chichi wa ishiatama de hontō ni komaru.
   My father is so <u>hardheaded</u>, I really don't know what to do.

5. 石けんで手をよく洗いなさい。
   Sekken de te o yoku arainasai.
   Wash your hands well with <u>soap</u>.

† *koku* is an old unit of measurement, approx.180 liters.

Common Compounds and Phrases

石油	**sekiyu**	petroleum; kerosene
宝石	**hōseki**	a precious stone; a jewel
一石二鳥	**isseki nichō**	killing two birds with one stone
石けん	**sekken**	soap
石炭	**sekitan**	coal
石川	**Ishikawa**	Ishikawa (a name)
*磁石	**jishaku**	a magnet

The second stroke does not protrude.

5　一 ア イ 石 石

石

EXERCISE 4 (37 – 48)

A. Give readings for the following using hiragana or rōmaji.

1. 日の出 _____
2. 生えている _____
3. 六月六日 _____
4. 左がわ _____
5. 外出 _____
6. 友だち _____
7. 木の下 _____
8. 古い _____
9. 水玉 _____
10. 四十円 _____

B. Write in English.

1. 六つ _____
2. 生ねん月日 _____
3. 四人 _____
4. 出す _____
5. 右うで _____
6. 大きな石 _____

7. 友人 _____
8. 生きる _____
9. 外に出る _____
10. 右から左へ _____

C. Match the following with their correct reading.

1. 木よう日　（　）　　a. ishikawa
2. 右手　　　（　）　　b. sayū
3. 石川　　　（　）　　c. rokkagetsu
4. 六ヶ月　　（　）　　d. shigatsu muika
5. 左右　　　（　）　　e. deguchi
6. 中古　　　（　）　　f. gohyakuen-dama
7. 四月六日　（　）　　g. ikebana
8. 五百円玉　（　）　　h. chūko
9. 出口　　　（　）　　i. migite
10. 生け花　　（　）　　j. mokuyōbi

49 白

white

ハク HAKU　*ビャク BYAKU
しろ shiro　しろ・い shiro(i)
*しら shira

Originally, the character 白 represented the *white* nut of an acorn.

GR1 N5 AP

Example Sentences

1. コピーの中に白紙が混ざっている。
   Kopii no naka ni hakushi ga mazatte iru.
   There is <u>a blank sheet</u> mixed in with the copies.

2. 理由を明白にする必要があった。
   Riyū o meihaku ni suru hitsuyō ga atta.
   We had <u>to clarify</u> the reason.

3. 白黒の写真が好きです。
   Shiro-kuro no shashin ga suki desu.
   I like <u>black and white</u> photographs.

4. あの白い車が私のです。
   Ano shiroi kuruma ga watashi no desu.
   That <u>white</u> car is mine.

5. 白髪が目立ってきた。
   Shiraga ga medatte kita.
   <u>The gray in my hair</u> has become noticeable.

Common Compounds and Phrases

白紙	**hakushi**	white paper; blank paper
明白	**meihaku**	clear; obvious
白人	**hakujin**	a Caucasian
白菜	**hakusai**	Chinese cabbage
白夜	**byakuya**	a night under the midnight sun
白黒	**shirokuro**	black-and-white; right or wrong
*白髪	**shiraga**	gray hair

The first stroke tapers down from right to left. Give the same spacing.

5 　′　亅　白　白　白

白

---

50 半

half

ハン HAN
なか・ば naka(ba)

The character 半 depicts a *cow* 牛 being *split* 八 in *half*.

GR2 N5 AP

Example Sentences

1. ケーキを半分に切った。
   Kēki o hanbun ni kitta.
   I cut the cake in <u>half</u>.

2. 番組の前半を見なかった。
   Bangumi no zenhan o minakatta.
   I missed <u>the first half</u> of the program.

3. 六時半に学校で会おう。
   Rokuji han ni gakkō de aō.
   Let's meet at school at <u>6:30</u>.

4. このリボン、中途半端な長さだなあ。
   Kono ribon, chūto hanpa na nagasa da nā.
   This ribbon is such an <u>awkward</u> length.

5. 七月の半ばに友だちが来る。
   Shichigatsu no nakaba ni tomodachi ga kuru.
   A friend is visiting <u>around the middle</u> of July.

Common Compounds and Phrases

半分	**hanbun**	half
前半	**zenhan**	the first half, period
後半	**kōhan**	the latter half
半島	**hantō**	a peninsula
下半身	**kahanshin**	the lower half of one's body
半額	**hangaku**	half the amount (price)
中途半端	**chūto hanpa**	halfway; incomplete

The first two strokes slant in and the fourth stroke is longer than the third stroke.

5 　丶　丷　ソ　半　半

半

51 母

mother

ボ BO *モ MO
はは haha

The character 母 derived from a pictograph of a *seated woman*. The two dots represent the breasts.

GR2 N5 AP

Example Sentences

1. 母国語は絶対に忘れないそうです。
   Bokokugo wa zettai ni wasurenai sō desu.
   They say that you can't possibly forget <u>your mother tongue</u>.

2. 保母さんになりたいと思います。
   Hobosan ni naritai to omoimasu.
   I'd like to become <u>a nursery school teacher</u>.

3. 母は五年前に亡くなりました。
   Haha wa gonen mae ni nakunarimashita.
   <u>My mother</u> died five years ago.

4. お母さん、私のお弁当はどこ？
   Okāsan, watashi no obentō wa doko?
   <u>Mom</u>, where's my box lunch?

5. 叔母に茶道を習っています。
   Oba ni sadō o naratte imasu.
   I'm learning the tea ceremony from <u>my aunt</u>.

Common Compounds and Phrases

母国語	**bokokugo**	one's mother tongue
保母（さん）	**hobo(san)**	a kindergarten teacher
祖母	**sobo**	one's grandmother
母校	**bokō**	one's *alma mater*
母親	**hahaoya**	one's mother
*お母さん	**okāsan**	mother; mom
*叔母	**oba**	an aunt

End the second stroke with a hook.

5 ㇄ 므 므 므 母

母

---

52 北

north

ホク HOKU
きた kita

The character 北 depicts two people sitting back-to-back, a reference to turning one's back and fleeing to the *north*.

GR2 N5 AP

Example Sentences

1. まっすぐ北に行けばその町に着きますよ。
   Massugu kita ni ikeba sono machi ni tsukimasu yo.
   If you go directly <u>north</u>, you'll reach that town.

2. 選挙ではじめて敗北した。
   Senkyo de hajimete haiboku shita.
   He <u>suffered</u> his first <u>defeat</u> in the election.

3. 北半球と南半球では季節が反対です。
   Kita-hankyū to minami-hankyū de wa kisetsu ga hantai desu.
   Seasons in <u>the Northern</u> and Southern <u>Hemispheres</u> are reversed.

4. 外は寒い北風が吹いている。
   Soto wa samui kitakaze ga fuite iru.
   There's a cold <u>north wind</u> blowing outside.

5. 温暖化の影響で北極の氷が溶け始めている。
   Ondanka no eikyō de hokkyoku no kōri ga tokehajimete iru.
   The ice in <u>the North Pole</u> has begun to melt because of global warming.

Common Compounds and Phrases

北上	**hokujō**	going north
敗北	**haiboku**	a defeat; a setback
北極	**hokkyoku**	the North Pole
北半球	**kita-hankyū**	the Northern Hemisphere
北風	**kitakaze**	a north wind
北向き	**kitamuki**	facing north
*北京	**Pekin**	Beijing (a place)

The third stroke sweeps upwards from left to right.

5 ㇐ ㇏ ㇉ ㇍ 北

北

53

ホン **HON**
もと **moto**

book; main;
origin

The character 本 represents a *tree* with a line marked at the base, suggesting the *most important part*. From this came the meaning *foundation*, *base*.

GR1 N5 AP

Example Sentences

1. 本屋で本を二冊買った。
   Honya de hon o nisatsu katta.
   I bought two <u>books</u> at <u>the bookstore</u>.

2. 何でも基本が大事。
   Nan demo kihon ga daiji.
   Knowing <u>the basics</u> is important for all things.

3. 本社は東京にあります。
   Honsha wa Tōkyō ni arimasu.
   <u>The head office</u> is in Tokyo.

4. これは本物の金だ。
   Kore wa honmono no kin da.
   This is <u>real</u> gold.

5. 雑草は根本から抜いた方がいい。
   Zassō wa nemoto kara nuita hō ga ii.
   It's better to pull weeds out by <u>the roots</u>.

Common Compounds and Phrases

本屋	**honya**	a bookseller; a bookstore
基本	**kihon**	a foundation; a basis
本当	**hontō**	true; real
本物	**honmono**	a real, genuine thing
見本	**mihon**	a sample
山本	**Yamamoto**	Yamamoto (a name)
根本	**nemoto** /	the root; the base;
	konpon	Nemoto (a name)

Leave space on either side of the last stroke.

5　一 十 オ 木 本

本

54

目

モク **MOKU**　*ボク **BOKU**
め **me**　*ま **ma**

eye

The character 目 represents a human eye, turned sideways.

GR1 N5 AP

Example Sentences

1. 新大統領に世界中が注目している。
   Shin-daitōryō ni sekaijū ga chūmoku shite iru.
   The new president is the focus of world <u>attention</u>.

2. まず、目的地までの切符を買いましょう。
   Mazu, mokutekichi made no kippu o kaimashō.
   Firstly, let's buy the tickets to <u>our destination</u>.

3. 目にごみが入った。
   Me ni gomi ga haitta.
   I've got a speck of dust in <u>my eye</u>.

4. 右から三番目の席に座ってください。
   Migi kara sanbanme no seki ni suwatte kudasai.
   Please sit in <u>the third</u> seat from the right.

5. 目印は駅前のコンビニです。
   Mejirushi wa ekimae no konbini desu.
   <u>Look out for</u> the convenience store in front of the station.

Common Compounds and Phrases

注目	**chūmoku**	attention; observation
目的地	**mokutekichi**	one's destination
目次	**mokuji**	a table of contents
三番目	**sanbanme**	the third (one)
目薬	**megusuri**	eye drops
目印	**mejirushi**	a mark; a sign
目安	**meyasu**	a standard; an aim

Give equal spacing.

5　｜ 冂 冃 月 目

目

55 立

リツ RITSU
た・つ ta(tsu)
た・てる ta(teru)

to stand;
to raise

GR1 N5 AP

The character 立 depicts a *person standing* with outstretched arms.

Example Sentences

1. 国立の大学に入りたいと思います。
   Kokuritsu no daigaku ni hairitai to omoimasu.
   I'd like to enter a <u>national</u> university.

2. アメリカはイギリスから独立した。
   Amerika wa Igirusu kara dokuritsu shita.
   America gained <u>independence</u> from Britain.

3. 今日は立春だ。
   Kyō wa risshun da.
   Today is <u>the first day of spring</u>.

4. 危険ですから、ここに立たないで下さい。
   Kiken desu kara, koko ni tatanai de kudasai.
   Please <u>don't stand</u> here. It's dangerous.

5. 次の予定を立てましょう。
   Tsugi no yotei o tatemashō.
   <u>Let's work out</u> the next schedule.

Common Compounds and Phrases

国立	**kokuritsu**	national; state
独立	**dokuritsu**	independence; freedom
立春	**risshun**	the beginning of spring
自立	**jiritsu**	self-reliance
成立	**seiritsu**	formation; conclusion
立派	**rippa**	splendid; magnificent
立ち話	**tachibanashi**	standing and chatting

The third and fourth strokes slant inward.

5 ′ 一 ナ 立 立

立

---

56 安

アン AN
やす・い yasu(i)

peaceful; cheap

GR3 N5 AP

The character 安 combines 宀 *house* and 女 *woman*, to suggest a woman at home, feeling at *ease*.

Example Sentences

1. 今週は交通安全週間です。
   Konshū wa kōtsū anzen shūkan desu.
   This week is 'Traffic <u>Safety</u> Week'.

2. 彼から電話がないのを不安に思っている。
   Kare kara denwa ga nai no o fuan ni omotte iru.
   His not having called makes me feel <u>ill at ease</u>.

3. そのやり方は安易な方法でしたね。
   Sono yarikata wa an'i na hōhō deshita ne.
   That was an <u>easy</u> way of dealing with the matter.

4. これとこれではどっちが安いですか。
   Kore to kore de wa dotchi ga yasui desu ka.
   Which is the <u>cheaper</u> of these two?

5. この曲を聴くと心が安らぐ。
   Kono kyoku o kiku to kokoro ga yasuragu.
   Whenever I hear this song, it <u>puts my mind at ease</u>.

Common Compounds and Phrases

安全	**anzen**	safety; security
不安	**fuan**	uneasiness; anxiety
安易	**an'i**	easy; careless
安心	**anshin**	peace of mind
安定	**antei**	stability; balance
安物	**yasumono**	a low-priced article
大安売り	**ōyasu-uri**	a big bargain sale
安らぐ	**yasuragu**	to put someone's mind at ease; to feel at ease

The first stroke is at an angle.

6 ′ ′′ 宀 灾 安 安

安

57 会

カイ KAI エ E
あ・う a(u)

society; to meet;
meeting

The character 会 combines *lid* 亼 and *pot of rice* 云, which possibly meant *put together*, and then *come together*.

GR2 N5 AP

Example Sentences

1. 今、課長は会議中です。
   Ima, kachō wa <u>kaigichū</u> desu.
   The section chief is <u>in a meeting</u> now.

2. 新人の歓迎会があった。
   Shinjin no <u>kangeikai</u> ga atta.
   There was <u>a welcoming party</u> for new employees.

3. 機会があったら、また会いましょう。
   <u>Kikai</u> ga attara, mata <u>aimashō</u>.
   <u>Let's get together</u> again when we get <u>the chance</u>.

4. 会費を忘れず支払って。
   <u>Kaihi</u> o wasurezu shiharatte.
   Remember to pay <u>your membership fee</u>.

5. 友だちと会う約束がある。
   Tomodachi to <u>au</u> yakusoku ga aru.
   I'm planning <u>to meet</u> a friend.

Common Compounds and Phrases

会議	**kaigi**	a conference; a meeting
歓迎会	**kangeikai**	a welcome (reception)
機会	**kikai**	an opportunity; a chance
運動会	**undōkai**	a field (sports) day
会話	**kaiwa**	conversation; speaking
会費	**kaihi**	a membership fee; dues
出会い	**deai**	a meeting; an encounter

Make the fourth stroke longer than the one above it.

6 ノ 人 ハ 스 会 会

会

---

58 気

キ KI ケ KE

spirit; mind;
heart

The character 気 combines 乂, which symbolizes *rice*, and 气, which represents the *steam* emitted when rice is cooked.

GR1 N5 AP

Example Sentences

1. 気をつけてね。
   <u>Ki o tsukete ne</u>.
   <u>Take care!</u>

2. 山の天気は、急に変わる事があります。
   Yama no <u>tenki</u> wa, kyū ni kawaru koto ga arimasu.
   <u>The weather</u> in the mountains can change suddenly.

3. この高原は空気がきれいだ。
   Kono kōgen wa <u>kūki</u> ga kirei da.
   <u>The air</u> is clean up on this plateau.

4. だんだん景気が良くなってきた。
   Dandan <u>keiki</u> ga yoku natte kita.
   <u>Business</u> has gradually picked up.

5. 人の気配がした。
   Hito no <u>kehai</u> ga shita.
   <u>I sensed someone nearby</u>.

Common Compounds and Phrases

天気	**tenki**	the weather; fine weather
空気	**kūki**	air; the atmosphere
景気	**keiki**	business activity; the market
病気	**byōki**	sickness; to be ill
気に入り	**kiniiri**	a favorite; a pet
短気	**tanki**	a short temper
気配	**kehai**	an indication; a hint

End the fourth stroke with a hook.

6 ノ ⺅ ⺫ 気 気 気

気

59 休

キュウ KYŪ
やす・む yasu(mu)
やす・める yasu(meru)
やす・まる yasu(maru)

to rest; to feel
at ease

The character 休 combines 亻 *person* and 木 *tree*, representing a person *resting* against a tree.

GR1 N5 AP

Example Sentences

1. 休日はテニスをします。
   Kyūjitsu wa tenisu o shimasu.
   I play tennis on <u>my days off</u>.

2. あの店は年中無休だ。
   Ano mise wa <u>nenjū mukyū</u> da.
   That store is <u>open all year round</u>.

3. 昨日、風邪で学校を休んだ。
   Kinō, kaze de gakkō o yasunda.
   I <u>was absent</u> from school yesterday because of a cold.

4. 体を休めたらどうですか。
   Karada o yasumetara dō desu ka.
   Why don't you <u>take a rest</u>?

5. 急がしすぎて、心が休まる時がない。
   Isogashi-sugite, kokoro ga yasumaru toki ga nai.
   I'm too busy to have time <u>to relax</u>.

Common Compounds and Phrases

休日	**kyūjitsu**	a holiday; a day off
連休	**renkyū**	consecutive holidays
休憩	**kyūkei**	a break; an intermission
年中無休	**nenjū mukyū**	open throughout the year
夏休み	**natsu-yasumi**	a summer holiday
昼休み	**hiru-yasumi**	a lunch break

The fifth and sixth strokes taper off.

6　ノ　イ　仁　什　休　休

休

---

60 行

コウ KŌ　ギョウ GYŌ
い・く i(ku)　ゆ・く yu(ku)
おこな・う okona(u)

to go; a row;
to carry out

The character 行 originated from a pictograph of an *intersection* 十, a point of stopping and *going*.

GR2 N5 AP

Example Sentences

1. この道は一方通行だ。
   Kono michi wa <u>ippō tsūkō</u> da.
   This is a <u>one-way</u> street.

2. 映画館の前に長い行列があった。
   Eigakan no mae ni nagai gyōretsu ga atta.
   There was a long <u>line</u> in front of the movie theater.

3. 今日は学校へ行かなくてよい。
   Kyō wa gakkō e ikanakute yoi.
   I <u>don't have to go</u> to school today.

4. 東京行きの電車に乗って下さい。
   Tōkyō-yuki no densha ni notte kudasai.
   Please take the train <u>bound for Tokyo</u>.

5. 明日は試験が行われる。
   Ashita wa shiken ga okonawareru.
   <u>There will be</u> an examination tomorrow.

Common Compounds and Phrases

通行	**tsūkō**	passing; traffic
銀行	**ginkō**	a bank
旅行	**ryokō**	travel; a trip
急行	**kyūkō**	an express train
行列	**gyōretsu**	a line; a queue; a parade
行事	**gyōji**	an event; a function
*行方	**yukue**	whereabouts

Make the fifth stroke longer than the one above it, and end the last stroke with a hook.

6　ノ　ク　彳　行　行　行

行

EXERCISE 5 (49 – 60)

A. **Write the readings for the following in hiragana or rōmaji.**

1. 休む _____
2. 行く _____
3. 母と父 _____
4. 気をつける _____
5. 半分 _____
6. 会います _____
7. 大きい目 _____
8. 日本 _____
9. 安い _____
10. 立っている _____

B. **Match the following with their correct readings.**

1. 安上がり　（　）　　a. hokujō
2. 天気　　　（　）　　b. nakaba
3. 北上　　　（　）　　c. futsukame
4. 本日　　　（　）　　d. hakujin
5. 半ば　　　（　）　　e. furuhon
6. クラス会　（　）　　f. okāsan

7. 二日目　　（　）　　g. honjitsu
8. 古本　　　（　）　　h. yasuagari
9. 白人　　　（　）　　i. kurasu-kai
10. お母さん　（　）　　j. tenki

C. **Write in kanji and kana.**

1. Let's go! _____
2. a tournament _____
3. a northern exit _____
4. Mother's Day _____
5. was cheap _____
6. to carry out _____
7. Ms. Yamamoto _____
8. a feeling, mood _____
9. an eye _____
10. a day off, holiday _____

---

61 糸

シ SHI
いと ito

a thread

Originally written as 絲, this character represents a double-stranded *thread*.

GR1　N2

Example Sentences

1. 針と糸、持ってない？
   Hari to ito, motte nai?
   Do you have a needle and <u>thread</u>?

2. 彼女は白い毛糸のセーターを着ていた。
   Kanojo wa shiroi keito no sētā o kite ita.
   She wore a white, <u>woolen</u> sweater.

3. 赤ちゃんの髪は絹糸のようだ。
   Akachan no kami wa kinu-ito no yō da.
   The baby's hair is like <u>silken thread</u>.

4. 彼は裏で糸を引いているらしい。
   Kare wa ura de ito o hiite iru rashii.
   He seems to be <u>manipulating things</u> behind the scenes.

5. 問題解決の糸口を探る。
   Mondai kaiketsu no itoguchi o saguru.
   We will search for <u>clues</u> to settle the question.

Common Compounds and Phrases

綿糸	**menshi**	cotton thread
毛糸	**keito**	wool; woolen yarn
糸を引く	**ito o hiku**	to have sticky threads; to pull strings
絹糸	**kinu-ito, kenshi**	silk thread
糸口	**itoguchi**	a beginning; a clue
生糸	**kiito**	raw silk
糸偏	**itohen**	the *ito* radical of a Chinese character

The first two strokes are single strokes.

6 　く　幺　幺　纟　糸　糸

糸

34

62 耳

ジ JI
みみ mimi

ear

The character 耳 depicts the shape of an *ear*.

GR1 N5

Example Sentences

1. 耳鼻科の先生に喉を診てもらった。
   Jibika no sensei ni nodo o mite moratta.
   I had <u>an ear, nose and throat specialist</u> have a look at my throat.

2. 耳に水が入った。
   Mimi ni mizu ga haitta.
   Some water got into <u>my ear</u>.

3. 祖父は少し耳が遠い。
   Sofu wa sukoshi mimi ga tōi.
   My grandfather is a little <u>hard of hearing</u>.

4. それは初耳だよ。
   Sore wa hatsumimi da yo.
   That's <u>news</u> to me!

5. パンの耳を切り落とさないで。
   Pan no mimi o kiri-otosanai de.
   Please don't cut <u>the crust</u> off the bread!

Common Compounds and Phrases

耳鼻科	**jibika**	the ear, nose and throat department
中耳炎	**chūjien**	a middle ear infection
初耳	**hatsumimi**	hearing something for the first time
耳が遠い	**mimi ga tōi**	hard of hearing
耳たぶ	**mimitabu**	an earlobe
耳鳴り	**miminari**	ringing in the ears
耳障り	**mimizawari**	rasping; harsh

Provide equal spacing, and end the last stroke firmly.

6 一 丁 丆 午 耳 耳

耳

---

63 西

セイ SEI サイ SAI
にし nishi

west

The character 西 depicted a *bird in a nest*. A bird returns to its nest when the sun sets in the *west*.

GR2 N5 AP

Example Sentences

1. 西洋の文化に興味があります。
   Seiyō no bunka ni kyōmi ga arimasu.
   I'm interested in <u>Western</u> culture.

2. 関西国際空港はいつ完成しましたか。
   Kansai Kokusai Kūkō wa itsu kansei shimashita ka.
   When was <u>the Kansai International Airport</u> completed?

3. 毎日、東西線に乗る。
   Mainichi, Tōzai-sen ni noru.
   I take <u>the Tōzai line</u> every day.

4. 西の空に太陽が沈む。
   Nishi no sora ni taiyō ga shizumu.
   The sun sets in the <u>west</u>.

5. この部屋は西日が射して暑い。
   Kono heya wa nishibi ga sashite atsui.
   This room is hot from <u>the afternoon sun</u>.

Common Compounds and Phrases

西洋	**seiyō**	the West; Europe
北西	**hokusei**	northwest
西部	**seibu**	the western part
西暦	**seireki**	the Christian era; A.D.
関西	**kansai**	the Kansai (Region)
東西	**tōzai**	east and west; East-West
西日	**nishibi**	the western (afternoon) sun

The fifth stroke bends.

6 一 厂 襾 西 西 西

西

64 先

セン SEN
さき saki

previous;
ahead; future

The character 先 combines *foot* 生 and leg 儿 to give the idea of a person *going forward*.

GR1 N5 AP

Example Sentences

1. 先月、ロンドンに出張した。
   Sengetsu, Rondon ni shutchō shita.
   I went to London <u>last month</u> on a business trip.

2. 先着順で受け付けます。
   Senchakujun de uketsukemasu.
   We will accept people on <u>a first-come, first-served basis</u>.

3. 先日、クラス会がありました。
   Senjitsu, kurasu-kai ga arimashita.
   I had a class reunion <u>the other day</u>.

4. お先にどうぞ。
   Osaki ni dōzo.
   Please go <u>ahead</u> of me.

5. タクシーの運転手に行き先を告げた。
   Takushii no untenshu ni <u>ikisaki</u> o tsugeta.
   We told the taxi driver <u>where we wanted to go</u>.

Common Compounds and Phrases

先月	**sengetsu**	last month
先生	**sensei**	a teacher; a doctor
先着順	**senchakujun**	the order of receipt (arrival)
先日	**senjitsu**	the other day
先輩	**senpai**	one's senior; one's superior
優先	**yūsen**	a priority; a preference
行き先	**ikisaki**	one's destination

End the last stroke with a hook.

6 ｜ ′ ⺧ ⺧ 生 牛 先

先

65 多

タ TA
おお・い ō(i)

many; much

The character 多 combines two moons to indicate *many*.

GR1 N5 AP

Example Sentences

1. 多分、明日は雨だね。
   Tabun, ashita wa ame da ne.
   It'll <u>probably</u> rain tomorrow.

2. あちこちでテロが多発している。
   Achikochi de tero ga <u>tahatsu</u> shite iru.
   Everywhere you go, acts of terrorism are becoming more <u>frequent</u>.

3. ご多忙のところおいで下さってありがとうございます。
   <u>Gotabō no tokoro</u> oide kudasatte arigatō gozaimasu.
   Thank you so much for <u>taking the time</u> to come.

4. 近頃外食が多い。
   Chikagoro gaishoku ga <u>ōi</u>.
   I've been eating out <u>a lot</u> lately.

5. 英語が多少話せます。
   Eigo ga <u>tashō</u> hanasemasu.
   I can speak <u>some</u> English.

Common Compounds and Phrases

多分	**tabun**	probably; likely
多発	**tahatsu**	a frequent occurrence
多忙	**tabō**	being busy
多少	**tashō**	more or less
多才	**tasai**	versatile; multi-talented
多種多様	**tashu tayō**	various; diverse
多目	**ōme**	a somewhat larger quantity

The bottom half is slightly larger than the top half.

6 ｜ ′ ⺈ 夕 夕 多 多

多

66 年
ネン NEN
とし toshi

a year

The character 年 combines 禾 *rice plant* and ㇒ a *person bent over*. This represented harvest, which occurred *every year*.

GR1 N5 AP

Example Sentences

1. 日本に来てから一年たちました。
   Nihon ni kite kara ichinen tachimashita.
   <u>One year</u> has passed since I came to Japan.

2. 近年、日本に住む外国人が増えてきた。
   Kinnen, Nihon ni sumu gaikokujin ga fuete kita.
   The number of foreigners living in Japan has been growing <u>in recent years</u>.

3. 犠牲者は十五歳の少年だった。
   Giseisha wa jūgosai no shōnen datta.
   The victim was a 15-year-old <u>boy</u>.

4. 今、60年代が注目されている。
   Ima, 60-nendai ga chūmoku sarete iru.
   Now, everyone is interested in <u>the 60's</u>.

5. 今年の秋に、インドへ旅行に行く予定です。
   Kotoshi no aki ni, Indo e ryokō ni iku yotei desu.
   I'm planning to travel to India <u>this autumn</u>.

Common Compounds and Phrases

一年	**ichi<u>nen</u>**	one year; twelve months
近年	**kin<u>nen</u>**	recent years
少年	**shō<u>nen</u>**	a boy; a lad
60年代	**rokujū-<u>nen</u>dai**	the sixties
今年	**ko<u>toshi</u>**	this year
年上	**<u>toshi</u>ue**	older; senior
毎年	**mai<u>toshi</u> / mai<u>nen</u>**	every year

The fourth stroke is vertical.

6　ノ　ヒ　モ　午　年　年

年

67 百
ヒャク HYAKU
もも momo

hundred

The character 百 combines *one* 一 and *white* 白. It is believed that 白 also once indicated *hundred*; adding 一 thus meant *one hundred*.

GR1 N5 AP

Example Sentences

1. 自動販売機に百円玉を入れた。
   Jidō hanbaiki ni hyakuen-dama o ireta.
   I put <u>a ¥100 coin</u> into a vending machine.

2. パーティーに三百人ぐらいの人が来た。
   Pātii ni sanbyaku-nin gurai no hito ga kita.
   About <u>three hundred people</u> came to the party.

3. 百科事典で調べよう。
   Hyakka jiten de shirabeyō.
   Let's look it up in <u>an encyclopedia</u>.

4. 百聞は一見にしかず。
   Hyakubun wa ikken ni shikazu.
   A picture is worth a thousand words. (a saying)

5. テストで百点をとった。
   Tesuto de hyakuten o totta.
   I got <u>full marks</u> for the exam.

Common Compounds and Phrases

百円	**<u>hyaku</u>en**	one hundred yen
三百人	**san<u>byaku</u>-nin**	three hundred people
百科事典	**<u>hyak</u>ka jiten**	an encyclopedia
百貨店	**<u>hyak</u>katen**	a department store
百点	**<u>hyaku</u>ten**	one hundred points; full marks
百個	**<u>hyak</u>ko**	one hundred pieces

The second stroke tapers down from right to left. Give equal spacing between horizontal strokes.

6　一　 T　T　百　百　百

百

68 毎 マイ MAI

every; each

The character 毎 depicts a *mother* 母 wearing a *headpiece* ⼇. The meaning of *every* perhaps stems from the frequency at which the mother gives birth.

GR2 N5 AP

Example Sentences

1. 毎日、同じことばかり考えている。
   Mainichi, onaji koto bakari kangaete iru.
   I think about the same thing <u>every day</u>.

2. この番組は毎回おもしろいね。
   Kono bangumi wa <u>maikai</u> omoshiroi ne.
   This program is <u>always</u> interesting.

3. この薬は毎食後に飲んでください。
   Kono kusuri wa <u>maishokugo</u> ni nonde kudasai.
   Please take this medication <u>after every meal</u>.

4. 毎朝、公園を散歩する。
   Maiasa, kōen o sanpo suru.
   I walk in the park <u>every morning</u>.

5. 毎月、東京へ出張する。
   Maitsuki, Tōkyō e shutchō suru.
   I make a business trip to Tokyo <u>every month</u>.

Common Compounds and Phrases

毎日	**mainichi**	every day; daily
毎朝	**maiasa**	every morning
毎晩	**maiban**	every evening; nightly
毎回	**maikai**	every time
毎食後	**maishokugo**	after every meal
毎度	**maido**	each time; always
毎月	**maitsuki /**	every month; monthly
	maigetsu	

Don't mistake 毎 for 母.

6　ノ　ケ　ヒ　勾　毎　毎

毎

---

69 名 メイ MEI ミョウ MYŌ
な na

a name; famous

The character 名 combines 夕 *evening* and 口 *mouth*. People at night would announce themselves to others by calling out their *names*.

GR1 N5 AP

Example Sentences

1. 彼はベストセラーを書いて有名になった。
   Kare wa besutoserā o kaite <u>yūmei</u> ni natta.
   He wrote a bestseller and became <u>well-known</u>.

2. レストランに八名で予約した。
   Resutoran ni <u>hachimei</u> de yoyaku shita.
   I made a reservation for <u>eight people</u> at the restaurant.

3. 東名高速を一時間半走った。
   Tōmei kōsoku o ichijikan-han hashitta.
   I drove along the <u>Tōmei</u> (Tokyo-Nagoya) Expressway for one and a half hours.

4. 結婚して、名字が変わった。
   Kekkon shite, <u>myōji</u> ga kawatta.
   Her <u>surname</u> changed when she married.

5. カタカナで名前をここに書いてください。
   Katakana de <u>namae</u> o koko ni kaite kudasai.
   Please write <u>your name</u> here in *katakana*.

Common Compounds and Phrases

有名	**yūmei**	famous; well-known
八名	**hachimei**	8 people, persons
氏名	**shimei**	a full name
名産	**meisan**	a noted product; a specialty
名字	**myōji**	a surname
本名	**honmyō**	one's real name
名前	**namae**	a name; one's first name

Make the second stroke long.

6　ノ　ク　夕　夕　名　名

名

70 何

what

カ KA
なに nani　なん nan

The character 何 combines *person* 亻 and *possibility* 可. Think of this character as a depiction of one's breath when asking *What?*

GR2　N5　AP

Example Sentences

1. 今、何時ですか。
   Ima, nanji desu ka.
   <u>What time</u> is it now?

2. 夕食は何がいい。
   Yūshoku wa nani ga ii.
   <u>What</u> would you like to have for dinner?

3. 何人ぐらい来る予定ですか。
   Nannin gurai kuru yotei desu ka.
   About <u>how many people</u> are you expecting?

4. それについては何も知りません。
   Sore ni tsuite wa nani mo shirimasen.
   I know <u>nothing</u> about it.

5. 遅くまで、何処へ行っていたの？
   Osoku made, doko e itte ita no?
   <u>Where</u> have you been until so late?

Common Compounds and Phrases

幾何学	**kikagaku**	geometry
何時	**nanji**	when; what time?
何人	**nannin**	How many people?
何も	**nani mo**	not anything; nothing
何曜日	**nanyōbi**	What day of the week?
何日	**nannichi**	How many days; What day of the month?
*何処	**doko**	Where?

End the seventh stroke with a hook.

7　ノ　亻　仁　仁　何　何　何

何

---

71 花

a flower

カ KA
はな hana

The character 花 combines *plants* 艹 and *change* 化 to indicate the *flowering* of a plant.

GR1　N5　AP

Example Sentences

1. 毎年、春先は花粉症になる。
   Maitoshi, harusaki wa kafunshō ni naru.
   I suffer from <u>hay fever</u> every year in early spring.

2. お祝いに花を贈ったらどう？
   Oiwai ni hana o okuttara dō?
   Why don't we send <u>flowers</u> to celebrate?

3. 花火を見に行こう。
   Hanabi o mi ni ikō.
   Let's go watch <u>the fireworks</u>.

4. 花嫁さんはきれいだなあ。
   Hanayome-san wa kirei da nā.
   <u>The bride</u> is so gorgeous!

5. アメリカで生け花を教えていました。
   Amerika de ikebana o oshiete imashita.
   I've been teaching *ikebana* (<u>flower arrangement</u>) in the U.S.

Common Compounds and Phrases

花粉症	**kafunshō**	hay fever
開花	**kaika**	blooming; to blossom
花瓶	**kabin**	a (flower) vase
花嫁	**hanayome**	a bride
生け花	**ikebana**	*ikebana*; Japanese flower arrangement
花見	**hanami**	cherry-blossom viewing
花束	**hanataba**	a bunch of flowers

End the fifth stroke firmly, and the last stroke with a hook.

7　一　十　サ　艹　艾　花　花

花

72 貝

かい kai

a seashell

The character 貝 originally depicted a *bivalve*, although it presently looks more like an overhead view of a single *shell with feelers*.

GR1 N2

Example Sentences

1. きれいな貝殻を拾った。
   Kirei na kaigara o hirotta.
   I picked up some beautiful <u>shells</u>.

2. 貝の刺身はあまり好きじゃない。
   Kai no sashimi wa amari suki ja nai.
   I don't like raw <u>shellfish</u> very much.

3. その話になると彼は貝のようにかたく口を閉ざした。
   Sono hanashi ni naru to kare wa <u>kai no yō ni</u> kataku kuchi o tozashita.
   When the subject came up, he <u>clammed right up</u>.

4. 縄文時代の貝塚が発掘された。
   Jōmon jidai no <u>kaizuka</u> ga hakkutsu sareta.
   They have excavated <u>shell mounds</u> from the Jōmon Period.

Common Compounds and Phrases

貝殻	**kaigara**	a shell; a seashell
貝柱	**kaibashira**	a shellfish (ligament)
巻き貝	**makigai**	a spiral shell; a conch
二枚貝	**nimai-gai**	a bivalve
赤貝	**akagai**	an ark shell
ほら貝	**horagai**	a trumpet shell
貝塚	**kaizuka**	a shell mound; a midden

Give equal spacing.

7 丨 冂 冂 冃 目 目 貝 貝

貝

EXERCISE 6 (61 – 72)

A. Give the readings for the following.

1. 二百 _____
2. 耳 _____
3. 名 _____
4. 貝 _____
5. 糸 _____
6. 何人 _____
7. 多かった _____
8. 西日 _____
9. 今年 _____
10. お先に _____

B. Rewrite the following using kanji and kana.

1. はな (flower) _____
2. いきさき _____
3. せんせい _____
4. としうえ _____
5. おおめ _____
6. ほくせい _____
7. なにも _____

8. まいにち _____
9. たぶん _____
10. さんびゃくねん _____

C. Give the English meanings for the following.

1. 百円玉 _____
2. パンの耳 _____
3. 生け花 _____
4. 毎月 _____
5. 糸口 _____
6. 多少 _____
7. 何日 _____
8. 先月 _____
9. 二十名 _____
10. 八百円 _____

Review 2 (1 – 72)

A. Give the readings for the following.

1. 貝 ＿＿＿＿＿＿＿＿＿＿
2. 西口 ＿＿＿＿＿＿＿＿＿
3. 先生 ＿＿＿＿＿＿＿＿＿
4. 千九百六十四年 ＿＿＿＿＿＿
5. 生年月日 ＿＿＿＿＿＿＿
6. 白い糸 ＿＿＿＿＿＿＿＿
7. 先月 ＿＿＿＿＿＿＿＿＿
8. 何もない ＿＿＿＿＿＿＿
9. 生け花 ＿＿＿＿＿＿＿＿
10. 何人 ＿＿＿＿＿＿＿＿＿
11. パンの耳 ＿＿＿＿＿＿＿
12. 多い ＿＿＿＿＿＿＿＿＿
13. お先に ＿＿＿＿＿＿＿＿
14. 毎日 ＿＿＿＿＿＿＿＿＿
15. 三百本 ＿＿＿＿＿＿＿＿

B. Give the English meanings of the following.

1. 六年生 ＿＿＿＿＿＿＿＿
2. 今日の天気 ＿＿＿＿＿＿
3. 空気 ＿＿＿＿＿＿＿＿＿
4. 多分 ＿＿＿＿＿＿＿＿＿
5. 四ヵ月 ＿＿＿＿＿＿＿＿
6. 白い ＿＿＿＿＿＿＿＿＿
7. 古い ＿＿＿＿＿＿＿＿＿
8. 国立 ＿＿＿＿＿＿＿＿＿
9. 会いたい ＿＿＿＿＿＿＿
10. バスで行く ＿＿＿＿＿＿
11. 今年 ＿＿＿＿＿＿＿＿＿
12. 五百円玉 ＿＿＿＿＿＿＿
13. 少し ＿＿＿＿＿＿＿＿＿
14. 三千六百円 ＿＿＿＿＿＿
15. 安い ＿＿＿＿＿＿＿＿＿

C. Fill in the kanji according to the meanings provided.

1. はなび (fireworks) ＿＿ ＿＿
2. まいとし (every year) ＿＿ ＿＿
3. はちねんめ (the eighth year) ＿＿ ＿＿ ＿＿
4. いとぐち (a beginning; a clue) ＿＿ ＿＿
5. はんとし (a half year) ＿＿ ＿＿
6. きのした (under a tree) ＿＿ の ＿＿
7. ともだち (friend) ＿＿ だち

8. ほんみょう (one's real name) ＿＿ ＿＿
9. みぎて (the right hand) ＿＿ ＿＿
10. なんにち (What day of the month?) ＿＿ ＿＿
11. しょうねん (a boy; a lad) ＿＿ ＿＿
12. しがつついたち (April 1st) 四 ＿＿ 一 ＿＿
13. じゅうえんだま (a ten-yen coin) ＿＿ ＿＿ ＿＿

D. Match the following with their readings.

1. 左へ　　（　）　　a. tadai na
2. 本日　　（　）　　b. nannenme
3. 年上　　（　）　　c. fubo
4. 名まえ　（　）　　d. happyaku
5. 右目　　（　）　　e. honjitsu
6. 多大な　（　）　　f. namae
7. 行き先　（　）　　g. migime
8. 中西先生（　）　　h. toshiue
9. 石川　　（　）　　i. Nakanishi-sensei
10. 左右　　（　）　　j. sayū
11. 西日本　（　）　　k. sekiyu
12. 父母　　（　）　　l. ikisaki
13. 八百　　（　）　　m. Ishikawa
14. 何年目　（　）　　n. hidari e
15. 石ゆ　　（　）　　o. Nishi Nihon

E. Match the following with their English meanings.

1. 休む　　　（　）　　a. the other day
2. 先日　　　（　）　　b. middle age
3. 外に出る　（　）　　c. to have a rest
4. 中年　　　（　）　　d. younger; junior
5. 生糸　　　（　）　　e. eight people
6. 八名　　　（　）　　f. raw silk
7. 母　　　　（　）　　g. to go outside
8. 北西　　　（　）　　h. my mother
9. 四分の一　（　）　　i. a petal
10. 耳たぶ　　（　）　　j. an earlobe
11. 多少　　　（　）　　k. Why; What for?
12. 何で　　　（　）　　l. born in March
13. 年下　　　（　）　　m. more or less
14. 花びら　　（　）　　n. northwest
15. 三月生まれ（　）　　o. one quarter

73 見

ケン **KEN**
み・る **mi(ru)**
み・せる **mi(seru)**

to see; to show;
to look; to watch

The character 見 combines the characters for *eye* 目 and *person* 人, and represents a person *looking* with his eyes.

GR1 N5 AP

Example Sentences

1. 自分の意見を言いなさい。
   Jibun no <u>iken</u> o iinasai.
   Express your own <u>opinion</u>!

2. 行方不明の美術品が発見された。
   Yukue fumei no bijutsuhin ga <u>hakken sareta</u>.
   The missing artwork <u>was found</u>.

3. 首相は記者会見した。
   Shushō wa <u>kisha kaiken</u> shita.
   The prime minister held <u>a press conference</u>.

4. 今、テレビで新番組を見ている。
   Ima, terebi de shinbangumi o <u>mite iru</u>.
   <u>I'm watching</u> a new program on TV.

5. 定期券を見せる必要はない。
   Teikiken o <u>miseru</u> hitsuyō wa nai.
   There's no need <u>to show</u> your commuter pass.

Common Compounds and Phrases

意見	**iken**	an opinion; an idea
発見	**hakken**	a discovery
記者会見	**kisha kaiken**	a press conference
見物	**kenbutsu**	sightseeing
見学	**kengaku**	a study tour; a visit
見当	**kentō**	a guess; an estimate
見本	**mihon**	a model; a sample

Give equal spacing and end the last stroke with a hook.

7 丨 冂 冃 冃 目 目 貝 見

---

74 言

ゲン **GEN**　ゴン **GON**
い・う **i(u)**
こと **koto**

word; to say

The character 言 depicted a *knife* pointing down at a *mouth*, suggesting the clear-cut pronunciation of sounds to form *words*.

GR2 N5 AP

Example Sentences

1. 裁判で証言することになった。
   Saiban de <u>shōgen suru</u> koto ni natta.
   I ended up <u>giving evidence</u> in the trial.

2. 大学で言語学を専攻した。
   Daigaku de <u>gengogaku</u> o senkō shita.
   I majored in <u>linguistics</u> at college.

3. 遺言を書いておきましょう。
   <u>Yuigon</u> o kaite okimashō.
   I'm going to draw up <u>a will</u>.

4. もう一度言って下さい。
   Mō ichido <u>itte</u> kudasai.
   <u>Please say</u> that again.

5. あの人の言葉は一生忘れられない。
   Ano hito no <u>kotoba</u> wa isshō wasurerarenai.
   I'll never forget <u>what he said to me</u>.

Common Compounds and Phrases

証言	**shōgen**	evidence; testimony
発言	**hatsugen**	a speech; a proposal
言語	**gengo**	language; speech
遺言	**yuigon**	one's will; dying words
言葉	**kotoba**	a word; a language; an expression
一言	**hitokoto**	a word; a comment
ひとり言	**hitori-goto**	talking to oneself; a soliloquy

The second stroke is the longest.

7 丶 亠 亍 亖 言 言 言

75 車

シャ SHA
くるま kuruma

a vehicle;
a car

The character 車 depicts the two wheels and carriage of a *palanquin* viewed from above.

GR1　N5　AP

Example Sentences

1. ここは駐車禁止です。
   Koko wa chūsha kinshi desu.
   No <u>parking</u> here.

2. 前から三両目の車両に乗っていた。
   Mae kara sanryōme no sharyō ni notte ita.
   He was in the third <u>carriage</u> from the front of the train.

3. 風車による発電をよく見かける。
   Fūsha ni yoru hatsuden o yoku mikakeru.
   <u>Windmills</u> being used to generate electricity are a common sight.

4. 車庫から車を出してあげましょうか。
   Shako kara kuruma o dashite agemashō ka.
   Shall I get <u>the car</u> out of <u>the garage</u> for you?

Common Compounds and Phrases

駐車	**chūsha**	parking
車両	**sharyō**	a railroad car; a coach
風車	**fūsha** / **kazaguruma**	a windmill / a pinwheel
自動車	**jidōsha**	an automobile
発車	**hassha**	the start / departure of a train
下車	**gesha**	getting off a train or bus
乳母車	**ubaguruma**	a baby carriage; a pram

The sixth stroke is longer than those above it.

7　一　一　一　戸　百　百　百　亘　車

車

---

76 社

シャ SHA
やしろ yashiro

a company;
a Shinto shrine

The character 社 combines *ground* 土 and *altar* ネ, the makings of a *shrine*.

GR2　N5　AP

Example Sentences

1. 中国も車社会になりつつある。
   Chūgoku mo kuruma shakai ni naritsutsu aru.
   China is also becoming <u>a society</u> that is increasingly dependent on cars.

2. 仲間と三人で小さな会社を作った。
   Nakama to sannin de chiisa na kaisha o tsukutta.
   Two colleagues and myself formed a small <u>company</u>.

3. 去年の四月に入社しました。
   Kyonen no shigatsu ni nyūsha shimashita.
   I <u>joined the firm</u> in April of last year.

4. 神社にお参りに行(い)った。
   Jinja ni omairi ni itta.
   I visited <u>a Shinto shrine</u>.

5. 春から本社へ転勤になりました。
   Haru kara honsha e tenkin ni narimashita.
   I was transferred to <u>the head office</u> this spring.

Common Compounds and Phrases

社会	**shakai**	society; the world
会社	**kaisha**	a company; a firm
入社	**nyūsha**	joining a company
本社	**honsha**	a head office
商社	**shōsha**	a trading company
新聞社	**shinbunsha**	a newspaper publishing company
神社	**jinja**	a *Shinto* shrine

The last stroke is longer than the one above it.

7　丶　ラ　ネ　ネ　ネ　社　社

社

77 足

ソク SOKU
あし ashi　た・りる ta(riru)
た・す ta(su)

foot; leg; to be enough; to add

The character 足 represents the shape of the lower part of the *leg*, beneath the knee joint.

GR1　N5　AP

Example Sentences

1. 来週、高尾山に遠足に行きます。
   Raishū, Takao-zan ni <u>ensoku</u> ni ikimasu.
   I'm going on <u>an excursion</u> to Mount Takao next week.

2. 最近の若い人は、足が長い。
   Saikin no wakai hito wa, <u>ashi</u> ga nagai.
   Young people these days have long <u>legs</u>.

3. 時間が足りない。
   Jikan ga <u>tarinai</u>.
   There <u>isn't enough</u> time.

4. 独身男性の多くは、野菜不足だ。
   Dokushin dansei no ōku wa, <u>yasai busoku</u> da.
   A lot of single men are <u>not eating enough vegetables</u>.

5. 父は田舎で自給自足の暮らしを始めた。
   Chichi wa inaka de <u>jikyū jisoku</u> no kurashi o hajimeta.
   My father started <u>living by himself</u> in the country.

Common Compounds and Phrases

遠足	**en<u>soku</u>**	an excursion; a trip
満足	**man<u>zoku</u>**	satisfaction
不足	**fu<u>soku</u>**	a shortage; a lack of
土足	**do<u>soku</u>**	with one's shoes on
三足	**san<u>soku</u>**	three pairs (of socks)
自給自足	**jikyū ji<u>soku</u>**	self-sufficiency
足首	**<u>ashi</u>kubi**	an ankle

The top half is somewhat smaller than the bottom half.

7 丨 冂 口 尸 尸 足 足

足

78 男

ダン DAN　ナン NAN
おとこ otoko　*お o

a man; a male

The character 男 combines characters for 田 *rice paddy* and 力 *strength* and indicates a *man* working.

GR1　N5　AP

Example Sentences

1. 男性用のかつらがよく売れている。
   <u>Dansei-yō</u> no katsura ga yoku urete iru.
   Wigs <u>for men</u> are selling well.

2. 歌舞伎は男優ばかりの芝居です。
   Kabuki wa <u>danyū</u> bakari no shibai desu.
   Kabuki is a form of drama involving only <u>male actors</u>.

3. 長男とは結婚したくないわ。
   <u>Chōnan</u> to wa kekkon shitakunai wa.
   I don't want to marry <u>an eldest son</u>!

4. あの背の高い男の人は誰？
   Ano se no takai <u>otoko no hito</u> wa dare?
   Who is that tall <u>man</u>?

5. 小さな男の子が迷子になっています。
   Chiisa na <u>otoko-no-ko</u> ga maigo ni natte imasu.
   A little <u>boy</u> is lost.

Common Compounds and Phrases

男性	**<u>dan</u>sei**	a man; a male; masculine
男優	**<u>dan</u>yū**	an actor
男女	**<u>dan</u>jo**	male and female
長男	**chō<u>nan</u>**	the eldest son
次男	**ji<u>nan</u>**	a second son
男の子	**<u>otoko</u> no ko**	a boy; a male child
大男	**ō-<u>otoko</u>**	a tall / large man

Provide equal spacing and end the sixth stroke with a hook.

7 丨 冂 冂 用 田 男 男

男

79 来

ライ RAI
く・る ku(ru)
きた・す kita(su)
きた・る kita(ru)

to come; to cause;
to bring about

The character 来 derived from a pictograph of *wheat*. The meaning of *come* perhaps was connected with wheat having been *brought* from a distant country.
GR2 N5 AP

Example Sentences

1. 未来のことはだれも知らない。
   Mirai no koto wa dare mo shiranai.
   No one knows what <u>the future</u> holds.

2. お正月以来会っていませんね。
   Oshōgatsu irai atte imasen ne.
   We haven't seen each other <u>since</u> New Year's.

3. 電車が来た。
   Densha ga kita.
   The train <u>has arrived</u>.

4. コンピューターがダウンして仕事に支障を来した。
   Konpyūtā ga daun shite shigoto ni shishō o kitashita.
   The computer being down <u>hindered</u> my work.

5. 大統領が来日した。
   Daitōryō ga rainichi shita.
   The President <u>came to Japan</u>.

Common Compounds and Phrases

未来	**mirai**	the future
以来	**irai**	since then; from that time
来日	**rainichi**	coming to Japan
来月	**raigetsu**	next month
本来	**honrai**	originally; naturally
由来	**yurai**	the origin; derived from
来客	**raikyaku**	a caller; a visitor

The fourth stroke is longer than the horizontal one above it.

7 一 ⼁ ⼧ ⼐ 平 来 来

来

---

80 雨

ウ U
あめ ame ＊あま ama
＊さめ same ＊ゆ yu

rain

The character 雨 combines three things: *heaven* 一, *clouds* 冂 and ⽶ *rain falling*.

GR1 N5 AP

Example Sentences

1. あそこは雨量が多い地方です。
   Asoko wa uryō ga ōi chihō desu.
   That region has high <u>rainfall</u>.

2. 急に雨が降ってきた。
   Kyū ni ame ga futte kita.
   It suddenly started <u>to rain</u>.

3. あしたの天気予報は大雨だ。
   Ashita no tenki yohō wa ōame da.
   <u>Heavy rain</u> is forecast for tomorrow.

4. 小雨なら傘は要らない。
   Kosame nara kasa wa iranai.
   I won't need an umbrella if it's just <u>drizzling</u>.

5. 梅雨の頃は蒸し暑い。
   Tsuyu no koro wa mushiatsui.
   It's muggy during <u>the rainy season</u>.

Common Compounds and Phrases

雨量	**uryō**	the amount of rainfall
豪雨	**gōu**	heavy rain; a downpour
暴風雨	**bōfūu**	a windy rainstorm
大雨	**ōame**	heavy rain
＊小雨	**kosame**	light rain; drizzle
＊雨漏り	**amamori**	a leak in the roof
＊梅雨	**tsuyu / baiu**	the rainy season

End the second stroke firmly, and the third stroke with a hook.

8 一 ⼂ ⼌ 币 币 雨 雨 雨

雨

81 学

learning; to study

ガク GAKU
まな・ぶ mana(bu)

The character 学 can be thought of as a child 子 under a roof 宀, to suggest *learning*.

GR1 N5 AP

Example Sentences

1. 大学で英語を勉強した。
   Daigaku de eigo o benkyō shita.
   I studied English at <u>university</u>.

2. 数学は苦手だった。
   Sūgaku wa nigate datta.
   I was poor at <u>mathematics</u>.

3. 三年間スウェーデンに留学した。
   Sannenkan Suēden ni ryūgaku shita.
   I <u>went</u> to Sweden <u>to study</u> for three years.

4. 医学博士の学位をとった。
   Igaku hakase no gakui o totta.
   I received <u>my doctorate</u> in medicine.

5. 少しドイツ語を学んだ。
   Sukoshi doitsugo o mananda.
   I <u>learned</u> a little German.

Common Compounds and Phrases

大学	**daigaku**	a university; a college
数学	**sūgaku**	mathematics
留学	**ryūgaku**	studying abroad
学位	**gakui**	an academic degree
学生	**gakusei**	a student
小学生	**shōgakusei**	elementary school student
学校	**gakkō**	a school

End the seventh stroke with a hook. The top element resembles the *katakana* ツ.

8 ` ゛ ゛ ゛ 学 学 学 学

---

82 金

money; gold

キン KIN   コン KON
かね kane   *かな kana

The character 金 represents *treasures* 丷 in the *ground* 土 with a *covering* 𠆢 over them. The treasures are *gold*.

GR1 N5 AP

Example Sentences

1. 現金で払います。
   Genkin de haraimasu.
   I'll pay in <u>cash</u>.

2. 弟は金属アレルギーがある。
   Otōto wa kinzoku arerugii ga aru.
   My younger brother is allergic to <u>metals</u>.

3. 来週の水木金は休みます。
   Raishū no sui-moku-kin wa yasumimasu.
   Next week I will take <u>Wednesday, Thursday and Friday</u> off.

4. あら！お金がない！
   Ara! Okane ga nai!
   Oh, no! I don't have any <u>money</u>!

5. バッグの金具が壊れた。
   Baggu no kanagu ga kowareta.
   <u>The clasp</u> on my handbag broke.

Common Compounds and Phrases

現金	**genkin**	cash
金属	**kinzoku**	a metal
金曜日	**kinyōbi**	Friday
税金	**zeikin**	a tax
料金	**ryōkin**	a fee; a charge; a fare
黄金	**ōgon**	(yellow) gold
金具	**kanagu**	metal parts

The slanted strokes do not touch the base.

8 ノ 人 人 仝 仐 全 金 金

83 空

クウ KŪ
そら sora　あ・く a(ku)
あ・ける a(keru)　から kara

sky; emptiness

The character 空 combines *hole* 穴 and *work upon* 工. This concept suggests a room, which encloses *space*. From this came the meaning of *sky* and *emptiness*.
GR1　N5　AP

Example Sentences

1. 成田空港は都心から遠い。
   Narita kūkō wa toshin kara tōi.
   Narita Airport is far from the city center.

2. 空がきれいだなあ。
   Sora ga kirei da nā.
   The sky is so beautiful!

3. あの歌を空で覚えている。
   Ano uta o sora de oboete iru.
   I know that song by heart.

4. この席は、空いてますか。
   Kono seki wa, aitemasu ka.
   Is this seat free?

5. 空き缶はくずかごに。
   Akikan wa kuzukago ni.
   Dispose of your empty cans in the trash bin.

Common Compounds and Phrases

空港	**kūkō**	an airport
空車	**kūsha**	an empty taxi
空白	**kūhaku**	a blank; an empty space
星空	**hoshizora**	a starry sky
空箱	**karabako**	an empty box, case
空手	**karate**	*karate*
空き缶	**akikan**	an empty can

The fifth stroke bends, and the last stroke is longer than the one above it.

8 ⟨strokes⟩ 空

---

84 国

コク KOKU
くに kuni

country

The character 国 combines *jewels* 玉 and *enclosure* 口, suggesting that a *country* is a land of treasures.

GR2　N5　AP

Example Sentences

1. 国際会議に出席する予定です。
   Kokusai kaigi ni shusseki suru yotei desu.
   I'm planning to attend an international conference.

2. 遠足で、日光国立公園に行く。
   Ensoku de, Nikkō kokuritsu kōen ni iku.
   I'm going to Nikkō National Park on an excursion.

3. 国産車に乗っています。
   Kokusansha ni notte imasu.
   I drive a Japanese-made car.

4. 国語の授業は好きだった。
   Kokugo no jugyō wa suki datta.
   I liked my Japanese language classes.

5. お国はどちらですか。
   Okuni wa dochira desu ka.
   Where are you from?

Common Compounds and Phrases

国産	**kokusan**	domestically produced / grown
国民	**kokumin**	the people; a national
国籍	**kokuseki**	nationality; citizenship
外国人	**gaikokujin**	foreigner; people from other countries
島国	**shimaguni**	an island country
国連	**kokuren**	the United Nations

Don't forget the dot.

8 ⟨strokes⟩ 国

EXERCISE 7 (73 – 84)

A. Give the readings for the following in hiragana or rōmaji.

1. 来る _____
2. 見える _____
3. 足りる _____
4. 社会 _____
5. 見学 _____
6. 空く _____
7. 車を出す _____
8. 大学生 _____
9. 男の子 _____
10. お金 _____

B. Give the English meanings of the following words.

1. 来月 _____
2. 下車 _____
3. 一言 _____
4. 外国人 _____
5. 男女 _____
6. 本社 _____
7. 見本 _____

8. 小学生 _____
9. 大雨 _____
10. 来日 _____

C. Match the following with their readings.

1. 四足 ( )   a. kūhaku
2. 空車 ( )   b. kuruma-shakai
3. 空手 ( )   c. karate
4. 男子 ( )   d. kūsha
5. 小雨 ( )   e. daigaku
6. 国産 ( )   f. kaisha
7. 本来 ( )   g. yonsoku
8. 中学生 ( )   h. ō-otoko
9. 車社会 ( )   i. danshi
10. 大学 ( )   j. honrai
11. 大男 ( )   k. ōame
12. 大雨 ( )   l. kokusan
13. 会社 ( )   m. chūgakusei
14. 国立 ( )   n. kokuritsu
15. 空白 ( )   o. kosame

---

85 長 long

チョウ CHŌ
なが・い naga(i)

The character 長 derived from a pictograph of a *long-haired old man* with a walking stick, suggesting a *long* passage of time.

GR2 N5 AP

Example Sentences

1. 部長の話はいつも長い。
   Buchō no hanashi wa itsumo nagai.
   The department chief is always long-winded.

2. 子供の成長が楽しみです。
   Kodomo no seichō ga tanoshimi desu.
   I enjoy watching the children grow up.

3. この製品の特長は小さいことです。
   Kono seihin no tokuchō wa chiisai koto desu.
   This product's best feature is its compactness.

4. 社長からお電話です。
   Shachō kara odenwa desu.
   The company president is on the line.

5. 長い髪を乾かすのに時間がかかる。
   Nagai kami o kawakasu no ni jikan ga kakaru.
   It takes some time to dry my long hair.

Common Compounds and Phrases

部長	**buchō**	a department/division chief
成長	**seichō**	growth
特長	**tokuchō**	a strong point; a strength
身長	**shinchō**	one's height
店長	**tenchō**	a store manager
長年	**naganen**	many years; a long time
長持ち	**nagamochi**	endurance; durability

End the sixth stroke with a hook and make the fifth stroke longer than those above it.

8 ｜ 厂 F F 토 투 長 長

長

86 店

テン TEN
みせ mise　*たな tana

a shop; a store

The character 店 combines *roof* 广 and *arrange* 占, suggesting a *place where objects are arranged and sold*; i.e., a *shop*.

GR2　N5　AP

Example Sentences

1. 売店で新聞を買った。
   Baiten de shinbun o katta.
   I bought a newspaper at <u>the kiosk</u>.

2. 閉店は七時です。
   Heiten wa shichiji desu.
   <u>The store closes</u> at 7:00.

3. 私は広告代理店に勤めています。
   Watashi wa kōkoku **dairiten** ni tsutomete imasu.
   I work for <u>an advertising agency</u>.

4. この店は何時まで開いていますか。
   Kono **mise** wa nanji made aite imasu ka.
   What time is this <u>store</u> open until?

5. 喫茶店で休んでいきませんか。
   Kissaten de yasunde ikimasen ka?
   Would you like to stop at <u>a coffee shop</u> for a break?

Common Compounds and Phrases

売店	**baiten**	a stand; a kiosk
閉店	**heiten**	closing a shop; shutting up shop
代理店	**dairiten**	an agency; an agent
本店	**honten**	the main store
喫茶店	**kissaten**	a café; a coffee shop
店員	**ten'in**	a store employee
店じまい	**mise-jimai**	closing a business (a store)

The inside portion is not 古.

8　｀　亠　广　广　庐　店　店　店

店

---

87 東

トウ TŌ
ひがし higashi

east

The character 東 combines *tree* 木 and *sun* 日, representing the morning sun rising in the *east* behind some tree branches.

GR1　N5　AP

Example Sentences

1. 中東に長く住んでいました。
   Chūtō ni nagaku sunde imashita.
   I lived in <u>the Middle East</u> for a long time.

2. 東洋といっても、様々な文化があります。
   Tōyō to itte mo samazama na bunka ga arimasu.
   <u>The Orient</u> actually consists of many cultures.

3. 関東地方のニュースをお伝えします。
   Kantō chihō no nyūsu o otsutae shimasu.
   And now for <u>the Kantō regional</u> news.

4. 東名高速を使うと早く着く。
   Tōmei kōsoku o tsukau to hayaku tsuku.
   Using the <u>Tōmei</u> (Tōkyō-Nagoya) Expressway will be quicker.

5. シルクロードの東の果てが日本です。
   Shiruku rōdo no **higashi** no hate ga Nihon / Nippon desu.
   The <u>eastern</u>most extremity of the Silk Road is Japan.

Common Compounds and Phrases

中東	**chūtō**	the Middle East
東洋	**tōyō**	the Orient; the East
関東	**Kantō**	the Kanto region
東海	**Tōkai**	the Tokai region
北東	**hokutō**	north-east
東西南北	**tōzai** **nanboku**	north, south, east and west
東風	**higashi-kaze**	an east wind

The seventh stroke ends firmly, and the eighth stroke tapers off.

8　一　厂　厅　គ　គ　車　東　東

東

88 後

after; behind; later; the back; to be late

ゴ GO　コウ KŌ
のち nochi　あと ato
うし・ろ ushi(ro)
おく・れる oku(reru)

The character 後 combines *advance* 彳, *little* 幺, and *foot* 夂, in reference to someone who is walking slowly, and thus falling *behind*.

GR2　N5　AP

Example Sentences

1. 午後なら時間があります。
   Gogo nara jikan ga arimasu.
   I'll have time <u>in the afternoon</u>.

2. 私達は試合の後半で逆転した。
   Watashitachi wa shiai no kōhan de gyakuten shita.
   The tables turned in our favor in <u>the second half</u> of the match.

3. 後ほどお電話いたします。
   Nochihodo odenwa itashimasu.
   I will call you <u>later</u>.

4. 後でまた掛け直します。
   Ato de mata kakenaoshimasu.
   I'll call you back <u>later</u>.

5. 列の後ろに並んで下さい。
   Retsu no <u>ushiro</u> ni narande kudasai.
   Please go to <u>the end</u> of the line.

Common Compounds and Phrases

最後	**saigo**	the last; the end
今後	**kongo**	in the future; from now on
後半	**kōhan**	the latter half
後輩	**kōhai**	one's junior
後世	**kōsei**	later ages; posterity
後味	**atoaji**	an aftertaste
後ろ足	**ushiroashi**	a hind leg, paw

The bottom portion is not 又.

9 ＇ ⺁ ⼻ ⼻ ⾏ ⾏ 祥 後 後

---

89 食

food; eating; to eat

ショク SHOKU　*ジキ JIKI
た・べる ta(beru)
く・う ku(u)

The character 食 derived from a pictograph of a tall vessel filled with *food* and covered by a lid.

GR2　N5　AP

Example Sentences

1. 食後に薬を飲んでいる。
   Shokugo ni kusuri o nonde iru.
   I take my medication <u>after meals</u>.

2. 今夜は月食が見られる。
   Konya wa gesshoku ga mirareru.
   We can see <u>a lunar eclipse</u> tonight.

3. 今晩は、何を食べようか。
   Konban wa, nani o tabeyō ka.
   What <u>shall we have to eat</u> this evening?

4. 蚊に食われてかゆい。
   Ka ni kuwarete kayui.
   I've <u>been bitten</u> by a mosquito and it's itchy.

5. 彼は厳格な菜食主義者だ。
   Kare wa genkaku na saishoku shugisha da.
   He is a strict <u>vegetarian</u>.

Common Compounds and Phrases

食後	**shokugo**	after meals; after eating
食事	**shokuji**	a meal; dining
食欲	**shokuyoku**	an appetite
定食	**teishoku**	a set-course meal
朝食	**chōshoku**	breakfast
食べ放題	**tabehōdai**	eating as much as one likes
菜食主義者	**saishoku shugisha**	a vegetarian

The eighth and ninth strokes connect.

9 ノ 人 𠆢 今 今 今 食 食 食

90 前

ゼン ZEN
まえ mae

**before;
the front**

The character 前 combines *boat* 月, *foot* ⺌ and *sword* リ. From the idea of cutting off the rope and pushing off from shore comes the meaning *advance*, which evolved to *before*.

GR2 N5 AP

Example Sentences

1. 前回はいつお越しになりましたか。
   Zenkai wa itsu okoshi ni narimashita ka.
   When was <u>the last time</u> you came?

2. その人とは前に会ったことがある。
   Sono hito to wa mae ni atta koto ga aru.
   I've met that person <u>before</u>.

3. 駅前にタクシー乗り場がある。
   Ekimae ni takushii noriba ga aru.
   There is a taxi stand <u>in front of</u> the station.

4. ラーメンを二人前出前して下さい。
   Rāmen o nininmae demae shite kudasai.
   Could I have <u>two bowls</u> of *ramen* <u>delivered</u>, please?

5. そのTシャツ後ろ前じゃない。
   Sono T-shatsu ushiromae ja nai.
   You have that T-shirt on <u>back to front</u>, don't you?

Common Compounds and Phrases

前回	**zenkai**	the last occasion
五日前	**itsuka-mae**	five days ago
直前	**chokuzen**	immediately before
駅前	**ekimae**	in front of (outside) a station
二人前	**nininmae**	two portions
出前	**demae**	a restaurant delivery service
後ろ前	**ushiromae**	back to front

The last stroke ends with a hook.

9 ` ⺍ ⺌ 广 广 首 首 前 前

前

91 南

ナン NAN　*ナ NA
みなみ minami

south

The character 南 can be thought of as *ten* 十 houses with *plants* ⺀ growing *inside* 冂, a reference to villages in *southern* areas.

GR2 N5 AP

Example Sentences

1. ペンギンはもともと南極の鳥です。
   Pengin wa motomoto nankyoku no tori desu.
   Penguins are from <u>Antarctica</u>.

2. 沖縄は日本の南西地方です。
   Okinawa wa Nippon no nansei chihō desu.
   Okinawa occupies the <u>southwestern</u> region of Japan.

3. 東南アジアの島でのんびり休暇を楽しんだ。
   Tōnan Ajia no shima de nonbiri kyūka o tanoshinda.
   I enjoyed my holiday relaxing on an island in <u>Southeast-Asia</u>.

4. 夜空に南十字星が輝いていた。
   Yozora ni minami jūjisei ga kagayaite ita.
   <u>The Southern Cross</u> shone in the night sky.

5. 南向きで2DKの部屋を探しています。
   Minami-muki de 2DK no heya o sagashite imasu.
   I'm looking for an apartment with two rooms and a kitchen-dining area, <u>facing the south</u>.

Common Compounds and Phrases

南極	**nankyoku**	the Antarctic; the South Pole
南西	**nansei**	southwest
東南	**tōnan**	southeast
南北	**nanboku**	north and south
南向き	**minami-muki**	facing south
南太平洋	**minami taiheiyō**	the South Pacific
南十字星	**minami jūjisei**	the Southern Cross

The bottom portion is not 半. End the fourth stroke with a hook.

9 一 十 广 冇 内 甪 南 南 南

南

92 高

コウ KŌ
たか・い taka(i)
たか・める taka(meru)

high; to increase;
to raise

GR2 N5 AP

The character 高 depicts a *high* lookout.

Example Sentences

1. 電車の中で女子高生が騒いでいた。
   Densha no naka de joshi kōsei ga sawaide ita.
   <u>Some senior high school girls</u> were making a commotion on the train.

2. あの人はいつも高圧的な態度をとる。
   Ano hito wa itsumo kōatsuteki na taido o toru.
   He is always <u>very overbearing</u>.

3. このビルは日本一高いビルです。
   Kono biru wa Nihonichi takai biru desu.
   This building is <u>the tallest in Japan</u>.

4. 口座の残高を教えて下さい。
   Kōza no zandaka o oshiete kudasai.
   Please tell me <u>the balance</u> of my account.

5. 彼はこの映画に出て、評判を高めた。
   Kare wa kono eiga ni dete, hyōban o takameta.
   His appearance in this movie <u>has added</u> to his reputation.

Common Compounds and Phrases

高校生	**kōkōsei**	a senior high-school student
高速道路	**kōsoku dōro**	an expressway; a freeway
最高	**saikō**	maximum; best; great
高価	**kōka**	high priced
高級	**kōkyū**	high-grade / class
背が高い	**se ga takai**	to be tall in stature
高山	**Takayama**	Takayama (a place, name)

The 口 above is larger than the one below. End the seventh stroke with a hook.

10 ` 亠 亠 亠 古 古 亨 高 高 高 高

高

93 校

コウ KŌ

a school

The character 校 combines 木 *tree* and 交 *a person sitting cross-legged*, and can be thought of as a place where people sit and study; i.e., a *school.*

GR1 N5 AP

Example Sentences

1. 希望の高校に合格した。
   Kibō no kōkō ni gōkaku shita.
   I was accepted into the <u>high school</u> I wanted to go to.

2. 一年間予備校に通った。
   Ichinenkan yobikō ni kayotta.
   I attended <u>a prep school</u> for one year.

3. 明日中に校正してください。
   Ashita-jū ni kōsei shite kudasai.
   Please <u>proofread</u> this by the end of tomorrow.

4. 彼は海軍の将校になった。
   Kare wa kaigun no shōkō ni natta.
   He became a naval <u>officer</u>.

5. 小学校のとなりに住んでいる。
   Shōgakkō no tonari ni sunde iru.
   I live next door to <u>an elementary school</u>.

Common Compounds and Phrases

高等学校	**kōtō gakkō**	a senior high school
予備校	**yobikō**	a preparatory (prep) school
小学校	**shōgakkō**	an elementary school
下校	**gekō**	going home from school
校門	**kōmon**	a school gate
校正	**kōsei**	proofreading
初校	**shokō**	first proofs

End the last stroke firmly.

10 ー 十 才 木 木 术 校 校 校 校

校

94 時

ジ JI
とき toki

time; hour

The character 時 combines 日 *sun* and 寺 *a place of work*, which suggests *moving the hands and feet to work*, hence the idea of continuous motion and by association, *time*.
GR2 N5 AP

Example Sentences

1. ちょっとお時間ありますか。
   Chotto ojikan arimasu ka.
   Do you have <u>a moment</u>?

2. 北京と東京の時差は何時間ですか。
   Pekin to Tōkyō no jisa wa nanjikan desu ka.
   <u>How many hours</u>' <u>time difference</u> is there between Beijing and Tōkyō?

3. 当時を知る人はおじいさんだけです。
   Tōji o shiru hito wa ojiisan dake desu.
   Only grandfather knows what life was like <u>then</u>.

4. うちの主人は時々夕食を作る。
   Uchi no shujin wa tokidoki yūshoku o tsukuru.
   My husband <u>sometimes</u> makes dinner.

5. いらいらして何度も時計を見た。
   Ira ira shite nando mo tokei o mita.
   He kept glancing impatiently at <u>his watch</u>.

Common Compounds and Phrases

時間	**jikan**	(the) time; an hour; a lesson
時差	**jisa**	a time difference
当時	**tōji**	at that time; in those days
時速	**jisoku**	speed per hour
五時十分	**goji juppun**	5:10; ten past five
時々	**tokidoki**	sometimes; every time
*時計	**tokei**	a clock; a watch

End the ninth stroke with a hook.

10 丨 冂 冂 日 日一 日十 旷 旷 時 時

時

95 書

ショ SHO
か・く ka(ku)

to write; writing

The character 書 combines *hand holding a brush* 聿 and *thing* 日 (a simple form of 者), to suggest *writing* something with a brush.
GR2 N5 AP

Example Sentences

1. 一緒に書店に行こうか。
   Issho ni shoten ni ikō ka.
   Let's go to the <u>bookshop</u> together.

2. 申込書を書くように言われた。
   Mōshikomisho o kaku yō ni iwareta.
   I was asked <u>to fill in</u> an <u>application form</u>.

3. 書道の先生に書いていただいた。
   Shodō no sensei ni kaite itadaita.
   I <u>had</u> my <u>Japanese calligraphy</u> teacher <u>write</u> it for me.

4. 漢字で名前を書いて下さい。
   Katakana de namae o kaite kudasai.
   Please <u>write</u> your name in *kanji*.

5. 小学校時代の友達から葉書が届いた。
   Shōgakkō jidai no tomodachi kara hagaki ga todoita.
   I had a <u>postcard</u> from a friend from elementary school days.

Common Compounds and Phrases

書店	**shoten**	a bookstore
申込書	**mōshikomi-sho**	a written application
書道	**shodō**	oriental calligraphy
書類	**shorui**	documents
辞書	**jisho**	a dictionary
読書	**dokusho**	reading (books)
手書き	**tegaki**	handwriting; one's hand
葉書	**hagaki**	a postcard

The second stroke is longer than those above and below it.

10 フ ﾌ ｺ ヨ 聿 聿 書 書 書 書

書

96 魚

ギョ GYO

うお uo　さかな sakana

fish

The character 魚 derived from a pictograph of a *fish* on its side, mouth pointing upwards.

GR2　N5　AP

Example Sentences

1. 金魚を五匹飼っています。
   Kingyo o gohiki katte imasu.
   I have five pet <u>goldfish</u>.

2. 魚座の人はどんな性格ですか。
   Uoza no hito wa donna seikaku desu ka.
   What kind of personalities do '<u>Pisces</u>' have?

3. 近所の魚屋でまぐろを買った。
   Kinjo no <u>sakanaya</u> de maguro o katta.
   I bought some tuna at the local <u>fish shop</u>.

4. 刺身もいいけど、焼き魚も好きだ。
   Sashimi mo ii kedo, **yakizakana** mo suki da.
   Raw fish is fine, but I like <u>grilled fish</u>, too.

5. 魚偏の漢字はたくさんある。
   Sakana-hen no kanji wa takusan aru.
   There are many Chinese characters with <u>the *sakana* radical</u>.

Common Compounds and Phrases

金魚	**kingyo**	a goldfish
熱帯魚	**nettaigyo**	a tropical fish
魚座	**uoza**	the Fishes; Pisces
魚市場	**uo-ichiba**	a fish market
魚屋	**sakana-ya**	a fishmonger; a fish shop
焼き魚	**yakizakana**	roast fish
魚釣り	**sakana-tsuri**	fishing

Note that there are four dots.

11　丿　ク　ケ　台　乃　角　負　角　魚　魚　魚

魚

EXERCISE 8 (85 – 96)

A. Give readings for the following.

1. 何時 _____
2. 食べる _____
3. 東北 _____
4. 南口 _____
5. 長年 _____
6. 店 _____
7. 後ろ _____
8. 女子高生 _____
9. 食べた後 _____
10. 書いて下さい _____

B. Write in kanji and kana.

1. a goldfish _____
2. handwriting _____
3. the latter half _____
4. the main store _____
5. a company president _____
6. a bookstore _____
7. three days before/earlier _____
8. 12:45 _____

C. Fill in the appropriate kanji.

1. しょくぜん _____ _____ (before meals)
2. あしがながい _____ が _____ い (to have long legs)
3. いとぐち _____ _____ (a beginning; a clue)
4. たちぐい _____ ち _____ い (to eat while standing)
5. てんちょう _____ _____ (a store manager)
6. したがき _____ き (a rough copy)
7. げっしょく _____ _____ (a lunar eclipse)
8. こざかな _____ _____ (a small fish)
9. しょうがっこう _____ _____ _____ (an elementary school)
10. たかやま _____ _____ (Takayama)
11. みせにはいる _____ に _____ る (to enter a store)
12. のちに _____ に (later on)
13. ににんまえ _____ _____ _____ (two portions)
14. こんご _____ _____ (from now on)
15. たべた _____ べた (ate)
16. うしろあし _____ ろ _____ (a hind leg)
17. しちじはん _____ _____ _____ (7:30)

97 週 シュウ SHŪ

week

The character 週 originally meant *going* 辶 around a *field* 周, i.e., making a circuit. This came to mean *cycle of time*, and then *week*.

GR2 N5 AP

Example Sentences

1. 一週間はあっという間だ。
   Isshūkan wa atto iu ma da.
   A <u>week</u> passes in no time.

2. 週刊誌を電車の中で読んだ。
   Shūkanshi o densha no naka de yonda.
   I read <u>a weekly magazine</u> in the train.

3. この会社は週休二日です。
   Kono kaisha wa shūkyū futsuka desu.
   This company has <u>a five-day working week</u>.

4. 週末には何をするつもりですか。
   Shūmatsu ni wa nani o suru tsumori desu ka.
   Do you have any plans for <u>the weekend</u>?

5. 来週はちょっと忙しいですね。
   Raishū wa chotto isogashii desu ne.
   We're going to be a little busy <u>next week</u>, aren't we?

Common Compounds and Phrases

一週間	**isshūkan**	a week
週刊誌	**shūkanshi**	a weekly (magazine)
週末	**shūmatsu**	a weekend
来週	**raishū**	next week
毎週	**maishū**	every week; weekly
先週	**senshū**	last week
週給	**shūkyū**	weekly pay

End the second stroke with a hook.

11 丿 冂 冃 冃 冎 冉 用 周 周 凋 週 週

週

---

98 飲 イン IN の・む no(mu)

to drink

The character 飲 combines 食, which originally suggested *pouring sake or water into a pot* with 欠, *a person with an open mouth*. From this came the idea of *drinking* with one's mouth open wide.

GR3 N5 AP

Example Sentences

1. いろいろな飲料水が売られている。
   Iroiro na inryōsui ga urarete iru.
   Various kinds of <u>drinking water</u> are being sold.

2. あの人は飲酒運転で逮捕された。
   Ano hito wa inshu unten de taiho sareta.
   He was arrested for <u>drunk driving</u>.

3. この水は、飲めますか。
   Kono mizu wa, nomemasu ka.
   Is this water <u>good for drinking</u>?

4. 一気に水を飲み干した。
   Ikki ni mizu o nomihoshita.
   I <u>drank</u> the water <u>down</u> in one gulp.

5. 医者に飲み薬をもらった。
   Isha ni nomigusuri o moratta.
   I got <u>some medicine</u> from the doctor.

Common Compounds and Phrases

飲料水	**inryōsui**	drinking water
飲酒	**inshu**	drinking alcohol
飲食店	**inshokuten**	a restaurant
飲み薬	**nomigusuri**	an internal medicine
飲み物	**nomimono**	a drink; liquor
飲み水	**nomimizu**	drinking water
湯飲み茶わん	**yunomi-jawan**	a teacup

End the second stroke firmly.

12 丿 𠆢 𠆢 今 今 今 食 食 食 飮 飲 飲

飲

99 間

カン KAN　ケン KEN
あいだ aida　ま ma

interval;
room; pause

The character 間 combines *gate* 門 and *sun* 日, to indicate light shining through a *space between* the gates.

GR2　N5　AP

Example Sentences

1. 時間がたつのは速いね。
   Jikan ga tatsu no wa hayai ne.
   <u>Time</u> flies, doesn't it?

2. 滞在期間を延長したい。
   Taizai kikan o enchō shitai.
   I want to extend the <u>duration</u> of my stay.

3. 母は隣の人とよく世間話をする。
   Haha wa tonari no hito to yoku seken-banashi o suru.
   My mother often <u>chats</u> with the person next door.

4. 会社は神田と銀座の間にあります。
   Kaisha wa Kanda to Ginza no aida ni arimasu.
   The company is located <u>between</u> Kanda and the Ginza.

5. 間に合いましたか。
   Ma ni aimashita ka.
   Did you <u>make it in time</u>?

Common Compounds and Phrases

期間	**kikan**	a term; a period of time
世間	**seken**	the world; society
人間	**ningen**	a human being
居間	**ima**	a living / sitting room
昼間	**hiruma**	the day; the daytime
間違い	**machigai**	a mistake; an accident
間に合う	**maniau**	to be in time; to be useful

End the first stroke firmly, and the sixth stroke with a hook.

12 丨 冂 冂 冂 冂 門 門 門 門 問 間 間

間

---

100 道

ドウ DŌ
みち michi

road; way

The character 道 combines *go* 辶 and *head, main* 首 to suggest going along a main path; i.e. a *road*.

GR2　N5　AP

Example Sentences

1. その店は国道246号線沿いにあります。
   Sono mise wa kokudō 246 gōsen-zoi ni arimasu.
   That store is located on <u>Highway</u> 246.

2. そんなこと道理に合わないよ。
   Sonna koto dōri ni awanai yo.
   That's a load of <u>nonsense</u>!

3. 道場は武道の稽古をするところです。
   Dōjō wa budō no keiko o suru tokoro desu.
   A *dojo* is a place to practice <u>martial arts</u>.

4. この道をまっすぐ行って下さい。
   Kono michi o massugu itte kudasai.
   Please go straight along this <u>street</u>.

5. 駅への近道を教えてください。
   Eki e no chikamichi o oshiete kudasai.
   Please tell me a <u>shortcut</u> to the station.

Common Compounds and Phrases

国道	**kokudō**	a national road (highway)
道理	**dōri**	reason; common sense
武道	**budō**	the martial arts
道具	**dōgu**	an implement; a tool; furniture
道路	**dōro**	a road; a street; a highway
北海道	**Hokkaidō**	Hokkaido (a place)
近道	**chikamichi**	a shortcut

The third stroke is longer than those below it, and the eleventh stroke is one single action.

12 丶 丷 丷 圵 产 首 首 首 首 首 道 道

道

101 買

バイ BAI
か・う ka(u)

to buy

The character 買 combines *net* 罒 and *shells* 貝. Since shells were used for money, netting lots of shells meant being able to *buy* things.

GR2 N5 AP

Example Sentences

1. A 社が B 社を買収した。
   A-sha ga B-sha o baishū shita.
   Company A <u>bought out</u> Company B.

2. ちょっと買い物に行ってきます。
   Chotto kaimono ni itte kimasu.
   I'm just going to do a bit of <u>shopping</u>.

3. 部長は彼の実績を買っている。
   Buchō wa kare no jisseki o katte iru.
   The department chief is <u>impressed with</u> his performance.

4. 彼は損な役を買って出た。
   Kare wa son na yaku o katte deta.
   He <u>volunteered for</u> the thankless job.

5. 買い占めによって株式市場は混乱した。
   Kaishime ni yotte kabushiki shijo wa konran shita.
   The stock market was in a frenzy with <u>the panic buying</u> of stocks.

Common Compounds and Phrases

買収	**baishū**	to purchase; to buy up (out)
売買	**baibai**	buying and selling; trade
買い物	**kaimono**	shopping; a purchase
買い出し	**kaidashi**	going out to buy
買い手	**kaite**	a buyer
買い占め	**kaishime**	to buy up; to corner the market
お買い得品	**okaidokuhin**	a good bargain

The top portion is not 四. End the last stroke firmly.

12 `丶 冂 冂 冂 四 四 罒 罒 胃 罒 冒 胃 買 買

買

---

102 新

シン SHIN
あたら・しい atara(shii)
あら・た ara(ta)　*にい nii

new

The character 新 can be thought of as using an *axe* 斤 to cut into a *standing* 立 *tree* 木, leaving a *fresh* or *new* mark.

GR2 N5 AP

Example Sentences

1. 今朝の新聞読んだ？
   Kesa no shinbun yonda?
   Have you read this morning's <u>newspaper</u>?

2. 新年に新しい手帳を使おう。
   Shinnen ni atarashii techō o tsukaō.
   I'll use my <u>new</u> daily planner for <u>the new year</u>.

3. ビザを更新する時期になった。
   Bisa o kōshin suru jiki ni natta.
   It's time <u>to renew</u> my visa.

4. あの会社は人事を一新した。
   Ano kaisha wa jinji o isshin shita.
   That firm has <u>reorganized</u> its personnel.

5. 新たな問題が起きた。
   Arata na mondai ga okita.
   A <u>new</u> problem has come up.

Common Compounds and Phrases

新聞	**shinbun**	a newspaper; a journal
新年	**shinnen**	the New Year; a new year
更新	**kōshin**	renewal; replacement; update
新鮮	**shinsen**	fresh
最新	**saishin**	the newest; the latest
新幹線	**shinkansen**	the *Shinkansen*; the Bullet Train
*新妻	**niizuma**	a newly married woman

The seventh stroke ends firmly, and the eleventh stroke tapers off.

13 `丶 亠 六 立 立 辛 辛 辛 亲 新 新 新

新

103 電

デン DEN

electricity

The character 電 shows *rain* 雨 with a flash of *lightning* 电 to represent *electricity*.

GR2 N5 AP

Example Sentences

1. 先月の電気代は高かった。
   Sengetsu no <u>denkidai</u> wa takakatta.
   Last month, the <u>electricity bill</u> was high.

2. 終電に間に合うかな。
   <u>Shūden</u> ni maniau ka na.
   I wonder if I'll make <u>the last train</u>.

3. 結婚式に行けないので祝電を打った。
   Kekkonshiki ni ikenai node <u>shukuden</u> o utta.
   As I couldn't attend the wedding reception, I sent <u>a congratulatory telegram</u>.

4. 暗闇に電光が走った。
   Kurayami ni <u>denkō</u> ga hashitta.
   <u>Lightning</u> flashed in the darkness.

5. このエリアは台風の影響で停電した。
   Kono eria wa taifū no eikyō de <u>teiden shita</u>.
   There was a <u>blackout</u> in this area because of the typhoon.

Common Compounds and Phrases

電気	**denki**	electricity; an electric light
電車	**densha**	a train
終電	**shūden**	the last train (of the day)
電力	**denryoku**	electric power
電池	**denchi**	a battery; a dry cell
停電	**teiden**	a power failure
祝電	**shukuden**	a congratulatory telegram
電光	**denkō**	lightning

The last stroke ends with a hook.

13 　一　厂　厂　雨　雨　雨　雨　雨　雨　雪　雪　雪　電

電

---

104 話

ワ WA
はなし hanashi
はな・す hana(su)

story;
to speak

The character 話 combines *words* 言 and *tongue* 舌 to give the meaning of *speak*.

GR2 N5 AP

Example Sentences

1. 車内で携帯電話で話すのは迷惑だ。
   Shanai de <u>keitai denwa</u> de <u>hanasu</u> no wa meiwaku da.
   People <u>talking</u> on <u>cell-phones</u> on the train annoy me.

2. 英会話学校に一年間通った。
   <u>Eikaiwa</u> gakkō ni ichinenkan kayotta.
   I attended <u>English conversation</u> classes for a year.

3. 「古事記」というのは日本の神話です。
   'Kojiki' to iu no wa Nihon no <u>shinwa</u> desu.
   The *Kojiki* is a collection of <u>Japanese myths</u>.

4. 彼は話のわかる人だよ。
   Kare wa <u>hanashi</u> no wakaru hito da yo.
   He is one who <u>understands the situation</u>.

5. 話し合いで解決しましょう。
   <u>Hanashiai</u> de kaiketsu shimashō.
   Let's <u>talk the matter over</u> to resolve it.

Common Compounds and Phrases

携帯電話	**keitai denwa**	a cell-phone; a mobile phone
英会話	**eikaiwa**	English conversation
神話	**shinwa**	a myth; mythology
話題	**wadai**	a topic; a subject
世話	**sewa**	assistance; to take care of
昔話	**mukashi-banashi**	a legend; a folk tale
話し合い	**hanashiai**	a consultation; an agreement; a discussion

The eighth stroke tapers down from right to left.

13 　丶　亠　亍　言　言　言　言　訂　話　話　話　話

話

105 駅

エキ EKI

station

Originally 驛, this character is a combination of *horse* 馬 and 睪, an ideograph meaning to *keep guard over prisoners*. Hence, a reference to *relay stations* where horses were changed. From this, the present meaning of *station* has developed.
GR3 N5 AP

Example Sentences

1. 次の駅で降ります。
   Tsugi no eki de orimasu.
   I'm getting off at the next <u>station</u>.

2. 始発駅なら座れます。
   Shihatsueki nara suwaremasu.
   If you use <u>the first station on the line</u>, you can get a seat.

3. 駅長に最終電車の出発時刻を聞いた。
   Ekichō ni saishū densha no shuppatsu jikoku o kiita.
   I asked <u>the station master</u> what time the last train left.

4. 東京駅は一日100万人以上もの乗客が利用する。
   Tōkyō-eki wa ichinichi 100 mannin ijō mo no jōkyaku ga riyō suru.
   More than one million passengers a day use <u>Tokyo Station</u>.

Common Compounds and Phrases

始発駅	**shihatsueki**	the first station (on a line)
駅長	**ekichō**	a stationmaster
各駅停車	**kakueki teisha**	a local train
駅員	**ekiin**	a station employee
駅弁	**ekiben**	a box lunch sold at stations
終着駅	**shūchakueki**	a terminal station; the last stop
東京駅	**Tōkyō-eki**	Tokyo Station

Be careful with the dots.

14 ｜ 冂 冖 厂 丆 馬 馬 馬 馬 馬 馬 馬 駅 駅 駅

駅

---

106 語

ゴ GO
かた・る kata(ru)
かた・らう kata(rau)

word; to talk

The character 語 can be thought of as a *mouth* 口 saying *five* 五 *words* 言, a reference to *talking*.

GR2 N5 AP

Example Sentences

1. 中国語を習い始めた。
   Chūgokugo o naraihajimeta.
   I've started learning <u>Chinese</u>.

2. あの人は語学力を買われている。
   Ano hito wa gogakuryoku o kawarete iru.
   He is highly valued for his <u>linguistic skill</u>.

3. 日本語には外来語がたくさん使われています。
   Nihongo ni wa gairaigo ga takusan tsukawarete imasu.
   Many <u>foreign loanwords</u> are used in <u>Japanese</u>.

4. 寝る前に父はおもしろい話を語ってくれた。
   Neru mae ni chichi wa omoshiroi hanashi o katatte kureta.
   My father <u>used to tell me</u> interesting stories at bed time.

5. 久しぶりに古い友達と語らった。
   Hisashiburi ni furui tomodachi to kataratta.
   I <u>chatted</u> with an old friend I hadn't seen for some time.

Common Compounds and Phrases

中国語	**Chūgokugo**	Chinese; Mandarin
日本語	**Nihongo**	the Japanese language
外来語	**gairaigo**	a loanword; a borrowing
外国語	**gaikokugo**	a foreign language
敬語	**keigo**	honorific language
語学力	**gogakuryoku**	linguistic ability
物語	**monogatari**	a story; a tale

Don't confuse 語 with 話.

14 ｀ ｀ 二 三 三 言 言 言 訂 訂 評 語 語 語 語

語

107 読
to read

ドク DOKU　トク TOKU
*トウ TŌ
よ・む yo(mu)

The character 読 combines *sell* 売 and *words* 言, perhaps referring to books, which are *read*.

GR2　N5　AP

Example Sentences

1. 読書をする人が減ってきている。
Dokusho o suru hito ga hette kite iru.
Fewer and fewer people enjoy reading these days.

2. 新聞を三紙読んでいる。
Shinbun o sanshi yonde iru.
I read three newspapers.

3. 音読みと訓読み、両方書いてください。
Onyomi to kunyomi, ryōhō kaite kudasai.
Please write both *on* and *kun* readings of the character.

4. 行間を読むのが難しい。
Gyōkan o yomu no ga muzukashii.
It's hard to read between the lines.

5. 彼は読みが深い。
Kare wa yomi ga fukai.
He possesses keen insight.

Common Compounds and Phrases

読書	**dokusho**	reading
読解力	**dokkairyoku**	reading comprehension
音読	**ondoku**	reading aloud
読み物	**yomimono**	reading matter
音読み	**on-yomi**	an *on* (Chinese) reading
訓読み	**kun-yomi**	a *kun* (native Japanese) reading
*句読点	**kutōten**	a punctuation mark

The thirteenth stroke tapers off, and the last stroke ends with a hook. The eighth stroke is longer than the tenth.

14 ｀ ｀ ⺀ ⻗ 訁 言 言 計 詰 読 読 読 読 読

読

---

108 聞
to hear; to listen

ブン BUN　モン MON
き・く ki(ku)
き・こえる ki(koeru)

The character 聞 combines *gate* 門 and *ear* 耳, and suggests *listening* at a gate.

GR2　N5　AP

Example Sentences

1. 見聞を広めるために旅行している。
Kenbun o hiromeru tame ni ryokō shite iru.
I'm traveling so as to add to my experience.

2. これは前代未聞の出来事だ。
Kore wa zendai mimon no dekigoto da.
This is an unprecedented event.

3. 満員電車で音楽を聞いている人が多い。
Man'in densha de ongaku o kiite iru hito ga ōi.
Many people listen to music on the crowded trains.

4. あまり人聞きの悪いことは言わないでよ。
Amari hitogiki no warui koto wa iwanai de yo.
You shouldn't bring up such gossipy things!

5. 山でカッコーの声が聞こえた。
Yama de kakkō no koe ga kikoeta.
I heard cuckoos calling in the mountains.

Common Compounds and Phrases

見聞	**kenbun**	information; knowledge
風聞	**fūbun**	a report; a rumor
前代未聞	**zendai mimon**	unprecedented
聴聞会	**chōmonkai**	a public hearing
人聞きが悪い	**hitogiki ga warui**	scandalous
聞き手	**kikite**	a listener
盗み聞き	**nusumigiki**	eavesdropping

The second last stroke does not protrude.

14 丨 ⺆ ⻔ ⻔ ⻔ ⻔ 門 門 門 門 門 聞 聞 聞

聞

EXERCISE 9 (97 – 108)

A. Give the readings for the following.

1. 新しくない ＿＿＿＿＿＿＿＿＿＿
2. 外国語 ＿＿＿＿＿＿＿＿＿＿
3. 国道 ＿＿＿＿＿＿＿＿＿＿
4. 駅ビル ＿＿＿＿＿＿＿＿＿＿
5. 話している ＿＿＿＿＿＿＿＿＿＿
6. 電気 ＿＿＿＿＿＿＿＿＿＿
7. 語る ＿＿＿＿＿＿＿＿＿＿
8. 長い間 ＿＿＿＿＿＿＿＿＿＿
9. 先週 ＿＿＿＿＿＿＿＿＿＿
10. 飲みたい ＿＿＿＿＿＿＿＿＿＿

B. Write in kanji and kana.

1. Japanese (language) ＿＿＿＿＿＿＿＿＿＿
2. a telephone ＿＿＿＿＿＿＿＿＿＿
3. two weeks ＿＿＿＿＿＿＿＿＿＿
4. going out to buy something ＿＿＿＿＿＿＿＿
5. the new year ＿＿＿＿＿＿＿＿＿＿
6. conversation ＿＿＿＿＿＿＿＿＿＿
7. a human being ＿＿＿＿＿＿＿＿＿＿
8. the Chinese language; Mandarin ＿＿＿＿＿＿＿
9. next week ＿＿＿＿＿＿＿＿＿＿
10. (the pastime of) reading ＿＿＿＿＿＿＿＿

C. Add kanji to the following according to the meanings provided.

1. ＿＿＿＿＿＿＿（じかん）がない (to have no time)
2. ＿＿＿＿＿＿＿（でんしゃ）で ＿＿＿（く）る (to come by train)
3. ＿＿＿（みち）で ＿＿＿（あ）う (to meet someone in the street)
4. ＿＿＿＿＿＿＿（しんぶん）を ＿＿＿（よ）む (to read a newspaper)
5. ＿＿＿（はなし）を ＿＿＿（き）く (to listen to someone talking)
6. ＿＿＿＿＿＿＿（まいしゅう）＿＿＿（い）きます。 (I go every week.)
7. ＿＿＿（えき）の ＿＿＿（まえ）に (in front of the station)
8. ＿＿＿（みず）を ＿＿＿（の）む (to drink some water)
9. よく＿＿＿（き）こえない (to not be able to hear well)
10. ＿＿＿（やす）く＿＿＿（か）う (to buy something cheaply)

Review 3 (1 – 108)

A. Give the readings for the following.

1. 長雨 ＿＿＿＿＿＿＿＿＿＿
2. 話を語る ＿＿＿＿＿＿＿＿＿＿
3. 読んでいる間に ＿＿＿＿＿＿＿＿
4. 電気 ＿＿＿＿＿＿＿＿＿＿
5. 空間 ＿＿＿＿＿＿＿＿＿＿
6. 外来語 ＿＿＿＿＿＿＿＿＿＿
7. 六週間 ＿＿＿＿＿＿＿＿＿＿
8. 四月二十日に出る ＿＿＿＿＿＿＿
9. 新しい車 ＿＿＿＿＿＿＿＿＿＿
10. 聞こえない ＿＿＿＿＿＿＿＿＿＿
11. 十分の三 ＿＿＿＿＿＿＿＿＿＿
12. 山道を下る ＿＿＿＿＿＿＿＿＿＿
13. 入り口の前 ＿＿＿＿＿＿＿＿＿＿
14. 安く買えた ＿＿＿＿＿＿＿＿＿＿
15. 話し中 ＿＿＿＿＿＿＿＿＿＿

B. Write in English.

1. ゴルフが下手である ＿＿＿＿＿＿＿
2. スペイン語 ＿＿＿＿＿＿＿＿＿＿
3. 買い出し ＿＿＿＿＿＿＿＿＿＿
4. CD を聞く ＿＿＿＿＿＿＿＿＿＿

5. 飲み水 ＿＿＿＿＿＿＿＿＿＿
6. 女の子が生まれる ＿＿＿＿＿＿＿
7. 会話 ＿＿＿＿＿＿＿＿＿＿
8. 電話で話す ＿＿＿＿＿＿＿＿＿＿
9. 九日間 ＿＿＿＿＿＿＿＿＿＿
10. 男子五人 ＿＿＿＿＿＿＿＿＿＿
11. 先々週 ＿＿＿＿＿＿＿＿＿＿
12. 駅長 ＿＿＿＿＿＿＿＿＿＿
13. 新聞 ＿＿＿＿＿＿＿＿＿＿
14. 来週 ＿＿＿＿＿＿＿＿＿＿

C. Write in Japanese.

1. a store in Roppongi ＿＿＿＿＿＿＿
2. to leave from the southern exit ＿＿＿＿＿＿
3. all day long ＿＿＿＿＿＿＿＿＿＿
4. today's newspaper ＿＿＿＿＿＿＿＿
5. 300,000 people ＿＿＿＿＿＿＿＿
6. under that tree ＿＿＿＿＿＿＿＿
7. 3:30 P.M. ＿＿＿＿＿＿＿＿＿＿
8. thirty minutes ＿＿＿＿＿＿＿＿
9. a secondhand car ＿＿＿＿＿＿＿＿
10. the right hand ＿＿＿＿＿＿＿＿

Review 3 (1 – 108) *continued*

11. heaven _____
12. your father _____
13. draft beer _____
14. this week _____
15. early summer rain _____

D. Add kana to the following, using the hints.

1. 見 _____ (is watching, looking at)
2. 白 _____ (was white)
3. 足 _____ (is not enough)
4. 入 _____ (entered)
5. 学 _____ (learned)
6. 会 _____ (to want to meet)
7. 出 _____ (to go out, leave)
8. 立 _____ (was standing)
9. 買 _____ (to buy)
10. 分 _____ (to divide; to share)
11. _____ 母 _____ (mother)
12. 言 _____ (said, was saying)
13. 生 _____ (to be alive, living)
14. 来 _____ (to come, will come)
15. 行 _____ (went)

E. Match the following with their readings.

1. 買い手 ( )	a. しんねん
2. 話が上手 ( )	b. はなしがじょうず
3. 一月八日 ( )	c. にゅうがくした
4. 週休二日 ( )	d. ちゅうごくご
5. 山口駅 ( )	e. どにちやすみ
6. 新たに ( )	f. いんしょくてん
7. 三ヶ月 ( )	g. ななせんねんまえ
8. 中間 ( )	h. しゅうきゅうふつか
9. 小田先生 ( )	i. いちがつようか
10. 大金 ( )	j. にじかんはん
11. 読書 ( )	k. おだせんせい
12. 二時間半 ( )	l. かいて
13. 新年 ( )	m. ちゅうかん
14. 中国語 ( )	n. たいきん
15. 飲食店 ( )	o. やまぐちえき
16. 七千年前 ( )	p. あらたに
17. 人間 ( )	q. にんげん
18. 入学した ( )	r. さんかげつ
19. 話し手 ( )	s. どくしょ
20. 土日休み ( )	t. はなして

---

109 力

power

リキ RIKI リョク RYOKU
ちから chikara

The character 力 originally represented a *flexed arm*.

GR1 N4 AP

Example Sentences

1. このエンジンは150馬力ある。
   Kono enjin wa hyaku gojū bariki aru.
   This engine develops 150 horsepower.

2. あの人は権力を持っている。
   Ano hito wa kenryoku o motte iru.
   That person possesses power (influence).

3. 目的のために努力しよう。
   Mokuteki no tame ni doryoku shiyō.
   Let's strive towards our goal.

4. 彼には実力がある。
   Kare ni wa jitsuryoku ga aru.
   He has ability.

5. 体力には自信があります。
   Tairyoku ni wa jishin ga arimasu.
   I am confident of my physical strength.

Common Compounds and Phrases

馬力	**bariki**	horsepower; energy
力士	**rikishi**	a *sumo* wrestler
権力	**kenryoku**	power; authority
努力	**doryoku**	effort; labor
実力	**jitsuryoku**	competence, ability
体力	**tairyoku**	physical strength
力仕事	**chikara-shigoto**	manual labor

Don't confuse 力 with 九. The first stroke ends with a hook, and the second stroke tapers off.

2	フ 力				
力					

110 工

コウ KŌ　ク KU

an artisan;
construction

GR2　N4　AP

The character 工 depicts an ancient carpenter's tool, from which derived the meaning of *work*.

Example Sentences

1. 自動車工場を見学した。
   Jidōsha kōjō o kengaku shita.
   I visited an automobile factory.

2. その道は工事中で通れない。
   Sono michi wa kōjichū de tōrenai.
   You can't get through because they're fixing the road.

3. 伝統工芸品に興味があります。
   Dentō kōgeihin ni kyōmi ga arimasu.
   I'm interested in traditional handicrafts.

4. 大工さんに家の改築を頼もう。
   Daiku-san ni ie no kaichiku o tanomō.
   Let's hire a carpenter to do some alterations on the house.

5. それは人工真珠です。
   Sore wa jinkō shinju desu.
   Those are artificial pearls.

Common Compounds and Phrases

工場	**kōjō**	a factory; a plant
工事	**kōji**	construction work
工芸品	**kōgeihin**	craftwork
工業	**kōgyō**	industry
人工	**jinkō**	human skill / work
大工	**daiku**	a carpenter
工夫	**kufū**	figuring out; planning; a scheme

The last stroke is longer than the one above.

3　一 丁 工

工

111 才

サイ SAI

talent, ability;
years old

GR2　N2

The character 才 originally depicted a *dam in a river*. Its present meanings resulted from phonetic borrowing.

Example Sentences

1. この子は絵の才能がある。
   Kono ko wa e no sainō ga aru.
   This child has a talent for drawing.

2. モーツァルトは天才だった。
   Mōtsuaruto wa tensai datta.
   Mozart was a genius.

3. お酒は二十才（歳）になってから。
   Osake wa nijussai ni natte kara.
   The drinking age is twenty.

4. 彼は多才な人だ。
   Kare wa tasai na hito da.
   He is a person of many talents.

5. あの親は、子供を英才教育している。
   Ano oya wa, kodomo o eisai kyōiku shite iru.
   That couple are having their child specially tutored.

Common Compounds and Phrases

才能	**sainō**	ability
天才	**tensai**	a genius
二十才（歳）	**nijussai /**	twenty years old
	*hatachi	
多才	**tasai**	many talents
商才	**shōsai**	business ability
英才	**eisai**	talent; genius
青二才	**aonisai**	an inexperienced youth; a novice

The last stroke protrudes slightly.

3　一 十 才

才

112 夕

セキ SEKI
ゆう yū

evening

The character 夕 depicts the *crescent moon*, viewed during the *evening*.

GR1 N4 AP

Example Sentences

1. これは一朝一夕にできることではない。
   Kore wa itchō isseki ni dekiru koto de wa nai.
   This isn't <u>something</u> that can be <u>done overnight</u>.

2. 夕食は六時に始まります。
   Yūshoku wa rokuji ni hajimarimasu.
   <u>Dinner</u> will be at 6:00.

3. きのうは、夕刊が来なかった。
   Kinō wa, yūkan ga konakatta.
   Yesterday's <u>evening paper</u> never came.

4. 夕方は忙しい。
   Yūgata wa isogashii.
   I'm busy in <u>the evening</u>.

5. 夕焼けで空が真っ赤になる。
   Yūyake de sora ga makka ni naru.
   The sky turns bright red with <u>the afterglow of the setting sun</u>.

Common Compounds and Phrases

一朝一夕	**itchō isseki**	in one day; overnight
夕食	**yūshoku**	supper; dinner
夕刊	**yūkan**	an evening paper
夕方	**yūgata**	evening; the dusk
夕焼け	**yūyake**	an evening glow
夕立	**yūdachi**	an evening squall
朝夕	**asayū**	morning and evening; day and night

Leave a slight space between the first and third strokes.

3 ノ ク タ

夕

---

113 引

イン IN
ひ・く hi(ku)
ひ・ける hi(keru)

to pull; to attract;
to close

The character 引 combines *bow* 弓 and *string* | to suggest *pulling*.

GR2 N4 AP

Example Sentences

1. 引退したら、海外旅行をしたい。
   Intai shitara, kaigai ryokō o shitai.
   I want to travel overseas <u>when I retire</u>.

2. 彼は、強引にその計画を決めてしまった。
   Kare wa gōin ni sono keikaku o kimete shimatta.
   He <u>forced</u> the plans through.

3. 海の近くに引っ越したい。
   Umi no chikaku ni hikkoshitai.
   <u>I'd like to move</u> (to a house) near the sea.

4. 二割引きでCDプレーヤーを買った。
   Niwari-biki de CD purēyā o katta.
   I bought a CD player at <u>a 20 percent discount</u>.

5. 風邪をひいて、早引けしました。
   Kaze o hiite, hayabike shimashita.
   I caught a cold and <u>left the office early</u>.

Common Compounds and Phrases

引退	**intai**	retirement
強引	**gōin**	by force; forcibly
引越し	**hikkoshi**	house-moving
二割引き	**niwaribiki**	20 percent discount
引き出し	**hikidashi**	a drawer (of a desk); a withdrawal
取引	**torihiki**	business; a transaction
値引き	**nebiki**	a discount

End the last stroke firmly.

4 ⁊ ⁊ 弓 引

引

114 牛

ギュウ GYŪ
うし ushi

a cow; an ox

The character 牛 derived from a pictograph of a *cow's head and horns*, viewed from the front.

GR2 N4 AP

Example Sentences

1. 毎日、牛乳を飲んでいる。
   Mainichi, gyūnyū o nonde iru.
   I drink <u>milk</u> every day.

2. 牛肉があるので、今夜はすきやきにしよう。
   Gyūniku ga aru node, konya wa sukiyaki ni shiyō.
   Since we have some <u>beef</u>, let's eat *sukiyaki* tonight.

3. このバッグは牛革ですか。
   Kono baggu wa gyūkawa desu ka.
   Is this handbag <u>leather</u>?

4. 昨夜、子牛が生まれた。
   Yūbe, koushi ga umareta.
   <u>A calf</u> was born last night.

5. 私の田舎では、牛をたくさん飼っている。
   Watashi no inaka de wa, ushi o takusan katte iru.
   We have a lot of <u>cows</u> back where I come from in the country.

Common Compounds and Phrases

牛乳	**gyūnyū**	cow's milk
牛肉	**gyūniku**	beef
牛革	**gyūkawa**	cowhide
狂牛病	**kyōgyūbyō**	mad cow disease
乳牛	**nyūgyū**	a dairy cow
水牛	**suigyū**	a water buffalo
子牛	**koushi**	a calf

The third stroke is longer than the one above, and the last stroke protrudes.

4 ノ ⺧ 二 牛

牛

---

115 区

ク KU

a district; a ward

Originally written as 區, this character indicated three small *enclosures* within a larger one. The idea of *section* or *ward* derived from this.

GR3 N4

Example Sentences

1. あの双子はまったく区別がつかない。
   Ano futago wa mattaku kubetsu ga tsukanai.
   I <u>can't tell</u> those twins <u>apart</u>.

2. 彼女は港区に住んでいる。
   Kanojo wa Minato-ku ni sunde iru.
   She lives in <u>Minato Ward</u>.

3. 子供部屋を二つに区切った。
   Kodomo-beya o futatsu ni kugitta.
   We <u>divided</u> the nursery in two.

4. 区役所で書類をもらって来て。
   Kuyakusho de shorui o moratte kite.
   Can you get the documents from <u>the ward office</u>?

5. この地区で空き巣が多発している。
   Kono chiku de akisu ga tahatsu shite iru.
   There have been a lot of burglaries in this <u>area</u>.

Common Compounds and Phrases

区別	**kubetsu**	a difference; a distinction
港区	**Minato-ku**	Minato Ward
区切る	**kugiru**	to punctuate; to partition off
区役所	**kuyakusho**	a ward office
地区	**chiku**	a district; an area
区間	**kukan**	a section; an interval
区域	**kuiki**	a boundary; a zone

End the third stroke firmly.

4 一 フ ㄡ 区

区

116 犬

ケン **KEN**
いぬ **inu**

dog

Greatly modified over time, the character 犬 originally depicted a *dog* standing on its hind legs.

GR1 N4 AP

Example Sentences

1. 番犬を飼っている。
   Banken o katte iru.
   I have <u>a watchdog</u>.

2. 庭に犬小屋を建てよう。
   Niwa ni inugoya o tateyō.
   I'll build <u>a doghouse</u> in the garden.

3. 子犬が五匹生まれた。
   Koinu ga gohiki umareta.
   Five <u>puppies</u> were born.

4. 野良犬が車にひかれた。
   Nora-inu ga kuruma ni hikareta.
   <u>A stray dog</u> was hit by a car.

5. 盲導犬が入れるお店はありますか。
   Mōdōken ga haireru omise wa arimasu ka.
   Are there any stores that allow <u>seeing eye dogs</u>?

Common Compounds and Phrases

番犬	**banken**	a watchdog
愛犬	**aiken**	one's pet dog
盲導犬	**mōdōken**	a seeing eye dog
子犬	**koinu**	a puppy
犬小屋	**inugoya**	a kennel; a doghouse
野良犬	**nora-inu**	a stray dog
飼い犬	**kaiinu**	a pet dog

Align the second and third strokes.

4 一 ナ 大 犬

犬

---

117 元

ゲン **GEN**　ガン **GAN**
もと **moto**

a source;
a root; an origin

The character 元 derived from a pictograph of a person's *head and neck*, symbolizing *origin* and *source*.

GR2 N4 AP

Example Sentences

1. どうしたの。元気がないね。
   Dōshita no. Genki ga nai ne.
   What's the matter? You seem <u>depressed</u>.

2. 私たちは平成元年に結婚した。
   Watashitachi wa Heisei gannen ni kekkon shita.
   We got married in <u>the first year</u> of the Heisei Era.

3. 使ったら元のところに返して下さい。
   Tsukattara moto no tokoro ni kaeshite kudasai.
   Once you've used it, please return it to <u>where it was</u>.

4. ガスの元栓を閉め忘れた。
   Gasu no motosen o shimewasureta.
   I forgot to turn off <u>the gas main</u>.

5. 元首相が来日しました。
   Moto-shushō ga rainichi shimashita.
   <u>The former prime minister</u> came to Japan.

Common Compounds and Phrases

元気	**genki**	health; vitality
お中元	**ochūgen**	summer gift-giving
復元	**fukugen**	restoration; reconstruction
平成元年	**Heisei gannen**	the first year of the Heisei Era
元金	**gankin / motokin**	a principal; capital
元栓	**motosen**	a main tap
火の元	**hi no moto**	a possible cause of a fire

The second stroke is longer than the one above it, and the last stroke ends with a hook.

4 一 二 テ 元

元

118 公

public

コウ KŌ
おおやけ ōyake

The character 公 derived from the *breaking up* 八 of *private property* ム; i.e., making it *public* property.

GR2 N3 AP

Example Sentences

1. そのスキー場は国立公園の中にあると聞いた。
   Sono sukii-jō wa kokuritsu kōen no naka ni aru to kiita.
   I heard that that ski resort was inside a national <u>park</u>.

2. 父は公務員でした。
   Chichi wa kōmuin deshita.
   My father was <u>a government official</u>.

3. 70年代から公害がひどくなってきた。
   Nanajū-nendai kara kōgai ga hidoku natte kita.
   <u>Pollution</u> has worsened since the 1970s.

4. 公平な裁判が行われた。
   Kōhei na saiban ga okonawareta.
   A <u>fair</u> trial was held.

5. 事件が公になった。
   Jiken ga ōyake ni natta.
   The case was made <u>public</u>.

Common Compounds and Phrases

公園	**kōen**	a public park
公務員	**kōmuin**	a public employee
公害	**kōgai**	environmental pollution
公平な	**kōhei na**	fair; just
公共	**kōkyō**	public society; the community
公式	**kōshiki**	formality; official
主人公	**shujinkō**	a main character

Leave a gap between the first two strokes. The third stroke bends sharply.

4 　ノ　ハ　公　公

公

---

119 止

to stop

シ SHI
と・まる to(maru)
と・める to(meru)

The character 止 originally depicted the *foot and toes*, from which later came the meaning of *stop*.

GR2 N4 AP

Example Sentences

1. ここは駐車禁止区域です。
   Koko wa chūsha kinshi kuiki desu.
   This is a <u>no-parking</u> area.

2. 雨で試合が中止になった。
   Ame de shiai ga chūshi ni natta.
   The match <u>was called off</u> because of rain.

3. 時計が止まっていて遅刻した。
   Tokei ga tomatte ite chikoku shita.
   My watch <u>had stopped</u> and so I was late.

4. なかなか煙草が止められない。
   Naka naka tabako ga yamerarenai.
   I just <u>can't manage to quit</u> smoking.

5. その道は行き止まりです。
   Sono michi wa ikidomari desu.
   That road is <u>a dead end</u>.

Common Compounds and Phrases

禁止	**kinshi**	prohibition; a ban
中止	**chūshi**	a suspension; a stoppage
休止	**kyūshi**	a pause; a suspension
防止	**bōshi**	prevention
急停止	**kyūteishi**	a sudden stop
行き止まり	**ikidomari**	a dead end; an impasse
通行止め	**tsūkō-dome**	road closed

The last stroke protrudes.

4 　丨　⺊　⺊　止

止

120 心

heart; mind

シン SHIN
こころ kokoro

The character 心 depicts the shape of the *heart*.

GR2 N4 AP

Example Sentences

1. ジョギング中に心臓の発作を起こした。
   Jogingu-chū ni <u>shinzō</u> no hossa o okoshita.
   He had a <u>heart</u> attack while jogging.

2. 大丈夫だから、もう心配しないで。
   Daijōbu da kara, mō <u>shinpai</u> shinai de.
   <u>Don't worry</u>—everything will be all right.

3. 大学で心理学を勉強した。
   Daigaku de <u>shinrigaku</u> o benkyō shita.
   I studied <u>psychology</u> at university.

4. 問題の核心を突く質問をされた。
   Mondai no <u>kakushin o tsuku</u> shitsumon o sareta.
   I was asked a question that <u>went to the heart of the matter</u>.

5. ご親切に心からお礼申し上げます。
   Goshinsetsu ni <u>kokoro kara</u> orei mōshiagemasu.
   I offer you my <u>heartfelt</u> gratitude for your kindness.

Common Compounds and Phrases

心臓	**shinzō**	the heart; nerve
心配	**shin<u>pai</u>**	anxiety; worry
中心	**chū<u>shin</u>**	the center
熱心	**nes<u>shin</u>**	enthusiasm
感心	**kan<u>shin</u>**	to be impressed by; to admire
決心	**kes<u>shin</u>**	determination
心がけ	**kokorogake**	an attitude; an approach

End the first stroke firmly, and the second stroke with a hook.

4	ノ 心 心 心				
心					

EXERCISE 10 (109 – 120)

A. Give the readings for the following.

1. 区 _____
2. 牛 _____
3. 心 _____
4. 犬 _____
5. 夕立 _____
6. 天才 _____
7. 引力 _____
8. 中止 _____
9. 元気 _____
10. 人工 _____

B. Give the English meanings for the following.

1. 子牛 _____
2. 元日 _____
3. 大工 _____
4. 区間 _____
5. 中心 _____
6. 北区 _____
7. 九才 (歳) _____

8. 夕がた _____
9. 引っこす _____
10. 行き止まり _____

C. Write the readings for the following kanji in hiragana.

1. 元のところ (the original place) _____
2. 二わり引き (a 20% discount) _____
3. 引き出しの中 (in the drawer) _____
4. 牛の大きい目 (a cow's big eyes) _____
5. 犬をかう (to have a dog) _____
6. 水を止める (to turn off the water) _____
7. 力がある (to be strong) _____
8. 公にする (to make public) _____
9. 引いて下さい (please pull) _____
10. 多才な人 (a versatile person) _____

121 切

セツ SETSU *サイ SAI

き・る ki(ru)
き・れる ki(reru)

to cut; sharp

The character 切 combines *sword* 刀 and the act of *cutting in two* 七, emphasizing the meaning of *cut*.

GR2 N4 AP

Example Sentences

1. こういう時、適切なアドバイスをする自信がない。
   Kō iu toki, tekisetsu na adobaisu o suru jishin ga nai.
   I'm not confident about giving <u>suitable</u> advice in this situation.

2. 髪を切ろうと思います。
   Kami o kirō to omoimasu.
   <u>I'll have</u> my hair <u>cut</u>.

3. 突然電話が切れた。
   Totsuzen denwa ga kireta.
   Suddenly the telephone <u>went dead</u>.

4. 本棚で部屋を二つに仕切る。
   Hondana de heya o futatsu ni shikiru.
   We'll <u>divide</u> the room in two with a bookcase.

5. 売り切れです。
   Urikire desu.
   We're <u>sold out</u>.

Common Compounds and Phrases

適切な	**tekisetsu na**	appropriate; suitable
切断	**setsudan**	cutting; amputation
切手	**kitte**	a (postage, revenue) stamp
切符	**kippu**	a ticket
期限切れ	**kigen-gire**	overdue; expired
切羽詰って	**seppa-tsumatte**	out of desperation
*一切	**issai**	entirely; all; everything

The second stroke bends sharply, and the third stroke ends with a hook.

4 一 七 切刀 切

切

---

122 太

タイ TAI タ TA

ふと・い futo(i)
ふと・る futo(ru)

fat; thick; to gain weight

The character 太 originally combined *big* 大 and *two* 二, emphasizing the idea of something *very large*. 二 was later simplified to one dot.

GR2 N4 AP

Example Sentences

1. 太陽が眩しい。
   Taiyō ga mabushii.
   <u>The sun</u> is dazzling.

2. 皇太子殿下がお見えになりました。
   Kōtaishi denka ga omie ni narimashita.
   His Highness <u>the Crown Prince</u> has arrived.

3. もう少し太い糸がありますか。
   Mō sukoshi futoi ito ga arimasu ka.
   Do you have a slightly <u>thicker</u> thread?

4. 最近、少し太った。
   Saikin, sukoshi futotta.
   I've <u>put on</u> a little <u>weight</u> lately.

5. 彼は太平洋をヨットで横断した。
   Kare wa Taiheiyō o yotto de ōdan shita.
   He crossed <u>the Pacific Ocean</u> in a yacht.

Common Compounds and Phrases

太陽	**taiyō**	the sun
皇太子	**kōtaishi**	the Crown Prince
太平洋	**Taiheiyō**	the Pacific Ocean
太鼓	**taiko**	a drum
丸太	**maruta**	a log
太刀	**tachi**	a sword
太もも	**futomomo**	a thigh

Don't mistake 太 for 大 or 犬.

4 一 ナ 大 太

太

123 内

ナイ NAI *ダイ DAI
うち uchi

inside; within

The character 内 combines *enclosure* 冂 and *go in* 入 to give the idea of *inside*.

GR2 N3 AP

Example Sentences

1. それは国内では売っていません。
   Sore wa kokunai de wa utte imasen.
   That isn't sold domestically.

2. 仕事の内容を教えて下さい。
   Shigoto no naiyō o oshiete kudasai.
   Please tell me about what the job entails.

3. 博物館の案内図をもらいましょうか。
   Hakubutsukan no annaizu o moraimashō ka.
   Shall we get a map of the museum?

4. 話は三分以内にして下さい。
   Hanashi wa sanpun inai ni shite kudasai.
   Please say what you have to say within three minutes.

5. 線の内側に並んでください。
   Sen no uchigawa ni narande kudasai.
   Please queue up behind the line.

Common Compounds and Phrases

国内	kokunai	domestic; the interior (of Japan)
内容	naiyō	contents; details
案内	annai	guidance; instructions
以内	inai	within; no more than
内科	naika	internal medicine
年内	nennai	within the year
内側	uchigawa	the inside; the interior

The second stroke ends with a hook, and the third stroke protrudes.

4 丨 冂 内 内

内

124 不

フ FU ブ BU

not

The character 不 is a pictograph of the round *bud of a flower*. The shape of the mouth when saying *no, not* is thought to derive from this idea.

GR4 N4 AP

Example Sentences

1. パソコンが壊れて、とても不便だ。
   Pasokon ga kowarete, totemo fuben da.
   It is so inconvenient with my PC out of order.

2. 今の仕事に不満を持っている。
   Ima no shigoto ni fuman o motte iru.
   I'm not satisfied with my present job.

3. 運転手の不注意で、事故が起きた。
   Untenshu no fuchūi de, jiko ga okita.
   The accident was caused by the driver's carelessness.

4. 彼はまだ行方不明のままだ。
   Kare wa mada yukue fumei no mama da.
   His whereabouts are still unknown.

5. 今年の夏は水不足だった。
   Kotoshi no natsu wa mizu-busoku datta.
   There was a water shortage this summer.

Common Compounds and Phrases

不便	fuben	inconvenience
不満	fuman	dissatisfaction; discontent
不注意	fuchūi	carelessness; inattention
不明	fumei	obscurity; ignorance
不足	fusoku	a shortage; a deficiency; discontent
不自由	fujiyū	inconvenience; poverty
不気味	bukimi	weird(ness); uncanny

The fourth stroke does not join.

4 一 プ 不 不

不

125 文

letter; sentence; writings

ブン **BUN** モン **MON**
ふみ **fumi**

The character 文 derived from a *pattern* used on ancient earthenware. It then took on the meaning of *character*, which was then extended to *writing*.

GR1 N4 AP

Example Sentences

1. 彼の文章はわかりにくい。
   Kare no bunshō wa wakari-nikui.
   His <u>writing</u> is difficult to understand.

2. 例文を考えてください。
   Reibun o kangaete kudasai.
   Please think of <u>an example sentence</u>.

3. エジプト文化に興味を持っている。
   Ejiputo-bunka ni kyōmi o motte iru.
   I am interested in Egyptian <u>culture</u>.

4. これは日本の伝統的な文様です。
   Kore wa Nihon no dentōteki na mōnyō desu.
   This is a traditional Japanese <u>pattern</u>.

5. 正しい文字を書いてみて。
   Tadashii moji o kaite mite.
   Try and write the correct <u>character</u>.

Common Compounds and Phrases

文章	**bunshō**	writing; a sentence
例文	**reibun**	an example (sentence)
文化	**bunka**	culture; civilization
文学	**bungaku**	literature
文様	**monyō**	a pattern; a design
文句	**monku**	a phrase; a complaint
*文字	**moji**	a letter; a character

The first stroke joins, and the last two strokes taper off.

4　 ` 亠 ナ 文

文

---

126 方

a direction; a person; a way of (doing)

ホウ **HŌ**
かた **kata**

The character 方 possibly derived from a pictograph of a *tethered boat*, floating in the *direction* of the current.

GR2 N4 AP

Example Sentences

1. 池袋方面行きの電車が参ります。
   Ikebukuro hōmen yuki no densha ga mairimasu.
   The approaching train is <u>bound for</u> Ikebukuro.

2. 早く予約した方がいいよ。
   Hayaku yoyaku shita hō ga ii yo.
   <u>You'd better</u> make a reservation soon.

3. その地方の方言はよく知らない。
   Sono chihō no hōgen wa yoku shiranai.
   I don't know much about that <u>region</u>'s <u>dialect</u>.

4. 森田さんという方からお電話です。
   Morita-san to iu kata kara odenwa desu.
   There is a telephone call from <u>a Mr. Morita</u>.

5. この漢字の読み方が分かりますか。
   Kono kanji no yomikata ga wakarimasu ka.
   Do you know <u>how to read</u> this Chinese character?

Common Compounds and Phrases

方面	**hōmen**	a direction; a way; an aspect
地方	**chihō**	a district; a region; the countryside
方言	**hōgen**	a dialect
両方	**ryōhō**	both (sides)
方法	**hōhō**	a method; a means
方向	**hōkō**	a direction; a course
読み方	**yomikata**	pronunciation of a character

The third stroke bends sharply.

4　 ` 亠 方 方

方

127 以　イ I

to the ... of;
using

The character 以 is a combination of a *wooden tool* ㇄ and *hand* 人, signifying *working with a tool*. From this came the idea of *using* or *holding* something.

GR4 N4 AP

Example Sentences

1. この車は六人以上は乗れない。
   Kono kuruma wa rokunin ijō wa norenai.
   This car seats no <u>more than</u> six.

2. 鉛筆以外は使わないで欲しい。
   Enpitsu igai wa tsukawanai de hoshii.
   I don't want you to use anything <u>other than</u> pencil.

3. 二分以内に答えなさい。
   Nifun inai ni kotaenasai.
   Please answer <u>within</u> two minutes.

4. 彼女には五月以来会っていません。
   Kanojo ni wa gogatsu irai atte imasen.
   I haven't seen her <u>since</u> May.

5. 以前どこかでお会いしましたか。
   Izen doko ka de oai shimashita ka.
   Have we met somewhere <u>before</u>?

Common Compounds and Phrases

以上	**ijō**	over; more than
以外	**igai**	except for; besides
以来	**irai**	since then; after that
以下	**ika**	under; not exceeding
以降	**ikō**	from that point forward; after that
以前	**izen**	before; since; the past
以後	**igo**	after this / that; from now / then on

End the last stroke firmly.

5 ｜ ㇄ ㇄ ㇄ 以

---

128 去　キョ KYO　コ KO
さ・る sa(ru)

to go away

The character 去 depicted a *rice container with a lid*. When the lid was put on the contents were hidden or *gone*.

GR3 N4 AP

Example Sentences

1. 彼は去年大学を卒業した。
   Kare wa kyonen daigaku o sotsugyō shita.
   He graduated from college <u>last year</u>.

2. これは過去に例がない。
   Kore wa kako ni rei ga nai.
   There is no <u>precedent</u> for this.

3. 都会を去ることにした。
   Tokai o saru koto ni shita.
   He decided <u>to leave</u> the city.

4. 家具のほこりを取り去った。
   Kagu no hokori o torisatta.
   I <u>dusted</u> the furniture.

5. 彼女は何も言わず立ち去った。
   Kanojo wa nani mo iwazu tachisatta.
   She <u>left</u> without saying a word.

Common Compounds and Phrases

去年	**kyonen**	last year
死去	**shikyo**	death
除去	**jokyo**	elimination
撤去	**tekkyo**	removal
退去	**taikyo**	leaving; withdrawal
過去	**kako**	the past; one's past
立ち去る	**tachisaru**	to leave; to depart

The third stroke is longer than the one above it.

5 一 十 土 去 去

129 兄

elder brother

ケイ KEI *キョウ KYŌ
あに ani

The character 兄 combines *person* 儿 and *mouth* 口, suggesting an *elder brother* who advises his younger siblings.

GR2 N4 AP

Example Sentences

1. 私の義兄は株で大もうけした。
   Watashi no gikei wa kabu de ōmōke shita.
   My <u>brother-in-law</u> made a killing on the stock exchange.

2. ご兄弟がいらっしゃいますか。
   Gokyōdai ga irasshaimasu ka.
   Do you have any <u>brothers or sisters</u>?

3. 兄が二人います。
   Ani ga futari imasu.
   I have two <u>older brothers</u>.

4. お兄ちゃん、遊ぼうよ。
   Oniichan, asobō yo.
   Come on, let's play! (said to an older brother / young boy)

5. 「兄弟仲良く」は、我が家のモットーです。
   'Kyōdai nakayoku' wa, wagaya no mottō desu.
   '<u>Be kind to each other</u>' is our family's motto.

Common Compounds and Phrases

義兄	**gikei**	a brother-in-law
長兄	**chōkei**	an eldest brother
次兄	**jikei**	one's second eldest brother
兄弟	**kyōdai**	brothers / sisters; a pal
兄弟げんか	**kyōdai-genka**	a quarrel between brothers (and sisters)
兄貴	**aniki**	an older brother; Buddy!
*(お)兄さん	**(o)niisan**	an older brother; 'Young man'

The last stroke ends with a hook.

5 ｜ ⼝ ⼝ ⼫ 兄

兄

130 広

broad; wide; to spread; to extend

コウ KŌ
ひろ・い hiro(i)
ひろ・まる hiro(maru)
ひろ・がる hiro(garu)

The character 広 combines *roof* 广 and *large* ム to indicate a *spacious* building.

GR2 N4 AP

Example Sentences

1. 新聞の求人広告に応募した。
   Shinbun no kyūjin kōkoku ni ōbo shita.
   I applied for a <u>Help Wanted ad</u> in the newspaper.

2. もっと広い家に住みたいなあ。
   Motto hiroi ie ni sumitai nā.
   I'd love to live in a more <u>spacious</u> house!

3. 噂はすぐ広まった。
   Uwasa wa sugu hiromatta.
   The rumor <u>spread</u> in no time.

4. 目の前に真っ青な海が広がる。
   Me no mae ni massao na umi ga hirogaru.
   The deep blue sea <u>stretches out</u> before me.

5. ボーナスで背広を新調した。
   Bōnasu de sebiro o shinchō shita.
   I had a new <u>suit</u> made with my bonus money.

Common Compounds and Phrases

広告	**kōkoku**	an advertisement; an announcement
広大な	**kōdai na**	vast; extensive
広々と	**hirobiro to**	spacious; open; wide
広場	**hiroba**	a public square
広間	**hiroma**	a hall; a spacious room
背広	**sebiro**	a business suit
広島	**Hiroshima**	Hiroshima (a place)

The first stroke connects, and the third one tapers off.

5 ｀ 亠 广 広 広

広

131 市

シ SHI
いち ichi

a city;
a market

The character 市 originally combined *stop* 止 and *balance* 平, indicating a place where people *stop and negotiate* goods.

GR2 N4 AP

Example Sentences

1. 都市に人口が集中する。
   Toshi ni jinkō ga shūchū suru.
   The population is concentrated in the <u>cities</u>.

2. 市民センターで生け花教室が始まります。
   Shimin sentā de ikebana kyōshitsu ga hajimarimasu.
   Flower arrangement classes will begin at the <u>civic center</u>.

3. 毎日、朝市が立つ。
   Mainichi, asaichi ga tatsu.
   A <u>morning market</u> is held every day.

4. 陶器市でいい茶碗を買った。
   Tōki-ichi de ii chawan o katta.
   I bought some nice rice bowls at <u>the pottery fair</u>.

5. 三人の候補者が市長選に立候補した。
   Sannin no kōhosha ga <u>shichō-sen</u> ni rikkōho shita.
   Three candidates ran for <u>the mayoral election</u>.

Common Compounds and Phrases

都市	**toshi**	a city; a town
市民	**shimin**	a citizen; a resident
市長	**shichō**	a mayor
市役所	**shiyakusho**	a city hall
名古屋市	**Nagoya-shi**	Nagoya City
朝市	**asaichi**	a morning market
市場	**ichiba**	a market (place)

The fourth stroke ends with a hook.

5 　丶 亠 亣 方 市

市

---

132 仕

シ SHI ＊ジ JI
つか・える tsuka(eru)

to serve; to do

The character 仕 combines *man* 亻 and *samurai* 士, indicating a *samurai serving* his master. *Do* is an associated meaning.

GR3 N4 AP

Example Sentences

1. 旅行の仕度をしましょう。
   Ryokō no shitaku o shimashō.
   <u>Let's get ready</u> for our trip.

2. 祖母は一日中畑仕事をしている。
   Sobo wa ichinichijū hatake-shigoto o shite iru.
   My grandmother spends the whole day <u>working in the fields</u>.

3. 値段を見て、仕入れてください。
   Nedan o mite, shiirete kudasai.
   Please check the prices before <u>ordering</u>.

4. 彼はあのお屋敷に長年仕えている。
   Kare wa ano oyashiki ni naganen <u>tsukaete iru</u>.
   He <u>has served</u> in that residence for many years.

5. 今日中にそれを仕上げてください。
   Kyōjū ni sore o shiagete kudasai.
   <u>Please finish</u> it by today.

Common Compounds and Phrases

仕度	**shitaku**	arrangements; preparations
仕事	**shigoto**	work; a job
畑仕事	**hatake-shigoto**	work(ing) in the fields
仕方	**shikata**	a way; a means
仕上げ	**shiage**	a finish; completion
仕切り	**shikiri**	a partition
給仕	**kyūji**	service; a waiter

The last stroke is shorter than the one above it.

5 　ノ 亻 仁 仕 仕

仕

EXERCISE 11 (121 – 132)

A. Give the readings for the following.

1. お兄さん _____
2. 以下 _____
3. 切手 _____
4. 行き方 _____
5. 山口市 _____
6. 太い _____
7. 広まる _____
8. 方言 _____
9. 以外 _____

B. Match the following with their meanings.

1. 水不足　（　）　　a. running out of time
2. 年内に　（　）　　b. important
3. 仕上げ　（　）　　c. last year
4. 時間切れ（　）　　d. vast
5. 文学　　（　）　　e. literature
6. 大切な　（　）　　f. within the year
7. 広大な　（　）　　g. completion
8. 去年　　（　）　　h. a water shortage

C. Fill in the blanks with an appropriate mixture of kanji and kana.

1. ____ (た) べた ____ (ほう) がいい (You'd better eat (it)).
2. ____ (さんじゅっぷん) ____ (いない) (within thirty minutes)
3. ____ (あに) が ____ (ひとり) いる (to have one older brother)
4. ____ (かねこ) さんという ____ (かた) (a person called Kaneko)
5. ____ (き) らないで ____ (くだ) さい。(Don't hang up.)
6. ____ (ご) の ____ (よ) み ____ (かた) (how to pronounce a word)
7. ____ (いちねん) の ____ (うち) で ____ (にかげつ) (two months of the year)
8. ____ (すこ) し ____ (ふと) る (to put on a little weight)
9. ____ (しかた) がない。(It can't be helped.)
10. ____ (ひ) が ____ (ひろ) がる (fire spreads)

133　写

シャ SHA
うつ・る utsu(ru)
うつ・す utsu(su)

to copy;
to photograph

Originally combining *house* 宀 and *magpie* 鵲, the character 写 suggested the idea of *sketching* a magpie indoors. Hence, the simplified form has the meaning of *copy*.

GR3　N4　AP

Example Sentences

1. 写生大会に出た。
   Shasei taikai ni deta.
   I entered a <u>sketching</u> contest.

2. 試写会の券が当たった。
   Shishakai no ken ga atatta.
   We won some tickets for a <u>preview</u>.

3. いつも写真うつりが悪い。
   Itsumo shashin-utsuri ga warui.
   I always <u>photograph</u> poorly.

4. 電車の時刻表をノートに写した。
   Densha no jikokuhyō o nōto ni utsushita.
   I <u>copied</u> the train timetable into my notebook.

5. 若い頃、写真家になるのが夢だった。
   Wakai koro, shashinka ni naru no ga yume datta.
   When I was a youngster, it was my ambition to become a <u>photographer</u>.

Common Compounds and Phrases

写生	shasei	sketching; portrayal
試写会	shishakai	a preview; a trade show
写真	shashin	a photograph; a picture
写真家	shashinka	a professional photographer
複写	fukusha	reproduction; a copy
映写	eisha	projecting (a movie)
生き写し	iki-utsushi	the spitting image of ...

The fourth stroke ends with a hook.

5　｀ 宀 宀 写 写

写

75

134 主

シュ SHU
ぬし nushi おも omo

a master; main

The character 主 depicted a *candle burning* indoors; a symbol of the *master* of the house.

GR3 N4 AP

Example Sentences

1. 店の主人に聞いた方がいい。
   Mise no shujin ni kiita hō ga ii.
   You'd better ask the store <u>owner</u>.

2. 我が家は米を主食にしている。
   Wagaya wa kome o shushoku ni shite iru.
   We eat rice as a <u>staple</u> at our house.

3. あの大きなたぬきはこの森の主です。
   Ano ōki na tanuki wa kono mori no nushi desu.
   That big raccoon is the <u>guardian</u> of this forest.

4. その国の主な産業は何ですか。
   Sono kuni no omo na sangyō wa nan desu ka.
   What is that country's <u>main</u> industry?

5. 主婦は毎日忙しい。
   Shufu wa mainichi isogashii.
   <u>A housewife</u> is busy every day.

Common Compounds and Phrases

主人	**shujin**	the master; the head; one's husband
主食	**shushoku**	the staple (food / diet)
主婦	**shufu**	a housewife; a hostess
主語	**shugo**	a / the subject (of a sentence)
主治医	**shujii**	a doctor in charge; one's usual doctor
持ち主	**mochinushi**	the owner; the proprietor
*坊主	**bōzu**	a Buddhist monk; a shaven head; a boy

Don't forget to angle the dot.

5 ` 二 十 丯 主

主

---

135 世

セイ SEI セ SE
よ yo

world; age

The character 世 was originally a combination of three lots of *ten* 十, representing thirty years or an average *generation*. Later this assumed the more general meaning of the *world at large*.

GR3 N4 AP

Example Sentences

1. 我々は二十一世紀を迎えた。
   Wareware wa nijūis-seiki o mukaeta.
   We've seen in the <u>twenty-first century</u>.

2. インターネットの普及で世界は狭くなった。
   Intānetto no fukyū de sekai wa semaku natta.
   <u>The world</u> has become a smaller place with the spread of the internet.

3. もうすぐ団塊の世代の人は退職する。
   Mō sugu dankai no sedai no hito wa taishoku suru.
   The <u>baby boomers</u> are approaching retirement.

4. 仕事中に世間話をするな。
   Shigoto-chū ni seken-banashi o suru na.
   Enough of that <u>small talk</u> while you're at work!

5. 世の中、暗いニュースばかりです。
   Yononaka, kurai nyūsu bakari desu.
   <u>The world</u> is just full of depressing news.

Common Compounds and Phrases

世紀	**seiki**	a century
二世	**nisei**	the second; second-generation (Korean / Japanese)
世界	**sekai**	the world; the earth; society
世代	**sedai**	a generation
世間	**seken**	the world; society; life
世話	**sewa**	care; recommendation
世論	**seron, yoron**	public opinion

The second stroke is slightly longer than the third, and the last one bends sharply.

5 一 十 丗 丗 世

世

136 正

セイ SEI　ショウ SHŌ
ただ・しい tada(shii)
まさ・に masa (ni)

correct; just; truly

The character 正 combines *bar* 一 and *leg* 止 to suggest reaching one's destination, or achieving a goal. The quickest way to reach a destination is by going straight; *correct* is a corollary meaning.
GR1　N4　AP

Example Sentences

1. 材料の重さを正確に量ってください。
   Zairyō no omosa o seikaku ni hakatte kudasai.
   Measure the weight of the ingredients <u>accurately</u>.

2. お正月のあいさつはもうすみましたか。
   Oshōgatsu no aisatsu wa mō sumimashita ka.
   Have you made your <u>New Year</u>'s greetings?

3. 正面玄関に車を止めた。
   Shōmen genkan ni kuruma o tometa.
   I parked the car in <u>the front of the house</u>.

4. 三つの中から正しい答えを選びなさい。
   Mittsu no naka kara tadashii kotae o erabinasai.
   Choose the <u>correct</u> answer from among the three.

5. 正にそのとおりです。
   Masa ni sono tōri desu.
   That's <u>certainly</u> right!

Common Compounds and Phrases

正確な	**seikaku na**	accurate, exact
正常	**seijō**	normal
正面	**shōmen**	a front part; a facade
正体	**shōtai**	one's true character; consciousness
賀正	**gashō**	Happy New Year! (a card greeting)
正義	**seigi**	justice
礼儀正しい	**reigi-tadashii**	well-mannered; polite

Make the fifth stroke the longest.

5　一　丁　下　正　正

正

---

137 台

ダイ DAI　タイ TAI

a stand; a base

Originally 臺, this character, meaning *platform*, comprised *tall* 高, *earth* 土 and *peak, arrive* 至. Now written 台, it is a combination of *self* ム and *mouth* 口, which in Chinese meant *to name oneself*.
GR2　N4　AP

Example Sentences

1. せっかくのチャンスが台無しになった。
   Sekkaku no chansu ga dainashi ni natta.
   A precious chance was <u>wasted</u>.

2. 夜行の寝台車で九州まで行った。
   Yakō no shindaisha de Kyūshū made itta.
   I went to Kyushu on the overnight <u>sleeper</u>.

3. 車が一台家の前に止まった。
   Kuruma ga ichidai ie no mae ni tomatta.
   <u>A car</u> stopped in front of my house.

4. 今日は、娘の初舞台だ。
   Kyō wa, musume no hatsubutai da.
   It is my daughter's <u>debut</u> today.

5. 屋台のラーメンを初めて食べた。
   Yatai no rāmen o hajimete tabeta.
   I ate *rāmen* at <u>a street stall</u> for the first time.

Common Compounds and Phrases

台本	**daihon**	a script; a text; a scenario
寝台車	**shindaisha**	a sleeper; a sleeping car
譜面台	**fumendai**	a music stand
台所	**daidokoro**	a kitchen
灯台	**tōdai**	a lighthouse
台無し にする	**dainashi ni suru**	to spoil; to ruin
屋台	**yatai**	a street stall
舞台	**butai**	a stage

Draw the first stroke as one stroke.

5　ノ　ム　台　台　台

台

138 代

ダイ DAI　タイ TAI
か・わる ka(waru)
か・える ka(eru)
よ yo　*しろ shiro

a generation; an age;
a fare; to substitute

The character 代 combines *person* 亻 and *wooden stake* 弋, originally suggesting the notion of *interchangeable*. The associated meaning of *generation* comes from the idea of people *replacing each other*.
GR3　N4

Example Sentences

1. タクシー代がまた上がる。
   Takushii-dai ga mata agaru.
   Taxi <u>fares</u> are going up again.

2. この土地は先祖代々の土地です。
   Kono tochi wa <u>senzo daidai</u> no tochi desu.
   This land has been <u>in the family for many generations</u>.

3. 30分たったら交代しましょう。
   Sanjuppun tattara <u>kōtai</u> shimashō.
   I will <u>change</u> with you in 30 minutes.

4. 母の代理でお葬式に出た。
   <u>Haha no dairi</u> de o-sōshiki ni deta.
   I went to the funeral as <u>my mother's representative</u>.

5. 担当者を代えて欲しいと言われた。
   Tantōsha o <u>kaete</u> hoshii to iwareta.
   I was asked <u>to change</u> the person-in-charge.

Common Compounds and Phrases

タクシー代	**takushii-<u>dai</u>**	a taxi fare
代々	**<u>daidai</u>**	for generations
時代	**ji<u>dai</u>**	a period; an age; the present
代表	**<u>dai</u>hyō**	representation; a representative; a model
交代	**kō<u>tai</u>**	a change; a substitution
お代わり	**o<u>ka</u>wari**	a second helping
身代金	**mino<u>shiro</u>kin**	a ransom

Don't forget the dot.

5　ノ　イ　仁　代　代

代

---

139 田

デン DEN
た ta

a rice field;
a paddy

田 represents an aerial view of a *rice paddy* neatly divided into quarters.

GR1　N5　AP

Example Sentences

1. 水田が道の両側に広がる。
   <u>Suiden</u> ga michi no ryōgawa ni hirogaru.
   <u>Paddy fields</u> extend from both sides of the road.

2. 海底油田が発見された。
   Kaitei <u>yuden</u> ga hakken sareta.
   <u>An offshore oilfield</u> was discovered.

3. もうすぐ、田んぼに苗を植える時期だ。
   Mō sugu, <u>tanbo</u> ni nae o ueru jiki da.
   It will soon be time to plant rice seedlings in <u>the paddies</u>.

4. 田植えのシーズンはいつですか。
   <u>Taue</u> no shiizun wa itsu desu ka.
   When is the <u>rice-planting</u> season?

5. 郊外には、田園風景が広がっている。
   Kōgai ni wa, <u>den'en</u> fūkei ga hirogatte iru.
   The suburbs feature a peaceful <u>rural scene</u>.

Common Compounds and Phrases

水田	**sui<u>den</u>**	a rice paddy
油田	**yu<u>den</u>**	an oil field (well)
田園	**<u>den</u>'en**	fields and gardens; the country
田植え	**<u>tau</u>e**	rice planting
田んぼ	**<u>tan</u>bo**	a rice field
田畑	**<u>ta</u>hata**	fields and rice paddies
*田舎	**inaka**	the country; rural areas

Make sure the character is divided into equal parts.

5　丨　冂　冂　甲　田

田

140 冬 winter

トウ TŌ
ふゆ fuyu

The character 冬 derived from a pictograph of *two bags hanging from a rope* with the two dots in the middle representing *ice*, indicating that it was *winter*.
GR2 N4 AP

Example Sentences

1. 次の冬期オリンピック開催地は、どこですか。
   Tsugi no tōki orinpikku kaisaichi wa, doko desu ka.
   Where will the next Winter Olympics be held?

2. 今年は、暖冬だと言われている。
   Kotoshi wa, dantō da to iwarete iru.
   It is said this year will be a mild winter.

3. 今年の冬は、何回か雪が降った。
   Kotoshi no fuyu wa, nankaika yuki ga futta.
   We have had a number of snowfalls this winter.

4. 冬山登山は危険が伴う。
   Fuyuyama-tozan wa kiken ga tomonau.
   It is dangerous to do mountain climbing in winter.

5. バーゲンで冬物を買った。
   Bāgen de fuyumono o katta.
   I bought some winter clothing at a sale.

Common Compounds and Phrases

冬季	**tōki**	the winter season
冬眠	**tōmin**	hibernation
初冬	**shotō**	the beginning of winter
暖冬	**dantō**	a mild (warm) winter
冬山	**fuyuyama**	winter mountains
冬物	**fuyumono**	winter clothing
冬休み	**fuyu-yasumi**	a winter vacation

Make the last two strokes parallel.

5 ノ ク タ 冬 冬

冬

---

141 民 people; race

ミン MIN
たみ tami

The character 民 is thought to combine *needle* 弋 and *eye* 目, to suggest the idea of *blind*. This ideograph symbolized *slaves*, which later came to mean common *people*.
GR4 N4

Example Sentences

1. 来年度から住民税が上がる。
   Rainendo kara jūminzei ga agaru.
   The residence tax will go up from the next fiscal year.

2. 彼はアメリカへの移民を認められた。
   Kare wa Amerika e no imin o mitomerareta.
   He has been recognized as an immigrant to the U.S.

3. 民芸品を売っている店は、この辺にありますか。
   Mingeihin o utte iru mise wa, kono hen ni arimasu ka.
   Is there a store that sells folk handicrafts near here?

4. この建物は植民地時代のものです。
   Kono tatemono wa shokuminchi jidai no mono desu.
   This building dates from the colonial period.

5. 政治家は国民の声に耳を傾けるべきだ。
   Seijika wa kokumin no koe ni mimi o katamukeru beki da.
   Politicians should listen to the voice of the people.

Common Compounds and Phrases

住民	**jūmin**	inhabitants; residents
移民	**imin**	emigration; an immigrant
民芸品	**mingeihin**	an article of folkcraft
植民地	**shokuminchi**	a colony; a settlement
民間	**minkan**	of the people; non-governmental
民宿	**minshuku**	a private house offering lodging
民主主義	**minshu shugi**	democracy

End the last stroke with a hook.

5 ヿ ⁊ ⼾ ⼾ 民

民

142 用

ヨウ YŌ
もち・いる mochi(iru)

business; an errand; to use

The character 用 depicts a square board with a stick passed through a hole in the center. The present meaning derived from the idea of people *making use of* tools to do things.
GR2 N4 AP

Example Sentences

1. 急いで用意しなさい。
   Isoide yōi shinasai.
   Hurry up and <u>get ready</u>!

2. ちょっと用事があるので、遅れます。
   Chotto yōji ga aru node, okuremasu.
   I <u>have something to do</u>, so I'll be late.

3. 今、会議室は使用中です。
   Ima, kaigishitsu wa shiyōchū desu.
   The conference room is presently <u>in use</u>.

4. 費用は、どれくらいかかりますか。
   Hiyō wa, dore kurai kakarimasu ka.
   What will it <u>cost</u>?

5. この用具は、何に用いますか。
   Kono yōgu wa, nani ni mochiimasu ka.
   What do you <u>use</u> this <u>appliance</u> for?

Common Compounds and Phrases

用意	**yōi**	preparation(s); arrangements
用事	**yōji**	business; an engagement; work
使用	**shiyō**	use; application
作用	**sayō**	action; operation; function
費用	**hiyō**	expense(s); cost
利用	**riyō**	use; to make use of
専用	**senyō**	personal use; exclusively for

The first stroke tapers off, and the last stroke ends with a hook.

5 丿 冂 月 月 用

用

143 回

カイ KAI *エ E
まわ・る mawa(ru)
まわ・す mawa(su)

times; to go around; to spin

The character 回 derived from a pictograph of a *whirl* to suggest *going around*.

GR2 N4 AP

Example Sentences

1. もう一回言って下さい。
   Mō ikkai itte kudasai.
   Please say that <u>again</u>.

2. プラスチック容器を回収し始めた。
   Purasuchikku yōki o kaishū shihajimeta.
   They've started <u>collecting</u> plastic containers (for recycling).

3. 工事中なので、迂回して下さい。
   Kōjichū na node, ukai shite kudasai.
   There is construction work going on, so please <u>take the detour</u>.

4. 年末は、目が回るほど忙しい。
   Nenmatsu wa, me ga mawaru hodo isogashii.
   I am <u>very busy</u> at year end.

5. そっちは遠回りだよ。
   Sotchi wa tōmawari da yo.
   That's <u>the long way around</u>.

Common Compounds and Phrases

一回	**ikkai**	once; one time; one round
回収	**kaishū**	collection; recovery
迂回	**ukai**	a detour; a circuit
今回	**konkai**	this time; lately
次回	**jikai**	next time
時計回り	**tokei-mawari**	clockwise
遠回り	**tōmawari**	a long way round; long-winded

Use equal spacing.

6 丨 冂 冂 冋 回 回

回

144 交	コウ KŌ	The character 交 depicts a person sitting with

144 交
to associate with;
to mix; to exchange
(greetings)

コウ KŌ
ま・じる ma(jiru) まじ・える maji(eru) ま・ぜる ma(zeru) か・う ka(u) ま・ざる ma(zaru) か・わす ka(wasu) まじ・わる maji(waru)

The character 交 depicts a person sitting with *crossed legs*, which took on the meaning of *mix* and *exchange*.

GR2 N3

Example Sentences

1. この所、交通事故が多い。
   Kono tokoro, kōtsū jiko ga ōi.
   There have been many <u>traffic</u> accidents lately.

2. 社交ダンスをちょっと習いました。
   Shakō dansu o chotto naraimashita.
   I learned <u>ballroom dancing</u> for a short while.

3. 髪の毛に白いものが交じってきた。
   Kami no ke ni shiroi mono ga majitte kita.
   My hair <u>is sprinkled</u> with gray.

4. 留学生による文化交流会が開催された。
   Ryūgakusei ni yoru <u>bunka kōryūkai</u> ga kaisai sareta.
   <u>A cultural exchange event</u> was held by international students.

5. おたがいに十分意見を交わした。
   Otagai ni jūbun iken o kawashita.
   We <u>exchanged</u> views at length.

Common Compounds and Phrases

交通	**kōtsū**	traffic; transportation
社交	**shakō**	socializing; society
交番	**kōban**	a police box
交換	**kōkan**	exchange; interchange
交差点	**kōsaten**	an intersection (point)
交流	**kōryū**	exchange; alternating current
片言交じり	**katakoto-majiri**	a mixture of correct and broken speech

The first stroke touches the second stroke. End the fourth stroke firmly.

6 ` 亠 ナ 亣 六 交

交

EXERCISE 12 (133 – 144)

A. Give the readings for the following.

1. 冬 _____
2. 代える _____
3. 主な _____
4. 用いる _____
5. 交ざる _____
6. 正しい _____
7. 回す _____
8. 写る _____
9. 三十円台 _____
10. 世代 _____

B. Rewrite the following in hiragana.

1. 交ざっている _____
2. 世の中 _____
3. 田んぼ _____
4. 主人 _____
5. 台本 _____
6. 二十回 _____
7. 写生 _____

8. 民間 _____
9. 交代 _____
10. 中学生用の _____

C. Give the meanings for the following.

1. 時代 _____
2. 今回 _____
3. 世話 _____
4. 水田 _____
5. お正月 _____
6. 写す _____
7. 用がある _____
8. 冬休み _____
9. タクシー代 _____
10. 社交ダンス _____

Review 4 (1 – 144)

A. Give the readings for the following.

1. 行き止まり _____
2. 不足 _____
3. 夕方 _____
4. 仕切り _____
5. 広々と _____
6. 写生 _____
7. 話し方 _____
8. 国民 _____
9. 世間話 _____
10. 電話台 _____

B. Write in kanji and kana.

1. ふゆやすみ _____
2. まじっている _____
3. たんぼ _____
4. まわる _____
5. おもに _____
6. もちいる _____
7. よのなか _____
8. ナポレオンにせい _____
9. うつす _____
10. ただしくない _____

C. Write in Japanese.

1. a citizen; a resident _____
2. except for; besides _____
3. the New Year _____
4. someone else's older brother _____
5. a second helping _____
6. the third time _____
7. a staple food _____
8. a carpenter _____
9. an eighty-yen stamp _____
10. the southern exit (of a station) _____

D. Match the following with their readings.

1. 水田 ( )　　a. せだい
2. 世代 ( )　　b. ゆくえ
3. 市長 ( )　　c. みんかん
4. 国内 ( )　　d. いらい
5. 主人 ( )　　e. じだい
6. 元気 ( )　　f. しちょう

7. 一切 ( )　　g. すいでん
8. 大田区 ( )　h. こんかい
9. 子牛 ( )　　i. げんき
10. 中心 ( )　　j. てんさい
11. 今回 ( )　　k. しゅじん
12. 行方 ( )　　l. おおたく
13. 台本 ( )　　m. いっさい
14. 民間 ( )　　n. ゆうしょく
15. 以来 ( )　　o. しゅじんこう
16. 時代 ( )　　p. ふゆやま
17. 天才 ( )　　q. こくない
18. 冬山 ( )　　r. こうし
19. 夕食 ( )　　s. だいほん
20. 主人公 ( )　t. ちゅうしん

E. Fill in the appropriate kanji and write in English.

1. ____(あに)と ____(こうたい)で ____(いぬ)の ____(せわ)をすることにした。
2. ____(しちょう)の ____(ふせい)が ____(おおやけ)になった。
3. ____(うちだ)さんはとても ____(こころ)の ____(ひろ)い ____(かた)です。
4. _____(きょうじゅう)にそのデザインを ____(しあ)げなさい。
5. ____(きょねん)の ____(ふゆ)____(いらい)____(ほんだ)さんに ____(あ)っていない。
6. ____(えき)の ____(みなみぐち)の ____(まえ)に ____(くるま)が____(にだい) ____(と)まっている。
7. ____(はは)は ____(たいせつ)なものを ____(ひ)き ____(だ)しにしまっている。
8. (しゅじん)は、____ (こんしゅう)ずっと ____ (げんき)がなかった。
9. ____(おおた)さん、この ____(てんもんだい)へ ____(き)たのは ____(なんかいめ)ですか。
10. ____(くみん)の ____(ちから)を ____(あ)わせて、ポイすてをなくそう。

145 好

コウ KŌ
この・む kono(mu)
す・く su(ku)

to like;
favorable

The character 好 is a combination of *woman* 女 and *child* 子, representing the *love* a mother has for her child.

GR4 N4 AP

Example Sentences

1. あの国々は友好条約を結んだ。
   Ano kuniguni wa yūkō jōyaku o musunda.
   Those two countries have signed <u>a friendship treaty</u>.

2. 笹の葉はパンダの大好物だ。
   Sasa no ha wa panda no daikōbutsu da.
   The <u>favorite food</u> of pandas is the leaves of bamboo grass.

3. 祖母はコーヒーより紅茶を好む。
   Sobo wa kōhii yori kōcha o konomu.
   My grandmother <u>prefers</u> tea to coffee.

4. 博覧会は好評のうちに幕を閉じた。
   Hakurankai wa kōhyō no uchi ni maku o tojita.
   The expo closed <u>on a good note</u>.

5. タデ食う虫も好き好き。
   Tade kū mushi mo sukizuki.
   There is no accounting for tastes. (a saying).

Common Compounds and Phrases

好物	**kōbutsu**	a favorite (food); a passion
好意	**kōi**	kindness; goodwill
絶好調	**zekkōchō**	excellent shape; top form
格好	**kakkō**	shape; form; suitable
好評	**kōhyō**	a good reputation; popularity
若者好み	**wakamono-gonomi**	popular with young people
大好き	**daisuki**	to love; to be very fond of

End the fifth stroke with a hook.

6　く　女　女　好　好　好

好

---

146 考

コウ KŌ
かんが・える kanga(eru)

to think;
to consider

The character 考 combines *old person* 耂 and *bent* 丂, a reference to *wisdom* that an old man bent with age has.

GR2 N4 AP

Example Sentences

1. 何かいい参考書はないかな。
   Nani ka ii sankōsho wa nai ka na.
   I wonder if there might be any good <u>reference books</u>.

2. 最近、思考力の低下を感じるよ。
   Saikin, shikōryoku no teika o kanjiru yo.
   Lately I've been finding it hard <u>to concentrate</u>.

3. 私は考古学に興味があります。
   Watashi wa kōkogaku ni kyōmi ga arimasu.
   I'm interested in <u>archeology</u>.

4. それはいい考えだね。
   Sore wa ii kangae da ne.
   That's a good <u>idea</u>!

5. 彼の考え方にはついて行けない。
   Kare no kangaekata ni wa tsuite ikenai.
   I cannot follow his <u>way of thinking</u>.

Common Compounds and Phrases

参考	**sankō**	reference; consultation
思考	**shikō**	thinking; thought
考古学	**kōkogaku**	archeology
選考	**senkō**	selection; choice
考慮	**kōryo**	consideration; reflection
考え方	**kangaekata**	a way of thinking; an opinion
考え過ぎ	**kangae-sugi**	thinking too much

The fourth stroke tapers down from right to left, and the last stroke is one continuous action.

6　一　十　土　耂　考　考

考

147 光

コウ KŌ
ひかり hikari
ひか・る hika(ru)

light; to shine

The character 光 shows a *person* 儿 carrying a *torch* 屮 giving off *light*.

GR2 N4

Example Sentences

1. イギリスへは観光旅行で行きました。
   Igirisu e wa kankō ryokō de ikimashita.
   I went to Britain on a sightseeing trip.

2. レーサーたちは栄光を目指して疾走した。
   Rēsā-tachi wa eikō o mezashite shissō shita.
   With their hopes set on glory, the drivers raced at full speed.

3. 美しい光景に目を奪われた。
   Utsukushii kōkei ni me o ubawareta.
   I was captivated by the beautiful landscape.

4. 彼女の目に涙が光っていた。
   Kanojo no me ni namida ga hikatte ita.
   Tears were glistening in her eyes.

5. 今月も光熱費が増えた。
   Kongetsu mo kōnetsuhi ga fueta.
   The cost of utilities increased again this month.

Common Compounds and Phrases

観光	**kankō**	sightseeing; tourism
栄光	**eikō**	glory; honor
光熱	**kōnetsu**	light and heat
光景	**kōkei**	a scene; a sight
日光	**nikkō**	sunlight; Nikkō (a place)
光化学	**kōkagaku**	photochemical
スモッグ	**sumoggu**	smog
光ファイバー	**hikari-faibā**	an optical fiber

The sixth stroke hooks up at the end.

6 丨 丬 丬 屮 屵 光

光

148 合

ゴウ GŌ ガッ GA'
あ・う a(u) あ・わす a(wasu)
あ・わせる a(waseru)

together; total; to combine

The character 合 shows a *lid* and a *bowl* being *put together*.

GR2 N4 AP

Example Sentences

1. 明日は朝八時に集合して下さい。
   Ashita wa asa hachiji ni shūgō shite kudasai.
   Please be there tomorrow morning at 8:00.

2. 富士山の五合目までは車で行けます。
   Fuji-san no gogōme made wa kuruma de ikemasu.
   You can go up to the fifth station on Mount Fuji by car.

3. なかなか意見が合わなかった。
   Naka naka iken ga awanakatta.
   We just couldn't see eye to eye.

4. とてもよくお似合いですよ。
   Totemo yoku oniai desu yo.
   That outfit really suits you!

5. 合わせていくらになりましたか。
   Awasete ikura ni narimashita ka
   How much did it come to in total?

Common Compounds and Phrases

集合	**shūgō**	gathering; meeting
合意	**gōi**	mutual consent; agreement
合計	**gōkei**	a total
合理的	**gōriteki**	rational; logical
合同	**gōdō**	combination; joint, united
割合	**wariai**	a proportion; a rate; a ratio
合図	**aizu**	a signal; a sign

The third stroke does not touch the outside strokes.

6 丿 人 亼 亽 合 合

合

149 死

シ SHI
し・ぬ shi(nu)

to die

The character 死 combines *bone* 歹 and *fallen person* ヒ. The association of these elements conveys the idea of the *death* of a person.

GR3　N4

Example Sentences

1. 妹は未だにペットの死を悲しんでいる。
   Imōto wa imada ni petto no <u>shi</u> o kanashinde iru.
   My younger sister is still grieving over the <u>death</u> of her pet.

2. 台風で大勢の死傷者が出た。
   Taifū de ōzei no <u>shishōsha</u> ga deta.
   Many <u>people</u> were either <u>killed or injured</u> in the typhoon.

3. 試験前に必死になって勉強した。
   Shiken-mae ni <u>hisshi</u> ni natte benkyō shita.
   I studied <u>frantically</u> right before the exam.

4. 同級生が交通事故で死亡した。
   Dōkyūsei ga kōtsū jiko de <u>shibō shita</u>.
   A classmate of mine <u>died</u> in a traffic accident.

5. 死因の第一位はガンです。
   <u>Shiin</u> no dai-ichii wa gan desu.
   The <u>primary cause of death</u> is cancer.

Common Compounds and Phrases

死傷者	**shishōsha**	casualties
必死	**hisshi**	frantic; desperate; certain death
死者	**shisha**	a dead person; the deceased
死因	**shiin**	the cause of someone's death
死体	**shitai**	a dead body
死亡	**shibō**	death
早死に	**hayajini**	a premature death

The last stroke sweeps upwards.

6　一　丆　歹　歹　歹　死

死

---

150 字

ジ JI

a character; a letter

The character 字, which combines *house* 宀 and *child* 子, can be thought of as a child in a house who is studying *characters*.

GR1　N4　AP

Example Sentences

1. 漢字は表意文字です。
   Kanji wa <u>hyōi moji</u> desu.
   <u>Chinese characters</u> are <u>ideographic</u>.

2. 名字を先に書いて下さい。
   <u>Myōji</u> o saki ni kaite kudasai.
   Please write your <u>surname</u> first.

3. 映画の字幕を読むのは、苦手です。
   Eiga no jimaku o yomu no wa, nigate desu.
   I am not good at reading <u>movie subtitles</u>.

4. 盲人のための点字が打ってあります。
   Mōjin no tame no <u>tenji</u> ga utte arimasu.
   <u>Braille</u> has been provided for the blind.

5. 今年も、多くの会社が赤字を出した。
   Kotoshi mo, ōku no kaisha ga <u>akaji</u> o dashita.
   A lot of companies suffered <u>a deficit</u> again this year.

Common Compounds and Phrases

字幕	**jimaku**	(movie) subtitles
点字	**tenji**	braille
字典	**jiten**	a character dictionary
赤字	**akaji**	a deficit; in the red
数字	**sūji**	a figure; a numeral
赤十字	**sekijūji**	the Red Cross
習字	**shūji**	calligraphy

The fifth stroke ends with a hook.

6　丶　丷　宀　宁　字　字

字

151 自

ジ JI　シ SHI
みずか・ら mizuka(ra)

self; by itself

The character 自 depicts the *nose*, which in Japan is a reference to *oneself*.

GR2　N4　AP

Example Sentences

1. もっと自信を持ちなさい。
   Motto jishin o mochinasai.
   Have more <u>confidence in yourself</u>!

2. どうぞご自由にお取り下さい。
   Dōzo gojiyū ni otori kudasai.
   Please <u>feel free</u> to help yourself.

3. あの人は自立した人ですよ。
   Ano hito wa jiritsu shita hito desu yo.
   He's a very <u>independent</u> person.

4. このままの自然を後世に残したい。
   Kono mama no shizen o kōsei ni nokoshitai.
   I'd like <u>nature</u> to be left as it is for future generations.

5. 自分から彼女に話した方がいいと思う。
   Jibun kara kanojo ni hanashita hō ga ii to omou.
   I think you'd better speak to her <u>yourself</u>.

Common Compounds and Phrases

自信	**jishin**	self-confidence
自由	**jiyū**	freedom; liberty
自立	**jiritsu**	independence; self-reliance
自宅	**jitaku**	one's home
自殺	**jisatsu**	suicide
自転車	**jitensha**	a bicycle
自給自足	**jikyū jisoku**	self-sufficiency

Use the same spacing between horizontal strokes.

6　′　丨　冂　白　自　自

自

---

152 色

ショク SHOKU　シキ SHIKI
いろ iro

color

While hard to discern, the character 色 originally depicted a person bending over another person, i.e., *having sex*.

GR2　N4　AP

Example Sentences

1. その小説家の文章には特色がある。
   Sono shōsetsuka no bunshō ni wa tokushoku ga aru.
   That novelist has <u>a distinctive</u> writing <u>style</u>.

2. どこかで見たことのある景色だなあ。
   Doko ka de mita koto no aru keshiki da nā.
   I know I've seen this <u>scene</u> somewhere before.

3. どうしたの？顔色が悪いよ。
   Dōshita no? Kao-iro ga warui yo.
   What's the matter? You <u>look pale</u>!

4. あの女優は才色兼備だ。
   Ano joyū wa saishoku kenbi da.
   That actress is <u>endowed with both intelligence and beauty</u>.

5. 若いうちは色々な経験をしたほうがいい。
   Wakai uchi wa iroiro na keiken o shita hō ga ii.
   You should try <u>various experiences</u> when you are young.

Common Compounds and Phrases

特色	**tokushoku**	a characteristic
無色	**mushoku**	colorless
才色	**saishoku**	wit and beauty
景色	**keshiki**	scenery; a scene
色々 (な)	**iroiro (na)**	various; assorted
水色	**mizu-iro**	light blue
十人十色	**jūnin toiro**	To each his own. (a saying)

End the last stroke with a hook.

6　′　ク　ク　ヶ　名　色

色

153 早

ソウ SŌ *サッ SA'
はや・い haya(i)
はや・める haya(meru)
はや・まる haya(maru)

early;
to accelerate

The character 早 depicted a *rising sun*, from which the meaning of *early* derived.

GR1 N4 AP

Example Sentences

1. 毎日、早朝ジョギングをしている。
   Mainichi, sōchō jogingu o shite iru.
   Every day, I've been taking <u>early morning</u> jogs.

2. 荷物が届いたので、早速空けてみよう。
   Nimotsu ga todoita node, sassoku akete miyō.
   A parcel has arrived, so let's open it <u>right away</u>.

3. 夕食にはまだ早い。
   Yūshoku ni wa mada hayai.
   It's still too <u>early</u> for dinner.

4. 明日、早起きしよう。
   Ashita, haya-oki shiyō.
   Let's <u>get up early</u> tomorrow!

5. 待ち合わせの時間を三十分早めてください。
   Machiawase no jikan o sanjuppun hayamete kudasai.
   <u>Could you move up</u> the meeting time by thirty minutes?

Common Compounds and Phrases

早朝	**sōchō**	early morning
早期	**sōki**	an early phase
早退	**sōtai**	leaving early
足早	**ashibaya**	quick; light-footed
早番	**hayaban**	an early shift
素早い	**subayai**	quick; agile
*早速	**sassoku**	immediately

Keep the spacing between the horizontal strokes equal.

6 ノ 口 日 日 旦 早

早

154 池

チ CHI
いけ ike

a pond

The character 池 combines *water* 氵 and *snake* 也, which came to mean *pond*.

GR2 N4

Example Sentences

1. そろそろ電池を取り換えた方がいいよ。
   Soro soro denchi o torikaeta hō ga ii yo.
   You'd better change the <u>batteries</u> soon.

2. 用水池の水が減っている。
   Yōsuichi no mizu ga hette iru.
   The water in the <u>reservoir</u> is dropping.

3. 池の鯉に餌をやった。
   Ike no koi ni esa o yatta.
   I fed the carp in the <u>pond</u>.

4. 水不足に備えて、貯水池が作られた。
   Mizubusoku ni sonaete, chosuichi ga tsukurareta.
   The <u>reservoir</u> was built in anticipation of a water shortage.

5. 週末に池袋へ買い物に行こうと思う。
   Shūmatsu ni Ikebukuro e kaimono ni ikō to omou.
   I think that I'll go shopping in <u>Ikebukuro</u> this weekend.

Common Compounds and Phrases

単三電池	**tansan-denchi**	an AA size battery
用水池	**yōsuichi**	a reservoir
貯水池	**chosuichi**	a reservoir
古池	**furuike**	an old pond
溜め池	**tameike**	a reservoir; a holding pond
池田	**Ikeda**	Ikeda (a name)
池袋	**Ikebukuro**	Ikebukuro (a place)

The fifth stroke protrudes, and the sixth stroke ends with a hook.

6 丶 丶 氵 汁 池 池

池

155 地

チ CHI
ジ JI

earth; land

The character 地 combines *soil* 土 and *snake* 也 to give the meaning of *earth*.

GR2 N4 AP

Example Sentences

1. 地下鉄は便利です。
   Chikatetsu wa benri desu.
   The subway is convenient.

2. 地球にやさしい製品を作ろう。
   Chikyū ni yasashii seihin o tsukurō.
   Let's create environmentally-friendly products.

3. 彼は、今の地位に満足している。
   Kare wa, ima no chii ni manzoku shite iru.
   He is satisfied with his present position.

4. その土地の地酒を飲むのが好きです。
   Sono tochi no jizake o nomu no ga suki desu.
   I'm fond of that region's locally brewed *sake*.

5. 日本は、とても地震が多い国です。
   Nihon wa, totemo jishin ga ōi kuni desu.
   Japan is a country where earthquakes occur frequently.

Common Compounds and Phrases

地下鉄	**chikatetsu**	a subway; an underground
地球	**chikyū**	the earth; the globe
地位	**chii**	a position; a status
地味	**jimi**	plain; simple; quiet
地獄	**jigoku**	hell
地元	**jimoto**	a local neighborhood
地震	**jishin**	an earthquake

The third stroke goes up from left to right, and the sixth stroke ends with a hook.

6 一 十 土 圠 地 地

地

156 同

ドウ DŌ
おな・じ ona(ji)

the same

The character 同 depicts a *plank* with a hole drilled in it. The hole is the *same* size on either side of the plank.

GR2 N4 AP

Example Sentences

1. 同時通訳でスピーチを聴いた。
   Dōji tsūyaku de supiichi o kiita.
   We listened to the speech done in simultaneous translation.

2. 私たちは同姓同名なので、よく間違われます。
   Watashitachi wa dōsei dōmei na node, yoku machigaware-masu.
   We have the same family and first names, so people often confuse us.

3. 二つの会社が合同で会議をした。
   Futatsu no kaisha ga gōdō de kaigi o shita.
   The two companies held a joint conference.

4. お正月には親戚一同が集まります。
   Oshōgatsu ni wa shinseki ichidō ga atsumarimasu.
   All of the relatives get together for New Year's.

5. 妹と同じ趣味を持っています。
   Imōto to onaji shumi o motte imasu.
   My sister and I share the same interest.

Common Compounds and Phrases

同時	**dōji**	the same time, hour
同姓同名	**dōsei dōmyō, dōsei dōmei**	a person with the same family and given name
同意	**dōi**	the same meaning / opinion
共同	**kyōdō**	cooperation; collaboration
同一	**dōitsu**	the same; equal
同級生	**dōkyūsei**	a classmate
同様	**dōyō**	the same; similar

End the second stroke with a hook.

6 丨 冂 冂 冋 同 同

同

EXERCISE 13 (145 – 156)

A. Give the readings for the following.

1. 池田さん _____
2. 名字 _____
3. 好む _____
4. 水色 _____
5. 光っている _____
6. 地元 _____
7. 間に合う _____
8. 死にました _____
9. 考え方 _____

B. Match the following.

1. じりつ ( )   a. 合同
2. ちほう ( )   b. 早死に
3. にっこう ( )   c. 用水池
4. とち ( )   d. 地方
5. もじ ( )   e. 日光
6. ようすいち ( )   f. 自立
7. ゆうこう ( )   g. 文字
8. ごうどう ( )   h. 友好
9. はやじに ( )   i. 土地

C. Fill in the blanks with an appropriate kanji according to the English.

1. ____（あし）が ____（はや）い (to be a fast walker)
2. いい ____（かんが）えがある (to have a good idea)
3. ____（いろいろ）な ____（さかな）(various kinds of fish)
4. ____（じぶん）で ____（い）く (to go by oneself)
5. ____（おな）じことを ____（い）う (to repeat oneself)
6. ____（だいす）きな ____（ひと）(the person one loves)
7. ローマ ____（じ）で ____（か）く (to write in Roman letters)
8. ____（て）を ____（あ）わせる (to join hands)
9. ____（でんち）が ____（き）れた (the battery is dead)
10. ____（どうじ）に ____（く）る (to come at the same time)

---

157   肉

ニク NIKU

meat

The character 肉 depicts a slice of *meat* showing the grains of flesh.

GR2 N4 AP

Example Sentences

1. ベジタリアンなので、肉は食べません。
   Bejitarian na node, niku wa tabemasen.
   I'm a vegetarian, so I don't eat meat.

2. このジュースの中には果肉が入っている。
   Kono jūsu no naka ni wa kaniku ga haitte iru.
   This fruit juice contains pulp.

3. あの星は肉眼では見えない。
   Ano hoshi wa nikugan de wa mienai.
   That star is invisible to the naked eye.

4. 彼女は肉親を失った。
   Kanojo wa nikushin o ushinatta.
   She suffered the loss of a relative.

5. その時彼は皮肉っぽく笑った。
   Sono toki kare wa hinikuppoku waratta.
   At that time, he laughed sarcastically.

Common Compounds and Phrases

果肉	**kaniku**	pulp; fruit flesh
肉親	**nikushin**	a blood relative
筋肉	**kinniku**	muscles
肉屋	**nikuya**	a meat shop; a butcher's
皮肉	**hiniku**	irony; sarcasm
焼き肉	**yakiniku**	grilled meat
肉体	**nikutai**	the body; one's physique

The third stroke protrudes. End the fourth and sixth strokes firmly.

6 | 丨 冂 内 内 肉 肉

89

158 有

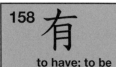

ユウ YŪ *ウ U
あ・る a(ru)

to have; to be

The character 有 combines a *clasping hand* ナ and *meat* 月, suggesting *having something important as one's own.*

GR3 N4 AP

Example Sentences

1. 有名な女優が逮捕された。
   Yūmei na joyū ga taiho sareta.
   A <u>well-known</u> actress was arrested.

2. 被告人は、有罪判決を受けた。
   Hikokunin wa, yūzai-hanketsu o uketa.
   The accused was given a judgment of '<u>guilty</u>'.

3. 軽井沢に別荘が有る。
   Karuizawa ni bessō ga aru.
   I <u>have</u> a villa in Karuizawa.

4. そんな話は有り得ない。
   Sonna hanashi wa arienai.
   I <u>can't believe</u> what I am hearing!

5. 絵を買うために、有り金をはたいた。
   E o kau tame ni, arigane o hataita.
   He <u>used all of his savings</u> to buy the painting.

Common Compounds and Phrases

有罪	**yūzai**	guilt; criminality
有害	**yūgai**	bad; harmful
有料	**yūryō**	for a charge / fee
有効	**yūkō**	valid; effective
有利	**yūri**	profitable; favorable
所有	**shoyū**	possession; ownership
*有無	**umu**	presence or absence; yes or no

The fourth stroke ends with a hook.

6 ノ ナ オ 有 有 有

有

---

159 医

イ I

medicine; a doctor

Originally the character 医 contained the elements of *rice wine pot*, *quiver* and *action*, which combined to suggest making medicinal spirits in a pot. The meanings of *healing* and *doctor* have derived from this.

GR3 N4 AP

Example Sentences

1. 将来の夢は医者になることだ。
   Shōrai no yume wa isha ni naru koto da.
   I have a dream of becoming <u>a doctor</u> one day.

2. 地方では医師不足が深刻な問題になっている。
   Chihō de wa ishi busoku ga shinkoku na mondai ni natte iru.
   <u>A shortage of doctors</u> is a serious problem in the provinces.

3. 専門医を紹介された。
   Senmon'i o shōkai sareta.
   I was referred to <u>a specialist</u>.

4. 年に一回ぐらいは歯医者に行った方がいいよ。
   Nen ni ikkai gurai wa haisha ni itta hō ga ii yo.
   You should see <u>a dentist</u> once a year.

5. この病気のせいで多額の医療費がかかった。
   Kono byōki no sei de tagaku no iryōhi ga kakatta.
   I have had huge <u>medical expenses</u> because of this illness.

Common Compounds and Phrases

医者	**isha**	a doctor; a physician
医院	**iin**	a doctor's clinic
専門医	**senmon'i**	a medical specialist
歯医者	**haisha**	a dentist
医療	**iryō**	medical treatment
医学	**igaku**	medical science; medicine
医師	**ishi**	a medical doctor; a physician

The fifth stroke does not protrude, and the last stroke is one motion.

7 一 ァ 𠄌 𠄌 𠥘 医 医

医

160 究

キュウ KYŪ
きわ・める kiwa(meru)

to study intensely

The character 究 is a combination of *cave* 穴 and *thrusting in the arm* 九, suggesting going to great lengths to *investigate* something.

GR3 N4 AP

Example Sentences

1. その科学者は地震を研究している。
   Sono kagakusha wa jishin o kenkyū shite iru.
   That scientist is doing research on earthquakes.

2. 警察は事件の究明に全力を注いだ。
   Keisatsu wa jiken no kyūmei ni zenryoku o sosoida.
   The police concentrated their efforts on investigating the case.

3. 化学研究室はどちらですか。
   Kagaku kenkyūshitsu wa dochira desu ka.
   Could you tell me where the Chemistry Office is?

4. 彼女は一生をかけて学問を究めた。
   Kanojo wa isshō o kakete gakumon o kiwameta.
   She spent her whole life mastering her field of study.

5. 留年か中退か、究極の選択を迫られた。
   Ryūnen ka chūtai ka, kyūkyoku no sentaku o semarareta.
   To repeat a year or to drop out—an ultimate selection had to be made.

Common Compounds and Phrases

研究	**kenkyū**	research; study
研究室	**kenkyūshitsu**	a study; an office; a lab
研究所	**kenkyūjo**	a research laboratory (institute)
追究	**tsuikyū**	a thorough investigation
究極	**kyūkyoku**	the final; the ultimate
探究	**tankyū**	research; investigation
究明	**kyūmei**	finding out the facts

The sixth stroke bends sharply.

7 ｀ ｀ ｀ 宀 宂 空 究 究

---

161 近

キン KIN
ちか・い chika(i)

near

The character 近 combines *movement* 辶 and *axe* 斤 suggesting a short movement. From this came the meaning of *near*.

GR2 N4 AP

Example Sentences

1. 最近、おもしろい映画見た？
   Saikin, omoshiroi eiga mita?
   Seen any interesting movies lately?

2. 台風が日本列島に接近している。
   Taifū ga Nihon rettō ni sekkin shite iru.
   A typhoon is approaching the Japanese Archipelago.

3. 家から駅が近い。
   Ie kara eki ga chikai.
   The station is close to my house.

4. 学校の近くに本屋がある。
   Gakkō no chikaku ni honya ga aru.
   There's a bookshop close to the school.

5. 遠くの親類より近くの他人。
   Tōku no shinrui yori chikaku no tanin.
   Better is a neighbor that is near than a brother far off. (a saying)

Common Compounds and Phrases

最近	**saikin**	recently; these days
接近	**sekkin**	an approach; an advance
近年	**kinnen**	in recent years
近郊	**kinkō**	suburbs; the outskirts
近所	**kinjo**	the neighborhood
付近	**fukin**	the neighborhood; the vicinity
間近	**majika**	the proximity; nearby

End the fourth stroke firmly, and take care with the sixth stroke.

7 ｀ ｢ ｢ 斤 斤 近 近

162 作

サク SAKU　サ SA
つく・る tsuku(ru)

work; production; to make

The character 作 combines *person* 亻 and *construct* 乍 to give the meaning of *make*.

GR2　N4　AP

Example Sentences

1. テレビ番組を制作している。
   Terebi bangumi o seisaku shite iru.
   They are producing a television program.

2. この作品は名作です。
   Kono sakuhin wa meisaku desu.
   This work is a masterpiece.

3. 編集作業がなかなか進まない。
   Henshū sagyō ga nakanaka susumanai.
   I haven't made much progress with the editing.

4. この薬は、眠くなる作用がありますか。
   Kono kusuri wa, nemuku naru sayō ga arimasu ka.
   Will this medicine make me drowsy?

5. 今夜は、カレーを作ろう。
   Konya wa, karē o tsukurō.
   I'll make curry this evening.

Common Compounds and Phrases

制作	**seisaku**	work; production
名作	**meisaku**	a masterpiece
作文	**sakubun**	a composition; writing
作曲家	**sakkyokuka**	a musical composer
作業	**sagyō**	work; operations
作法	**sahō**	manners; etiquette
手作り	**tezukuri**	handmade; self-produced

The fourth stroke is the longest horizontal one.

7　ノ　イ　イ′　仁　仨　作　作

作

---

163 私

シ SHI
わたくし watakushi, watashi

private; I

The character 私 is a combination of *harvested crops* 禾 and *hold in one's arms* 厶, suggesting *holding one's portion*. The meanings of *pertaining to oneself* or *one's own* derived from this.

GR6　N4　AP

Example Sentences

1. 娘は私立の学校に通っています。
   Musume wa shiritsu no gakkō ni kayotte imasu.
   My daughter attends a private school.

2. 今日は私用で休ませていただきます。
   Kyō wa shiyō de yasumasete itadakimasu.
   I'm having today off on personal business.

3. 家は私鉄の駅に近い。
   Ie wa shitetsu no eki ni chikai.
   My house is close to a private railway station.

4. 彼女の私生活は、誰も知らなかった。
   Kanojo no shiseikatsu wa, dare mo shiranakatta.
   Nobody knew about her private life.

5. 私達にお任せください。
   Watashitachi ni omakase kudasai.
   Please leave it up to us.

Common Compounds and Phrases

私立	**shiritsu**	private; non-government
私用	**shiyō**	private use / business
私鉄	**shitetsu**	a private railway (line)
公私	**kōshi**	public and private matters
私服	**shifuku**	ordinary / informal clothes
私生活	**shiseikatsu**	one's private life
私達	**watashitachi**	we; us; ourselves

The sixth stroke bends sharply.

7　一　二　千　チ　禾　私　私

私

164 住

to live

ジュウ JŪ
す・む su(mu)
す・まう su(mau)

The character 住 combines *person* 亻 and *staying in the same place* 主, suggesting a person living in that place. Hence, the present sense of *live* and *residence*.
GR3 N4 AP

Example Sentences

1. 新しい住所を教えてくれない？
   Atarashii jūsho o oshiete kurenai?
   Could you tell me your new <u>address</u>?

2. あんな高級住宅地に住んでみたいものだ。
   Anna kōkyū jūtakuchi ni sunde mitai mono da.
   I'd really like to live in an upmarket <u>residential area</u> like that.

3. 永住権を申請した。
   Eijūken o shinsei shita.
   I applied for <u>the right to permanent residence</u>.

4. 公園に野良猫が住み着いている。
   Kōen ni nora-neko ga sumitsuite iru.
   A stray cat <u>has taken up residence</u> in the park.

5. 住めば都。
   Sumeba miyako.
   Anywhere is home <u>once you get used to it</u>. (a saying)

Common Compounds and Phrases

住所	**jūsho**	one's address / residence
住宅	**jūtaku**	a house; a residence
住居	**jūkyo**	a house; a dwelling
住まい	**sumai**	a dwelling; a residence; living
居住者	**kyojūsha**	a resident
永住	**eijū**	permanent residence
移住	**ijū**	migration; immigration

Be careful with the angle of the third stroke.

7 ノ 亻 亻 亻 仁 什 住 住

住

---

165 図

a drawing; a diagram; to plan

ズ ZU ト TO
はか・る haka(ru)

The character 図 combines *enclosure* 囗 and a very stylized pictograph of a *rice granary* 㐄, suggesting an enclosed granary drawn on a *map*.
GR2 N4 AP

Example Sentences

1. 地図を見てから出かけた。
   Chizu o mite kara dekaketa.
   We set off, after looking at the <u>map</u>.

2. 用意ができたら合図して下さい。
   Yōi ga dekitara aizu shite kudasai.
   Please <u>indicate</u> when you are ready.

3. 図書館で調べものをする。
   Toshokan de shirabemono o suru.
   I'll do some research in the <u>library</u>.

4. どうも、彼の意図がはっきりしない。
   Dōmo, kare no ito ga hakkiri shinai.
   <u>What he intends to do</u> just isn't clear.

5. まず、身の安全を図ろう。
   Mazu, mi no anzen o hakarō.
   <u>Let's look to</u> safety, first.

Common Compounds and Phrases

合図	**aizu**	a signal; a sign
図表	**zuhyō**	a chart; a diagram
図形	**zukei**	a diagram; a figure
設計図	**sekkeizu**	a plan; a blueprint
天気図	**tenkizu**	a weather map
図書	**tosho**	books
意図	**ito**	an intention; a purpose

End the sixth stroke firmly.

7 丨 冂 冂 冈 図 図 図

図

166 声

セイ SEI *ショウ SHŌ
こえ koe *こわ kowa

voice

The character 声 derived from a pictograph of an instrument made up of suspended stones. *Voice* came from its former meaning of *sound*.

GR2 N4

Example Sentences

1. 首相は声明を発表した。
   Shushō wa seimei o happyō shita.
   The prime minister made an official statement.

2. 彼はデザイナーとしての名声を得た。
   Kare wa dezainā to shite no meisei o eta.
   He gained fame as a designer.

3. 電話の声は、いつもと違うね。
   Denwa no koe wa, itsumo to chigau ne.
   Your voice on the telephone sounds different from the usual.

4. そんな大声を出さないで。
   Sonna ōgoe o dasanai de.
   Stop yelling!

5. 突然、テレビの音声が途絶えた。
   Totsuzen, terebi no onsei ga todaeta.
   The sound on the television suddenly died.

Common Compounds and Phrases

声明	**seimei**	a statement; an announcement
名声	**meisei**	a reputation
音声	**onsei**	the voice; audio
声色	**kowairo**	vocal sound; a voice
声優	**seiyū**	a voice actor
声帯	**seitai**	the vocal chords
大声	**ōgoe**	a loud voice
歌声	**utagoe**	a singing voice

The third stroke is shorter than the first, and the last stroke tapers off.

7　一 十 士 声 声 声 声

声

---

167 赤

セキ SEKI *シャク SHAKU
あか aka あか・い aka(i)
あか・らめる aka(rameru)

red; to redden

The character 赤 used to be written 烾 which combined *big* 大 and *fire* 火. A big fire was, of course, *red*.

GR1 N4 AP

Example Sentences

1. インドネシアは赤道をまたいでいる。
   Indoneshia wa sekidō o mataide iru.
   Indonesia sits astride the equator.

2. 信号は赤です。
   Shingō wa aka desu.
   The traffic light is red.

3. その 赤いセーターを見せて下さい。
   Sono akai sētā o misete kudasai.
   Please show me that red sweater.

4. あの人は赤の他人です。
   Ano hito wa aka no tanin desu.
   That person is a complete stranger.

5. 彼は、恥ずかしそうに顔を赤らめた。
   Kare wa, hazukashisō ni kao o akarameta.
   He blushed shyly.

Common Compounds and Phrases

赤道	**sekidō**	the equator
赤外線	**sekigaisen**	infrared rays
赤飯	**sekihan**	rice cooked with red beans
赤信号	**aka-shingō**	a red traffic signal (light)
赤ちゃん	**akachan**	a baby
赤ん坊	**akanbō**	a baby; an infant
*真っ赤	**makka**	deep red; crimson

The fifth stroke ends with a hook.

7　一 十 土 キ 赤 赤 赤

赤

走
to run

ソウ SŌ
はし・る hashi(ru)

The character 走 depicts a *person running*, taking long strides and with arms outstretched.

GR2 N4 AP

Example Sentences

1. 車が暴走してけが人が出た。
   Kuruma ga bōsō shite keganin ga deta.
   People were injured because the car <u>was being driven recklessly</u>.

2. 飛行機が滑走しはじめた。
   Hikōki ga kassō shihajimeta.
   The airplane began to <u>taxi out</u>.

3. 銀行強盗はまだ逃走中です。
   Ginkō gōtō wa mada tōsōchū desu.
   The bank robber is still <u>at large</u>.

4. 百メートルを十一秒で走った。
   Hyaku-mētoru o jūichi-byō de hashitta.
   I <u>ran</u> the one hundred meters in 11 seconds.

5. 向こうの大きな木まで競走しよう。
   Mukō no ōki na ki made kyōsō shiyō.
   <u>I'll race</u> you to that big tree over there.

Common Compounds and Phrases

暴走	**bōsō**	reckless driving; speeding
滑走路	**kassōro**	a runway; an airstrip
逃走	**tōsō**	a flight; an escape
脱走	**dassō**	to escape; to flee
競走	**kyōsō**	a race; a run
走行距離	**sōkō kyori**	the distance covered; mileage
一走り	**hitoppashiri,**	a run; a dash
	hitohashiri	

The third stroke is longer than the one above it.

7   一 十 土 キ キ 走 走

走

EXERCISE 14 (157 – 168)

A. Give the readings for the following.

1. 私 _____
2. 近く _____
3. 究める _____
4. 作文 _____
5. 住まい _____
6. 医学 _____
7. 赤ちゃん _____
8. 肉食 _____
9. 合図 _____
10. 赤十字 _____

B. Give the English for the following.

1. 走っている車 _____
2. 夕食を作る _____
3. 天気図を読む _____
4. 近道をする _____
5. 大声を出さないで下さい _____
6. 肉を毎日食べる _____
7. 赤いソックスを買う _____

8. あまり有名ではない人 _____
9. 私立の学校 _____
10. 駅の近くに住んでいる _____

C. Rewrite the following using a mixture of kanji and kana.

1. あからめる _____
2. まぢか _____
3. はしった _____
4. ちず _____
5. ぎゅうにく _____
6. てづくりの _____
7. わたしたちの _____
8. ある _____
9. あかくなる _____
10. ちいさいこえ _____

169 村

ソン SON
むら mura

a village

The character 村 combines *tree* 木 and *measure* 寸, and can be thought of as measuring wood to make buildings for a *village*.

GR1 N4 AP

Example Sentences

1. あの農村の人口が大分減った。
   Ano nōson no jinkō ga daibu hetta.
   The population of that <u>rural community</u> has dropped considerably.

2. 僕は小さな漁村で育った。
   Boku wa chiisa na gyoson de sodatta.
   I was raised in a small <u>fishing village</u>.

3. 村上さんは村長でした。
   Murakami san wa sonchō deshita.
   <u>Mr. Murakami</u> used to be the <u>village leader</u>.

4. 山奥の村は地震で大きな被害を受けた。
   Yamaoku no mura wa jishin de ōki na higai o uketa.
   <u>The mountain village</u> suffered great damage in the earthquake.

5. 村人のほとんどはお年寄りだ。
   Murabito no hotondo wa otoshiyori da.
   Most of <u>the villagers</u> are elderly.

Common Compounds and Phrases

農村	**nōson**	a farming village; a rural community
漁村	**gyoson**	a fishing village
村長	**sonchō**	a village chief
市町村	**shichōson**	cities, towns and villages
無医村	**muison**	a village without a doctor
村人	**murabito**	a villager
村八分	**mura-hachibu**	ostracism

The third stroke is longer than the fourth. The sixth stroke ends with a hook.

7　一　十　才　木　木　村　村

村

170 体

タイ TAI　テイ TEI
からだ karada

the body; an object

The character 体 combines *person* 亻 and *foundation* 本 suggesting that the foundation of a person is the *body*.

GR2 N4 AP

Example Sentences

1. 近頃、体重を計っていない。
   Chikagoro, taijū o hakatte inai.
   I haven't <u>weighed myself</u> recently.

2. この作家は独特の文体を持っている。
   Kono sakka wa dokutoku no buntai o motte iru.
   This writer has a distinctive <u>literary style</u>.

3. 外国生活を体験してみたい。
   Gaikoku seikatsu o taiken shite mitai.
   I <u>want to experience</u> life abroad.

4. 世間体ばかり気にしていては何もできない。
   Sekentei bakari ki ni shite ite wa nani mo dekinai.
   If you keep worrying about <u>what other people think</u>, you won't be able to get anything done.

5. 一日中テニスをしたら、体中が痛くなった。
   Ichinichijū tenisu o shitara, karadajū ga itaku natta.
   After playing tennis all day, I ached <u>all over</u>.

Common Compounds and Phrases

体重	**taijū**	one's weight
文体	**buntai**	a literary style
体験	**taiken**	(personal) experience
大体	**daitai**	generally; on the whole
体調	**taichō**	physical condition
世間体	**sekentei**	appearances; decency
体付き	**karadatsuki**	one's build; one's figure

End the second and fourth strokes firmly.

7　ノ　亻　仁　什　休　休　体

体

171 町

チョウ CHŌ
まち machi

a town; a city

The character 町 combines *rice paddy* 田 and *step* 丁 to mean edge of the rice fields—the place where people congregate, hence *town*.

GR1 N4 AP

Example Sentences

1. 先日、町長選挙があった。
   Senjitsu, chōchō senkyo ga atta.
   The election for <u>town mayor</u> took place the other day.

2. 新しい家は南町三丁目です。
   Atarashii ie wa <u>minami-machi</u> sanchōme desu.
   Our new house is in <u>Minami-machi</u>, in the third section.

3. この町は住み心地がよい。
   Kono <u>machi</u> wa sumigokochi ga yoi.
   This <u>town</u> is comfortable to live in.

4. 本町通りの喫茶店で待ち合わせをした。
   Honchō-dōri no kissaten de machi-awase o shita.
   We arranged to meet at a café on <u>Honchō Street</u>.

5. 京都の美しい町並みが印象に残った。
   Kyōto no utsukushii <u>machi-nami</u> ga inshō ni nokotta.
   I was impressed by the beauty of <u>the streets</u> of Kyoto.

Common Compounds and Phrases

町長	**chōchō**	a town mayor
町会	**chōkai**	a town council
町並み	**machinami**	a row of stores and houses
田舎町	**inaka-machi**	a country town
町角	**machikado**	a street corner
港町	**minato-machi**	a port city
町外れ	**machi-hazure**	the outskirts of a town

End the last stroke with a hook.

7 　丨 冂 冂 田 田 町 町

町

172 弟

テイ TEI ＊ダイ DAI
＊デ DE

younger brother; pupil; disciple

The character 弟 depicted *stakes bound with twine*. The lower ノ represents *low*, and from this came *younger brother*, who is low in position and short in height.

GR2 N4 AP

Example Sentences

1. あの二人は師弟でもあり友人でもある。
   Ano futari wa <u>shitei</u> de mo ari yūjin de mo aru.
   The two of them are <u>master and pupil</u> as well as friends.

2. 兄弟げんかはやめなさい。
   <u>Kyōdai</u> genka wa yamenasai.
   Stop <u>fighting with your brother</u>!

3. あの先生には三十人の弟子がいる。
   Ano sensei ni wa sanjūnin no <u>deshi</u> ga iru.
   That teacher has thirty <u>pupils</u>.

4. 四つ違いの弟がいます。
   Yottsu chigai no <u>otōto</u> ga imasu.
   I have <u>a brother</u> who is four years younger than me.

5. 従兄弟が隣の町に住んでいる。
   <u>Itoko</u> ga tonari no machi ni sunde iru.
   <u>My cousin</u> lives in the next town.

Common Compounds and Phrases

師弟	**shitei**	master and pupil
子弟	**shitei**	children
高弟	**kōtei**	one's best student
徒弟	**totei**	an apprentice
兄弟	**kyōdai**	brothers / sisters; a pal
＊弟子	**deshi**	a pupil; a disciple
＊従兄弟	**itoko**	a cousin

The fifth stroke ends with a hook, and the sixth stroke does not protrude.

7 　丶 䒑 䒑 肖 弔 弟 弟

弟

173 低

low; to lower

テイ TEI
ひく・い hiku(i)
ひく・める hiku(meru)
ひく・まる hiku(maru)

The character 低 comprises the elements *person* イ, *hill* 氏 and *base line* 一, indicating the *lowly commoners* at the bottom of the hill. From this, the meaning of *low* derived.

GR4 N4 AP

Example Sentences

1. 昨年度の出生率は過去最低だった。
   Sakunendo no shusshōritsu wa kako saitei datta.
   Last year's birth rate was the <u>lowest on record</u>.

2. 今週は、低気圧の影響で雨が多い。
   Konshū wa, teikiatsu no eikyō de ame ga ōi.
   This week there will be heavy downpours due to the influence of <u>a low-pressure area</u>.

3. 今朝は、低温で霜が降りた。
   Kesa wa, teion de shimo ga orita.
   This morning <u>the low temperature</u> produced a frost.

4. 妹は私より背が低い。
   Imōto wa watashi yori se ga hikui.
   My younger sister is <u>shorter than me</u>.

5. 近年の大学生の学力の低下は著しい。
   Kinnen no daigakusei no gakuryoku no teika wa ichijirushii.
   There has been a marked <u>decline</u> in the scholastic attainment of university students in recent years.

Common Compounds and Phrases

最低	**saitei**	minimum; lowest; worst
低気圧	**teikiatsu**	low atmospheric pressure
低温	**teion**	a low temperature
低下	**teika**	a fall; a decline; a drop
高低	**kōtei**	unevenness; a fluctuation
低血圧	**teiketsuatsu**	low blood pressure
腰が低い	**koshi ga hikui**	modest; unpretentious

Don't forget to add the last stroke.

7 　ノ　イ　イ　仁　任　低　低

低

174 売

to sell

バイ BAI
う・る u(ru)

The character 売 combines *put out* 士 (from 出) and 兀 *buy* (from 買). *To sell* comes from the idea of *put out for buying*.

GR2 N4 AP

Example Sentences

1. この雑誌は、毎週水曜日発売です。
   Kono zasshi wa, maishū suiyōbi hatsubai desu.
   This magazine <u>goes on sale</u> every Wednesday.

2. あの店では切手も売っている。
   Ano mise de wa kitte mo utte iru.
   They also <u>sell</u> stamps at that store.

3. 彼は情報をライバル会社に売った。
   Kare wa jōhō o raibaru gaisha ni utta.
   He <u>leaked information</u> to a rival company.

4. あの子は今売り出し中の歌手です。
   Ano ko wa ima uridashi-chū no kashu desu.
   That girl is an <u>up-and-coming</u> singer.

5. 話題の映画の前売り券はすでに完売だった。
   Wadai no eiga no maeuriken wa sude ni kanbai datta.
   Advance tickets for the talked-about movie had already <u>sold out</u>.

Common Compounds and Phrases

発売	**hatsubai**	offering for sale
販売	**hanbai**	sales; selling
商売	**shōbai**	trade; business
前売り	**maeuri**	advance sale
安売り	**yasu-uri**	to sell cheaply; a bargain sale
売り物	**urimono**	things for sale
売り切れ	**urikire**	sold out

The first stroke is longer than the one below it, and the seventh stroke ends with a hook.

7 　一　十　土　吉　声　売　売

売

175 別

ベツ BETSU
わか・れる waka(reru)

another;
to separate

The character 別 is a combination of a derivate of *bones* 另 and *sword* 刂, suggesting *splitting bones with a sword*. The more general meaning of *divide* came from this.
GR4 N4 AP

Example Sentences

1. それは、別な問題だと思う。
   Sore wa, betsu na mondai da to omou.
   I think that that is quite a <u>different</u> matter.

2. 特別扱いは必要ない。
   Tokubetsu atsukai wa hitsuyō nai.
   There is no call for <u>special</u> treatment.

3. 昨日は、同僚の送別会があった。
   Kinō wa, dōryō no sōbetsukai ga atta.
   <u>A farewell party</u> for a co-worker was held yesterday.

4. 銭湯は男女別になっている。
   Sentō wa danjo-betsu ni natte iru.
   The public bath has <u>separate sections for men and women</u>.

5. 友達と駅で別れた。
   Tomodachi to eki de wakareta.
   My friend and I <u>parted</u> at the station.

Common Compounds and Phrases

特別な	**tokubetsu na**	particular; special
別人	**betsujin**	a different person
男女別	**danjo-betsu**	separated by gender
差別	**sabetsu**	discrimination; a distinction
送別会	**sōbetsukai**	a farewell party
別世界	**bessekai**	another world
別々 (に)	**betsubetsu (ni)**	separately; respectively

End the fourth stroke with a hook.

7 　丶 冂 口 号 另 別 別

別

---

176 英

エイ EI

superb; England

The character 英 combines *plant* ⺿ and *center* 央, to express the notion of *bloom*. Originally meaning a blossoming flower that had great beauty, the sense of *superior* derived from this. A phonetic association has given it the meaning of *England*.
GR4 N4 AP

Example Sentences

1. アキレスはギリシャ神話の英雄だった。
   Akiresu wa girisha shinwa no eiyū datta.
   Achilles was <u>a hero</u> of Greek mythology.

2. この技術は世界中の英知を集めて作られた。
   Kono gijutsu wa sekai-jū no eichi o atsumete tsukurareta.
   The <u>wisdom</u> of people from around the world was brought together to develop this technology.

3. 毎週火曜日に、英会話の授業がある。
   Maishū kayōbi ni, eikaiwa no jugyō ga aru.
   I have an <u>English conversation</u> class every Tuesday.

4. その言葉はまだ和英辞典に載っていなかった。
   Sono kotoba wa mada waei jiten ni notte inakatta.
   The word wasn't listed yet in the <u>Japanese-English dictionary</u>.

Common Compounds and Phrases

英雄	**eiyū**	a hero
英知	**eichi**	wisdom; intelligence
英会話	**eikaiwa**	English conversation
英語	**eigo**	the English language
和英	**waei**	Japanese-English
英国	**eikoku**	Britain; the United Kingdom
英訳	**eiyaku**	an English translation

The seventh stroke protrudes.

8 　一 十 艹 艹 芒 苎 英 英

英

177 画

ガ GA　カク KAKU

a picture; a drawing;
a kanji stroke

The character 画 shows a *hand holding a brush* 一, over a *rice paddy* 田 that is surrounded by a *partition* 凵. This suggested dividing fields with a brush, which then came to mean *draw*.
GR2　N4　AP

Example Sentences

1. 映画を見に行かない。
   Eiga o mi ni ikanai.
   Would you like to go see a movie?

2. 将来は画家になりたい。
   Shōrai wa gaka ni naritai.
   I'd like to become an artist in the future.

3. 旅行の計画はありますか。
   Ryokō no keikaku wa arimasu ka.
   Do you have any travel plans?

4. 街の区画整理が行われる。
   Machi no kukaku seiri ga okonawareru.
   A readjustment of town lots will be undertaken.

5. 「字」の画数は六画です。
   Ji no **kakusū** wa rokkaku desu.
   The character 字 has six strokes.

Common Compounds and Phrases

映画	**eiga**	a movie; a film
画家	**gaka**	a painter; an artist
漫画	**manga**	a cartoon; comics
画面	**gamen**	a picture; a screen
録画	**rokuga**	videotape recording
計画	**keikaku**	a plan; a project
画数	**kakusū**	a *kanji* stroke count

The fourth stroke does not protrude (top and bottom).

8　一 厂 厂 币 冊 面 面 画 画

画

178 京

キョウ KYŌ　ケイ KEI

the capital

The character 京 derived from a pictograph of a *house on a hill*, a reference to the residences of nobles, who spent much of their time in the *capital*.
GR2　N4　AP

Example Sentences

1. 上京して十年たつ。
   Jōkyō shite jūnen tatsu.
   Ten years have passed since I came to Tokyo.

2. 兄は京大を去年卒業した。
   Ani wa Kyōdai o kyonen sotsugyō shita.
   My elder brother graduated from Kyoto University last year.

3. 妻の料理は京風の味付けだ。
   Tsuma no ryōri wa kyōfū no ajitsuke da.
   My wife uses Kyoto-style seasoning in her cooking.

4. 第三京浜を使って家へ帰る。
   Daisan Keihin o tsukatte ie e kaeru.
   I'll go back home using the Daisan Keihin Expressway.

Common Compounds and Phrases

上京	**jōkyō**	going up to the capital
東京	**Tōkyō**	Tokyo (a place)
京風	**kyōfū**	Kyoto-style
京都	**Kyōto**	Kyoto (a place)
京人形	**kyō-ningyō**	a Kyoto doll
京阪	**Keihan**	the Kyoto-Osaka area
*北京	**Pekin**	Beijing (a place)

The second stroke is longer than those below it, and the sixth stroke ends with a hook.

8　' 亠 亠 古 古 宁 京 京

京

179 姉

シ SHI
あね ane

an elder sister

The character 姉 combines *woman* 女 and a *vine winding around a stake* 市, symbolizing growth and the associated meaning of *starting point*. From this character derives the meaning of *female first born*.
GR2 N4 AP

Example Sentences

1. あの姉妹はよく似ていますね。
   Ano shimai wa yoku nite imasu ne.
   Those sisters look alike, don't they?

2. 京都とボストンは姉妹都市です。
   Kyōto to Bosuton wa shimai toshi desu.
   Kyoto and Boston are sister cities.

3. 三つ上の姉がいる。
   Mittsu ue no ane ga iru.
   I have a sister who is three years older than me.

4. お姉ちゃん、ちょっとこれ貸して。
   Onēchan, chotto kore kashite.
   Lend me this, will you? (said to an older sister).

5. 彼の奥さんは姉さん女房だ。
   Kare no okusan wa anesan nyōbō da.
   His wife is older than him.

Common Compounds and Phrases

姉妹	**shimai**	sisters
姉妹都市	**shimai toshi**	a sister city
姉妹品	**shimai-hin**	a companion product
姉妹校	**shimaikō**	a sister school
長姉	**chōshi**	the eldest daughter
姉さん女房	**anesan nyōbō**	a wife older than her husband
*お姉さん	**onēsan**	an older sister; young lady

The first stroke is one fluid motion, and the seventh stroke ends with a hook.

8 く 夕 女 女' 圹 圹 圹 姉

姉

180 使

シ SHI
つか・う tsuka(u)

**to use;
an envoy**

Combining *person* 亻 and *doing work* 吏, the character 使 originally meant *having a person work*. Hence the meanings *use* and *messenger*.
GR3 N4 AP

Example Sentences

1. 最初の一ヶ月の使用料は無料です。
   Saisho no ikkagetsu no shiyōryō wa muryō desu.
   The first month's rental is free of charge.

2. 先週、新しい駐日大使が任命された。
   Senshū, atarashii chūnichi taishi ga ninmei sareta.
   The new U.S. ambassador to Japan was appointed last week.

3. この機械の使い方を教えてくれる。
   Kono kikai no tsukaikata o oshiete kureru.
   Could you show me how to use this machine?

4. 若者たちは、最新の携帯電話を使いこなしている。
   Wakamonotachi wa, saishin no keitai denwa o tsukaikonashite iru.
   Young people have mastered the use of the latest cellular phones.

5. 「オズの魔法使い」を見たことがありますか。
   'Ozu no mahōzukai' o mita koto ga arimasu ka.
   Have you seen 'The Wizard of Oz'?

Common Compounds and Phrases

使用料	**shiyōryō**	a rental fee, charge
大使	**taishi**	an ambassador
使役	**shieki**	employment; service
使い方	**tsukaikata**	how to use, handle
使い道	**tsukaimichi**	a use
使い捨て	**tsukaisute**	disposable; throwaway
召使	**meshitsukai**	a servant; a domestic help

The seventh stroke protrudes.

8 丿 亻 亻 仁 仃 乍 乍 使

使

101

EXERCISE 15 (169 – 180)

A. Give the readings for the following.

1. お姉さん _____
2. 使い方 _____
3. 売り切れ _____
4. 別れる _____
5. 英会話 _____
6. 村人 _____
7. 別々に _____
8. 北京 _____
9. 町長 _____
10. 低くない _____

B. Rewrite using kanji where possible.

1. えいこく _____
2. まえうり _____
3. とうきょう _____
4. まちはずれ _____
5. からだじゅう _____
6. にほんたいし _____
7. ていかする _____

8. つかわないでください _____
9. きょうだい _____
10. くべつ _____

C. Give the meanings for the following.

1. 弟さん _____
2. 電話を使用する _____
3. 町に住む _____
4. 声を低める _____
5. 小さな村 _____
6. 安く売る _____
7. 別れの時 _____
8. 人の体 _____
9. 姉が二人いる _____
10. 上京する _____

Review 5 (1 – 180)

A. Give the readings for the following.

1. 低い _____
2. 大体 _____
3. 姉 _____
4. 兄弟 _____
5. 使わない _____
6. 村長 _____
7. 別れる _____
8. 下町 _____
9. 売っている _____
10. 英語 _____

B. Write in kanji and kana.

1. a villager _____
2. English conversation _____
3. a distinction _____
4. your younger brother _____
5. an ambassador _____
6. physical strength _____
7. going up to the capital _____
8. a town mayor _____
9. early _____
10. an advance sale _____

C. Match the following.

1. 男女別 (　)　　a. つかいかた
2. 長姉　 (　)　　b. なかむら
3. 体中　 (　)　　c. みょうじ
4. 名字　 (　)　　d. やすうり
5. 低下　 (　)　　e. えいぶん
6. 安売り (　)　　f. ちょうし
7. 東京　 (　)　　g. からだじゅう
8. 中村　 (　)　　h. だんじょべつ
9. 使い方 (　)　　i. とうきょう
10. 英文　 (　)　　j. ていか

D. Write in English.

1. 色々な _____
2. 売り出し中 _____
3. 死体 _____
4. 低い声 _____
5. 市町村 _____
6. 使い道 _____
7. 町外れ _____
8. 文体 _____
9. 好み _____
10. 別人 _____

E. Match the following.

1. oneself ( )
2. different, another ( )
3. a disciple ( )
4. use, employment ( )
5. sold out ( )
6. a store ( )
7. separately ( )
8. ostracism ( )
9. to divide up ( )
10. children ( )
11. English literature ( )
12. a town council ( )
13. Beijing ( )
14. a fluctuation ( )
15. Britain ( )
16. an angel ( )
17. buying and selling ( )
18. a way of thinking ( )
19. your older sister ( )
20. death by drowning ( )

a. お姉さん
b. 高低
c. 英文学
d. 町会
e. 売買
f. 天使
g. 子弟
h. 北京
i. 考え方
j. 売店
k. 別の
l. 水死
m. 弟子
n. 使用
o. 売り切れ
p. 村八分
q. 自分
r. 別々に
s. 別ける
t. 英国

F. Rewrite the following using kanji where possible.

1. (あね)の(め)の(いろ)は(おとうと)と(おな)じではない。

2. (いけだ)(い院)が(わたし)の家に(いち番)(ちか)い。

3. (ゆうしょく)に(わたし)の(す)きな(にく料理)を(つく)ろうと(かんが)えている。

4. (ありむら)さんは(からだ)が(おお)きくて、(こえ)が(ひく)い。

5. (送べつかい)に(ま)に(あ)うように(はやめ)に家を(で)た。

6. (いま)、(じぶん)の(す)んでいる(まち)を(ちず)で探してみた。

7. (こう告)の「ペキン」の(もじ)が(あか)く(ひか)っていた。

8. (えいかいわ)に遅れそうなので、(必し)に(はし)った。

9. この(はな)を(つく)るのに(おお)くの(研きゅう費)が(つか)われた。

10. (ゆうめい)な(が家)の絵が(う)りに(だ)された。

181

始

シ SHI

はじ・める haji(meru)
はじ・まる haji(maru)

to begin

The character 始 combines *woman* 女 and *plow* 台, suggesting *first-born daughter* and *starting point*.

GR3 N4 AP

Example Sentences

1. この店は年末年始はお休みです。
   Kono mise wa <u>nenmatsu nenshi</u> wa oyasumi desu.
   This store will be closed <u>over the New Year</u>.

2. 一学期の始業式は、何日ですか。
   Ichigakki no <u>shigyōshiki</u> wa, nannichi desu ka.
   What is the date of <u>the opening ceremony</u> for the first semester?

3. さあ、始めましょう。
   Sā, <u>hajimemashō</u>.
   Okay, <u>let's begin!</u>

4. 午後から雨が降り始めた。
   Gogo kara ame ga <u>furihajimeta</u>.
   It <u>began raining</u> in the afternoon.

5. 試合は、何時から始まりますか。
   Shiai wa, nanji kara <u>hajimarimasu</u> ka.
   What time <u>will</u> the game <u>begin</u>?

Common Compounds and Phrases

年末年始	nenmatsu nenshi	the year-end and New Year holidays
始業式	shigyōshiki	an opening (inauguration) ceremony
開始	kaishi	the beginning; the opening
原始的	genshiteki	primitive
始発	shihatsu	the starting station
始末	shimatsu	managing; dealing with
始まり	hajimari	the beginning

End the first stroke firmly.

8 ㄑ 女 女 如 奶 始 始 始

始

182 事

ジ JI
こと koto

affair; abstract thing

Originally, the character 事 was a pictograph of a *hand gripping a flag*, suggesting the beginning of work in a public office. From this, the meanings *work* and *affair* have derived.
GR3 N4 AP

Example Sentences

1. 事実が明らかになった。
   Jijitsu ga akiraka ni natta.
   The facts became clear.

2. 水道工事がまだ終わらない。
   Suidō kōji ga mada owaranai.
   The water-service work is yet to be completed.

3. 大事な約束を破ってしまった。
   Daiji na yakusoku o yabutte shimatta.
   I failed to keep an important appointment.

4. 仕事の帰りに事故にあった。
   Shigoto no kaeri ni jiko ni atta.
   He met with an accident on the way home from work.

5. 物事には裏と表がある。
   Monogoto ni wa ura to omote ga aru.
   There are two sides to everything.

Common Compounds and Phrases

事実	**jijitsu**	a fact; a reality
事故	**jiko**	an accident; a mishap
返事	**henji**	a reply; an answer
大事な	**daiji na**	important; essential; vital
無事な	**buji na**	safe; uneventful; quiet
物事	**monogoto**	things; everything
出来事	**dekigoto**	a happening; an event

The first and sixth strokes are longer.

8 一 丁 币 币 写 写 写 事

事

183 者

シャ SHA
もの mono

person

Formerly the character 者 was a depiction of a *box for kindling* and later referred to *various things*. From this, the unflattering reference to *person*, in general, has derived.
GR3 N4 AP

Example Sentences

1. 早く医者に診てもらいなさい。
   Hayaku isha ni mite morainasai.
   Go and see a doctor as soon as you can!

2. 彼は記者会見で罪を認めた。
   Kare wa kisha kaiken de tsumi o mitometa.
   He admitted his guilt at the press conference.

3. 阪神淡路大震災では多数の死者が出た。
   Hanshin-Awaji daishinsai de wa tasū no shisha ga deta.
   There were many fatalities in the Great Hanshin-Awaji Earthquake.

4. この機材は初心者にも使いやすい。
   Kono kizai wa shoshinsha ni mo tsukaiyasui.
   This equipment is easy for beginners to handle.

5. 兄は働き者です。
   Ani wa hatarakimono desu.
   My older brother is a hard worker.

Common Compounds and Phrases

記者	**kisha**	a reporter; a journalist
初心者	**shoshinsha**	a beginner; a novice
作者	**sakusha**	a writer; an author; a playwright
役者	**yakusha**	an actor; a performer
著者	**chosha**	an author; a writer
責任者	**sekininsha**	a person responsible
人気者	**ninkimono**	a favorite; a popular person

The third stroke is longer than the first.

8 一 十 土 耂 耂 者 者 者

者

184 所

place

ショ SHO
ところ tokoro

The character 所 is a combination of *wooden door* 戸 and *axe* 斤, suggesting the sound of wood being chopped. Through phonetic borrowing this character came to be associated with the one for *place* 処.
GR3 N4 AP

Example Sentences

1. この近所に図書館がありますか。
   Kono kinjo ni toshokan ga arimasu ka.
   Is there a library in the neighborhood?

2. あの車の所有者を知っていますか。
   Ano kuruma no shoyūsha o shitte imasu ka.
   Do you know who owns that car?

3. また発電所で事故が起きたそうです。
   Mata hatsudensho de jiko ga okita sō desu.
   Apparently there's been another accident in a power station.

4. 京都には見所がたくさんある。
   Kyōto ni wa midokoro ga takusan aru.
   There are lots of good sightseeing spots in Kyoto.

5. 今の所、明日は出掛ける予定はない。
   Ima no tokoro, asu wa dekakeru yotei wa nai.
   At the moment, I don't have any plans to go out tomorrow.

Common Compounds and Phrases

所有者	**shoyūsha**	an owner; a proprietor
発電所	**hatsudensho**	a power station (plant)
長所	**chōsho**	a strong point; a forté
事務所	**jimusho**	an office; business premises
所得	**shotoku**	income; earnings
見所	**midokoro**	a good scene; promise
所々	**tokoro-dokoro**	here and there; in places

The sixth stroke sweeps down.

8 　一　ㄱ　ㅋ　戸　戸　所　所　所

所

---

185 青

blue; green; unripe; new

セイ SEI ＊ショウ SHŌ
あお ao あお・い ao(i)

The character 青 depicted *plant life* 生 by a *well* 井, which was *green*. Some believe that *blue* comes from the color of the water in the well.
GR1 N4 AP

Example Sentences

1. その映画を見て、青春時代を思い出した。
   Sono eiga o mite, seishun jidai o omoidashita.
   Seeing that movie reminded me of my younger days.

2. 信号が青に変わった。
   Shingō ga ao ni kawatta.
   The traffic light changed to green.

3. どうしたの、顔が真っ青だよ。
   Dōshita no, kao ga massao da yo.
   What's the matter? You're very pale.

4. なに青くさいことを言ってるの。
   Nani aokusai koto o itteru no.
   What an immature thing to say!

5. 青空に白い雲が浮かんでいる。
   Aozora ni shiroi kumo ga ukande iru.
   White clouds are floating in the blue sky.

Common Compounds and Phrases

青春	**seishun**	youth; one's prime
青年	**seinen**	a youth
青天の ヘキレキ	**seiten no hekireki**	a bolt from the blue
＊真っ青な	**massao na**	deep blue; deadly pale
青白い	**aojiroi**	pale; pallid
青空	**aozora**	blue sky
青信号	**ao-shingō**	a green traffic signal (light)

The last stroke ends with a hook.

8 　一　十　キ　主　丰　青　青　青

青

186 知

チ CHI
し・る shi(ru)
し・らせる shi(raseru)

to know; to notify; to inform

The character 知 combines *mouth* 口 and *arrow* 矢, suggesting *straightforward* answers are a sign of *wisdom*.

GR2 N4 AP

Example Sentences

1. 一を聞いて十を知る。
   Ichi o kiite jū o shiru.
   A word is enough to the wise. (a saying) (lit. Hear one, <u>know</u> ten.)

2. 試験の結果は郵便で通知します。
   Shiken no kekka wa yūbin de tsūchi shimasu.
   We will <u>notify</u> you of your exam results by mail.

3. 新聞でその事件を知った。
   Shinbun de sono jiken o shitta.
   I <u>learned</u> of that incident from the newspaper.

4. 彼とはパーティーで知り合いました。
   Kare to wa pātii de shiriaimashita.
   I <u>got to know</u> him at a party.

5. メールアドレスを知らせるように言われた。
   Mēru adoresu o shiraseru yō ni iwareta.
   I was asked <u>to provide</u> my e-mail address.

Common Compounds and Phrases

知識	**chishiki**	knowledge; information
通知	**tsūchi**	a notice; communication
無知	**muchi**	ignorance
知事	**chiji**	a governor
知人	**chijin**	an acquaintance
知った かぶり	**shittakaburi**	pretending to know things one does not
知り合い	**shiriai**	an acquaintance

The fourth stroke does not protrude. End the fifth stroke firmly.

8 ノ 匸 午 矢 矢 知 知 知

知

187 注

チュウ CHŪ
そそ・ぐ soso(gu)
*さ・す sa(su)
*つ・ぐ tsu(gu)

to pour; to concentrate

The character 注 combines *water* シ and a *steady candle flame* 主. The sense of *pour* derives from the idea of steadily *pouring* water from above, with *pay attention* being a figurative association.

GR3 N4 AP

Example Sentences

1. お昼におそばを注文しよう。
   Ohiru ni osoba o chūmon shiyō.
   <u>Let's order</u> *soba* (buckwheat noodles) for lunch!

2. 事故の原因はパイロットの不注意だった。
   Jiko no gen'in wa pairotto no fuchūi datta.
   The cause of the accident was put down to pilot <u>error</u>.

3. 彼の演説は人々の注目を集めた。
   Kare no enzetsu wa hitobito no chūmoku o atsumeta.
   His speech gained public <u>attention</u>.

4. コップに水を注いだ。
   Koppu ni mizu o sosoida.
   I <u>poured</u> some water into a glass.

5. この部屋には太陽がさんさんと降り注いでいる。
   Kono heya ni wa taiyō ga sansan to furisosoide iru.
   Sunlight <u>is streaming into</u> the room.

Common Compounds and Phrases

注文	**chūmon**	an order; a request
飛び出し 注意!	**Tobidashi chūi!**	Watch out for children!
注射	**chūsha**	an injection; a shot
注入	**chūnyū**	pouring into; injection; cramming
発注	**hatchū**	placing an order
注意を 注ぐ	**chūi o sosogu**	to pay attention
注ぎ口	**sosogiguchi**	a spout; an opening

The sixth stroke does not protrude.

8 ヽ ヽ シ シ 汁 汁 注 注

注

188 直

チョク CHOKU　ジキ JIKI
ただ・ちに tada(chi ni)
なお・す nao(su)
なお・る nao(ru)

straight; direct; imme-
diately; to fix/be fixed

The character 直 combines *direct* 十, *eye* 目 and *hidden* ∟, suggesting taking a *direct* look at something concealed.

GR2 N3

Example Sentences

1. 彼と直接話して下さい。
   Kare to chokusetsu hanashite kudasai.
   Please speak to him directly.

2. 赤道直下の国に滞在した。
   Sekidō chokka no kuni ni taizai shita.
   He visited a country lying right on the equator.

3. あの人は正直な人ですよ。
   Ano hito wa shōjiki na hito desu yo.
   He's an honest kind of person.

4. 電話を受け、直ちに病院に向かった。
   Denwa o uke, tadachi ni byōin ni mukatta.
   After receiving the call, I headed straight to the hospital.

5. 日本語の発音を直してもらいたい。
   Nihongo no hatsuon o naoshite moraitai.
   I'd like you to correct my Japanese pronunciation.

Common Compounds and Phrases

直接に	**chokusetsu ni**	directly; straight
直下	**chokka**	directly (right) under
直後	**chokugo**	immediately after
直感	**chokkan**	intuition
直通	**chokutsū**	a direct line; a non-stop service
正直な	**shōjiki na**	honest; frank
仲直り	**nakanaori**	reconciliation

The last stroke bends sharply.

8　一　十　ナ　方　古　吉　肖　直

直

189 服

フク FUKU

clothes;
dress

Originally a combination of *boat* 舟 and *a hand working* 殳, the sense of *serve* possibly derives from the idea of working on boat repairs. The related meaning of *clothes* remains unclear.

GR3 N4 AP

Example Sentences

1. 服はきちんとたたんでしまいなさい。
   Fuku wa kichinto tatande shimainasai.
   Fold your clothes properly and put them away.

2. 姉は服装にうるさい。
   Ane wa fukusō ni urusai.
   My older sister is fussy about what she wears.

3. 一服してから仕事を始めよう。
   Ippuku shite kara shigoto o hajimeyō.
   Let's start work after we've had a break!

4. 上官の命令には服従しなければいけない。
   Jōkan no meirei ni wa fukujū shinakereba ikenai.
   We have to obey the orders of our superiors.

5. 新しい制服を着ると気持ちが引き締まる。
   Atarashii seifuku o kiru to kimochi ga hikishimaru.
   When I put on a new uniform, I feel refreshed.

Common Compounds and Phrases

服装	**fukusō**	the style of dress; attire
一服	**ippuku**	a dose; a cup of tea; a smoke; a rest
服従	**fukujū**	obedience; submission
洋服	**yōfuku**	(Western) clothes, dress
衣服	**ifuku**	clothes; clothing
制服	**seifuku**	a uniform
感服	**kanpuku**	admiration; wonder

Be careful with the fifth stroke.

8　丿　刀　月　月　肝　服　服　服

服

190 物

thing

ブツ BUTSU　モツ MOTSU
もの mono

The character 物 combines *cow* 牛 and a *multi-colored cloth streamer* 勿, suggesting the various colors of a cow's coat. Later this came to refer to various *things*.
GR3　N4　AP

Example Sentences

1. 苺は私の大好物です。
   Ichigo wa watashi no daikōbutsu desu.
   Strawberries are my favorite.

2. もっと食物繊維を取るべきだ。
   Motto shokumotsu sen'i o toru beki da.
   I should eat more dietary fiber.

3. 祖母は物を大切にする人です。
   Sobo wa mono o taisetsu ni suru hito desu.
   My grandmother takes good care of things.

4. その絵は本物ですか。
   Sono e wa honmono desu ka.
   Is that picture an original?

5. 早くこの物語の最後が知りたい。
   Hayaku kono monogatari no saigo ga shiritai.
   I'm dying to know how this story ends.

Common Compounds and Phrases

好物	**kōbutsu**	a favorite; a passion
見物	**kenbutsu**	sightseeing
食物/	**shokumotsu /**	food; foodstuffs
食べ物	**tabemono**	
荷物	**nimotsu**	a load; baggage; luggage
本物	**honmono**	a real thing
物覚え	**monooboe**	memory; retentiveness
果物	**kudamono**	fruit

End the sixth stroke with a hook.

8 　丿　ㇰ　牛　牛　牜　物　物　物

物

---

191 歩

a step; rate;
to walk

ホ HO　ブ BU　*フ FU
ある・く aru(ku)
あゆ・む ayu(mu)

The character 歩 can be thought of as *right foot* 止 and *left foot* 少, suggesting placing one foot after the other, in other words, *walking*.
GR2　N4　AP

Example Sentences

1. 進歩しても分からないことは多い。
   Shinpo shite mo wakaranai koto wa ōi.
   In spite of progress, many things remain unknown.

2. セールスマンの給料は歩合制です。
   Sērusuman no kyūryō wa buaisei desu.
   A salesman earns his salary by commission.

3. 駅まで歩いて十分かかります。
   Eki made aruite juppun kakarimasu.
   It's a ten-minute walk to the station.

4. 彼は苦難の道を歩んできた人です。
   Kare wa kunan no michi o ayunde kita hito desu.
   He is a person who has followed a path beset with difficulties.

5. 千里の道も一歩から。
   Senri no michi mo ippo kara.
   A journey of a thousand miles begins with a single step.
   (a saying)

Common Compounds and Phrases

散歩	**sanpo**	a walk; a stroll
一歩	**ippo**	one step
歩行者	**hokōsha**	a pedestrian; a walker
横断歩道	**ōdan hodō**	a pedestrian crossing
徒歩	**toho**	walking
山歩き	**yama-aruki**	mountain hiking
歩み	**ayumi**	walking; progress

The eighth stroke tapers off. The top portion is not 上.

8 　丨　上　止　歩　歩　歩　歩　歩

歩

192 妹

マイ MAI
いもうと imōto

a younger sister

The character 妹 combines *woman* 女 and *immature* 未 to mean *younger sister*.

GR2 N4 AP

Example Sentences

1. あの姉妹は本当に仲がいい。
   Ano shimai wa hontō ni naka ga ii.
   Those <u>sisters</u> really get along well.

2. かわいい妹さんですね。
   Kawaii imōto-san desu ne.
   <u>Your younger sister</u> is cute.

3. 義理の妹は東京に住んでいます。
   Giri no imōto wa Tōkyō ni sunde imasu.
   My <u>sister-in-law</u> lives in Tokyo.

4. 妹分としてかわいがってください。
   Imōtobun to shite kawaigatte kudasai.
   Please treat her kindly as <u>your junior</u>.

5. 事故にあったのは先生の実の妹だそうだ。
   Jiko ni atta no wa sensei no jitsu no imōto da sō da.
   I heard that it was <u>my teacher's actual sister</u> who was in the accident.

Common Compounds and Phrases

義妹	**gimai**	a sister-in-law
義理の妹	**giri no imōto**	one's sister-in-law
弟妹	**teimai**	younger brothers and sisters
実妹	**jitsumai**	one's true (younger) sister
妹さん	**imōtosan**	a person's younger sister
妹分	**imōtobun**	a protegée

The fifth stroke is longer than the fourth.

8	㇒	㇄	女	女	女	妹	妹	妹

妹

EXERCISE 16 (181–192)

A. Give the readings for the following.

1. 青白い _____
2. 好物 _____
3. 所々 _____
4. 知らない _____
5. 始まる _____
6. 直ちに _____
7. 妹さん _____
8. 人気者 _____
9. 歩行者 _____
10. 注文 _____

B. Give the English meanings for the following.

1. 一服する _____
2. 弟がいる所 _____
3. 食事を始める _____
4. 道を歩く _____
5. 古くからの、知り合い _____
6. 大事なこと _____
7. 正直なやり方 _____

8. 医者に来てもらう _____
9. 水を注ぐ _____
10. 青空が広がる _____

C. Match the following.

1. 出来事 ( )　　a. さくしゃ
2. 姉妹 ( )　　b. こうじ
3. 青年 ( )　　c. きんじょ
4. 注目 ( )　　d. ちょくぜん
5. 工事 ( )　　e. しまい
6. 見物 ( )　　f. できごと
7. 直前 ( )　　g. けんぶつ
8. 作者 ( )　　h. ちじ
9. 知事 ( )　　i. ちゅうもく
10. 近所 ( )　　j. せいねん

193 味

ミ MI
あじ aji　あじ・わう aji(wau)

taste

The character 味 combines *mouth* 口 and *unfinished* 未, here suggesting lingering in the mouth, hence, a nice *taste*.

GR3　N4　AP

Example Sentences

1. 何か趣味をお持ちですか。
   Nani ka shumi o omochi desu ka.
   Do you have some kind of <u>hobby</u>?

2. 彼を味方につけたら。
   Kare o mikata ni tsuketara.
   How about <u>trying to get him on your side</u>?

3. もう少し塩味をつけて下さい。
   Mō sukoshi shioaji o tsukete kudasai.
   <u>Add</u> a little more <u>salt</u>.

4. この小説には、味がある。
   Kono shōsetsu ni wa, aji ga aru.
   This novel <u>has a certain appeal</u>.

5. みんなで優勝の喜びを味わった。
   Minna de yūshō no yorokobi o ajiwatta.
   We all <u>savored</u> the joy of taking the championship.

Common Compounds and Phrases

趣味	**shumi**	a hobby; an interest; a taste
味方	**mikata**	a friend; an ally
興味	**kyōmi**	an interest; curiosity
意味	**imi**	a meaning; value; significance
風邪気味	**kaze-gimi**	coming down with a cold
賞味期限	**shōmi kigen**	an expiration date; a use-by date
塩味	**shioaji**	a salty taste

The fifth stroke is longer than the one above it.

8　丨 冂 口 口 ⼝⼀ ⼝⼆ 咔 味 味

味

---

194 明

メイ MEI　ミョウ MYŌ
あか・るい aka(rui)　あき・らか aki(raka)　あ・く a(ku)　あ・かす a(kasu)　あ・かり a(kari)　あか・るむ aka(rumu)　あか・らむ aka(ramu)　あ・ける a(keru)　あ・くる a(kuru)

light; clear; to pass (the night)

The character 明 combines *sun* 日 and *moon* 月, both of which represent *light*.

GR2　N4　AP

Example Sentences

1. 英語の説明書はありますか。
   Eigo no setsumeisho wa arimasu ka.
   Do you have <u>a manual</u> in English?

2. 明日の十時に伺います。
   Ashita (myōnichi, asu) no jūji ni ukagaimasu.
   I'll visit at 10:00 <u>tomorrow</u>.

3. 明るいうちに帰ろう。
   Akarui uchi ni kaerō.
   Let's go home while it's still <u>light</u>.

4. ちょっと明かりをつけてくれる？
   Chotto akari o tsukete kureru?
   Would you please turn <u>the light</u> on?

5. 明け方はまだ少し寒いね。
   Akegata wa mada sukoshi samui ne.
   It's still a little cold at <u>dawn</u>.

Common Compounds and Phrases

説明書	**setsumeisho**	an explanation; a description
証明	**shōmei**	proof; certification
発明	**hatsumei**	an invention
明日	**myōnichi, *ashita, *asu**	tomorrow; the future
明朝	**myōchō**	tomorrow morning
明け方	**akegata**	daybreak; dawn
梅雨明け	**tsuyu-ake**	the end of the rainy season

Take care to use the same spacing with the horizontal strokes.

8　丨 冂 月 日 明 明 明 明

明

195 門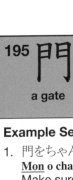

モン MON
かど kado

a gate

The character 門 depicts a *double door* that is closed.

GR2 N4 AP

Example Sentences

1. 門をちゃんと閉めて。
   Mon o chanto shimete.
   Make sure you shut the <u>gate</u>!

2. 彼は名門の出だ。
   Kare wa meimon no de da.
   He comes <u>from a distinguished family</u>.

3. 私は田中先生の門下生でした。
   Watashi wa Tanaka-sensei no monkasei deshita.
   I was <u>a pupil</u> of Professor Tanaka.

4. 池の水門を開けて、放水した。
   Ike no suimon o akete, hōsui shita.
   I opened the pond's <u>sluice gate</u> to drain the water.

5. 囲碁の入門書がありますか。
   Igo no nyūmonsho ga arimasu ka.
   Do you have any <u>introductory books</u> on *go*?

Common Compounds and Phrases

名門	**meimon**	a distinguished family
門下生	**monkasei**	one's pupil, follower
水門	**suimon**	a flood (sluice) gate
入門書	**nyūmonsho**	a guide; a manual
専門	**senmon**	specialty
門限	**mongen**	a closing time; a curfew
部門	**bumon**	a class; a category

End the first stroke firmly, and the sixth stroke with a hook.

8 丨 冂 冂 冂 冂 門 門 門

門

196 夜

ヤ YA
よ yo　よる yoru

night

Although originally derived from different characters, 夜 now combines *person* 人, *roof* 亠 and *evening* 夕, suggesting a person inside at *night*.

GR2 N4 AP

Example Sentences

1. 夜行列車でスキーに出かけた。
   Yakō ressha de sukii ni dekaketa.
   We took an <u>overnight train</u> to go skiing.

2. 大学の夜間部に通っている。
   Daigaku no yakanbu ni kayotte iru.
   I attend the <u>evening sessions</u> of a university.

3. 頂きから見る香港の夜景は美しいです。
   Itadaki kara miru Honkon no yakei wa utsukushii desu.
   The <u>night view</u> of Hong Kong from the peak is lovely.

4. 夜中に変な電話がかかってきた。
   Yonaka ni hen na denwa ga kakatte kita.
   I got a strange phone call <u>in the middle of the night</u>.

5. ここは夏でも夜になると涼しい。
   Koko wa natsu de mo yoru ni naru to suzushii.
   Even in summer it's cool here <u>in the evening</u>.

Common Compounds and Phrases

夜行列車	**yakō ressha**	a night train
夜間部	**yakanbu**	a school's evening session
夜景	**yakei**	a night view
昨夜	**sakuya**	last night
深夜	**shinya**	late at night
夜中に	**yonaka ni**	in the dead of night
夜空	**yozora**	the night sky

Be careful with the balance of this character.

8 ㇀ 亠 广 广 疒 夜 夜 夜

夜

197 林

リン RIN
はやし hayashi

**woods;
a forest**

The character 林 combines two of the characters for *tree* 木, suggesting trees or bamboo growing together in the *woods*.

GR1 N4 AP

Example Sentences

1. 山の奥まで林道が通っている。
   Yama no oku made rindō ga tōtte iru.
   A forest road runs deep into the mountains.

2. 新宿副都心には、高層ビルが林立している。
   Shinjuku Fukutoshin ni wa, kōsō biru ga rinritsu shite iru.
   The Shinjuku subcenter of Tokyo bristles with high-rise office buildings.

3. 林の中を散歩した。
   Hayashi no naka o sampo shita.
   I went for a stroll through the woods.

4. 放火による森林火災が発生した。
   Hōka ni yoru shinrin kasai ga hassei shita.
   The forest fire that occurred was a case of arson.

5. 森で森林浴をした。
   Mori de shinrinyoku o shita.
   I enjoyed a walk through the woods.

Common Compounds and Phrases

林道	**rindō**	a forest path, road
林立	**rinritsu**	standing close together
森林	**shinrin**	woods; a forest
林業	**ringyō**	forestry
森林浴	**shinrinyoku**	walking in the woods
雑木林	**zōkibayashi**	a thickly wooded area
小林	**Kobayashi**	Kobayashi (a name)

The fourth stroke ends firmly, and the eighth stroke tapers off.

8 一 十 才 木 木 村 材 林

林

198 映

エイ EI
うつ・る utsu(ru)
うつ・す utsu(su)
*は・える ha(eru)

**to reflect;
to project**

The character 映 is a combination of *sun* 日 and *center* 央, indicating the bright center of the sun. From this the meanings of *shine* and *reflect* have derived.

GR6 N4 AP

Example Sentences

1. 音楽にはその時代がよく反映されている。
   Ongaku ni wa sono jidai ga yoku han'ei sarete iru.
   The music captures the period quite well.

2. 鏡に映った姿を見てがっかりした。
   Kagami ni utsutta sugata o mite gakkari shita.
   I was disappointed when I saw myself in the mirror.

3. 湖に山の景色が映し出されている。
   Mizuumi ni yama no keshiki ga utsushidasarete iru.
   The mountain scenery is reflected in the lake.

4. 彼の言う事は、毎度代わり映えがしないね。
   Kare no iu koto wa, maido kawaribae ga shinai ne.
   He's always talking about the same old thing.

5. 我ながらいい出来映えだ。
   Ware nagara ii dekibae da.
   I did well if I do say so myself.

Common Compounds and Phrases

反映	**han'ei**	influence; reflection
映画館	**eigakan**	a movie theater; a cinema
上映	**jōei**	screening
映写	**eisha**	projection
映像	**eizō**	an image (on a screen)
放映	**hōei**	televising; broadcasting
*出来映え	**dekibae**	workmanship; the result

Make sure the eighth stroke protrudes.

9 丨 冂 日 日 日 日' 旷 肕 映 映

映

199 屋

オク OKU
や ya

a house;
a small shop

The character 屋 is a combination of a *hanging cloth* 尸 and *arrive/stop* 至, which is used to represent *room*. A roof covering a *house* is the associated meaning.

GR3 N4 AP

Example Sentences

1. この小学校には屋内プールがある。
   Kono shōgakkō ni wa okunai pūru ga aru.
   This elementary school has an <u>indoor</u> pool.

2. この時期は、屋根の雪下ろしが大変だ。
   Kono jiki wa, yane no yukioroshi ga taihen da.
   It's hard work removing the snow from the <u>roof</u> at this time of year.

3. 近所の魚屋で新鮮な魚を買った。
   Kinjo no sakana-ya de shinsen na sakana o katta.
   I bought some fresh fish at the local <u>fish shop</u>.

4. 恥ずかしがり屋にしては、大胆な行動を取った。
   Hazukashigariya ni shite wa, daitan na kōdō o totta.
   For someone so <u>shy</u>, it was a daring act.

5. 部屋を探しているんですが...
   Heya o sagashite iru n desu ga...
   Excuse me, but I'm looking for <u>a room</u>...

Common Compounds and Phrases

屋内	**okunai**	the inside of a building
屋上	**okujō**	a rooftop
屋根	**yane**	a roof; roofing
部屋	**heya**	a room; a sumo stable
魚屋	**sakana-ya**	a fishmonger; a fish shop
恥ずかしがり屋	**hazukashigariya**	a shy person
一軒屋 / 一軒家	**ikken'ya**	a detached (isolated) house

The third stroke sweeps down.

9　一　コ　尸　尸　尸　居　居　屋　屋

屋

200 音

オン ON　イン IN
おと oto　ね ne

sound

The character 音 is a derivation of 言 *speak*, with a line in 口 *mouth* to represent the tongue making a *sound*.

GR1 N4 AP

Example Sentences

1. どんな音楽が好きですか。
   Donna ongaku ga suki desu ka.
   What kind of <u>music</u> do you like?

2. 発音がいいですね。
   Hatsuon ga ii desu ne.
   You have good <u>pronunciation</u>.

3. 自分の声を録音してみた。
   Jibun no koe o rokuon shite mita.
   I tried <u>recording</u> my own voice.

4. 今、大きな音が隣の部屋から聞こえた。
   Ima, ōki na oto ga tonari no heya kara kikoeta.
   I heard a loud <u>noise</u> from the room next door, just now.

5. 彼から何の音沙汰もない。
   Kare kara nan no otosata mo nai.
   I haven't had <u>any word</u> from him at all.

Common Compounds and Phrases

音楽	**ongaku**	music
発音	**hatsuon**	pronunciation; sound production
録音	**rokuon**	recording
雑音	**zatsuon**	noise; static
音読み	**on-yomi**	an *on* (Chinese) reading
子音	**shiin**	a consonant
物音	**monooto**	a noise; a sound

Take care to space out the horizontal strokes equally.

9　丶　亠　亠　立　立　产　咅　音　音

音

201 海　カイ KAI　うみ umi
the sea; the ocean

The character 海 combines *water* 氵 and *every, always* 毎, suggesting that water always returns to the *sea*.

GR2 N4 AP

Example Sentences

1. 時々、海岸を散歩する。
   Tokidoki, kaigan o sanpo suru.
   I sometimes go for a walk along the <u>seashore</u>.

2. 夏休みに海水浴をした。
   Natsuyasumi ni kaisuiyoku o shita.
   I <u>swam in the sea</u> during the summer holidays.

3. きれいな海だね。
   Kirei na umi da ne.
   The <u>ocean</u> is beautiful, isn't it?

4. 山は一面火の海となった。
   Yama wa ichimen hi no umi to natta.
   The whole mountain <u>became engulfed in flames</u>.

5. 一年に二度は海外旅行に行きます。
   Ichinen ni nido wa kaigai ryokō ni ikimasu.
   I <u>travel abroad</u> twice a year.

Common Compounds and Phrases

海岸	**kaigan**	the seashore; the coast; the beach
海水浴	**kaisuiyoku**	swimming in the sea
海外	**kaigai**	overseas; abroad
瀬戸内海	**setonaikai**	the Inland Sea
海産物	**kaisanbutsu**	a marine product; seafood
海辺	**umibe**	the beach; the seashore
*海老	**ebi**	a shrimp; a prawn; a lobster

The seventh stroke protrudes and ends with a hook.

9　丶丶氵汀汀沔沔海海

海

---

202 界　カイ KAI
world; bounds

The character 界 is a combination of *rice field* 田 and a person *intervening and dividing* 介. The sense of *boundary* developed from the idea of the division of rice fields.

GR3 N4 AP

Example Sentences

1. 両親は、先月から世界一週の旅に出ている。
   Ryōshin wa, sengetsu kara sekai isshū no tabi ni dete iru.
   My parents have been off on an <u>around-the-world</u> trip since last month.

2. 小さい頃から芸能界にあこがれていた。
   Chiisai koro kara geinōkai ni akogarete ita.
   She had been drawn to <u>the entertainment business</u> since she was a child.

3. この川が二つの県の境界になっている。
   Kono kawa ga futatsu no ken no kyōkai ni natte iru.
   This river marks the <u>boundary</u> between two prefectures.

4. もう体力の限界だ！
   Mō tairyoku no genkai da!
   I'm at the <u>limits</u> of my strength!

Common Compounds and Phrases

世界中に	**sekai-jū ni**	all over the world
芸能界	**geinōkai**	show business
境界	**kyōkai**	a boundary; a border
限界	**genkai**	a boundary; a limit
視界	**shikai**	a field of vision
学界	**gakkai**	academic circles
自然界	**shizenkai**	the natural world

End the eighth stroke with a sweeping motion.

9　丨冂冂甲田甼界界界

界

203 急

キュウ KYŪ
いそ・ぐ iso(gu)

urgent; sudden;
steep; to hurry; vital

The character 急 combines 刍, a derivative of 及, indicating a *hand trying to catch a person running away* and *heart* 心. The idea of *hurrying* to try and catch up derived from this.
GR3 N4 AP

Example Sentences

1. 急に風が吹いてきた。
   Kyū ni kaze ga fuite kita.
   The wind picked up <u>suddenly</u>.

2. あそこの山道は急カーブが続いている。
   Asoko no yamamichi wa **kyū kābu** ga tsuzuite iru.
   That mountain pass has <u>sharp bends</u>, one after the other.

3. 野球のボールが急所に当たったらしい。
   Yakyū no bōru ga **kyūsho** ni atatta rashii.
   The baseball hit him in <u>the groin</u>, apparently.

4. 応急手当を受けた方がいいよ。
   Ōkyū teate o uketa hō ga ii yo.
   You'd better get some <u>first-aid</u> treatment.

5. 電車に間に合うように急ぎなさい。
   Densha ni maniau yō ni **isoginasai**.
   <u>Hurry</u> so that you can make the train!

Common Compounds and Phrases

急カーブ	**kyū kābu**	a sharp bend
急所	**kyūsho**	a vital part; the groin
応急手当	**ōkyū teate**	first aid
急行	**kyūkō**	hurrying; an express train
急激な	**kyūgeki na**	sudden; abrupt
救急車	**kyūkyūsha**	an ambulance
大急ぎ	**ōisogi**	a great hurry; at top speed

The fourth stroke does not protrude.

9 ′ ″ ″ 刍 刍 刍 急 急 急

急

---

204 計

ケイ KEI
はか・る haka(ru)
はか・らう haka(rau)

to plan; to measure;
to arrange

The character 計 combines *say* 言 and *ten* 十 to suggest *measuring* in units of ten.

GR2 N4 AP

Example Sentences

1. あの時計は五分遅れているみたい。
   Ano **tokei** wa gofun okurete iru mitai.
   That <u>clock</u> seems to be five minutes slow.

2. 合計で三千六百六十円です。
   Gōkei de sanzen roppyaku rokujū-en desu.
   That comes to <u>a total</u> of ¥3,660.

3. ちょっと計算してくれますか。
   Chotto **keisan shite** kuremasu ka.
   Would you mind <u>calculating</u> this?

4. 彼女は毎晩体重計にのっている。
   Kanojo wa maiban **taijūkei** ni notte iru.
   She <u>weighs herself</u> every evening.

5. どのぐらい速く走れるか計ってみよう。
   Dono gurai hayaku hashireru ka **hakatte miyō**.
   <u>I'm going to time myself</u> to see how fast I can run.

Common Compounds and Phrases

合計	**gōkei**	the (sum) total
計算	**keisan**	calculation; counting
体重計	**taijūkei**	a scale; scales
温度計	**ondokei**	a thermometer
会計	**kaikei**	the account(s); a bill
統計	**tōkei**	statistics
設計	**sekkei**	a design; planning

The second stroke is longer than those above and below it.

9 ` ﹅ ﹅ ﹅ ﹅ 言 言 計 計

計

EXERCISE 17 (193 – 204)

A. Give the readings for the following.

1. 海 _____
2. 夜 _____
3. 小林 _____
4. 魚屋 _____
5. 日本海 _____
6. 味わう _____
7. 急ぎなさい _____
8. 明日 _____
9. 計る _____
10. 校門 _____

B. Write in kanji and kana.

1. all over the world _____
2. a movie, film _____
3. overseas _____
4. a friend, ally _____
5. an express (train) _____
6. a forest road _____
7. a clock, watch _____

8. a flower shop _____
9. a plan, scheme _____
10. a consonant _____

C. Fill in the blanks with appropriate kanji.

1. _____(おお)きな _____(おと)が _____(き)こえる。
2. _____(よなか)の _____(にじ)ごろ
3. _____(まち)の _____(あ)かりが _____(み)える。
4. _____(じょうえい) _____(じかん)
5. _____(あか)るい _____(ところ)に _____(た)つ。
6. シェイクスピア _____(ぶんがく)の _____(にゅうもんしょ)
7. _____(せかい) _____(ちず)を _____(み)る。
8. _____(はやし)の _____(なか)を _____(はし)る。
9. _____(でんしゃ)が _____(きゅう)に _____(と)まる 。
10. _____(しょうがっこう)の _____(おくない)プール

---

205 研

ケン **KEN**

*と・ぐ **to(gu)**

**to grind;
to do research**

The character 研 combines *stone* 石 and *the alignment of two objects* 开, suggesting scraping the surface of stones to make them flat, hence *grind*.

GR3 N4

Example Sentences

1. 忙しくて、自分の研究が進まない。
   Isogashikute, jibun no kenkyū ga susumanai.
   I've been busy, not getting on with my own research.

2. 砥石で包丁を研ぐ人が少なくなった。
   Toishi de hōchō o togu hito ga sukunakunatta.
   There aren't many people who sharpen knives using a grindstone now.

3. お米を研ぎ終わった。
   Okome o togiowatta.
   I have finished washing the rice.

4. あの先生はがん研究の第一人者だ。
   Ano sensei wa gan-kenkyū no dai-ichininsha da.
   That doctor is an authority on cancer research.

5. 新人たちは、1週間研修を受けた。
   Shinjin-tachi wa, isshūkan kenshū o uketa.
   The new recruits had a week's training.

Common Compounds and Phrases

研修	**kenshū**	(study and) training
研磨	**kenma**	grinding; polishing
研削	**kensaku**	grinding
研究会	**kenkyūkai**	a research society (group)
研究所	**kenkyūjo**	a research laboratory
がん研究	**gan-kenkyū**	cancer research
研究家	**kenkyūka**	a researcher

The seventh stroke is longer than the sixth.

9 　一　　丆　　石　　石　　石　　石　　研　研

研

206 県 ケン KEN
prefecture

The character 県 originally suggested a severed head being attached to a tree. From this, perhaps, derived the meaning of the power of the authorities and by extension, the *prefectural government*.
GR3 N4

Example Sentences

1. 日本には四十七の都道府県がある。
   Nihon ni wa yonjūnana no todōfuken ga aru.
   There are forty-seven <u>prefectures</u> in Japan.

2. 弟は県立の高校に通っています。
   Otōto wa kenritsu no kōkō ni kayotte imasu.
   My younger brother attends a <u>prefectural</u> senior high school.

3. 山口県の県庁所在地はどこですか。
   Yamaguchi-ken no kenchō shozaichi wa doko desu ka.
   Where is <u>the seat of</u> the <u>Yamaguchi prefectural government</u>?

4. あの県知事は元タレントだった。
   Ano kenchiji wa moto tarento datta.
   That <u>prefectural governor</u> was a former TV personality.

Common Compounds and Phrases

県知事	**kenchiji**	a prefectural governor
県境	**kenzakai**	a prefectural border
県民	**kenmin**	a resident of a prefecture
県立	**kenritsu**	prefectural
都道府県	**todō-fuken**	the 47 prefectures of Japan (43 + 4)
神奈川県	**Kanagawa-ken**	Kanagawa Prefecture
青森県	**Aomori-ken**	Aomori Prefecture

End the seventh stroke firmly.

9 丨 冂 冃 冃 目 目 県 県 県

県

---

207 建 ケン KEN
た・てる ta(teru)
た・つ ta(tsu)
to build

The character 建 combines *writing brush* 聿, held erect in the hand and *move forward* 廴, suggesting to *make erect* or *build*.

GR4 N4

Example Sentences

1. 市長が建築現場の視察に見えた。
   Shichō ga kenchiku genba no shisatsu ni mieta.
   The mayor came to inspect the <u>construction</u> site.

2. 今、小学校が建設中です。
   Ima, shōgakkō ga kensetsu-chū desu.
   The elementary school is <u>under construction</u> at present.

3. 来年、新しい家を建てるつもりだ。
   Rainen, atarashii ie o tateru tsumori da.
   I intend <u>to build</u> a new house next year.

4. この辺りの住宅はほとんど二階建てです。
   Kono atari no jūtaku wa hotondo nikai-date desu.
   Most of the dwellings around here are <u>two-storied</u>.

5. 公園に銅像が建った。
   Kōen ni dōzō ga tatta.
   A bronze statue <u>was erected</u> in the park.

Common Compounds and Phrases

建築	**kenchiku**	construction; architecture
建設	**kensetsu**	construction; building
建国記念日	**kenkoku kinenbi**	a national foundation day
建造	**kenzō**	building; construction
二階建て	**nikai-date**	two-story (storied)
建物	**tatemono**	a building; a structure
建て売り	**tateuri**	to build and sell a house

The second stroke protrudes.

9 フ ㇕ ㋤ ㋤ 㸤 聿 肂 建 建

建

208 思

シ SHI
おも・う omo(u)

to think

The character 思 combines *heart* 心 and *brain* 田 (although now written using the character for *field*) to give the idea of *thought*.

GR2 N4 AP

Example Sentences

1. それは現実とは思えない不思議な話だ。
   Sore wa genjitsu to wa omoenai fushigi na hanashi da.
   It is an <u>incredible</u> and <u>seemingly unreal</u> story.

2. 彼とは意思が通じ合わない。
   Kare to wa ishi ga tsūjiawanai.
   The two of us <u>don't see eye to eye</u>.

3. ときどき亡くなった母のことを思い出す。
   Tokidoki nakunatta haha no koto o omoidasu.
   I sometimes <u>reminisce</u> about my late mother.

4. 突然いい考えを思い付いた。
   Totsuzen ii kangae o omoitsuita.
   I suddenly <u>hit upon</u> a good idea.

5. 彼女は本当にお母さん思いだ。
   Kanojo wa hontō ni okāsan-omoi da.
   She certainly <u>takes good care of her mother</u>.

Common Compounds and Phrases

不思議	**fushigi**	a wonder; a mystery; strangeness
意思	**ishi**	an intention; a wish; a purpose
思考	**shikō**	thinking; a thought
思想	**shisō**	a thought; an idea
思春期	**shishunki**	puberty; adolescence
思い出	**omoide**	a memory; a remembrance
思い込み	**omoikomi**	an assumption; a preconception

The seventh stroke ends with a hook.

9 丨 冂 冂 田 田 甲 思 思 思

思

---

209 持

ジ JI
も・つ mo(tsu)

to hold

The character 持 contains the elements of *hand* 扌 and 寺, signifying *moving the hands and feet*, as well as *standing still*. From this we have the meaning of *holding* something in the hand.

GR3 N4 AP

Example Sentences

1. 試験には筆記用具を持参すること。
   Shiken ni wa hikki-yōgu o jisan suru koto.
   <u>Bring</u> something to write with to the examination.

2. 古い車は維持費がかかる。
   Furui kuruma wa ijihi ga kakaru.
   Old cars are <u>expensive to maintain</u>.

3. 荷物を持って、こちらへどうぞ。
   Nimotsu o motte, kochira e dōzo.
   <u>Bring</u> your luggage and come this way, please.

4. このまま天気が持ってくれればいい。
   Kono mama tenki ga motte kurereba ii.
   I hope the weather <u>stays fine</u> like this.

5. この小説には作者の持ち味が生かされている。
   Kono shōsetsu ni wa sakusha no mochiaji ga ikasarete iru.
   This novel brings out the <u>distinctive qualities</u> of the author.

Common Compounds and Phrases

持参	**jisan**	bringing; taking
維持	**iji**	maintenance; upkeep
持続	**jizoku**	to continue; to last
支持	**shiji**	to support; to maintain
持ち味	**mochiaji**	a distinctive quality
気持ち	**kimochi**	a feeling; slightly
金持ち	**kanemochi**	a wealthy person

Don't confuse the 土 element with 土.

9 一 十 扌 扌 扩 扩 持 持 持

持

210 室
room

シツ SHITSU
むろ muro

The character 室 combines *arrow* ∠, *earth* 土 and *roof* 宀. The arrow hitting earth suggests *arrive*, so with roof, this came to mean a place to come to, i.e., a *room*.

GR2 N4 AP

Example Sentences

1. 室内では禁煙です。
   Shitsunai de wa kin'en desu.
   The indoor area is a nonsmoking area.

2. 温室でランを育てている。
   Onshitsu de ran o sodatete iru.
   I am growing orchids in a greenhouse.

3. 603号室の鍵を下さい。
   603 gōshitsu no kagi o kudasai.
   Could I have the key to room 603, please?

4. ここは昔、氷を貯蔵しておく氷室でした。
   Koko wa mukashi, kōri o chozō shite oku himuro deshita.
   This was once a room used to store ice.

5. 皇室に親王様がお生まれになりました。
   Kōshitsu ni shinnō-sama ga oumare ni narimashita.
   A prince was born in the Imperial Family.

Common Compounds and Phrases

室内	**shitsunai**	indoors; in a room
温室	**onshitsu**	a greenhouse
皇室	**kōshitsu**	the (Japanese) Imperial Family
教室	**kyōshitsu**	a classroom
寝室	**shinshitsu**	a bedroom
和室	**washitsu**	a Japanese-style room
病室	**byōshitsu**	a hospital room; a ward

The ninth stroke is longer than the seventh.

9 　｀ 丶 宀 宀 宓 宏 宏 室 室 室

室

211 首
head; neck; first

シュ SHU
くび kubi

The character 首 originally depicted a person's *head* with hair on top.

GR2 N4

Example Sentences

1. 東京は日本の首都です。
   Tōkyō wa Nippon no shuto desu.
   Tōkyō is the capital of Japan.

2. 今度の首脳会談は北海道で行われるそうです。
   Kondo no shunō kaidan wa Hokkaidō de okonawareru sō desu.
   I hear that the next summit will be held in Hokkaidō.

3. 百人一首をやったことある。
   Hyakunin isshu o yatta koto aru.
   Have you ever played the game 'Hyakunin isshu'?

4. きりんは首が長い。
   Kirin wa kubi ga nagai.
   Giraffes have long necks.

5. テニスをして、手首を痛めた。
   Tenisu o shite, tekubi o itameta.
   I hurt my wrist playing tennis.

Common Compounds and Phrases

首都	**shuto**	a capital city
首脳	**shunō**	a head; a (top) leader
党首	**tōshu**	a party leader
部首	**bushu**	a kanji radical
手首	**tekubi**	a wrist
首輪	**kubiwa**	a necklace; a collar
首になる	**kubi ni naru**	to lose one's job
百人一首	**hyakunin isshu**	one hundred verses by one hundred poets, a Japanese card game

The first two strokes slant inwards.

9 　｀ ゛ 艹 艹 宀 首 首 首 首

首

119

212 秋

シュウ SHŪ
あき aki

autumn, fall

The character 秋 combines *rice plant* 禾 and *fire* 火, a reference to drying the rice stalks after the *fall* harvesting.

GR2 N4 AP

Example Sentences

1. 秋分の日は祝日です。
   Shūbun no hi wa shukujitsu desu.
   <u>Autumnal Equinox Day</u> is a national holiday.

2. 彼と会える日を一日千秋の思いで待っていた。
   Kare to aeru hi o <u>ichijitsu senshū</u> no omoi de matte ita.
   I <u>waited impatiently</u> for the day when I would be able to meet him.

3. 秋が一番好きな季節です。
   <u>**Aki**</u> **ga ichiban suki na kisetsu desu.**
   <u>Fall</u> is my favorite season.

4. 秋雨前線が各地で大雨を降らせています。
   <u>**Akisame**</u> **zensen ga kakuchi de ōame o furasete imasu.**
   <u>The autumn rain</u> front is bringing heavy rain to various parts of the country.

Common Compounds and Phrases

秋分	**shūbun**	autumnal equinox
晩秋	**banshū**	late autumn
秋晴れ	**akibare**	clear autumn weather
秋雨	**akisame**	autumn rain
秋田県	**Akita-ken**	Akita Prefecture (a place)
読書の秋	**dokusho no** <u>**aki**</u>	autumn, the best season for reading
*秋刀魚	**sanma**	mackerel

End the third stroke firmly, and be sure to align the eighth and ninth strokes.

9 `ノ 二 千 禾 禾 禾 禾 秋 秋`

秋

213 重

ジュウ JŪ チョウ CHŌ
おも・い omo(i) *え e
かさ・ねる kasa(neru)
かさ・なる kasa(naru)

heavy;
to duplicate

The character 重 combines *person* 人, *ground* 土 and *east* 東, with its literal meaning of *heavy sack*. Thus, we have a person standing on the ground carrying a heavy sack. The general meanings of *heavy* and later, *pile up*, derived from this.

GR3 N4 AP

Example Sentences

1. 今朝の会議で重要な連絡があった。
   Kesa no kaigi de <u>jūyō</u> na renraku ga atta.
   There was an <u>important</u> announcement in the meeting this morning.

2. 昨日の事故で重症の人がたくさん出た。
   Kinō no jiko de <u>jūshō</u> no hito ga takusan deta.
   Many were <u>seriously injured</u> in the accident yesterday.

3. 老人ホームの手伝いは貴重な経験だった。
   Rōjin-hōmu no tetsudai wa <u>kichō</u> na keiken datta.
   Helping out in the old people's home was a <u>valuable</u> experience.

4. 生と死は紙一重だ。
   Sei to shi wa <u>kami hitoe</u> da.
   There is <u>only a fine line</u> between life and death.

5. ここに洗濯物を重ねておいて。
   Koko ni sentakumono o <u>kasanete</u> oite.
   Just <u>pile</u> the laundry here.

Common Compounds and Phrases

重症	**jūshō**	a serious condition
重大な	**jūdai na**	important; serious
重労働	**jūrōdō**	hard labor / work
重要文化財	**jūyō bunkazai**	an important cultural property
貴重な	**kichō na**	precious; valuable
尊重	**sonchō**	to respect; to esteem
紙一重	**kami hitoe**	a fine line

The second stroke is the longest horizontal one.

9 `ノ 二 千 台 台 台 重 重 重`

重

214 春
spring

シュン SHUN
はる haru

GR2 N4 AP

The character 春 combines *budding plant* 夫 and *sun* 日, a reference to *spring*.

Example Sentences

1. 来春、社会人になります。
   Raishun, shakaijin ni narimasu.
   I'll start my first full-time job <u>this spring</u>.

2. 青春時代は二度と訪れない。
   Seishun jidai wa nido to otozurenai.
   There's no reliving <u>one's youth</u>.

3. 子供が思春期を迎える年頃になった。
   Kodomo ga shishunki o mukaeru toshigoro ni natta.
   My child has reached <u>puberty</u>.

4. 春になると、花粉症に悩まされる。
   Haru ni naru to, kafunshō ni nayamasareru.
   When <u>spring</u> comes round, my hay fever gets me down.

5. 今日、春一番が吹いた。
   Kyō, haruichiban ga fuita.
   <u>The first winds of spring</u> blew today.

Common Compounds and Phrases

来春	**raishun**	next spring
春分	**shunbun**	vernal equinox
初春	**shoshun**	the beginning of spring
青春	**seishun**	(the bloom of) youth
思春期	**shishunki**	puberty
春雨	**harusame**	spring rain; vermicelli
小春日和	**koharu biyori**	balmy autumn weather; Indian summer

The third stroke is longer than those above it, and the fifth stroke tapers off.

9 一 二 三 耂 夫 耒 春 春 春

春

215 乗
to ride;
to get on

ジョウ JŌ
の・る no(ru)
の・せる no(seru)

GR3 N4 AP

In its original form, the character 乗 depicted a person climbing a tree, using both hands. From this, the sense of *get on*, *ride* has derived. *Multiplication* is an associated meaning.

Example Sentences

1. うちの乗用車は七人乗りです。
   Uchi no jōyōsha wa shichinin-nori desu.
   Our <u>car</u> is a <u>seven-seater</u>.

2. これはきっと便乗値上げだよ。
   Kore wa kitto binjō neage da yo.
   This is definitely a case of <u>price gouging</u>.

3. 台風の影響で多くの乗客が駅で足止めされた。
   Taifū no eikyō de ōku no jōkyaku ga eki de ashidome sareta.
   A lot of <u>passengers</u> were forced to stay at the station because of the typhoon.

4. 駅まで自転車に乗っていこう。
   Eki made jitensha ni notte ikō.
   <u>I'll ride</u> my bicycle to the station.

5. 昨夜、友達の相談に乗ってあげました。
   Yūbe, tomodachi no sōdan ni notte agemashita.
   I <u>gave some advice</u> to a friend last night.

Common Compounds and Phrases

乗用車	**jōyōsha**	a passenger car
便乗	**binjō**	taking a ride; taking advantage
乗客	**jōkyaku**	a passenger; a fare
乗車	**jōsha**	riding on a train, car, bus
乗り物	**norimono**	a vehicle; transport; a ride
乗り換え	**norikae**	changing trains; conversion
乗組員	**norikumiin**	a crew

The third stroke is slightly longer.

9 一 二 三 千 禾 乖 垂 乗 乗 乗

乗

216 洗

to wash

セン SEN
あら・う ara(u)

The character 洗 combines *water* 氵 and *toes* 先, suggesting the *washing* of one's feet.

GR6 N4 AP

Example Sentences

1. お天気がいいから、洗濯しよう。
   Otenki ga ii kara, <u>sentaku shiyō</u>.
   <u>Let's do the laundry</u> since it's such a nice day.

2. 食器を洗うのに時間がかかった。
   <u>Shokki o arau</u> no ni jikan ga kakatta.
   It took me quite a while <u>to do the dishes</u>.

3. 警察は容疑者の身元を洗っている。
   Keisatsu wa yōgisha no <u>mimoto o aratte iru</u>.
   The police are <u>looking into the</u> suspect's <u>background</u>.

4. お手洗いはどこですか。
   <u>Otearai</u> wa doko desu ka.
   Could you tell me where the <u>bathroom</u> is?

5. 彼女は洗練されたユーモアの持ち主だ。
   Kanojo wa <u>senren sareta yūmoa</u> no mochinushi da.
   She has <u>a sophisticated sense of humor</u>.

Common Compounds and Phrases

洗濯	**sentaku**	washing; laundry
洗顔	**sengan**	washing one's face
洗剤	**senzai**	a cleaner; a detergent
洗面所	**senmenjo**	a washroom; a bathroom
水洗	**suisen**	flushing; washing
洗練	**senren**	refinement; elegance
手洗い	**tearai**	a toilet; a washstand

The sixth stroke protrudes at the top.

9 丶 冫 氵 氵 汁 汼 汼 洗

洗

EXERCISE 18 (205 – 216)

A. Give the readings for the following.

1. 首 _____
2. 思わない _____
3. 乗り物 _____
4. 気持ち _____
5. 重い _____
6. 研究室 _____
7. 青春時代 _____
8. 秋田県 _____
9. 持ってくる _____
10. ビルが建った _____

B. Write in Japanese using kanji and kana.

1. an autumn sky _____
2. a building; a structure _____
3. a memory; a remembrance _____
4. a wrist _____
5. a research laboratory _____
6. a wealthy person _____

7. spring rain; vermicelli _____
8. prefectural _____
9. to ride on a train, car, bus _____
10. hand-washing; a toilet _____

C. Write in kanji and kana.

1. しゅうぶん の ひ _____
2. でんしゃ に のる _____
3. ホテルを たてる _____
4. しつない プール _____
5. じゅうだい な _____
6. ナイフを とぐ _____
7. て を よく あらう _____
8. やまぐちけん に すむ _____
9. ときどき おもいだす _____
10. きょねん の はるやすみ _____

Review 6 (1–216)

A. Write the readings for the following.

1. 気持ち _____
2. 建てる _____
3. 洗い物 _____
4. 首 _____
5. 思わない _____
6. 乗せる _____
7. 秋 _____
8. 重ねる _____
9. 山口県 _____
10. 来春 _____

B. Write in English.

1. 電車に乗る _____
2. 去年の春 _____
3. 県立の高校 _____
4. 父のことを思い出す _____
5. 高知県に住む _____
6. 首の長い人 _____
7. 研究をする _____
8. 石を持ち上げる _____
9. マンションが建つ _____
10. 重そうな物 _____

C. Write in kanji and kana.

1. すいせんトイレ _____
2. どくしょのあき _____
3. いしかわけん _____
4. もちぬし _____
5. おもいもの _____
6. もちあじ _____
7. てくび _____
8. けんきゅうかい _____
9. せいしゅんじだい _____
10. しつがい _____

D. Match the following.

1. a library ( )   a. 金持ち
2. a prefectural resident ( )   b. 研究室
3. a building ( )   c. 思い出
4. a wealthy person ( )   d. 図書室
5. spring rain ( )   e. 県民
6. a study ( )   f. 二重
7. a toilet ( )   g. 建物

8. autumnal equinox day ( )   h. 手洗い
9. a memory ( )   i. 春雨
10. doubly; twice ( )   j. 秋分の日

E. Match the following with their readings.

1. 乗車 ( )   a. たてうり
2. 県知事 ( )   b. ほっかいどう
3. 秋雨 ( )   c. あしくび
4. 研究者 ( )   d. ちからもち
5. 建て売り ( )   e. みえけん
6. 春休み ( )   f. そうしゅん
7. 早春 ( )   g. あきさめ
8. 北海道 ( )   h. ながもち
9. 重力 ( )   i. はるやすみ
10. 乗用車 ( )   j. じょうしゃ
11. 足首 ( )   k. おおいたけん
12. 大分県 ( )   l. おうしつ
13. 室内 ( )   m. しこう
14. 研究所 ( )   n. じゅうりょく
15. 力持ち ( )   o. けんちじ
16. 王室 ( )   p. あきたけん
17. 秋田県 ( )   q. けんきゅうじょ
18. 思考 ( )   r. しつない
19. 三重県 ( )   s. じょうようしゃ
20. 長持ち ( )   t. けんきゅうしゃ

F. Add *furigana* to the kanji in the following and translate into English.

1. 来年の春には新しい研究室が建つ。

2. 妹の知り合いが会社を首になった。

3. 今夜は乗り物に乗らずに海まで歩くことにしよう。

4. 秋になったら、三重県に住む姉の家^{いえ}に行こうと思う。

5. 林さんは映画の世界には興^{きょう}味を持っていない。

6. 見事な時計台が急に目の前に現^{あらわ}れた。

7. 直ぐ服を洗いなさい。

8. 本屋で「青春の門」という本を注文した。

9. 耳に水が入ったので、近所の医者にみてもらった。

10. 明らかに青木さんは本音で語っていなかった。

217 送

ソウ SŌ
おく・る oku(ru)

to send

The character 送 contains the elements of *go* 辶 and *holding in the hands* 关, to suggest the idea of taking something from one place to another; hence, to *send*.
GR3 N4 AP

Example Sentences

1. この金額には送料が含まれていますか。
   Kono kingaku ni wa sōryō ga fukumarete imasu ka.
   Does this amount include shipping?

2. 昨夜の映画を再放送してほしい。
   Yūbe no eiga o saihōsō shite hoshii.
   I hope they show a repeat of last night's movie.

3. 空港まで荷物を宅配便で送ろうかな。
   Kūkō made nimotsu o takuhaibin de okurō ka na.
   I think I'll send my luggage to the airport by courier.

4. 友達を駅まで見送りに行ってきた。
   Tomodachi o eki made miokuri ni itte kita.
   I've been to the station to see a friend off.

5. 明日の送別会は会費三千円だって。
   Ashita no sōbetsukai wa kaihi sanzen-en datte.
   I heard it costs 3,000 yen each to attend tomorrow's farewell party.

Common Compounds and Phrases

送料	**sōryō**	shipping; postage
放送	**hōsō**	(radio, television) broadcasting
送金	**sōkin**	a remittance
送別会	**sōbetsukai**	a farewell party
郵送	**yūsō**	sending by mail
送り仮名	**okurigana**	*kana* affixes
見送り	**miokuri**	seeing someone off

End the sixth stroke firmly.

9 　丶　ソ　ソ　ヱ　ヱ　关　关　送　送

送

218 待

タイ TAI
ま・つ ma(tsu)

to wait

The character 待 combines *road* 彳 and 寺, *moving the hands and feet* or *remaining in one place*. This association gives the character its meaning of *wait for*.
GR3 N4 AP

Example Sentences

1. あまり彼に期待しない方がいい。
   Amari kare ni kitai shinai hō ga ii.
   You'd better not expect too much from him.

2. 待ちに待った試合の日が来た。
   Machi ni matta shiai no hi ga kita.
   The day of the long-awaited match finally arrived.

3. 今度の連休が待ち遠しい。
   Kondo no renkyū ga machidōshii.
   I can't wait until the next long holiday.

4. 待ち合わせの時間に遅れそう。
   Machiawase no jikan ni okuresō.
   It looks like I'm going to be late for that appointment.

5. お待ちどうさまです。
   Omachidōsama desu.
   Sorry to have kept you waiting.

Common Compounds and Phrases

期待	**kitai**	expectation; anticipation
招待	**shōtai**	an invitation
待機	**taiki**	being on stand by; holding
待遇	**taigū**	treatment; salary
待ち合わせ	**machiawase**	waiting for someone at an appointed place
待合室	**machiai-shitsu**	a waiting room

The last stroke ends with a hook.

9 　ノ　ク　彳　彳　行　休　待　待　待

待

219 茶

チャ CHA　サ SA

tea; light brown

The character 茶 combines *plant* ⁺⁺ and *ample* 余, suggesting one's ample, or relaxed feelings when drinking *tea*.

GR2　N4　AP

Example Sentences

1. 紅茶にしますか。
   Kōcha ni shimasu ka.
   Would you like some <u>tea</u>?

2. 昨日、茶会に行った。
   Sakujitsu, chakai ni itta.
   I went to <u>a tea ceremony</u> yesterday.

3. 彼女は黒い髪を茶色に染めた。
   Kanojo wa kuroi kami o chairo ni someta.
   She dyed her black hair <u>light brown</u>.

4. あまり焦って無茶をするなよ。
   Amari asette mucha o suru na yo.
   Don't <u>be</u> so impatient and <u>reckless</u>!

5. どこの喫茶店で待ち合わせをしましょうか。
   Doko no kissaten de machiawase o shimashō ka.
   Which <u>coffee shop</u> shall we meet at?

Common Compounds and Phrases

紅茶	**kōcha**	(black) tea
茶会	**chakai**	a tea ceremony
茶色	**chairo**	brown
無茶な	**mucha na**	absurd; reckless; excessive
緑茶	**ryokucha**	green tea
茶室	**chashitsu**	a tea-ceremony room
喫茶店	**kissaten**	a café

The bottom portion is not 木.

9 一 十 艹 艻 犬 苂 苂 茶 茶

茶

220 昼

チュウ CHŪ
ひる hiru

daytime; noon

The character 昼 consists of *measure* 尺, *sun* 日 and *one* 一, suggesting the largest amount of sun is at *noon*.

GR2　N4　AP

Example Sentences

1. 昼食はまだですか。
   Chūshoku wa mada desu ka.
   Isn't <u>lunch</u> ready yet?

2. 夏は昼が長い。
   Natsu wa hiru ga nagai.
   <u>The days</u> are long in summer.

3. 昼間は仕事で忙しいのです。
   Hiruma wa shigoto de isogashii no desu.
   <u>During the day</u> I'm busy with work.

4. お昼前に一仕事済ませよう。
   Ohiru-mae ni hito-shigoto sumaseyō.
   Let's get one job over and done with <u>before noon</u>.

5. 子供は、すやすやと昼寝をしていた。
   Kodomo wa, suyasuya to hirune o shite ita.
   The child <u>was napping</u> peacefully.

Common Compounds and Phrases

昼夜	**chūya**	day and night
昼食	**chūshoku**	lunch
昼飯	**hirumeshi**	lunch
昼間	**hiruma**	(the) daytime
昼寝	**hirune**	a nap; sleeping in the day
真昼	**mahiru**	broad daylight; midday
昼下がり	**hirusagari**	early afternoon

The third and fourth strokes do not touch 日.

9 一 コ コ ア 尺 尺 尽 昼 昼 昼

昼

221 点 テン TEN

a point; a dot

The character 点 now combines *occupy* 占 and *fire* 灬, suggesting a black *mark* left by fire.

GR2 N3 AP

Example Sentences

1. 彼の欠点は怒りっぽいところだ。
   Kare no ketten wa okorippoi tokoro da.
   His shortcoming is a short temper.

2. 次は終点です。
   Tsugi wa shūten desu.
   The next stop is the end of the line.

3. 要点を先に言いなさい。
   Yōten o saki ni iinasai.
   State the main points first!

4. あと一点で満点だったのに。
   Ato itten de manten datta no ni.
   One more point and your score would have been perfect.

5. 写真を十五点選んだ。
   Shashin o jūgoten eranda.
   I selected fifteen photographs.

Common Compounds and Phrases

終点	**shūten**	the terminus; the last stop
要点	**yōten**	the gist; the main point
満点	**manten**	a perfect score; full marks
点数	**tensū**	points; a score
点検	**tenken**	an inspection
点字	**tenji**	Braille
欠点	**ketten**	a defect; a flaw

Note the way the dots are written.

9 ｜ ト 卜 占 占 点 点 点 点

点

---

222 度 ド DO ト TO タク TAKU たび tabi

degree; time

The character 度 combines a simplified form of *various* 庶 and *hand* 又, suggesting measuring with the hand. From this, the sense of *counting the number of times* was derived.

GR3 N4 AP

Example Sentences

1. 何度言っても聞いてくれない。
   Nando itte mo kiite kurenai.
   He won't listen, no matter how many times you tell him.

2. 今年の夏は、三十度以上の日が続いた。
   Kotoshi no natsu wa, sanjūdo ijō no hi ga tsuzuita.
   This summer the temperature stayed over thirty degrees for days on end.

3. 今度の日曜日は暇ですか。
   Kondo no nichiyōbi wa hima desu ka.
   Are you free this Sunday?

4. お父さん、夕飯の仕度を手伝ってよ。
   Otōsan, yūhan no shitaku o tetsudatte yo.
   Dad, come and help get dinner ready!

5. 雨が降る度になくした傘を思い出す。
   Ame ga furu tabi ni nakushita kasa o omoidasu.
   Whenever it rains, I think of the umbrella I lost.

Common Compounds and Phrases

何度	**nando**	how many times (degrees)
態度	**taido**	an attitude; a manner
限度	**gendo**	a limit; bounds
年度	**nendo**	a year; a fiscal year; a term
度合い	**doai**	a degree; an extent
仕度・支度	**shitaku**	arrangements; preparations
度々	**tabitabi**	often

Make sure the element 廿 is not 丗.

9 ｀ 宀 广 广 庐 庐 序 度 度

度

223

発

to start;
to emit

ハツ HATSU　ホツ HOTSU
*た・つ ta(tsu)

The original form of the character 発 was a combination of *two planted feet* 癶 and *an arrow being shot from a bow* 設. From this the various meanings of *leave, discharge* and *start* have derived.
GR3 N4 AP

Example Sentences

1. 出発時刻は八時です。
   Shuppatsu jikoku wa hachiji desu.
   <u>Departure</u> time is eight o'clock.

2. この時期、発表会の練習で忙しい。
   Kono jiki, happyōkai no renshū de isogashii.
   We are busy at this time of year with practice for
   <u>a concert</u>.

3. その政治家は、問題発言が多い。
   Sono seijika wa, mondai hatsugen ga ōi.
   That politician often makes <u>controversial statements</u>.

4. 地震の影響で発電所が被害を受けた。
   Jishin no eikyō de hatsudensho ga higai o uketa.
   The <u>power station</u> suffered damage from the
   earthquake.

5. 明日、中国へ発つ予定です。
   Ashita (Asu), Chūgoku e tatsu yotei desu.
   I'm planning <u>to leave</u> for China tomorrow.

Common Compounds and Phrases

出発	**shuppatsu**	departure
発表	**happyō**	an announcement; a statement
発言	**hatsugen**	a statement; a remark
発電	**hatsuden**	the generation of electricity
発展	**hatten**	expansion; development
発生	**hassei**	an occurrence; an outbreak
発作	**hossa**	an attack; a fit

The last stroke sweeps upwards.

9　フ　フ　ブ　癶　癶　癶　癶　発

発

224

品

an article

ヒン HIN
しな shina

The character 品 depicts three square *articles* placed together.

GR3 N4 AP

Example Sentences

1. 先月、新製品が発売されたばかりです。
   Sengetsu, shinseihin ga hatsubai sareta bakari desu.
   <u>The new products</u> went on sale only last month.

2. 母は食品の安全に気を配っている。
   Haha wa shokuhin no anzen ni ki o kubatte iru.
   My mother is careful about <u>food</u> safety.

3. この頃、品格と言う言葉をよく耳にする。
   Kono goro, hinkaku to iu kotoba o yoku mimi ni suru.
   You often hear the word '<u>dignity</u>' being used recently.

4. あそこの専門店にはいい品物が揃っている。
   Asoko no senmonten ni wa ii shinamono ga sorotte iru.
   That specialty store has a good range of <u>products</u>.

5. あの人気のゲームソフトは、もう品切れだって。
   Ano ninki no gēmusofuto wa, mō shinagire datte.
   I hear that popular game has already <u>sold out</u>.

Common Compounds and Phrases

製品	**seihin**	manufactured goods; a product
食品	**shokuhin**	food products
品格	**hinkaku**	grace; dignity
作品	**sakuhin**	a work; a piece
上品	**jōhin**	elegant; stylish
下品	**gehin**	vulgar; crude
品切れ	**shinagire**	being out of stock

The top element is slightly larger than those below it.

9　丨　口　口　口　吊　吊　品　品　品

品

225

風

フウ FŪ　*フ FU
かぜ kaze

wind; appear-
ance; style

The character 風 combines *sail* 几 and *insect*
虫, suggesting insects blown against a sail by
the *wind*.

GR2 N4 AP

Example Sentences

1. 夕べは何時間も強風が吹いていた。
   Yūbe wa nanjikan mo kyōfū ga fuite ita.
   There was <u>a strong wind</u> blowing for hours last night.

2. その地方には独特の風習がある。
   Sono chihō ni wa dokutoku no fūshū ga aru.
   That region has its distinctive <u>customs</u>.

3. イギリスの風景画が好きだ。
   Igirisu no fūkeiga ga suki da.
   I'm fond of English <u>landscape paintings</u>.

4. 日本の家は和風と洋風が混ざっている。
   Nippon no ie wa wafū to yōfū ga mazatte iru.
   Japanese houses are a mixture of <u>Japanese</u> and
   <u>Western styles</u>.

5. 寝冷えで風邪を引いた。
   Nebie de kaze o hiita.
   I <u>caught a chill</u> while asleep.

Common Compounds and Phrases

強風	**kyōfū**	a strong wind
風習	**fūshū**	manners and customs; ways
風景	**fūkei**	a scene; a landscape
洋風	**yōfū**	European (Western) style
台風	**taifū**	a typhoon
*風呂	**furo**	a (hot) bath
*風邪	**kaze**	a cold

The second stroke ends with a hook.

9 ノ 几 几 凡 凨 凬 風 風 風

風

226

便

ベン BEN　ビン BIN
たより tayori

convenient;
mail; excrement

The character 便 combines *person* 亻 and
servant 更, suggesting *service* and by
extension, *convenience*. Mail is an associated
idea from service.

GR4 N4 AP

Example Sentences

1. 交通の便は、どうですか。
   Kōtsū no ben wa, dō desu ka.
   How are the <u>public transport facilities</u>?

2. 実家は駅に近くて便利です。
   Jikka wa eki ni chikakute benri desu.
   My parents' house is <u>conveniently</u> located near the
   station.

3. 航空便だといくらになりますか。
   Kōkūbin da to ikura ni narimasu ka.
   How much will that be if it is <u>air mail</u>?

4. うそも方便。
   Uso mo hōben.
   A lie is sometimes <u>justified</u>. (a saying)

5. 便りのないのはよい知らせ。
   Tayori no nai no wa yoi shirase.
   No news is good <u>news</u>. (a saying)

Common Compounds and Phrases

便利な	**benri na**	convenient; useful
航空便	**kōkūbin**	air transport; air mail
郵便	**yūbin**	the mail; the post
宅配便	**takuhaibin**	a courier (delivery) service
便所	**benjo**	a toilet; a lavatory
便秘	**benpi**	constipation
小便	**shōben**	urine

The eighth stroke does not protrude at the top. Don't
confuse 便 with 使.

9 ノ 亻 仁 仁 仹 佰 佰 便 便

便

227 洋

ヨウ YŌ

ocean; Western

The character 洋 is a combination of *water* 氵 and *sheep* 羊. The latter is thought to represent great size, hence, a large body of water or *ocean*.

GR3 N4 AP

Example Sentences

1. あの人は太平洋をヨットで横断した。
   Ano hito wa <u>taiheiyō</u> o yotto de ōdan shita.
   That man crossed <u>the Pacific</u> in a yacht.

2. 明治時代に西洋の習慣が数多く導入された。
   Meiji jidai ni <u>seiyō no</u> shūkan ga kazu-ōku dōnyū sareta.
   Many <u>Western</u> practices were introduced during the Meiji era.

3. 祖母が洋服を着ることはまれだ。
   Sobo ga <u>yōfuku</u> o kiru koto wa mare da.
   My grandmother rarely wears <u>Western clothing</u>.

4. 1975年に沖縄で海洋博覧会がありました。
   Senkyūhyaku nanajūgonen ni Okinawa de <u>kaiyō hakurankai</u> ga arimashita.
   In 1975 <u>a marine exposition</u> was held in Okinawa.

Common Compounds and Phrases

太平洋	**Taiheiyō**	the Pacific Ocean
大西洋	**Taiseiyō**	the Atlantic Ocean
洋服	**yōfuku**	Western clothes
海洋	**kaiyō**	the sea; the ocean
洋食	**yōshoku**	foreign (Western) food
洋画	**yōga**	Western painting; a foreign film
洋物	**yōmono**	a foreign article; an imported article

The last stroke does not protrude at the top.

9 ` ⼎ 氵 氵 氵 氵 浐 浐 洋 洋

洋

228 員

イン IN

a member

The character 員 combines a *circle* 口 and a *three-legged kettle* 貝, apparently suggesting officials gathered round, counting. The meaning of *member* has derived from this.

GR3 N4 AP

Example Sentences

1. この映画館の定員は二百十名です。
   Kono eigakan no <u>teiin</u> wa nihyaku jūmei desu.
   This movie theater has <u>a seating capacity</u> of two hundred and ten.

2. 朝の満員電車には乗りたくない。
   Asa no <u>man'in</u> densha ni wa noritaku nai.
   I don't wish to ride on a <u>jam-packed</u> train in the morning.

3. 職業欄に「会社員」と書けばいいんですか。
   Shokugyō-ran ni '<u>kaishain</u>' to kakeba ii n desu ka.
   Is it OK to write '<u>company employee</u>' in the space for occupation?

4. 必要な時に店員がいない。
   Hitsuyō na toki ni <u>ten'in</u> ga inai.
   You can never find <u>a shop assistant</u> when you need one.

Common Compounds and Phrases

満員	**man'in**	full house; packed
会社員	**kaishain**	a company employee
全員	**zen'in**	everybody; all the people
係員	**kakariin**	a person in charge
会員	**kaiin**	a member of a society
銀行員	**ginkōin**	a bank employee
乗務員	**jōmuin**	a member of a crew

End the last stroke firmly.

10 ` ⼎ 冂 冋 曱 貝 肙 肙 冒 員 員

員

EXERCISE 19 (217 – 228)

A. Write the readings for the following.

1. 何度 _____
2. お茶 _____
3. 品物 _____
4. 見送る _____
5. 不便な _____
6. 昼休み _____
7. 待たない _____
8. 洋食 _____
9. 五十点 _____
10. 発売 _____

B. Write in kanji and kana.

1. a discovery _____
2. a spring breeze _____
3. a waiting room _____
4. Western style _____
5. a station employee _____
6. daytime _____
7. elegant; tasteful _____

8. a farewell party _____
9. the Atlantic Ocean _____
10. a letter; news _____

C. Choose a character from the list to add to the following, to match the English meanings.
  LIST: 茶、風、度、発、洋、送、品、昼、員、便

1. 店 ____ (a shop assistant)
2. ____ 食 (lunch)
3. 今 ____ (the latest; next time)
4. 海 ____ (the ocean)
5. ____ 金 (a remittance)
6. 出 ____ (a departure)
7. ____ 所 (a lavatory; a WC)
8. ____ 色 (brown)
9. 台 ____ (a typhoon)
10. 作 ____ (a piece of work; a product)

---

229 院

institution

イン IN

The character 院 combines *hill, mound* 阝 and *complete* 完, which originally meant *a building with a surrounding wall*, to give us the present meaning of *institute*.
GR3 N4 AP

Example Sentences

1. 隣のおじいさんが救急車で病院に運ばれた。
   Tonari no ojiisan ga kyūkyūsha de byōin ni hakobareta.
   The old man next door was taken to <u>hospital</u> by ambulance.

2. 美容院の予約を取らなくちゃ。
   Biyōin no yoyaku o toranakucha.
   I'll have to make an appointment for <u>the hairdresser's</u>.

3. 兄は大学院に行きたがっている。
   Ani wa daigakuin ni ikitagatte iru.
   My older brother is keen to go to <u>graduate school</u>.

4. 政治家は衆議院へ辞職願を提出した。
   Seijika wa shūgiin e jishoku-negai o teishutsu shita.
   The politician tendered his resignation to <u>the House of Representatives</u>.

Common Compounds and Phrases

病院	**byōin**	a hospital; a clinic
美容院	**biyōin**	a beauty salon; a hairdresser's
大学院	**daigakuin**	graduate school
衆議院	**shūgiin**	the House of Representatives
参議院	**sangiin**	the House of Councillors
修道院	**shūdōin**	a monastery; a convent
退院	**taiin**	discharge from a hospital

The last stroke sweeps upward.

10	⁷	３	阝	阝'	阝'	阝宀	阼	阼	陀	院

院

230 夏

summer

カ KA *ゲ GE
なつ natsu

The character 夏 derived from a pictograph of a masked person dancing, perhaps in a *summer* festival.

GR2 N4 AP

Example Sentences

1. 初夏の海辺でバーベキューをして楽しんだ。
   Shoka no umibe de bābekyū o shite tanoshinda.
   We enjoyed a barbecue at the beach in <u>early summer</u>.

2. 明日から学校は夏休みだ。
   Ashita kara gakkō wa <u>natsuyasumi</u> da.
   School <u>summer vacation</u> begins tomorrow.

3. 夏ばてしてだるいなあ。
   <u>**Natsubate shite darui nā.**</u>
   This <u>summer heat</u> has worn me out.

4. 日本には夏時間はありません。
   Nippon ni wa <u>natsujikan</u> wa arimasen.
   Japan has no <u>daylight saving time</u>.

5. ハワイは「常夏の島」と言われている。
   Hawai wa '<u>Tokonatsu</u> no shima' to iwarete iru.
   Hawaii is known as 'the land of <u>eternal summer</u>'.

Common Compounds and Phrases

初夏	**shoka**	early summer
夏ばて	**natsubate**	summer fatigue
夏時間	**natsu-jikan**	daylight saving time
常夏	**tokonatsu**	everlasting summer
夏痩せ	**natsuyase**	summer weight loss
夏物	**natsumono**	summer goods, clothing
*夏至	**geshi**	the summer solstice

The bottom portion is not 又.

10 一 丆 丆 币 币 百 百 百 戸 夏 夏

夏

---

231 家

house

カ KA ケ KE
いえ ie や ya

The character 家 combines *roof* 宀 and *pig* 豕, suggesting a place where pigs and humans are together, i.e., a *house*.

GR2 N4 AP

Example Sentences

1. 台風で民家に被害が出た。
   Taifū de <u>minka</u> ni higai ga deta.
   <u>Houses</u> were damaged by the typhoon.

2. 古い家具を直せば、また使える。
   Furui <u>kagu</u> o naoseba, mata tsukaeru.
   If you repair old <u>furniture</u>, it can be reused.

3. 川端康成はノーベル賞作家でした。
   Kawabata Yasunari wa Nōberu-shō <u>sakka</u> deshita.
   Yasunari Kawabata was a Nobel prize-winning <u>author</u>.

4. 私の店は大阪にありますが、家は神戸です。
   Watashi no mise wa Ōsaka ni arimasu ga, <u>ie</u> wa Kōbe desu.
   I have a store in Osaka, but <u>my house</u> is in Kobe.

5. 月々、十万円の家賃を払っています。
   Tsukizuki, jūman-en no <u>yachin</u> o haratte imasu.
   I'm paying ¥100,000 a month in <u>rent</u>.

Common Compounds and Phrases

民家	**minka**	a private house
家具	**kagu**	furniture
作家	**sakka**	an author; a writer
専門家	**senmonka**	a specialist; an expert
家内	**kanai**	a family; my wife
家賃	**yachin**	house (apartment) rent
大家	**ōya**	a landlord

The sixth stroke ends with a hook.

10 ' ⺌ 宀 宀 宁 宇 字 家 家 家

家

131

232 記

キ KI
しる・す shiru(su)

to write down;
to note

The character 記 combines *words* 言 and *winding thread* 己, which can be thought of as tying words together in *writing*.

GR2 N3 AP

Example Sentences

1. ここに名前と住所を記入して下さい。
   Koko ni namae to jūsho o kinyū shite kudasai.
   Please <u>write</u> your name and address here.

2. この記号は何ですか。
   Kono kigō wa nan desu ka.
   What does this <u>symbol</u> represent?

3. 新聞の面白い記事を読んだ。
   Shinbun no omoshiroi kiji o yonda.
   I read an interesting newspaper <u>article</u>.

4. あの人の名前は記憶していない。
   Ano hito no namae wa kioku shite inai.
   I <u>don't remember</u> that person's name.

5. 右側の空欄に答えを記しなさい。
   Migigawa no kūran ni kotae o shirushinasai.
   <u>Write</u> your answer in the space on the right.

Common Compounds and Phrases

記号	**kigō**	a symbol; a sign
記事	**kiji**	a (news) story; an article
記憶	**kioku**	a recollection; a memory
記録	**kiroku**	a record
記念	**kinen**	commemoration
明記	**meiki**	to clearly state; to specify
書記	**shoki**	a clerk; a secretary

The last stroke ends with a hook.

10 ` ゛ ー ゠ ゠ 言 言 訁 記 記

記

---

233 帰

キ KI
かえ・る kae(ru)
かえ・す kae(su)

to return;
to send back

The character 帰 combines *broom* 帚 and *foot* リ, and can be thought of as a place where sweeping is done, i.e., the *home*. Home is an associated meaning of *return*.

GR2 N4 AP

Example Sentences

1. ご帰国はいつですか。
   Gokikoku wa itsu desu ka.
   When do you <u>return to your home country</u>?

2. 箱根へ日帰り旅行に行って来た。
   Hakone e higaeri ryokō ni itte kita.
   We took <u>a day trip</u> to Hakone.

3. 彼はアメリカ人だったが日本に帰化した。
   Kare wa Amerikajin datta ga Nihon ni kika shita.
   He <u>changed his citizenship</u> from American to Japanese.

4. 雨が降りそうだから早く帰ろう。
   Ame ga furisō da kara hayaku kaerō.
   <u>Let's hurry home</u> because it looks like it's going to rain.

5. 暗くなってきたので、子供たちを家に帰した。
   Kuraku natte kita node, kodomotachi o ie ni kaeshita.
   It had gotten dark, so we <u>sent</u> the children <u>home</u>.

Common Compounds and Phrases

帰国	**kikoku**	returning to one's country
帰化	**kika**	naturalization
帰宅	**kitaku**	to return; to come home
復帰	**fukki**	a return; a comeback
帰省	**kisei**	returning to one's hometown
日帰り	**higaeri**	to go and return in one day
帰り道	**kaerimichi**	the way home; a return trip

The fourth stroke doesn't protrude, and the ninth stroke ends with a hook.

10 ' リ リ゛ リ゛ リ゛ リ゛ 帰 帰 帰

帰

234 起

キ KI
お・きる o(kiru)
お・こる o(koru)
お・こす o(kosu)
*た・つ ta(tsu)

to get up; to rise;
to occur; to cause

Formerly, 起 this character combined *run* 走 and *serpent* 巳, which suggested the notion of *to stop running and rear up*. The associated meanings of *rise* and *occur* developed from this.

GR3 N4 AP

Example Sentences

1. 起床時間は朝六時です。
   Kishō jikan wa asa rokuji desu.
   We get up at 6:00 A.M.

2. あの水泳選手は怪我から再起した。
   Ano suiei senshu wa kega kara saiki shita.
   That swimmer made a comeback after being injured.

3. 朝早く起きて、犬の散歩に行く。
   Asa hayaku okite, inu no sanpo ni iku.
   I get up early in the morning and take the dog for a walk.

4. 一体何が起きてるの。
   Ittai nani ga okiteru no.
   What on earth is going on?

5. 娘は、夜中に喘息の発作を起こした。
   Musume wa, yonaka ni zensoku no hossa o okoshita.
   My daughter had an asthma attack in the night.

Common Compounds and Phrases

起床	**kishō**	getting up in the morning
再起	**saiki**	a comeback; a recovery
起立	**kiritsu**	to stand up; to rise
起点	**kiten**	a starting point; a terminus
起源	**kigen**	the origin; the beginning
縁起	**engi**	an omen; an origin
早起き	**hayaoki**	early rising

Make sure you do not write 己 as 巳.

10 一 十 土 キ キ キ 走 走 起 起

起

---

235 紙

シ SHI
かみ kami

paper

The character 紙 combines *threads* 糸 and *ladle* 氏, and can be thought of as stirring boiled threads to make *paper*.

GR2 N4 AP

Example Sentences

1. コピー用紙、ある。
   Kopii yōshi, aru.
   Do you have any photocopy paper?

2. 父は業界紙を読むのがすきです。
   Chichi wa gyōkaishi o yomu no ga suki desu.
   My father likes to read trade journals.

3. 会社では五紙取っている。
   Kaisha de wa goshi totte iru.
   We subscribe to five newspapers at our company.

4. 折り紙で鶴を折った。
   Origami de tsuru o otta.
   I folded a piece of origami paper into a crane.

5. この電気の笠は、紙で出来ている。
   Kono denki no kasa wa, kami de dekite iru.
   This lamp shade is made from paper.

Common Compounds and Phrases

用紙	**yōshi**	a blank form; stationery
包装紙	**hōsōshi**	wrapping paper
紙幣	**shihei**	paper money; notes
新聞紙	**shinbunshi**	newspaper
再生紙	**saiseishi**	recycled paper
紙袋	**kamibukuro**	a paper bag
手紙	**tegami**	a letter
折り紙	**origami**	origami folding paper

The last stroke ends with a hook.

10 乡 幺 幺 幺 糸 糸 紅 紙 紙 紙

紙

236 借

to borrow

シャク SHAKU
か・りる ka(riru)

The character 借 combines *person* 亻 and *duplicate* 昔, hence it conveys the meaning of *to imitate a person*. The sense of *not really one's own* and thus, *borrow*, developed from this.
GR4 N4

Example Sentences

1. 借金してでもあの車を買いたい。
   Shakkin shite de mo ano kuruma o kaitai.
   I want to buy that car even if I have <u>to take out a loan</u>.

2. 真向かいの借家は、なかなか人が入らない。
   Mamukai no shakuya wa, nakanaka hito ga hairanai.
   There have been no takers for <u>the house for rent</u> across the street.

3. 友達から今話題の本を借りた。
   Tomodachi kara ima wadai no hon o karita.
   I <u>borrowed</u> a book that is being much talked about from a friend.

4. この問題については専門家の知恵を借りるべきだろう。
   Kono mondai ni tsuite wa senmonka no chie o kariru beki darō.
   We might <u>have to ask for</u> expert advice about this matter.

Common Compounds and Phrases

借金	**shakkin**	a debt; a loan
借家	**shakuya**	a rented house
借用	**shakuyō**	borrowing; a loan
拝借	**haishaku**	borrowing
貸し借り	**kashikari**	lending and borrowing
前借	**maegari**	getting an advance
借り物	**karimono**	a borrowed (rented) item

The sixth stroke is longer than the one above it.

10 ノ　イ　イ゠　イ゠　イ゠　件　借　借　借　借

借

---

237 弱

weak;
to weaken

ジャク JAKU
よわ・い yowa(i)
よわ・る yowa(ru)
よわ・まる yowa(maru)

The character 弱 depicted two decorative *bows*, not of any practical use, thus symbolizing *weakness*.
GR2 N4

Example Sentences

1. 駅までバスで一時間弱かかった。
   Eki made basu de ichijikan jaku kakatta.
   It took <u>a little less than an hour</u> to get to the station by bus.

2. あなたの最大の弱点は何ですか。
   Anata no saidai no jakuten wa nan desu ka.
   What is your greatest <u>weakness</u>?

3. 彼は気が弱くて、友達ができない。
   Kare wa ki ga yowakute, tomodachi ga dekinai.
   He's so <u>timid</u>, he's unable to make friends.

4. 母は機械に弱い。
   Haha wa kikai ni yowai.
   My mother <u>isn't mechanically minded</u>.

5. やっと雨足が弱まった。
   Yatto amaashi ga yowamatta.
   Finally this pouring rain <u>has lightened up</u>.

Common Compounds and Phrases

弱点	**jakuten**	a weak point; a weakness
弱冠	**jakkan**	20 years old; youth
病弱	**byōjaku**	a delicate constitution
貧弱	**hinjaku**	shabby; meager
強弱	**kyōjaku**	(relative) strength
弱虫	**yowamushi**	a weakling; a coward
弱気	**yowaki**	weakness; bearish

The third and seventh strokes end with a hook.

10 ⁊　⁊　弓　弓　弓゙　弓゙　弱　弱　弱　弱

弱

238 真

true; truth

シン SHIN
ま ma

Originally 眞, the origins of this character are unclear, but it is said to represent an image of filling a container with food, suggesting *not false* or *true*.

GR2 N4 AP

Example Sentences

1. 真実から目を背けるな。
   Shinjitsu kara me o somukeru na.
   Don't close your eyes to <u>the truth</u>.

2. 純真な心を持ったまま大人になった。
   Junshin na kokoro o motta mama otona ni natta.
   He grew to adulthood with a <u>pure and simple</u> heart.

3. もっと真剣に取り組みなさい。
   Motto shinken ni torikuminasai.
   Deal with the matter <u>more seriously</u>!

4. 矢が的の真ん中に当たった。
   Ya ga mato no mannaka ni atatta.
   The arrow struck the target <u>dead in the center</u>.

5. 真っ白な雪景色が広がっていた。
   Masshiro na yukigeshiki ga hirogatte ita.
   A <u>pure-white</u> snowy scene stretched out before me.

Common Compounds and Phrases

純真な	**junshin na**	pure; genuine; sincere
真実	**shinjitsu**	truth; reality; truly
真剣な	**shinken na**	earnest; serious
真新しい	**maatarashii**	brand new
真ん中	**mannaka**	the middle; the center
真夏	**manatsu**	midsummer
*真っ白	**masshiro**	pure white

The eighth stroke is longer than those above it.

10 一 十 广 古 古 直 直 直 真 真

真

---

239 通

to go through; to pass; to commute

ツウ TSŪ
とお・る tō(ru)
かよ・う kayo(u)

The character 通 combines *go* 辶 and *fence* 甬 to give the meaning of *pass through*.

GR2 N4 AP

Example Sentences

1. 通勤電車の混み方は最悪だ。
   Tsūkin densha no komikata wa saiaku da.
   The crowds on the <u>commuter trains</u> are horrible!

2. 彼は音楽通です。
   Kare wa ongaku-tsū desu.
   He <u>has a thorough knowledge of music</u>.

3. 最近、彼女から手紙が一通も来ない。
   Saikin, kanojo kara tegami ga ittsū mo konai.
   I haven't received <u>a single letter</u> from her lately.

4. 目白通りを通って下さい。
   Mejiro-dōri o tōtte kudasai.
   <u>Please go along</u> Mejiro Avenue.

5. 娘は二人とも近所の学校に通っています。
   Musume wa futari to mo kinjo no gakkō ni kayotte imasu.
   Both of my daughters <u>attend</u> the local school.

Common Compounds and Phrases

通勤	**tsūkin**	commuting
一方通行	**ippō tsūkō**	one-way traffic
共通	**kyōtsū**	common; shared
通過	**tsūka**	to pass by (through)
通訳	**tsūyaku**	interpreting; an interpreter
普通	**futsū**	normal; ordinary
通り道	**tōrimichi**	a passage; a route

The fourth stroke ends with a hook.

10 フ マ ア 丙 丙 甬 甬 浦 通 通

通

240 特

トク TOKU

special

The character 特 combines *cow*, *bull* 牛 and *temple* 寺, a reference to a sacrificial bull of *special* quality kept in the temple precinct.

GR4 N4 AP

Example Sentences

1. この印は特別な意味を持っています。
   Kono shirushi wa tokubetsu na imi o motte imasu.
   This symbol has a <u>special</u> significance.

2. 特に注意する事はありますか。
   Toku ni chūi suru koto wa arimasu ka.
   Is there anything <u>in particular</u> I need to look out for?

3. ゴーヤ（にがうり）には独特の苦みがある。
   Gōya (nigauri) ni wa dokutoku no nigami ga aru.
   Goya (bitter gourd) has a <u>distinctive bitter taste</u>.

4. 東京行きの特急電車は一時間に一本しかない。
   Tōkyō-yuki no tokkyū densha wa ichijikan ni ippon shika nai.
   There is only one <u>limited express train</u> bound for Tokyo every hour.

5. あの地方の特産物と言えばミカンでしょう。
   Ano chihō no tokusanbutsu to ieba mikan deshō.
   The <u>local specialty</u> in that region would have to be mandarin oranges.

Common Compounds and Phrases

独特	**dokutoku**	special; original
特急	**tokkyū**	a limited express train
特徴	**tokuchō**	a distinctive feature
特価	**tokka**	a bargain price
特許	**tokkyo**	a patent; a concession
特技	**tokugi**	a special ability, talent
特定	**tokutei**	specific; particular

Take care to use the same spacing with the horizontal strokes.

10 ′ 广 ヒ 牛 牜 牜 牜 牜 特 特

特

EXERCISE 20 (229 – 240)

A. Write the readings for the following.

1. 起こす _____
2. 特別な _____
3. 帰り道 _____
4. 真っ白な _____
5. 夏時間 _____
6. 弱まっている _____
7. 民家 _____
8. 借金 _____
9. 大学院生 _____
10. 白紙 _____

B. Write in kanji and kana.

1. まなつ の ひ _____
2. さっか に なる _____
3. でんしゃ で かえる _____
4. ろくじ はん に おきる _____
5. なつやすみ ちゅう に _____
6. がっこう に かよう _____
7. しんぶん の きじ _____

8. とく に やすい _____
9. のりもの に よわい _____
10. はやく かえろう _____

C. Give the English meanings for the following.

1. 一方通行の道 _____
2. 記入して下さい _____
3. 手紙を読む _____
4. 入院する _____
5. 真新しいシャツ _____
6. 毎日日記を書く _____
7. 起立する _____
8. 夏ばてする _____
9. 自分の家 _____
10. 本を借りる _____

241 病

illness

ビョウ BYŌ　*ヘイ HEI
や・む ya(mu)　やまい yamai

The character 病 combines *sickness* 疒 and *immobility* 丙, suggesting a crippling *illness*.

GR3 N4 AP

Example Sentences

1. 病気のため、会議を欠席させてください。
   Byōki no tame, kaigi o kesseki sasete kudasai.
   Because of my <u>illness</u>, you'll have to excuse me from attending the conference.

2. 狂牛病は社会問題になりつつある。
   Kyōgyūbyō wa shakai mondai ni naritsutsu aru.
   <u>Mad cow disease</u> continues to be a problem at large.

3. そんなこと、気に病む必要はない。
   Sonna koto, ki ni yamu hitsuyō wa nai.
   There's no need <u>to worry</u> about such a thing.

4. 病は気から。
   Yamai wa ki kara.
   <u>Illness</u> originates from the mind. (a saying)

5. 知人が先日不治の病で亡くなった。
   Chijin ga senjitsu fuji no yamai de nakunatta.
   An acquaintance died recently of <u>an incurable illness</u>.

Common Compounds and Phrases

病人	**byōnin**	a patient; an invalid
仮病	**kebyō**	feigned illness
病状	**byōjō**	a patient's condition
狂牛病	**kyōgyūbyō**	mad cow disease
熱射病	**nesshabyō**	heatstroke
うつ病	**utsubyō**	depression; melancholy
おく病な	**okubyō na**	cowardly, timid

The eighth stroke ends with a hook.

10 　丶　亠　广　广　疒　疒　疒　病　病　病

病

---

242 勉

to endeavor

ベン BEN
つと・める tsuto(meru)

The character 勉 is comprised of the elements 免, *a mother in childbirth* and 力, *strength, effort*, representing a sense of *striving with great effort*.

GR3 N4 AP

Example Sentences

1. 毎日家で二時間勉強をしている。
   Mainichi ie de nijikan benkyō o shite iru.
   I <u>study</u> for two hours every day at home.

2. あの科学者は子供の頃から勉強家だったそうです。
   Ano kagakusha wa kodomo no koro kara benkyōka datta sō desu.
   I read that that scientist was <u>hard-working</u> from his youth.

3. 受験生は休み中も必死に受験勉強をしている。
   Jukensei wa yasumi-chū mo hisshi ni juken benkyō o shite iru.
   Students preparing for exams <u>are busy studying</u> even during the holidays.

4. 彼はとても勤勉な青年だ。
   Kare wa totemo kinben na seinen da.
   He is a very <u>diligent</u> young person.

Common Compounds and Phrases

勉強	**benkyō**	study; selling cheaply
勤勉	**kinben**	diligent; hard-working
勉学	**bengaku**	study
勉強家	**benkyōka**	a hard-working student
勉強の虫	**benkyō no mushi**	a grind; a nerd
ガリ勉	**gariben**	studying hard; a grind
受験勉強	**juken benkyō**	studying for (entrance) examinations

The eighth stroke sweeps upwards.

10 　丿　ク　ゲ　名　各　岳　免　免　勉　勉

勉

243 旅

リョ RYO
たび tabi

to travel

The character 旅 brings together the elements of *flag, banner* 方, 亠 and *rallied warriors* 氏, suggesting a military campaign. From this, the idea of *traveling far* has developed.
GR3 N4 AP

Example Sentences

1. 三日後に旅に出る。
   Mikka-go ni <u>tabi</u> ni deru.
   I'll be leaving on <u>a trip</u> in three days.

2. 大抵の旅館は、朝食付きです。
   Taitei no <u>ryokan</u> wa, chōshoku-tsuki desu.
   <u>Japanese inns</u> usually include breakfast in the tariff.

3. 旅客機のエンジントラブルで出発時間が遅れた。
   <u>Ryokakki</u> no enjin toraburu de shuppatsu jikan ga okureta.
   Our departure was delayed due to a mechanical problem with <u>the plane</u>.

4. 船旅は、旅費が高くつくと聞いている。
   <u>Funatabi</u> wa, <u>ryohi</u> ga takaku tsuku to kiite iru.
   I hear that <u>sea voyages</u> are <u>expensive</u>.

5. よい旅をお楽しみください。
   Yoi <u>tabi</u> o otanoshimi kudasai.
   Have a good <u>trip</u>!

Common Compounds and Phrases

旅館	**ryokan**	a Japanese inn
旅費	**ryohi**	traveling expenses
修学旅行	**shūgaku**	a school excursion;
	ryokō	a study tour
新婚旅行	**shinkon**	a honeymoon
	ryokō	
旅券	**ryoken**	a passport
旅先	**tabisaki**	one's destination
一人旅	**hitori-tabi**	traveling alone

End the eighth stroke firmly.

10	'	ﾗ	ｫ	方	ｶﾞ	ｶﾞ	扩	抃	旅	旅

旅

244 料

リョウ RYŌ

a fee; materials

The character 料 combines *rice* 米 and *to measure* 斗, suggesting the measuring of rice or any *material*, as well as the quantity. *Fee* is an associated meaning.
GR4 N4 AP

Example Sentences

1. たまには家庭料理を味わいたい。
   Tama ni wa <u>katei ryōri</u> o ajiwaitai.
   There are times when I just want to enjoy <u>a home-cooked meal</u>.

2. コンクリートの原料は何ですか。
   Konkuriito no <u>genryō</u> wa nan desu ka.
   What are the <u>raw materials</u> used in concrete?

3. 六十五歳以上の方は入場料は無料になります。
   Rokujūgo-sai ijō no kata wa <u>nyūjōryō</u> wa muryō ni narimasu.
   <u>Admission</u> is free for those people over the age of sixty-five.

4. この料金には手数料が含まれています。
   Kono <u>ryōkin</u> ni wa <u>tesūryō</u> ga fukumarete imasu.
   This <u>price</u> includes a <u>commission</u>.

5. ペットボトルの飲料水を持ち歩く人が増えた。
   Petto botoru no <u>inryōsui</u> o mochiaruku hito ga fueta.
   The number of people who carry bottled <u>water</u> has increased.

Common Compounds and Phrases

材料	**zairyō**	material; matter
資料	**shiryō**	materials; data
燃料	**nenryō**	fuel
衣料	**iryō**	clothing; clothes
給料	**kyūryō**	a salary; wages
食料	**shokuryō**	food; foodstuffs
使用量	**shiyōryō**	a rental fee
手数料	**tesūryō**	a commission

Do not put a hook on the last stroke.

10	'	'	立	半	米	米	米	米	料	料

料

245 悪

アク AKU *オ O
わる・い waru(i)

bad; evil; poor

The character 悪 originally combined *heart* 心 and *the hollow created by the pillars of a house* 亞, suggesting a *bad* feeling one might have as if being crushed by heavy pillars.

GR3 N4 AP

Example Sentences

1. 父親の病気が悪化した。
   Chichioya no byōki ga akka shita.
   Their father's illness became more serious.

2. さっきから、悪寒がする。
   Sakki kara, okan ga suru.
   I've been feeling a chill since a while ago.

3. 小さい時から目が悪い。
   Chiisai toki kara me ga warui.
   I've had bad eyesight since childhood.

4. ごめんなさい。私が悪かった。
   Gomen nasai. Watashi ga warukatta.
   I'm sorry. I'm to blame.

5. 人の悪口を言うと嫌われますよ。
   Hito no warukuchi o iu to kirawaremasu yo.
   If you speak ill of a person, you will be disliked.

Common Compounds and Phrases

悪化	**akka**	getting worse; deterioration
悪意	**akui**	malicious intent
悪質	**akushitsu**	malicious; malignant
最悪	**saiaku**	the worst
必要悪	**hitsuyō-aku**	a necessary evil
意地悪	**ijiwaru**	spitefulness; malice
悪口	**warukuchi**	slander; foul language

The fifth and sixth strokes do not protrude.

11 一 丆 冖 冖 五 再 亜 严 恶 悪 悪

悪

246 強

キョウ KYŌ ゴウ GŌ
つよ・い tsuyo(i)
つよ・める tsuyo(meru)
し・いる shi(iru)

strong

The character 強 combines *bow* 弓 which represents *strength*, and 虫, which originally meant *horsefly*, a *strong*, persistent bug.

GR2 N4 AP

Example Sentences

1. 反テロ対策の重要性を強調すべきだ。
   Han-tero taisaku no jūyōsei o kyōchō subeki da.
   It is necessary to emphasize the importance of anti-terrorism measures.

2. その荷物は十キロ強ある。
   Sono nimotsu wa jukkiro kyō aru.
   That baggage weighs a little over ten kilograms.

3. 強引にお酒を飲まされた。
   Gōin ni osake o nomasareta.
   They forced me to drink alcohol.

4. 彼は数学に強い。
   Kare wa sūgaku ni tsuyoi.
   He's good at mathematics.

5. 大臣のコメントは両国の緊張を強める恐れがあります。
   Daijin no komento wa ryōkoku no kinchō o tsuyomeru osore ga arimasu.
   There is a concern that the Minister's comment will increase tensions between the two countries.

Common Compounds and Phrases

強調	**kyōchō**	emphasis; stress
強力	**kyōryoku**	strength; power
強制	**kyōsei**	compulsory; forced
補強	**hokyō**	reinforcement; strengthening
銀行強盗	**ginkō gōtō**	a bank robber(y)
強いて言えば	**shiite ieba**	if I had to say...
力強い	**chikarazuyoi**	strong; powerful

The third stroke is one continuous stroke.

11 フ ㇇ 弓 弣 弨 弨 弨 弨 強 強 強

強

247 教

キョウ KYŌ
おし・える oshi(eru)
おそ・わる oso(waru)

to teach;
lesson; doctrine

The character 教 combines *stick* 攵, *adult* 耂, and *child* 子, to represent a person holding a stick and *teaching* a child.

GR2 N4 AP

Example Sentences

1. 教科書と漢和辞典を買った。
   Kyōkasho to kanwa jiten o katta.
   I bought myself <u>a textbook</u> and a Japanese *kanji* dictionary.

2. 毎週、日曜日には教会へ行きます。
   Maishū, nichiyōbi ni wa kyōkai e ikimasu.
   I go to <u>church</u> every Sunday.

3. 一応、仏教徒です。
   Ichiō, bukkyōto desu.
   Technically, I'm <u>Buddhist</u>.

4. 電話番号を教えて。
   Denwa bangō o oshiete.
   <u>Could you tell me</u> your telephone number?

5. 小学生の頃ピアノを教わっていた。
   Shōgakusei no koro piano o osowatte ita.
   I <u>was taught</u> piano as an elementary student.

Common Compounds and Phrases

教科書	**kyōkasho**	a (school) textbook
教会	**kyōkai**	a church
仏教	**bukkyō**	Buddhism
キリスト教	**kirisuto-kyō**	Christianity
教科	**kyōka**	a subject; a curriculum
教授	**kyōju**	a professor
宗教	**shūkyō**	a religion

The sixth stroke ends with a hook.

11 一 十 土 耂 耂 孝 孝 孝 孝 教 教

教

---

248 黒

コク KOKU
くろ kuro　くろ・い kuro(i)

black

The character 黒 was originally a pictograph of a cooking stove on a blazing fire. The suggestion of the color *black* derives from the soot on the stove.

GR2 N4 AP

Example Sentences

1. 黒板の字が小さくて、よく読めない。
   Kokuban no ji ga chiisakute, yoku yomenai.
   The writing on <u>the blackboard</u> is too small for me to make out.

2. 白黒の写真をたくさん撮った。
   Shirokuro no shashin o takusan totta.
   I took a lot of <u>black and white</u> photographs.

3. しばらく掃除をサボったら、床が真っ黒だった。
   Shibaraku sōji o sabottara, yuka ga makkuro datta.
   When I neglected cleaning for a while, the floor became <u>quite filthy</u>.

4. あいつは腹黒い奴で、信用できないよ。
   Aitsu wa haraguroi yatsu de, shinyō dekinai yo.
   That jerk is <u>malicious</u>. He can't be trusted.

5. 事件の黒幕は彼だと言われている。
   Jiken no kuromaku wa kare da to iwarete iru.
   He is the one who is said to have <u>masterminded</u> the incident.

Common Compounds and Phrases

黒板	**kokuban**	a blackboard; a chalkboard
黒人	**kokujin**	a black; an Afro-American
暗黒	**ankoku**	darkness
真っ黒	**makkuro**	jet-black
腹黒い	**haraguroi**	scheming; treacherous
黒字	**kuroji**	in the black
*黒子	**hokuro**	a mole (facial)

The sixth stroke is longer than those above it, and the seventh stroke is the longest.

11 丿 冂 冃 日 甲 甲 里 里 黒 黒 黒

黒

249 菜

サイ SAI
な na

vegetable

The character 菜 combines *grass* ⺾ (草) and *picking leaves by hand* 采, a reference to hand-picked grasses. From this the sense of greens or *vegetables* has derived.
GR4 N4

Example Sentences

1. 今日の昼は野菜炒めにしよう。
   Kyō no hiru wa <u>yasai-itame</u> ni shiyō.
   I feel like having <u>stir-fried vegetables</u> for lunch today!

2. 祖母とよく山菜を取りに行ったものだ。
   Sobo to yoku <u>sansai</u> o tori ni itta mono da.
   I often used to go with my grandma to collect <u>edible wild plants</u>.

3. そろそろ菜の花の季節だ。
   Soro soro <u>nanohana</u> no kisetsu da.
   <u>The rape</u> will be blossoming soon.

4. 肉ばかりじゃなく野菜も食べなさい。
   Niku bakari ja naku <u>yasai</u> mo tabenasai.
   Eat some <u>vegetables</u>, not just meat.

5. 趣味は家庭菜園で野菜を作ることです。
   Shumi wa <u>katei saien</u> de <u>yasai</u> o tsukuru koto desu.
   My hobby is growing <u>vegetables</u> in my <u>kitchen garden</u>.

Common Compounds and Phrases

野菜	**yasai**	(green) vegetables
山菜	**sansai**	an edible wild plant
お惣菜	**osōzai**	ready-prepared food
前菜	**zensai**	an appetizer
菜食	**saishoku**	a vegetable diet
青菜	**aona**	greens
菜の花	**nanohana**	rape; canola

Don't forget the fourth stroke.

11 一 十 艹 艹 艹 艹 芏 芏 莁 菜 菜

菜

---

250 産

サン SAN
う・む u(mu)
う・まれる u(mareru)
*うぶ ubu

to give birth;
to produce

Originally 產, the character 産 combined *pattern* 文, *cliff* 厂 and *the growth of new grass* 生, suggesting the idea of something being clearly separated from its origin, hence being *born*. The sense of *being produced* from the earth or business derives from this.
GR4 N4

Example Sentences

1. 母は妹のお産の手伝いをする予定です。
   Haha wa imōto no <u>osan</u> no tetsudai o suru yotei desu.
   My mother intends to assist when my sister <u>has her baby</u>.

2. 不動産屋に、新しい部屋を探してもらっている。
   <u>Fudōsan</u>ya ni, atarashii heya o sagashite moratte iru.
   I'm having <u>a real estate agent</u> find a new apartment for me.

3. 彼女は子供を四人産んだ。
   Kanojo wa kodomo o yonin <u>unda</u>.
   She <u>has given birth to</u> four children.

4. 子猫が三匹産まれた。
   Koneko ga sanbiki <u>umareta</u>.
   Three kittens <u>were born</u>.

5. あなたの街の産業は何ですか。
   Anata no machi no <u>sangyō</u> wa nan desu ka.
   What <u>industry</u> is there in your town?

Common Compounds and Phrases

お産	**osan**	childbirth; birth
不動産	**fudōsan**	real estate
産地	**sanchi**	place of production, birth
産業	**sangyō**	industry
外国産	**gaikokusan**	produced overseas; foreign-born
遺産	**isan**	an inheritance; a heritage
*産毛	**ubuge**	fine soft hair

The fifth and sixth strokes join.

11 ' 二 千 宁 立 产 产 产 斉 産 産

産

251 進

to advance

シン SHIN
すす・む susu(mu)
すす・める susu(meru)

The character 進 is a combination of *to go* 辶 and a *bird* 隹, suggesting the flight of a bird and from this, *proceeding* straight ahead.

GR3 N4 AP

Example Sentences

1. コンピューター技術の進歩は目覚しい。
   Konpyūtā gijutsu no shinpo wa mezamashii.
   The progress that computer technology is making is remarkable.

2. 先進国の金融不安が全世界に広まった。
   Senshinkoku no kin'yū fuan ga zensekai ni hiromatta.
   The financial turmoil of the developed nations spread throughout the entire globe.

3. 工事が予定通りに進んでいる。
   Kōji ga yotei-dōri ni susunde iru.
   Construction is proceeding according to schedule.

4. 姉は大学へ進む決心をした。
   Ane wa daigaku e susumu kesshin o shita.
   My older sister made up her mind to go on to college.

5. 夏時間に備えて、時計を一時間進めなさい。
   Natsujikan ni sonaete, tokei o ichijikan susumenasai.
   Put your watches forward an hour to be ready for daylight saving time.

Common Compounds and Phrases

進歩	**shinpo**	progress; improvement
先進国	**senshinkoku**	advanced (developed) nations
進学	**shingaku**	to advance a grade; to enter a higher-level school
進行	**shinkō**	progress; development
前進	**zenshin**	an advance; progress
進入	**shinnyū**	entry; admission
進化	**shinka**	evolution; progress

Keep uniform spacing between the horizontal strokes.

11 ノ　亻　彳　彳　什　件　隹　隹　谁　進　進

進

252 習

to learn; a custom

シュウ SHŪ
なら・う nara(u)

The character 習 combines *wings of a bird* 羽 and 白, formerly *oneself* 自 to suggest doing something by oneself. The repeated action of a bird moving its wings to fly represents the idea of *learning* by repetition.

GR3 N4 AP

Example Sentences

1. 毎朝、ジョギングするのが習慣になった。
   Maiasa, jogingu suru no ga shūkan ni natta.
   It has become my practice to jog every morning.

2. 八時から十時まで学習塾へ行っている。
   Hachiji kara jūji made gakushūjuku e itte iru.
   I study at a private preparatory school from 8 until 10.

3. 今日の三時間目は自習になった。
   Kyō no sanjikan-me wa jishū ni natta.
   My third class today became a self-study period.

4. 彼女は小さい頃からバレエを習っている。
   Kanojo wa chiisai koro kara baree o naratte iru.
   She has been learning ballet since she was a child.

5. この店で見習いとして三年間働いた。
   Kono mise de minarai to shite sannenkan hataraita.
   I worked in this store as an apprentice for three years.

Common Compounds and Phrases

習慣	**shūkan**	a habit; a custom
自習	**jishū**	studying by oneself
復習	**fukushū**	a review (lesson)
習得	**shūtoku**	learning; acquisition
実習	**jisshū**	practice; practical training
見習い	**minarai**	an apprentice(ship); a learner
習い事	**naraigoto**	an accomplishment; lessons

Be careful when writing the four dots.

11 ㄱ　ㄱ　ㅋ　ㅋㄱ　ㅋㄱ　羽　羽　羽　習　習　習

習

EXERCISE 21 (241 – 252)

A. Give the readings for the following.

1. 強い _____
2. 産まれる _____
3. 食料 _____
4. 教わる _____
5. 進む _____
6. 勉める _____
7. 習っている _____
8. 悪い _____
9. 旅 _____
10. 黒い _____

B. Match the following compounds with the corresponding hiragana.

1. 教会　（　）　　a. しろくろ
2. 悪口　（　）　　b. びょうき
3. 白黒　（　）　　c. しんぽ
4. 産地　（　）　　d. しようりょう
5. 病気　（　）　　e. がくしゅう
6. 前菜　（　）　　f. りょこう
7. 学習　（　）　　g. さんち

8. 進歩　（　）　　h. わるくち
9. 旅行　（　）　　i. きょうかい
10. 使用料（　）　　j. ぜんさい

C. Choose the correct kanji from the LIST to complete the following, according to the hint.
　　LIST: 勉強、料金、青菜、強引、病、外国産、
　　先進国、黒字、悪、教

1. 中国語を _____ える (to teach Chinese)
2. 世界一の _____ (the most advanced nation)
3. 日本語の _____ (Japanese study)
4. 目が _____ い (to have poor eyesight)
5. _____ である (to be in the black)
6. 心を _____ んでいる (to have psychological problems)
7. _____ を食べる (to eat some greens)
8. バスの _____ (a bus fare)
9. _____ の車 (a foreign-made car)
10. _____ に飲ませる (to force someone to drink)

Review 7 (1 – 252)

A. Write the readings for the following.

1. 料金 _____
2. 悪い _____
3. 習っている _____
4. 真っ黒 _____
5. 終わる _____
6. 借りる _____
7. 一人旅 _____
8. 産む _____
9. 強める _____
10. 進む _____

B. Write in English.

1. 習い事 _____
2. 旅先 _____
3. 力強い _____
4. 前菜 _____
5. 病院 _____
6. 家に帰る _____
7. 早起きする _____

8. 目が悪い _____
9. 去年の夏 _____
10. 英語を教える _____

C. Write in kanji and kana.

1. おおどおり _____
2. ガリべん _____
3. しんがくする _____
4. しようりょう _____
5. まんなか _____
6. きもちわるい _____
7. ひがえり _____
8. やまい _____
9. みおくり _____
10. さいしょく _____

D. Choose an appropriate kanji from the list to complete the following.

LIST: 勉、料、産、黒、進、強、病、旅、悪、弱

1. ＿＿ 引に (by force)
2. ＿＿ 行する (to travel)
3. ＿＿ 口を言う (to speak ill of)
4. ＿＿ 気になる (to become ill)
5. ＿＿ 字 (in the black)
6. ＿＿ 点 (a weak point)
7. ＿＿ 強する (to study)
8. ＿＿ 歩する (to progress)
9. 入場 ＿＿ (an entrance fee)
10. りんごの ＿＿ 地 (an apple-growing area)

E. Match the following with the corresponding kanji.

1. びょうにん　　（　）
2. せんしんこく　（　）
3. しょくりょう　（　）
4. じいん　　　　（　）
5. きょうりょく　（　）
6. かいがいりょこう（　）
7. とっきゅう　　（　）

a. 飲料水
b. 海外旅行
c. 茶色
d. 山菜
e. 新聞紙
f. 勉強家
g. 強力

8. キリストきょう　（　）
9. ちゃいろ　　　　（　）
10. こくさん　　　　（　）
11. そうりょう　　　（　）
12. しんぶんし　　　（　）
13. いんりょうすい　（　）
14. べんきょうか　　（　）
15. さんさい　　　　（　）

h. 送料
i. 先進国
j. キリスト教
k. 病人
l. 食料
m. 寺院
n. 国産
o. 特急

F. Rewrite using as many kanji as possible.
1. あに を びょういん に おくって いった。
2. まなつ の べんきょう は あつくて つらい。
3. たびさき で とくさんひん を かった。
4. ひる、いえ に かえって おちゃ を のんだ。
5. つぎ の びん の しゅっぱつ を またなければ ならない。

G. Rewrite the following in kana.
1. 洋服屋 の 店員 が 黒いコートを 売った。
2. 進学教室 で 習った字を 日記 に 書いた。
3. 「悪いけど、通行料 を 借りていいですか。」
4. 電気 が 点く 度 に 起こされた。
5. 青菜 は 紙につつむと 長持ちする。

---

253 終

シュウ SHŪ
お・わる o(waru)
お・える o(eru)

an end;
to end

The character 終 is a combination of *thread* 糸 and *storing food* 冬. A reference to the *end* of the thread that has been wound on to a spool, the character has taken on the general meaning of *end*.
GR3 N4 AP

Example Sentences

1. 本日の営業は終了いたしました。
   Honjitsu no eigyō wa shūryō itashimashita.
   We are now <u>closed</u> for the day.

2. 駅のホームでは終日禁煙です。
   Eki no hōmu de wa shūjitsu kinen desu.
   Station platforms are non-smoking <u>at all times</u>.

3. コンサートは、何時に終わりますか。
   Konsāto wa, nanji ni owarimasu ka.
   What time does the concert <u>finish</u>?

4. この長編小説をようやく読み終えた。
   Kono chōhen shōsetsu o yōyaku yomioeta.
   I finally <u>finished reading</u> this full-length novel.

5. 飲み過ぎて終電に乗り遅れた。
   Nomisugite shūden ni nori okureta.
   I had drunk too much and missed <u>the last train</u>.

Common Compounds and Phrases

終了	**shūryō**	an end; completion; expiry
終日	**shūjitsu**	all day long
最終	**saishū**	the last
終止	**shūshi**	termination; an end
終業式	**shūgyōshiki**	a closing ceremony
終止符	**shūshifu**	a full stop; a period
終わり	**owari**	an ending; a finish

The top element in the right-hand radical is not 又.

11 `⟨ 乡 幺 幺 糸 糸 紗 紗 終 終 終`

終

254 組

ソ SO
くみ kumi
く・む ku(mu)

class; to put together

The character 組 combines *threads* 糸 and *piled up* 且, perhaps suggesting threads intertwined, which led to the meaning of *put together*.

GR2 N3

Example Sentences

1. 委員会は十人の委員で組織されている。
   Iinkai wa jūnin no iin de soshiki sarete iru.
   The committee is made up of ten members.

2. 彼とは同じ組でした。
   Kare to wa onaji kumi deshita.
   He and I were in the same class.

3. 労働組合が二十四時間ストをしている。
   Rōdō kumiai ga nijūyo-jikan suto o shite iru.
   The labor union is holding a 24-hour strike.

4. ここは液晶テレビの組み立て工場です。
   Koko wa ekishō terebi no kumitate kōjō desu.
   This is an assembly plant for liquid crystal televisions.

5. 少年は彼女と腕を組んで道を歩いていた。
   Shōnen wa kanojo to ude o kunde michi o aruite ita.
   The boy was walking along the street, arm in arm with his girlfriend.

Common Compounds and Phrases

組織	**soshiki**	organization; constitution
組閣	**sokaku**	the formation of a cabinet
組合	**kumiai**	an association; a union
組み立て	**kumitate**	assembling; construction
組み合わせ	**kumiawase**	a combination; matching
骨組み	**honegumi**	a skeleton; a framework
組曲	**kumikyoku**	a suite (music)

Keep the same spacing with the element on the right.

11 `く 幺 幺 幺 糸 糸 紀 組 組 組 組`

組

255 族

ソク ZOKU

family

The character 族 combines *arrow* 矢 and *banner* 方, representing many arrows being collected beneath a banner. From this, the sense of the assembling of one *family* has derived.

GR3 N4 AP

Example Sentences

1. うちは四人家族です。
   Uchi wa yonin kazoku desu.
   There are four members in my family.

2. あの地方では民族文化を守る努力をしている。
   Ano chihō de wa minzoku bunka o mamoru doryoku o shite iru.
   That region is making efforts to protect the ethnic culture.

3. 次の遠足で水族館に行くことに決まった。
   Tsugi no ensoku de suizokukan ni iku koto ni kimatta.
   We decided to go to an aquarium on the next excursion.

4. 彼はグレて暴走族の一員になった。
   Kare wa gurete bōsōzoku no ichiin ni natta.
   He went off the rails and became a member of a motorcycle gang.

Common Compounds and Phrases

家族	**kazoku**	a family; a household
民族	**minzoku**	a race; a nation
貴族	**kizoku**	nobility; a noble
親族	**shinzoku**	a relative
一族	**ichizoku**	a relative; one's family
水族館	**suizokukan**	an aquarium
暴走族	**bōsōzoku**	a gang of reckless motorcyclists; reckless drivers

The tenth stroke does not protrude.

11 `丶 亠 方 方 方 扩 扩 放 族 族`

族

256 鳥

チョウ CHŌ
とり tori

bird

GR2 N4 AP

The character 鳥 evolved from a pictograph of a *bird* with a long tail drooping down.

Example Sentences

1. シベリアから日本へ白鳥が渡ってきます。
   Shiberia kara Nihon e hakuchō ga watatte kimasu.
   Swans migrate from Siberia to Japan.

2. きじは日本の国鳥です。
   Kiji wa Nihon no kokuchō desu.
   The pheasant is Japan's national bird.

3. 一石二鳥を狙うなんて不可能だよ。
   Isseki nichō o nerau nante fukanō da yo.
   It is impossible to kill two birds with one stone.

4. 子供のころ、小鳥を飼いたくてしようがなかった。
   Kodomo no koro, kotori o kaitakute shiyō ga nakatta.
   As a child I desperately wanted to have a small bird as a pet.

5. 寒くて鳥肌が立っている。
   Samukute torihada ga tatte iru.
   I've got goose bumps from the cold.

Common Compounds and Phrases

白鳥	**hakuchō**	a swan
国鳥	**kokuchō**	a national bird
一石二鳥	**isseki nichō**	killing two birds with one stone (a saying)
小鳥	**kotori**	a (small) bird
鳥肌	**torihada**	goose bumps
焼鳥	**yakitori**	grilled skewered chicken
渡り鳥	**wataridori**	a migratory bird

The sixth stroke is longer than those above it. Keep the spacing equal between the horizontal strokes.

11 ′ ′ ′ ′ ′ ′ 自 鳥 鳥 鳥 鳥 鳥

鳥

257 転

テン TEN
ころ・がる koro(garu)
ころ・げる koro(geru)
ころ・がす koro(gasu)
ころ・ぶ koro(bu)

to turn; to revolve;
to shift; to roll over

GR3 N4 AP

The original character 轉 was a combination of a *spinning spool of thread* 專 and *wheel, vehicle* 車, suggesting the *turning* of a wheel.

Example Sentences

1. 十八歳になったら運転免許を取りたい。
   Jūhassai ni nattara unten menkyo o toritai.
   I want to get a driver's license when I turn eighteen.

2. あの店は駅の南口に移転する予定です。
   Ano mise wa eki no minamiguchi ni iten suru yotei desu.
   That store is planning to move to near the southern entrance of the station.

3. どこかおいしい回転寿司を知らない。
   Doko ka oishii kaiten-zushi o shiranai.
   Do you know of any good conveyor-belt sushi bars?

4. 坂道をボールが転がっている。
   Sakamichi o bōru ga korogatte iru.
   A ball is rolling down a hill.

5. おばあさんが、バスを降りようとして転んでしまった。
   Obāsan ga, basu o oriyō to shite koronde shimatta.
   The old lady fell over as she was getting off the bus.

Common Compounds and Phrases

運転	**unten**	operation; driving; working
移転	**iten**	a move; moving; a transfer
回転	**kaiten**	rotation; a revolution
転勤	**tenkin**	a job transfer
横転	**ōten**	rolling over onto one side
転校	**tenkō**	moving to a new school
寝転ぶ	**nekorobu**	to lie down

End the seventh stroke firmly.

11 ′ ′ ′ ′ ′ 車 車 車 転 転

転

258 都

ト TO　ツ TSU
みやこ miyako

metropolis

The character 都 combines *person, gather* 者 and *village* 阝, suggesting a village where many people gather, hence, a *big town* or *capital*.

GR3　N4　AP

Example Sentences

1. こんな大都会だなんて思いも寄らなかった。
   Konna daitokai da nante omoi mo yoranakatta.
   I never imagined that it would be such <u>a big city</u>.

2. オーストラリアの首都はどこですか。
   Ōsutoraria no shuto wa doko desu ka.
   What is <u>the capital</u> of Australia?

3. 都合のいい日を教えてください。
   Tsugō no ii hi o oshiete kudasai.
   Please let me know a day that is <u>convenient for you</u>.

4. キャッシュ・オン・デリバリーはその都度お金を払えばいい。
   Kyasshu on deribarii wa sono tsudo okane o haraeba ii.
   C.O.D. means you pay <u>each time</u> upon delivery.

5. 住めば都。
   Sumeba miyako.
   Anywhere is home once you get used to it. (a saying)

Common Compounds and Phrases

都心	toshin	the center of the city
首都	shuto	a capital city
都会	tokai	a city; a town
東京都	Tōkyō-to	the Metropolis of Tokyo
京都	Kyōto	Kyoto (a place)
都合	tsugō	convenience; circumstances
都度	tsudo	whenever; each time

The fourth stroke protrudes.

11　一　十　土　耂　耂　者　者　者　者ˀ　者ß　都

都

259 堂

ドウ DŌ

hall

The character 堂 comprises the elements of *air escaping from a window* 尚 and *foundation* 土, suggesting a *large building* resting on its foundations.

GR4　N4

Example Sentences

1. ただ今、食堂は満席です。
   Tadaima, shokudō wa manseki desu.
   <u>The dining hall</u> is full at present.

2. 生徒の皆さん、十時に講堂に集まってください。
   Seito no minasan, jūji ni kōdō ni atsumatte kudasai.
   All students please meet in <u>the lecture hall</u> at 10 o'clock.

3. 二人の選手は正々堂々と戦った。
   Futari no senshu wa seisei dōdō to tatakatta.
   The two players fought <u>openly and squarely</u>.

4. 公会堂でクラシック・コンサートが開催された。
   Kōkaidō de kurasshiku konsāto ga kaisai sareta.
   A classical music concert was performed in the <u>public hall</u>.

5. 礼拝堂に来るといつも落ち着いた気持ちになる。
   Reihaidō ni kuru to itsumo ochitsuita kimochi ni naru.
   Whenever I am in <u>a chapel</u>, I feel at peace.

Common Compounds and Phrases

食堂	shokudō	a dining room; a cafeteria
講堂	kōdō	a lecture hall (auditorium)
本堂	hondō	the main temple
礼拝堂	reihaidō	a chapel
公会堂	kōkaidō	a public hall
国会議事堂	kokkai gijidō	the Diet (National Assembly) Building
正々堂々と	seisei dōdō to	fairly; openly

The last stroke is longer than those above it.

11　丨　⺍　⺌　⺌　⺍　尚　尚　尚　堂　堂　堂

堂

260 動

ドウ DŌ
うご・く ugo(ku)
うご・かす ugo(kasu)

to move

The character 動 combines *heavy* 重 and *strength* 力, suggesting the idea of applying strength to something, causing it to *move*.

GR3 N4 AP

Example Sentences

1. 長年、動物学の研究をしてきた。
   Naganen, dōbutsugaku no kenkyū o shite kita.
   He has been doing <u>zoological</u> research for many years.

2. 全自動洗濯機はかなり進化した。
   Zenjidō sentakki wa kanari shinka shita.
   <u>Fully automatic</u> washing-machines have made great advances.

3. 自分の行動に責任を持ちなさい。
   Jibun no kōdō ni sekinin o mochinasai.
   Be responsible for your own <u>action</u>.

4. 映画を見て感動したのは初めてだ。
   Eiga o mite kandō shita no wa hajimete da.
   This is the first time I've <u>felt moved</u> watching a movie.

5. このテレビをそこに動かすのを手伝って。
   Kono terebi o soko ni ugokasu no o tetsudatte.
   Could you help me <u>move</u> this TV over there?

Common Compounds and Phrases

動物	**dōbutsu**	an animal; a living creature
自動	**jidō**	automatic movement (operation)
行動	**kōdō**	behavior; action
動作	**dōsa**	an action; movement; operation
活動	**katsudō**	activity; function
移動	**idō**	movement; transfer
感動	**kandō**	strong emotion; inspiration

The tenth stroke ends with a hook.

11 `一 一 一 一 一 一 一 一 一 一 一`

動

---

261 問

モン MON
と・う to(u)　と・い to(i)
*とん ton

to question

The character 問 is a pictograph of *two closed gates* 門 with a person's *mouth* 口 asking for someone. The associated meanings are *enquire*, *ask* and *visit*.

GR3 N4 AP

Example Sentences

1. この問題は難しくて分からない。
   Kono mondai wa muzukashikute wakaranai.
   This <u>problem</u> is too difficult for me to understand.

2. 彼女の言ったことには疑問を持っている。
   Kanojo no itta koto ni wa gimon o motte iru.
   I <u>have some doubts</u> about what she said.

3. 質問がある人はいませんか。
   Shitsumon ga aru hito wa imasen ka.
   Doesn't anyone have any <u>questions</u>?

4. その会社の住所を問い合わせた。
   Sono kaisha no jūsho o toiawaseta.
   I <u>enquired about</u> that company's address.

5. 問屋で欲しかった洋服が安く売っていた。
   Ton'ya de hoshikatta yōfuku ga yasuku utte ita.
   They were selling clothes I wanted at <u>the wholesaler's</u> cheaply.

Common Compounds and Phrases

問題	**mondai**	a question; a problem; a topic
疑問	**gimon**	a doubt; a question
質問	**shitsumon**	a question; a query
訪問	**hōmon**	a visit; a call
学問	**gakumon**	study; learning
問い合わせ	**toiawase**	an enquiry; a request
*問屋	**ton'ya**	a wholesaler

End the sixth stroke with a hook, and don't confuse 問 with 間.

11 `丨 冂 冂 冂 冂 門 門 門 門 問 問`

問

262 野

ヤ YA
の no

field; wild

The character 野 combines *village* 里 and *loose* 予, suggesting a spacious *rural* community.

GR2 N4 AP

Example Sentences

1. 野菜をもっと食べた方がいいよ。
   Yasai o motto tabeta hō ga ii yo.
   You ought to eat more <u>vegetables</u>!

2. 様々な分野の人がセミナーに参加した。
   Samazama na bun'ya no hito ga seminā ni sanka shita.
   People from various <u>fields</u> attended the seminar.

3. 山には野生のサルが住んでいる。
   Yama ni wa yasei no saru ga sunde iru.
   <u>Wild</u> monkeys live in the mountains.

4. どうもあの人は粗野で困るね。
   Dōmo ano hito wa soya de komaru ne.
   There's something <u>vulgar</u> about that man that bothers me.

5. 向こうの広々とした野原でお弁当を食べましょう。
   Mukō no hirobiro to shita nohara de obentō o tabemashō.
   Let's have lunch in that open <u>field</u> over there.

Common Compounds and Phrases

分野	**bun'ya**	a field; a branch; a sphere
野生の	**yasei no**	wild; savage
平野	**heiya**	a plain; an open field
野球	**yakyū**	baseball
野党	**yatō**	an opposition party
野原	**nohara**	a field; a plain
上野	**Ueno**	Ueno (a place, name)

The seventh stroke goes up from left to right, and the last stroke ends with a hook.

11 　丨 冂 冂 日 甲 甲 里 里' 野 野 野

野

---

263 理

リ RI

reason; truth; principle

The character 理 combines *jewel* 王 and *village* 里, which acts phonetically to express split. From cutting a jewel came the meaning of *acting carefully*, and then *reason*.

GR2 N4 AP

Example Sentences

1. とても料理がお上手ですね。
   Totemo ryōri ga ojōzu desu ne.
   You're a very <u>good cook</u>.

2. 靴のかかとを修理しないとだめだ。
   Kutsu no kakato o shūri shinai to dame da.
   I need the heel of my shoe <u>repaired</u>.

3. ビザの申請をてきぱきと処理してくれた。
   Biza no shinsei o tekipaki to shori shite kureta.
   They promptly <u>processed</u> my visa application.

4. アインシュタインの相対性理論を勉強している。
   Ainshutain no sōtaisei riron o benkyō shite iru.
   I'm studying Einstein's <u>Theory</u> of Relativity.

5. 大学の理系の学部に進むつもりです。
   Daigaku no rikei no gakubu ni susumu tsumori desu.
   I intend to study in <u>the science faculty</u> at university.

Common Compounds and Phrases

料理	**ryōri**	cooking; handling
修理	**shūri**	repair(s); fixing
処理	**shori**	management; dealing
理論	**riron**	a theory
理系	**rikei**	the sciences
理解	**rikai**	understanding; comprehension
総理大臣	**sōri daijin**	the prime minister

The fourth stroke goes up from left to right.

11 　一 丁 王 王 珇 珇 理 理 理 理

理

264 運　ウン UN　はこ・ぶ hako(bu)

fortune;
to carry; to move

The character 運 is a combination of *movement* 辶 and *army* 軍; thus, the meaning of an army on the *move* and by extension, *transportation* has derived. *Fortune* is a related meaning.
GR3　N4　AP

Example Sentences

1. なんて私は運が悪いんだろう。
   Nante watashi wa un ga warui n darō.
   Why am I always so <u>unlucky</u>?

2. 毎日、軽い運動をすることにしている。
   Mainichi, karui undō o suru koto ni shite iru.
   I make it a rule to do light <u>exercise</u> every day.

3. あまりに運賃が高かったので驚いた。
   Amari ni unchin ga takakatta node odoroita.
   I was surprised at how expensive <u>the fare</u> was.

4. 倉庫から家具を運び出すのに相当時間がかかった。
   Sōko kara kagu o hakobidasu no ni sōtō jikan ga kakatta.
   It took quite some time to <u>carry</u> the furniture <u>out</u> of the store-room.

5. わざわざ足をお運びいただき、ありがとうございました。
   Waza waza ashi o ohakobi itadaki, arigatō gozaimashita.
   Thank you so much for <u>taking the trouble to come</u>.

Common Compounds and Phrases

運動	**undō**	motion; movement; exercise
運賃	**unchin**	a (passenger) fare; freight
幸運	**kōun**	good luck, fortune
不運	**fuun**	misfortune; bad luck
運送	**unsō**	shipping; transportation
運命	**unmei**	one's destiny, fate
運河	**unga**	a canal; a waterway

Write the eleventh stroke with one single motion.

12 ｀ 一 一 一 一 冖 冃 冒 冒 軍 軍 運 運

運

EXERCISE 22 (253 – 264)

A. Give the readings for the following.
1. 野菜 _____
2. 転がる _____
3. 持ち運ぶ _____
4. 都合 _____
5. 分野 _____
6. 終わり _____
7. 心理学 _____
8. 小鳥 _____
9. 動き出す _____
10. 問い合わせ _____

B. Write in kanji and kana.
1. うえの _____
2. うんどう _____
3. よみおわる _____
4. ごにんかぞく _____
5. かいてんドア _____
6. じてんしゃ _____
7. だいとかい _____
8. はくちょう _____

9. くみたてる _____
10. いっせきにちょう _____

C. Fill in the blanks with kanji and kana.
1. _____ (りょうり) が _____ (じょうず)
   (a good cook)
2. _____ (でんしゃ) の _____ (うんてんしゅ)
   (a train driver)
3. _____ (とうきょうと) に ____ (す) む (to live in the Tokyo Metropolis)
4. _____ (うんそう) _____ (がいしゃ)
   (a transport company)
5. _____ (がくもん) の ____ (みち) に ____ (すす) む (to choose an academic career)
6. _____ (さんにんぐみ) の ____ (ゆうじん)
   (a group of three friends)
7. _____ (かぞく) _____ (りょこう) (a family trip)
8. _____ (しょくどう) で _____ (しょくじ) する
   (to eat in a cafeteria)

150

265 開

カイ KAI
ひら・く hira(ku)
ひら・ける hira(keru)
あ・く a(ku)
あ・ける a(keru)

opening;
to open

The character 開 is a combination of *gate* 門 and 开, originally *two hands*, as if reaching out to *open* the gate.

GR3 N4 AP

Example Sentences

1. 駅前に新しい店が開店するそうです。
   Ekimae ni atarashii mise ga kaiten suru sō desu.
   I hear a new store is opening in front of the station.

2. 開発によって森が消えた。
   Kaihatsu ni yotte mori ga kieta.
   The forest has disappeared with encroaching development.

3. 会議が開かれたが欠席した。
   Kaigi ga hirakareta ga kesseki shita.
   The conference was held but I didn't attend.

4. ビンのふたが硬くて開かない。
   Bin no futa ga katakute akanai.
   The lid on the bottle is too tight for me to open it.

5. 窓を開けっぱなしにしないでください。
   Mado o akeppanashi ni shinai de kudasai.
   Please don't leave the window open.

Common Compounds and Phrases

開店	**kaiten**	the opening of a store
開発	**kaihatsu**	development; growth
公開	**kōkai**	opening; disclosure
展開	**tenkai**	deployment; development
満開	**mankai**	full bloom
開会式	**kaikaishiki**	an opening ceremony
海開き	**umibiraki**	the start of the swimming season

The sixth stroke ends with a hook. Don't confuse 開 with 閉.

12 丨 冂 冂 冃 冐 門 門 門 門 閂 閈 開 開

開

---

266 寒

カン KAN
さむ・い samu(i)

cold

The character 寒 contains 寒, with a person building a stone wall for a house, to keep out the *cold* wind and 冫, suggesting *icy cold*, giving us the general meaning of *cold*.

GR3 N4 AP

Example Sentences

1. この季節になると防寒具が欲しくなる。
   Kono kisetsu ni naru to bōkangu ga hoshiku naru.
   When this season arrives, I feel the need for cold weather protective gear.

2. 寒冷前線が南下してくるらしい。
   Kanrei zensen ga nanka shite kuru rashii.
   Apparently a cold front is moving south.

3. アラスカと北海道ではどちらの冬が寒いですか。
   Arasuka to Hokkaidō de wa dochira no fuyu ga samui desu ka.
   Which is colder, Alaska's winter or Hokkaidō's?

4. 母は非常に寒がりです。
   Haha wa hijō ni samugari desu.
   My mother really feels the cold.

5. その話を聞いて、背筋が寒くなった。
   Sono hanashi o kiite, sesuji ga samuku natta.
   When I heard that story, a chill ran down my spine.

Common Compounds and Phrases

防寒	**bōkan**	protection against the cold
寒冷前線	**kanrei zensen**	a cold front
寒流	**kanryū**	a cold current
寒々しい	**samuzamushii**	looking very cold, bleak
寒気	**samuke**	a chill
肌寒い	**hadazamui**	chilly
寒がり	**samugari**	a person sensitive to the cold

Be careful with the angle of the dots.

12 丶 丷 宀 宀 宀 宀 宯 宲 実 寒 寒 寒

寒

267 軽 light

ケイ KEI
かる・い karu(i)
*かろ・やか karo(yaka)

Originally 輕, this character combined *vehicle* 車 and the *warp of a loom* 巠, suggesting the weaving was not yet complete. Hence, the character has the sense of an *unladen vehicle*. From this, the meaning of *light* is derived.
GR3 N4

Example Sentences

1. ガソリン代が高くなるにつれて、軽自動車の人気も上がる。
   Gasorin-dai ga takaku naru ni tsurete, keijidōsha no ninki mo agaru.
   As the price of gasoline has increased, so too, the popularity of mini-cars has grown.

2. 小腹が空いたので軽食を取ろうかな。
   Kobara ga suita node keishoku o torō ka na.
   I'm feeling a bit hungry, so I'll have a quick bite.

3. 軽い荷物の方が送料が安い。
   Karui nimotsu no hō ga sōryō ga yasui.
   It's cheaper to send light packages.

4. いつでも気軽に立ち寄ってください。
   Itsu de mo kigaru ni tachiyotte kudasai.
   Please feel free to call in any time.

5. 軽やかな足取りで帰ってきた。
   Karoyaka na ashidori de kaette kita.
   She came back home as if walking on air.

Common Compounds and Phrases

軽自動車	**kei-jidōsha**	a light vehicle
軽食	**keishoku**	a light meal; a snack
軽蔑	**keibetsu**	contempt; scorn
軽率な	**keisotsu na**	rash; careless
気軽な	**kigaru na**	lighthearted; carefree
手軽な	**tegaru na**	simple; casual
軽々と	**karugaru to**	lightly; with ease

Be careful not to write 土 as 土.

12 一 厂 戸 戸 百 亘 車 軯 軯 軽 軽 軽

軽

268 集 to collect

シュウ SHŪ
あつ・まる atsu(maru)
あつ・める atsu(meru)
*つど・う tsudo(u)

The character 集 was originally a pictograph of *three birds gathered* together in a tree. Thus, the meaning of many things *gathering* together is derived from this.
GR3 N4 AP

Example Sentences

1. 集合時間は何時ですか。
   Shūgō jikan wa nanji desu ka.
   What time are we supposed to meet?

2. 自分で作った旅行の写真集を友達に見せた。
   Jibun de tsukutta ryokō no shashinshū o tomodachi ni miseta.
   I showed a friend a collection of photos I made of my trip.

3. 下町には古い住宅が密集している。
   Shitamachi ni wa furui jūtaku ga misshū shite iru.
   Old houses stand close together in the downtown area.

4. みんなで公園に集まって、掃除をした。
   Minna de kōen ni atsumatte, sōji o shita.
   We all got together in the park and did a clean-up.

5. 会費を集めるのは私の担当です。
   Kaihi o atsumeru no wa watashi no tantō desu.
   I'm in charge of collecting the fees.

Common Compounds and Phrases

集合	**shūgō**	a gathering; a meeting
写真集	**shashinshū**	a photographic collection
密集	**misshū**	a mass; a concentration
特集	**tokushū**	a special edition
集中	**shūchū**	concentration; convergence
集団	**shūdan**	a group; a mass
集会	**shūkai**	a meeting; an assembly

Make the eighth stroke a little longer than those above.

12 ノ イ イ 扩 什 仹 隹 隹 隼 集 集 集

集

269 暑

ショ SHO
あつ・い atsu(i)

summer heat; hot

The character 暑 brings together the elements *sun* 日 and 者, representing a *person burning firewood* in a brazier, suggesting *burning heat*. Consequently, we have the association of *summer heat* and *hot*.

GR3 N4 AP

Example Sentences

1. 暑中お見舞い申し上げます。
   Shochū omimai mōshiagemasu.
   How are you getting along <u>in this hot season</u>?

2. 今年の残暑は厳しい。
   Kotoshi no zansho wa kibishii.
   <u>The lingering heat</u> this year is severe.

3. 今日の午後は暑くなるそうだ。
   Kyō no gogo wa atsuku naru sō da.
   <u>It's going to be hot</u> this afternoon, I hear.

4. 真夏にその格好では暑苦しいよ。
   Manatsu ni sono kakkō de wa atsukurushii yo.
   Seeing you dressed like that in mid-summer makes me feel <u>uncomfortably hot</u>.

5. 軽井沢の別荘へ避暑に行く。
   Karuizawa no bessō e hisho ni iku.
   I'll go to the villa in Karuizawa <u>for the summer</u>.

Common Compounds and Phrases

暑中	**shochū**	midsummer; high summer
残暑	**zansho**	the lingering summer heat
猛暑	**mōsho**	fierce heat
避暑	**hisho**	escaping the summer heat
暑がり	**atsugari**	(someone) sensitive to the heat
蒸し暑い	**mushiatsui**	muggy; sticky
暑苦しい	**atsukurushii**	stifling; stuffy; sultry

The eighth stroke extends beyond the seventh stroke.

12 亅 冂 冂 冃 日 旦 昦 昦 昦 暑 暑 暑

暑

---

270 場

ジョウ JŌ
ば ba

place

The character 場 depicts the *sun* 日 *shining down* 勿 on the *ground* 土, perhaps suggesting a *place* in the sun.

GR2 N4 AP

Example Sentences

1. コンサートの開場は六時です。
   Konsāto no kaijō wa rokuji desu.
   The <u>doors</u> for the concert <u>open</u> at six o'clock.

2. 工場の場所を教えてください。
   Kōjō no basho o oshiete kudasai.
   Please tell me <u>where</u> <u>the factory</u> <u>is</u>.

3. 雨の場合は、試合は中止になる。
   Ame no baai wa, shiai wa chūshi ni naru.
   <u>If it rains</u>, the game will be called off.

4. この言葉は、どんな場面で使われますか。
   Kono kotoba wa, donna bamen de tsukawaremasu ka.
   What kind of <u>situation</u> is this word used in?

5. 今日、初めて競馬場で競馬を見た。
   Kyō, hajimete keibajō de keiba o mita.
   Today, I saw horse racing for the first time <u>at a race track</u>.

Common Compounds and Phrases

開場	**kaijō**	opening the doors of a hall
牧場	**bokujō**	a pasture; a ranch; a meadow
競馬場	**keibajō**	a race track
場所	**basho**	a place; a seat; room
場合	**baai**	an occasion; a case; a situation
場面	**bamen**	a scene; a place
立場	**tachiba**	a standpoint; a position

The third stroke goes up from left to right, and the tenth stroke ends with a hook.

12 一 十 扌 圹 圹 圹 垣 垣 垣 場 場 場

場

271 森

forest

シン SHIN
もり mori

GR1 N4 AP

The character 森 consists of three *trees* 木 to give the idea of *forest*.

Example Sentences

1. 森林資源を守るべきだ。
   Shinrin shigen o mamoru beki da.
   We should protect our <u>timber resources</u>.

2. 神社は森閑としていた。
   Jinja wa shinkan to shite ita.
   The shrine was <u>very quiet</u>.

3. あの小さな森に行ってみよう。
   Ano chiisa na mori ni itte miyō.
   Let's go over to that <u>grove</u>.

4. 私の古里は青森です。
   Watashi no furusato wa Aomori desu.
   My birthplace is <u>Aomori</u>.

5. 森林伐採は、地球温暖化の一因である。
   Shinrin basai wa, chikyū ondanka no ichiin de aru.
   <u>Deforestation</u> is a cause of global warming.

Common Compounds and Phrases

森林	**shinrin**	woods; a forest
森林浴	**shinrinyoku**	walking in the woods
森林開発	**shinrin kaihatsu**	forest development
森林伐採	**shinrin basai**	deforestation
森閑とした	**shinkan to shita**	still; quiet; deserted
森田	**Morita**	Morita (a name)
青森	**Aomori**	Aomori (a place)

The inner stroke of the bottom left 木 is short. Don't confuse 森 with 林.

12 一 十 才 木 木 朮 森 森 森 森 森 森

森

---

272 貸

to lend

タイ TAI
か・す ka(su)

GR5 N4 AP

The character 貸 combines *substitution* 代 and *money, goods* 貝. The meaning of *lend* is derived from the idea of people providing money in dealing with goods.

Example Sentences

1. 駅の西側に賃貸マンションが建った。
   Eki no nishigawa ni chintai manshon ga tatta.
   <u>An apartment building with rental apartments</u> was built on the western side of the station.

2. 弟に読み終わった本を貸してやった。
   Otōto ni yomiowatta hon o kashite yatta.
   I <u>lent</u> my brother a book I had finished reading.

3. 本日はパーティーのため貸切です。
   Honjitsu wa pātii no tame kashikiri desu.
   We are <u>reserved for the whole day</u> due to a private function.

4. それは貸し出し禁止です。
   Sore wa kashidashi kinshi desu.
   That <u>can't be lent out</u>.

5. 開業するため貸店舗を探しています。
   Kaigyō suru tame kashi-tenpo o sagashite imasu.
   I am searching for <u>a store to lease</u> to start a business.

Common Compounds and Phrases

賃貸	**chintai**	leasing; letting
貸与	**taiyo**	lending; a loan
貸し出し	**kashidashi**	lending; a loan; rental
貸切	**kashikiri**	(full) booking; chartering
貸し借り	**kashikari**	lending and borrowing
（貸借）	**(taishaku)**	
貸家	**kashiya**	a house for rent
貸し店舗	**kashi-tenpo**	a store for lease

The fourth stroke ends with a hook.

12 ノ イ 仁 代 代 代 侍 貸 貸 貸 貸 貸

貸

273 短

short

タン TAN
みじか・い mijika(i)

The character 短 combines *arrow* 矢 and *food vessel* 豆, both used as crude measures when comparing things that were rather small or *short*.
GR3 N4 AP

Example Sentences

1. 来年の春から短期大学に通い始める。
   Rainen no haru kara tanki daigaku ni kayoihajimeru.
   She'll start attending a junior college next spring.

2. あなたの長所と短所は、何だと思いますか。
   Anata no chōsho to tansho wa, nan da to omoimasu ka.
   What do you think your strengths and weaknesses are?

3. 父は気が短くてすぐ怒る。
   Chichi wa ki ga mijikakute sugu okoru.
   My father is impatient and loses his temper easily.

4. 忙しいので手短に話してください。
   Isogashii node temijika ni hanashite kudasai.
   I'm busy so could you please be brief?

5. 意外と短時間で着いた。
   Igai to tanjikan de tsuita.
   We arrived there in a surprisingly short time.

Common Compounds and Phrases

短期	**tanki**	a short time
短気	**tanki**	a short, hot temper
短時間	**tanjikan**	a brief time
短所	**tansho**	a weak point; a weakness
短縮	**tanshuku**	shortening; contraction
短編	**tanpen**	a short piece of fiction; a sketch
手短に	**temijika ni**	shortly; briefly

End the fifth stroke firmly.

12 ′ ト ヒ チ 矢 矢 短 短 短 短 短 短

短

---

274 着

to put on; to arrive; to stick

チャク CHAKU *ジャク JAKU
き・る ki(ru) き・せる ki(seru)
つ・く tsu(ku) つ・ける tsu(keru)

Originally written as 著, this character combined *grass* ⺾ and *burning firewood* 者 to suggest writing things down on wooden name plates. From this, the meanings of *put on* and *wear* have derived.
GR3 N4 AP

Example Sentences

1. そろそろ、飛行機が到着する時間だ。
   Soro soro, hikōki ga tōchaku suru jikan da.
   The plane should arrive any moment.

2. 卒業式に着物を着るつもりです。
   Sotsugyōshiki ni kimono o kiru tsumori desu.
   I intend to wear a *kimono* at my graduation ceremony.

3. 子供に新しい上着を着せた。
   Kodomo ni atarashii uwagi o kiseta.
   I put a new jacket on my child.

4. 時間通りに会社に着きました。
   Jikan-dōri ni kaisha ni tsukimashita.
   I arrived at the office on time.

5. 名札を着けてください。
   Nafuda o tsukete kudasai.
   Please put your name tag on.

Common Compounds and Phrases

到着	**tōchaku**	an arrival
着席	**chakuseki**	taking a seat
着実な	**chakujitsu na**	steady; solid; reliable
一着	**itchaku**	the first to finish; one suit
着替え	**kigae**	a change of clothes
水着	**mizugi**	a swimsuit
落ち着く	**ochitsuku**	to calm (settle) down; to become stable

The seventh stroke does not protrude.

12 ′ ′ ′ ″ ″ 羊 羊 羊 着 着 着 着

着

275 朝

チョウ CHŌ
あさ asa

morning;
dynasty

The character 朝 shows the *sun rising behind plants* 卓 and the *moon* 月, which perhaps is being displaced by the *morning* sun.

GR2 N4 AP

Example Sentences

1. ハイキングの日は、早朝に家を出ます。
   Haikingu no hi wa, sōchō ni ie o demasu.
   On days when I go hiking, I leave home early in the morning.

2. 朝刊はまだ来てないよ。
   Chōkan wa mada kite nai yo.
   The morning paper hasn't arrived yet.

3. 源氏物語は王朝文化の代表作です。
   'Genji Monogatari' wa ōchō bunka no daihyōsaku desu.
   'The Tale of Genji' is a representative work of Heian-period culture.

4. 高山の朝市は有名です。
   Takayama no asaichi wa yūmei desu.
   The morning market in Takayama is famous.

5. 朝早く散歩するのは気持がいいですね。
   Asa hayaku sanpo suru no wa kimochi ga ii desu ne.
   It feels great to go for an early morning walk.

Common Compounds and Phrases

朝刊	**chōkan**	a morning paper
平安朝	**heian-chō**	the Heian Period
朝廷	**chōtei**	the Imperial court
朝ご飯	**asagohan**	breakfast
朝晩	**asaban**	day and night
朝寝坊	**asanebō**	sleeping in; oversleeping
翌朝	**yokuasa /**	the next (following)
	yokuchō	morning

The seventh stroke is longer than those above it, and the tenth stroke ends with a hook.

12　一　十　す　古　吉　吉　直　卓　訓　朝　朝　朝

朝

276 答

トウ TŌ
こた・える kota(eru)
こた・え kota(e)

an answer;
to answer

The character 答 combines *bamboo* 竹 and *fit, match* 合, which suggests that a bamboo cover that exactly matches its container is similar to a statement that directly *answers* a question.

GR2 N4 AP

Example Sentences

1. ファックスで問い合わせたが返答がない。
   Fakkusu de toiawaseta ga hentō ga nai.
   I made an enquiry by fax, but there has been no response.

2. 解答用紙には鉛筆を使わなければなりません。
   Kaitō yōshi ni wa enpitsu o tsukawanakereba narimasen.
   You have to use a pencil for the answer sheet.

3. 講演の後で、質疑応答の時間を設けます。
   Kōen no ato de, shitsugi ōtō no jikan o mōkemasu.
   A question period will be held after the lecture.

4. 彼は質問に答えなかった。
   Kare wa shitsumon ni kotaenakatta.
   He didn't answer the question.

5. 問題の答えがわからない。
   Mondai no kotae ga wakaranai.
   I don't know the answers to the questions.

Common Compounds and Phrases

返答	**hentō**	a reply; an answer
解答	**kaitō**	an answer; a solution
回答	**kaitō**	a reply
応答	**ōtō**	a response; an answer
即答	**sokutō**	a prompt reply
答案	**tōan**	an answer paper (script)
口答え	**kuchigotae**	talking back; a retort

Nothing touches the 𠆢 element.

12　ノ　ト　ケ　ケ　ヶ　竹　竹　竺　笅　笣　答　答

答

EXERCISE 23 (265 – 276)

A. Give the readings for the following.

1. 短くない _____
2. 寒気 _____
3. 着く _____
4. 集める _____
5. 会場 _____
6. 開ける _____
7. 暑い _____
8. 寒くなる _____
9. 貸家 _____
10. 手軽な _____

8. 短時間 _____
9. 集中する _____
10. 場合 _____

C. Write in kanji and kana.

1. かしきり _____
2. みずぎ _____
3. とくしゅう _____
4. あおもり _____
5. あつがり _____
6. うんどうじょう _____
7. かいはつ _____
8. うわぎをきる _____
9. うりば _____
10. ちょうしょく _____

B. Write in English.

1. 森林 _____
2. 電話を貸す _____
3. 軽自動車 _____
4. 明朝 _____
5. 外で集まる _____
6. 答えて下さい。_____
7. 海開き _____

---

277 飯

ハン **HAN**
めし **meshi**

**cooked rice;
a meal**

The character 飯 combines *food* 食 and *bend back and scatter* 反, referring to so many grains of *rice* after being cooked.

GR4 N4 AP

Example Sentences

1. ご飯ですよ。
   Gohan desu yo.
   <u>Dinner</u> (breakfast, lunch) is ready!

2. お母さんは夕飯の仕度で忙しい。
   Okāsan wa yūhan no shitaku de isogashii.
   Mother is busy getting <u>dinner</u> ready.

3. そんなことは朝飯前だ。
   Sonna koto wa asameshi-mae da.
   That'll be <u>a piece of cake</u>!

4. 釜飯を食べた事がありますか。
   Kama-meshi o tabeta koto ga arimasu ka.
   Have you ever eaten <u>kama-meshi</u> (Japanese pilaf in a small pot)?

5. 電気炊飯器はとても便利だ。
   Denki suihanki wa totemo benri da.
   Electric <u>rice cookers</u> are very convenient.

Common Compounds and Phrases

ご飯	**gohan**	(boiled) rice; a meal; food
夕飯	**yūhan**	an evening meal; dinner
晩飯	**banmeshi**	dinner; supper
朝飯	**asameshi**	breakfast
炊飯器	**suihanki**	a rice cooker
残飯	**zanpan**	leftover rice (food)
日常茶飯事	**nichijō**	an everyday
	sahanji	occurrence

End the second stroke firmly.

12 ノ 𠂉 𠂊 今 今 今 食 食 飣 飣 飯 飯

飯

157

278 番

バン BAN

keeping watch; one's turn; number; order

The character 番 combines *come* 来 and *field* 田, which can be thought of as coming to plant seedlings in a specific *order*.

GR2 N3 AP

Example Sentences

1. 今日は留守番がいないんです。
   Kyō wa rusuban ga inai n desu.
   There's no one <u>looking after the house</u> today.

2. この犬は吠えないから番犬にならないよ。
   Kono inu wa hoenai kara banken ni naranai yo.
   This dog is useless as <u>a watchdog</u>—it doesn't bark!

3. 次はあなたの番ですよ。
   Tsugi wa anata no ban desu yo.
   It's your <u>turn</u> next.

4. 待合室で順番を待った。
   Machiaishitsu de junban o matta.
   I waited for <u>my turn</u> in the waiting room.

5. 何番ゲートから搭乗するのですか。
   Nanban gēto kara tōjō suru no desu ka.
   <u>What gate</u> do I board at?

Common Compounds and Phrases

留守番	**rusuban**	house-sitting; a caretaker
番組	**bangumi**	a program
順番	**junban**	order; a turn
何番	**nanban**	what number (size)
交番	**kōban**	a police box
二番目	**nibanme**	the second (one)
当番	**tōban**	being on duty (watch)

The top section is slightly larger than the bottom section.

12 ノ ⺌ �☆ ⼧ ⼲ 平 乎 来 番 番 番 番

番

279 暗

アン AN
くら・い kura(i)

dark

The character 暗 is a combination of *sun* 日 and *sound* 音, a reference to a sound from the throat, suggesting to *hide, be confined*. From this idea came the meaning of a place which is *dark*, where the sun doesn't shine.

GR3 N4 AP

Example Sentences

1. 彼の字は暗号のようで読みにくい。
   Kare no ji wa angō no yō de yominikui.
   His writing is like <u>a code</u> and is unreadable.

2. 私は暗算が速い。
   Watashi wa anzan ga hayai.
   I'm quick at doing <u>mental arithmetic</u>.

3. 暗闇で石につまずいた。
   Kurayami de ishi ni tsumazuita.
   I tripped on a stone in the <u>darkness</u>.

4. ここは暗くて字が読めない。
   Koko wa kurakute ji ga yomenai.
   It's too <u>dark</u> for me to read here.

5. 彼は数学には明るいが文学には暗い。
   Kare wa sūgaku ni wa akarui ga bungaku ni wa kurai.
   He knows a lot about math but is <u>ignorant</u> when it comes to literature.

Common Compounds and Phrases

暗号	<u>**angō**</u>	a secret language; a code
暗算	<u>**anzan**</u>	mental arithmetic
暗記	<u>**anki**</u>	learning by heart
暗黒	<u>**ankoku**</u>	darkness; blackness
暗殺	<u>**ansatsu**</u>	an assassination
暗闇	<u>**kurayami**</u>	darkness; gloominess
薄暗い	**usugurai**	gloomy; somber

The ninth stroke is longer than the sixth stroke.

13 丨 冂 日 日 日' 日立 日立 日立 昢 晬 暗 暗 暗

暗

280 意　イ I
mind; meaning

The character 意 brings together *sound* 音 and *heart* 心. The 音 element suggests hiding away, thus there is the association of *thoughts* hidden away in the heart.
GR3 N4 AP

Example Sentences

1. 強い意志で禁煙に成功した。
   Tsuyoi ishi de kin'en ni seikō shita.
   He succeeded in quitting smoking through <u>strong will power</u>.

2. 無意識にやってしまった。
   Muishiki ni yatte shimatta.
   I did it <u>unconsciously</u>.

3. ぬれた床は滑りやすいので、注意しなさい。
   Nureta yuka wa suberiyasui node, chūi shinasai.
   <u>Take care</u>! The wet floor's slippery.

4. 今更そんなことを言っても無意味だよ。
   Imasara sonna koto o itte mo muimi da yo.
   It's <u>meaningless</u> to say something like that at this stage.

5. 得意科目は何ですか。
   Tokui kamoku wa nan desu ka.
   What is your <u>strongest</u> subject (at school)?

Common Compounds and Phrases

意志	**ishi**	will; determination
意識	**ishiki**	consciousness; awareness
注意	**chūi**	attention; care; interest
無意味な	**muimi na**	meaningless; pointless
得意	**tokui**	pride; one's strong point
意義	**igi**	meaning; importance
意欲	**iyoku**	an interest; a desire

The fifth stroke is longer than the second stroke.

13　丶 一 亠 立 产 音 音 音 音 意 意 意

意

---

281 遠　エン EN　*オン ON　とお・い tō(i)
far; distant

The character 遠 combines *go* 辶 and *kimono-clad woman* 袁, perhaps referring to how *far* one must go to find a beautiful woman.

GR4 N4 AP

Example Sentences

1. 遠慮しないで、召し上がって下さい。
   Enryo shinai de, meshiagatte kudasai.
   Please <u>help yourself</u> to the food.

2. 誕生日に望遠鏡を買ってもらいました。
   Tanjōbi ni bōenkyō o katte moraimashita.
   They bought me a <u>telescope</u> for my birthday.

3. 思ったより駅から遠いなあ。
   Omotta yori eki kara tōi nā.
   It's <u>further</u> from the station than I thought.

4. ちょっと、電話が遠いんですが。
   Chotto, denwa ga tōi n desu ga.
   (on the telephone) <u>I can't hear you very well</u>.

5. 世界中の戦争が永遠になくなればいいと思う。
   Sekaijū no sensō ga eien ni nakunareba ii to omou.
   I think that it would be good if all wars in the world could cease <u>forever</u>.

Common Compounds and Phrases

遠慮	**enryo**	reserve; abstaining
遠大な	**endai na**	far-reaching; ambitious
永遠	**eien**	eternity; immortality
遠近感	**enkinkan**	a sense of perspective
望遠鏡	**bōenkyō**	a telescope
遠い昔	**tōi mukashi**	the distant past
遠く	**tōku**	a great distance; long ago

End the eighth and tenth strokes firmly.

13　一 十 土 卉 吉 吉 孛 吏 贡 袁 袁 读 遠

遠

282 楽

ガク GAKU　ラク RAKU
たの・しい tano(shii)
たの・しむ tano(shimu)

music; fun; to look forward to

The character 楽 shows a tree 木 with lots of *white acorns* 白, indicating an oak tree. Perhaps musical instruments were made from oak; *fun* evolved from making *music*.
GR2　N4　AP

Example Sentences

1. 何か楽器が演奏できますか。
   Nani ka gakki ga ensō dekimasu ka.
   Can you play any <u>instruments</u>?

2. 色々な新しい発明のおかげで家事が楽になった。
   Iroiro na atarashii hatsumei no okage de kaji ga raku ni natta.
   Various modern inventions have <u>made</u> housework <u>easier</u>.

3. そこでは映画が最大の娯楽です。
   Soko de wa eiga ga saidai no goraku desu.
   Movies are the main form of <u>entertainment</u> there.

4. 旅行は楽しかった。
   Ryokō wa tanoshikatta.
   Did you <u>have a good time</u> on your trip?

5. わたしは友達と会っておしゃべりを楽しんだ。
   Watashi wa tomodachi to atte oshaberi o tanoshinda.
   I met up with a friend and we <u>had an enjoyable chat</u>.

Common Compounds and Phrases

楽器	**gakki**	a musical instrument
楽譜	**gakufu**	sheet music
娯楽	**goraku**	a pleasure; an amusement
気楽な	**kiraku na**	relaxed; carefree
楽勝	**rakushō**	an easy victory
楽観的	**rakkanteki**	optimistic; hopeful
楽しみ	**tanoshimi**	enjoyment; anticipation

Take care with the dots. Don't confuse 楽 with 薬.

13　`′ ′ ′ 自 自 自 泊 泊 泊 渉 渉 楽 楽`

楽

---

283 漢

カン KAN

Chinese; fellow

The character 漢 combines *water* 氵 and *drying animal skins* 莫, a reference to the *Han* River, one with little water. *Han* (漢) referred to the upper reaches of the river but later assumed the general meaning of *China*.
GR3　N4　AP

Example Sentences

1. 漢字字典で漢字の成り立ちを調べてみた。
   Kanji jiten de kanji no naritachi o shirabete mita.
   I looked up the derivation of a Chinese character in a *kanji* dictionary.

2. 胃薬として、漢方薬を飲むことにした。
   Igusuri to shite, kanpōyaku o nomu koto ni shita.
   I decided to take some <u>herbal medicine</u> for my stomach.

3. 夜道の一人歩きは痴漢に注意しましょう。
   Yomichi no hitori-aruki wa chikan ni chūi shimashō.
   Please beware of <u>molesters</u> when walking alone at night.

4. 彼は相撲取り並みの大食漢だね。
   Kare wa sumōtori nami no taishokukan da ne.
   He <u>has a large appetite</u>—like that of a *sumo* wrestler, doesn't he?

Common Compounds and Phrases

漢字字典	**kanji jiten**	a *kanji* (character) dictionary
漢和辞典	**kanwa jiten**	a Japanese character dictionary
漢数字	**kansūji**	a Chinese numeral
漢方薬	**kanpōyaku**	a herbal medicine
暴漢	**bōkan**	a ruffian; a thug
痴漢	**chikan**	a molester; a groper
大食漢	**taishokukan**	a big eater; a glutton

The twelfth stroke does not protrude.

13　`丶 冫 氵 汀 汁 汁 洼 洪 淓 淓 漢 漢`

漢

284 業

ギョウ GYŌ *ゴウ GŌ
わざ waza

work; business; industry

The character 業 is a pictograph of a stand used to support a heavy musical instrument. From the association of supporting something, the meaning of *work*—that which supports one's existence has derived.
GR3 N4 AP

Example Sentences

1. 日曜日も営業をしております。
   Nichiyōbi mo eigyō o shite orimasu.
   We <u>are</u> also <u>open</u> on Sundays.

2. ここに職業を書いてください。
   Koko ni shokugyō o kaite kudasai.
   Please write your <u>profession</u> here.

3. あのデパートは従業員を募集しているよ。
   Ano depāto wa jūgyōin o boshū shite iru yo.
   That department store is recruiting <u>staff</u>.

4. この仕事は容易な作業じゃない。
   Kono shigoto wa yōi na sagyō ja nai.
   It will be no easy <u>work</u> getting through this business.

5. 寝坊で遅刻したのは自業自得だ。
   Nebō de chikoku shita no wa jigō jitoku da.
   It is <u>your own fault</u> that you overslept and came late.

Common Compounds and Phrases

営業	**eigyō**	business; trade; sales
職業	**shokugyō**	an occupation
従業員	**jūgyōin**	an employee; a worker; staff
農業	**nōgyō**	agriculture; farming
実業家	**jitsugyōka**	a business person
仕業	**shiwaza**	an act; an action; a deed
*自業自得	**jigō jitoku**	reaping as one sowed (a saying)

The eleventh stroke does not protrude.

13 丨 丷 丷 丱 业 业 业 业 丵 荢 荢 業 業

業

285 試

シ SHI
こころ・みる kokoro(miru)
ため・す tame(su)

trial; test; to try

The character 試 combines *words* 言 and *building with a stick* 式. When having someone make something, one uses words to ask about the work to *try* and ensure quality.
GR4 N4 AP

Example Sentences

1. 今度の土曜日は柔道の試合だ。
   Kondo no doyōbi wa jūdō no shiai da.
   I have a judo <u>match</u> this Saturday.

2. 来年の今頃は入試の準備で忙しいだろう。
   Rainen no imagoro wa nyūshi no junbi de isogashii darō.
   This time next year I'll be busy preparing for <u>college entrance exams</u>.

3. 何度も試みた。
   Nando mo kokoromita.
   I <u>tried</u> time after time.

4. 全く新しい試みだったから、少し不安だった。
   Mattaku atarashii kokoromi datta kara, sukoshi fuan datta.
   It was a bold new <u>venture</u>, so I felt a little uneasy.

5. この新製品をお試しになりませんか。
   Kono shinseihin o otameshi ni narimasen ka.
   <u>Would you like to try</u> this new product?

Common Compounds and Phrases

試合	**shiai**	a match; a game; an event
入試	**nyūshi**	entrance exams
試食	**shishoku**	sampling; tasting
試案	**shian**	a tentative plan (draft)
試行錯誤	**shikō sakugo**	trial and error
試み	**kokoromi**	an attempt; a test
力試し	**chikara-dameshi**	a test of one's strength

Don't forget the dot.

13 丶 二 言 言 言 言 言 訂 訂 試 試

試

286 数

スウ SŪ *ス SU
かず kazu
かぞ・える kazo(eru)

number;
to count

The character 数 combines *woman* 女, *rice* 米 and *stick in hand* 攵 and can be thought of as a woman *counting* rice with a stick.

GR2 N3 AP

Example Sentences

1. 多数決で議長を決めた。
   Tasūketsu de gichō o kimeta.
   The chairperson was elected by a <u>majority decision</u>.

2. 本が届くのに数週間かかります。
   Hon ga todoku no ni sūshūkan kakarimasu.
   It takes <u>several weeks</u> for the books to arrive.

3. コピーの枚数を数えて。
   Kopii no maisū o kazoete.
   <u>Count</u> the <u>number of copies</u>.

4. 棚卸しで商品の数を調べた。
   Tanaoroshi de shōhin no kazu o shirabeta.
   During inventory, we checked the <u>number</u> of items in stock.

5. 私は数学より英語が得意です。
   Watashi wa sūgaku yori eigo ga tokui desu.
   I am better at English than <u>mathematics</u>.

Common Compounds and Phrases

多数決	**ta<u>sū</u>ketsu**	a majority vote
数週間	**<u>sū</u>shūkan**	a few weeks
数日	**<u>sū</u>jitsu**	a few days
人数	**nin<u>zū</u> / nin<u>zu</u>**	the number of people
少数	**shō<u>sū</u>**	a few; a minority
奇数	**ki<u>sū</u>**	an odd number
偶数	**gū<u>sū</u>**	an even number

The tenth and thirteenth strokes do not join, and the last stroke tapers off.

13 | ` ´ ⺊ ⺀ ⺘ ⺘ ⺘ 娄 娄 娄 数 数

数

287 働

ドウ DŌ
はたら・く hatara(ku)

to work

The character 働 is a combination of *person* イ and *move* 動, to indicate a person *being busy, working*.

GR4 N4 AP

Example Sentences

1. 労働時間を短縮するよう努力している。
   Rōdō jikan o tanshuku suru yō doryoku shite iru.
   We are endeavoring to shorten <u>working hours</u>.

2. 父は毎日遅くまで働いています。
   Chichi wa mainichi osoku made hataraite imasu.
   My father <u>works</u> until late every day.

3. あの人は今が働き盛りだ。
   Ano hito wa ima ga hataraki-zakari da.
   He is now <u>in the prime of</u> his <u>working life</u>.

4. 彼女のところは共働きだ。
   Kanojo no tokoro wa tomobataraki da.
   She and her husband <u>both work</u>.

5. その仕事は思ったより重労働だった。
   Sono shigoto wa omotta yori jūrōdō datta.
   It was <u>harder</u> <u>work</u> than I imagined.

Common Compounds and Phrases

労働	**rō<u>dō</u>**	(manual) labor, work
重労働	**jūrō<u>dō</u>**	heavy labor; hard work
労働組合	**rō<u>dō</u> kumiai**	a labor (trade) union
働き者	**hatarakimono**	a hard worker
働き盛り	**hataraki-zakari**	in the prime of one's working life
共働き	**tomobataraki**	both husband and wife working
働き手	**hatarakite**	a (good) worker; a provider

The twelfth stroke ends with a hook.

13 | ノ イ イ´ 仁 仁 伶 伶 伶 俥 俥 働 働

働

288 歌

カ KA
うた uta　うた・う uta(u)

song; to sing

The character 歌 combines *open mouth* 欠 and two 可, pronounced 'ka'. 'Ka-ka' was the Chinese version of 'tra-la-la', which suggests *singing*.
GR2　N4　AP

Example Sentences

1. 私の好きな歌手が来日した。
   Watashi no suki na <u>kashu</u> ga rainichi shita.
   <u>A singer</u> that I like came to Japan.

2. 試合の前に国歌が演奏されていた。
   Shiai no mae ni <u>kokka</u> ga ensō sarete ita.
   <u>The national anthem</u> was played before the game.

3. 母は和歌に興味があります。
   Haha wa <u>waka</u> ni kyōmi ga arimasu.
   My mother is interested in *waka* poems.

4. 鼻歌を歌いながら運転していた。
   <u>Hanauta o utainagara</u> unten shite ita.
   He <u>was humming</u> while he was driving.

5. ビートルズの歌は曲も歌詞もいい。
   Biitoruzu no <u>uta</u> wa kyoku mo kashi mo ii.
   Both the music and lyrics in the Beatles' <u>songs</u> are good.

Common Compounds and Phrases

歌手	**ka<u>shu</u>**	a singer
国歌	**kokka**	a national anthem
和歌	**wa<u>ka</u>**	a 31-syllable Japanese poem
歌詞	**ka<u>shi</u>**	lyrics
賛美歌	**sanbika**	a hymn
歌舞伎	**kabuki**	Kabuki (drama)
鼻歌	**hana<u>uta</u>**	humming; crooning

The fifth and tenth strokes end with a hook.

14　一　ㄅ　ㄅ　ਰ　可　可　哥　哥　哥　哥　哥　歌　歌

歌

EXERCISE 24 (277 – 288)

A. Give the readings for the following.

1. 意味 _____
2. 楽な _____
3. 数 _____
4. 暗い _____
5. 試みる _____
6. 遠くに _____
7. 試食 _____
8. 歌っている _____
9. ご飯 _____
10. 楽しい _____

B. Rewrite using a mixture of kanji and kana.

1. ためしてみる _____
2. ちゅういする _____
3. はたらきもの _____
4. あさめしまえ _____
5. あんきする _____
6. きらくな _____
7. とおまわり _____

8. ごばんめ _____
9. さんぎょう _____
10. すうしゅうかん _____

C. Match the following kanji with their readings.

1. 音楽 （　） 　　a. えんそく
2. 試合 （　） 　　b. ばんぐみ
3. 暗号 （　） 　　c. かんじ
4. 数学 （　） 　　d. さぎょう
5. 遠足 （　） 　　e. いけん
6. 歌手 （　） 　　f. しあい
7. 番組 （　） 　　g. すうがく
8. 漢字 （　） 　　h. あんごう
9. 意見 （　） 　　i. かしゅ
10. 作業 （　） 　　j. おんがく

289 銀

ギン GIN

silver

The character 銀 combines *metal* 金 and *permanent tattooing around the eye* 艮, a reference to *silver*, which, unlike iron, does not rust, but lasts forever.

GR3 N4

Example Sentences

1. 日本の紙幣は日本銀行で発行している。
   Nihon no shihei wa <u>Nihon Ginkō</u> de hakkō shite iru.
   Japanese banknotes are issued by <u>the Bank of Japan</u>.

2. 銀婚式の祝いに純銀のブローチを夫にもらった。
   <u>Ginkonshiki</u> no iwai ni <u>jungin</u> no burōchi o otto ni moratta.
   I received a <u>pure silver</u> brooch from my husband, when celebrating our <u>silver wedding anniversary</u>.

3. グレタ・ガルボは銀幕の女王だった。
   Gureta Garubo wa <u>ginmaku</u> no joō datta.
   Greta Garbo was a queen of <u>the silver screen</u>.

4. 銀座には、一流店が揃っている。
   <u>Ginza</u> ni wa, ichiryūten ga sorotte iru.
   Prestigious stores are all to be found in <u>the Ginza district</u>.

Common Compounds and Phrases

日本銀行	**Nihon <u>Gin</u>kō**	the Bank of Japan
銀行口座	**<u>gin</u>kō kōza**	a bank account
純銀	**jun<u>gin</u>**	pure silver
銀婚式	**<u>gin</u>konshiki**	a silver (25th) wedding anniversary
銀幕	**<u>gin</u>maku**	the silver screen
銀座	**<u>Gin</u>za**	the Ginza district (in Tokyo)
銀色	**<u>gin</u>-iro**	the color silver

The eighth stroke sweeps up from left to right.

14 丿 八 △ △ 牟 牟 金 金 金﹃ 金﹃ 釒 銀 銀

銀

---

290 説

セツ SETSU ＊ゼイ ZEI
と・く to(ku)

to explain; theory

The character 説 contains *words* 言 and *strip off, liberate* 兑, suggesting an attempt to unravel that which is difficult to understand, hence *explain*.

GR4 N4 AP

Example Sentences

1. この携帯の機能を説明してくれる？
   Kono keitai no kinō o <u>setsumei</u> shite kureru?
   <u>Could you explain</u> this cell-phone's functions to me?

2. 今朝読んだ記事には説得力があった。
   Kesa yonda kiji ni wa <u>settoku</u>ryoku ga atta.
   The article I read this morning was <u>written convincingly</u>.

3. 彼の失踪の原因については、いろいろな説がある。
   Kare no shissō no gen'in ni tsuite wa, iroiro na <u>setsu</u> ga aru.
   There are various <u>theories</u> as to the reason for his disappearance.

4. この推理小説の結末を早く知りたい。
   Kono <u>suiri shōsetsu</u> no ketsumatsu o hayaku shiritai.
   I can't wait to find out how this <u>detective story</u> ends.

5. ガンジーは平和の大切さを説いて回った。
   Ganjii wa heiwa no taisetsusa o <u>toite</u> mawatta.
   Gandhi traveled widely, <u>advocating</u> the importance of peace.

Common Compounds and Phrases

説明	**<u>setsu</u>mei**	an explanation; a description
説得	**<u>setsu</u>toku**	persuasion
小説	**shō<u>setsu</u>**	a novel; a work of fiction
解説	**kai<u>setsu</u>**	a commentary; an explanation
伝説	**den<u>setsu</u>**	a legend; a tradition
演説	**en<u>zetsu</u>**	a public speech; an address
＊遊説	**yū<u>zei</u>**	canvassing; stumping

The last stroke ends with a hook.

14 丶 亠 亠 言 言 言 訃 訟 説 説 説 説

説

291 質

シツ SHITSU　シチ SHICHI
***チ CHI**

quality; matter; pawn

The character 質 combines *shell, money* 貝 and two *axes* 斤, expressing equivalence. The suggestion is that a thing whose monetary value is known is either something of *quality* or something to be *pawned*.
GR5　N4

Example Sentences

1. 量より質だ。
   Ryō yori shitsu da.
   <u>Quality</u>, rather than quantity.

2. ちょっと、質問していいですか。
   Chotto, shitsumon shite ii desu ka.
   Is it okay if I ask you <u>a question</u>?

3. 姉妹でも性質が全く異なる。
   Shimai de mo seishitsu ga mattaku kotonaru.
   They are sisters, but are totally different <u>kinds of people</u>.

4. その工場は品質管理に問題があった。
   Sono kōjō wa hinshitsu kanri ni mondai ga atta.
   That factory had a problem with <u>quality control</u>.

5. この時計を質屋に入れたら、いくらになるかな。
   Kono tokei o shichiya ni iretara, ikura ni naru ka na.
   I wonder how much I'd get for this watch at <u>a pawnshop</u>?

Common Compounds and Phrases

性質	**seishitsu**	nature; character
品質	**hinshitsu**	quality
質素	**shisso**	simplicity; modesty
神経質	**shinkeishitsu**	a nervous temperament
たんぱく質	**tanpakushitsu**	protein
質屋	**shichiya**	a pawnshop
人質	**hitojichi**	a hostage; a prisoner

Give the two elements at the top the same shape.

15 ｒ ｆ ｆ ｆ' ｆ'' ｆ''' ｆ'''' 竹 竹 竹 竹 皙 皙 質 質

質

---

292 線

セン SEN

line

The character 線 combines *thread* 糸 and *water spring* 泉 to suggest a *thin stream of water*. From this came the meaning of *line*.

GR2　N3　AP

Example Sentences

1. 台風で電線が切れた。
   Taifū de densen ga kireta.
   <u>The power lines</u> were severed in the typhoon.

2. 点線のところで紙を折って下さい。
   Tensen no tokoro de kami o otte kudasai.
   Fold the paper along <u>the dotted line</u>.

3. 線路に靴が落ちた。
   Senro ni kutsu ga ochita.
   A shoe fell onto <u>the railway track</u>.

4. ここからだと、水平線がよく見える。
   Koko kara da to, suiheisen ga yoku mieru.
   There's a good view of <u>the horizon</u> from here.

5. その線で交渉してみよう。
   Sono sen de kōshō shite miyō.
   Let's try and negotiate <u>along these lines</u>.

Common Compounds and Phrases

電線	**densen**	an electric wire; telegraph wires
点線	**tensen**	a dotted (broken) line
線路	**senro**	a railway track
水平線	**suiheisen**	the horizon
直線	**chokusen**	a straight line
曲線	**kyokusen**	a curve
視線	**shisen**	one's gaze; a line of vision

The center stroke in 泉 ends with a hook.

15 ｚ ｚ ｚ 糸 糸 糸' 糸' 紗 絆 絆 綿 綿 線 線 線

線

293 館

カン KAN
*やかた yakata
public building *たて tate *たち tachi

The character 館 brings together *food* 食 and *officials in a meeting hall* 官, later assuming the broader meaning of *building*.

GR3 N4 AP

Example Sentences

1. 大学時代によく図書館に通ったものだ。
   Daigaku jidai ni yoku toshokan ni kayotta mono da.
   I often used to go to the library when I was a college student.

2. 館内放送で今名前を呼ばれたよ。
   Kannai hōsō de ima namae o yobareta yo.
   Your name was just announced over the public address system.

3. 旅行会社に勧められた旅館は思ったほどよくなかった。
   Ryokō gaisha ni susumerareta ryokan wa omotta hodo yokunakatta.
   The Japanese inn recommended to us by the travel agency wasn't as good as we had hoped.

4. 大使館の入館には厳しいチェックがある。
   Taishikan no nyūkan ni wa kibishii chekku ga aru.
   There is a strict security check when entering the embassy.

Common Compounds and Phrases

図書館	**toshokan**	a library
館内	**kannai**	in the building
映画館	**eigakan**	a movie theater
大使館	**taishikan**	an embassy
美術館	**bijutsukan**	an art gallery
入館料	**nyūkanryō**	an admission fee
体育館	**taiikukan**	a gymnasium

End the second stroke firmly.

16 亼 亽 亽 亽 食 食 食' 飠' 飠 館 館 館 館 館

館

---

294 親

シン SHIN
おや oya
した・しい shita(shii)
した・しむ shita(shimu)
parent; close; intimate

The character 親 combines *stand* 立, *tree* 木 and *look* 見, which can be thought of as standing to look *closely* at a tree.

GR2 N4 AP

Example Sentences

1. ご両親はお元気ですか。
   Goryōshin wa ogenki desu ka.
   Are your parents well?

2. お正月には親類が大勢集まった。
   Oshōgatsu ni wa shinrui ga ōzei atsumatta.
   We had a large family get-together on New Year's.

3. 親指にけがをして、何もできない。
   Oyayubi ni kega o shite, nani mo dekinai.
   I've hurt my thumb and can't do anything.

4. 親しい友だちが外国に行ってしまった。
   Shitashii tomodachi ga gaikoku ni itte shimatta.
   A close friend of mine went overseas.

5. 先生は、とても親しみやすい人だった。
   Sensei wa, totemo shitashimi-yasui hito datta.
   My teacher was very approachable.

Common Compounds and Phrases

親類	**shinrui**	a relative; a relation
親切な	**shinsetsu na**	kind; friendly
親愛なる	**shin'ai naru**	dear; beloved
親会社	**oyagaisha**	a parent company
親指	**oyayubi**	the thumb
父親	**chichioya**	one's father
親ばか	**oya-baka**	foolish parental doting

The last stroke ends with a hook.

16 亠 亠 立 立 辛 亲 亲 新 新 新 新 親 親

親

295 頭

トウ TŌ　ズ ZU　*ト TO
あたま atama
*かしら kashira

head; top; leader

GR2　N4　AP

The character 頭 combines *head* 頁 and *stand* 豆. The stand suggests a vessel, which due to its shape reinforced the meaning of *head*.

Example Sentences

1. 彼は列の先頭に立っていた。
   Kare wa retsu no sentō ni tatte ita.
   He was standing at the front of the line.

2. 頭取というのは銀行の社長のことです。
   Tōdori to iu no wa ginkō no shachō no koto desu.
   Tōdori refers to the president of a bank.

3. 牧場には馬が八頭いる。
   Bokujō ni wa uma ga hattō iru.
   There are eight horses in the meadow.

4. 老後のことは頭痛の種です。
   Rōgo no koto wa zutsū no tane desu.
   Life after retirement is a worry.

5. 頭が痛い。
   Atama ga itai.
   I have a headache.

Common Compounds and Phrases

先頭	**sentō**	the front; the head; the top
頭取	**tōdori**	a bank president
店頭	**tentō**	a shop front (window)
頭脳	**zunō**	brains; the head
頭痛	**zutsū**	a headache; a worry
頭金	**atamakin**	a deposit; a down payment
頭文字	**kashira-moji**	initials; capitals; the first letter

The seventh stroke goes up from left to right.

16　一 口 口 豆 豆 豆 豆 頭 頭 頭 頭 頭 頭 頭 頭

頭

---

296 薬

ヤク YAKU
くすり kusuri

drug; medicine

GR3　N4　AP

The character 薬 combines *plant* ⧾ and *pleasure* 楽, suggesting soothing. From this, the idea of a *medicinal* herb or plant has derived.

Example Sentences

1. この薬品は危険ですから、子供の手が届かないところに置いてください。
   Kono yakuhin wa kiken desu kara, kodomo no te ga todokanai tokoro ni oite kudasai.
   This is a dangerous drug, so please keep it out of the reach of young children.

2. 九世紀ごろ中国で火薬が始めて作られたそうだ。
   Kyūseiki goro Chūgoku de kayaku ga hajimete tsukurareta sō da.
   Gunpowder was apparently first manufactured in China in around the 9th century.

3. 腹痛によく利く薬を教えて下さい。
   Fukutsū ni yoku kiku kusuri o oshiete kudasai.
   Please give me the name of a medication good for a stomach ache.

4. その風邪薬には副作用があるかどうか確認した方がいい。
   Sono kaze-gusuri ni wa fukusayō ga aru ka dō ka kakunin shita hō ga ii.
   You'd better check to see if that cold medicine has any side effects.

Common Compounds and Phrases

薬品	**yakuhin**	a medicine; a drug
製薬会社	**seiyaku-gaisha**	a pharmaceutical company
薬局	**yakkyoku**	a pharmacy; a chemist's
麻薬	**mayaku**	a narcotic; a drug
風邪薬	**kaze-gusuri**	a cold remedy (medicine)
胃薬	**igusuri**	stomach medicine
薬指	**kusuri-yubi**	the third (ring) finger

End the fourteenth stroke firmly.

16　艹 艹 艹 芢 芢 芢 苩 苩 莖 蓮 蓮 蓮 薬 薬

薬

297 顔

ガン GAN
かお kao

face

The character 顔 combines *head* 頁 and *handsome* 彦, which came from a pictograph of a forehead and three hairs. Handsome head took on the meaning of *face*.

GR2 N4 AP

Example Sentences

1. あの人は童顔だが、すでに高校生の息子がいる。
   Ano hito wa dōgan da ga, sude ni kōkōsei no musuko ga iru.
   That person has <u>a youthful face</u> but already has a child in high school.

2. 顔を洗ってクリームをつけた。
   Kao o aratte kuriimu o tsuketa.
   I washed <u>my face</u> and applied some cream.

3. 顔色が悪いけど、大丈夫？
   Kaoiro ga warui kedo, daijōbu?
   You <u>look pale</u>. Are you all right?

4. 彼女は知らん顔で通りすぎて行った。
   Kanojo wa shirankao de tōrisugite itta.
   She <u>ignored me</u> and walked right past me.

5. 彼に顔をつぶされた。
   Kare ni kao o tsubusareta.
   He <u>caused me to lose face</u>.

Common Compounds and Phrases

童顔	**dōgan**	a youthful (childlike) face
洗顔	**sengan**	facial cleansing
顔色	**kao-iro**	a complexion; a face; a look
知らん顔	**shiran-kao**	feigned ignorance; indifference
笑顔	**egao**	a smile; a smiling face
顔負け	**kaomake**	to put to shame; to be outdone
顔つき	**kaotsuki**	looks; an expression

The three strokes for 彡 taper down from right to left.

18 立 产 产 彦 彦 彦 彦 節 顔 顔 顔 顔 顔 顔

顔

298 験

ケン KEN *ゲン GEN

test; experience

The character 験 was originally made up of *horse* 馬 and *gather together and examine* 僉, suggesting rounding up horses and riding them to *test* the quality.

GR4 N4 AP

Example Sentences

1. やっと試験が終わって、ほっとした。
   Yatto shiken ga owatte, hotto shita.
   I feel relieved now that the <u>tests</u> are finally over.

2. 京都の旅行は貴重な体験になるだろう。
   Kyōto no ryokō wa kichō na taiken ni naru darō.
   Our trip to Kyoto will be a valuable <u>experience</u>.

3. この製品を作るためには、動物実験は行われていない。
   Kono seihin o tsukuru tame ni wa, dōbutsu jikken wa okonawarete inai.
   No <u>animal testing</u> was carried out in the manufacture of this product.

4. その仕事は、経験不足でうまくいかなかった。
   Sono shigoto wa, keiken busoku de umaku ikanakatta.
   I <u>did not have enough experience</u> to make the project succeed.

Common Compounds and Phrases

試験	**shiken**	an examination; an experiment
検定試験	**kentei shiken**	a certification examination
受験	**juken**	sitting for an examination
経験	**keiken**	an experience
実験	**jikken**	an experiment; a test
実験室	**jikkenshitsu**	a laboratory
験を担ぐ	**gen o katsugu**	for good luck

Make sure the eleventh and twelfth strokes connect.

18 馬 馬 馬 馬 馬 馬 駒 験 験 験 験 験 験

験

299 題　ダイ DAI

title; topic; problem

The character 題 combines *a straight spoon handle* 是 and *head* 頁, perhaps referring to the straight, flat part of the head, namely the forehead. By extension, this came to refer to the first part of a piece of writing, ie., the *title* or *topic*.
GR3　N4　AP

Example Sentences

1. 作文に題をつけるのを忘れずに。
   Sakubun ni dai o tsukeru no o wasurezu ni.
   Don't forget to give your essay a title.

2. また、政治家の汚職問題が話題になっている。
   Mata, seijika no oshoku mondai ga wadai ni natte iru.
   A corruption case involving a politician is in the news again.

3. 宿題の期限が明日に迫っている。
   Shukudai no kigen ga ashita ni sematte iru.
   The deadline for the homework—due tomorrow—is fast approaching.

4. 緊急の課題が山済みされている。
   Kinkyū no kadai ga yamazumi sarete iru.
   Pressing matters have piled up, one after the other.

5. 辞めるなんて大問題だよ。
   Yameru nante daimondai da yo.
   Your resignation will create serious problems.

Common Compounds and Phrases

題名	**daimei**	a title
大問題	**daimondai**	a serious problem; a pressing question
問題集	**mondaishū**	a book of drills
議題	**gidai**	a topic for discussion
課題	**kadai**	a task; an assignment; a problem
難題	**nandai**	a difficult problem
題材	**daizai**	subject matter; a theme

The sixth stroke does not protrude.

18 旦 早 早 昻 是 尟 尟 𡖊 題 題 題 題 題

題

---

300 曜　ヨウ YŌ

day of the week

The character 曜 combines *sun* 日, *bird* 隹 and *two wings* ヨ彐, suggesting the sun flying like a bird; i.e., the passing of a *day*.

GR2　N4　AP

Example Sentences

1. やっと金曜日だね。
   Yatto kinyōbi da ne.
   Friday is here at last.

2. 今日は、何曜日だっけ？
   Kyō wa, nanyōbi dakke?
   What day (of the week) is it today?

3. 第二・第四土曜日はお休みです。
   Daini daiyon doyōbi wa oyasumi desu.
   The second and fourth Saturdays are holidays.

4. 「火曜定休」と書いてあった。
   'Kayō teikyū' to kaite atta.
   'Closed on Tuesdays,' the sign said.

5. 今度の土曜日に、映画に行きませんか。
   Kondo no doyōbi ni, eiga ni ikimasen ka.
   Would you like to go to the movies next Saturday?

Common Compounds and Phrases

曜日	**yōbi**	a day of the week
月曜日	**getsuyōbi**	Monday
火曜日	**kayōbi**	Tuesday
土曜日	**doyōbi**	Saturday
先週の日曜日	senshū no nichiyōbi	last Sunday
今度の水曜日	kondo no suiyōbi	this (next) Wednesday
第一木曜日	daiichi mokuyōbi	the first Thursday (of the month)

The 日 radical is narrow.

18 月 日 日丨 日彐 日彐 日彐丿 日彐丿 日彐彐 日彐彐 日彐彐 日彐彐 𣇵 𣇵 曜

曜

EXERCISE 25 (289 – 300)

A. Give the readings for the following.
1. 顔 _____
2. 親 _____
3. 土曜日 _____
4. 薬 _____
5. 質屋 _____
6. 銀 _____
7. 説明する _____
8. 頭 _____
9. 説く _____
10. 映画館 _____

B. Write the following using kanji and kana.
1. しけん _____
2. てんせん _____
3. かおいろ _____
4. だいめい _____
5. しつもんする _____
6. やくひん _____
7. げつようび _____

8. としょかん _____
9. ちちおや _____
10. したしい _____

C. Write the English meanings for the following.
1. 電線 _____
2. 旅館 _____
3. 体験 _____
4. 日本銀行 _____
5. 頭金 _____
6. 火曜日 _____
7. 小説 _____
8. 人質 _____
9. 親切な人 _____
10. 大問題 _____

Review 8 (1 – 300)

A. Give the readings for the following.
1. 題名 _____
2. 大使館 _____
3. 楽な _____
4. 親しい _____
5. 品質 _____
6. 体験 _____
7. 暗い _____
8. 薬 _____
9. 歌わない _____
10. 入試 _____

B. Write in English.
1. 漢方薬 _____
2. 会館 _____
3. 話題 _____
4. 頭金 _____
5. 火曜日 _____
6. 電線 _____
7. 人数 _____

8. 試験 _____
9. 父親 _____
10. 目薬 _____

C. Add an appropriate kanji to complete the following.
1. 注 _____ する (to be careful)
2. 知らん _____ をする (to feign ignorance)
3. 今度の木 _____ 日 (next Thursday)
4. _____ 明する (to explain; to show)
5. _____ 犬にいい犬 (a good guard dog)
6. 入 _____ 料 (an admission fee)
7. 問 _____ をとく (to solve a problem)
8. 先 _____ に立つ (to stand at the front of a line)
9. 電話が _____ い (to have a poor line)
10. 洗 _____ クリーム (facial cleansing cream)

Review 8 (1 – 300) *continued*

D. Write in kanji and kana.

1. おやこ (parent and child) _____
2. きんようび (Friday) _____
3. しちや (a pawnshop) _____
4. ゆうはん (an evening meal) _____
5. かおいろ (a complexion) _____
6. かしらもじ (initials; capitals) _____
7. きがるな (lighthearted) _____

E. Rewrite using appropriate kanji and translate into English.

1. _____(せんしゅう)の _____(にちようび)
2. _____(しつもん)に _____(こた)える
3. _____(しんせつ)な _____(かた)に _____
   (みち)を _____(おし)えてもらった。
4. _____(てんせん)の _____(ところ)から
   _____(き)り _____(と)る
5. _____(あたま)がいい _____(しょうねん)
6. _____(ぎんこう)で、お _____(かね)を _____
   (お)ろす

7. _____(にほんご)の _____(しけん)
8. _____(しょうせつ)を ___(か)く
9. _____(まいしゅう) _____(どようび)
10. _____(としょかん)で ____(ほん)を _____
   (か)りる

F. Add *furigana* to the kanji in the following and translate the sentences into English.

1. 朝、遠くの森で野鳥をたくさん見た。
2. 数学の問題集をやっとやり終えた。
3. 昨夜は家族で歌番組を楽しんだ。　　（ゆうべ）
4. 親しい友達と食堂で軽くご飯を食べた。　　（だち）
5. 今日は暑すぎて頭が働かない。
6. 自転車なら図書館の帰りに銀行に行ける。
7. 薬屋には、ここから一直線に行けば着きますよ。
8. これは母の料理と同じ味だ。
9. この薬を毎食後に飲んで下さい。
10. 今夜は寒くなるからセーターを着ていきなさい。

---

301 刀

トウ TŌ
かたな katana

sword

The character 刀 depicts a *sword* with a bent blade.

GR2 N1

Example Sentences

1. 日本刀は美術品として価値がある。
   Nihontō wa bijutsuhin to shite kachi ga aru.
   <u>Japanese swords</u> are valued as works of art.

2. 記者は大統領に単刀直入に質問した。
   Kisha wa daitōryō ni <u>tantō chokunyū ni</u> shitsumon shita.
   The journalists questioned the president <u>in a direct manner.</u>

3. 刀は武士の命と言われた。
   Katana wa bushi no inochi to iwareta.
   <u>The sword</u> was said to be the 'life' of the samurai.

4. 小刀で鉛筆を削った。
   Kogatana de enpitsu o kezutta.
   I sharpened a pencil with my <u>pocket knife.</u>

5. 毎朝、電気剃刀でひげを剃る。
   Maiasa, denki <u>kamisori</u> de hige o soru.
   I shave with an electric <u>razor</u> every morning.

Common Compounds and Phrases

日本刀	**Nihon-tō**	a Japanese sword
木刀	**bokutō**	a wooden sword
短刀	**tantō**	a short sword; a dagger
単刀直入の	**tantō chokunyū no**	frank, direct
小刀	**kogatana**	a knife; a penknife
*剃刀	**kamisori**	a razor
*竹刀	**shinai**	a bamboo sword (used in *kendo*)

The second stroke does not protrude. Don't confuse 刀 with 力.

| 2 | フ 刀 |

刀

171

302 丸

ガン GAN
まる maru　まる・い maru(i)
まる・める maru(meru)

round; to
make round

The character 丸 was originally written showing a *person huddled* メ at the base of a *cliff* 乁. From this came the meaning of *round*.

GR2 N2

Example Sentences

1. 市民は一丸となってゴミ処理場の建設に反対した。
   Shimin wa ichigan to natte gomi shorijō no kensetsu ni hantai shita.
   The citizens <u>were united</u> in their opposition to the construction of the refuse disposal plant.

2. 猫は、寒さに背中を丸くした。
   Neko wa, samusa ni senaka o maruku shita.
   The cat <u>was hunched up</u> against the cold.

3. 京都に引っ越してから、丸一年になる。
   Kyōto ni hikkoshite kara, maru-ichinen ni naru.
   It has been <u>a full year</u> since I moved to Kyoto.

4. 港に日本丸が停泊している。
   Minato ni Nippon-maru ga teihaku shite iru.
   The *Nippon Maru* is moored in the harbor.

5. 彼は紙を丸めてゴミ箱に投げた。
   Kare wa kami o marumete gomibako ni nageta.
   He <u>crumpled up</u> a piece of paper and threw it into the trash can.

Common Compounds and Phrases

一丸となる	**ichigan** to naru	to be united (as a body)
弾丸	**dangan**	a bullet
丸薬	**ganyaku**	a pill
丸一年	**maru-ichinen**	a full (whole) year
丸ごと	**marugoto**	whole; entirely
丸見え	**maru-mie**	in plain sight
丸暗記	**maru-anki**	rote memorization

The second stroke ends with a hook. Don't confuse 丸 with 九.

3 ノ 九 丸

丸

303 弓

キュウ KYŪ
ゆみ yumi

a bow

The character 弓 derives from a pictograph of a *bow*.

GR2 N1

Example Sentences

1. 姉は弓道を習っている。
   Ane wa kyūdō o naratte iru.
   My older sister is learning <u>Japanese archery</u>.

2. バイオリンは弓で弾く楽器です。
   Baiorin wa yumi de hiku gakki desu.
   The violin is an instrument played with <u>a bow</u>.

3. その建物には弓形の窓がいくつもある。
   Sono tatemono ni wa yumigata no mado ga ikutsu mo aru.
   That building has numerous <u>arched windows</u>.

4. 胡弓の音色は、とても美しい。
   Kokyū no neiro wa, totemo utsukushii.
   The tone of <u>the Chinese fiddle</u> is very beautiful.

Common Compounds and Phrases

弓道	**kyūdō**	Japanese archery
洋弓	**yōkyū**	Western archery
弓状の	**kyūjō no**	bow-shaped; arched
胡弓	**kokyū**	a Chinese fiddle
弓矢	**yumiya**	bow and arrow
弓なり	**yuminari**	an arch; a curve
真弓	**Mayumi**	Mayumi (a name)

The third stroke ends with a hook.

3 ㄱ ㄢ 弓

弓

304 化

カ KA　*ケ KE
ば・ける ba(keru)
ば・かす ba(kasu)

to change into;
to bewitch

The character 化 comprises a *standing person* 亻 and *a fallen person* ヒ, suggesting a change in appearance or state. *Deceive* and *bewitch* are associated meanings.

GR3 N3 AP

Example Sentences

1. この頃、変化しやすい天候が続いている。
   Kono goro, <u>henka shiyasui</u> tenkō ga tsuzuite iru.
   The weather has been <u>changeable</u> of late.

2. 日本、中国、韓国は、箸を使う文化があります。
   Nippon, Chūgoku, Kankoku wa, hashi o tsukau <u>bunka</u> ga arimasu.
   Japan, China and Korea have <u>a culture</u> of using chopsticks.

3. 肌の老化を防ぐには、あまり日光に当たらない方がいいらしい。
   Hada no <u>rōka</u> o fusegu ni wa, amari nikkō ni ataranai hō ga ii rashii.
   Apparently, it's better not to expose your skin to too much sunlight, to prevent premature <u>ageing</u>.

4. 彼女は厚化粧だね。
   Kanojo wa <u>atsu-geshō</u> da ne.
   She is <u>heavily made-up</u>.

5. 夏のボーナスが全部洋服に化けた。
   Natsu no bōnasu ga zenbu yōfuku ni <u>baketa</u>.
   I <u>blew</u> (spent) my entire summer bonus on clothing.

Common Compounds and Phrases

変化	**henka**	a change; conjugation
化学	**kagaku**	chemistry
強化	**kyōka**	strengthening; a buildup
老化	**rōka**	ageing; senility
化粧	**keshō**	makeup
化け物	**bakemono**	a goblin; a monster
お化け屋敷	**obake-yashiki**	a haunted house

The third stroke sweeps down from the right.

4 ｀ 亻 仁 化

化

---

305 戸

コ KO
と to　*べ be

door; household

The character 戸 derived from a pictograph of one half of a double *door* or *gate*.

GR2 N3

Example Sentences

1. 一戸建ての家に住みたいなあ。
   <u>Ikko-date</u> no ie ni sumitai nā.
   I'd like to live in <u>my own house</u>.

2. 役所に戸籍謄本を取りにいった。
   Yakusho ni <u>koseki</u> tōhon o tori ni itta.
   I went to a government office to get <u>a copy of the family register</u>.

3. その戸は押して下さい。
   Sono <u>to</u> wa oshite kudasai.
   Please push that <u>door</u> open.

4. 出かける時は、きちんと戸締りしてね。
   Dekakeru toki wa, kichinto <u>tojimari</u> shite ne.
   Make sure you <u>lock up</u> when you go out.

5. 戸棚の奥にへそくりがしまってある。
   <u>Todana</u> no oku ni hesokuri ga shimatte aru.
   My secret savings are hidden at the very back of <u>the cupboard</u>.

Common Compounds and Phrases

一戸建て	**ikko-date**	a detached house
戸籍	**koseki**	a household register
雨戸	**amado**	a shutter; a storm door
戸棚	**todana**	a closet; a cupboard
引き戸	**hikido**	a sliding door
戸締り	**tojimari**	locking up
*神戸	**Kōbe**	Kobe (a place)

The last stroke tapers off.

4 一 ラ ヨ 戸

戸

306 反

to counter; to oppose

ハン HAN　*ホン HON
*タン TAN
そ・る so(ru)
そ・らす so(rasu)

The character 反 combines *thin board*, *cloth* 厂 and *hands* 又, suggesting the motion of lightly tapping a board with the hand. The board then bends back or returns to its original shape, representing the notion of *countering* or *opposition*.
GR3　N3　AP

Example Sentences

1. 両親は、彼との結婚に反対している。
   Ryōshin wa, kare to no kekkon ni hantai shite iru.
   My parents <u>are opposed to</u> my marrying him.

2. 冗談を言っても、彼女は反応がなかった。
   Jōdan o itte mo, kanojo wa hannō ga nakatta.
   Jokes <u>were lost</u> on her.

3. 息子はもう中学生で、反抗期を迎えている。
   Musuko wa mō chūgakusei de, hankōki o mukaete iru.
   Our son is now a junior high school student and about to enter <u>the rebellious phase</u>.

4. 反省するまで、おこづかいはなしですよ。
   Hansei suru made, okozukai wa nashi desu yo.
   Your allowance will be stopped until you <u>have adequately reflected on your behavior</u>.

5. 彼はスピード違反で捕まった。
   Kare wa supiido ihan de tsukamatta.
   He was caught <u>speeding</u>.

Common Compounds and Phrases

反対	**hantai**	opposition; the opposite
反応	**hannō**	a reaction; a response
反抗	**hankō**	resistance; rebellion
反則	**hansoku**	a rules violation
違反	**ihan**	a violation; an offense
反省	**hansei**	self-examination; reflection
反乱	**hanran**	rebellion; revolt

The first and second strokes join.

4　一 厂 万 反

反

---

307 夫

husband; male laborer

フ FU　*フウ FŪ
おっと otto

The original form of 夫 suggested a mature (adult) male, wearing a hairpin, an ancient sign of adulthood. From this comes the association of *husband*.
GR4　N3　AP

Example Sentences

1. フランスの大統領夫妻が来日した。
   Furansu no daitōryō fusai ga rainichi shita.
   The <u>president</u> of France <u>and his wife</u> came to Japan.

2. 彼らは似合いの夫婦だ。
   Karera wa niai no fūfu da.
   They are <u>a perfect match for each other</u>.

3. 顔が青いよ。大丈夫?
   Kao ga aoi yo. Daijōbu?
   You look pale. Do you feel <u>all right</u>?

4. その新しい車には様々な工夫がこらしてある。
   Sono atarashii kuruma ni wa samazama na kufū ga korashite aru.
   They've come up with all kinds of <u>ideas</u> for that new car.

5. 姉の夫は弁護士です。
   Ane no otto wa bengoshi desu.
   My sister's <u>husband</u> is a lawyer.

Common Compounds and Phrases

夫妻	**fusai**	husband and wife
夫婦	**fūfu**	man and wife; a married couple
夫人	**fujin**	a wife; a married woman
工夫	**kufū**	figuring out; planning; a scheme
農夫	**nōfu**	a farmer; a countryman
丈夫な	**jōbu na**	strong; solid
大丈夫な	**daijōbu na**	all right; OK; fine; surely

The third stroke protrudes.

4　一 二 三 夫

夫

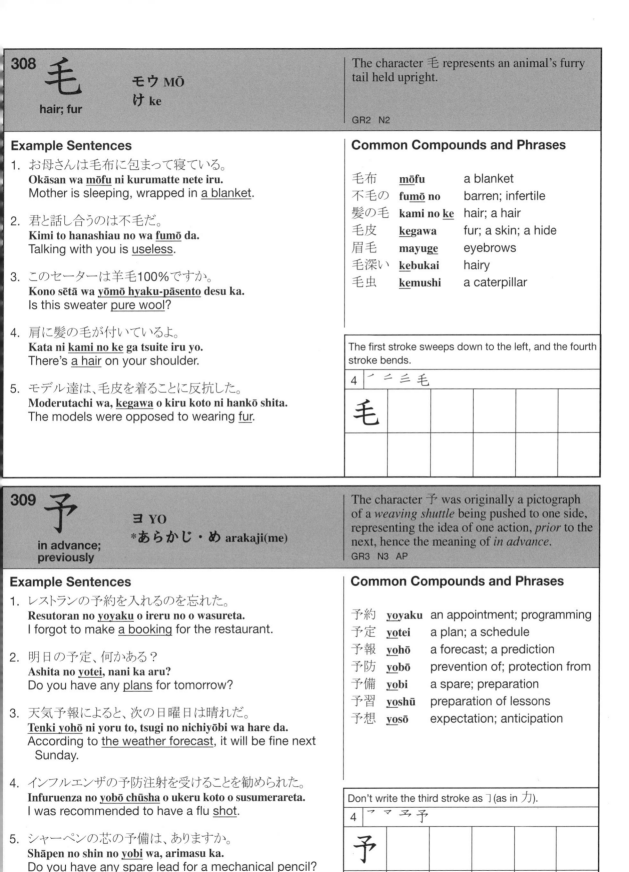

308 毛

モウ MŌ
け ke

hair; fur

GR2 N2

The character 毛 represents an animal's furry tail held upright.

Example Sentences

1. お母さんは毛布に包まって寝ている。
   Okāsan wa <u>mōfu</u> ni kurumatte nete iru.
   Mother is sleeping, wrapped in <u>a blanket</u>.

2. 君と話し合うのは不毛だ。
   Kimi to hanashiau no wa <u>fumō</u> da.
   Talking with you is <u>useless</u>.

3. このセーターは羊毛100%ですか。
   Kono sētā wa <u>yōmō</u> hyaku-pāsento desu ka.
   Is this sweater <u>pure wool</u>?

4. 肩に髪の毛が付いているよ。
   Kata ni <u>kami no ke</u> ga tsuite iru yo.
   There's <u>a hair</u> on your shoulder.

5. モデル達は、毛皮を着ることに反抗した。
   Moderutachi wa, <u>kegawa</u> o kiru koto ni hankō shita.
   The models were opposed to wearing <u>fur</u>.

Common Compounds and Phrases

毛布	**<u>mōfu</u>**	a blanket
不毛の	**<u>fumō</u> no**	barren; infertile
髪の毛	**kami no <u>ke</u>**	hair; a hair
毛皮	**<u>kegawa</u>**	fur; a skin; a hide
眉毛	**<u>mayuge</u>**	eyebrows
毛深い	**<u>kebukai</u>**	hairy
毛虫	**<u>kemushi</u>**	a caterpillar

The first stroke sweeps down to the left, and the fourth stroke bends.

4 ノ 二 三 毛

毛

309 予

ヨ YO
*あらかじ・め arakaji(me)

in advance; previously

GR3 N3 AP

The character 予 was originally a pictograph of a *weaving shuttle* being pushed to one side, representing the idea of one action, *prior* to the next, hence the meaning of *in advance*.

Example Sentences

1. レストランの予約を入れるのを忘れた。
   Resutoran no <u>yoyaku</u> o ireru no o wasureta.
   I forgot to make <u>a booking</u> for the restaurant.

2. 明日の予定、何かある？
   Ashita no <u>yotei</u>, nani ka aru?
   Do you have any <u>plans</u> for tomorrow?

3. 天気予報によると、次の日曜日は晴れだ。
   Tenki <u>yohō</u> ni yoru to, tsugi no nichiyōbi wa hare da.
   According to <u>the weather forecast</u>, it will be fine next Sunday.

4. インフルエンザの予防注射を受けることを勧められた。
   Infuruenza no <u>yobō</u> chūsha o ukeru koto o susumerareta.
   I was recommended to have a flu <u>shot</u>.

5. シャーペンの芯の予備は、ありますか。
   Shāpen no shin no <u>yobi</u> wa, arimasu ka.
   Do you have any <u>spare</u> lead for a mechanical pencil?

Common Compounds and Phrases

予約	**<u>yoyaku</u>**	an appointment; programming
予定	**<u>yotei</u>**	a plan; a schedule
予報	**<u>yohō</u>**	a forecast; a prediction
予防	**<u>yobō</u>**	prevention of; protection from
予備	**<u>yobi</u>**	a spare; preparation
予習	**<u>yoshū</u>**	preparation of lessons
予想	**<u>yosō</u>**	expectation; anticipation

Don't write the third stroke as フ (as in 力).

4 フ マ ヌ 予

予

310

永

エイ EI
なが・い naga(i)

eternal; long;
permanent

The character 永 represents the *merging of rivers*, suggesting an extensive river system. From this, the meanings of *long* and *enduring* have derived.

GR5　N2

Example Sentences

1. この安定した状態は永遠には続かないでしょう。
   Kono antei shita jōtai wa eien ni wa tsuzukanai deshō.
   These stable conditions won't last <u>forever</u>.

2. 二国間の争いは永久に終わりそうもない。
   Nikokukan no arasoi wa eikyū ni owarisō mo nai.
   There <u>seems to be no end</u> to the conflict between those two nations.

3. 有名な映画俳優が昨日永眠された。
   Yūmei na eiga haiyū ga kinō eimin sareta.
   A well-known movie actor <u>passed away</u> yesterday.

4. 末永くお幸せに。
   Suenagaku oshiawase ni.
   Wishing you <u>everlasting</u> happiness.

5. アメリカの永住権を得た。
   Amerika no eijūken o eta.
   I got <u>permanent resident status</u> for the United States.

Common Compounds and Phrases

永久	**eikyū**	permanence; eternity
永眠	**eimin**	death; eternal sleep
永住	**eijū**	permanent residence
永続	**eizoku**	permanency; perpetuity
永年	**einen**	a long time; many long years
永久歯	**eikyūshi**	the second (permanent) teeth
末永く	**suenagaku**	forever; everlastingly

Be careful with the second stroke. Note the difference from 水.

5 ｜ 丶 丁 汀 永 永

永

311

号

ゴウ GŌ

number; issue;
designation; sign

The character 号 is a combination of *mouth* 口 and *gathering in the breath* 丂, indicating a loud, drawn out *call*. The meanings of *number* and *sign* derived from this.

GR3　N3　AP

Example Sentences

1. 夫の事故死の連絡を受けて、号泣した。
   Otto no jikoshi no renraku o ukete, gōkyū shita.
   She <u>wept bitterly</u> upon receiving the news of her husband's accidental death.

2. 青信号を待たずに渡った。
   Aoshingō o matazu ni watatta.
   He crossed the street without waiting for <u>the green light</u>.

3. キャッシュカードの暗証番号を忘れてしまった。
   Kyasshu kādo no anshō bangō o wasurete shimatta.
   I forgot the <u>PIN</u> for my bankcard.

4. ひかり二号は、何時に京都に着きますか。
   Hikari nigō wa, nanji ni Kyōto ni tsukimasu ka.
   What time does <u>the Hikari No 2 bullet train</u> get into Kyoto?

5. 株価の大暴落を伝える号外を道角で配っていた。
   Kabuka no daibōraku o tsutaeru gōgai o michikado de kubatte ita.
   They were handing out <u>newspaper extras</u> about the stock price crash on the street corner.

Common Compounds and Phrases

号泣	**gōkyū**	wailing; crying bitterly
信号	**shingō**	a (traffic) signal
番号	**bangō**	a number
暗証番号	**anshō bangō**	a PIN (personal identification number)
号外	**gōgai**	a newspaper extra; a special (edition)
符号	**fugō**	a sign; a symbol
年号	**nengō**	the era name

Don't write the fourth and fifth strokes as 万.

5 ｜ 丶 ロ ロ 므 号

号

矢

arrow

シ SHI
や ya

The character 矢 derived from a pictograph of an *arrow* with a broad tip.

GR2　N1

Example Sentences

1. 次の試合で一矢を報いたい。
   Tsugi no shiai de <u>isshi o mukuitai</u>.
   I <u>want to get back at</u> the other team next time we play them.

2. 矢で的を射った。
   Ya de mato o itta.
   I <u>shot an arrow</u> at the target.

3. 矢印に沿って進んでください。
   Yajirushi ni sotte susunde kudasai.
   Please follow the direction of <u>the arrow</u>.

4. 光陰矢のごとし。
   Kōin <u>ya no gotoshi</u>.
   Time <u>flies</u>. (a saying)

5. 出かけようとした矢先に宅配便が届いた。
   Dekakeyō to <u>shita yasaki ni</u> takuhaibin ga todoita.
   <u>Just as I was about to</u> go out, a home delivery arrived.

Common Compounds and Phrases

一矢を報いる	**isshi o mukuiru**	to get back at somebody
吹き矢	**fukiya**	a blowpipe dart
毒矢	**dokuya**	a poisoned arrow
矢印	**yajirushi**	an arrow symbol
矢先(に)	**yasaki (ni)**	an arrowhead; just as one is about to
矢面に立つ	**yaomote ni tatsu**	to become the target of (criticism)

The fourth stroke does not protrude. Align the fourth and fifth strokes.

5　ノ　ヒ　ヒ　チ　矢

矢

EXERCISE 26 (301 – 312)

A. Give the readings for the following.

1. 化学 _____
2. 反っている _____
3. 刀 _____
4. 永い _____
5. 文化 _____
6. 引き戸 _____
7. 丸める _____
8. 工夫 _____
9. 真弓 _____
10. 矢先に _____

B. Rewrite using a mixture of kanji and kana.

1. いし で できた みち

   _____

2. にほんとう の もちぬし

   _____

3. きゅうどう を ならう

   _____

4. えいえん に

5. いっこだて の いえ に すむ

   _____

6. すうがく の きごう

   _____

7. まる いちねん に なる

   _____

8. おっと と わかれる

   _____

C. Choose kanji from the list to complete the following compounds.
   LIST: 丸、予、化、永、夫、刀、戸

1. _____ 人 (a wife; a married woman)
2. 雨 _____ (a shutter)
3. _____ 習 (preparation for lessons)
4. 木 _____ (a wooden sword)
5. _____ 住 (permanent residence)
6. 強 _____ (strengthening)
7. _____ 見え (fully exposed to view)

313 失

シツ SHITSU
うしな・う ushina(u)

error; to lose;
to slip (up)

The character 失 originally depicted something *slipping* ╲ from one's *hand* 手 to suggest the idea of *lose* and by association, a *mistake*.

GR4 N3 AP

Example Sentences

1. お先に、失礼します。
   Osaki ni, <u>shitsurei shimasu</u>.
   I'll be leaving now. (lit. <u>I'm sorry</u> to leave early.)

2. 兄は二ヶ月前から失業保険をもらっている。
   Ani wa nikagetsu mae kara <u>shitsugyō hoken</u> o moratte iru.
   My brother has been on <u>unemployment relief</u> for the past two months.

3. 一度ぐらい失敗してもがっかりするんじゃないよ。
   Ichido gurai <u>shippai shite</u> mo gakkari suru n ja nai yo.
   Don't let one <u>failure</u> get you down.

4. 彼は交通事故で息子を失った。
   Kare wa kōtsū jiko de musuko o <u>ushinatta</u>.
   He <u>lost</u> his son in a traffic accident.

5. あの大臣はよく失言をする。
   Ano daijin wa yoku <u>shitsugen</u> o suru.
   That minister often makes <u>slips of the tongue</u>.

Common Compounds and Phrases

失業	**shitsugyō**	unemployment
失敗	**shippai**	failure; an error
失恋	**shitsuren**	lost love
過失	**kashitsu**	a mistake; negligence
失格	**shikkaku**	disqualification
紛失	**funshitsu**	a loss
失言	**shitsugen**	a slip of the tongue

The fourth stroke protrudes.

5 ╱ ┌ 二 牛 失

失

314 打

ダ DA
う・つ u(tsu)

to strike;
to hit

The character 打 combines *hand* 扌 and *nail* 丁 to signify the action of *striking*. Now, there is a more general meaning of *hit with the hand*.

GR3 N2 AP

Example Sentences

1. その火災は彼には大きな打撃であった。
   Sono kasai wa kare ni wa ōki na <u>dageki</u> de atta.
   The fire was a heavy <u>blow</u> to him.

2. 彼はいつも打算的に物事を考える。
   Kare wa itsumo <u>dasanteki</u> ni monogoto o kangaeru.
   His way of thinking is always <u>self-centered</u>.

3. 遠くで太鼓を打つ音が聞こえた。
   Tōku de taiko o <u>utsu</u> oto ga kikoeta.
   Drums could be heard <u>beating</u> in the distance.

4. 病院で痛み止めの注射を打った。
   Byōin de itamidome no <u>chūsha o utta</u>.
   They gave me a pain-killing <u>injection</u> at the hospital.

5. 打ち合わせの時間に間に合いませんよ。
   <u>Uchiawase</u> no jikan ni maniaimasen yo.
   We won't make it in time for <u>the meeting</u>.

Common Compounds and Phrases

打撃	**dageki**	a blow; damage; batting
打算的	**dasanteki**	calculating; selfish
打楽器	**dagakki**	a percussion instrument
打撲	**daboku**	a blow
打者	**dasha**	a batter; a hitter
打ち合わせ	**uchiawase**	preliminary discusssions
舌打ち	**shitauchi**	clicking one's tongue

The second and the fifth strokes end with hooks.

5 ┌ 十 扌 扌 打

打

315 必

ヒツ HITSU
かなら・ず kanara(zu)

**without fail;
necessarily; surely**

The character 必 depicts a pole supported by sticks on either side, bound with rope, *necessary* to keep the pole stable. The sense of *always*, *without fail* derives from this idea.
GR4 N3 AP

Example Sentences

1. 彼は働く必要がない。
   Kare wa hataraku hitsuyō ga nai.
   He doesn't need to work.

2. ゴールを目指して選手は必死に泳いでいた。
   Gōru o mezashite senshu wa hisshi ni oyoide ita.
   The swimmers swam toward the finish for all they were worth.

3. 高校生の必修科目は多い。
   Kōkōsei no hisshū kamoku wa ōi.
   Senior high school students have a lot of compulsory subjects.

4. 必ず六時に来てください。
   Kanarazu rokuji ni kite kudasai.
   Be sure to be there at six o'clock.

5. 必ずしもそうとは限らない。
   Kanarazu shi mo sō to wa kagiranai.
   That isn't necessarily so.

Common Compounds and Phrases

必要	**hitsuyō**	a necessity; a need
必死	**hisshi**	desperate; inevitable
必須(の)	**hissu (no)**	indispensable; necessary
必修	**hisshū**	a requirement; compulsory
不必要 (な)	**fuhitsuyō (na)**	unnecessary; needless
必需品	**hitsujuhin**	necessities
必見	**hikken**	a must-see

The third stroke ends with a hook, and the fourth stroke ends firmly.

5 丶 ソ 必 必 必

必

316 付

フ FU
つ・ける tsu(keru)
つ・く tsu(ku)

**to attach;
attached**

The character 付 is a combination of *person* 亻 and *hand* 寸, suggesting holding up a person from behind. The sense of *attach*, *add to* derived from this.
GR4 N3 AP

Example Sentences

1. この付近にごみ焼却場ができるそうです。
   Kono fukin ni gomi shōkyakujō ga dekiru sō desu.
   I hear they're going to build a garbage incinerator near here.

2. 姉は私立大学の付属高校に通っている。
   Ane wa shiritsu daigaku no fuzoku kōkō ni kayotte iru.
   My sister attends the affiliated high school of a private university.

3. 食卓の皿を片付けましょう。
   Shokutaku no sara o katazukemashō.
   Let's clear the dishes from the table.

4. 切符を買おうと思ったら、財布がないのに気付いた。
   Kippu o kaō to omottara, saifu ga nai no ni kizuita.
   When I went to buy my ticket, I noticed that my wallet was missing.

5. 彼は付き合って面白い男だ。
   Kare wa tsukiatte omoshiroi otoko da.
   I enjoy his company.

Common Compounds and Phrases

付属	**fuzoku**	attached; affiliated
寄付	**kifu**	a contribution; a donation
受付	**uketsuke**	a reception(ist); a counter
後片付け	**atokatazuke**	tidying up; clearing away
身に付ける	**mi ni tsukeru**	to wear; to carry; to acquire
付き合う	**tsukiau**	to be friends with; to accompany
気付く (気が付く)	**kizuku (ki ga tsuku)**	to see; to notice

The fourth stroke ends with a hook.

5 丿 亻 亻 付 付

付

317 払

フツ FUTSU

はら・う hara(u)

to clear away; to pay

Formerly the character 払 combined *hand* 手 and *unwind, disperse* 弗, to express the idea of removing something with the hand. Later it was used to mean *rid* and *pay*.

JK N3 AP

Example Sentences

1. 政府は食に関する不安を払拭しようとしている。
   Seifu wa shoku ni kan suru fuan o <u>fusshoku shiyō to shite iru</u>.
   The government <u>is trying to remove</u> people's uneasiness about food.

2. 野良猫は公園から追い払われた。
   Noraneko wa kōen kara <u>oiharawareta</u>.
   The stray cat <u>was driven out of</u> the park.

3. 君は、その本にいくら払ったの。
   Kimi wa, sono hon ni ikura <u>haratta</u> no.
   How much <u>did you pay</u> for that book?

4. お支払いは、分割払いにしますか。
   <u>Oshiharai</u> wa, <u>bunkatsu barai</u> ni shimasu ka.
   Would you like the <u>payment</u> to be <u>in installments</u>?

5. パソコンの画面のほこりを払った。
   Pasokon no gamen no hokori o <u>haratta</u>.
   I <u>removed</u> the dust from my computer screen.

Common Compounds and Phrases

払拭	**fusshoku**	wipe out; eradication
追い払う（追っ払う）	**oiharau** (**opparau**)	beat off; brush off; drive off (away); get rid of
注意を払う	**chūi o harau**	to pay attention; to keep close watch
支払い	**shiharai**	a payment; a payout
払い戻し	**haraimodoshi**	a refund; a repayment
分割払い	**bunkatsu barai**	payment in installments
酔っ払い	**yopparai**	a drunkard

The fourth stroke bends sharply.

5 　一　十　オ　払　払

払

---

318 平

ヘイ HEI　ビョウ BYŌ

たい・ら tai(ra)

ひら hira

flat; calm; ordinary

The character 平 describes water weed floating *flat* on the surface of the water. From this, the meanings of *flat, calm* have derived.

GR3 N2 AP

Example Sentences

1. 行っても行かなくても平気です。
   Itte mo ikanakute mo <u>heiki</u> desu.
   <u>I don't mind</u> whether I go or not.

2. クラスの男子の身長の平均は160センチです。
   Kurasu no danshi no shinchō no <u>heikin</u> wa hyaku rokujussenchi desu.
   The boys in the class <u>average</u> 160 cm in height.

3. 法の下ではすべての人は平等だ。
   Hō no moto de wa subete no hito wa <u>byōdō</u> da.
   Everyone is <u>equal</u> under the law.

4. 昔の人は地球が平らだと信じていた。
   Mukashi no hito wa chikyū ga <u>taira</u> da to shinjite ita.
   People used to believe that the earth was <u>flat</u>.

5. 私は平泳ぎが得意です。
   Watashi wa <u>hira-oyogi</u> ga tokui desu.
   I'm a strong <u>breaststroke</u> swimmer.

Common Compounds and Phrases

平気な	**heiki na**	calm; indifferent
平均	**heikin**	an average; the mean
平日	**heijitsu**	a weekday; a workday
平等な	**byōdō na**	equal; impartial
平泳ぎ	**hira-oyogi**	the breaststroke
平たい（平べったい）	**hiratai** (**hirabettai**)	flat; easy-to-understand
平仮名	**hiragana**	the *hiragana* syllabary

The fourth stroke is longer than the first.

5 　一　一　ワ　立　平

平

319 末

マツ MATSU　*バツ BATSU
すえ sue

the last part; end(ing)

The character 末 depicts a *tree* 木 with *one* 一 stroke added to suggest the topmost branches and hence *end, tip*.

GR4　N3　AP

Example Sentences

1. 月末に休暇を取りたいと思っています。
   Getsumatsu ni kyūka o toritai to omotte imasu.
   I'm planning to take some time off towards <u>the end of the month</u>.

2. その事件はまだ結末がつかないんですか。
   Sono jiken wa mada ketsumatsu ga tsukanai n desu ka.
   Has<u>n't</u> that incident been <u>settled</u> yet?

3. 錠剤をくだいて、粉末にしてもいいですか。
   Jōzai o kudaite, funmatsu ni shite mo ii desu ka.
   Is it OK if I crush the tablet into <u>powder</u> (before I take it)?

4. 首相は、よく考えた末に辞任することにした。
   Shushō wa, yoku kangaeta sue ni jinin suru koto ni shita.
   <u>After</u> careful consideration, the prime minister decided to resign.

Common Compounds and Phrases

月末	**getsumatsu**	the end of the month
結末	**ketsumatsu**	an end; a conclusion
年末	**nenmatsu**	year's end
粉末	**funmatsu**	powder; dust
始末	**shimatsu**	management; the outcome
粗末な	**somatsu na**	coarse; careless
末っ子	**suekko**	the youngest child

The second stroke is shorter than the first.

5　一 二 キ 才 末

末

---

320 未

ミ MI
***いま・だ ima(da)**

not yet; un-

The character 未 is a depiction of a smaller branch at the top of a tree, *not yet* fully grown, giving it the sense of *not yet*.

GR4　N3　AP

Example Sentences

1. 六歳未満の子供は無料です。
   Rokusai miman no kodomo wa muryō desu.
   It is free for children <u>under</u> six years of age.

2. 若者には、明るい未来が待っている。
   Wakamono ni wa, akarui mirai ga matte iru.
   A bright <u>future</u> awaits all young people.

3. 深海は本当に未知の世界ですね。
   Shinkai wa hontō ni michi no sekai desu ne.
   The deep sea really is an <u>unknown</u> world.

4. 「未成年」とは、何歳までですか。
   'Miseinen' to wa, nansai made desu ka.
   At what age does one cease to be '<u>a minor</u>'?

5. この件は前代未聞の不祥事だ。
   Kono ken wa zendai mimon no fushōji da.
   This matter is an <u>unprecedented</u> scandal.

Common Compounds and Phrases

未満	**miman**	less than
未定	**mitei**	unsettled; undecided
未知の	**michi no**	unknown; strange
未成年	**miseinen**	a minor; underage
未婚の	**mikon no**	unmarried; single
未完成の	**mikansei no**	incomplete; unfinished
前代未聞の	**zendai mimon no**	unprecedented; unparalleled

The second stroke is longer than the first. Don't confuse 未 with 末.

5　一 二 キ 才 未

未

321 由

reason

ユ YU　ユウ YŪ　*ユイ YUI
よし yoshi

The character 由 depicts a pot with a narrow neck. The idea of drops falling *from* the pot gives us the sense of *cause* and *reason*.

GR3　N3　AP

Example Sentences

1. 大阪経由の飛行機でヨーロッパへ行った。
   Ōsaka keiyu no hikōki de Yōroppa e itta.
   I flew to Europe via Osaka.

2. 彼女が来た理由ははっきりしない。
   Kanojo ga kita riyū wa hakkiri shinai.
   The reason she came is not clear.

3. その女優は自由奔放に生きた。
   Sono joyū wa jiyū honpō ni ikita.
   The actress lived as she liked.

4. ここは由緒ある町です。
   Koko wa yuisho aru machi desu.
   This town has a glorious history.

5. 何が起こるか知る由もない。
   Nani ga okoru ka shiru yoshi mo nai.
   There is no knowing what may happen.

Common Compounds and Phrases

経由	**keiyu**	by way of; via
理由	**riyū**	a reason; a cause
事由	**jiyū**	a reason; a cause
由来	**yurai**	origin; derivative; pedigree
目の不自由な人	**me no fujiyū na hito**	a visually-disabled person
由緒	**yuisho**	a history; an origin
自由奔放な	**jiyū honpō na**	fancy-free; free-spirited

The third stroke protrudes. Don't confuse 由 with 田.

5 ｜ 冂 冋 由 由

由

---

322 礼

courtesy; gratitude; rite

レイ REI　ライ RAI

The character 礼 combines *altar* ネ and *kneeling figure* ㇄, suggesting kneeling at the altar, an act of *propriety* or *rite*.

GR3　N3　AP

Example Sentences

1. お礼を言う間もなく、電話を切られた。
   Orei o iu ma mo naku, denwa o kirareta.
   I was cut off even before I had time to say thank you.

2. なんて失礼な人なんだろう。
   Nante shitsurei na hito nan darō.
   What a rude person!

3. 父は礼儀にやかましい人です。
   Chichi wa reigi ni yakamashii hito desu.
   Father is very particular about manners.

4. 謝礼の印に田中さんにワインを一本贈った。
   Sharei no shirushi ni Tanaka-san ni wain o ippon okutta.
   We gave Mr. Tanaka a bottle of wine as a token of our thanks.

5. 無礼な発言は、つつしんでください。
   Burei na hatsugen wa, tsutsushinde kudasai.
   Be careful about making impolite remarks.

Common Compounds and Phrases

失礼	**shitsurei**	rude; impolite
礼儀	**reigi**	courtesy; etiquette
謝礼	**sharei**	thanks; a fee
朝礼	**chōrei**	a morning meeting
無礼な	**burei na**	impolite; rude
礼拝	**reihai, raihai**	worship; a church service
礼状	**reijō**	a letter of thanks

The fifth stroke hooks upwards.

5 ` ラ ネ ネ 礼

礼

323 羽

ウ U
はね hane は ha

feather; wing; a counter
for birds, rabbits

GR2 N2

The character 羽 represents the long feathers of a bird's *wing*.

Example Sentences

1. 羽毛布団はとても保温性が高い。
   Umōfuton wa totemo ho'onsei ga takai.
   <u>Down-filled quilts</u> have a very high heat-retaining property.

2. あのあひるは羽をけがしている。
   Ano ahiru wa <u>hane</u> o kega shite iru.
   That duck has hurt its <u>wing</u>.

3. おじさんは赤い羽根を上着のえりに付けていた。
   Ojisan wa akai <u>hane</u> o uwagi no eri ni tsukete ita.
   The man was wearing a red <u>feather</u> on his jacket lapel.

4. 家でインコを二羽飼っています。
   Ie de inko o <u>niwa</u> katte imasu.
   We have <u>two</u> parakeets at home.

5. 子供達は羽目を外して夜中まで騒いでいた。
   Kodomotachi wa <u>hame o hazushite</u> yonaka made sawaide ita.
   The children <u>went wild</u> and were making a racket well into the night.

Common Compounds and Phrases

羽毛	**umō**	feathers; down
羽化	**uka**	to grow wings
羽根	**hane**	a shuttlecock; a fan
羽音	**haoto**	the sound of flapping wings
羽目を外す	**hame o hazusu**	to step over the line
羽田空港	**Haneda kūkō**	Haneda Airport
羽を伸ばす	**hane o nobasu**	to spread one's wings

The first and fourth strokes end with hooks.

6 フ フ ヲ 羽 羽 羽

羽

---

324 向

コウ KŌ
む・く mu(ku)
む・ける mu(keru)
む・かう mu(kau)
む・こう mu(kō)

to turn toward

GR3 N3 AP

The character 向 combines *house* 冂 and *air vent* 口, referring to air escaping from a house's air vent, a reference to *moving toward, facing*.

Example Sentences

1. 弟の成績は、最近向上してきている。
   Otōto no seiseki wa, saikin <u>kōjō</u> shite kite iru.
   My brother's school record has been <u>improving</u> lately.

2. 私の部屋は南向きで冬でも暖かい。
   Watashi no heya wa <u>minami-muki</u> de fuyu de mo atatakai.
   My room <u>faces south</u> and is warm even in winter.

3. その言葉は、彼に向けられたものだった。
   Sono kotoba wa, kare ni <u>mukerareta</u> mono datta.
   That remark <u>was directed</u> at him.

4. いとこは、アメリカへ向かって日本を出発した。
   Itoko wa, Amerika e <u>mukatte</u> Nihon o shuppatsu shita.
   My cousin left Japan <u>for</u> the United States.

5. 向こうに見えるのは東京タワーです。
   <u>Mukō</u> ni mieru no wa Tōkyō tawā desu.
   That is Tokyo Tower that you can see <u>over there</u>.

Common Compounds and Phrases

向上	**kōjō**	improvement; an upgrading
意向	**ikō**	an intention; an inclination
傾向	**keikō**	a tendency; a disposition
外向的な	**gaikōteki na**	extroverted; outgoing
対向車	**taikōsha**	an oncoming vehicle
子供向け	**kodomo-muke**	suitable for children
向かい風	**mukai-kaze**	a head wind

The third stroke ends with a hook.

6 ' 丨 冂 冋 向 向

向

EXERCISE 27 (313 – 324)

A. Give the readings for the following.

1. 羽 _____
2. 打つ _____
3. 向いていない _____
4. 付き合う _____
5. 平らな _____
6. 失う _____
7. 向き合う _____
8. 失礼な _____
9. 必死 _____
10. 末っ子 _____

B. Rewrite using kanji and kana.

1. でんきだい を はらう _____
2. はめ を はずす _____
3. うちあわせ の じかん _____
4. め の ふじゆうな かた _____
5. かならず いく _____
6. みち の ひと (a stranger) _____
7. しつげん を する _____

8. おれい を いう _____
9. きづかなかった _____
10. ねんまつ おおうりだし _____

C. Match the following kanji with their correct readings.

1. 週末　（　）　　a. みらい
2. 平気　（　）　　b. ひづけ
3. 向上　（　）　　c. うもう
4. 打者　（　）　　d. てのひら
5. 手の平（　）　　e. ちょうれい
6. 朝礼　（　）　　f. しゅうまつ
7. 日付　（　）　　g. こうじょう
8. 方向　（　）　　h. ほうこう
9. 未来　（　）　　i. だしゃ
10. 羽毛　（　）　　j. へいき

---

325 寺

ジ JI
てら tera

temple

The character 寺 combines *hand* 寸 and *foot* 土 and referred to a *place of work*, especially a governmental office. The character later took on the meaning of *temple*.
GR2 N3 AP

Example Sentences

1. 東大寺に日本で一番大きい大仏がある。
   Tōdaiji ni Nihon de ichiban ōkii daibutsu ga aru.
   The largest statue of the Buddha in Japan is in the Todaiji Temple.

2. 京都にはお寺がたくさんある。
   Kyōto ni wa otera ga takusan aru.
   There are many temples in Kyoto.

3. この山寺は紅葉の季節になると観光客で大変込み合う。
   Kono yamadera wa kōyō no kisetsu ni naru to kankōkyaku de taihen komiau.
   When the autumn foliage is at its best, this mountain temple is crowded with visitors.

4. 四国には寺を巡る「遍路」というものがある。
   Shikoku ni wa tera o meguru 'henro' to iu mono ga aru.
   There is a pilgrimage of the Buddhist temples in Shikoku, known as 'henro.'

Common Compounds and Phrases

寺院	**jiin**	a temple
東大寺	**Tōdaiji**	Todaiji Temple
薬師寺	**Yakushiji**	Yakushiji Temple
寺参り	**teramairi**	visiting a temple
寺町	**teramachi**	a town with a lot of temples
山寺	**yamadera**	a mountain temple
清水寺	**Kiyomizu-dera**	Kiyomizu Temple

The third stroke is the longest, and the fifth stroke ends with a hook.

6	一 十 土 圭 寺 寺				
寺					

326 次

next

ジ JI　シ SHI
つ・ぐ tsu(gu)　つぎ tsugi

The character 次 symbolized a person bent over, arranging things in order. The meanings of *order*, *one after the other* have derived from this.
GR3　N3　AP

Example Sentences

1. 教科書には目次がついていなかった。
   Kyōkasho ni wa <u>mokuji</u> ga tsuite inakatta.
   There was no <u>table of contents</u> in the textbook.

2. 生徒の相次ぐ不祥事に関係者は頭を抱えていた。
   Seito no <u>aitsugu</u> fushōji ni kankeisha wa atama o kakaete ita.
   <u>A succession of</u> scandals involving students was causing the people involved a good deal of worry.

3. 決定は君次第だ。
   Kettei wa <u>kimi shidai</u> da.
   It's <u>up to you</u> to decide.

4. あのテニス選手は、昨年に次いで優勝した。
   Ano tenisu senshu wa, sakunen <u>ni tsuide</u> yūshō shita.
   That tennis player has won the championship for a second year <u>in a row</u>.

5. 友人は次から次へと職を変えている。
   Yūjin wa <u>tsugi kara tsugi e to</u> shoku o kaete iru.
   A friend of mine changes jobs <u>one after the other</u>.

Common Compounds and Phrases

三次元	**sanjigen**	three dimensions
順次	**junji**	successively; gradually
二次会	**nijikai**	a second party
次第	**shidai**	order; circumstances; as soon as
相次ぐ	**aitsugu**	to come one after another
次の日	**tsugi no hi**	the next day
次々に	**tsugitsugi ni**	one after another

Don't write ⼎ as ⼑.

6 ⼃ ⼆ ⼅ ⼎ 次 次

次

327 式

style, ceremony

シキ SHIKI

The character 式 combines *measure* 工 and *stake* 弋, indicating a set *format* when doing something. The associated meanings are *style* and *ceremony*.
GR3　N3　AP

Example Sentences

1. 結婚式は、午後二時から行われる予定です。
   <u>Kekkonshiki</u> wa, gogo niji kara okonawareru yotei desu.
   The <u>wedding ceremony</u> is scheduled for 2 P.M.

2. H₂O は水の化学式です。
   H₂O wa mizu no <u>kagakushiki</u> desu.
   H_2O is the <u>formula</u> for water.

3. 卒業式で友達ばかりか先生も泣いていた。
   <u>Sotsugyōshiki</u> de tomodachi bakari ka sensei mo naite ita.
   At <u>the graduation ceremony</u>, not only were my friends crying, but my teacher, too.

4. 来月から、申込書の形式が変わります。
   Raigetsu kara, mōshikomisho no <u>keishiki</u> ga kawarimasu.
   <u>The format</u> of the application form will change next month.

5. 昨日、近所で葬式があった。
   Kinō kinjo de <u>sōshiki</u> ga atta.
   There was <u>a funeral</u> in the neighborhood yesterday.

Common Compounds and Phrases

結婚式	**kekkonshiki**	a wedding ceremony
化学式	**kagakushiki**	a chemical formula
和式	**washiki**	Japanese style
形式	**keishiki**	form; formality; a style
卒業式	**sotsugyōshiki**	a graduation ceremony
正式な	**seishiki na**	formal; official
葬式	**sōshiki**	a funeral ceremony

Don't forget the dot.

6 ⼀ ⼆ ⼅ ⼅ 式 式

式

328 州

シュウ SHŪ
す su

state

The character 州 originally depicted *sand* gradually building up *in a river* to form a small island. From this, the character has come to refer to large areas of land or *states*.
GR3 N2 AP

Example Sentences

1. 妹は、二年前州立大学を卒業した。
   Imōto wa, ninenmae shūritsu daigaku o sotsugyō shita.
   My younger sister graduated from a <u>state</u> university two years ago.

2. 本州は日本の中央部を成している。
   Honshū wa Nihon no chūōbu o nashite iru.
   <u>Honshu</u> constitutes the central part of Japan.

3. 今は、欧州各国が失業問題に直面している。
   Ima wa, ōshū kakkoku ga shitsugyō mondai ni chokumen shite iru.
   Presently, <u>all European nations</u> are facing the unemployment problem.

4. 先週は、九州へ出張していた。
   Senshū wa, Kyūshū e shutchō shite ita.
   I went to <u>Kyushu</u> on a business trip last week.

Common Compounds and Phrases

州立	**shūritsu**	state(-run)
本州	**Honshū**	Honshu (a place)
九州	**Kyūshū**	Kyushu (a place)
欧州	**Ōshū**	Europe(an)
カリフォルニア州	**Kariforunia-shū**	California (a place)
州議会	**shūgikai**	a state legislature
砂州	**sasu**	a sandbar; a sandbank

Be careful with the dots.

6 丶 丿 小 州 州 州

州

329 成

セイ SEI *ジョウ JŌ
な・る na(ru)
な・す na(su)

**to form;
to achieve**

The character 成 combines *halberd* 戈, suggesting a tool used to make things, and *hitting a nail* 丁. Thus, the character has come to mean *to bring together*, *to be just so* or *to form*.
GR4 N3 AP

Example Sentences

1. 今学期は数学の成績が上がった。
   Kongakki wa sūgaku no seiseki ga agatta.
   I received a better <u>grade</u> for mathematics this term.

2. 成長するにつれて、彼女はますます母親に似てきた。
   Seichō suru ni tsurete, kanojo wa masumasu hahaoya ni nite kita.
   As she <u>grew older</u>, she became more and more like her mother.

3. 彼は、何一つ成就できない。
   Kare wa, nani hitotsu jōju dekinai.
   He <u>can't succeed</u> at anything.

4. 父は私が医者になることに賛成しなかった。
   Chichi wa watashi ga isha ni naru koto ni sansei shinakatta.
   My father <u>did not agree</u> to my becoming a doctor.

5. バッファローは群れを成して移動している。
   Baffarō wa mure o nashite idō shite iru.
   The buffalo are moving <u>in herds</u>.

Common Compounds and Phrases

成績	**seiseki**	results; a record
作成	**sakusei**	preparing (a report)
賛成	**sansei**	approval; agreement
成果	**seika**	a result; a product
成分	**seibun**	an ingredient; a component
完成	**kansei**	completion; perfection
成就	**jōju**	accomplishment; achievement

The fifth stroke protrudes.

6 丿 厂 厂 成 成 成

成

330 全

whole

ゼン ZEN
まった・く matta(ku)

The character 全 is a combination of *cover* ヘ and *jewel* 王. From the idea of protecting a precious, perfect jewel, we have the association of *whole* or *complete*.

GR3 N3 AP

Example Sentences

1. その投手は完全試合を達成した。
   Sono tōshu wa kanzen jiai o tassei shita.
   The pitcher threw a <u>perfect game</u>.

2. 全部でいくらになりましたか。
   Zenbu de ikura ni narimashita ka.
   How much did it come to <u>altogether</u>?

3. 決勝戦で皆が全力をつくした。
   Kesshōsen de mina ga zenryoku o tsukushita.
   Everyone <u>gave it their best</u> in the deciding game.

4. 全くおっしゃる通りです。
   Mattaku ossharu tōri desu.
   You're <u>quite</u> right!

5. その二人は全然似ていない。
   Sono futari wa zenzen nite inai.
   The two of them are <u>not at all</u> similar.

Common Compounds and Phrases

全身	**zenshin**	the whole body
全部	**zenbu**	all; the whole; entirely
全力	**zenryoku**	all one's strength
全国	**zenkoku**	the whole country
全体	**zentai**	the whole (body)
完全な	**kanzen na**	perfect; complete; entire
全速力	**zensokuryoku**	full (maximum) speed

The sixth stroke is longer than those above it.

6 ノ 入 ム 仐 仐 全

全

---

331 竹

bamboo

チク CHIKU
たけ take

The character 竹 represents growing *bamboo*.

GR1 N2

Example Sentences

1. お祝いには松竹梅がつきものだ。
   Oiwai ni wa shō-chiku-bai ga tsukimono da.
   Pine, <u>bamboo</u> and plum are associated with celebrations.

2. スペインチームは、破竹の勢いで連勝した。
   Supein chiimu wa, hachiku no ikioi de renshō shita.
   The Spanish team won victory after victory, <u>gaining momentum as they went</u>.

3. 彼は竹を割ったようなさっぱりした性格だ。
   Kare wa take o watta yō na sappari shita seikaku da.
   He has a <u>candid</u>, straightforward personality.

4. 裏山で竹の子を掘ってきた。
   Urayama de take no ko o hotte kita.
   We've been digging for <u>bamboo shoots</u> on the hill out back.

5. 剣道の竹刀を片付けましょう。
   Kendō no shinai o katazukemashō.
   Let's put the *kendo* <u>bamboo swords</u> away.

Common Compounds and Phrases

松竹梅	**shō-chiku-bai**	pine, bamboo and plum (top, middle and bottom grade)
爆竹	**bakuchiku**	a firecracker
青竹	**aodake**	green bamboo
竹串	**take-gushi**	a bamboo skewer
竹薮	**take-yabu**	a bamboo thicket
竹の子	**take no ko**	a bamboo shoot
竹馬	**takeuma**	a pair of stilts

End the third stroke firmly, and the sixth one with a hook.

6 ノ ト ケ ゲ ゲ 竹

竹

332 虫

チュウ CHŪ
むし mushi

insect

The character 虫 originally depicted a cobra-like *snake* partially coiled up. In the past snakes and *insects* were grouped together.

GR1 N3

Example Sentences

1. 幼い頃から昆虫に興味があった。
   Osanai koro kara konchū ni kyōmi ga atta.
   I've been interested in insects since my childhood.

2. 今日はボスの虫の居所が悪い。
   Kyō wa bosu no mushi no idokoro ga warui.
   The boss got up on the wrong side of the bed today.

3. 泣き虫はきらいよ。
   Nakimushi wa kirai yo.
   I hate crybabies!

4. うちの本の虫は、一日中図書館にいる。
   Uchi no hon no mushi wa, ichinichi-jū toshokan ni iru.
   Our 'bookworm' spends all day in the library.

5. 虫歯が痛くて一睡も出来なかった。
   Mushiba ga itakute issui mo dekinakatta.
   I couldn't sleep a wink because a decayed tooth was aching.

Common Compounds and Phrases

昆虫	**konchū**	an insect
害虫	**gaichū**	a harmful insect; a pest
防虫剤	**bōchūzai**	insecticide
爬虫類	**hachūrui**	a reptile
泣き虫	**nakimushi**	a crybaby
虫眼鏡	**mushi-megane**	a magnifying glass
虫歯	**mushiba**	a decayed tooth

The fourth stroke does not protrude. End the sixth stroke firmly.

6 ｜ 丨 丁 口 中 虫 虫

虫

---

333 伝

デン DEN
つた・わる tsuta(waru)
つた・える tsuta(eru)
つた・う tsuta(u)

to transmit

The character 伝 originally combined *person* 亻 and *spinning weight* 専, to suggest *rotation*. The idea of *convey* or *transmit* has derived from this.

GR4 N3 AP

Example Sentences

1. 私は、あなたへ伝言を頼まれた。
   Watashi wa, anata e dengon o tanomareta.
   I was asked to give you a message.

2. あくびは伝染する。
   Akubi wa densen suru.
   Yawning is catching.

3. 仏教は、中国から日本に伝わった。
   Bukkyō wa, Chūgoku kara Nihon ni tsutawatta.
   Buddhism was introduced into Japan from China.

4. 皆様によろしくお伝え下さい。
   Mina-sama ni yoroshiku otsutae kudasai.
   Please give my best regards to your family.

5. 老人は手すりを伝ってよたよた歩いていた。
   Rōjin wa tesuri o tsutatte yota yota aruite ita.
   The old man was shuffling along, holding on to the handrail.

Common Compounds and Phrases

伝言	**dengon**	a (verbal) message
伝染	**densen**	infection; communication
伝記	**denki**	a life; a biography
自伝	**jiden**	an autobiography
遺伝	**iden**	heredity; inheritance
宣伝	**senden**	publicity; promotion
手伝う	**tetsudau**	to help; to assist

The fourth stroke is longer than the third.

6 ノ 亻 仁 仁 伝 伝

伝

334 当

トウ TŌ
あ・たる a(taru)
あ・てる a(teru)

appropriate; to hit; to guess at; to confront

The character 当 combines *rice field* 彐 (from 田) and *in proportion* ⼍, originally a depiction of a suitably placed house. From this came the meaning of *appropriate* and then *hit*.
GR2　N3

Example Sentences

1. この件の担当はどなたですか。
   Kono ken no tantō wa donata desu ka.
   Who is <u>in charge of</u> this matter?

2. 見当が外れた。
   Kentō ga hazureta.
   I <u>guessed</u> wrongly.

3. お金はパーティーの当日持ってきて下さい。
   Okane wa pātii no tōjitsu motte kite kudasai.
   Please bring the money on <u>the day</u> of the party.

4. ボールがバッターの頭に当たった。
   Bōru ga battā no atama ni atatta.
   The ball <u>hit</u> the batter in the head.

5. この植物はなるべく雨に当てないように。
   Kono shokubutsu wa narubeku <u>ame ni atenai yō ni.</u>
   Try to <u>keep</u> this plant <u>out of the rain</u> as much as possible.

Common Compounds and Phrases

担当	**tantō**	being in charge (of)
当日	**tōjitsu**	the (that) day
適当	**teki<u>tō</u>**	suitable; proper
弁当	**ben<u>tō</u>**	a packed lunch
相当な(の)	**sō<u>tō</u> na (no)**	considerable; sizable
当たり前の	**atari<u>mae</u> (no)**	proper; right; average
割り当て	**wari<u>ate</u>**	an allotment; a quota

Dont't write ⼍ as ⼞.

6　'　⼍　⼍　当　当　当

当

---

335 米

ベイ BEI　マイ MAI
こめ kome　*よね yone

rice; America

The character 米, depicts the tip of a *stalk of rice*.

GR2　N3　AP

Example Sentences

1. おみやげは米国製のビーフジャーキーだった。
   Omiyage wa <u>beikokusei</u> no biifujākii datta.
   It was a gift of <u>American-made</u> beef jerky.

2. 中南米の音楽が好きです。
   <u>Chūnanbei</u> no ongaku ga suki desu.
   I like <u>Latin American</u> music.

3. 日本の「マンガ」は今や欧米でも大変な人気だ。
   Nihon no 'manga' wa ima ya <u>ōbei</u> de mo taihen na ninki da.
   Japanese 'manga' are now very popular in <u>Europe and the United States</u>, too.

4. 新米のおまわりさんが交通整理をしている。
   Shinmai no omawarisan ga kōtsū seiri o shite iru.
   The police officer, <u>new at the job</u>, is doing traffic duty.

5. お米はといでから炊きます。
   Okome wa toide kara takimasu.
   You cook <u>rice</u> after washing it.

Common Compounds and Phrases

米国	**Beikoku**	the United States of America
南米	**Nanbei**	South America
欧米	**Ōbei**	Europe and the United States
白米	**haku<u>mai</u>**	polished (white) rice
玄米	**gen<u>mai</u>**	unmilled (brown) rice
新米	**shin<u>mai</u>**	new rice; a novice
米屋	**kome<u>ya</u>**	a rice dealer

The first two strokes slant in. Don't confuse 米 with 光 or 来.

6　'　'ヽ　ゞ　半　米　米

米

忙

ボウ BŌ
いそが・しい isoga(shii)
*せわ・しい sewa(shii)

busy;
occupied

The character 忙 combines *heart, feelings* 忄 and *die* 亡, originally meaning *being so flustered one could die*. From this the general meaning of *busy* has derived.
JK　N3　AP

Example Sentences

1. あの人は引越しの準備で多忙のようだ。
   Ano hito wa hikkoshi no junbi de <u>tabō</u> no yō da.
   He seems <u>to be busy</u> getting ready to move house.

2. 繁忙期は休みが取りにくい。
   <u>Hanbōki</u> wa yasumi ga torinikui.
   It's hard to take holidays in <u>the busy period</u>.

3. 今月中は試験勉強で忙しいだろう。
   Kongetsuchū wa shiken benkyō de <u>isogashii</u> darō.
   I'll be <u>busy</u> preparing for examinations all this month.

4. 忙しさのあまり、家賃を払うのを忘れた。
   <u>Isogashisa</u> no amari, yachin o harau no o wasureta.
   I was <u>so occupied</u> that I forgot to pay the rent.

5. 開店準備で大忙しだ。
   Kaiten junbi de <u>ōisogashi</u> da.
   I'm <u>rushed off my feet</u>, getting ready to open a new store.

Common Compounds and Phrases

多忙な	**tabō na**	busy; hectic
繁忙期	**hanbōki**	a busy period
忙殺される	**bōsatsu sareru**	to be swamped with work
大忙し	**ōisogashi**	very busy
忙しない	**sewashinai**	busy; restless
仕事で忙しい	**shigoto de isogashii**	to be busy with one's work
気忙しい	**kizewashii**	restless; fidgety

The sixth stroke is one continuous motion.

6 丶 丶 忄 忄 忙 忙

忙

EXERCISE 28 (325 – 336)

A. Give the readings for the following.

1. 伝える ＿＿＿＿＿＿＿＿＿＿
2. 米 ＿＿＿＿＿＿＿＿＿＿
3. 全く ＿＿＿＿＿＿＿＿＿＿
4. 当たり前の ＿＿＿＿＿＿＿＿＿＿
5. お寺 ＿＿＿＿＿＿＿＿＿＿
6. 竹 ＿＿＿＿＿＿＿＿＿＿
7. 九州 ＿＿＿＿＿＿＿＿＿＿
8. 成る ＿＿＿＿＿＿＿＿＿＿
9. 忙しい ＿＿＿＿＿＿＿＿＿＿
10. 次の ＿＿＿＿＿＿＿＿＿＿

B. Write the following using kanji and kana.

1. the day in question ＿＿＿＿＿＿＿＿
2. the whole country ＿＿＿＿＿＿＿＿
3. formal; official ＿＿＿＿＿＿＿＿
4. a (verbal) message ＿＿＿＿＿＿＿＿
5. the United States of America ＿＿＿＿＿＿
6. a table of contents ＿＿＿＿＿＿＿＿
7. a rice dealer ＿＿＿＿＿＿＿＿

8. to grow up; to be brought up ＿＿＿＿＿＿
9. to be busy with one's work ＿＿＿＿＿＿
10. a 'bookworm' ＿＿＿＿＿＿＿＿

C. Match up the following kanji with their correct readings.

1. たけのこ （ 　） a. 東大寺
2. かがくしき （ 　） b. 全力
3. さくせい （ 　） c. 州立大学
4. とうだいじ （ 　） d. 化学式
5. てつだう （ 　） e. 竹の子
6. ぜんりょく （ 　） f. 見当
7. なんべい （ 　） g. 寺院
8. じいん （ 　） h. 作成
9. けんとう （ 　） i. 南米
   (a direction; a guess)
10. しゅうりつ　だいがく （ 　） j. 手伝う

Review 9 (1 – 336)

A. Give the readings for the following.

1. 虫 _____
2. 丸める _____
3. 番号 _____
4. 東大寺 _____
5. 反映する _____
6. 工夫する _____
7. 未来 _____
8. 打つ _____
9. 伝わる _____
10. 本州 _____

B. Write in kanji and kana.

1. a telephone number _____
2. South America _____
3. formal; official _____
4. a caterpillar _____
5. a bookworm _____
6. a mountain temple _____
7. strengthening _____
8. the whole (body) _____
9. a life; a biography _____
10. Japanese archery _____

C. Add furigana to the kanji in the following.

1. 当日 _____
2. 多忙な _____
3. 安全な _____
4. 新米 _____
5. 二次会 _____
6. 自伝 _____
7. テキサス州 _____
8. 丸見え _____
9. 成長する _____
10. 一平米 _____

D. Match the following.

1. 化学式　（　）　a. きゅうしゅう
2. 竹刀　　（　）　b. もくじ
3. 本当　　（　）　c. ぜんいん
4. 九州　　（　）　d. せいぶん
5. 東大寺　（　）　e. でんごん
6. 全員　　（　）　f. かがくしき
7. 米国　　（　）　g. しない
8. 伝言　　（　）　h. ほんとう
9. 目次　　（　）　i. とうだいじ
10. 成分　　（　）　j. べいこく

E. Select an appropriate kanji to complete the following.

LIST: 成、次、夫、永、米、当、平、州、竹、戸、刀、忙、号、予、付、院、払、全、伝、失

1. _____国 (the whole country)
2. 手_____う (to help; to assist)
3. _____しい一日 (a busy day)
4. 雨_____ (a storm door; a shutter)
5. 寺_____ (a temple)
6. 青_____ (green bamboo)
7. 前_____い (payment in advance)
8. 作_____ (preparing a report)
9. 白_____ (polished white rice)
10. _____言 (a prophecy; a forecast)
11. 末_____く（すえながく）
12. _____日（へいじつ）
13. 見_____（けんとう）
14. _____礼（しつれい）
15. 三_____元（さんじげん）
16. 小_____（こがたな）
17. _____人（ふじん）
18. _____立（しゅうりつ）
19. 気_____く（きづく）
20. 記_____（きごう）

F. Rewrite the following, changing the kana in brackets into kanji. Then translate into English.

1. 「(にわ) の (とり) (two birds) がお (てら) の (たけばやし) に (す) み (つ) いているらしい。」「あそこには、えさになる(むし) が たくさんいるからだ。」
2. 「(つぎ) の (しゅうまつ)、(あ) いていますか。」「ごめんなさい。(せいじんしき) に (い)くことになっています。」
3. (きゅうしゅう) のお(てら) で (ふる)くから(つた)わる (ゆみや) と (かたな) を (み)ることが (でき)た。
4. 「(かなら)ずしも (たか)いお(こめ) が おいしいとはかぎりません。」「(ほんとう)ですね。(りょうり) の (しかた) によります。」
5. 「(へいき) でそんな(しつれい)なことを (い)うなんて (かんが)えられない。」「(まった)くだ。(りゆう) が (わ)からない。」
6. 「(いそが)しくて、(かがく) の (よしゅう) をする(じかん) が なかった。」「(きょう)、(かがくきごう) の (しょう)テストもあるよ。」
7. (みらい)に(む)けて、(あたら)しい (いけん) が (はんえい)されている。

337 両 リョウ RYŌ

both; pair

GR3 N3 AP

The character 両 has often been assumed to be a *set of scales*, suggesting equality. A *pair* of things, *both* being balanced is the association.

Example Sentences

1. あの子は両親を失った。
   Ano ko wa ryōshin o ushinatta.
   That child has lost his parents.

2. 少女は転んで両手をすりむいた。
   Shōjo wa koronde ryōte o surimuita.
   The little girl fell over and grazed both her hands.

3. 紙の両面に氏名を書くこと。
   Kami no ryōmen ni shimei o kaku koto.
   Write your full name on both sides of the paper.

4. それは両方とも私の物です。
   Sore wa ryōhō to mo watashi no mono desu.
   They both belong to me.

5. この一万円札を、千円札に両替できますか。
   Kono ichiman'en-satsu o, sen'en-satsu ni ryōgae dekimasu ka.
   Can you change this ten-thousand yen note into one-thousand yen notes for me?

Common Compounds and Phrases

両親	**ryōshin**	one's parents
両手	**ryōte**	both hands
両立	**ryōritsu**	coexistence; compatibility
両側	**ryōgawa**	either side; both sides
両替	**ryōgae**	exchange of money
両手に花	**ryōte ni hana**	to have a double advantage
賛否両論	**sanpi ryōron**	pros and cons

The third stroke ends with a hook.

6 一 丆 历 両 両 両

両

338 角 カク KAKU / かど kado / つの tsuno

angle; corner; horn

GR2 N3

The character 角 depicts a beast's *horns*.

Example Sentences

1. この紙は直角に切れていない。
   Kono kami wa chokkaku ni kirete inai.
   This paper hasn't been cut squarely.

2. 二人の選手は互角の力だ。
   Futari no senshu wa gokaku no chikara da.
   The two players are evenly-matched.

3. 窓のこの角度から、海が見えます。
   Mado no kono kakudo kara, umi ga miemasu.
   You can see the sea when you look from this window from this angle.

4. 最初の角を右に曲がって下さい。
   Saisho no kado o migi ni magatte kudasai.
   Turn right at the first corner.

5. このバックルは、水牛の角でできています。
   Kono bakkuru wa, suigyū no tsuno de dekite imasu.
   This buckle is made from water buffalo horn.

Common Compounds and Phrases

直角	**chokkaku**	a right angle
互角	**gokaku**	equal; even; level
三角の	**sankaku no**	triangular
方角	**hōgaku**	a direction
角度	**kakudo**	an angle
広角レンズ	**kōkaku renzu**	a wide-angle lens
四つ角	**yottsukado**	a crossroads

The third stroke tapers off, and the fourth stroke ends with a hook.

7 ′ ″ 冂 角 角 角 角

角

339 汽　キ KI

steam

The character 汽 combines *water* 氵 and *vapor* 气 to give the meaning of *steam*.

GR2　N1

Example Sentences

1. 今も観光用の汽車が走っているところがある。
   Ima mo kankōyō no kisha ga hashitte iru tokoro ga aru.
   Even now, <u>steam trains</u> are used for sightseeing.

2. 港のそばなので、汽笛が聞こえる。
   Minato no soba na node, kiteki ga kikoeru.
   Because it's near the harbor, you can hear the <u>ships'</u> <u>whistles</u>.

3. 叔父は四十年間汽船会社に勤めていた。
   Oji wa yonjū nenkan kisen gaisha ni tsutomete ita.
   My uncle worked for <u>a steamship company</u> for forty years.

4. 青森まで夜汽車に乗ることにした。
   Aomori made yogisha ni noru koto ni shita.
   I decided to take <u>the night train</u> to Aomori.

Common Compounds and Phrases

汽車	**kisha**	a steam train
汽笛	**kiteki**	a (steam) whistle
汽船	**kisen**	a steamship
夜汽車	**yogisha**	a night train
汽圧	**kiatsu**	steam pressure
汽缶室	**kikanshitsu**	a boiler room

Don't write 乁 as 乙 (おつ).

7　丶　冫　氵　氵　汽　汽　汽

汽

---

340 局　キョク KYOKU

bureau; segment

The original form of this character was a small square, surrounded by brackets 「 」, suggesting the idea of a house being divided into different rooms. The meanings of *office* and *section* derived from this.

GR3　N3

Example Sentences

1. 戦争は今や最終局面に入った。
   Sensō wa imaya saishū kyokumen ni haitta.
   The war now entered <u>a final phase</u>.

2. 結局、どうなりましたか。
   Kekkyoku dō narimashita ka.
   What happened <u>in the end</u>?

3. 郵便局から大きな小包を海外に送った。
   Yūbinkyoku kara ōki na kozutsumi o kaigai ni okutta.
   I sent a large parcel overseas from <u>the post office</u>.

4. 彼は元々放送局のアナウンサーだった。
   Kare wa motomoto hōsōkyoku no anaunsā datta.
   He was originally an announcer at <u>a broadcasting station</u>.

5. 今夜から局地的な大雨が降る恐れがある。
   Konya kara kyokuchiteki na ōame ga furu osore ga aru.
   There is a possibility of heavy <u>isolated</u> showers overnight.

Common Compounds and Phrases

局面	**kyokumen**	an aspect; a position
結局	**kekkyoku**	after all; finally
郵便局	**yūbinkyoku**	a post office
電話局	**denwakyoku**	a telephone exchange
放送局	**hōsōkyoku**	a broadcasting station
テレビ局	**terebi-kyoku**	a TV station
局地的	**kyokuchiteki**	localized; isolated

The fourth stroke ends with a hook.

7　コ　コ　尸　尸　吊　局　局

局

341 形

ケイ KEI　ギョウ GYŌ

かたち katachi　かた kata

form; shape

The character 形 depicts a window with a *grid pattern* 开 and *brushwork* 彡, suggesting *copying a pattern.*

GR2　N3　AP

Example Sentences

1. 紙を三角形に折った。
   Kami o <u>sankakukei</u> ni otta.
   I folded the paper into a <u>triangular shape</u>.

2. この辺は、地形が複雑です。
   Kono hen wa, <u>chikei</u> ga fukuzatsu desu.
   The <u>topography</u> of this area is complex.

3. この人形は母の形見です。
   Kono <u>ningyō</u> wa haha no <u>katami</u> desu.
   This <u>doll</u> is <u>a keepsake</u> from my mother.

4. 形のおもしろい石を集めている。
   <u>Katachi</u> no omoshiroi ishi o atsumete iru.
   I collect stones with interesting <u>shapes</u>.

5. 彼女からもらった手編みのセーターは形くずれしてきた。
   Kanojo kara moratta teami no sētā wa <u>katakuzure</u> shite kita.
   The hand-knitted sweater she gave me has started to <u>lose its shape</u>.

Common Compounds and Phrases

三角形	**sankakukei**	a triangle
	(sankakkei)	
整形	**seikei**	cosmetic surgery
地形	**chikei**	topography
形容詞	**keiyōshi**	an adjective
長方形	**chōhōkei**	a rectangle; rectangular
人形	**ningyō**	a doll; a puppet
形見	**katami**	a keepsake

The second stroke is longer than the first.

7　一 二 テ 开 开 形 形

形

342 決

ケツ KETSU

き・める ki(meru)

き・まる ki(maru)

to decide

The character 決 combines *water* 氵 and *to gouge* 夬 suggesting water breaking through a levee. From the idea of *breaking through*, we have the association of *deciding upon* a solution.

GR3　N3　AP

Example Sentences

1. 彼はもっと勉強しようと決心した。
   Kare wa motto benkyō shiyō to <u>kesshin shita</u>.
   He <u>made up his mind</u> to study harder.

2. 明日、会議があるかどうかはまだ決定していない。
   Ashita, kaigi ga aru ka dō ka wa mada <u>kettei shite inai</u>.
   It is <u>yet to be determined</u> whether there will be a meeting tomorrow or not.

3. 両国間の国境問題は、いつ解決するんだろう。
   Ryōkokukan no kokkyō mondai wa, itsu <u>kaiketsu suru n darō</u>.
   I wonder when the border issue between the two countries <u>will be settled</u>.

4. じゃんけんで順番を決めよう。
   Janken de junban o <u>kimeyō</u>.
   <u>Let's decide</u> the order by doing *janken* ('paper, scissors and stone').

5. 結婚式の日取りが4月28日に決まりました。
   Kekkonshiki no hidori ga shigatsu nijūhachi-nichi ni <u>kimarimashita</u>.
   The wedding <u>has been fixed</u> for April twenty-eighth.

Common Compounds and Phrases

決定	**kettei**	a decision; a conclusion
解決	**kaiketsu**	a solution; a resolution
決断	**ketsudan**	a clear-cut decision (determination)
決意	**ketsui**	a resolution; a determi-nation
決して... ない	**kesshite... nai**	never; not at all
決め手	**kimete**	a decisive fact
決まり 文句	**kimari monku**	a set phrase (expression)

The sixth stroke protrudes.

7　丶 冫 氵 汀 汀 決 決

決

343 谷

コク KOKU

たに tani　*や ya

valley; ravine; canyon

The character 谷 depicts *splitting* 八 and *opening* 口, a reference to a *valley*.

GR2　N2

Example Sentences

1. 気圧の谷が通過するので、天気が悪くなるでしょう。
   Kiatsu no tani ga tsūka suru node, tenki ga waruku naru deshō.
   A <u>trough</u> of low atmospheric pressure will pass through, so the weather will be unfavorable.

2. カヌーで谷川を下った。
   Kanū de tanigawa o kudatta.
   I went down a <u>mountain stream</u> in a canoe.

3. ビルの谷間に小さな公園がある。
   Biru no tanima ni chiisa na kōen ga aru.
   There's a little park <u>between</u> the buildings.

4. いつこの渓谷は国立公園になったんですか。
   Itsu kono keikoku wa kokuritsu kōen ni natta n desu ka.
   When was this <u>gorge</u> made into a national park?

5. 渋谷のハチ公前で待ち合わせましょう。
   Shibuya no Hachikō-mae de machiawasemashō.
   Let's meet in front of the *Hachikō* statue in <u>Shibuya</u>.

Common Compounds and Phrases

谷川	**tanigawa**	a mountain stream
谷間	**tanima**	a valley; a ravine; cleavage
谷底	**tanizoko**	a valley floor
小谷	**Kotani**	Kotani (a name)
渓谷	**keikoku**	a ravine; a gorge
峡谷	**kyōkoku**	a gorge; a canyon
*渋谷	**Shibuya**	Shibuya (a place)

The third and fourth strokes taper off.

7　ノ　ハ　グ　グ　グ　谷　谷

---

344 困

コン KON

こま・る koma(ru)

to be in trouble

The character 困 combines *tree* 木 and *confined area* 口, symbolizing *being restricted* or *in difficulty*.

GR6　N3　AP

Example Sentences

1. この先相当の困難が予想される。
   Kono saki sōtō no konnan ga yosō sareru.
   A significant amount of <u>hardship</u> is anticipated from now on.

2. その国は昔貧困だった。
   Sono kuni wa mukashi hinkon datta.
   That country was once <u>impoverished</u>.

3. どうしたらいいのか困惑してしまった。
   Dō shitara ii no ka konwaku shite shimatta.
   I <u>was puzzled</u> as to what to do.

4. 長い間水不足で困っている。
   Nagai aida mizu busoku de komatte iru.
   They <u>have been suffering</u> from a shortage of water for quite some time.

5. 彼はクビになって、生活に困っている。
   Kare wa kubi ni natte, seikatsu ni komatte iru.
   He was fired and <u>is finding it hard to make ends meet</u>.

Common Compounds and Phrases

困難	**konnan**	difficulty; hardship
貧困	**hinkon**	poverty; a shortage
困惑	**konwaku**	perplexity; confusion
困苦	**konku**	hardship; adversity
困り者	**komarimono**	a nuisance; a good-for-nothing
困り果てる	**komarihateru**	to be at one's wit's end
生活に困る	**seikatsu ni komaru**	to find it hard to make a living

The fourth stroke does not end with a hook. Don't confuse 困 with 因 (いん).

7　｜　冂　冂　冃　困　困　困

345 初

first

ショ SHO
はじ・め haji(me)
はじ・めて haji(mete)
はつ hatsu　うい ui
そ・める so(meru)

The character 初 is a combination of *clothing* ネ and *to cut* 刀. In order to make clothing one *first* has to cut the cloth. The meaning of *beginning* comes from this idea.

GR4　N3　AP

Example Sentences

1. まだ初心者だから、ゆっくり行きましょう。
   Mada <u>shoshinsha</u> da kara, yukkuri ikimashō.
   I'm still <u>a beginner</u>, so let's take it slowly.

2. そんなことは、初めから分かっていた。
   Sonna koto wa, <u>hajime kara</u> wakatte ita.
   I knew it <u>all along</u>.

3. 彼女に初めて会ったのはいつでしたか。
   Kanojo ni <u>hajimete</u> atta no wa itsu deshita ka.
   When did you <u>first</u> meet her?

4. 今の話はまったく初耳だ。
   Ima no hanashi wa mattaku <u>hatsumimi da</u>.
   What you've just told me is <u>the first I've heard of it</u>.

5. 昨晩、初雪が降りました。
   Sakuban, <u>hatsuyuki</u> ga furimashita.
   The <u>first snow of the season</u> fell last night.

Common Compounds and Phrases

初日	**shonichi**	the first (opening) day
初級	**shokyū**	a beginners' (introductory) class
初め	**hajime**	the start; the beginning
初めて	**hajimete**	(for the) first (time)
初雪	**hatsuyuki**	the first snow(fall) of the season
初産	**uizan**	one's first childbirth
初々しい	**uiuishii**	innocent; naïve; fresh

Don't forget the fifth stroke.

7 ｀ ゔ ネ ネ ネ 初 初

初

---

346 身

body; self

シン SHIN
み mi

The character 身 depicts the *body* of a pregnant woman.

GR3　N3　AP

Example Sentences

1. ご出身はどちらですか。
   <u>Goshusshin</u> wa dochira desu ka.
   Where <u>are you from</u>?

2. 母はダイエットに成功して、見事に変身した。
   Haha wa daietto ni seikō shite, migoto ni <u>henshin shita</u>.
   My mother <u>was a new person</u> after a successful diet.

3. 独身者向けのマンションは今販売中です。
   <u>Dokushinsha</u>-muke no manshon wa ima hanbaichū desu.
   Apartments for <u>single people</u> are selling at the moment.

4. 身に覚えのない事件だ。
   <u>Mi ni oboe no nai</u> jiken da.
   I <u>have no personal knowledge of</u> that incident.

5. 彼女はいつも同じネックレスを身に付けている。
   Kanojo wa itsumo onaji nekkuresu o <u>mi ni tsukete iru</u>.
   She always <u>wears</u> the same necklace.

Common Compounds and Phrases

変身	**henshin**	a transformation; a metamorphosis
独身	**dokushin**	celibacy; bachelorhood
身体検査	**shintai kensa**	a medical (examination); a body search
出身	**shusshin**	to come (hail) from
中身	**nakami**	content(s); substance
身分	**mibun**	one's position in society; circumstances
身に付ける	**mi ni tsukeru**	to wear; to carry; to learn

The seventh stroke protrudes.

7 ´ ｢ 竹 竹 身 身 身

身

196

347 対

タイ TAI ツイ TSUI

opposite;
to oppose

The original character for 対 combined *musical instrument* and *regulate*. From the idea of adjusting the instrument's *opposing* bells, we have the sense of *oppose* and, by association, *pair*.

GR3 N3 AP

Example Sentences

1. 直接対決で決着をつけた。
   Chokusetsu taiketsu de ketchaku o tsuketa.
   They settled the matter through a direct <u>confrontation</u>.

2. 被害を小さくするためには何らかの対策が必要だ。
   Higai o chiisaku suru tame ni wa nanraka no taisaku ga hitsuyō da.
   Some kind of <u>countermeasure</u> is necessary to lessen the damage.

3. 彼は強い言葉で反対した。
   Kare wa tsuyoi kotoba de hantai shita.
   He <u>objected</u> in strong language.

4. その秘密は誰にも絶対もらしてはいけない。
   Sono himitsu wa dare ni mo zettai morashite wa ikenai.
   You must <u>on no condition</u> divulge the secret to anybody.

5. このカップとソーサーは一対になっていない。
   Kono kappu to sōsā wa ittsui ni natte inai.
   This cup and saucer <u>don't match</u>.

Common Compounds and Phrases

対決	**taiketsu**	a confrontation; a showdown
対策	**taisaku**	a measure; a step
対象	**taishō**	an object; a subject; a target
一対一	**ittai ichi**	one on (to) one
反対語	**hantaigo**	an antonym; an opposite
絶対に	**zettai ni**	absolutely; totally; cannot possibly
一対	**ittsui**	a pair; a twosome

End the fourth stroke firmly.

7 ` ー ナ 文 文 対 対

対

---

348 麦

**バク BAKU
むぎ mugi**

wheat; barley;
rye; oats

The character 麦 combines *stalk of wheat* 丰 and *foot* 夂, in reference to people carrying *wheat* from distant places.

GR2 N2

Example Sentences

1. このビールは麦芽百パーセントだ。
   Kono biiru wa bakuga hyaku- pāsento da.
   This is one hundred percent <u>malt</u> beer.

2. 小麦粉と卵、牛乳でケーキを焼いた。
   Komugiko to tamago, gyūnyū de kēki o yaita.
   I baked a cake using <u>flour</u>, eggs and milk.

3. 夏は麦茶がおいしい。
   Natsu wa mugicha ga oishii.
   <u>Barley tea</u> is delicious in summer.

4. あの麦わら帽子をかぶった人が祖父だ。
   Ano mugiwara bōshi o kabutta hito ga sofu da.
   That man wearing the <u>straw hat</u> is my grandfather.

5. 「ライ麦畑でつかまえて」を読んだ。
   'Raimugi-batake de tsukamaete' o yonda.
   I read *The Catcher in the Rye*.

Common Compounds and Phrases

麦芽	**bakuga**	malt
冷や麦	**hiyamugi**	iced wheat noodles
大麦	**ōmugi**	barley
小麦	**komugi**	wheat
麦茶	**mugicha**	barley water (tea)
麦わら	**mugiwara**	wheat (barley) straw
麦畑	**mugi-batake**	a wheat field

The bottom part is not 又 (また).

7 ー 十 キ 主 丰 麦 麦

麦

EXERCISE 29 (337 – 348)

A. Give the readings for the following.

1. 形 _____
2. 谷川 _____
3. 汽車 _____
4. 電話局 _____
5. 初めて _____
6. 四つ角 _____
7. 決めていない _____
8. 困る _____
9. 反対語 _____
10. 中身 _____

B. Rewrite using kanji and kana.

1. しょしんしゃ (a beginner; a novice)
2. しんちょう を はかる (to measure someone's height)
3. さんかく の (triangular)
4. たにま (a valley; a ravine; cleavage)
5. けっしん する (to decide; to resolve)
6. こむぎ (wheat)

7. りょうしん (one's parents)
8. ずけい (a diagram; a figure)
9. こまりもの (a nuisance; a good-for-nothing)
10. にんぎょう (a doll; a puppet)

C. Write the following in English.

1. 九州の出身である _____
2. 両手を使う _____
3. 決して言っていない _____
4. 両方好きである _____
5. 初耳です。 _____
6. 直角に切る _____
7. 一対一で話し合う _____
8. テレビ局 _____
9. 角で待つ _____
10. 麦茶を飲む _____

---

349 忘

to forget

ボウ BŌ
わす・れる wasu(reru)

The character 忘 combines heart 心 and *to die* 亡, suggesting something which is no longer present in the heart; hence, a *forgotten* thing.

GR6 N3 AP

Example Sentences

1. 近所の居酒屋はこの時期忘年会でにぎわっている。
   Kinjo no izakaya wa kono jiki bōnenkai de nigiwatte iru.
   The local bar is busy at this time with <u>year-end parties</u>.

2. 祖母は物忘れがひどくなった。
   Sobo wa monowasure ga hidoku natta.
   My grandmother has become awfully <u>forgetful</u>.

3. 初心忘るべからず。
   Shoshin wasuru bekarazu.
   Remember your <u>first resolution</u>. (a saying)

4. 梅雨に入ると傘の忘れ物が増える。
   Tsuyu ni hairu to kasa no wasuremono ga fueru.
   The number of people who <u>leave</u> their umbrellas <u>behind</u> increases in the rainy season.

5. 知ってるのに度忘れしてしまった。
   Shitte iru no ni dowasure shite shimatta.
   I know it but I <u>just can't remember</u>.

Common Compounds and Phrases

忘年会	**bōnenkai**	a year-end party (gathering)
健忘症	**kenbōshō**	forgetfulness; amnesia
物忘れ	**monowasure**	forgetfulness
忘れ物	**wasuremono**	a lost article; lost property
度忘れ	**dowasure**	a lapse of memory
忘れっぽい	**wasureppoi**	forgetful
忘れん坊	**wasurenbō**	a forgetful person

The third stroke is one fluid motion.

7 | ` 一 亡 亡 亡 忘 忘

忘

350 利

リ RI
き・く ki(ku)

advantage;
profit

The character 利 depicts a *rice plant* 禾 and *sword* or *to cut* 刂. The idea of reaping the harvest has the association of *profit* or *gain*.

GR4　N3　AP

Example Sentences

1. 出来るだけ時間を有効に利用しなくてはならない。
   Dekiru dake jikan o yūkō ni riyō shinakute wa naranai.
   We <u>must make the most of the time we have</u>.

2. 郵便貯金の利子はいくらですか。
   Yūbin chokin no <u>rishi</u> wa ikura desu ka.
   What is the rate of <u>interest</u> for postal savings?

3. 日本は何歳から投票する権利がありますか。
   Nihon wa nansai kara tōhyō suru <u>kenri</u> ga arimasu ka.
   From what age do Japanese have the <u>right</u> to vote?

4. お医者さんからもらった薬はよく利いた。
   Oisha-san kara moratta kusuri wa <u>yoku kiita</u>.
   The medication I received from the doctor <u>worked wonders</u>.

5. 左利きの人は、器用なんですか。
   <u>Hidari-kiki no hito</u> wa, kiyō nan desu ka.
   Is it true that <u>left-handed people</u> are good with their hands?

Common Compounds and Phrases

利子	**rishi**	(an) interest (rate)
権利	**kenri**	a right; a privilege; power
利益	**rieki**	profit; benefit
不利	**furi**	a disadvantage; a handicap
利口な	**rikō na**	clever; wise; smart
利点	**riten**	an advantage
腕利き	**udekiki**	a person of ability; a skillful person

The seventh stroke ends with a hook.

7　丿 二 千 チ 禾 利 利

利

351 里

リ RI
さと sato

village;
countryside

The character 里 combines *field* 田 and *earth* 土, indicating an area of land where people lived, i.e., a *village*.

GR2　N1

Example Sentences

1. 郷里の素朴な料理が懐かしい。
   Kyōri no soboku na ryōri ga natsukashii.
   I miss the simple cooking of <u>my hometown</u>.

2. 万里の長城を見てみたい。
   <u>Banri</u> no chōjō o mite mitai.
   I'd like to see <u>the Great Wall of China</u>.

3. 食べ物を求めて、熊が里に下りてきた。
   Tabemono o motomete, kuma ga <u>sato</u> ni orite kita.
   The bears came down into the <u>village</u>, looking for food.

4. 私は孤児の里親になった。
   Watashi wa koji no <u>sato-oya</u> ni natta.
   I became <u>a foster-parent</u> to an orphan.

5. 駅は里帰りの人々で混雑していた。
   Eki wa <u>sato-gaeri</u> no hitobito de konzatsu shite ita.
   The station was crowded with people <u>coming home for a visit</u>.

Common Compounds and Phrases

郷里	**kyōri**	one's birthplace
海里	**kairi**	a nautical mile
里帰り	**sato-gaeri**	a visit to one's (parents') home
里心	**satogokoro**	homesickness; nostalgia
里親	**sato-oya**	a foster parent
里子	**satogo**	a foster child
村里	**murazato**	villages

The seventh stroke is longer than the sixth.

7　丨 口 曰 日 甲 里 里

里

352 冷

レイ REI
つめ・たい tsume(tai)　ひ・える hi(eru)
ひ・や hi(ya)　ひ・やす hi(yasu)
ひ・やかす hi(yakasu)　さ・める sa(meru)　さ・ます sa(masu)

cold; cool; to cool (down)

The character 冷 combines *ice* 冫 and *to rule* 令 to express the sense of *to tremble* and also *to prevail*. From this, the meanings of *ice-cold* and *to freeze* have derived.
GR4 N3 AP

Example Sentences

1. この部屋には冷房が付いていない。
   Kono heya ni wa reibō ga tsuite inai.
   This room does not have air-conditioning.

2. 近頃、彼女の態度が冷たくなった。
   Chikagoro, kanojo no taido ga tsumetaku natta.
   Her attitude towards me has cooled recently.

3. 海からあがって、体がすっかり冷えてしまった。
   Umi kara agatte, karada ga sukkari hiete shimatta.
   I came up out of the water, chilled to the bone.

4. 冷やかさないで下さい。
   Hiyakasanai de kudasai.
   Don't make fun of me!

5. 食事が冷めないうちに食べましょう。
   Shokuji ga samenai uchi ni tabemashō.
   Let's eat our food before it gets cold.

Common Compounds and Phrases

冷房	**reibō**	air-conditioning
冷水	**reisui**	cold water
冷静な	**reisei na**	calm; cool
冷蔵庫	**reizōko**	a refrigerator
寒冷前線	**kanrei zensen**	a cold front
お冷	**ohiya**	a glass of cold water
冷や汗	**hiyaase**	a cold sweat

Don't write 冫 as 八.

7 `丶 冫 冫 冸 冸 冷 冷`

冷

---

353 育

イク IKU
そだ・つ soda(tsu)
そだ・てる soda(teru)

to breed; to raise

The character 育 combines an *inverted child* 𠫓 and *flesh* 月, suggesting the *flesh of a newborn child*. From this, we have the sense of *to raise* children.
GR3 N3 AP

Example Sentences

1. 彼女は来月まで育児休暇中です。
   Kanojo wa raigetsu made ikuji kyūka-chū desu.
   She is on childcare leave until the end of next month.

2. 子供の教育にずいぶんお金をかけた。
   Kodomo no kyōiku ni zuibun okane o kaketa.
   We spent a great deal of money on our children's education.

3. 体育着に着替えて、グラウンドに集合した。
   Taiikugi ni kigaete, guraundo ni shūgō shita.
   After changing into our gym uniforms, we assembled on the sports' field.

4. 大阪で生まれたけれども、東京で育った。
   Ōsaka de umareta keredomo, Tōkyō de sodatta.
   I was born in Osaka but raised in Tokyo.

5. 彼は医者になるように育てられた。
   Kare wa isha ni naru yō ni sodaterareta.
   He was brought up to be a doctor.

Common Compounds and Phrases

育児	**ikuji**	childcare
教育	**kyōiku**	education; culture
義務教育	**gimu kyōiku**	compulsory education
体育	**taiiku**	physical education
保育園	**hoikuen**	a day-care center; a preschool
都会（田舎）育ち	**tokai (inaka)-sodachi**	raised in the city (country)
育て方	**sodatekata**	a child-rearing method

End the fifth stroke firmly.

8 `丶 亠 ㄊ 充 充 育 育 育`

育

354 泳

to swim

エイ EI
およ・ぐ oyo(gu)

The character 泳 is a combination of water 氵 and long 永, suggesting *flowing water*. The meanings of *float in the current* and later, *swim* derived from this.

GR3 N2 AP

Example Sentences

1. 小学生達は一キロの遠泳に挑戦した。
   Shōgakusei-tachi wa ichikiro no en'ei ni chōsen shita.
   The elementary school students attempted a one kilometer <u>swim</u>.

2. 僕は水泳があまり上手ではない。
   Boku wa suiei ga amari jōzu de wa nai.
   I'm not a very good <u>swimmer</u>.

3. あそこまで泳いでいけますか。
   Asoko made oyoide ikemasu ka.
   Can you <u>swim</u> out to there?

4. 一泳ぎしてこようかな。
   Hito-oyogi shite koyō ka na.
   I think I'll go for <u>a bit of a swim</u>.

5. どのくらい立ち泳ぎが出来ると思いますか。
   Dono kurai tachi-oyogi ga dekiru to omoimasu ka.
   How long do you think you can <u>tread water</u> for?

Common Compounds and Phrases

遠泳	**en'ei**	a long-distance swim
遊泳	**yūei**	swimming; bathing
競泳	**kyōei**	a swimming competition
水泳教室	**suiei kyōshitsu**	a swimming class
水泳大会	**suiei taikai**	a swimming meet
立ち泳ぎ	**tachi-oyogi**	treading water
背泳ぎ	**se-oyogi**	the backstroke

Leave a space between the fifth and sixth strokes.

8 ゛ ゛ 氵 氵 沪 沬 泳 泳

泳

355 岩

rock

ガン GAN
いわ iwa

The character 岩 combines *mountain* 山 and *stone* 石 to suggest large *rocks*.

GR2 N2

Example Sentences

1. 火山から、溶岩が流れ出した。
   Kazan kara, yōgan ga nagaredashita.
   <u>Lava</u> began to flow from the volcano.

2. 地滑りで家が岩や土で押しつぶされた。
   Jisuberi de ie ga iwa ya tsuchi de oshi-tsubusareta.
   The house was crushed by the landslide of <u>rock and soil</u>.

3. 登山家は岩がごろごろした斜面を下りてきた。
   Tozanka wa iwa ga goro goro shita shamen o orite kita.
   The climber came down the <u>rock-strewn</u> slope.

4. その山はごつごつした岩山で木がほとんどない。
   Sono yama wa gotsu gotsu shita iwayama de ki ga hotondo nai.
   That <u>mountain is rugged</u> and has hardly any trees on it.

5. あの力士は岩手県出身です。
   Ano rikishi wa Iwate-ken shusshin desu.
   That sumo wrestler is from <u>Iwate Prefecture</u>.

Common Compounds and Phrases

溶岩	**yōgan**	lava
岩石	**ganseki**	rock
削岩機	**sakuganki**	a jackhammer
花崗岩	**kakōgan**	granite
岩山	**iwayama**	a rocky mountain
岩場	**iwaba**	a rocky tract; a wall
岩手県	**Iwate-ken**	Iwate Prefecture (a place)

The fifth stroke does not protrude.

8 ' 屮 屮 屵 屵 岩 岩 岩

岩

356 泣

キュウ KYŪ

な・く na(ku)

to cry

The character 泣 depicts *water* 氵 and *stand* 立, referring to *falling tears* and, by association, *to weep, cry*.

GR4 N3 AP

Example Sentences

1. こんなドラマで号泣するとは思わなかった。
   Konna dorama de gōkyū suru to wa omowanakatta.
   I hadn't expected the TV drama to make me blubber so.

2. 借金が返せなくて、親に泣きついた。
   Shakkin ga kaesenakute, oya ni nakitsuita.
   He was not able to pay off his debts and threw himself on his parents' mercy.

3. 小さい女の子がしくしくと泣いていた。
   Chiisai onna no ko ga shikushiku to naite ita.
   The little girl sobbed to herself.

4. あんな泣き上戸は始めて見た。
   Anna naki-jōgo wa hajimete mita.
   This is the first time I've ever come across a drinker who becomes so maudlin.

5. どこかで子供の泣き声がする。
   Doko ka de kodomo no nakigoe ga suru.
   I can hear a child crying somewhere.

Common Compounds and Phrases

号泣	**gōkyū**	wailing
泣きつく	**nakitsuku**	to beg; to plead for
泣き上戸	**naki-jōgo**	a maudlin drunk
泣き声	**nakigoe**	a tearful voice; a cry
大泣き	**ōnaki**	loud crying
うそ鳴き	**usonaki**	to pretend to cry
泣き出す	**nakidasu**	to burst into tears

The eighth stroke is longer than those above.

8 丶 丶 氵 氵 汀 汁 泣 泣

泣

357 治

ジ JI　チ CHI

おさ・める osa(meru)
おさ・まる osa(maru)
なお・る nao(ru)
なお・す nao(su)

**to govern;
to cure**

The character 治 combines *water* 氵 and *platform* or *self* 台, suggesting *providing water for oneself*. From this, we have the associations of *control* or *to govern, rule*.

GR4 N3 AP

Example Sentences

1. 現在、最も必要なのは強力な政治である。
   Genzai, mottomo hitsuyō na no wa kyōryoku na seiji de aru.
   What is needed most at present is a strong government.

2. ガンには確かな治療法がない。
   Gan ni wa tashika na chiryōhō ga nai.
   There is no certain cure for cancer.

3. 頭痛がやっと治まった。
   Zutsū ga yatto osamatta.
   My headache has finally gone.

4. 病気はすっかり治った。
   Byōki wa sukkari naotta.
   I've made a complete recovery.

5. この病気は現代の医学では治せない。
   Kono byōki wa gendai no igaku de wa naosenai.
   Modern medicine cannot cure this disease.

Common Compounds and Phrases

政治	**seiji**	politics; government
政治家	**seijika**	a statesman; a politician
主治医	**shujii**	a doctor in charge; someone's usual doctor
治療	**chiryō**	treatment; medical care
治安	**chian**	law and order; public safety
自治	**jichi**	self-government
統治	**tōchi**	rule; government

The fourth stroke is written with one fluid motion.

8 丶 丶 氵 汁 治 治 治 治

治

358 実

ジツ JITSU
み mi みの・る mino(ru)

**real; fruit;
to bear fruit**

The original form of the character 実 combined *house, field full of crops* and *money*, suggesting a *house made wealthy through bumper crops*. From this, the meanings of *crop, substance* and *bear fruit* have derived.
GR3 N3 AP

Example Sentences

1. 実はヨーロッパに行ったことがないのです。
   Jitsu wa Yōroppa ni itta koto ga nai no desu.
   To tell the truth, I've never been to Europe.

2. 優勝した実感がまだない。
   Yūshō shita jikkan ga mada nai.
   I still can't believe we've won.

3. 実物を見てから、判断してください。
   Jitsubutsu o mite kara, handan shite kudasai.
   Save your judgment until you've seen the real thing.

4. あのりんごの木には実がたくさんなっている。
   Ano ringo no ki ni wa mi ga takusan natte iru.
   There are lots of fruit on that apple tree.

5. 彼の長年の努力がついに実った。
   Kare no naganen no doryoku ga tsui ni minotta.
   His long years of effort were at last rewarded with success.

Common Compounds and Phrases

実に	jitsu ni	truly; really; indeed
実感	jikkan	a real feeling, sensation
実物	jitsubutsu	the real thing; the original
実行	jikkō	practice; action; execution
現実	genjitsu	reality; a fact of life
実家	jikka	one's parents' home, house
ヤシの実	yashi no mi	a coconut

The sixth stroke is longer than those above it.

8 ｀ 丶 ⼧ ⼧ ⼧ 宔 実 実

実

---

359 若

ジャク JAKU　ニャク NYAKU
わか・い waka(i)
も・しくは mo(shiku wa)

young

Formerly, the character 若 was a pictograph of a *young* girl brushing her hair, combined with *mouth*. The present meaning of *lithesome* and *young* has derived from this.
GR5 N3 AP

Example Sentences

1. バーゲン品なので若干傷があります。
   Bāgen-hin na node jakkan kizu ga arimasu.
   Being a sale item, there are a few scratches.

2. この番組は若年層に人気がある。
   Kono bangumi wa jakunensō ni ninki ga aru.
   This program is popular with young people.

3. 若い時は二度と来ない。
   Wakai toki wa nido to konai.
   You are only young once.

4. 数字の若い方が先だ。
   Sūji no wakai hō ga saki da.
   The lower numbers come first.

5. 22日、若しくは25日にいらっしゃってください 。
   Nijūni-nichi, moshiku wa nijūgo-nichi ni irasshatte kudasai.
   Please come on either the 22nd or the 25th of the month.

Common Compounds and Phrases

若干	jakkan	a number of; a few; some
若年	jakunen	youth; an early age
老若男女	rōnyaku nannyo	men and women of all ages
若者	wakamono	a young man / woman; the young
若手	wakate	a young man, woman, clerk
若葉	wakaba	new leaves; young foliage
若々しい	wakawakashii	youthful; fresh

The fifth stroke is longer than the one above it.

8 一 十 艹 艻 芋 若 若 若

若

203

取

シュ SHU
と・る to(ru)

to take; to get;
to remove

The character 取 combines *ear* 耳 and *to take hold of* 又, possibly a reference to the way animals were taken by the ear to control them. Hence, the meanings of *to take* and *to control*.

GR3 N3 AP

Example Sentences

1. 彼は運転免許を二十歳で取得した。
   Kare wa unten menkyo o hatachi de <u>shutoku shita</u>.
   He <u>got</u> his driver's license at the age of twenty.

2. 新聞記者はその事故現場を取材している。
   Shinbun kisha wa sono jiko <u>genba o shuzai shite iru</u>.
   The journalist <u>is reporting from</u> the accident scene.

3. そのナイフを取って下さい。
   Sono naifu o <u>totte kudasai</u>.
   <u>Will you hand me</u> that knife, <u>please</u>?

4. 年を取るにつれて、だんだん物忘れをする。
   Toshi o toru ni tsurete, dan dan monowasure o suru.
   I'm getting more and more forgetful as I <u>grow older</u>.

5. ワイシャツのボタンが取れた。
   Waishatsu no botan ga <u>toreta</u>.
   A button <u>came off</u> my shirt.

Common Compounds and Phrases

取得	**shutoku**	acquisition; purchase
取材	**shuzai**	data collection; doing research
年を取る	**toshi o toru**	to grow older; to age
連絡を取る	**renraku o toru**	to get into contact with
書き取り	**kakitori**	transcribing spoken material
取り消し	**torikeshi**	cancellation; withdrawal
取り除く	**torinozoku**	to remove; to take away

The fifth stroke does not protrude on the right.

8 一 丁 F F 耳 耳 取 取

取

EXERCISE 30 (349 – 360)

A. Give the readings for the following.

1. 実家 _____
2. 利子 _____
3. 岩石 _____
4. 泣き出す _____
5. 里帰り _____
6. 治安 _____
7. 冷たい _____
8. 水泳 _____
9. 忘年会 _____
10. 教育 _____

B. Match the following.

1. 体育 　(　) 　　a. a foster parent
2. 忘れ物 (　) 　　b. the young
3. 主治医 (　) 　　c. the truth
4. 左利き (　) 　　d. cold water
5. 若者 　(　) 　　e. lost property
6. 里親 　(　) 　　f. treading water
7. 真実 　(　) 　　g. left-handed
8. 書き取り (　) 　　h. physical education

9. 立ち泳ぎ (　) 　　i. transcription
10. 冷水 　　(　) 　　j. somebody's usual doctor

C. Write in kanji and kana.

1. じゆう に とる

   _____

2. あたま を ひやす

   _____

3. およぐ の に よい ところ

   _____

4. にさんにち で なおる

   _____

5. ひと の なまえ を わすれる

   _____

6. わかい しゃちょう

   _____

7. あきじかん を りよう する

   _____

8. まだ、みのって いない

   _____

361 受 to receive

ジュ JU
う・ける u(keru)
う・かる u(karu)

The character 受 combines *a hand reaching down* ⺶ and *a hand reaching up* 又, with an *object* in between 冖, being *received*.

GR3 N3 AP

Example Sentences

1. 大学の受験生の数が年々減ってきている。
   Daigaku no jukensei no kazu ga nennen hette kite iru.
   The numbers of <u>examination candidates</u> for college are dropping year on year.

2. あなたからメールを受信していないと思います。
   Anata kara mēru o jushin shite inai to omoimasu.
   I don't believe <u>I've had</u> an e-mail message from you.

3. 十時から英語の試験を受けなければならない。
   Jūji kara eigo no shiken o ukenakereba naranai.
   I <u>have to do</u> an English test at ten o'clock.

4. 大学の入学試験に受かったかどうかは明日分かる。
   Daigaku no nyūgaku shiken ni ukatta ka dō ka wa ashita wakaru.
   I'll know tomorrow whether <u>I've passed</u> the entrance examination for the university.

5. 今年度のアカデミー賞の受賞者が発表された。
   Konnendo no Akademii-shō no jushōsha ga happyō sareta.
   The names of this year's Academy Awards' <u>recipients</u> have been announced.

Common Compounds and Phrases

受験生	**jukensei**	a student preparing for an entrance examination
受信する	**jushin suru**	to receive a message (e-mail)
受話器	**juwaki**	a telephone receiver; headphones
受賞	**jushō**	receiving a prize (reward)
感受性	**kanjusei**	sensitivity; sensibility
受け身	**ukemi**	passiveness; passive
受け取り	**uketori**	receipt; a receipt, voucher

Don't join the seventh and eighth strokes.

8 ⺶ ⺶ ⺶ ⺶ 严 受

---

362 制 system; to control

セイ SEI

The character 制 is a combination of *tree with many branches* 朱 and *to cut* 刂, indicating the *pruning of a tree*. From this, the sense of *put in order* or *control* has derived.

GR5 N2 AP

Example Sentences

1. 九月から、新しい制度に変わります。
   Kugatsu kara, atarashii seido ni kawarimasu.
   We will be changing to a new <u>system</u> from September.

2. 時間制限があるからゆっくり見物出来ない。
   Jikan seigen ga aru kara yukkuri kenbutsu dekinai.
   I can't go sightseeing leisurely as my time is <u>limited</u>.

3. ご出席は強制ではありません。
   Goshusseki wa kyōsei de wa arimasen.
   Attendance is not <u>obligatory</u>.

4. 制服姿の警察が家の前に現れた。
   Seifuku sugata no keisatsu ga ie no mae ni arawareta.
   A <u>uniformed</u> police officer turned up in front of my house.

5. 空港では植物の持ち込みが厳しく規制されている。
   Kūkō de wa shokubutsu no mochikomi ga kibishiku kisei sarete iru.
   The importation of plant materials is strictly <u>controlled</u> at the airport.

Common Compounds and Phrases

制度	**seido**	a system; an organization
制限	**seigen**	a restriction; a limit
強制的な	**kyōseiteki na**	compulsory; mandatory
制服姿で	**seifuku sugata de**	uniformed
規制	**kisei**	regulation; control
体制	**taisei**	structure; a (the) system
無制限に	**museigen ni**	without any restriction; freely

The fifth and eighth strokes end with hooks.

8 ノ 二 二 午 与 制 制 制

363 昔

セキ SEKI　*シャク SHAKU
むかし mukashi

former /
ancient times

The character 昔 is thought to combine *sun* 日 and *piling up* 龸, suggesting the *passing of days*. This gives us the meanings of *history* or *the past*.
GR3　N3　AP

Example Sentences

1. その町には昔年の面影は残っていない。
   Sono machi ni wa sekinen no omokage wa nokotte inai.
   The look of the town has changed completely from the old days.

2. とっくの昔に彼とは別れたわ。
   Tokku no mukashi ni kare to wa wakareta wa.
   I broke up with my boyfriend ages ago.

3. 子供の頃、母がよく昔話を読んでくれた。
   Kodomo no koro, haha ga yoku mukashi-banashi o yonde kureta.
   My mother often read fairy tales to me when I was a child.

4. 昔々、ある所に、おじいさんとおばあさんが住んでいました。
   Mukashimukashi, aru tokoro ni, ojiisan to obāsan ga sunde imashita.
   Long, long ago, in a certain place, there lived an old man and woman.

5. この前、昔なじみと偶然に出会った。
   Kono mae, mukashi-najimi to gūzen ni deatta.
   I bumped into an old acquaintance the other day.

Common Compounds and Phrases

昔年	**sekinen**	old times; long ago
昔日	**sekijitsu**	former times
今昔	**konjaku**	past and present
昔々	**mukashi-mukashi**	long, long ago
昔なじみ	**mukashi-najimi**	an old friend (acquaintance)
昔話	**mukashi-banashi**	an old tale; a legend; reminiscences
とっくの昔に	**tokku no mukashi ni**	ages ago; long before

The fourth stroke is longer than the one above it.

8　一 十 卅 卅 井 昔 昔 昔

昔

364 卒

ソツ SOTSU

to graduate

The character 卒 incorporates an early form of *clothing* and *ten* 十, a reference to groups of ten people. From this, the idea of *soldier* has derived with *end*, being a borrowed meaning.
GR4　N2　AP

Example Sentences

1. 君はいつ中学校を卒業しましたか。
   Kimi wa itsu chūgakkō o sotsugyō shimashita ka.
   When did you graduate from junior high school?

2. 来年度は、新卒が9名採用される予定です。
   Rainendo wa, shinsotsu ga kyūmei saiyō sareru yotei desu.
   We are planning to employ nine new college graduates next year.

3. 彼は東大卒を鼻にかけている。
   Kare wa Tōdai sotsu o hana ni kakete iru.
   He is a proud graduate of the University of Tokyo.

4. 彼女はまだ若いのに脳卒中で倒れた。
   Kanojo wa mada wakai no ni nōsotchū de taoreta.
   She had a stroke, even though she was still young.

5. この資格を取るには高卒が条件です。
   Kono shikaku o toru ni wa kōsotsu ga jōken desu.
   To obtain this qualification, you need to have graduated from high school.

Common Compounds and Phrases

卒業	**sotsugyō**	graduation; outgrowing
卒業生	**sotsugyōsei**	a graduate; an alumnus
新卒	**shinsotsu**	a new graduate
大卒	**daisotsu**	a university graduate; graduation
高卒	**kōsotsu**	a senior high-school graduate
脳卒中	**nōsotchū**	a stroke
卒倒	**sottō**	a faint; fainting

Don't write 人人 as 入入.

8　' 亠 亠 太 卒 卒 卒 卒

卒

365

定
to fix

テイ TEI　ジョウ JŌ
さだ・める sada(meru)
さだ・まる sada(maru)
さだ・か sada(ka)

The character 定 contains the elements of *roof* 宀 and *correct* 疋/正, referring to the construction of a building. The more general meaning of *fix* derived from this.

GR3　N3　AP

Example Sentences

1. 応募者はまだ定員に達していないそうです。
   Ōbosha wa mada teiin ni tasshite inai sō desu.
   Apparently, they are still short of the designated number of applicants.

2. 洋服は定価の二割引で売っているんですか。
   Yōfuku wa teika no niwaribiki de utte iru n desu ka.
   Are the clothes on sale at a discount of 20% off the list price?

3. 案の定、彼女はまだ寝ていた。
   An no jō, kanojo wa mada nete ita.
   Sure enough, she was still in bed.

4. それは法律で定めるべき事だ。
   Sore wa hōritsu de sadameru beki koto da.
   It is something which the law has to determine.

5. あの出来事の記憶は定かでない。
   Ano dekigoto no kioku wa sadaka de nai.
   My memory of that event is unclear.

Common Compounds and Phrases

定員	**teiin**	a quota; the seating capacity
定期	**teiki**	regular; a rail pass; a fixed-term deposit
指定する	**shitei suru**	to appoint; to assign
定価	**teika**	a marked (list) price
固定する	**kotei suru**	to fix; to settle
案の定	**an no jō**	as one expected
勘定	**kanjō**	calculation; one's bill, account

Don't write 疋 as 正.

8 `〃 宀 宀 宀 宇 定 定`

定

366

的
target

テキ TEKI
まと mato

The character 的 combines *white* or *conspicuous* 白 and *ladle* or *choose* 勺. The suggestion is that a thing which is conspicuous and set aside is a *target*.

GR3　N3　AP

Example Sentences

1. 留学する目的で、フランス語を勉強中です。
   Ryūgaku suru mokuteki de, Furansugo o benkyō-chū desu.
   I am studying French in order to study abroad.

2. 知的な女性にあこがれます。
   Chiteki na josei ni akogaremasu.
   I'm attracted to intellectual women.

3. このセンサーに近づくと明かりが自動的に点く。
   Kono sensā ni chikazuku to akari ga jidōteki ni tsuku.
   When you approach this sensor, the lights come on automatically.

4. 近代的な建物は、何か冷たい感じがします。
   Kindaiteki na tatemono wa nani ka tsumetai kanji ga shimasu.
   Modern buildings strike me as being somewhat cold.

5. 玉は的を外れた。
   Tama wa mato o hazureta.
   The bullet missed its target.

Common Compounds and Phrases

目的	**mokuteki**	a purpose; an aim; a goal
知的	**chiteki**	intellectual; intelligent
自動的	**jidōteki**	self-moving; automatic
近代的	**kindaiteki**	modern
積極的	**sekkyokuteki**	positive; active; aggressive
比較的	**hikakuteki**	comparatively; relatively
的外れ	**matohazure**	to be off the mark; amiss

The seventh stroke ends with a hook.

8 `〃 亻 白 白 白 白 的 的`

的

367 非　ヒ HI

not; not good

The character 非 originally indicated a *bird spreading its wings and flying away*. The meanings of *opposite direction* and *not* or *un-* have derived from this.
GR5 N3 AP

Example Sentences

1. 非常の際は赤いボタンを押してください。
   Hijō no sai wa akai botan o oshite kudasai.
   In case of an emergency, please press the red button.

2. 彼には非難すべき点がない。
   Kare ni wa hinan subeki ten ga nai.
   I find no fault with him.

3. 非行少年は万引の疑いで逮捕された。
   Hikō shōnen wa manbiki no utagai de taiho sareta.
   A juvenile delinquent was arrested on suspicion of shoplifting.

4. 是非、あの展覧会を見るべきだ。
   Zehi, ano tenrankai o miru beki da.
   You should, by all means, see that exhibition.

5. そんな非常識な考えは止めてください。
   Sonna hijōshiki na kangae wa yamete kudasai.
   Put such a preposterous idea out of your head!

Common Compounds and Phrases

非常口	**hijōguchi**	an emergency (fire) exit
非常に	**hijō ni**	very; extremely
非常識	**hijōshiki**	thoughtlessness; lack of common sense
非難	**hinan**	criticism; blame
非行	**hikō**	misconduct; delinquent behavior
是非	**zehi**	right and wrong; by all means
非公開の	**hikōkai no**	exclusive; private; secret

End the fifth stroke firmly.

8　ノ　ゔ　ゔ　ヺ　非　非　非　非

非

368 表　ヒョウ HYŌ
あらわ・す arawa(su)
おもて omote
あらわ・れる arawa(reru)

surface; table; to show

The character 表 is a combination of *clothing* and *hair* or *fur* 毛. *Fur clothing* is worn on the outer *surface*. *To show* and *list* are associated meanings.
GR3 N3 AP

Example Sentences

1. 食品の表示をよく読んでおいた方がいい。
   Shokuhin no hyōji o yoku yonde oita hō ga ii.
   You ought to always read the labels carefully when buying food.

2. この気持ちは言葉でうまく表現できない。
   Kono kimochi wa kotoba de umaku hyōgen dekinai.
   I can't express this feeling properly in words.

3. 本の裏表紙に面白い写真が載っている。
   Hon no urabyōshi ni omoshiroi shashin ga notte iru.
   There is an interesting photograph on the back cover of the book.

4. 赤は危険を表す。
   Aka wa kiken o arawasu.
   Red represents danger.

5. 出席カードは、表を上にして机の上に置いてください。
   Shusseki kādo wa, omote o ue ni shite tsukue no ue ni oite kudasai.
   Put your attendance card face up on your desk.

Common Compounds and Phrases

表示	**hyōji**	indication; (a) display
表現	**hyōgen**	an expression; representation
表紙	**hyōshi**	a cover; a binding
時刻表	**jikokuhyō**	a timetable;
表情	**hyōjō**	an expression; an appearance; a look
表向き	**omotemuki**	the outward appearance; formally
裏表	**uraomote**	a back and (a) front; inside out

The fourth stroke is longer than those above it.

8　一　十　キ　主　丰　声　表　表

表

369 法

ホウ HŌ　*ハッ HA'　*ホッ HO'

law; method

The character 法 contains *water* 氵 and *to leave* 去, indicating a *tight-lidded container*. This is thought to be a figurative description of *the law*, constraining human behavior.

GR4　N3　AP

Example Sentences

1. 未成年者の喫煙は法律で禁じられている。
   Miseinensha no kitsuen wa hōritsu de kinjirarete iru.
   Smoking by minors is prohibited by law.

2. この文章の文法が間違っている。
   Kono bunshō no bunpō ga machigatte iru.
   This sentence is grammatically incorrect.

3. 日本語を簡単にマスターする方法はありません。
   Nihongo o kantan ni masutā suru hōhō wa arimasen.
   There is no simple way of mastering Japanese.

4. 病院での飲酒はご法度だ。
   Byōin de no inshu wa gohatto da.
   The consumption of alcohol is banned in hospitals.

5. 父は食事の作法にやかましい。
   Chichi wa shokuji no sahō ni yakamashii.
   My father is very particular about table manners.

Common Compounds and Phrases

法律	**hōritsu**	a (the) law
文法	**bunpō**	grammar; rules of composition
法案	**hōan**	a bill; a measure
憲法	**kenpō**	a constitution
寸法	**sunpō**	length; size; a scheme
法王	**hōō**	a pope; the Pope
ご法度	**gohatto**	banned; prohibited

The sixth stroke is longer than the fourth stroke.

8　丶 シ 氵 氵 汁 汪 法 法

法

---

370 枚

マイ MAI

counter for sheets

The character 枚 has the elements of *wood* 木 and *hand holding a stick* 攵. This is a reference to a thin, flat stick used with horses, later becoming a *general counter* for similar objects.

GR6　N3　AP

Example Sentences

1. 80年代にCDの生産枚数はレコードを抜きました。
   Hachijū nendai ni CD no seisan maisū wa rekōdo o nukimashita.
   In the 1980's, the number of CDs produced exceeded that of records.

2. 相手のほうが一枚上手だ。
   Aite no hō ga ichimai uwate da.
   You are no match for the other party in such matters.

3. あの社長は二枚舌なので、信用できない。
   Ano shachō wa nimai-jita na node shinyō dekinai.
   That president is deceitful and can't be trusted.

4. このプリントを一枚ずつ取って回してください。
   Kono purinto o ichimai zutsu totte mawashite kudasai.
   Please take one copy each of the handout and pass the rest on.

5. 大枚をはたいて外車を買った。
   Taimai o hataite gaisha o katta.
   I spent a fortune on an imported car.

Common Compounds and Phrases

枚数	**maisū**	the number of pages, sheets
一枚上手	**ichimai uwate**	be a notch above others
二枚舌の	**nimaijita no**	double-tongued; dishonest
二枚重ね	**nimai-gasane**	two-ply
二枚目	**nimaime**	a good-looking man
三枚目	**sanmaime**	a clown; a comedian; a flip
大枚	**taimai**	good money; a large sum

End the fourth stroke firmly.

8　一 十 オ 木 杧 杧 枚 枚

枚

209

371 和

ワ WA　オ O
やわ・らぐ yawa(ragu)
やわ・らげる yawa(rageru)
なご・む nago(mu)
なご・やか nago(yaka)

peace; sum;
Japan

The character 和 combines rice plant 禾 and *mouth* or *to say* 口. The association here is *softness in speech*. The meanings of *harmony* and *peace* derived from this.

GR3　N2　AP

Example Sentences

1. 今夜の夕食は和食にしますか。
   Konya no yūshoku wa washoku ni shimasu ka.
   Would you like Japanese-style food for dinner tonight?

2. じゅうたんとカーテンが調和しない。
   Jūtan to kāten ga chōwa shinai.
   The carpet does not go well with the curtains.

3. 暑さがやっと和らいだ。
   Atsusa ga yatto yawaraida.
   It has cooled down at last.

4. この薬があなたの痛みを和らげるでしょう。
   Kono kusuri ga anata no itami o yawarageru deshō.
   This medicine will ease your pain.

5. あのバーの和やかな雰囲気が気に入っている。
   Ano bā no nagoyaka na fun'iki ga ki ni itte iru.
   I like that bar's friendly atmosphere.

Common Compounds and Phrases

和食	**washoku**	Japanese-style food
調和	**chōwa**	harmony; accord; agreement
和風	**wafū**	a light wind; Japanese style
英和辞典	**eiwa jiten**	an English-Japanese dictionary
平和	**heiwa**	peace; harmony
*和え物	**aemono**	marinated food
*大和	**yamato**	*Yamato*; (old) Japan

Write the first stroke from right to left.

8　ノ　二　千　禾　禾　和　和

和

372 科

カ KA
*しな shina

branch;
department

The character 科 combines *rice* 禾 and *ladle for measuring* 斗, suggesting the act of sorting rice into *different categories*.

GR2　N2　AP

Example Sentences

1. 科学者たちは新しい研究を始めたばかりです。
   Kagakushatachi wa atarashii kenkyū o hajimeta bakari desu.
   Those scientists have just begun a new research project.

2. 百科事典で調べてみよう。
   Hyakka jiten de shirabete miyō.
   I'll look it up in an encyclopedia.

3. 桜はバラ科の植物です。
   Sakura wa bara-ka no shokubutsu desu.
   The Japanese cherry belongs to the rose family.

4. 姉のだんなさんは歯科医です。
   Ane no danna-san wa shikai desu.
   My sister's husband is a dentist.

5. 彼には窃盗の前科が二度あります。
   Kare ni wa settō no zenka ga nido arimasu.
   He has two previous convictions for robbery.

Common Compounds and Phrases

科学	**kagaku**	science
学科	**gakka**	a (school) subject; a university department
理科系	**rika-kei**	a science major
文科系	**bunka-kei**	a liberal arts major
歯科医	**shikai**	a dentist
小児科	**shōnika**	pediatrics
前科	**zenka**	a previous offense; a criminal history

End the third and ninth strokes firmly.

9　ノ　二　千　禾　禾　禾　科　科

科

EXERCISE 31 (361 – 372)

A. Give the readings for the following.

1. 定める _____
2. 文法 _____
3. 新卒 _____
4. 一枚 _____
5. 非行 _____
6. 受かる _____
7. 表す _____
8. 今昔 _____
9. 制服 _____
10. 目的 _____

B. Choose an appropriate kanji from the LIST to complete the expressions below.

LIST: 和、制、卒、昔、法、受、的、表、枚、科

1. ____ 々、ある所に
2. 近代 ____
3. シャツ三 ____
4. 新しい ____ 度

5. 本の ____ 紙
6. ____ 学者
7. 試験を ____ ける
8. ____ 食のレストラン
9. ____ 業生
10. いい方 ____ が見つからない

C. Add *furigana* to the following.

1. 和風 _____
2. 作法 _____
3. 昔話 _____
4. 非行少年 _____
5. 卒業式 _____
6. 枚数 _____
7. 的外れ _____
8. 強制的な _____
9. 定員 _____
10. 表向き _____

Review 10 (1 – 372)

A. Give the readings for the following.

1. 決め手 _____
2. 育てる _____
3. 定まる _____
4. 忘れっぽい _____
5. 失う _____
6. 和らげる _____
7. 形見 _____
8. 忘れ物 _____
9. 外科 _____

B. Write in English.

1. 平泳ぎ _____
2. 方法 _____
3. 大泣き _____
4. 表面 _____
5. 非公開の _____
6. 何枚 _____
7. 教育 _____
8. 和服 _____
9. 近代的な _____

C. Write in kanji and kana.

1. youthful; fresh _____
2. the number of pages _____
3. long, long ago _____
4. peace; harmony _____
5. an examination candidate _____
6. a quota; a fixed capacity _____
7. a confrontation; a showdown _____
8. a system; an organization _____
9. a glass of cold water _____

D. Add *furigana* to the following.

1. 初めての時 _____
2. 教科書を買う _____
3. 受信する _____
4. 四つ角 _____
5. 科学的 _____
6. 制服を着る _____
7. 卒業する _____
8. 人を困らせる _____
9. 和風 _____

E. Match the following.

1. 文法 ( )   a. じどうてき
2. 昔話 ( )   b. さんまい
3. 発表 ( )   c. ひこう
4. 知的 ( )   d. さほう
5. 英文科 ( )   e. わしょく
6. 体制 ( )   f. むかしばなし
7. 和食 ( )   g. はっぴょう
8. 利口 ( )   h. ひとむかしまえ
9. 大麦 ( )   i. やっきょく
10. 中身 ( )   j. がっか
11. 作法 ( )   k. ひょうし
12. 薬局 ( )   l. なかみ
13. 自動的 ( )   m. たいせい
14. 非行 ( )   n. おおむぎ
15. 表紙 ( )   o. りょうほう
16. 学科 ( )   p. ちてき
17. 三枚 ( )   q. えいぶんか
18. 一昔前 ( )   r. りこう
19. 両方 ( )   s. ぶんぽう
20. 岩場 ( )   t. いわば

F. Add the appropriate readings in kana to the following, then translate into English.

1. 昔＿＿＿、谷＿＿＿さんは、よく夜汽車＿＿＿に乗＿＿＿って、里帰＿＿＿りをしていた。
2. 卒業式＿＿＿の日取り＿＿＿が決定＿＿＿した。
3. 角田＿＿＿さんは、若＿＿＿い時＿＿＿、非行＿＿＿に走＿＿＿って、親＿＿＿を困＿＿＿らせていたそうだ。
4. 実＿＿＿は、今回＿＿＿初＿＿＿めて和服＿＿＿を着＿＿＿ます。
5. 山形県＿＿＿と岩手県＿＿＿は、両方＿＿＿とも東北＿＿＿地方＿＿＿にあります。
6. 体育＿＿＿の時間＿＿＿に泳＿＿＿いだ後＿＿＿、冷＿＿＿たい麦茶＿＿＿を飲＿＿＿んだ。
7. 法科＿＿＿大学＿＿＿の新＿＿＿しい受験＿＿＿制度＿＿＿が発表＿＿＿された。
8. 薬局＿＿＿で買＿＿＿った薬＿＿＿を飲んだら、一時的＿＿＿に治＿＿＿った。
9. 少女＿＿＿は大切＿＿＿にしていた一枚＿＿＿のカードを電車＿＿＿に忘＿＿＿れた。

---

373 皆

カイ KAI
みな mina　*みんな minna

all; everyone

The character 皆 was originally made up of *people in a line* 比 and *to speak* 曰, giving us the present-day sense of *all* the people.

JK N2 AP

Example Sentences

1. 彼らの行方は皆目分からない。
   Karera no yukue wa kaimoku wakaranai.
   Nobody has any idea where they are.

2. 今年度、山田君が皆勤賞を受けた。
   Konnendo, Yamada-kun ga kaikinshō o uketa.
   Yamada received a prize for perfect attendance this year.

3. 「皆さん、おはようございます。」
   'Minasan, ohayō gozaimasu.'
   'Good morning, everybody.'

4. 母の生け花は免許皆伝の腕前だ。
   Haha no ikebana wa menkyo kaiden no udemae da.
   My mother is highly skilled in Japanese flower arrangement.

5. テロリストは村の男を皆殺しにしました。
   Terorisuto wa mura no otoko o minagoroshi ni shimashita.
   The terrorists killed every man in the village.

Common Compounds and Phrases

皆目	**kaimoku**	altogether; wholly
皆勤	**kaikin**	perfect attendance
免許皆伝	**menkyo kaiden**	full proficiency
皆無	**kaimu**	nothing; (not) at all
皆さん／皆様	**mina-san / mina-sama**	everyone; ladies and gentlemen / all of you; everybody
皆殺し	**mina-goroshi**	massacre; annihilation

Make the bottom element slightly narrower.

9   ⌐   ㇏   ㇏   比   比   皆   皆   皆

皆

374 活

カツ KATSU
いき iki

life; activity

The character 活 combines *water* 氵 and *tongue* 舌 to convey the idea of wetting the tongue to become *active* and *full of life*.

GR2 N3 AP

Example Sentences

1. あの人はとても活動的な人だ。
   Ano hito wa totemo katsudōteki na hito da.
   He's a very active person.

2. 人口が増えて、町は活性化した。
   Jinkō ga fuete, machi wa kasseika shita.
   The population grew and injected new life into the town.

3. 新しい生活にやっと慣れてきた。
   Atarashii seikatsu ni yatto narete kita.
   I've finally become used to this new lifestyle.

4. 落ち込んでいた友人に活を入れた。
   Ochikonde ita yūjin ni katsu o ireta.
   I cheered up a friend who was feeling depressed.

5. あの商店街はいつもにぎやかで活気がある。
   Ano shōtengai wa itsumo nigiyaka de kakki ga aru.
   That shopping district is always lively and full of people.

Common Compounds and Phrases

活動的な	**katsudōteki na**	active; energetic
活発な	**kappatsu na**	lively; active
活性化	**kasseika**	activation; stimulation
生活	**seikatsu**	living; life
活気	**kakki**	liveliness; vigor
活力	**katsuryoku**	vitality; vigor
復活	**fukkatsu**	revival; resurrection

The fourth stroke sweeps down from right to left.

9 ` ｀ ｀ 氵 氵 汗 沽 活 活

活

---

375 係

ケイ KEI
かか・る kaka(ru)
かかり kakari

to connect; in charge

The character 係 combines *person* 亻 and *joined threads* 系, indicating connected. From this, the meaning of a person *connected* or *involved* has derived.

GR3 N3 AP

Example Sentences

1. これは君と何の関係もない。
   Kore wa kimi to nan no kankei mo nai.
   This has nothing to do with you.

2. 国民の健康に係る新しい法律が作られた。
   Kokumin no kenkō ni kakaru atarashii hōritsu ga tsukurareta.
   A new law relating to people's health has been enacted.

3. 係の者はただ今席を外しております。
   Kakari no mono wa tadaima seki o hazushite orimasu.
   The person in charge is not available at the moment.

4. ご不明な点は、係員までお問い合わせください。
   Gofumei na ten wa, kakariin made otoiawase kudasai.
   If you have any questions, please contact the clerk in charge.

5. 案内係に呼び出しを頼んだ。
   Annai-gakari ni yobidashi o tanonda.
   I asked the clerk at the information desk to page someone for me.

Common Compounds and Phrases

関係	**kankei**	a relation(ship); a connection
国際関係	**kokusai kankei**	international relations
連係	**renkei**	a connection; a liaison
係数	**keisū**	a co-efficient
係員	**kakariin**	a person (clerk) in charge
案内係	**annai-gakari**	a desk clerk; an usher(ette)
図書係	**tosho-gakari**	a librarian

The third stroke sweeps from right to left. End the seventh stroke firmly.

9 ノ 亻 亻 俘 俘 伾 係 係 係

係

376 昨

サク SAKU

yesterday; last

The character 昨 consists of *day* 日 and *to make* 乍, used phonetically to indicate to *build up*. The idea of the accumulation of days gives us the sense of the passage of time and hence, the *past*.
GR4 N3 AP

Example Sentences

1. 昨日の新聞は読んでいない。
   Kinō no shinbun wa yonde inai.
   I haven't read <u>yesterday's</u> newspaper.

2. ひょうが降ったのは昨夜だったと思います。
   Hyō ga futta no wa sakuya datta to omoimasu.
   I think it was <u>last night</u> that there was a hailstorm.

3. 昨年の夏は猛暑が何日も続いた。
   Sakunen no natsu wa mōsho ga nannichi mo tsuzuita.
   <u>Last summer</u> we had many days of fierce heat.

4. 一昨日、久しぶりに映画を見に行った。
   Ototoi (issakujitsu), hisashiburi ni eiga o ni mi ni itta.
   <u>The day before yesterday</u> was the first time I had been to the movies in ages.

5. 昨今のコンピューター・ゲームの進化には目を見張る。
   Sakkon no konpyūtā gēmu no shinka ni wa me o miharu.
   The evolution of computer games <u>these days</u> is amazing.

Common Compounds and Phrases

昨年	**sakunen**	last year
一昨年	**issakunen /**	the year before last
	*ototoshi	
昨日	**sakujitsu /**	yesterday
	*kinō	
昨晩	**sakuban**	last evening
一昨夜	**issakuya**	the night before last
一昨日	**issakujitsu /**	the day before yesterday
	*ototoi	
昨今	**sakkon**	these days

Do not end the seventh stroke with a hook.

9 丨 冂 日 日 日' 旿 昨 昨 昨

昨

---

377 指

シ SHI
ゆび yubi さ・す sa(su)

finger;
to point

The character 指 is a combination of *hand* 扌 and *good* 旨, used phonetically to suggest *branch*. The branches of the hand are the *fingers*. *To point* is a related meaning.
GR3 N3 AP

Example Sentences

1. 子供たちは指示された通り、おもちゃを片付けた。
   Kodomotachi wa shiji sareta tōri, omocha o katazuketa.
   The children put the toys away, <u>as</u> they were <u>told to do</u>.

2. 今後とも、よろしくご指導お願いします。
   Kongo to mo, yoroshiku goshidō onegai shimasu.
   I look to you for <u>guidance</u>.

3. この車両は全席指定となります。
   Kono sharyō wa zenseki shitei to narimasu.
   All the seats in this carriage are <u>reserved</u>.

4. 婚約指輪を左手の薬指にはめていた。
   Konyaku yubiwa o hidarite no kusuriyubi ni hamete ita.
   She wore her engagement <u>ring</u> on the <u>ring finger</u> of her left hand.

5. 人を指差すのは失礼だ。
   Hito o yubisasu no wa shitsurei da.
   It is rude <u>to point</u> at somebody.

Common Compounds and Phrases

指示	**shiji**	an indication; instructions
指導	**shidō**	guidance; direction
指摘	**shiteki**	pointing out; indication
指名	**shimei**	nomination; designation
指輪	**yubiwa**	a (finger) ring
人差し指	**hitosashi-**	the forefinger; the index
	yubi	finger
目指す	**mezasu**	to aim at; to have an eye to

The second stroke ends with a hook.

9 一 十 扌 扩 拃 拃 指 指 指

指

378 信　シン SHIN

to believe;
message

GR4　N3　AP

The character 信 is made up of *person* 亻 and *word* 言. A person's word is something which can be *believed* and *trusted*.

Example Sentences

1. あの人のことはほとんど信頼出来ない。
   Ano hito no koto wa hotondo shinrai dekinai.
   One can hardly rely upon him.

2. 僕の言うことを信用しないんですか。
   Boku no iu koto o shinyō shinai n desu ka.
   Don't you believe me?

3. 模擬試験の成績が良くて、少し自信がついた。
   Mogi shiken no seiseki ga yokute, sukoshi jishin ga tsuita.
   I gained a little confidence after receiving a good grade in the trial exam.

4. 迷信というものはなかなか無くならないものだ。
   Meishin to iu mono wa naka naka nakunaranai mono da.
   Superstitions die hard.

5. 彼がこんな事件を起こすなんて、信じられない！
   Kare ga konna jiken o okosu nante, shinjirarenai!
   I can't believe that he would be to blame for such an incident!

Common Compounds and Phrases

信頼	**shinrai**	trust; confidence
信用	**shinyō**	confidence; trust; credit
迷信	**meishin**	superstition
信じる	**shinjiru**	to believe; to trust (in)
信仰	**shinkō**	faith; (religious) belief
送信	**sōshin**	transmission (of a message)
通信販売	**tsūshin hanbai**	(a) mail order sale(s)

The fourth stroke is longer than the other horizontal ones.

9　ノ　亻　亻　亻　信　信　信　信　信

---

379 神　シン SHIN　ジン JIN
かみ kami　*かん kan
*こう kō

god; spirit;
mind

GR3　N3　AP

The character 神 combines *altar* ネ (and by extension, *pertaining to the gods*) and *to say* 申 (here lit. *lightning*). Lightning was thought to be the voice of the gods. *Spirit* is a related meaning.

Example Sentences

1. あの山は神秘的な場所として知られている。
   Ano yama wa shinpiteki na basho to shite shirarete iru.
   That mountain is known as a mystical place.

2. 彼は他人の気持ちに対して無神経だ。
   Kare wa hito no kimochi ni taishite mushinkei da.
   He is insensitive to other people's feelings.

3. 神社の境内は禁煙となっている。
   Jinja no keidai wa kin'en to natte iru.
   There is no smoking within the precincts of the shrine.

4. 結果は神のみぞ知ることだ。
   Kekka wa kami nomi zo shiru koto da.
   Only God knows how things will turn out.

5. 彼は神経症で精神科に通院していたことがある。
   Kare wa shinkeishō de seishin-ka ni tsūin shite ita koto ga aru.
   He has been seeing a psychiatrist for treatment for his neuroses.

Common Compounds and Phrases

神秘的	**shinpiteki**	mysterious; miraculous
神経	**shinkei**	a nerve; sensitivity; a worry
精神	**seishin**	mind; (the) spirit; an intention
失神	**shisshin**	a faint; a blackout
神様	**kamisama**	a god; a deity; God; Allah
*神主	**kannushi**	a *Shintō* priest
*神々しい	**kōgōshii**	divine; heavenly; holy

The last stroke protrudes.

9　ゝ　ラ　ネ　ネ　ネ　初　初　袔　神

380 星

star

セイ SEI　*ショウ SHŌ
ほし hoshi

The character 星 combines *sun*, *light* 日 and *seedling* 生, a reference to *emerging light*. This then took on the meaning of *star*.

GR2 N2

Example Sentences

1. 星占いによると今日は金運がいいらしい。
   Hoshiuranai ni yoru to kyō wa kin'un ga ii rashii.
   According to <u>your horoscope</u>, it says that today you're going to be lucky with money.

2. 北極星は動かないので、道しるべになる。
   Hokkyokusei wa ugokanai node, michishirube ni naru.
   Since <u>the North Star</u> is stationary, it can be used as a guide.

3. 今夜は、星がよく見える。
   Konya wa, hoshi ga yoku mieru.
   The <u>stars</u> are very bright tonight.

4. やっと契約できる目星がついた。
   Yatto keiyaku dekiru meboshi ga tsuita.
   It <u>seems likely</u> that we will finally be able to get the contract.

5. 大関は星を落とした。
   Ōzeki wa hoshi o otoshita.
   The champion sumo wrestler <u>lost his bout</u>.

Common Compounds and Phrases

火星	**kasei**	Mars
北極星	**hokkyokusei**	the North (polar) Star
星座	**seiza**	a constellation
人工衛星	**jinkō eisei**	an artificial satellite
星印	**hoshijirushi**	a star (symbol); an asterisk
星占い	**hoshi-uranai**	astrology; a horoscope
図星	**zuboshi**	a bull's eye

The last stroke is longer than those above it.

9 ` ⼞ ⼞ 日 ⼾ ⼽ 尸 星 星

星

381 専

exclusive; sole

セン SEN
もっぱ・ら moppa(ra)

The character 専 has obscure origins, however it is thought to be a combination of *hand* and *toy*. The way a child holds on to a toy gives the character its meaning of *exclusive* or *sole*.

GR6 N3 AP

Example Sentences

1. この記事には専門用語が多くて分かり難い。
   Kono kiji ni wa senmon yōgo ga ōkute wakarinikui.
   There are so many <u>technical terms</u> in this article that it is hard to understand.

2. 駐車場に社長専用車が停まっていた。
   Chūshajō ni shachō senyōsha ga tomatte ita.
   The company president's <u>private car</u> was parked in the parking lot.

3. 大学でのご専攻は何でしたか。
   Daigaku de no gosenkō wa nan deshita ka.
   What did you <u>major</u> in at college?

4. コーチは選手に専任のアドバイザーを付けた。
   Kōchi wa senshu ni sennin no adobaizā o tsuketa.
   The coach appointed an <u>exclusive</u> advisor to the player.

5. あの子は、専らサッカーの練習にはげんでいる。
   Ano ko wa moppara sakkā no renshū ni hagende iru.
   That child <u>devotes</u> most of his time to soccer practice.

Common Compounds and Phrases

専門用語	**senmon yōgo**	a technical term (terminology)
専門学校	**senmon gakkō**	a technical school
専攻	**senkō**	a special study; one's major
専売	**senbai**	a monopoly
専念する	**sennen suru**	to devote oneself to
専有する	**sen'yū suru**	to monopolize
専任	**sennin**	full-time work

The seventh stroke is the longest.

9 ⼀ ⼚ ⼀ ⼕ 百 車 車 専 専

専

382 相

ソウ SŌ　ショウ SHŌ
あい ai

phase; mutual;
minister

The character 相 is made up of *tree* 木 and *eye* 目, a reference to careful observation. The idea of the person watching being watched, as well, suggests the sense of *mutual*.
GR3　N3　AP

Example Sentences

1. リーダーたちは会談で相互に意見を出し合った。
   Riidā-tachi wa kaidan de sōgo ni iken o dashiatta.
   The leaders <u>exchanged</u> opinions at the talks.

2. そのことについては両親と相談した方がよい。
   Sono koto ni tsuite wa ryōshin to sōdan shita hō ga yoi.
   You had better <u>consult</u> with your parents over the matter.

3. 当時、小泉さんが首相だった。
   Tōji, Koizumi-san ga shushō datta.
   At that time, Mr. Koizumi was <u>prime minister</u>.

4. 皆はもう彼女を相手にしなかった。
   Mina wa mō kanojo o aite ni shinakatta.
   Nobody <u>took</u> any further <u>notice of</u> her.

5. 相変わらず、忙しそうですね。
   Aikawarazu, ishogashisō desu ne.
   You look as busy <u>as ever</u>.

Common Compounds and Phrases

相互に	<u>sōgo ni</u>	mutually; reciprocally
相談	<u>sōdan</u>	consultation; a talk; an offer
相違	<u>sōi</u>	a difference; a disagreement
首相	shu<u>shō</u>	a prime minister
相手	<u>aite</u>	one's companion (opponent); the other party
相変わらず	<u>aikawarazu</u>	as usual; as ever
相席	<u>aiseki</u>	sharing a table with somebody

End the second stroke firmly.

9　一 十 オ オ 木 机 相 相 相

相

---

383 草

ソウ SŌ
くさ kusa

grass

The character 草 combines *plant* ⺿ and *early* 早, a reference to *seedlings* and *small plants*.

GR1　N2

Example Sentences

1. 料理に香草を少し入れるとおいしくなった。
   Ryōri ni kōsō o sukoshi ireru to oishiku natta.
   I added a few <u>herbs</u>, improving the taste.

2. スピーチの草稿を手直しした。
   Supiichi no sōkō o tenaoshi shita.
   I touched up <u>the draft</u> of my speech.

3. 庭の草むしりが大変だ。
   Niwa no kusa-mushiri ga taihen da.
   It's hard work <u>weeding</u> the garden.

4. 僕は草野球チームに入っている。
   Boku wa kusa-yakyū chiimu ni haitte iru.
   I'm a member of an <u>amateur baseball</u> team.

5. 彼はCGの草分けである。
   Kare wa shii-jii no kusawake de aru.
   He is <u>a pioneer</u> in computer graphics.

Common Compounds and Phrases

香草	<u>kōsō</u>	(fragrant) herbs
草稿	<u>sōkō</u>	a rough draft; notes
海草	kai<u>sō</u>	seaweed
雑草	zas<u>sō</u>	a weed
道草を食う	michi<u>kusa</u> o kū	to loiter; to dawdle
草花	<u>kusabana</u>	a flowering plant
*煙草	**tabako**	tobacco; a cigarette

The eighth stroke is the longest.

9　一 十 艹 艹 芒 莒 草 草

草

384 単　タン TAN

unit; single;
simple

Originally the character 単 showed a *forked weapon*, combined with *to guard* and *binding*. Through phonetic borrowing, we have the associated meanings of *simple*, *single* and *unit*.
GR4　N3　AP

Example Sentences

1. 今学期は、英語を四単位取ってみよう。
   Kongakki wa, eigo o yon-tan'i totte miyō.
   I think I'll take four <u>credits</u> of English this semester.

2. 今、新しい単語を単語帳に写している。
   Ima, atarashii tango o tangochō ni utsushite iru.
   I'm copying the new <u>words</u> into my <u>vocabulary book</u> at the moment.

3. 簡単にやせられる方法はないでしょうか。
   Kantan ni yaserareru hōhō wa nai deshō ka.
   Is there no <u>easy</u> way to lose weight?

4. 単なる風邪に過ぎなかった。
   Tan' naru kaze ni suginakatta.
   It was <u>merely</u> a cold.

5. 単純に考えてみよう。
   Tanjun ni kangaete miyō.
   Let us consider the matter <u>simply</u>.

Common Compounds and Phrases

単位	**tan'i**	a unit; a credit
単語	**tango**	a word
簡単な	**kantan na**	simple; easy
単なる	**tan' naru**	mere; simple
単純な	**tanjun na**	simple; uncomplicated
単身赴任	**tanshin funin**	a single transfer; a job relocation
単行本	**tankōbon**	a single volume

Be careful with the dots at the top.

9　`丶丶丷丷冂冂峃峃単

単

EXERCISE 32 (373 – 384)

A. Give the readings for the following.

1. 活発な ＿＿＿＿＿＿＿＿＿＿＿
2. 相変わらず ＿＿＿＿＿＿＿＿＿
3. 草花 ＿＿＿＿＿＿＿＿＿＿＿＿
4. 昨日 ＿＿＿＿＿＿＿＿＿＿＿＿
5. 神戸 ＿＿＿＿＿＿＿＿＿＿＿＿
6. 指す ＿＿＿＿＿＿＿＿＿＿＿＿
7. 専ら ＿＿＿＿＿＿＿＿＿＿＿＿
8. 皆さん ＿＿＿＿＿＿＿＿＿＿＿
9. 単なる ＿＿＿＿＿＿＿＿＿＿＿
10. 信じる ＿＿＿＿＿＿＿＿＿＿＿

B. Select an appropriate kanji from the list to complete the following.

　　LIST: 係、星、単、信、指、活、専、相、昨、神

1. ＿＿＿ 語 (a word; vocabulary)
2. ＿＿＿ 員 (a person in charge)
3. ＿＿＿ 手 (a partner; an opponent)
4. 中 ＿＿＿ (the middle finger)
5. ＿＿＿ 力 (vitality; vigor)
6. ＿＿＿ 社 (a *Shinto* shrine)
7. ＿＿＿ 空 (a starry sky)
8. ＿＿＿ 夜 (last night)
9. ＿＿＿ 有する (to monopolize)
10. 自 ＿＿＿ (self-confidence)

C. Add *furigana* to the kanji in the following.

1. 赤信号 ＿＿＿＿＿＿＿＿＿＿＿
2. 単行本 ＿＿＿＿＿＿＿＿＿＿＿
3. 生活する ＿＿＿＿＿＿＿＿＿＿
4. 専門学校 ＿＿＿＿＿＿＿＿＿＿
5. 火星 ＿＿＿＿＿＿＿＿＿＿＿＿
6. 昨年度 ＿＿＿＿＿＿＿＿＿＿＿
7. 道草を食う ＿＿＿＿＿＿＿＿＿
8. 指定された ＿＿＿＿＿＿＿＿＿
9. 海草 ＿＿＿＿＿＿＿＿＿＿＿＿
10. 首相 ＿＿＿＿＿＿＿＿＿＿＿＿

385 背

back; to defy

ハイ HAI
せ se せい sei
そむ・く somu(ku)
そむ・ける somu(keru)

The character 背 is made up of *meat, body* 月 and *north* (persons sitting *back to back*) 北, suggesting *the back* of the body. Now, this character also refers to *stature* and *to turn one's back*.

GR6 N2 AP

Example Sentences

1. 山を背景にして、写真を撮ったらどうですか。
   Yama o haikei ni shite, shashin o tottara dō desu ka.
   How about I take a picture <u>with</u> the mountain <u>in the background</u>?

2. 背の高い男が背後から私に近づいて来た。
   Se no takai otoko ga haigo kara watashi ni chikazuite kita.
   A <u>tall</u> man approached me from <u>behind</u>.

3. 背くらべをしようよ。
   Sei-kurabe o shiyō yo.
   Let's compare <u>heights</u>!

4. 彼女は両親の意思に背いた。
   Kanojo wa ryōshin no ishi ni somuita.
   She went <u>against</u> her parents' wishes.

5. 彼は顔を背けて通った。
   Kare wa kao o somukete tōtta.
   He <u>looked away</u> as he passed by.

Common Compounds and Phrases

背景	**haikei**	a background; a setting
背後	**haigo**	the back; behind the scenes
背比べ	**sei-kurabe**	seeing who is taller
背が高い	**se ga takai**	to be tall, large
背中	**senaka**	one's (the) back
背筋	**sesuji / haikin**	the spine / the back muscles
背骨	**sebone**	a backbone; a spine

The seventh stroke ends with a hook.

9 ｜ 丬 ｊ ｊ 北 北 背 背 背

背

386 飛

to fly

ヒ HI
と・ぶ to(bu)
と・ばす to(basu)

Formerly, the character 飛 depicted a crane with wings spread in *flight*.

GR4 N3 AP

Example Sentences

1. 香港まで飛行時間は、何時間ですか。
   Honkon made hikō jikan wa, nanjikan desu ka.
   How many hours is <u>the flight</u> to Hong Kong?

2. 飛行機は滑走路に着陸した。
   Hikōki wa kassōro ni chakuriku shita.
   <u>The airplane</u> touched down on the runway.

3. 空に飛んでいるのは何ですか。
   Sora ni tonde iru no wa nan desu ka.
   What is that <u>flying</u> in the sky?

4. 飛んで火に入る夏の虫。
   Tonde hi ni iru natsu no mushi.
   It is like a moth <u>drawn</u> to a flame. (a saying)

5. 紙飛行機は勢いよく飛んで行った。
   Kamihikōki wa ikioi yoku tonde itta.
   The <u>paper plane</u> flew away, gaining momentum.

Common Compounds and Phrases

飛行	**hikō**	flight; flying; aviation
飛行機	**hikōki**	an airplane
飛行場	**hikōjō**	an airport; an airfield
宇宙飛行士	**uchū hikōshi**	an astronaut
飛び魚	**tobiuo**	a flying fish
高飛び込み	**taka-tobikomi**	high (platform) diving
飛躍する	**hiyaku suru**	to vault

The first and seventh strokes end with hooks, and the sixth stroke sweeps down.

9 乁 乁 乁 飞 飞 飛 飛 飛

飛

387 美

beautiful

ビ BI
うつく・しい utsuku(shii)

The character 美 combines *sheep* 羊 and *big* 大, representing a highly prized possession and hence, suggests desirable appearance and thus, *beautiful*.
GR3 N3 AP

Example Sentences

1. 美ははかないものだ。
   Bi wa hakanai mono da.
   <u>Beauty</u> is fragile.

2. もう二十年間、美術品を集めている。
   Mō nijū-nenkan, bijutsuhin o atsumete iru.
   I have been collecting <u>artworks</u> for twenty years.

3. 来月、校内美化運動が行われる。
   Raigetsu, kōnai bika undō ga okonawareru.
   A school <u>clean-up campaign</u> will be held next month.

4. あの女優さんは美人だと思いますか。
   Ano joyū-san wa bijin da to omoimasu ka.
   Do you find that actress <u>beautiful</u>?

5. オペラ歌手は美しい声で歌った。
   Opera kashu wa utsukushii koe de utatta.
   The opera singer sang with a <u>beautiful</u> voice.

Common Compounds and Phrases

美化	**bika**	beautification
美人	**bijin**	a beautiful woman
美女	**bijo**	a beauty; a pretty girl
美容	**biyō**	beauty culture; cosmetics
美徳	**bitoku**	a virtue; a fine trait
美味な	**bimi na**	nice; delicious; tasty
美しさ	**utsukushisa**	beauty; charm

End the fourth stroke firmly.

9 丶 丷 䒑 丷 羊 羊 美 美 美

美

---

388 変

to change; abnormal

ヘン HEN
か・わる ka(waru)
か・える ka(eru)

Formerly, the character 変 combined *striking hand* and *tied together*, suggesting *reverse* and *complicated*. Eventually, the character took on the general sense of *to change*.
GR4 N3 AP

Example Sentences

1. それには別に変なところがない。
   Sore ni wa betsu ni hen na tokoro ga nai.
   There is nothing particularly <u>strange</u> about it.

2. 父を納得させるのは大変なことだ。
   Chichi o nattoku saseru no wa taihen na koto da.
   It is <u>no easy task</u> to persuade my father.

3. もしかすると、異変が起きたかも知れない。
   Moshi ka suru to, ihen ga okita ka mo shirenai.
   <u>Something</u> must have <u>gone wrong</u>.

4. 近頃、天気が変わりやすい。
   Chikagoro, tenki ga kawari-yasui.
   The weather has been <u>unsettled</u> lately.

5. 彼は仕事を変えてばかりいる。
   Kare wa shigoto o kaete bakari iru.
   He is <u>always changing</u> jobs.

Common Compounds and Phrases

変な	**hen na**	strange; peculiar; unusual
大変	**taihen**	very; most; greatly; an emergency
異変	**ihen**	an accident; something strange
変更	**henkō**	an alteration; a change
変わりやすい	**kawari-yasui**	changeable; unsettled; fickle
変わり者	**kawarimono**	an eccentric; an oddball

Don't write 夂 as 又 (また).

9 丶 亠 ㇒ 亣 夻 亦 亦 変 変

変

389 面

メン MEN
おも omo　おもて omote
つら tsura

face; aspect; mask

Originally, the character 面 was made up of *face* and *enclosure*, suggesting the idea of something which encloses the *face*, like a *mask*. Later, this came to refer to outer appearance, hence *aspect*.
GR3　N3　AP

Example Sentences

1. ペーパーテストの他に面接もあります。
   Pēpā tesuto no hoka ni mensetsu mo arimasu.
   Besides the written examination, there is an interview as well.

2. その問題を、あらゆる方面から考えなければならない。
   Sono mondai o, arayuru hōmen kara kangaenakereba naranai.
   You must consider the question from all possible angles.

3. 彼には父親の面影がある。
   Kare ni wa chichioya no omokage ga aru.
   He reminds me of his father.

4. 日本人は、あまり感情を面に表さないと言われている。
   Nihonjin wa, amari kanjō o omote ni arawasanai to iwarete iru.
   It is said that Japanese rarely show their feelings.

5. この映画のどこが面白いのか分からない。
   Kono eiga no doko ga omoshiroi no ka wakaranai.
   I don't see what there is that is so funny about this movie.

Common Compounds and Phrases

面接	**mensetsu**	interviewing; an interview
表面	**hyōmen**	a surface; the outside
両面	**ryōmen**	both (two) faces (sides)
地面	**jimen**	the surface of the earth; the ground
一面の	**ichimen no**	an aspect; all over
面影	**omokage**	an image; a face; a reminder
面白い	**omoshiroi**	enjoyable; funny; interesting

Don't write 日 as 口 (くち).

9　一 ナ 丆 丙 而 而 面 面 面

面

---

390 要

ヨウ YŌ
い・る i(ru)

to require; to summarize; vital

The character 要 originally combined *hands*, *waist* and *legs*, the *woman* element 女 being added later. The meaning of waist gives us the sense of that which is the pivot of the body, thus *essential*.
GR4　N3　AP

Example Sentences

1. 完成するのに、いくらぐらいお金が必要ですか。
   Kansei suru no ni, ikura gurai okane ga hitsuyō desu ka.
   How much money will be needed to complete it?

2. 会社は賃金値上げの要求を受け入れた。
   Kaisha wa chingin neage no yōkyū o ukeireta.
   The company accepted the demand for higher wages.

3. 山田君はチームの重要なメンバーである。
   Yamada-kun wa chiimu no jūyō na menbā de aru.
   Yamada is a valuable member of the team.

4. 会社までの所要時間は、どのくらいですか。
   Kaisha made no shoyō jikan wa, dono kurai desu ka.
   How long does it take you to get to the office?

5. このケーキを作るにはどんな材料が要りますか。
   Kono kēki o tsukuru ni wa donna zairyō ga irimasu ka.
   What ingredients are needed to make this cake?

Common Compounds and Phrases

要求	**yōkyū**	a requirement; a demand; needs
重要な	**jūyō na**	important, essential
要約する	**yōyaku suru**	to summarize; to condense
所要時間	**shoyō jikan**	the time required
要点	**yōten**	the gist; the main point
不要な	**fuyō na**	useless; unnecessary
要するに	**yō suru ni**	in a word; in short

Don't write 覀 as 西 (にし).

9　一 厂 冂 币 币 覀 覀 要 要

要

391 荷

カ KA
に ni

load; baggage

The character 荷 combines *plant* 艹 and *what?* 何 (originally meaning *to bear a heavy load*). The latter part gives us the present meaning.

GR3 N3 AP

Example Sentences

1. あの人たちはその陰謀に荷担した。
   Ano hitotachi wa sono inbō ni <u>katan shita</u>.
   Those people <u>were a party to</u> the conspiracy.

2. その知らせで肩の荷が下りた。
   Sono shirase de <u>kata no ni ga orita</u>.
   The news <u>took a load off my mind</u>.

3. 早く車に荷物を積んで下さい。
   Hayaku kuruma ni <u>nimotsu</u> o tsunde kudasai.
   Please hurry and put your <u>luggage</u> in the car.

4. 荷造りはもう終わりましたか。
   <u>Nizukuri</u> wa mō owarimashita ka.
   Have you finished <u>packing</u> yet?

5. 積荷を降ろすのに丸一日かかった。
   <u>Tsumini</u> o orosu no ni maru ichinichi kakatta.
   It took the whole day <u>to unload the ship</u>.

Common Compounds and Phrases

荷担	**katan**	assistance; support; help
出荷	**shu<u>kka</u>**	a shipment; a consignment
手荷物	**te<u>ni</u>motsu**	(hand) luggage
荷造り	**<u>ni</u>zukuri**	packing; packaging; crating
荷車	**<u>ni</u>guruma**	a cart; a wagon; a van
積荷	**tsu<u>mini</u>**	a load; freight; shipping
重荷	**o<u>moni</u>**	a heavy load; a burden

The last stroke ends with a hook.

10 一 十 艹 艹 艹 艹 苻 苻 荷 荷

荷

392 原

ゲン GEN
はら hara

original; field; plain

The character 原 combines *cliff* 厂 and *spring* 泉, suggesting the *origin* of a stream and the edge of a *field*.

GR2 N3

Example Sentences

1. 事故の原因はまだ分かっていない。
   Jiko no <u>gen'in</u> wa mada wakatte inai.
   The <u>cause</u> of the accident remains unknown.

2. 原油の値上がりで物価が上がった。
   <u>Genyu</u> no neagari de bukka ga agatta.
   Because of the rise in the price of <u>crude oil</u>, commodity prices rose.

3. カタログの宝石は原寸大です。
   Katarogu no hōseki wa <u>gensundai</u> desu.
   The gems in the catalogue are shown in <u>actual size</u>.

4. 1945年8月6日に、広島市に原子爆弾が投下されました。
   1945-nen hachigatsu muika ni, Hiroshima-shi ni <u>genshi bakudan</u> ga tōka saremashita.
   <u>An atomic bomb</u> was dropped on Hiroshima City on August 6th, 1945.

5. 原っぱで昼寝をした。
   <u>Harappa</u> de hirune o shita.
   I took a nap in <u>an open field</u>.

Common Compounds and Phrases

原因	**<u>gen'in</u>**	a cause; a reason
原油	**<u>gen'yu</u>**	crude oil
原料	**<u>genryō</u>**	raw materials
原稿	**<u>genkō</u>**	a manuscript
原子爆弾	**genshi bakudan**	an atom bomb
河原	**ka<u>wara</u>**	a dry river bed
原っぱ	**<u>harappa</u>**	an open field

The eighth stroke ends with a hook.

10 一 厂 厂 厂 原 原 原 原 原 原

原

393 個

コ KO

individual; a counter
for objects

GR5 N3 AP

The character 個 combines *person* 亻 and *hard* 固, originally referring to an *individual* wearing hard armor.

Example Sentences

1. 洗面所に石けんが二個置いてある。
   Senmenjo ni sekken ga <u>niko</u> oite aru.
   There are <u>two cakes</u> of soap on the sink.

2. 個人的に知っているわけではない。
   Kojinteki ni shitte iru wake de wa nai.
   I don't know him <u>personally</u>.

3. この絵には画家の個性がはっきり出ている。
   Kono e ni wa gaka no <u>kosei</u> ga hakkiri dete iru.
   The artist's <u>personality</u> comes across clearly in this painting.

4. この映画について個々の意見を聞いてみた。
   Kono eiga ni tsuite <u>koko no</u> iken o kiite mita.
   I asked <u>each of them separately</u> how they felt about the movie.

5. もう少ししたら、個室が空くと思います。
   Mō sukoshi shitara, <u>koshitsu</u> ga aku to omoimasu.
   <u>A private room</u> should become available shortly.

Common Compounds and Phrases

石けん二個	**sekken niko**	two pieces of soap
個人	**kojin**	an individual
個性	**kosei**	individuality; originality
個々に	**koko ni**	separately; one by one
別個の	**bekko no**	separate; different
個室	**koshitsu**	a single (private) room, ward
個別の	**kobetsu no**	individual; separate

The fourth stroke is written in one fluid motion.

10 ノ 亻 亻 们 伜 佃 佃 個 個 個

個

---

394 降

コウ KŌ
お・りる o(riru)
お・ろす o(rosu)
ふ・る fu(ru)

to descend; to
alight; to fall

GR6 N3 AP

The character 降 is made up of *hill* 阝 and originally, *two inverted feet*, suggesting to *come down* (a hill) from above. The meanings of *to fall* and *alight* are related.

Example Sentences

1. 会社の株価は見る見る下降している。
   Kaisha no kabuka wa miru miru <u>kakō shite iru</u>.
   Our company's share price <u>is dropping</u> rapidly.

2. あそこは降水量の多い地方だ。
   Asoko wa kōsuiryō no ōi chihō da.
   That is a region of high <u>rainfall</u>.

3. ここで降ります。
   Koko de <u>orimasu</u>.
   I'm getting off here.

4. 次の角で降ろしてください。
   Tsugi no kado de <u>oroshite kudasai</u>.
   <u>Please let me off</u> at the next corner.

5. 雨が一晩中降っていた。
   Ame ga hitobanjū <u>futte ita</u>.
   It <u>rained</u> all night.

Common Compounds and Phrases

下降	**kakō**	a descent; a fall; a drop
降水量	**kōsuiryō**	an amount of precipitation
乗降口	**jōkōguchi**	an entrance; a hatch(way)
電車を降りる	**densha o oriru**	to get off (leave) a train
霜が降りる	**shimo ga oriru**	to have a frost
雪が降る	**yuki ga furu**	It snows; to have snow

The last stroke protrudes. Note that the left element is made up of 3 strokes.

10 �㇍ ㇌ 阝 阝 阝 阽 陉 陉 降

降

395 残

ザン ZAN
のこ・る noko(ru)

to remain;
cruel; harm

The character 残 combines *bare bones*, *death* 歹 and *halberd*, *to cut* 戋 suggesting killing someone *cruelly* by cutting them so that only the bones *remain*.

GR4　N3　AP

Example Sentences

1. あの映画は残酷な場面で話題になっている。
   Ano eiga wa <u>zankoku na</u> bamen de wadai ni natte iru.
   That movie is the talk of the town for its <u>brutal</u> scenes.

2. 残念なことに、彼女は来られなかった。
   <u>Zannen na</u> koto ni, kanojo wa korarenakatta.
   <u>To my disappointment</u>, she was unable to come.

3. 明日、残業で帰りが遅くなるかも知れない。
   Ashita, <u>zangyō</u> de kaeri ga osoku naru ka mo shirenai.
   I may be late getting home tomorrow because I have to work <u>overtime</u>.

4. まだ牛乳が残っていたら猫にやりなさい。
   Mada gyūnyū ga <u>nokotte itara</u> neko ni yarinasai.
   <u>If there is any</u> milk <u>left</u>, give it to the cat.

5. 赤ワインを一滴も残さずに飲んでしまった。
   Akawain o <u>itteki mo nokosazu</u> ni nonde shimatta.
   He drank the bottle of red wine <u>to the last drop</u>.

Common Compounds and Phrases

残酷な	**zankoku na**	cruel; ruthless
残念な	**zannen na**	regrettable; disappointing
残業	**zangyō**	overtime; extra work
残高	**zandaka**	the balance; the remainder
残り物	**nokorimono**	leftovers; remains; scraps
生き残る	**ikinokoru**	to survive
*名残	**nagori**	the sorrow of parting; remains

The ninth stroke protrudes.

10　一　丁　歹　歹　歹　歹　歼　残　残　残

残

---

396 酒

シュ SHU
さけ sake　*さか saka

alcohol; *sake*

The character 酒 consists of *water* or *liquid* 氵 and *wine jar* or *alcohol* 酉. The liquid in the wine jar is *alcohol*, or *sake* in Japanese.

GR3　N3　AP

Example Sentences

1. 酒造場の見学は10時から始まります。
   <u>Shuzōjō</u> no kengaku wa jūji kara hajimarimasu.
   The tour of <u>the brewery</u> will begin at 10:00.

2. 若者は飲酒運転で人身事故を起こした。
   Wakamono wa <u>inshu unten</u> de jinshin jiko o okoshita.
   The young man knocked a person down while <u>driving under the influence</u> of liquor.

3. 毎晩、風呂上りに日本酒を一杯飲んでいる。
   Maiban, furo-agari ni <u>nihonshu</u> o ippai nonde iru.
   Every evening, I've taken to having a drink of <u>Japanese sake</u> after my bath.

4. お父さん、酒臭いよ！
   Otōsan, <u>sake-kusai</u> yo!
   Dad, I can <u>smell liquor</u> on your breath!

5. あの酒場の主人とはもう二十年来の知り合いだ。
   Ano <u>sakaba</u> no shujin to wa mō nijūnen-rai no shiriai da.
   I've known the bartender in that <u>tavern</u> for the past twenty years or so.

Common Compounds and Phrases

酒造場	**shuzōjō**	a brewery; a distillery
飲酒運転	**inshu unten**	drunken driving; drinking and driving
日本酒	**nihonshu**	sake; rice wine
酒臭い	**sake-kusai**	smelling of liquor
酒好き	**sakezuki**	a love of drink
*酒場	**sakaba**	a bar; a pub
*酒屋	**sakaya**	a sake dealer; a liquor store

Don't write the right-hand side as 西 (にし).

10　丶　冫　氵　汀　汀　沪　洒　洒　酒　酒

酒

EXERCISE 33 (385 – 396)

A. Give the readings for the following.

1. 降りる _____
2. 飛ばす _____
3. 変な _____
4. 方面 _____
5. 飲酒運転 _____
6. 荷物 _____
7. 背中 _____
8. 飛行場 _____
9. 残り物 _____
10. 原っぱ _____

B. Write in English.

1. 面白い話 _____
2. 顔色を変える _____
3. 背の高い少年 _____
4. 何も残っていない _____
5. 美しい思い出 _____
6. 酒が飲めない _____
7. 青空を飛ぶ _____

8. お金が要る _____
9. 変わりやすい天気 _____
10. 大雨が降る _____

C. Match the following.

1. じめん　　　（　）　　a. 乗降口
2. げんりょう　（　）　　b. 美人
3. べっこ　　　（　）　　c. 個人的
4. はいご　　　（　）　　d. 日本酒
5. ざんだか　　（　）　　e. 重要
6. じゅうよう　（　）　　f. 地面
7. にほんしゅ　（　）　　g. 原料
8. こじんてき　（　）　　h. 別個
9. びじん　　　（　）　　i. 背後
10. じょうこうぐち（　）　　j. 残高

397　笑

ショウ SHŌ
え・む e(mu)
わら・う wara(u)

to laugh;
to smile

The origin of the character 笑 is obscure, however, it is thought to have combined *bamboo* 竹 and *a person with a bowed head* 夭, suggesting someone bent over (like bamboo), *laughing*.
GR4　N3　AP

Example Sentences

1. 談笑のうちに会談は幕を閉じた。
   Danshō no uchi ni kaidan wa maku o tojita.
   The meeting was closed with <u>a friendly chat</u>.

2. 微笑を浮かべて、賞を受け取った。
   Bishō o ukabete, shō o uketotta.
   She accepted the award, her face <u>all smiles</u>.

3. 彼は最後に微笑みながら去って行った。
   Kare wa saigo ni <u>hohoeminagara</u> satte itta.
   In the end, he left <u>with a smile on his face</u>.

4. 彼は笑わずにはいられなかった。
   Kare wa <u>warawazu ni wa irarenakatta</u>.
   He <u>couldn't help laughing</u>.

5. 島田さんは私たちを笑顔で迎えてくれた。
   Shimada san wa watashitachi o <u>egao de</u> mukaete kureta.
   Ms. Shimada greeted us <u>with a</u> welcoming <u>smile</u>.

Common Compounds and Phrases

談笑	**danshō**	a chat; a friendly conversation
微笑	**bishō**	a smile
微笑み	**hohoemi**	a smile
笑顔	**egao**	a smile; a smiling face
大笑い	**ōwarai**	a loud laugh; a guffaw; silliness
笑い声	**waraigoe**	laughter; a laughing voice
笑い話	**waraibanashi**	a funny story; a minor matter

The seventh stroke sweeps down from right to left.

10　ノ　ト　ゲ　゛ゲ　ゲ　竹　竹　竺　竿　笑

笑

398 速

ソク SOKU
はや・い haya(i)
はや・める haya(meru)
すみ・やか sumi(yaka)

quick; fast

The character 速 is a combination of *movement* 辶 and *to bundle* or *to manage* 束, here used phonetically to suggest *to hurry*. Thus, you have the sense of *hurrying movement*.
GR3 N3 AP

Example Sentences

1. 手紙を英国に速達で出した。
   Tegami o Eikoku ni sokutatsu de dashita.
   I sent a letter to England by <u>express delivery post</u>.

2. イーメールが届いたら、早速お知らせします。
   Ii-mēru ga todoitara, sassoku oshirase shimasu.
   I'll let you know <u>as soon as</u> I receive an e-mail.

3. あのサッカー選手は足が速い。
   Ano sakkā senshu wa ashi ga hayai.
   That soccer player <u>is a fast runner</u>.

4. テレビに事故のニュース速報が出た。
   Terebi ni jiko no nyūsu sokuhō ga deta.
   There was a <u>news flash</u> of the accident on TV.

5. 校内に残っている生徒は、速やかに帰りなさい。
   Kōnai ni nokotte iru seito wa, sumiyaka ni kaerinasai.
   Would all students still within the school grounds return home <u>without delay</u>!

Common Compounds and Phrases

速達	**sokutatsu**	express delivery
速度	**sokudo**	speed; velocity
高速道路	**kōsoku dōro**	an expressway; a freeway
急速に	**kyūsoku ni**	rapidly; swiftly; fast
速報	**sokuhō**	a quick report; a news flash
全速力で	**zensokuryoku de**	at full speed; as fast as one can
速歩で	**haya-ashi de**	(to walk) fast; at a trot

End the fifth stroke firmly.
10 一 戸 戸 戸 百 申 束 束 涑 速速

速

399 庭

テイ TEI
にわ niwa

court; garden

The character 庭 consists of a *large building* or *palace* 广 and *court* 廷, representing the place where people wait at court, namely a *courtyard* or *garden*.
GR3 N2 AP

Example Sentences

1. この季節になるとあそこの庭園がきれいです。
   Kono kisetsu ni naru to asoko no teien ga kirei desu.
   Those <u>gardens</u> are beautiful at this time of year.

2. 彼は家庭を大事にする人だ。
   Kare wa katei o daiji ni suru hito da.
   He takes good care of <u>his family</u>.

3. 家庭教師に、英会話のレッスンを受けている。
   Katei kyōshi ni, eikaiwa no ressun o ukete iru.
   I'm having English conversation lessons with <u>a private tutor</u>.

4. 子供が犬と庭で遊んでいる。
   Kodomo ga inu to niwa de asonde iru.
   The children are playing with the dog in <u>the garden</u>.

5. 中庭でおじいさんは日向ぼっこしていた。
   Nakaniwa de ojiisan wa hinata bokko shite ita.
   The old man was sunning himself in <u>the courtyard</u>.

Common Compounds and Phrases

庭園	**teien**	a garden; a park
家庭	**katei**	a home; a family; a household
家庭教師	**katei kyōshi**	a home (private) tutor
前庭	**zentei**	a front garden (yard); a forecourt
校庭	**kōtei**	a schoolyard; school grounds; a campus
中庭	**nakaniwa**	a courtyard; a quadrangle
裏庭	**uraniwa**	a back garden; a backyard

The last stroke protrudes.
10 ` 亠 广 广 庐 庄 庄 庭 庭 庭

庭

400 島

island

トウ TŌ
しま shima

Formerly written as 嶋, the character 島 combined *bird* 鳥 and *mountain* 山. A mountain where birds gather is a reference to *islands* in the sea.
GR3 N3 AP

Example Sentences

1. 今度の土曜日に伊豆半島にドライブに行こう。
   Kondo no doyōbi ni Izu-hantō ni doraibu ni ikō.
   Let's go for a drive to <u>the Izu Peninsula</u> this Saturday.

2. 無人島だが、野生のヤギがたくさんいる。
   Mujintō da ga, yasei no yagi ga takusan iru.
   The island is <u>uninhabited</u>, but there are many wild goats there.

3. 日本列島は、この冬、大雪に見舞われています。
   Nihon rettō wa, kono fuyu, ōyuki ni mimawarete imasu.
   <u>The Japanese archipelago</u> is having heavy snowfall this winter.

4. 伊豆大島は火山島です。
   Izu Ōshima wa kazantō desu.
   The island of Izu Ōshima is <u>volcanic</u>.

5. 日本は、アジア大陸の東側に位置する島国である。
   Nihon wa, Ajia tairiku no higashigawa ni itchi suru shimaguni de aru.
   Japan is <u>an island nation</u> lying off the east coast of the Asian continent.

Common Compounds and Phrases

無人島	**mujintō**	an uninhabited island
列島	**rettō**	an archipelago; a group of islands
火山島	**kazantō**	a volcanic island
諸島	**shotō**	a group of islands; an archipelago
島民	**tōmin**	the islanders
本島	**hontō**	the main island; this island
島国	**shimaguni**	an island country

The seventh stroke ends with a hook.

10 ′ 冖 宀 户 户 自 鸟 鸟 島 島

島

401 馬

horse

バ BA
うま uma　*ま MA

The character 馬 derived from a pictograph of a *horse*, showing its four legs and a tail drooping downwards.
GR2 N3

Example Sentences

1. 半年前から乗馬を始めました。
   Hantoshi mae kara jōba o hajimemashita.
   I took up <u>horse-riding</u> six months ago.

2. 女性にも競馬は人気がある。
   Josei ni mo keiba wa ninki ga aru.
   <u>Horse racing</u> is popular with women, as well.

3. 馬術はオリンピックの正式な競技種目です。
   Bajutsu wa orinpikku no seishiki na kyōgi shumoku desu.
   <u>Horsemanship</u> is an official Olympic sporting event.

4. 馬の耳に念仏。
   Uma no mimi ni nenbutsu.
   Preaching to <u>deaf ears</u> (*lit.* A sutra in <u>a horse's ear</u>—a saying)

5. 子供に、木馬を作ってあげた。
   Kodomo ni, mokuba o tsukutte ageta.
   I made <u>a rocking horse</u> for my child.

Common Compounds and Phrases

乗馬	**jōba**	riding on horseback; a mount
競馬	**keiba**	horse racing; the races
馬車	**basha**	a horse-drawn carriage
木馬	**mokuba**	a rocking horse, a vaulting horse
馬術	**bajutsu**	horseback riding; horsemanship
馬面	**umazura**	horse-faced; a long face
馬小屋	**umagoya**	a stable

Try to keep equal spacing between the horizontal strokes. Don't confuse 馬 with 鳥 (とり).

10 丨 厂 冂 丏 丐 馬 馬 馬 馬 馬

馬

402 配

ハイ HAI

くば・る kuba(ru)

to distribute

Of obscure origin, the character 配 is thought to combine *wine jar* 酉 and a *kneeling person* 己, representing a person pouring or *distributing* wine.
GR3 N3 AP

Example Sentences

1. これはいつ配達してもらえますか。
   Kore wa itsu haitatsu shite moraemasu ka.
   When can this <u>be delivered</u>?

2. お金は彼らに平等に配分された。
   Okane wa karera ni byōdō ni haibun sareta.
   The money <u>was</u> evenly <u>distributed</u> among them.

3. 生徒は試験の点数が心配だった。
   Seito wa shiken no tensū ga shinpai datta.
   The students <u>were worried</u> about their test marks.

4. 居間の家具の配置は何となく悪い。
   Ima no kagu no haichi wa nantonaku warui.
   There's something about <u>the arrangement</u> of the furniture in the living room that doesn't look right.

5. 間違えないように気を配ってください。
   Machigaenai yō ni ki o kubatte kudasai.
   <u>Be careful</u> not to make any mistakes.

Common Compounds and Phrases

配達	**haitatsu**	delivery
配分	**haibun**	distribution; division
支配人	**shihainin**	a manager; an executive
分配	**bunpai**	division; distribution
手配	**tehai**	arrangement; preparations
気を配る	**ki o kubaru**	to pay attention (to)
心配り	**kokoro-kubari**	thoughtful attention; care

The last stroke hooks upwards.

10 一 厂 冂 币 酉 酉 酉 酉ˀ 配ˀ 配

配

403 留

リュウ RYŪ *ル RU

と・める to(meru)

と・まる to(maru)

to keep; to stay

The character 留 formerly combined *horse's bit* and *reason* (here referring to *the link between the bit and the reins*.) To fasten to the bit came to mean *to fasten* or *stop*, in a general sense.
GR5 N3 AP

Example Sentences

1. 大学生だった頃、留学するチャンスはなかった。
   Daigakusei datta koro, ryūgaku suru chansu wa nakatta.
   I didn't have a chance <u>to study overseas</u> when I was at college.

2. 最終決定は来月まで保留された。
   Saishū kettei wa raigetsu made horyū sareta.
   The final decision <u>was deferred</u> until next month.

3. その言葉は心に留めておこう。
   Sono kotoba wa kokoro ni tomete okō.
   I'll <u>keep</u> what he said <u>in mind</u>.

4. 天井にハエが一匹留まっている。
   Tenjō ni hae ga ippiki tomatte iru.
   There <u>is</u> a fly <u>on</u> the ceiling.

5. 誰かが来たら、留守だと言いなさい。
   Dare ka ga kitara, rusu da to iinasai.
   If anyone comes, say I <u>am not at home</u>.

Common Compounds and Phrases

保留	**horyū**	to put on hold, defer
留年する	**ryūnen suru**	to repeat a year at school (college)
留守	**rusu**	absence; being away from the house
留守番電話	**rusuban denwa**	an answering machine
気に留める	**ki ni tomeru**	to pay attention to; to take something to heart
書留	**kakitome**	registered mail

The fourth stroke ends with a hook.

10 ´ ⺅ ⺊ ⺤ 卯 卯 叴 留 留 留

留

404 経

ケイ KEI　キョウ KYŌ
へ・る he(ru)

to manage;
passage

Formerly written as 經, the character 経 combined *long threads on a loom* 巠 and *thread* 糸 giving us the meanings of *passing through* and *longitude*.
GR5　N3　AP

Example Sentences

1. その会社はいくつかの鉄道とホテルを経営している。
   Sono kaisha wa ikutsu ka no tetsudō to hoteru o keiei shite iru.
   That company operates several railroads and hotels.

2. 二人とも海外生活の経験がある。
   Futari to mo kaigai seikatsu no keiken ga aru.
   The two of them have both lived abroad.

3. 十年があっという間に経過した。
   Jūnen ga atto iu ma ni keika shita.
   The ten years flew by in a twinkling.

4. 彼女は経済的理由で大学進学をあきらめた。
   Kanojo wa keizaiteki riyū de daigaku shingaku o akirameta.
   She gave up going on to college for economic reasons.

5. 必要な手続きを経て、ようやく永住権を与えられた。
   Hitsuyō na tetsuzuki o hete, yōyaku eijūken o ataerareta.
   After going through the necessary formalities, he was finally granted permanent residence.

Common Compounds and Phrases

経営	keiei	management; administration
経過する	keika suru	to elapse; to pass by
経済	keizai	(an) economy; economics
経費	keihi	expense(s); cost(s)
経理	keiri	accounting
経営者	keieisha	the CEO; management
お経	okyō	a sutra; the Buddhist scriptures

The eleventh stroke is longer than the ninth.

11 　く　纟　纟　纟　糸　糸　紅　終　経　紣　経

経

---

405 現

ゲン GEN
あらわ・れる arawa(reru)
あらわ・す arawa(su)

actual;
to appear

The character 現 is made up of *jewel* 王 and *to see* 見. Thus, from the sense of *to see a jewel* the meaning of *to be visible* or *appear* has derived. *To exist* and *now* are associated meanings.
GR5　N3　AP

Example Sentences

1. 価格表は2010年9月1日現在となっている。
   Kakakuhyō wa nisen jūnen kugatsu tsuitachi genzai to natte iru.
   Prices listed in the table are as of today, September 1st, 2010.

2. 母親からもらった小切手を現金にした。
   Hahaoya kara moratta kogitte o genkin ni shita.
   I cashed the check I received from my mother.

3. 長年の教員になる夢がやっと実現する。
   Naganen no kyōin ni naru yume ga yatto jitsugen suru.
   My long-cherished dream of becoming a teacher will be realized at last.

4. 壮大な景色が目の前に現れた。
   Sōdai na keshiki ga me no mae ni arawareta.
   A magnificent sight appeared in front of my eyes.

5. 友達が突然姿を現した。
   Tomodachi ga totsuzen sugata o arawashita.
   My friend appeared suddenly.

Common Compounds and Phrases

現在	genzai	presently; the present
実現	jitsugen	realization; actualization
現代	gendai	the present day, generation
現地	genchi	the actual place
現象	genshō	a phenomenon
現場	genba	the actual spot; the scene
現役	gen'eki	active service; at work

The last stroke hooks upwards.

11 　一　Ｔ　Ｆ　王　玌　玑　珇　珇　珇　玥　現

現

406 黄
yellow

コウ KŌ　オウ Ō
き ki　*こ ko

The character 黄 derived from a pictograph of a burning oil-tipped arrow, whose flames were *yellow*.

GR2　N3

Example Sentences

1. 山は黄色く色づき始めた。
   Yama wa kiiroku irozuki hajimeta.
   The leaves on the mountain trees have begun to turn a golden yellow.

2. ツタンカーメンの黄金のマスクを見た。
   Tsutankāmen no ōgon no masuku o mita.
   I saw King Tut's golden mask.

3. 青と黄色を混ぜると、緑になる。
   Ao to kiiro o mazeru to, midori ni naru.
   If blue and yellow are mixed, it becomes green.

4. 卵の黄身と白身を分けよう。
   Tamago no kimi to shiromi o wakeyō.
   I'll separate the egg yolk from the white.

5. 白いTシャツが黄ばんできた。
   Shiroi T-shatsu ga kibande kita.
   My white T-shirt has yellowed.

Common Compounds and Phrases

黄金	**ōgon**	gold
黄砂	**kōsa**	yellow sand
黄色人種	**ōshoku jinshu**	the yellow race
卵黄/黄身	**ran'ō / kimi**	the yolk (yellow) of an egg
黄色	**kiiro**	yellow
浅黄色	**asagiiro**	pale yellow
*黄昏	**tasogare**	dusk, twilight

The seventh stroke protrudes, touching the stroke above.

11　一 十 卄 芒 芦 芦 节 黹 萗 黄 黄

黄

407 婚
to marry

コン KON

The character 婚, of obscure origins, is believed to be made up of *woman* 女 and 昏, a reference to the *sunset*. This is presumed to reflect the practice of *marriages* taking place at sunset.
JK　N3　AP

Example Sentences

1. 結婚して二十年になります。
   Kekkon shite nijūnen ni narimasu.
   We have been married twenty years.

2. 婚約指輪が抜けなくなった。
   Konyaku yubiwa ga nukenaku natta.
   I can't get my engagement ring off my finger.

3. 婚礼の祝いの品物は、何がいいでしょうか。
   Konrei no iwai no shinamono wa, nani ga ii deshō ka.
   What would be a suitable gift to give as a wedding present?

4. 日本では、90%以上が「恋愛結婚」である。
   Nihon de wa, kyūjuppāsento ijō ga 'ren'ai kekkon' de aru.
   In Japan these days, more than 90% of all marriages are 'love-based marriages'.

5. 離婚することは「バツイチ」と呼ばれ珍しくなくなった。
   Rikon suru koto wa 'batsuichi' to yobare mezurashiku nakunatta.
   Being divorced, referred to as 'batsuichi', is no longer uncommon.

Common Compounds and Phrases

結婚記念日	**kekkon kinenbi**	one's wedding anniversary
国際結婚	**kokusai kekkon**	an international marriage
婚約	**konyaku**	an engagement; a betrothal
婚礼	**konrei**	a wedding (ceremony)
離婚	**rikon**	a divorce
再婚	**saikon**	remarriage
新婚さん	**shinkon-san**	newlyweds

The fourth stroke sweeps down from right to left.

11　く 女 女 女' 妒 妒 娇 娇 婚 婚 婚

婚

408 祭

サイ SAI
まつ・る matsu(ru)
まつ・り matsu(ri)

festival;
to honor

The character 祭 is a combination of *hand* 又, *meat* 月 and *altar* 示, a reference to a religious sacrifice during a ceremony. From this, the meanings of *festival* and *to worship* have derived.

GR3 N3 AP

Example Sentences

1. 月曜日は祭日なので、三連休になります。
   Getsuyōbi wa saijitsu na node, sanrenkyū ni narimasu.
   As Monday is a national holiday, we will have three consecutive days off.

2. 文化祭の準備で、毎日帰りが遅い。
   Bunkasai no junbi de, mainichi kaeri ga osoi.
   I've been getting home late every day because we're getting ready for the school festival.

3. 出雲大社は大国主命を祭っている。
   Izumo Taisha wa Ōkuninushi-no-Mikoto o matsutte iru.
   The Izumo Shrine is dedicated to Ō-kuninushi-no-Mikoto.

4. 今頃、後悔しても後の祭りだ。
   Imagoro, kōkai shite mo ato no matsuri da.
   It's too late now to feel sorry for what you did.

5. 毎年二月に、札幌で雪祭りが行われます。
   Maitoshi nigatsu ni, Sapporo de yuki-matsuri ga okonawaremasu.
   Every year, a snow festival is held in February in Sapporo.

Common Compounds and Phrases

祭日	**saijitsu**	a public holiday
文化祭	**bunka-sai**	a cultural (school) festival
体育祭	**taiiku-sai**	a field day; a sports day
祭典	**saiten**	a festival
冠婚葬祭	**kankon sōsai**	ceremonial occasions
雪祭り	**yuki-matsuri**	a snow festival
夏祭り	**natsu-matsuri**	a summer festival

The ninth stroke ends with a hook.

11 ノ ク タ タ 夕 夗 癶 癶 祭 祭 祭

祭

EXERCISE 34 (397 – 408)

A. Give the readings for the following.

1. 留まる _____
2. 馬小屋 _____
3. 島国 _____
4. 黄色い _____
5. 夏祭り _____
6. 速い _____
7. 経る _____
8. 手配 _____
9. 現れる _____
10. 祭日 _____

B. Write the following in English.

1. 書留 _____
2. 後の祭り _____
3. 馬車 _____
4. 黄身 _____
5. 経理 _____
6. 笑わずにいられなかった _____
7. 現場 _____
8. 心配です _____
9. 家庭 _____
10. 早速お知らせする _____

C. Write in kanji and kana.

1. きを くばる _____
2. りゅうがく せいかつ _____
3. すみやか に かえる _____
4. おもしろい けいけん _____
5. ひろしま に すんでいる _____
6. うま に のる _____
7. えがお に なる _____
8. しんこん りょこう に でかける _____
9. にわ しごとを する _____
10. げんきん で はらう _____

Review 11 (1 – 408)

A. Give the readings for the following.

1. 目指している _____
2. 留まる _____
3. 速やかに _____
4. 現す _____
5. 黄色 _____
6. 配る _____
7. 島 _____
8. 中庭 _____
9. 笑う _____
10. 馬面 _____

B. Write in English.

1. 後の祭りだ。_____
2. 不必要な物 _____
3. 馬小屋で火事があった。_____
4. 紙が黄ばんできている。_____
5. 心配しないで下さい。_____
6. 計画が実現する _____
7. 早速知らせる _____
8. 現地へ行く _____
9. 乗馬をする _____
10. 新婚生活 _____

C. Write in kanji and kana.

1. なつまつり _____
2. しないきょくばん _____
3. しんぶん　はいたつ _____
4. とうきょう　ほうめん _____
5. わらい　ばなし _____
6. はやく　できる　りょうり _____
7. けいりぶ _____
8. めだった　へんか _____
9. かざんとう _____
10. えいご　てきな　ひょうげん _____

D. Write in kanji and kana.

1. a specialist; an expert _____
2. registered mail _____
3. the year before last _____
4. a family; a household _____
5. a field day; a sports day _____
6. a peninsula _____
7. to appear _____
8. express delivery _____
9. an experience _____
10. a student studying abroad _____

E. Select the most appropriate word from the list to complete the expressions below:

LIST: 相手、広島、祭日、速度、神話、馬車、
酒場、現金、単語、新婚、小降り、笑い声、飛行、
手配、正面、お経、信号、前庭、残業、黄身

1. ＿＿＿＿＿ が聞こえる (laughter)
2. ＿＿＿＿＿ の意味が分からない (a word)
3. ＿＿＿＿＿ 払い (cash)
4. ＿＿＿＿＿ 待ちする (a traffic light)
5. 白身と ＿＿＿＿＿ (the yolk)
6. ＿＿＿＿＿ でキャッチボールをする (a front garden)
7. 雨が ＿＿＿＿＿ になった (light rain)
8. 宿を ＿＿＿＿＿ する (the arrangement)
9. 建物の ＿＿＿＿＿ (the front)
10. 月曜日は ＿＿＿＿＿ になる (a public holiday)
11. 強そうな ＿＿＿＿＿ (an opponent)
12. ＿＿＿＿＿ で育った (Hiroshima)
13. ＿＿＿＿＿ をはしごする (a bar)
14. ＿＿＿＿＿ を読む (a sutra)
15. 120 キロの ＿＿＿＿＿ を出す (a speed)
16. ＿＿＿＿＿ の多い会社 (overtime)
17. ＿＿＿＿＿ 旅行に出かける (newlyweds)
18. ＿＿＿＿＿ に乗ってみた (a carriage)
19. ギリシャ ＿＿＿＿＿ の中の人物 (a myth)
20. ロンドンまでの ＿＿＿＿＿ 時間 (a flight)

F. Add *furigana* to the kanji in the following and translate into English.

1. 馬が草原を速く走るすがたが美しい。
2. 昨日、経験したことの無いような大雨が降った。
3. 姉は新婚旅行で、南の島へ飛び立った。
4.「皆さんは、明日の祭日に何をしますか。」「私は、庭仕事をします。」「私は、家で面白い本でも読みましょう。」
5. 相変わらず、金曜日になるとあの人は酒屋に現れる。
6.「専門医にみてもらう必要がありますが、あまり心配しないで下さい。」
7. 係員は、荷物一個一個に黄色いステッカーをはっていた。
8.「残り少ない留学生活に何をする予定ですか。」
9. 小さかった時、火星人は背が低い、みどり色の生き物だと信じていた。
10. 人を指差して笑うのは失礼です。

409 細

サイ SAI
ほそ・い hoso(i)
ほそ・る hoso(ru)
こま・か koma(ka)
こま・かい koma(kai)

slender; detailed

The character 細 combines *thread* 糸 and *head seen from above* 田, suggesting the *fine* lines of the bones in the head.

GR2 N3

Example Sentences

1. 見積もりの明細書をくれますか。
   Mitsumori no <u>meisaisho</u> o kuremasu ka.
   Could you give me an estimate with the <u>details clearly listed</u>, please?

2. 彼女は細い割によく食べる。
   Kanojo wa <u>hosoi</u> wari ni yoku taberu.
   She eats a lot for someone so <u>thin</u>.

3. 年を取ると、だんだん食が細る。
   Toshi o toru to, dandan <u>shoku ga hosoru</u>.
   As people grow older, they gradually <u>lose their appetites</u>.

4. 何が起きたのか事細かに話してくれた。
   Nani ga okita no ka <u>kotokomaka ni</u> hanashite kureta.
   He gave me a <u>detailed</u> account of what happened.

5. 彼の字は細かいから、読むのが疲れる。
   Kare no ji wa <u>komakai</u> kara, yomu no ga tsukareru.
   He writes in <u>small</u> letters, so it's a strain to read his writing.

Common Compounds and Phrases

明細書	**meisaisho**	a detailed statement; details
詳細	**shōsai**	details; particulars
繊細な	**sensai na**	delicate; fine; subtle
細胞	**saibō**	a cell (biological)
細工	**saiku**	workmanship; a trick
細長い	**hosonagai**	long and narrow; slender
事細かに	**kotokomaka ni**	in detail; minutely

The 糸 element is slightly longer at both ends than the 田 element.

11 〈 幺 幺 幺 糸 糸 糸 糸 細 細 細

細

---

410 授

ジュ JU
さず・ける sazu(keru)
さず・かる sazu(karu)

to confer, to teach

The character 授 shows *hand* 手 with *to convey* 受, suggesting *to confer* or *bestow*, in particular, to confer knowledge or *teach*.

GR5 N3 AP

Example Sentences

1. 月曜日は午後四時まで授業がある。
   Getsuyōbi wa gogo yoji made <u>jugyō</u> ga aru.
   I have <u>classes</u> until four on Monday afternoon.

2. 川村先生は物理学の教授をしていた。
   Kawamura-sensei wa butsurigaku no <u>kyōju</u> o shite ita.
   Professor Kawamura was <u>a professor</u> of physics.

3. 三人の日本人科学者がノーベル賞の授賞式に出席しました。
   Sannin no Nihonjin kagakusha ga Nōberushō no <u>jushōshiki</u> ni shusseki shimashita.
   Three Japanese scientists attended the Nobel Prize <u>awards ceremony</u>.

4. 母は娘に「おふくろの味」を伝授した。
   Haha wa musume ni 'ofukuro-no-aji' o <u>denju shita</u>.
   The mother <u>instructed</u> her daughter in 'home cooking recipes'.

5. 結婚して七年目でようやく子供を授かった。
   Kekkon shite nananenme de yōyaku kodomo o <u>sazukatta</u>.
   In their seventh year of marriage, they <u>were</u> at last <u>blessed</u> with a child.

Common Compounds and Phrases

授業	**jugyō**	teaching; instruction; a lesson
教授	**kyōju**	teaching; a professor
授賞式	**jushōshiki**	an awards ceremony
授乳	**junyū**	breast-feeding
授与	**juyo**	presentation; awarding
伝授	**denju**	instruction; initiation
授受	**juju**	giving and receiving

The tenth and eleventh strokes do not connect at the top.

11 一 十 才 扌 扩 押 押 押 挼 授

授

411 宿

シュク SHUKU
やど yado　やど・る yado(ru)
やど・す yado(su)

lodge; inn

The character 宿 originally combined *building* 宀, *person* 亻 and a *rush mat* 丙 (this later becoming 百), a reference to resting, suggesting a building where a person can rest, namely a *house* or *inn*.

GR3　N3　AP

Example Sentences

1. 明日の夜、あのホテルに宿泊する予定です。
   Ashita no yoru, ano hoteru ni <u>shukuhaku suru</u> yotei desu.
   We're planning <u>to stay</u> at that hotel tomorrow night.

2. 兄はまだ宿題をしている。
   Ani wa mada <u>shukudai</u> o shite iru.
   My older brother is still working on <u>his homework</u>.

3. 宿に着いて、すぐにお風呂に入った。
   <u>Yado</u> ni tsuite, sugu ni ofuro ni haitta.
   As soon as I got to the <u>hotel</u>, I took a bath.

4. 健全な精神は健全な肉体に宿る。
   Kenzen na seishin wa kenzen na nikutai ni <u>yadoru</u>.
   A sound mind <u>in</u> a sound body. (a saying)

5. にわか雨が降ったので、雨宿りをした。
   Niwaka-ame ga futta node, <u>amayadori</u> o shita.
   I <u>took shelter</u> from a sudden shower.

Common Compounds and Phrases

宿泊	**shukuhaku**	lodging; accommodation
宿題	**shukudai**	homework; an assignment; a pending issue
合宿	**gasshuku suru**	to lodge (board) together; to go to a training camp
下宿	**geshuku**	boarding; lodging
寄宿学校	**kishuku gakkō**	a boarding school
雨宿り	**amayadori**	to take shelter from the rain

The seventh stroke is written at an angle.

11　丶 丶 宀 宀 宀 宁 宁 宿 宿 宿 宿

宿

412 術

ジュツ JUTSU

practical art; means; tactics

The character 術 is made up of *to go* (or *roads*) 行 with *to adhere* (or *twisting*) 朮 in the middle, suggesting adhering to a twisting road, referring to the *means* one employs to reach one's goal.

GR5　N3　AP

Example Sentences

1. 彼の手術後の回復はきわめて良好です。
   Kare no <u>shujutsugo</u> no kaifuku wa kiwamete ryōkō desu.
   He has made an excellent recovery <u>since his operation</u>.

2. あの絵は芸術的価値の高い作品だ。
   Ano e wa <u>geijutsuteki</u> kachi no takai sakuhin da.
   That picture is a work of great <u>artistic</u> value.

3. その調理師はイタリアで優れた技術を身につけた。
   Sono chōrishi wa Itaria de sugureta <u>gijutsu</u> o mi ni tsuketa.
   That chef acquired his superior <u>technique</u> in Italy.

4. この新聞社で美術評論家を募集している。
   Kono shinbunsha de <u>bijutsu</u> hyōronka o boshū shite iru.
   This newspaper is looking for <u>an art critic</u>.

5. 美術館へ行くには、どのバスに乗ればいいんですか。
   <u>Bijutsukan</u> e iku ni wa, dono basu ni noreba ii n desu ka.
   Which bus do I take to get to <u>the art museum</u>?

Common Compounds and Phrases

手術	**shujutsu**	an operation; surgery
芸術	**geijutsu**	art; artwork
技術	**gijutsu**	technique; technology
美術	**bijutsu**	art; fine art
催眠術	**saiminjutsu**	hypnosis
学術調査	**gakujutsu chōsa**	a scientific investigation
戦術	**senjutsu**	tactics; strategy

Don't forget the dot.

11　丿 彳 彳 彳 忰 忦 㣼 徆 術 術 術

術

413 商

ショウ SHŌ
あきな・う akina(u)

business;
to trade

Of obscure origin, however, the character 商 is thought to be a reference to the *vagina* and thus, an association with prostitution—the oldest *trade* in the world.

GR3 N3 AP

Example Sentences

1. 彼の商売は八百屋だ。
   Kare no shōbai wa yaoya da.
   He is a green-grocer by <u>trade</u>.

2. この店は色々な商品を扱っている。
   Kono mise wa iroiro na shōhin o atsukatte iru.
   This store carries many kinds of <u>merchandise</u>.

3. 主人は商社マンです。
   Shujin wa shōsha-man desu.
   My husband <u>works for a trading company</u>.

4. 商業区域内の歩道ではスケートボードは禁止されています。
   Shōgyō kuikinai no hodō de wa sukēto bōdo wa kinshi sarete imasu.
   The riding of skateboards is prohibited on sidewalks <u>in the business district</u>.

5. 実家はお米を商っている。
   Jikka wa okome o akinatte iru.
   My parents are <u>rice dealers</u>.

Common Compounds and Phrases

商品	**shōhin**	an article; a product
商業	**shōgyō**	commerce; business
商店街	**shōtengai**	a shopping arcade, street
商人	**shōnin**	a merchant; a trader
貿易商	**bōekishō**	a trading merchant
商工業	**shōkōgyō**	commerce and industry
商い	**akinai**	business; trading

The sixth stroke ends with a hook.

11 ` ー 亠 亠 产 产 产 商 商 商 商

商

---

414 接

セツ SETSU
つ・ぐ tsu(gu)

to contact;
to touch

The character 接 is a combination of *hand* 扌 and *concubine* 妾, the latter element being associated with the meaning of *to join*. Thus, joining hands suggests *contact* in a broader sense.

GR5 N3 AP

Example Sentences

1. うちは幼稚園にすぐ隣に接している。
   Uchi wa yōchien ni sugu tonari ni sesshite iru.
   Our house is <u>adjacent to</u> a kindergarten.

2. 台風が南から接近している。
   Taifū ga minami kara sekkin shite iru.
   A typhoon <u>is approaching</u> from the south.

3. あの交差点で接触事故を起こした。
   Ano kōsaten de sesshoku jiko o okoshita.
   I was involved in <u>a minor collision</u> at that intersection.

4. 客を応接室に通した。
   Kyaku o ōsetsushitsu ni tōshita.
   I showed the guest into <u>the drawing room</u>.

5. 病院で骨を接いでもらった。
   Byōin de hone o tsuide moratta.
   I <u>had</u> my broken bone <u>set</u> at the hospital.

Common Compounds and Phrases

接する	**sessuru**	to come into contact with; to touch
接触	**sesshoku**	contact; touch
応接室	**ōsetsushitsu**	a parlor; a drawing room
接続	**setsuzoku**	(a) connection; union
面接試験	**mensetsu shiken**	an oral test; an interview
間接に	**kansetsu ni**	indirectly
接待	**settai**	entertaining; a reception

Watch the order of strokes with the 女 element (く、ノ、一).

11 ー 十 扌 扩 扩 护 护 按 接 接

接

415 雪

snow

セツ SETSU
ゆき yuki

The character 雪 combines *rain* 雨 and *broom* ヨ, suggesting that what has fallen can be swept, namely, *snow*.

GR2 N3 AP

Example Sentences

1. 積雪が三メートルある。
   Sekisetsu ga sanmētoru aru.
   <u>The snow</u> is three meters deep.

2. この先除雪作業中。
   Kono saki josetsu sagyōchū.
   <u>Snow removal</u> underway ahead.

3. 雪が降って、一面真っ白だ。
   Yuki ga futte, ichimen masshiro da.
   It <u>has snowed</u> and blanketed everything in white.

4. 大雪のため、電車は30分ほど遅れて運転しています。
   Ōyuki no tame, densha wa sanjuppun hodo okurete unten shite imasu.
   The trains are running about thirty minutes late because of <u>heavy snowfalls</u>.

5. 春先は雪崩が多い。
   Harusaki wa nadare ga ōi.
   There are frequent <u>avalanches</u> in early spring.

Common Compounds and Phrases

積雪	**sekisetsu**	(fallen) snow
除雪	**josetsu**	snow removal
新雪	**shinsetsu**	fresh snow
大雪	**ōyuki**	a heavy snowfall
雪国	**yukiguni**	a snowy district
雪だるま	**yuki-daruma**	a snowman
*吹雪	**fubuki**	a blizzard; a snowstorm

The tenth stroke does not protrude. Note the differences between 雨、雪 and 曇.

11 ｜ 一 厂 厅 而 雨 雨 雪 雪 雪 雪

雪

416 船

ship

セン SEN
ふね fune　ふな funa

The character 船 combines *boat* 舟 and *flowing water in a ravine* 㕣, suggesting a *large boat* capable of going against a current.

GR2 N3

Example Sentences

1. 父は漁船の事故で亡くなりました。
   Chichi wa gyosen no jiko de nakunarimashita.
   My father died in <u>a fishing boat</u> accident.

2. ここは造船業で栄えた町です。
   Koko wa zōsengyō de sakaeta machi desu.
   This town has prospered due to the <u>shipbuilding industry</u>.

3. 祖父は船で英国へ渡った。
   Sofu wa fune de eikoku e watatta.
   My grandfather went to England <u>by ship</u>.

4. 港は船出を見送る人でいっぱいだった。
   Minato wa funade o miokuru hito de ippai datta.
   The harbor was full of people <u>seeing off the ship</u>.

5. 船便で荷物が届いた。
   Funabin de nimotsu ga todoita.
   A parcel arrived by <u>sea mail</u>.

Common Compounds and Phrases

漁船	**gyosen**	a fishing boat
造船	**zōsen**	shipbuilding
風船	**fūsen**	a balloon
船長	**senchō**	a ship's captain
貨物船	**kamotsusen**	a freighter
船出	**funade**	the departure of a ship
船便	**funabin**	a shipping service; sea mail

The sixth stroke sweeps up from left to right.

11 ′ 丿 丬 月 月 舟 舟 舯 船 船 船

船

417 側

ソク SOKU
かわ kawa

side

The character 側 combines *person* イ and *rule* or *model* 則 and is thought to express the idea of *to lean*, hence there is the sense of a person leaning to one *side*.
GR4 N3 AP

Example Sentences

1. この建物は、側面から光が入るよう設計されている。
   Kono tatemono wa, sokumen kara hikari ga hairu yō sekkei sarete iru.
   This building is designed such that light may come in from the side.

2. 左側によってください。
   Hidarigawa ni yotte kudasai.
   Please keep to the left.

3. 窓の外側に、大きなチョウ[チョウチョ]が止まっている。
   Mado no sotogawa ni, ōki na chō [chōcho] ga tomatte iru.
   There is a large butterfly on the outside of the window.

4. 道の両側でたくさんの人がマラソンの応援していた。
   Michi no ryōgawa de takusan no hito ga marason no ōen shite ita.
   Lots of people were cheering the marathon runners from both sides of the road.

5. 反対側を開けてください。
   Hantai-gawa o akete kudasai.
   Open the other end please.

Common Compounds and Phrases

側面	**sokumen**	the side; an aspect
側近	**sokkin**	a (close) aide
右側通行	**migigawa tsūkō**	keeping to the right
外側	**sotogawa**	the outside
反対側	**hantai-gawa**	the other (opposite) side
裏側	**uragawa**	the back (reverse) side
西側	**nishigawa**	the west(ern) side

The last stroke ends with a hook.

11 ノ イ 仴 仴 佀 侀 侀 側 側 側 側

側

---

418 第

ダイ DAI

rank; No.~

The character 第 is made up of *bamboo (tablets)* 竹 and 弔, a variant of *younger brother*, here meaning *sequence*. Putting bamboo tablets in order gives us the general sense of *order*, or *sequence*.
GR3 N3 AP

Example Sentences

1. 第一に時間を守ること。
   Daiichi ni jikan o mamoru koto.
   Above all, be punctual.

2. 何事も、まず第一歩を踏み出すのが一番大変だ。
   Nanigoto mo, mazu dai-ippo o fumidasu no ga ichiban taihen da.
   The hardest part in anything you do is taking the first step.

3. 私は第二職員住宅に長く住んでいた。
   Watashi wa daini shokuin jūtaku ni nagaku sunde ita.
   I lived in Staff Residence No. 2 for quite some time.

4. 雨が上がり次第出かけよう。
   Ame ga agari shidai dekakeyō.
   We'll leave as soon as it stops raining.

5. 大学二年のとき、落第した。
   Daigaku ninen no toki, rakudai shita.
   When I was a sophomore, I had to do another year.

Common Compounds and Phrases

第一に	**daiichi ni**	firstly; first of all
第一印象	**daiichi inshō**	one's first impression
第一人者	**daiichi ninsha**	the top-ranking player; the leading authority
次第に	**shidai ni**	gradually; bit by bit
落第	**rakudai**	failure; repeating a grade
第三者	**daisansha**	a third party (person)
第六感	**dairokkan**	a sixth sense; intuition

The ninth stroke ends with a hook.

11 ノ ト ホ 竹 竺 竺 竹 笃 笃 第 第

第

419 婦　フ FU

adult; woman

The character 婦 is a combination of *woman* 女 and *hand holding a broom* 帚, evoking the idea of *woman* or *wife*.

GR5　N3　AP

Example Sentences

1. 婦人服売り場で、かわいいブラウスを買った。
   Fujinfuku uriba de, kawaii burausu o katta.
   I bought myself a cute blouse in the <u>women's clothing</u> department.

2. 夫婦揃って、ゴルフが大好きだそうです。
   Fūfu sorotte, gorufu ga daisuki da sō desu.
   I hear that <u>both husband and wife</u> are keen golfers.

3. 多くの新郎新婦は、海外での結婚式にあこがれています。
   Ōku no shinrō shinpu wa, kaigai de no kekkonshiki ni akogarete imasu.
   Many <u>brides and grooms</u> long for a wedding ceremony overseas.

4. 母は専業主婦です。
   Haha wa sengyō shufu desu.
   My mother is a <u>full-time homemaker</u>.

5. 婦人科医になるため、何年ぐらい勉強しましたか。
   Fujinkai ni naru tame, nannen gurai benkyō shimashita ka.
   How many years of study did it take to become <u>a gynecologist</u>?

Common Compounds and Phrases

婦人	**fujin**	a wife; a married woman; Mrs.
婦人物	**fujinmono**	women's items
夫婦げんか	**fūfu genka**	a quarrel between husband and wife
新郎新婦	**shinrō shinpu**	a bride and groom
専業主婦	**sengyō shufu**	a full-time housewife
婦人科医	**fujinkai**	a gynecologist
産婦人科	**sanfujinka**	obstetrics and gynecology

The eight and tenth strokes end with hooks.

11 く 女 女 女' 妒 妒 妒 婦 婦 婦 婦

婦

420 部　ブ BU

section; part

The character 部 is of obscure origin, however it is thought to combine *to divide* 咅 and *people living in a village* 阝, a village being a smaller division or *part* of a larger district.

GR3　N3　AP

Example Sentences

1. その実験は部分的には成功した。
   Sono jikken wa bubunteki ni wa seikō shita.
   The experiment was a <u>partial</u> sucess.

2. 教室には全部で39人の生徒がいた。
   Kyōshitsu ni wa zenbu de sanjūkyū-nin no seito ga ita.
   <u>All together</u>, there were thirty-nine students in the classroom.

3. あの教員は昨年から柔道部のこもんをしている。
   Ano kyōin wa sakunen kara jūdōbu no komon o shite iru.
   That teacher has been the adviser for <u>the Judo Club</u> since last year.

4. 渋谷の本部に転勤するらしい。
   Shibuya no honbu ni tenkin suru rashii.
   Apparently, she's being transferred to <u>the head office</u> in Shibuya.

5. 十階に空き部屋が三つあります。
   Jukkai ni akibeya ga mittsu arimasu.
   There are three <u>rooms available</u> on the tenth floor.

Common Compounds and Phrases

全部で	**zenbu de**	in all; all together
本部	**honbu**	head office; the headquarters
営業部	**eigyōbu**	the business department
北部	**hokubu**	the northern part; the North
文学部	**bungakubu**	the department of literature
大部分	**daibubun**	the majority; most (of)
部分的に	**bubunteki ni**	partly

Don't write 阝 as 卩.

11 ' ㇗ ㇉ ㇌ 立 产 咅 咅 咅' 咅^阝 部

部

EXERCISE 35 (409 – 420)

A. Give the readings for the following.
1. 次第に _____
2. 教授 _____
3. 部屋 _____
4. 手術 _____
5. 船 _____
6. 接する _____
7. 細かい _____
8. 新雪 _____
9. 宿 _____
10. 商う _____

B. Write the following in kanji and kana according to the English.
1. ひだり がわ つうこう (keeping to the left)
   _____
2. めんせつ しけん を うける (to be interviewed)
   _____
3. しゅくはく りょう を はらう (to pay a hotel bill)
   _____
4. ぶんがく ぶちょう (the dean of the faculty of literature)
   _____

5. ほそながい かたち (a long, narrow shape)
   _____
6. しょうひん の うりあげ (sales of a product)
   _____
7. たいふう の せっきん (the approach of a typhoon)
   _____
8. じゅぎょう が はじまる (classes start)
   _____
9. おおゆき が ふる (to have a heavy snowfall)
   _____

C. Match the following.

1. 美術品 ( )	a. りょうがわ
2. 風船 ( )	b. だいさんしゃ
3. 商人 ( )	c. しんじゅく
4. 全部 ( )	d. あまやどり
5. 雨宿り ( )	e. ぜんぶ
6. 夫婦 ( )	f. びじゅつひん
7. 両側 ( )	g. ふうせん
8. 新宿 ( )	h. めいさいしょ
9. 明細書 ( )	i. しょうにん
10. 第三者 ( )	j. ふうふ

---

421 雲

ウン **UN**
くも **kumo**

cloud

GR2 N3

The character 雲 combines *rain* 雨 and *billowing* 云 to represent *clouds*.

Example Sentences

1. 天体望遠鏡でアンドロメダ星雲を見た。
   Tentai bōenkyō de Andoromeda seiun o mita.
   I observed the Andromeda <u>Nebula</u> using a telescope.

2. 雲泥の差がある。
   Undei no sa ga aru.
   The two things are as different as <u>chalk and cheese</u>.
   (lit. clouds and mud).

3. 空は雲一つない晴天だ。
   Sora wa kumo hitotsu nai seiten da.
   There's not a <u>cloud</u> in the sky.

4. 月が雲間から現れた。
   Tsuki ga kumoma kara arawareta.
   The moon peeked out from <u>between the clouds</u>.

5. 雨雲が出てきた。
   Amagumo ga dete kita.
   <u>Rain clouds</u> have appeared.

Common Compounds and Phrases

星雲	**seiun**	a nebula
雲海	**unkai**	a sea of clouds
積乱雲	**sekiran'un**	cumulonimbus clouds
雲間	**kumoma**	a break between clouds
雨雲	**amagumo**	a rain cloud
入道雲	**nyūdō-gumo**	a thunderhead
夕焼け雲	**yūyake-gumo**	sunset clouds

The tenth stroke is longer than the ninth.

12 一 гヮ 戸 戸 帀 帀 雨 雪 雪 雲 雲 雲

雲

422 温

オン ON
あたた・か atata(ka)
あたた・かい atata(kai)
あたた・まる atata(maru)
あたた・める atata(meru)

warm;
temperature

Originally written 溫, the character 温 referred to the *warm* act of kindness of giving a *prisoner* 囚 a *bowl* 皿 of *water* 氵, the figurative meaning of *warm* being retained.
GR3 N3 AP

Example Sentences

1. 今度の週末、海に行くか温泉に行くか迷っている。
   Kondo no shūmatsu, umi ni iku ka onsen ni iku ka mayotte iru.
   I can't decide whether I'll go to the seaside this weekend, or go to a hot spring.

2. 気温は零度に下がった。
   Kion wa reido ni sagatta.
   The temperature dropped to freezing point.

3. 田舎で心温まるもてなしを受けた。
   Inaka de kokoro-atatamaru motenashi o uketa.
   I was given a heart-warming reception in the country.

4. スズメたちは日光で温まっていた。
   Suzumetachi wa nikkō de nukumatte ita.
   The sparrows were warming themselves in the sun.

5. 牛乳を電子レンジで温めましょうか。
   Gyūnyū o denshi-renji de atatamemashō ka.
   Shall I warm the milk up for you in the microwave?

Common Compounds and Phrases

温泉	**onsen**	a hot spring
気温	**kion**	(atmospheric) temperature
温度	**ondo**	a temperature
体温	**taion**	body temperature
温水プール	**onsui pūru**	a heated swimming pool
地球温暖化	**chikyū ondanka**	global warming
心温まる	**kokoro-atatamaru**	heartwarming

Don't write 皿 as 皿.

12 `⼂ ⼃ 氵 汩 汩 沮 渭 渭 温 温 温

温

423 絵

カイ KAI エ E

picture

The character 絵 combines *thread* 糸 and *to come together* 会 to suggest an embroidered *picture*.

GR2 N3 AP

Example Sentences

1. 印象派の絵画展を見に行こう。
   Inshōha no kaigaten o mi ni ikō.
   Let's go and see the exhibition of Impressionist paintings.

2. 子供の時から、絵を描くのが好きだ。
   Kodomo no toki kara, e o kaku no ga suki da.
   I've liked drawing since my childhood.

3. この絵葉書を受け取る頃には、私は休暇から戻っているだろう。
   Kono ehagaki o uketoru koro ni wa, watashi wa kyūka kara modotte iru darō.
   By the time you receive this postcard, I'll be back from my holiday.

4. 趣味で油絵を描いている。
   Shumi de aburae o kaite iru.
   I do oil painting as a hobby.

5. 浮世絵は木版画です。
   Ukiyoe wa mokuhanga desu.
   Ukiyoe pictures are woodblock prints.

Common Compounds and Phrases

絵画	**kaiga**	pictorial arts; a painting
絵葉書	**ehagaki**	a picture postcard
油絵	**aburae**	(an) oil painting
似顔絵	**nigaoe**	a portrait
絵本	**ehon**	a picture book
絵の具	**enogu**	paint; colors
絵描き	**ekaki**	a painter; an artist

The first two strokes are each written as one fluid motion. End the last stroke firmly.

12 ⼂ ⼥ ⼦ ⼿ 糸 糸 糹 紵 給 紩 絵 絵

絵

424 階

カイ KAI

floor; rank; step

The character 階 is made up of *terraced hill* 阝 and *all* 皆, here suggesting a *row*. From the idea of a row of terraces on a hillside, the meaning of *step* has derived.
GR3 N3 AP

Example Sentences

1. 遅刻しそうだったので、階段を駆け上がった。
   Chikoku shisō datta node, kaidan o kakeagatta.
   Worried about being late, I ran up <u>the stairs</u>.

2. 今の段階では成功の見込みが薄い。
   Ima no dankai de wa seikō no mikomi ga usui.
   <u>At this stage</u>, there's not much likelihood of success.

3. 階級のない社会は実現できるだろうか。
   Kaikyū no nai shakai wa jitsugen dekiru darō ka.
   Is a <u>classless</u> society possible?

4. 事務所は6階にあります。
   Jimusho wa rokkai ni arimasu.
   The office is on <u>the sixth floor</u>.

5. となりの子は音階練習ばかりしている。
   Tonari no ko wa onkai renshū bakari shite iru.
   That child next door is <u>practicing</u> her <u>scales</u> over and over.

Common Compounds and Phrases

階段	**kaidan**	stairs; a step
段階	**dankai**	a step; a stage; a rank
階級	**kaikyū**	class; rank; position
一階	**ikkai**	a first (ground) floor
二階建て	**nikai-date**	two stories (-storied)
地階	**chikai**	a basement; a cellar
音階	**onkai**	a musical scale

Don't write ㇏ as 七.

12 ㇂ ㇂ 阝 阝 阝 阝 阝 阝 阝 階 階 階

階

---

425 期

キ KI
＊ゴ GO

term; to expect

Formerly written 朞 the *sun* or *day* element 日 became *moon* or *month* 月, indicating *time*. 其 was a *winnowing device*, suggesting a cycle of *time*, hence a *term*. To expect is a derived meaning.
GR3 N3 AP

Example Sentences

1. 比較的短い期間だったけど、楽しかった。
   Hikakuteki mijikai kikan datta kedo, tanoshikatta.
   It was a relatively short <u>period of time</u>, but it was fun.

2. このチーズは賞味期限が切れている。
   Kono chiizu wa shōmi kigen ga kirete iru.
   This cheese is past its <u>expiration date</u>.

3. 出発を一ヶ月延期した。
   Shuppatsu o ikkagetsu enki shita.
   We <u>postponed</u> our departure for a month.

4. 定期預金が二十日で満期になります。
   Teiki yokin ga hatsuka de manki ni narimasu.
   My <u>term deposit</u> <u>matures</u> on the twentieth of the month.

5. 期待したほど面白くなかった。
   Kitai shita hodo omoshirokunakatta.
   It wasn't as interesting as I <u>had expected</u>.

Common Compounds and Phrases

期間	**kikan**	a term; a period of time
期限	**kigen**	a term; a time limit
延期	**enki**	postponement; deferment
定期預金	**teiki yokin**	a term (time) deposit
時期	**jiki**	a time (of year); a season
二学期	**nigakki**	the second term (semester)
短期	**tanki**	a short time (term)

The seventh and eighth strokes do not connect.

12 一 十 卄 卄 卅 甘 其 其 期 期 期 期

期

426 結

to tie; to conclude

ケツ KETSU
むす・ぶ musu(bu)
ゆ・う yu(u)
ゆ・わえる yu(waeru)

The character 結 combines *thread* 糸 and *good luck* 吉, here expressing *to entwine*. Hence, we have the meaning of to *tie* threads together and by extension, *to tie up* or *conclude*.

GR4 N3 AP

Example Sentences

1. 試合の結果はどうだった？
   Shiai no kekka wa dō datta?
   What was the <u>result</u> of the match?

2. 田中さんは結婚したばかりです。
   Tanaka-san wa kekkon shita bakari desu.
   Ms. Tanaka is newly <u>married</u>.

3. 迷ったけれど、結局いつもと同じレストランに行った。
   Mayotta keredo, kekkyoku itsumo to onaji resutoran ni itta.
   I was in two minds but <u>ended up</u> going to the same restaurant as always.

4. 何歳で靴ひもが結べるようになりましたか。
   Nansai de kutsuhimo ga musuberu yō ni narimashita ka.
   How old were you when you were <u>able to tie</u> your shoelaces?

5. 彼女は成人式のため、髪を結ってもらった。
   Kanojo wa seijinshiki no tame, kami o yutte moratta.
   She <u>had</u> her hair <u>done</u> for the *Coming of Age* ceremony.

Common Compounds and Phrases

結果	**kekka**	a result; an outcome
結婚	**kekkon**	marriage; matrimony
結論	**ketsuron**	a conclusion; a judgment
完結	**kanketsu**	conclusion; completion
終結	**shūketsu**	a conclusion; an end
結晶	**kesshō**	a crystal; crystallization
結び目	**musubime**	a knot; a tie

The ninth stroke is shorter than the seventh.

12 　乙 幺 幺 糸 糸 糸 糸 紵 結 結 結 結

結

---

427 港

port

コウ KŌ
みなと minato

The character 港 is made up of *water* 氵 and *forking road* 巷, suggesting a forking river or delta, a suitable place for a *port*.

GR3 N3 AP

Example Sentences

1. 客船はシドニーを出港して五日経った。
   Kyakusen wa Shidonii o shukkō shite itsuka tatta.
   The passenger ship was five days <u>out from</u> Sydney.

2. 航空料金に空港使用料が含まれている。
   Kōkū ryōkin ni kūkō shiyōryō ga fukumarete iru.
   The airfare includes the <u>airport service charge</u>.

3. 港には小さい漁船がたくさん停泊していた。
   Minato ni wa chiisai gyosen ga takusan teihaku shite ita.
   There were many little fishing vessels anchored in <u>the harbor</u>.

4. 福岡県に新北九州空港が開港しました。
   Fukuoka-ken ni shin-kitakyūshū kūkō ga kaikō shimashita.
   The new Kita-Kyushu <u>Airport</u> has <u>opened</u> in Fukuoka Prefecture.

5. 横浜は活気のある港町だ。
   Yokohama wa kakki no aru minato-machi da.
   Yokohama is a <u>port town</u>, bustling with activity.

Common Compounds and Phrases

出港	**shukkō**	leaving port (harbor)
入港	**nyūkō**	entry into port
国際空港	**kokusai kūkō**	an international airport
開港	**kaikō**	the opening of a(n) (air)port
神戸港	**Kōbe-kō**	Kobe Harbor (Port)
港町	**minato-machi**	a port (town)
*香港	**Honkon**	Hong Kong (a place)

Don't write 己 as 巳 (み).

12 　丶 丶 氵 汀 汫 汫 洪 洪 洪 港 港

港

428 最

サイ SAI
もっと・も motto(mo)

most; the best

The character 最 combines 日, a variant of 冒, *warrior's helmet*, here representing to attack and 取, *to take*, suggesting to take by extreme force. The sense of *most* has derived from this.
GR4 N3 AP

Example Sentences

1. 今日の最高気温は35度でした。
   Kyō no saikō kion wa sanjūgo-do deshita.
   The <u>maximum temperature</u> today was thirty-five degrees.

2. 最初は日本語が難しかった。
   Saisho wa Nihongo ga muzukashikatta.
   Japanese was difficult <u>at first</u>.

3. 最終電車は何時ですか。
   Saishū densha wa nanji desu ka.
   What time is <u>the last train</u>?

4. 最近、何か変わったことはありませんか。
   Saikin, nani ka kawatta koto wa arimasen ka.
   Any news, <u>lately</u>?

5. グレート・バリア・リーフは世界で最も大きいサンゴ礁である。
   Gurēto Baria Riifu wa sekai de <u>mottomo ōkii</u> sangoshō de aru.
   The Great Barrier Reef is <u>the largest</u> system of coral reefs in the world.

Common Compounds and Phrases

最初	saisho	the start; the first time
最中に	saichū ni	in the midst of
最善をつくす	saizen o tsukusu	to do one's best
最強の	saikyō no	the most powerful
最新の	saishin no	the newest; the most recent
最大の	saidai no	the greatest; the largest
*最寄の	moyori no	the nearest; nearby

The ninth stroke sweeps up from left to right.

12 丨 冂 冂 冃 旦 旦 � 昻 昂 昻 最 最

最

429 晴

セイ SEI
は・れる ha(reru)
は・らす ha(rasu)

fine weather

The character 晴 combines *sun* 日 and *blue* 青 to suggest *clear weather*.

GR2 N3 AP

Example Sentences

1. 晴天が週末いっぱい持ってくれるといいですね。
   Seiten ga shūmatsu ippai motte kureru to ii desu ne.
   I hope the <u>clear weather</u> stays for the weekend.

2. 日曜日の運動会は快晴に恵まれた。
   Nichiyōbi no undōkai wa <u>kaisei</u> ni megumareta.
   We were blessed with <u>fine weather</u> for Sunday's sports day.

3. 明日もきっと晴れでしょう。
   Ashita mo kitto hare deshō.
   I'm sure the weather will be <u>fine</u> tomorrow too!

4. 彼の疑いが晴れた。
   Kare no <u>utagai ga hareta</u>.
   He was <u>cleared of all suspicion</u>.

5. 美味しい物でも食べて、気分を晴らそう。
   Oishii mono de mo tabete, <u>kibun o harasō</u>.
   Let's enjoy some fine food and <u>cheer ourselves up</u>.

Common Compounds and Phrases

晴天	seiten	clear weather
快晴	kaisei	fine (clear) weather
晴れ間	harema	an interval of clear weather
晴れ着	haregi	one's best clothes
晴れ晴れ	harebare	cloudless; bright; cheerful
日本晴れ	Nihon-bare	glorious weather
素晴らしい	subarashii	wonderful; excellent; superb

The eighth stroke is longer than those above it, and the tenth ends with a hook. Don't confuse 晴 with 青 (あお) or 清 (せい).

12 丨 冂 月 日 日⁻ 日⁺ 日垂 晴 晴 晴 晴 晴

晴

430 然

ゼン ZEN　ネン NEN

exactly; certainly;
however; so

The character 然 is a combination of *fire* 灬,
meat 月 and *dog* 犬, meaning *to roast dog meat*.
From this, it has assumed the meaning of *as
things should be*, through phonetic borrowing.
GR4　N2　AP

Example Sentences

1. そんな事は全然問題にならない。
   Sonna koto wa zenzen mondai ni naranai.
   It doesn't matter in the slightest.

2. 街からは自然が年々失われていく。
   Machi kara wa shizen ga nennen ushinawarete iku.
   The town is losing more of its natural environment year
   by year.

3. 私は彼に偶然新宿で会った。
   Watashi wa kare ni gūzen Shinjuku de atta.
   I met him in Shinjuku by chance.

4. 借りた物を返すのは当然だ。
   Karita mono o kaesu no wa tōzen da.
   It is only natural to return what you have borrowed.

5. この魚は天然のものですか。
   Kono sakana wa tennen no mono desu ka.
   Is this a wild (not farmed) fish?

Common Compounds and Phrases

全然	**zenzen**	not at all; totally; very
自然	**shizen**	nature; naturalness
自然保護	**shizen hogo**	environmental protection
偶然	**gūzen**	by chance; unexpectedly
当然	**tōzen**	naturally; of course
突然の	**totsuzen no**	sudden; unexpected
平然と	**heizen to**	calmly; matter-of-factly

Don't forget the dot at the top.

12　ノ　ク　タ　タ　タ　外　然　然　然　然　然　然

然

431 達

タツ TATSU

to attain;
plural suffix

The character 達 is made up of *movement* 辶
and *ease* 幸 (originally *big* 大 and *sheep* 羊).
Easy movement is a reference to the *attainment*
of a goal without difficulty.
GR4　N3　AP

Example Sentences

1. もう少しで目的地に達するだろう。
   Mō sukoshi de mokutekichi ni tassuru darō.
   We'll arrive at our destination shortly.

2. 祖父は八十歳を越えても、まだまだ達者です。
   Sofu wa hachijussai o koete mo, madamada tassha desu.
   My grandfather is over eighty, but he still keeps good
   health.

3. やっと論文を書き終えて、大きな達成感を味わった。
   Yatto ronbun o kakioete, ōki na tasseikan o ajiwatta.
   I felt a great sense of achievement when I completed my
   thesis.

4. 君は日本語の上達が早いですね。
   Kimi wa Nihongo no jōtatsu ga hayai desu ne.
   You're making rapid progress in Japanese, aren't you?

5. 友達と映画を見に行った。
   Tomodachi to eiga o mi ni itta.
   I went to see a movie with a friend.

Common Compounds and Phrases

達する	**tassuru**	to reach; to attain
達者な	**tassha na**	fit; healthy
達成	**tassei**	achievement; attainment
上達	**jōtatsu**	progress; improvement
達人	**tatsujin**	an expert; a master; a philosopher
発達	**hattatsu**	development; growth; progress
達筆な	**tappitsu na**	having good handwriting

Make the third and eighth strokes longer.

12　一　十　十　去　未　查　查　幸　幸　達　達

達

432 遅 slow; late; to be late; to be delayed	チ CHI おく・れる oku(reru) おく・らす oku(rasu) おそ・い oso(i)	The character 遅 originally consisted of *movement* 辶, *tail* 犀 and *cow* 牛, referring to bovine animals. Through phonetic borrowing the general meaning of *slow* movement has been adopted. JK N3 AP	

Example Sentences

1. 今朝、学校に三十分遅刻した。
   Kesa, gakkō ni sanjuppun chikoku shita.
   I <u>was</u> thirty minutes <u>late</u> for school this morning.

2. 会議は一時間遅れて始まった。
   Kaigi wa ichijikan okurete hajimatta.
   The conference began <u>an hour later than scheduled</u>.

3. 急がないと電車に乗り遅れますよ。
   Isoganai to densha ni noriokuremasu yo.
   If we don't hurry, we'll <u>miss</u> the train!

4. 台風のため、沖縄へ行くのを遅らせることにした。
   Taifū no tame, Okinawa e iku no o okuraseru koto ni shita.
   We decided <u>to put off</u> going to Okinawa due to the typhoon.

5. 今からでは遅すぎる。
   Ima kara de wa oso-sugiru.
   It <u>is too late</u> now.

Common Compounds and Phrases

遅刻	**chikoku**	lateness; tardiness
遅延	**chien**	a delay; retardation
遅れ	**okure**	being late; going slow
乗り遅れる	**noriokureru**	to miss (a train)
遅生まれ	**oso-umare**	being born after April 1st
遅咲き	**osozaki**	late blooming
遅かれ早	**osokare**	sooner or later;
かれ	**hayakare**	at some stage

Watch the stroke order— コ, ノ, then 羊 (ひつじ).

12	⁻	⁻	尸	尸	尸	尸	犀	屏	犀	犀	遅	遅

遅

EXERCISE 36 (421 – 432)

A. Give the readings for the following.

1. 結ぶ _____
2. 遅れる _____
3. 温かい _____
4. 全然 _____
5. 絵本 _____
6. 最も _____
7. 港 _____
8. 雲海 _____
9. 晴れる _____
10. 期待 _____

B. Write the following in kanji and kana.

1. getting home late _____
2. a basement; a cellar _____
3. a wedding ceremony _____
4. one's best clothes _____
5. to improve; to progress _____
6. the (atmospheric) temperature drops _____
7. an airport service charge _____

8. the beauty of nature _____
9. the second semester (term) _____
10. a delay of two hours _____

C. Match the following.

1. かいが （ ）   a. 温度
2. ともだち （ ）   b. 晴天
3. はったつ （ ）   c. 期間
4. あまぐも （ ）   d. 友達
5. にかい （ ）   e. 雨雲
6. さいしょ （ ）   f. 結局
7. おんど （ ）   g. 絵画
8. けっきょく （ ）   h. 最初
9. せいてん （ ）   i. 二階
10. きかん （ ）   j. 発達

433 痛

pain; to hurt

ツウ TSŪ
いた・い ita(i)
いた・む ita(mu)
いた・める ita(meru)

The character 痛 consists of *sickness* or *affliction* 疒 and *to burst through* 甬, here used to express the idea of *to pass through* or *pierce*. Hence, the suggestion is of a piercing *pain*.
GR6　N3　AP

Example Sentences

1. お医者さんにもらった薬で痛みが取れた。
   Oisha-san ni moratta kusuri de itami ga toreta.
   The medication I received from the doctor relieved my pain.

2. パズルを完成するのは痛快だ。
   Pazuru o kansei suru no wa tsūkai da.
   It gives me great pleasure to complete a crossword puzzle.

3. 市販の痛み止めは、ちっとも効かなかった。
   Shihan no itamidome wa, chittomo kikanakatta.
   I took an over-the-counter pain killer, but it had absolutely no effect.

4. 腕のやけどは良くなったが、まだ痛む。
   Ude no yakedo wa yoku natta ga, mada itamu.
   The burn on my arm is much better, but it still hurts.

5. 彼女はすっかり痩せて痛々しく見えた。
   Kanojo wa sukkari yasete itaitashiku mieta.
   She looked painfully thin.

Common Compounds and Phrases

苦痛	**kutsū**	suffering; pain
痛快な	**tsūkai na**	exhilarating; delightful
筋肉痛	**kinnikutsū**	muscular pain
腹痛	**fukutsū**	a stomachache; cramps
痛み	**itami**	a pain; an ache
痛み止め	**itamidome**	a pain-killer
痛々しい	**itaitashii**	pitiful; touching

Don't forget the fourth and fifth strokes.

12 ｀ 亠 广 广 疒 疒 疗 疗 痈 痛 痛 痛

434 登

to climb

トウ TŌ　ト TO
のぼ・る nobo(ru)

The character 登, obscure in origin, is thought to have formerly combined *two feet*, *hands* and a *food vessel* 豆 to depict a child *climbing* up onto a food vessel.
GR3　N3　AP

Example Sentences

1. 生徒は午前8時15分までに、登校しなくてはならない。
   Seito wa gozen hachiji jūgo-fun made ni, tōkō shinakute wa naranai.
   The students must be at school by eight fifteen.

2. 来年、外国人登録証を更新する必要がある。
   Rainen, gaikokujin tōrokushō o kōshin suru hitsuyō ga aru.
   I need to renew my alien registration card next year.

3. 吹雪の中で、登山者たちはそうなんした。
   Fubuki no naka de, tozansha-tachi wa sōnan shita.
   The climbers met with disaster in the midst of a blizzard.

4. このドラマは登場人物が多すぎる。
   Kono dorama wa tōjō jinbutsu ga ōsugiru.
   There are too many characters in this drama.

5. あの山にはまだ誰も登ったことがない。
   Ano yama ni wa mada dare mo nobotta koto ga nai.
   No one has ever reached the summit of that mountain.

Common Compounds and Phrases

登校	**tōkō**	going to school
登録	**tōroku**	registration; recording
登場	**tōjō**	an entrance (on the stage); appearance
登竜門	**tōryūmon**	a gateway to success
登山	**tozan**	mountain-climbing; mountaineering
木登り	**kinobori**	tree climbing
山登り	**yama-nobori**	mountain climbing

The sixth stroke does not touch the sides.

12 ㇀ 癶 癶 癶 癶 癶 癶 脊 脊 登 登 登

435 晩

バン BAN

evening; late

The character 晩 combines *sun* or *light* 日 and *to escape* 免, here used to express *obscure* and by extension, *striving with difficulty*. Striving hard to see when the light is obscure refers to *evening*.
GR6 N3 AP

Example Sentences

1. 毎日、朝晩これを練習しなさい。
   Mainichi, asa-ban kore o renshū shinasai.
   Practice this morning and night, every day!

2. お母さん、晩ご飯はまだ？
   Okāsan, bangohan wa mada?
   Mom, isn't dinner ready yet?

3. 今晩、九時に遊びに来たら。
   Konban, kuji ni asobi ni kitara.
   Why don't you come over at nine this evening!

4. この絵はピカソの晩年の作品です。
   Kono e wa Pikaso no bannen no sakuhin desu.
   This painting is a late work of Picasso.

5. 晩秋の紅葉はなんとも言えない美しさだ。
   Banshū no kōyō wa nan to mo ienai utsukushisa da.
   The late autumn foliage is indescribably beautiful.

Common Compounds and Phrases

晩ご飯	bangohan	the evening meal; dinner
今晩	konban	this evening; tonight
晩年	bannen	one's twilight years
晩春	banshun	late spring
晩方に	bangata ni	toward evening
明晩	myōban	tomorrow evening (night)
朝から晩まで	asa kara ban made	from morning till night

The last stroke hooks upwards.

12 丨 冂 日 日 日' 日ク 日ク 晩 晩 晩 晩 晩

晩

436 無

ム MU ブ BU
な・い na(i)

without; nothing

The character 無, was formerly a combination of *dancer with tassled sleeves* 無 and *to die* ⺗. Through phonetic borrowing the character came to express *not, to cease to be*.
GR4 N3 AP

Example Sentences

1. 彼がそう言うのも無理もない。
   Kare ga sō iu no mo muri mo nai.
   It is natural that he should say so.

2. 山頂の先発隊と無線で連絡を取っている。
   Sanchō no senpatsutai to musen de renraku o totte iru.
   We are in radio contact with the advance party from the summit of the mountain.

3. 柔道家は無差別級で金メダルを取った。
   Jūdōka wa musabetsu-kyū de kin-medaru o totta.
   The *judoist* won the gold medal in the open-weight division.

4. 母親は息子さんの無事な顔を見て安心した。
   Hahaoya wa musuko-san no buji na kao o mite anshin shita.
   The mother was relieved to see her son in good health.

5. この町では仕事が何も無い。
   Kono machi de wa shigoto ga nani mo nai.
   There's no work in this town.

Common Compounds and Phrases

無理	muri na	unreasonable; impossible; excessive
無線	musen	a radio; a wireless
無差別に	musabetsu ni	indiscriminately; equally
無口な	mukuchi na	silent; quiet; taciturn
無料	muryō	no charge
無意識な	muishiki na	unconscious; involuntary
無我夢中で	muga muchū de	wholeheartedly

The third stroke is longer than the others.

12 ノ 二 二 仁 午 無 無 無 無 無 無 無

無

247

437 遊

ユウ YŪ　ユ YU

あそ・ぶ aso(bu)

to play;
to relax

The character 遊 is often thought of as *children* 子 *gathering under a flag* 方, *moving around* 辶, to suggest *playing* or *relaxing*.

GR3　N3　AP

Example Sentences

1. 日曜日に遊園地に行こう。
   Nichiyōbi ni yūenchi ni ikō.
   Let's go to an amusement park on Sunday!

2. 何年も前からあの方と交遊がある。
   Nannen mo mae kara ano kata to kōyū ga aru.
   I've been associating with that person for a number of years.

3. 海水浴場は高波のため、遊泳禁止になった。
   Kaisui yokujō wa takanami no tame, yūei kinshi ni natta.
   The public beach was closed (lit. no swimming allowed) due to high waves.

4. 子供たちは隠れん坊をして、遊んでいた。
   Kodomotachi wa kakurenbō o shite, asonde ita.
   The children were playing hide-and-seek.

5. 時間をつぶすために友達と言葉遊びをした。
   Jikan o tsubusu tame ni tomodachi to kotoba-asobi o shita.
   I played word games with a friend to kill time.

Common Compounds and Phrases

遊園地	**yūenchi**	an amusement park
交遊	**kōyū**	friendship; acquaintance
遊泳禁止	**yūei kinshi**	No Swimming!
回遊する	**kaiyū suru**	to make an excursion (round trip)
遊び場	**asobiba**	a playground; an amusement area
言葉遊び	**kotoba-asobi**	a word game
火遊び	**hi-asobi**	playing with fire (matches)

The third and the eighth strokes both end with a hook.

12　丶　亠　方　方　扩　扩　於　斿　斿　斿　遊　遊

遊

438 絡

ラク RAKU

から・む kara(mu)

から・まる kara(maru)

to entwine;
to interlink

The character 絡 combines *thread* 糸 and *each* 各, here used to suggest *tangled*. The idea of tangled threads becoming *entwined* is associated with the meaning of *connect*.

JK　N3　AP

Example Sentences

1. この電話番号で、彼女に連絡できる。
   Kono denwa bangō de, kanojo ni renraku dekiru.
   You can reach her at this phone number.

2. あなたの話には脈絡が無い。
   Anata no hanashi ni wa myakuraku ga nai.
   There is no coherence in what you are saying.

3. 事件の裏には意外な絡繰りがあった。
   Jiken no ura ni wa igai na karakuri ga atta.
   There was an unexpected twist involved in the case.

4. お金が絡んだ問題がある。
   Okane ga karanda mondai ga aru.
   I'm saddled with a money–related problem.

5. この件には、色々な事情が絡み合っている。
   Kono ken ni wa, iroiro na jijō ga karamiatte iru.
   Various circumstances are involved in this matter.

Common Compounds and Phrases

連絡	**renraku**	a connection; a contact; communication
連絡先	**renrakusaki**	one's contact address
脈絡	**myakuraku**	a logical connection
短絡	**tanraku**	a short circuit
絡み	**karami**	an entanglement; an involvement
絡繰り	**karakuri**	a gimmick; magic
絡み合う	**karamiau**	to entangle; to intertwine with

End the fourth stroke firmly.

12　く　纟　纟　纟　糸　糹　紒　紒　終　絡　絡

絡

439 落

ラク RAKU
お・ちる o(chiru)
お・とす o(tosu)

to fall

The character 落 is a combination of *plant* ⁺⁺, *water* 氵 and *each* 各, the latter two meaning *falling water*. The notion of plants falling like water gives us the general sense of *to fall*.
GR3 N2 AP

Example Sentences

1. 人工衛星は砂漠に落下した。
   Jinkō eisei wa sabaku ni rakka shita.
   An artificial satellite fell into the desert.

2. 初めて寄席で落語を聞いた。
   Hajimete yose de rakugo o kiita.
   I listened to comic stories for the first time in a variety theater.

3. 行方不明の小型飛行機は、墜落しているのが発見された。
   Yukue fumei no kogata hikōki wa, tsuiraku shite iru no ga hakken sareta.
   The missing light aircraft was found crashed.

4. 日は地平線の下に落ちた。
   Hi wa chiheisen no shita ni ochita.
   The sun sank below the horizon.

5. 通勤電車の中で財布を落としてしまった。
   Tsūkin densha no naka de saifu o otoshite shimatta.
   I dropped my wallet on the commuter train.

Common Compounds and Phrases

落下	**rakka**	falling; descent
落語	**rakugo**	comic storytelling
墜落	**tsuiraku**	a fall; a crash
落書き	**rakugaki**	graffiti; scribbling
転落	**tenraku**	a fall; a plunge; a descent
落ち込む	**ochikomu**	to fall (in); to sink; to feel down
落とし穴	**otoshiana**	a pitfall; a trap

Don't write the 夂 element as 又 (また).

12 一 十 艹 艹 艹 艹 艹 芦 莎 莎 茨 落 落 落

落

---

440 園

エン EN
その sono

garden

The character 園 combines *enclosure* 囗 and 袁, originally a pictograph of a *kimono-clad woman*. The perfect place for such a woman is a *garden*.
GR2 N3 AP

Example Sentences

1. 果樹園でりんご狩りをした。
   Kajuen de ringo-gari o shita.
   I picked some apples at an orchard.

2. 園芸用品は何階ですか。
   Engei yōhin wa nankai desu ka.
   What floor are the gardening supplies on?

3. 金沢の兼六園に行った。
   Kanazawa no Kenrokuen ni itta.
   I went to Kenrokuen Garden in Kanazawa.

4. 毎朝、お母さんは子供を幼稚園に連れていきます。
   Maiasa, okāsan wa kodomo o yōchien ni tsurete ikimasu.
   Mothers take their children to kindergartens every morning.

5. かつて砂漠だった所は今や花園になっている。
   Katsute sabaku datta tokoro wa ima ya hanazono ni natte iru.
   Places that were once deserts are now flower gardens.

Common Compounds and Phrases

果樹園	**kajuen**	an orchard; a fruit farm
園芸	**engei**	gardening; horticulture
幼稚園	**yōchien**	a kindergarten; a preschool
動物園	**dōbutsuen**	a zoo
遊園地	**yūenchi**	an amusement park
保育園	**hoikuen**	a preschool; a day-care center
花園	**hanazono**	a flower garden

End the tenth stroke firmly.

13 丨 冂 冂 冃 罔 罔 罔 罔 罔 睘 闌 園 園

園

441 歳

サイ SAI　*セイ SEI

year; age suffix

The old form of the character 歲 combined *to walk* and *halberd* to express the idea of a *circuit*. Walking one circuit represented a cycle of time, a *year* to be specific.
JK　N3　AP

Example Sentences

1. 祖父は七十一歳で亡くなった。
   Sofu wa <u>nanajūissai</u> de nakunatta.
   My grandfather died at the age of <u>seventy-one</u>.

2. 歳月人を待たず。
   <u>Saigetsu</u> hito o matazu.
   <u>Time and tide</u> wait for no man. (a proverb)

3. 合格発表で万歳と叫んでいた。
   Gōkaku happyō de <u>banzai</u> to sakende ita.
   People were shouting <u>hurrah</u> at the announcement of the successful exam candidates.

4. 息子は、来年二十歳になります。
   Musuko wa rainen <u>hatachi</u> ni narimasu.
   My son turns <u>twenty</u> next year.

5. 今年のお歳暮で人気の品物は、産地直送品でした。
   Kotoshi no <u>oseibo</u> de ninki no shinamono wa, sanchi chokusōhin deshita.
   Local products were popular items for <u>year-end gifts</u> this year.

Common Compounds and Phrases

一歳	**issai**	one year old
何歳	**nansai**	How old? What age?
歳月	**saigetsu**	time
歳末	**saimatsu**	the end of the year
歳入	**sainyū**	annual revenue
歳出	**saishutsu**	annual expenditure
*お歳暮	**oseibo**	a year-end gift; the year-end

Note the order of the fifth and sixth strokes.

13 ｜ ｜ ｜ ｜ ｜ 广 广 卢 芦 芦 岁 歳 歳 歳

---

442 辞

ジ JI

＊や・める ya(meru)

word; to resign

The character 辭 combines *tongue* 舌, originally meaning *to judge*, and *sharp* 辛, the suggestion being *of sharp insight*. From the idea of speaking to the point, the meaning of *word* has derived.
GR4　N3　AP

Example Sentences

1. 電子辞書の電池が切れそうだ。
   <u>Denshi jisho</u> no denchi ga kiresō da.
   The batteries in my <u>electronic dictionary</u> are going flat.

2. 副社長は病気を理由に、辞職した。
   Fukushachō wa byōki o riyū ni, <u>jishoku shita</u>.
   The vice president <u>resigned</u> for reasons of health.

3. 校長の式辞は三十分も続いた。
   Kōchō no <u>shikiji</u> wa sanjuppun mo tsuzuita.
   The principal's <u>address</u> went on for thirty minutes.

4. 心から祝辞を述べたいと思います。
   Kokoro kara <u>shukuji</u> o nobetai to omoimasu.
   I'd like to extend my sincere <u>congratulations</u>.

5. 会社を辞めて、自営業を始めた。
   Kaisha o <u>yamete</u>, jieigyō o hajimeta.
   I <u>resigned</u> from the firm and am now self-employed.

Common Compounds and Phrases

辞職	**jishoku**	resignation; stepping down
式辞	**shikiji**	an address; a speech
辞退	**jitai**	declining; a refusal
国語辞典	**kokugo jiten**	a Japanese dictionary
辞任	**jinin**	a resignation
祝辞	**shukuji**	a congratulatory speech (address)
お世辞	**oseji**	an insincere comment; flattery

The twelfth stroke is shorter than the eleventh.

13 ｜ ｜ 千 千 舌 舌 舌 舌 舌 舌 辞 辞 辞

443 寝

シン SHIN
ね・る ne(ru)
ね・かす ne(kasu)

to go to sleep;
to lie down

The character 寝 is made up of *building* 宀, *bed* 爿 and *hands holding a broom* 㑴 to suggest *sweeping away sickness*. The idea of people being laid out to be 'healed' in a temple building gives this character its meaning of *rest* and *sleep*.

JK N3 AP

Example Sentences

1. となりの寝室から兄のイビキが聞こえる。
   Tonari no shinshitsu kara ani no ibiki ga kikoeru.
   I can hear my brother's snoring from the next <u>bedroom</u>.

2. そろそろ寝る時間ですよ。
   Soro soro neru jikan desu yo.
   It's getting near <u>bed</u> time!

3. こういう寒い朝は、寝床から出るのがいやだ。
   Kō iu samui asa wa, nedoko kara deru no ga iya da.
   On cold mornings like this, I dislike having to get out of <u>bed</u>.

4. 私はこの二三日風邪で寝込んでいた。
   Watashi wa kono nisan-nichi kaze de nekonde ita.
   I <u>have been in bed</u> with a cold for the last few days.

5. 子供たちは九時半には寝かすようにしている。
   Kodomo-tachi wa kuji-han ni wa nekasu yō ni shite iru.
   We <u>have</u> the children <u>in bed</u> at nine thirty.

Common Compounds and Phrases

就寝時間	**shūshin jikan**	bedtime
寝具	**shingu**	bedding; bedclothes
寝台車	**shindaisha**	a sleeping car; a sleeper
寝床	**nedoko**	a bed; a bedroom
寝言	**negoto**	talking in one's sleep; nonsense
寝坊	**nebō**	oversleeping; a late riser
寝起きが悪い	**neoki ga warui**	to wake in a bad temper

Note the order of the fourth, fifth and sixth strokes.

13 ` ´ ゙ 宀 宁 宁 宁 宕 宕 宕 寝 寝 寝

寝

---

444 節

セツ SETSU   *セチ SECHI
ふし fushi

tune; joint;
season

The character 節 combines *bamboo* 竹 and *namely* 即, here meaning *division* or *order*. The ordered look of the sections of a bamboo stem suggests the meanings of *period*, *verse* and *tune*.

GR4 N2 AP

Example Sentences

1. 彼は学校まで歩いて、バス代を節約した。
   Kare wa gakkō made aruite, basu-dai o setsuyaku shita.
   He walked to school and <u>saved</u> <u>spending money on</u> the bus fare.

2. 階段で転んで、足首の関節をくじいた。
   Kaidan de koronde, ashikubi no kansetsu o kujiita.
   I fell on the stairs and <u>sprained</u> my ankle.

3. 季節の変わり目だから、風邪を引かないように。
   Kisetsu no kawarime da kara, kaze o hikanai yō ni.
   Be careful not to catch a cold now that the <u>season</u> is changing.

4. 母は、お節料理の準備で忙しい。
   Haha wa osechi ryōri no junbi de isogashii.
   Mother has been busy preparing the traditional <u>foods for New Year</u>.

5. この柱は節が無くて、なかなか立派なものです。
   Kono hashira wa fushi ga nakute, naka naka rippa na mono desu.
   The timber in this post (pillar) does not have any <u>knots</u> and is just magnificent!

Common Compounds and Phrases

節約	**setsuyaku**	saving; thrift
関節	**kansetsu**	a joint; a knuckle
季節	**kisetsu**	a season
調節	**chōsetsu**	regulation; adjustment; control
節水	**sessui**	saving water
*お節料理	**osechi ryōri**	traditional New Year food
節穴	**fushiana**	a knothole; a joint

The twelfth stroke ends with a hook.

13 ´ ⺊ ⺅ ⺮ ⺮ 笁 竺 笞 笞 笞 節 節 節

節

EXERCISE 37 (433 – 444)

A. Give the readings for the following.

1. 無料 _____
2. 落し物 _____
3. 明晩 _____
4. 動物園 _____
5. 痛む _____
6. 絡まっている _____
7. 万歳 _____
8. 登校 _____
9. 節水 _____
10. 遊んでいる _____

B. Match the following.

1. 寝室　　（　）　　a. every evening
2. 無理　　（　）　　b. a painkiller
3. 火遊び　（　）　　c. How old? What age?
4. 木登り　（　）　　d. falling; dropping
5. 花園　　（　）　　e. an electronic dictionary
6. 毎晩　　（　）　　f. unreasonableness
7. 何歳　　（　）　　g. playing with fire
8. 痛み止め（　）　　h. tree climbing
9. 落下　　（　）　　i. a bedroom
10. 電子辞書（　）　　j. a flower garden

C. Write in kanji and kana.

1. でんしゃ　で　ねてしまう _____
2. まいばん　さけを　のむ _____
3. こうえん　で　あそぶ _____
4. かいしゃを　やめる _____
5. あたま　が　いたい _____
6. ぶじ　に　かえる _____
7. ろくじゅっさい　に　なる _____
8. やま　に　のぼる _____
9. ゆうえんち　で　デートを　する

_____

10. たかい　ところ　から　おちる

_____

Review 12 (1 – 444)

A. Give the readings for the following.

1. 寝る _____
2. 落下する _____
3. 遅い _____
4. 今晩は _____
5. 二十歳 _____
6. 遊び場 _____
7. 辞める _____
8. 痛々しい _____
9. 絡まる _____
10. 無線 _____

6. 目が痛む

_____

7. 無理なことを試みる

_____

8. 高い山に登る

_____

9. 金が絡んだ問題

_____

10. 痛みが少し落ち着く

_____

B. Write in English.

1. 病人をベッドに寝かす

_____

2. その単語は辞書には出ていない。

_____

3. 小説の場面に登場する

_____

4. 歌を歌って遊ぶ

_____

5. 朝から晩まで働く

C. Match the following.

1. 私達　　（　）　　a. こうえん
2. 登山家　（　）　　b. みょうばん
3. 節水　　（　）　　c. じき
4. 明晩　　（　）　　d. ずつう
5. 公園　　（　）　　e. むち
6. 寝室　　（　）　　f. わたしたち
7. 最近　　（　）　　g. せっすい
8. 頭痛　　（　）　　h. とざんか
9. 時期　　（　）　　i. さいきん
10. 無知　　（　）　　j. しんしつ

D. Rewrite the following in kana.

1. 落下 _____
2. 晩年 _____
3. 無事に _____
4. 昼寝 _____
5. 日本庭園 _____
6. 登校する _____
7. 天然の _____
8. 花園 _____
9. 遊園地 _____
10. 万歳 _____

E. Select the *most* appropriate kanji from the following list to complete the expressions below.
LIST: 園、痛、無、歳、寝、節、晩、遊、落、辞

1. 来年の _____ 分は二月三日になる。
2. 家に _____ びに来て下さい。
3. 動物 _____ でライオンを見た。
4. よく歩いたから足が _____ い。
5. うちの兄は _____ 言が多い。
6. _____ 語を聞いて、大笑いをした。
7. 毎 _____ お酒を飲む。
8. 卒業式で校長の式 _____ を聞く。
9. 手荷物は 20 キロまで _____ 料です。

10. 何 _____ ですか。

F. Rewrite the following using kanji and kana, and translate into English.

1. あした の てんき は、はれ の ちくもり、ところ によって、よる おそく ゆき が ふる でしょう。
2. 「あべさん は、にじゅうさんさい で けっこんする ために、かいしゃ を やめるらしい。さいきん では めずらしい ですね。」
3. しだい に かんせつ の いたみ が ひどく なってきたので、しゅじゅつ を うける けっしん を した。
4. こんばん、ともだち が のった ふね が、はちじはん に しゅっこうした。
5. 「おかあさん、こうえん で あそんでいる とき、たこ の いと が からんで、き の うえ に おちちゃった。き に のぼって、とっても いい？」
6. わたくし の しんしつ は、にかい の みなみがわ なので、いつも しぜん に あたたまる。
7. にがっき の はじめ の えいご の じゅぎょう で、この しゅくだい を はっぴょうする はず です。
8. きんじょ の しゅふ が あつまって、この しょうひん を つくっています。
9. この うえ に、ちょくせつ ふれないでください。
10. 「わるいけど、こまかい おかね が ない。」「じゃあ、あした で いいよ。」

445	続		
	to continue	ソク ZOKU つづ・く tsuzu(ku) つづ・ける tsuzu(keru)	The original character 續 combined *continuation* 賣 and *connecting things* 糸, to suggest an uninterrupted *continuation*. GR4 N3 AP

Example Sentences

1. あの方は相続により、その家を受け取った。
   Ano kata wa sōzoku ni yori, sono ie o uketotta.
   That person received the house by <u>inheritance</u>.

2. いろいろな問題が続出した。
   Iroiro na mondai ga zokushutsu shita.
   Various problems <u>cropped up one after another</u>.

3. その小説は十週間連続でベストセラーの第一位だった。
   Sono shōsetsu wa jusshūkan renzoku de besutoserā no dai-ichii datta.
   That novel was the No. 1 best seller <u>for ten weeks straight</u>.

4. 試験は二日間続いた。
   Shiken wa futsukakan tsuzuita.
   The examination <u>lasted</u> two days.

5. 何事も無かったように私は仕事を続けた。
   Nanigoto mo nakatta yō ni wata(ku)shi wa shigoto o tsuzuketa.
   I <u>continued</u> to work as if nothing had happened.

Common Compounds and Phrases

相続	**sōzoku**	succession; inheritance
連続	**renzoku**	continuation; succession; a series
続々	**zokuzoku**	successively; one after another
続編	**zokuhen**	a sequel; a follow-up
続出する	**zokushutsu suru**	to appear one after another
手続き	**tetsuzuki**	a procedure; a process
引き続き	**hikitsuzuki**	continuously; next; then

The last stroke ends with a hook.

13　乄 乡 幺 幺 糸 糸 紆 紆 紆 続 続 続 続

続

446 置

チ CHI
お・く o(ku)

**to place;
to put**

The character 置 combines *net* 罒 and *straight ahead* 直, referring to a net set in a fixed place to catch birds. From this, the sense of *putting something* in a certain place has derived.
GR4 N3 AP

Example Sentences

1. 私は舞台が良く見える位置にいた。
   Wata(ku)shi wa butai ga yoku mieru ichi ni ita.
   I was in a good <u>position</u> to see the stage.

2. 駅の近くに放置自転車をよく見かけます。
   Eki no chikaku ni hōchi jitensha o yoku mikakemasu.
   You often come across <u>abandoned bicycles</u> near the station.

3. 監督は俳優たちに配置につくよう命じた。
   Kantoku wa haiyū-tachi ni haichi ni tsuku yō meijita.
   The director told the actors to take their <u>positions</u>.

4. 待合室に携帯電話を置き忘れた。
   Machiaishitsu ni keitai denwa o oki-wasureta.
   I <u>left</u> my cell-phone in the waiting room.

5. 二日置きに本土から連絡船が到着する。
   Futsuka-oki ni hondo kara renrakusen ga tōchaku suru.
   A ferryboat arrives from the mainland <u>every three days</u>.

Common Compounds and Phrases

位置	**ichi**	a situation; a position
放置	**hōchi suru**	to let *something* stand; to abandon
配置	**haichi**	arrangement; placement
装置	**sōchi**	equipment; a device; a gadget
物置き	**monooki**	a closet; a storeroom; a shed
置き場	**okiba**	a place to put something in; a shed; a yard
三年置き	**sannen-oki**	every fourth year

Don't write the top element as 四.

13 丨 冖 冂 罒 罒 罒 罩 罩 罩 罩 罩 置

置

447 関

カン KAN
せき seki

**to concern;
a barrier**

The original character for 関 depicted a bolt passing through two gates to lock them. Thus, the association of the meaning of *controlling the coming and going of the people*, i.e., *a checkpoint.*
GR4 N3 AP

Example Sentences

1. 「お母さん、玄関に誰か来てるよ。」
   'Okāsan, genkan ni dare ka kiteru yo.'
   'Mom, there is someone <u>at the door</u>!'

2. 日本に関するフランス人記者の印象だそうです。
   Nihon ni kan suru Furansujin kisha no inshō da sō desu.
   They are apparently a French reporter's impressions <u>of Japan</u>.

3. 僕はそんなに歴史に関心がありません。
   Boku wa sonna ni rekishi ni kanshin ga arimasen.
   I'm <u>not</u> all that <u>interested in</u> history.

4. この二つの問題はまるで関連が無い。
   Kono futatsu no mondai wa marude kanren ga nai.
   The two questions are quite <u>separate</u>.

5. 交通機関が先ほどの大雨で止まっている。
   Kōtsū kikan ga sakihodo no ōame de tomatte iru.
   <u>Transport facilities</u> have been disrupted due to the recent heavy rain.

Common Compounds and Phrases

玄関	**genkan**	the entrance of a house; the front door
関心	**kanshin**	interest; concern; attention
関連	**kanren**	connection; relation; association
機関	**kikan**	an engine; a system; an organization
税関	**zeikan**	customs; a customs house
関西	**Kansai**	the Kansai region
大関	**ōzeki**	a sumo champion

End the last stroke firmly.

14 丨 冂 冂 門 門 門 門 門 門 門 閇 関 関

関

448 際

サイ SAI
きわ kiwa

verge; occasion; contact

The character 際 is made up of *earthen rampart* 阝 and *festival* 祭, here expressing *to come into contact*. People coming into contact with each other at a festival gives us the meaning of *contact*.
GR5 N3 AP

Example Sentences

1. 「ご乗車の際は携帯電話のスイッチをお切り下さい。」
   'Gojōsha <u>no sai</u> wa keitai denwa no suitchi o okiri kudasai.'
   'Please switch off your cell-phones <u>whilst</u> on the train (bus).'

2. 実際にこの目で確かめたい。
   <u>Jissai ni</u> kono me de tashikametai.
   I want to <u>actually</u> see it for myself.

3. 「国際線の乗り場に行きたいんですが...」
   '<u>Kokusaisen</u> no noriba ni ikitai n desu ga...'
   'I would like to know where the <u>international flights</u> leave from.'

4. 彼と交際して五年になります。
   Kare to <u>kōsai shite</u> gonen ni narimasu.
   I've been <u>going out with</u> him for five years.

5. 窓際の席はまぶしくて、集中出来ない。
   <u>Madogiwa</u> no seki wa mabushikute, shūchū dekinai.
   It's so glary <u>sitting next to the window</u> that I can't concentrate.

Common Compounds and Phrases

実際に	**jissai ni**	really; actually; in reality
国際的な	**kokusaiteki na**	international; universal
交際	**kōsai**	friendship; association; company
際限なく	**saigen naku**	endlessly; infinitely
窓際に	**madogiwa ni**	at (by) the window
間際	**magiwa**	a point just before; the point of doing
手際が よい	**tegiwa ga yoi**	to be skillful, adept (at) doing something

The radical on the left 阝 is written in three strokes.

14 ｀ ⻏ 阝 阝' 阝ア 阝ワ 阝ワ 阝ワ 阝欠 際 際 際 際 際

際

---

449 雑

ザツ ZATSU　ゾウ ZŌ

rough; mixed

Formerly 雜, the character 雑 combined *cloth* 衤, tree 木 and *birds gathering in a tree* 隹 to express the idea of gathering pieces of cloth to suggest *miscellany*. *Cloth* later became *nine* 九.
GR5 N3 AP

Example Sentences

1. あなたの掃除のやり方はいつも雑だ。
   Anata no sōji no yarikata wa itsumo <u>zatsu</u> da.
   You're always so <u>slipshod</u> with the way you do the cleaning.

2. 物事を複雑に考えるのは、やめた方がいい。
   Monogoto o <u>fukuzatsu ni</u> kangaeru no wa yameta hō ga ii.
   You oughtn't to consider matters <u>in such a complex way</u>.

3. その店は日曜日特に混雑する。
   Sono mise wa nichiyobi toku ni <u>konzatsu suru</u>.
   That store <u>becomes</u> particularly <u>crowded</u> on Sundays.

4. この雑誌は、次の号からページが減るそうだ。
   Kono <u>zasshi</u> wa, tsugi-no-gō kara pēji ga heru sō da.
   Apparently, this <u>magazine</u> is going to reduce the number of its pages from the next issue.

5. 汚れを雑巾でふき取ってください。
   Yogore o <u>zōkin</u> de fukitotte kudasai.
   Please use <u>a cleaning rag</u> to remove that dirty mark.

Common Compounds and Phrases

複雑な	**fukuzatsu na**	complicated; complex
混雑する	**konzatsu suru**	to be congested (full, crowded)
雑誌	**zasshi**	a magazine; a journal
乱雑な	**ranzatsu na**	confused; cluttered
雑用	**zatsuyō**	miscellaneous affairs; chores
雑貨	**zakka**	miscellaneous goods; groceries
雑巾	**zōkin**	a cleaning rag; a floor cloth

Make sure the right-hand side is evenly spaced.

14 ノ 九 九 杂 杂 杂 朵 刹 刹' 刹 雜 雜 雑 雑

雑

450 算　サン SAN

to calculate

The character 算 originated from a pictograph of *two hands* 廾 holding a *bamboo* 竹 *abacus* 目, a reference to *calculating*.

GR2 N2

Example Sentences

1. 来年度の予算が決まった。
   Rainendo no <u>yosan</u> ga kimatta.
   <u>The budget</u> for the coming year has been finalized.

2. その生徒はあっという間に暗算で答えを出した。
   Sono seito wa atto iu ma ni <u>anzan</u> de kotae o dashita.
   The student worked the answer out <u>in his head</u> in an instant.

3. 計算が速いので、私にやらせて下さい。
   Keisan ga hayai node, watashi ni yarasete kudasai.
   I'm <u>quick with figures</u>, so let me work it out.

4. 小学生時代は算数が得意でした。
   Shōgakusei jidai wa <u>sansū</u> ga tokui deshita.
   I used to be good at <u>arithmetic</u> when I was in elementary school.

5. 失業者が増える公算が大きい。
   Shitsugyōsha ga fueru <u>kōsan ga ōkii</u>.
   <u>There is a strong possibility</u> that the number of unemployed people will increase.

Common Compounds and Phrases

予算	**yosan**	an estimate; a budget
計算機	**kei<u>san</u>ki**	a calculator; a computer
算数	**<u>san</u>sū**	arithmetic; calculation
足し算	**tashi<u>zan</u>**	addition; adding up
引き算	**hiki<u>zan</u>**	subtraction
掛け算	**kake<u>zan</u>**	multiplication
割り算	**wari<u>zan</u>**	division

The thirteenth stroke tapers off.

14 〳 〵 〵 𠂉 𥫗 𥫗 竹 竹 竿 笪 笪 算 算 算

算

451 静

セイ SEI　ジョウ JŌ
しず・か shizu(ka)
しず・まる shizu(maru)
しず shizu
しず・める shizu(meru)

quiet; calm; to become quiet; to calm

The character 静 is thought to be made up of *fresh* or *pure* 青 and *to stop* or *stay* 争, suggesting staying pure. *Quiet* or *calm* has derived from the idea of a desirable lack of movement.

GR4 N2 AP

Example Sentences

1. 手術の後はしばらく安静にしていなさいと言われた。
   Shujutsu no ato wa shibaraku <u>ansei ni shite</u> inasai to iwareta.
   After my surgery I was ordered <u>to rest</u> for a while.

2. この件について、もう一度冷静に考えてみよう。
   Kono ken ni tsuite, mō ichido <u>reisei ni</u> kangaete miyō.
   Let us reconsider this matter <u>calmly</u>.

3. 静かにしろ！
   <u>Shizuka ni shiro</u>!
   <u>Silence</u>!

4. 司会者の登場で、場内が静まった。
   Shikaisha no tōjō de, jōnai ga <u>shizumatta</u>.
   <u>A hush fell over</u> the auditorium when the MC appeared.

5. 水でも飲んで、気を静めなさい。
   Mizu de mo nonde, <u>ki o shizumenasai</u>.
   Have a drink of water and <u>calm down</u>.

Common Compounds and Phrases

安静	**an<u>sei</u>**	rest; quiet; repose
静止	**<u>sei</u>shi**	stillness; a standstill
鎮静剤	**chin<u>sei</u>zai**	a sedative (drug)
静電気	**<u>sei</u>denki**	static electricity
静脈	**<u>jō</u>myaku**	a vein
物静かな	**mono<u>shizuka</u> na**	quiet; tranquil; still
静岡県	**<u>Shizuoka</u>-ken**	Shizuoka Prefecture (a place)

The twelfth stroke protrudes.

14 一 十 ⺫ ⺫ 丰 青 青 青 青 靜 靜 靜 靜 静

静

452 鼻

ビ BI
はな hana

nose

The character 鼻 is a combination of *self* or *nose* 自 and *to give* 畀, here indicating *prominent*. The idea of a prominent nose has given the character the general meaning of *nose*.
GR3 N3 AP

Example Sentences

1. 花粉症の薬を耳鼻咽喉科でもらった。
   Kafunshō no kusuri o jibiinkōka de moratta.
   I got some medication for my hay fever at the <u>ear, nose and throat specialist's</u>.

2. 鼻炎で鼻をかむ回数が増えた。
   Bien de hana o kamu kaisū ga fueta.
   I seem <u>to be blowing my nose</u> more than usual because of my <u>rhinitis</u>.

3. 郵便局は目と鼻の先ですよ。
   Yūbinkyoku wa me to hana no saki desu yo.
   The post office is <u>just around the corner</u>.

4. 妹はお風呂でのぼせて、鼻血を出した。
   Imōto wa ofuro de nobosete, hanaji o dashita.
   My sister stayed in the bath too long and <u>suffered a nosebleed</u>.

5. そんな風にほめられて、私も鼻が高いです。
   Sonna fū ni homerarete, wata(ku)shi mo hana ga takai desu.
   If I were to receive such praise, I would <u>feel proud</u>, too.

Common Compounds and Phrases

耳鼻咽喉科	**jibiinkōka**	the ear, nose and throat department of a hospital
鼻炎	**bien**	rhinitis
鼻声	**hanagoe**	a nasal voice (tone)
鼻づまり	**hanazumari**	a blocked nose
目と鼻の先	**me to hana no saki**	just around the corner
鼻高々	**hana-takadaka**	proud; haughty
鼻をほじる	**hana o hojiru**	to pick one's nose

The thirteenth and fourteenth strokes both protrude.

14 ′ ′ ′ ′ ′ ′ ′ ′ ′ ′ ′ ′ ′ ′

鼻

453 鳴

メイ MEI
な・く na(ku) な・る na(ru)
な・らす na(rasu)

to cry; to sing (by animals); to ring

The character 鳴 combines *mouth* 口 and *bird* 鳥 to represent a bird *singing*.

GR2 N3

Example Sentences

1. 初めてジェット・コースターに乗った時、悲鳴を上げた。
   Hajimete jetto kosutā ni notta toki, himei o ageta.
   When I first rode on a roller coaster, I <u>screamed</u>.

2. 猫の鳴き声がうるさくて、眠れなかった。
   Neko no nakigoe ga urusakute, nemurenakatta.
   I couldn't sleep because of the cat's <u>yowling</u>.

3. 今朝は、目覚まし時計が鳴らなかった。
   Kesa wa, mezamashi-dokei ga naranakatta.
   My alarm clock <u>didn't go off</u> this morning.

4. 今朝から、耳鳴りがしている。
   Kesa kara, miminari ga shite iru.
   <u>My ears have been ringing</u> since this morning.

5. 誰がこんな時間にチャイムを鳴らしてるんだろう。
   Dare ga konna jikan ni chaimu o narashiteru n darō?
   Who could <u>be ringing the front door bell</u> at this hour?

Common Compounds and Phrases

悲鳴	**himei**	a scream, a yell
共鳴	**kyōmei**	resonance; empathy
鳴動	**meidō**	rumbling
雷鳴	**raimei**	thunder; a thunderclap
鳴き声	**nakigoe**	a cry; a call; chirping
耳鳴り	**miminari**	ringing in the ears; tinnitus
*鳴門海峡	**naruto kaikyō**	Naruto Strait

Note the position of the dots.

14 ′ ′ ′ ′ ′ ′ ′ ′ ′ ′ ′ ′ ′ ′

鳴

257

454 様

ヨウ YŌ
さま sama

mode; appearance;
formal title

Of unclear origins, the character 様 combines
tree 木, *tributary* or *long* 水 and *sheep* 羊, the
latter two representing a fully-grown sheep. A
tree growing to full height suggests *appearance*.
GR3 N3 AP

Example Sentences

1. 雨の様だ。
   Ame no yō da.
   It looks <u>like</u> rain.

2. 様子を教えてください。
   Yōsu o oshiete kudasai.
   Please tell me <u>what you saw</u>.

3. あの異様な臭いは何ですか。
   Ano iyō na nioi wa nan desu ka.
   What is that <u>strange</u> smell?

4. この食堂には様々な種類の料理が用意されている。
   Kono shokudō ni wa samazama na shurui no ryōri ga yōi sarete iru.
   This cafeteria has a <u>wide</u> variety of food available.

5. 山田様、いらっしゃいますか。
   Yamada-sama, irasshaimasu ka?
   Is <u>Mr./Ms.</u> Yamada (t)here?

Common Compounds and Phrases

異様な	**iyō na**	strange; peculiar; odd
生活様式	**seikatsu yōshiki**	a way of life
同様の (な)	**dōyō no (na)**	the same; similar to
様々な	**samazama na**	various; diverse
有様	**arisama**	a state; a condition, a scene
奥様	**okusama**	a married lady; a housewife; Mrs.
ご苦労様。	**Gokurō-sama.**	Keep up the good work; Well done!

The tenth stroke does not protrude.

14 　一 十 オ オ オ ギ ギ ギ 栏 栏 样 样 样 様

様

455 練

レン REN
ね・る ne(ru)

to refine; to
knead; to train

Originally 練, this character combines 糸 *thread*
and 柬 *removing selected items from a bundle*,
referring to the preparation of raw silk. From this,
we have the association in meaning of *to knead*, *to
improve* and *to train*.
GR3 N3 AP

Example Sentences

1. 試合のために練習にはげんでいる。
   Shiai no tame ni renshū ni hagende iru.
   <u>I'm practicing hard</u> for an upcoming match.

2. 彼は別れた恋人に未練があるらしい。
   Kare wa wakareta koibito ni miren ga aru rashii.
   Apparently he still has <u>a lingering affection</u> for his ex-girlfriend.

3. その会社の洗練されたデザインが話題になっている。
   Sono kaisha no senren sareta dezain ga wadai ni natte iru.
   The <u>tasteful</u> designs of that company are the talk of the town.

4. パンの生地を練るのに力が要る。
   Pan no kiji o neru no ni chikara ga iru.
   You need strength to be able <u>to knead</u> the dough for bread.

5. 次の旅行の計画を練ろう。
   Tsugi no ryokō no keikaku o nerō.
   Let's <u>work out</u> our <u>plans</u> for our next trip.

Common Compounds and Phrases

練習	**renshū**	practice; training; exercise
未練	**miren**	lingering attachment
訓練	**kunren**	training; drill
熟練	**jukuren**	expertise; proficiency
修練	**shūren**	practice; training
試練	**shiren**	a test; a trial
練乳	**rennyū**	condensed milk

End the twelfth stroke firmly.

14 　乞 幺 幺 牟 糸 糸 糽 紅 紅 綀 綀 練 練 練

練

456 横

オウ Ō
よこ yoko

sideways; side

The character 横 is a combination of *wood* 木 and *yellow* (originally *flaming arrow*) 黄, a reference to a piece of wood placed across a gate to keep it closed. The meanings of *crossways* and *side* have derived from this.
GR3 N3 AP

Example Sentences

1. そこの道は危険ですから、横断歩道を渡ってください。
   Soko no michi wa kiken desu kara, ōdan hodō o watatte kudasai.
   That is a dangerous street, so cross at the <u>pedestrian crossing</u>.

2. あの人の横着な態度に腹が立つ。
   Ano hito no ōchaku na taido ni hara ga tatsu.
   His <u>impudent</u> attitude makes me angry.

3. 孫がおばあさんの横で料理を手伝っていた。
   Mago ga obāsan no <u>yoko</u> de ryōri o tetsudatte ita.
   The little girl was at her grandmother's <u>side</u>, helping with the cooking.

4. 彼の話に友達が横やりを入れた。
   Kare no hanashi ni tomodachi ga <u>yokoyari o ireta</u>.
   His friend <u>interrupted</u> him while he was talking.

5. 黒猫が目の前を横切った。
   Kuroneko ga me no mae o <u>yokogitta</u>.
   A black cat <u>crossed</u> right in front of me.

Common Compounds and Phrases

横断	**ōdan**	crossing; intersecting
横着な	**ōchaku na**	brazen; impudent; lazy
横顔	**yokogao**	a silhouette; a sketch
横書き	**yokogaki**	to write from left to right
縦横	**tateyoko (jūō)**	length and breadth
横やりを 入れる	**yokoyari o ireru**	to interrupt; to interfere
横浜	**Yokohama**	Yokohama (a place)

The eleventh stroke protrudes.

15 十 オ 木 杧 杧 枡 栉 栉 桔 楷 横 横 横 横

横

EXERCISE 38 (445 – 456)

A. Give the readings for the following.

1. 鳴く _____
2. 雑な _____
3. 引き算 _____
4. 置く _____
5. 静かな _____
6. 関心 _____
7. 鼻声 _____
8. 続ける _____
9. 様々な _____
10. 実際に _____

B. Write the following in kanji and kana, adding *furigana* to the kanji.

1. practice; training _____
2. a closet; a storeroom _____
3. an ear, nose and throat department _____
4. a relation(ship); an effect _____
5. a way of life _____
6. to become quiet, still _____

7. a procedure; a process _____
8. a silhouette; a sketch _____
9. miscellaneous affairs; chores _____
10. ringing in the ears; tinnitus _____

C. Choose an appropriate item from the following list to complete the expressions below.
LIST: 予算、配置、安静、関西、鳴き声、様、続々、横、国際、鼻

1. 母親はいつも子どもの ＿＿＿ に寝る。
2. 牛の ＿＿＿ が遠くから聞こえてくる。
3. 新東京 ＿＿＿ 空港
4. 人が ＿＿＿ と集まって来る。
5. その買い物をするには ＿＿＿ が足りない。
6. 銀行は目と ＿＿＿ の先だ。
7. 商品の ＿＿＿ を変える
8. 中島 ＿＿＿ 、いらっしゃいますか。
9. ＿＿＿ 地方へ旅行に行く
10. 手術後は一週間の ＿＿＿ が必要だった。

457 選

セン SEN
えら・ぶ era(bu)

to choose

The character 選 combines *to go* 辶 and *to arrange in order* 巽, suggesting the action of lining up a number of things, to *choose* from among them.
GR4 N3 AP

Example Sentences

1. 色々な選択が可能です。
   Iroiro na sentaku ga kanō desu.
   There are several possible options.

2. 選手入場に大きな歓声が上がった。
   Senshu nyūjō ni ōki na kansei ga agatta.
   When the players entered the stadium, a cheer went up from the crowd.

3. あの知事は人気者なので、再選されるだろう。
   Ano chiji wa ninkimono na node, saisen sareru darō.
   Owing to that governor's popularity, he will most probably be re-elected.

4. 選挙権は、二十歳以上の男女全員にあります。
   Senkyoken wa, hatachi ijō no danjo zen'in ni arimasu.
   All men and women over the age of twenty have the right to vote.

5. この中から、お好きなものをお選び下さい。
   Kono naka kara, osuki na mono o oerabi kudasai.
   Please choose any one that you like from among these.

Common Compounds and Phrases

選択	**sentaku**	a selection; a choice; an option
選手	**senshu**	an athlete (player)
再選	**saisen**	re-election
選挙	**senkyo**	an election
市長選挙	**shichō senkyo**	a mayoral election
当選	**tōsen**	election; winning (a prize)
予選	**yosen**	a preliminary (match, trial, round)

The tenth stroke is longer than the seventh.

15 丷 ユ 己 コ 弖 弖 巽 巽 巽 巽 巽 選 選

選

458 調

チョウ CHŌ
しら・べる shira(beru)
*ととの・う totono(u)
*ととの・える totono(eru)

tone; to investigate; to prepare

The character 調 is a combination of *to speak, words* 言 and *around a rice field* 周. The original meaning of *to discuss thoroughly* gives us the associated ideas of *to investigate* and *condition*.
GR3 N3 AP

Example Sentences

1. 温度調節する必要がある。
   Ondo chōsetsu suru hitsuyō ga aru.
   We need to adjust the temperature.

2. 試験勉強が順調に進んでいる。
   Shiken benkyō ga junchō ni susunde iru.
   Everything is going well with my preparation for the examinations.

3. 激しい口調で叱られた。
   Hageshii kuchō de shikarareta.
   I was reprimanded severely.

4. 電子辞書を使って、調べたらどうですか。
   Denshi jisho o tsukatte, shirabetara dō desu ka.
   Why don't you use your electronic dictionary to look the word up?

5. 転職のための書類を調えた。
   Tenshoku no tame no shorui o totonoeta.
   I got all the necessary documentation together for my career change.

Common Compounds and Phrases

順調な	**junchō na**	favorable; satisfactory
調査	**chōsa**	an investigation; a survey
調子	**chōshi**	a tone; a pitch; a manner; a condition
調整	**chōsei**	adjustment; control
強調	**kyōchō**	emphasis; stress; a tone
調理	**chōri**	cooking; cuisine
取調べ	**torishirabe**	an investigation; an inquiry

The ninth stroke ends with a hook.

15 丶 亠 言 言 言 言 訓 訊 訊 訊 調 調 調 調

調

459 熱

heat; hot

ネツ NETSU
あつ・い atsu(i)

The character 熱 combines *fire* 灬 and *a person bending down to plant a tree* 埶. Thus, we have the meaning of *heat* from the association of a person holding a stick, trying to make a fire.
GR4 N3 AP

Example Sentences

1. 娘が夜中に発熱した。
   Musume ga yonaka ni hatsunetsu shita.
   My daughter came down with a fever in the night.

2. 熱帯雨林を守る運動に参加したいと思っている。
   Nettai urin o mamoru undō ni sanka shitai to omotte iru.
   I'm thinking of joining a movement that is trying to protect the tropical rainforests.

3. 子供の頃はサッカーばかりに熱中したものだ。
   Kodomo no koro wa sakkā bakari ni netchū shita mono da.
   When I was a boy, I used to be absolutely crazy about soccer.

4. そんなに熱心になるほどのことではない。
   Sonna ni nesshin ni naru hodo no koto de wa nai.
   It's nothing to be all that enthusiastic about.

5. このお茶は熱すぎて飲めない。
   Kono ocha wa atsusugite nomenai.
   This green tea is too hot for me to drink.

Common Compounds and Phrases

発熱する	hatsunetsu suru	to develop a fever
熱帯	nettai	the tropics
熱中する	netchū suru	to be enthusiastic (wild) about
熱気	nekki	hot air; a heated atmosphere
光熱費	kōnetsuhi	heat and lighting charges
情熱	jōnetsu	passion; enthusiasm
熱々の	atsuatsu no	piping hot; passionate

Don't forget the eleventh stroke.

15 　十　土　产　去　去　幸　幸　刲　刲　埶　埶　執　執　熱　熱

熱

---

460 機

machine; loom; opportunity

キ KI
*はた hata

The character 機 combines *tree, wood* 木 and *how many?* (originally, *loom*) 幾. From *wooden loom* the sense of *machine*, in general, has developed. *Opportunity* is an associated meaning.
GR4 N3 AP

Example Sentences

1. 青空に飛行機がきらっと光った。
   Aozora ni hikōki ga kiratto hikatta.
   The flash of a plane in the blue sky caught my eye.

2. 機会があればそこに行きたい。
   Kikai ga areba soko ni ikitai.
   I'd like to go there if I had the chance.

3. 新しい携帯電話の機能が使いこなせない。
   Atarashii keitai denwa no kinō ga tsukai-konasenai.
   I haven't been able to master the functions on my new cellphone.

4. いとこの赤ちゃんはいつも機嫌がいい。
   Itoko no akachan wa itsumo kigen ga ii.
   My cousin's baby has a lovely nature.

5. 角のスーパーは有機野菜の品揃えが豊富だ。
   Kado no sūpā wa yūki yasai no shinazoroe ga hōfu da.
   The corner supermarket has a good range of organic vegetables.

Common Compounds and Phrases

機械	kikai	a machine; a mechanism
掃除機	sōjiki	a vacuum cleaner
機能	kinō	a function; a feature
機嫌がいい	kigen ga ii	to be in a good mood
有機野菜	yūki yasai	organic vegetables
危機	kiki	a crisis; a pinch
臨機応変	rinki ōhen	adaptation to circumstances

Don't forget the last stroke.

16 　才　木　栌　栌　栌　栌　栌　栌　機　機　機　機　機

機

461 橋 bridge

キョウ KYŌ
はし hashi

The character 橋 combines *tree*, *wood* 木 and *a structure with a curved roof* 喬. The meaning of a curved wooden structure or *bridge* developed from this.
GR3 N3 AP

Example Sentences

1. 歩道橋の上を走らないでください。
   Hodōkyō no ue o hashiranai de kudasai.
   Please don't run over the <u>pedestrian bridge</u>.

2. あの桟橋には有名な豪華客船が停泊する。
   Ano sanbashi ni wa yūmei na gōka kyakusen ga teihaku suru.
   Famous luxury liners berth at that <u>pier</u>.

3. この橋を渡れば、すぐ兄の家です。
   Kono hashi o watareba, sugu ani no ie desu.
   My brother lives just over this <u>bridge</u>.

4. 石橋はたたいて渡れ。
   Ishibashi wa tataite watare.
   Think well before you decide. (Lit: Strike <u>a stone bridge</u> before you cross it—a saying.)

5. 彼の望みは、人々の橋渡しをすることだった。
   Kare no nozomi wa, hitobito no hashiwatashi o suru koto datta.
   His hope was to <u>build bridges</u> between people.

Common Compounds and Phrases

歩道橋	**hodōkyō**	a pedestrian bridge; a footbridge
鉄橋	**tekkyō**	an iron (railway) bridge
桟橋	**sanbashi**	a pier; a wharf
つり橋	**tsuribashi**	a suspension bridge
橋渡し	**hashiwatashi**	mediation; good offices
橋本	**Hashimoto**	Hashimoto (a name)

The thirteenth stroke ends with a hook.

16 才 木 栌 栌 栌 杯 栌 栌 栌 棒 棒 橋 橋

橋

462 贈 to give; to present

ゾウ ZŌ   ソウ SŌ
おく・る oku(ru)

The character 贈 is a combination of *shell*, *money* 貝 and *build up* or *send*, *give* 曽, the suggestion being to give valuable items. Hence the meaning of *to present* or *give*.
JK N2 AP

Example Sentences

1. アカデミー賞の贈呈式はいつですか。
   Akademii-shō no zōteishiki wa itsu desu ka.
   When is the Academy <u>Awards ceremony</u> to be held?

2. 貴重な書類が資料館に寄贈されました。
   Kichō na shorui ga shiryōkan ni kizō saremashita.
   Some precious papers <u>were donated</u> to the museum.

3. 結婚祝いの贈答品は何がおすすめですか。
   Kekkon iwai no zōtōhin wa nani ga osusume desu ka.
   What do you recommend for a wedding <u>gift</u>?

4. 贈り物用にしてください。
   Okurimono-yō ni shite kudasai.
   Could you <u>gift</u> wrap it for me, please?

5. 父は結婚記念日に、母へバラの花束を贈た。
   Chichi wa kekkon kinenbi ni haha e bara no hanataba o okutta.
   My father <u>gave</u> my mother a bouquet of roses on their wedding anniversary.

Common Compounds and Phrases

贈呈式	**zōteishiki**	a presentation (award) ceremony
寄贈する	**kizō / kisō suru**	to contribute; to donate
贈与する	**zōyo suru**	to give; to present
贈答	**zōtō**	an exchange of gifts
贈賄	**zōwai**	bribery
贈り物	**okurimono**	a present; a gift

The left-hand side is slightly thinner than the right. Space equally on the left.

18 目 貝 貝 貝 貯 貯 貯 贮 贈 贈 贈 贈 贈

贈

463 難

difficult; trouble

ナン NAN
むずか・しい muzuka(shii)
*かた・い kata(i)
*にく・い niku(i)

The character 難 combines *roasting an animal over a flame* 堇 and *bird* 隹. A roasted bird suggests *misfortune*, as if being roasted alive and, by extension, *difficult*.
GR6 N3 AP

Example Sentences

1. 旅行中に災難に会った。
   Ryokōchū ni sainan ni atta.
   I met with an accident while traveling.

2. あの人の行為を非難するべきだ。
   Ano hito no kōi o hinan suru beki da.
   His behavior is reprehensible.

3. 国連は難民問題に取り組んでいる。
   Kokuren wa nanmin mondai ni torikunde iru.
   The United Nations is having to deal with the refugee issue.

4. 連休中の指定席を手に入れるのは難しい。
   Renkyūchū no shiteiseki o te ni ireru no wa muzukashii.
   It will be difficult to get reserved seats during the long holiday.

5. そういう大きなチャンスはなかなか得難い。
   Sō iu ōki na chansu wa naka naka egatai.
   You would rarely have such a great opportunity.

Common Compounds and Phrases

災難	**sainan**	a disaster; an accident; a mishap
難民	**nanmin**	a refugee
難病	**nanbyō**	a serious (intractable) disease
無難な	**bunan** na	safe; secure; acceptable
得難い	**egatai**	hard to obtain; unapproachable
有り難い	**arigatai**	moving; to be thankful, grateful
答え難い	**kotae-nikui**	difficult to answer, respond to

Use equal spacing on the right.

18 艹 艹 芑 莒 莫 莫 莫 葟 蓳 鄞 鄞 鞃 難 難

難

---

464 願

to wish; to ask a favor

ガン GAN
ねが・う nega(u)

Combining *spring water flowing from a round hole* 原 and *head* 頁, the character 願 represents a round head. From this, the sense of earnestly *wishing* for something has derived.
GR4 N3 AP

Example Sentences

1. 本日より願書の受付を始めました。
   Honjitsu yori gansho no uketsuke o hajimemashita.
   We have begun accepting written applications from today.

2. 出願者の中には大勢の主婦がいます。
   Shutsugansha no naka ni wa ōzei no shufu ga imasu.
   The applicants include a large number of homemakers.

3. ようやく、悲願がかなった。
   Yōyaku, higan ga kanatta.
   At long last, my dream came true.

4. 休職願いを会社に出した。
   Kyūshoku negai o kaisha ni dashita.
   I applied for a leave of absence from my company.

5. 若い人たちにはあまり結婚願望はないようだ。
   Wakai hitotachi ni wa amari kekkon ganbō wa nai yō da.
   Young people don't seem to have much of a desire to get married.

Common Compounds and Phrases

願書	**gansho**	a written application
出願者	**shutsugansha**	an applicant
念願	**nengan**	one's heart's desire; one's prayer
悲願	**higan**	a long-felt wish; a dream
志願	**shigan**	volunteering; a desire; an application
願望	**ganbō**	a wish; a desire; an ambition
願い	**negai**	a desire; a wish; a request

The eighth stroke ends with a hook.

19 厃 厈 厡 厡 原 原 原 願 願 願 願 願 願

願

EXERCISE 39 (457 – 464)

A. Give the readings for the following.
1. 読み難い _____
2. 調べる _____
3. 難しかった _____
4. 飛行機 _____
5. お願いします。 _____
6. 選ぶ _____
7. 橋 _____
8. 有り難い _____
9. 熱い _____
10. 贈る _____

B. Write the following in kanji and kana.
1. emphasis; stress _____
2. a pedestrian bridge _____
3. to be full of enthusiasm about something _____
4. an athlete; a player _____
5. transportation facilities _____
6. to adjust; to regulate _____
7. Mr. Hashimoto (polite) _____
8. a written application _____
9. a preliminary match, round _____
10. a present; a gift _____

C. Rewrite in kanji and kana, according to the hints provided.
1. けっこん あいてを えらぶ (to choose one's marriage partner)
2. あじを ととのえる (to refine the taste of something)
3. この さき こんなんが まっている。(Hard times are ahead.)
4. はは の ひ に はなを おくる (to give flowers on Mother's Day)
5. ジェットき の じだい (the jet age)
6. いかないで！おねがい。(Please don't go!)
7. さけを あつくして、のむ (to heat sake up and drink it)
8. しごとを みつける のが むずかしい (to have difficulty in finding work)
9. はし が おちた (a bridge collapsed)
10. あつあつの りょうりが あまり すきじゃない。(I don't much like piping hot food.)

Review 13 (1 – 464)

A. Give the readings for the following.
1. 失われている _____
2. 難しい _____
3. 熱い _____
4. 単なる _____
5. 橋 _____
6. 選ぶ _____
7. 化ける _____
8. 続く _____
9. 調べる _____
10. 送る _____

B. Write in English.
1. 公平な _____
2. 足し算 _____
3. 無難な _____
4. 不必要な _____
5. 強調 _____
6. 冷静な _____
7. 有機野菜 _____
8. 番号 _____
9. 同様の _____
10. 出願者 _____

C. Rewrite the following in kana.
1. 困難な _____
2. 間際 _____
3. 取り調べ _____
4. 置き場 _____
5. 贈り物 _____
6. 熱中する _____
7. 横書き _____
8. 飛行機 _____
9. 使い難い _____
10. 引き続き _____

D. Choose an appropriate item from the following list to complete the expressions below.
LIST: 歩道橋、受付、調、贈答、熱心、未成年、願、選手、変化、機関車

1. 次第に ＿＿＿ する
2. まだ ＿＿＿ の少年たち
3. 研究 ＿＿＿ な人
4. ＿＿＿ の下をくぐる
5. テニスの ＿＿＿
6. 結婚の ＿＿＿ 品

7. 必要な物が全部 _____ っている
8. _____ の係員に質問する
9. _____ を運転する人
10. お _____ いします。

17. 大関　　（　）
18. 熱気　　（　）
19. 日本橋　（　）
20. 静止　　（　）

q. あんざん
r. なんみん
s. えいじゅう
t. りゆう

E.　Match the following.

1. 永住　（　）
2. 難病　（　）
3. 結末　（　）
4. 暗算　（　）
5. 予選　（　）
6. 理由　（　）
7. 願書　（　）
8. 神戸　（　）
9. 雑音　（　）
10. 竹刀　（　）
11. 丸薬　（　）
12. 難民　（　）
13. 鳴動　（　）
14. 調子　（　）
15. 機会　（　）
16. 未練　（　）

a. ちょうし
b. ねっき
c. せいし
d. おおぜき
e. めいどう
f. なんびょう
g. よせん
h. きかい
i. けつまつ
j. みれん
k. ざつおん
l. しない
m. にほんばし
n. がんしょ
o. こうべ
p. がんやく

F.　Write the readings for the kanji in the following and then translate the sentences into English.

1. 明日までに算数の練習問題を終えなさい。
2. 熱が出たので、横になってしばらく休んだ。
3. オリンピック代表選手に、花を贈ってはげました。
4. あの国は国際社会から非難されている。
5. あの人は国家試験に合格（ごうかく）して、とても鼻が高いでしょう。
6. この都市の交通機関は発達していて、住むのに大変便利です。
7. 指を鳴らすのを止めて、静かに待っていなさい。
8. それに関しては、橋本様にお願いしてはいかがですか。
9. 調味料は台所のキャビネットの一番上に置いてあります。
10. そんな雑なやり方を続けても無意味だ。

Answers

Exercise 1 (1–12) p7

A.
1. やま (yama)
2. くち (kuchi)
3. はち (hachi)
4. ひと (hito)
5. さん (san)
6. く、きゅう (ku / kyū)
7. した (shita)
8. しち、なな (shichi / nana)
9. に (ni)
10. じゅう、とお (jū / tō)

B.
1. twenty-one
2. eight people
3. a mountain
4. seventy-nine
5. a mouth; speech
6. a multiplication table
7. thirty-eight
8. ninety-two
9. bottom; below; under
10. one person; on one's own

C.
1. ひとつ
2. ください
3. ここのつ
4. いれる
5. さがる
6. きゅうにん
7. みっつ
8. いりぐち
9. ななつ
10. じんこう

Exercise 2 (13–24) p13

A.
1. おんな (onna)
2. かわ (kawa)
3. せん (sen)
4. うえ 、かみ、じょう (ue, kami, jō)
5. まん (man)
6. ひ、か (hi, ka)
7. えん (en)
8. つち、ど (tsuchi, do)
9. ちいさな (chiisa na)
10. おおきい (ōkii)

B.
1. 大人
2. 八千
3. 上げる
4. 三千七十三円
5. 二千万
6. 女の子
7. 上がる、上る
8. 山口さん
9. 九千人
10. 七千二十

C.
1. 女子
2. 大 (きくない)
3. 小川
4. 八千円
5. 火山
6. 三万人
7. 女 (の) 人
8. 千円
9. 女王
10. 川上 (さん)

Exercise 3 (25–36) p20

A.
1. みず (mizu)
2. ごじゅっぷん、ごじっぷん (gojuppun, gojippun)
3. つき (tsuki)
4. ちちのひ (chichi no hi)
5. ななかげつ (nanakagetsu)
6. すこし (sukoshi)
7. いつつ (itsutsu)
8. てのなか (te no naka)
9. いつか (itsuka)
10. きょう、こんにち (kyō, konnichi)

B.
1. I'm home.
2. water skiing
3. a father, Father
4. I don't understand / know.
5. five people / persons
6. to place in one's hand; to acquire
7. Wednesday
8. five thousand yen
9. few; little
10. November

C.
1. 分ける
2. 少女
3. 三日
4. 三分の二
5. 十五日
6. 一日中
7. 今
8. 大きい手
9. 今月
10. ある日

Review 1 (1–36) pp20–21

A.
1. to climb down a mountain
2. January, one month
3. this month
4. a new moon
5. population
6. (a) hand(s)
7. ninety yen
8. a queen
9. a mountain
10. an entrance; an outset

B.
1. 小 (さい)
2. 女 (の) 子
3. 十月
4. 土
5. 手 (に) 入 (れる)
6. 今月
7. 一日
8. 今
9. 下 (がる)
10. 少 (ない)

266

C.
1. きょう、こんにち (kyō, konnnichi)
2. ふつか (futsuka)
3. いちにちじゅう (ichinichijū)
4. みず (mizu)
5. かわしも (kawashimo)
6. おうじ (ōji)
7. じゅうがつ (jūgatsu)
8. じょし (joshi)
9. ごぶごぶ (gobu gobu)
10. かざん (kazan)

D.
1. 三月二日	6. 分ける
2. 三ヶ月	7. 三分の二
3. 父の日	8. 三つ
4. 五十分	9. 五月五日
5. 少女	10. 水上スキー

E.
1. おおきなかわ
2. てのなか
3. みかみさんのこ
4. かわかみさんとたぐちさん
5. ちいさなおんなのこ
6. つちだというひと
7. 「こんにちは」
8. ごがつみっか
9. みずをください
10. じょしふたり
11. はっせんにじゅうえん
12. かわぐちさんにあげた。
13. まるいつき
14. おとうさん
15. すこしおおきい
16. ひとつすくない
17. さんがつにじゅうはちにち
18. かわださんとやましたさん
19. きゅうせんえん
20. すこしください。

F.
1. f	6. i
2. h	7. b
3. j	8. c
4. e	9. d
5. a	10. g

Exercise 4 (37 – 48)   p27

A.
1. ひので (hi no de)
2. はえている (haete iru)
3. ろくがつむいか (rokugatsu muika)
4. ひだりがわ (hidari-gawa)
5. がいしゅつ (gaishutsu)
6. ともだち (tomodachi)
7. きのした (ki no shita)
8. ふるい (furui)
9. みずたま (mizutama)
10. よんじゅうえん (yonjūen)

B.
1. six things	6. a big stone
2. date of birth	7. a friend
3. four people	8. to live
4. to take, put out; to send	9. to go outside
5. the right arm	10. from right to left

C.
1. j	6. h
2. i	7. d
3. a	8. f
4. c	9. e
5. b	10. g

Exercise 5 (49 – 60)   p34

A.
1. やすむ (yasumu)
2. いく、ゆく (iku, yuku)
3. ははとちち (haha to chichi)
4. きをつける (ki o tsukeru)
5. はんぶん (hanbun)
6. あいます (aimasu)
7. おおきいめ (ōkii me)
8. にほん、にっぽん (Nihon, Nippon)
9. やすい (yasui)
10. たっている (tatte iru)

B.
1. h	6. i
2. j	7. c
3. a	8. e
4. g	9. d
5. b	10. f

C.
1. 行きましょう、行こう
2. 大会
3. 北口
4. 母の日
5. 安かった
6. 行う
7. 山本さん
8. 気分
9. 目
10. 休日、休み

Exercise 6 (61–72)   p40

A.
1. にひゃく (nihyaku)
2. みみ (mimi)
3. な (na)
4. かい (kai)
5. いと (ito)
6. なんにん (nannin)
7. おおかった (ōkatta)
8. にしび (nishibi)
9. ことし (kotoshi)
10. おさきに (osaki ni)

B.
1. 花
2. 行き先
3. 先生
4. 年上
5. 多め
6. 北西
7. 何も
8. 毎日
9. 多分
10. 三百年

C.
1. a one-hundred yen coin
2. bread crust
3. *ikebana*; Japanese flower arrangement
4. every month
5. a clue; a beginning
6. more or less; rather
7. How many days? What day of the month?
8. last month
9. twenty people (persons)
10. eight hundred yen

Review 2 (1–72)   p41

A.
1. かい (kai)
2. にしぐち (nishiguchi)
3. せんせい (sensei)
4. せんきゅうひゃくろくじゅうよねん (sen kyūhyaku rokujū yonen)
5. せいねんがっぴ (seinen gappi)
6. しろいいと (shiroi ito)
7. せんげつ (sengetsu)
8. なにもない (nani mo nai)
9. いけばな (*ikebana*)
10. なんにん (nannin)
11. パンのみみ (pan no mimi)
12. おおい (ōi)
13. おさきに (osaki ni)
14. まいにち (mainichi)
15. さんびゃっぽん (sanbyappon)

B.
1. a sixth grader
2. today's weather
3. air; the atmosphere
4. perhaps
5. four months
6. white
7. old
8. national; state
9. to want to meet
10. to go by bus
11. this year
12. a five-hundred yen coin
13. a little; a few
14. ¥3,600
15. cheap

C.
1. 花火
2. 毎年
3. 八年目
4. 糸口
5. 半年
6. 木(の)下
7. 友(だち)
8. 本名
9. 右手
10. 何日
11. 少年
12. 四月一日
13. 十円玉

D.
1. n
2. e
3. h
4. f
5. g
6. a
7. l
8. i
9. m
10. j
11. o
12. c
13. d
14. b
15. k

E.
1. c
2. a
3. g
4. b
5. f
6. e
7. h
8. n
9. o
10. j
11. m
12. k
13. d
14. i
15. l

Exercise 7 (73–84)   p48

A.
1. くる (kuru)
2. みえる (mieru)
3. たりる (tariru)
4. しゃかい (shakai)
5. けんがく (kengaku)
6. あく (aku)
7. くるまをだす (kuruma o dasu)
8. だいがくせい (daigakusei)
9. おとこのこ (otoko no ko)
10. おかね (okane)

B.
1. next month
2. getting off a train
3. a word, a comment
4. a foreigner, a non-Japanese
5. male and female
6. a head office
7. a sample, a specimen
8. an elementary school student
9. heavy rain
10. coming to Japan

C.
1. g	9. b
2. d	10. e
3. c	11. h
4. i	12. k
5. o	13. f
6. l	14. n
7. j	15. a
8. m	

Exercise 8 (85–96)   p54

A.
1. なんじ (nanji)
2. たべる (taberu)
3. とうほく (tōhoku)
4. みなみぐち (minami-guchi)
5. ながねん (naganen)
6. みせ (mise)
7. うしろ (ushiro)
8. じょしこうせい (joshi kōsei)
9. たべたあと (tabeta ato)
10. かいてください (kaite kudasai)

B.
1. 金魚	5. 社長
2. 手書き	6. 書店
3. 後半	7. 三日前に
4. 本店	8. 十二時四十五分

C.
1. 食前	10. 高山
2. 足（が）長（い）	11. 店（に）入（る）
3. 糸口	12. 後（に）
4. 立（ち）食（い）	13. 二人前
5. 店長	14. 今後
6. 下書（き）	15. 食（べた）
7. 月食	16. 後（ろ）足
8. 小魚	17. 七時半
9. 小学校	

Exercise 9 (97–108)   p61

A.
1. あたらしくない (atarashiku nai)
2. がいこくご (gaikokugo)
3. こくどう (kokudō)
4. えきビル (eki biru)
5. はなしている (hanashite iru)
6. でんき (denki)
7. かたる (kataru)
8. ながいあいだ (nagai aida)
9. せんしゅう (senshū)
10. のみたい (nomitai)

B.
1. 日本語	6. 会話
2. 電話	7. 人間
3. 二週間	8. 中国語
4. 買い出し	9. 来週
5. 新年	10. 読書

C.
1. 時間（がない）	6. 毎週行（きます）。
2. 電車（で）来（る）	7. 駅（の）前（に）
3. 道（で）会（う）	8. 水（を）飲（む）
4. 新聞（を）読（む）	9. （よく）聞（こえない）
5. 話（を）聞（く）	10. 安（く）買（う）

Review 3 (1–108)   pp61-62

A.
1. ながあめ	9. あたらしいくるま
2. はなしをかたる	10. きこえない
3. よんでいるあいだに	11. じゅうぶんのさん
4. でんき	12. やまみちをくだる
5. くうかん	13. いりぐちのまえ
6. がいらいご	14. やすくかえた
7. ろくしゅうかん	15. はなしちゅう
8. しがつはつかにでる	

B.
1. to be a poor golf player	8. to talk on the phone
2. Spanish	9. nine days
3. going out to buy	10. five boys
4. to listen to a CD	11. the week before last
5. drinking water	12. the station master
6. a (baby) girl is born	13. a newspaper
7. conversation	14. next week

C.
1. 六本木の店
2. 南口を(から)出る
3. 一日中
4. 今日の新聞
5. 三十万人(の人々)
6. あの木の下に
7. 午後三時半(に)
8. 三十分
9. 中古車
10. 右手
11. 天国
12. お父さん
13. 生ビール
14. 今週
15. 五月雨

D.
1. 見ています、見ている
2. 白かった
3. 足りません、足りない
4. 入りました、入った
5. 学びました、学んだ
6. 会いたい
7. 出ます、出る
8. 立っていました、立っていた
9. 買います、買う
10. 分けます、分ける
11. お母さん
12. 言っていました，言っていた
13. 生きています、生きている
14. 来ます、来る
15. 行きました、行った

E.
1. l
2. b
3. i
4. h
5. o
6. p
7. r
8. m
9. k
10. n
11. s
12. j
13. a
14. d
15. f
16. g
17. q
18. c
19. t
20. e

Exercise 10 (109–120)　　　　p68

A.
1. く
2. うし
3. こころ
4. いぬ
5. ゆうだち
6. てんさい
7. いんりょく
8. ちゅうし
9. げんき
10. じんこう

B.
1. a calf
2. New Year's Day
3. a carpenter
4. a section; an interval
5. the center
6. Kita Ward
7. 9 years old
8. evening
9. to move (house)
10. a dead end

C.
1. もとのところ
2. にわりびき
3. ひきだしのなか
4. うしのおおきいめ
5. いぬをかう
6. みずをとめる
7. ちからがある
8. おおやけにする
9. ひいてください
10. たさいなひと

Exercise 11 (121–132)　　　　p75

A.
1. おにいさん
2. いか
3. きって
4. いきかた
5. やまぐちし
6. ふとい
7. ひろまる
8. ほうげん
9. いがい

B.
1. h
2. f
3. g
4. a
5. e
6. b
7. d
8. c

C.
1. 食(べた)方(がいい)
2. 三十分以内
3. 兄(が)一人(いる)
4. 金子(さんという)方
5. 切(らないで)下(さい)。
6. 語(の)読(み)方
7. 一年(の)内(で)二ヶ月
8. 少(し)太(る)
9. 仕方(がない)。
10. 火(が)広(がる)

Exercise 12 (133–144)　　　　p81

A.
1. ふゆ
2. かえる
3. おもな
4. もちいる
5. まざる
6. ただしい
7. まわす
8. うつる
9. さんじゅうえんだい
10. せだい

B.
1. まざっている
2. よのなか
3. たんぼ
4. しゅじん
5. だいほん
6. にじゅっかい
7. しゃせい
8. みんかん
9. こうたい
10. ちゅうがくせいようの

C.
1. a period; an age
2. this time; now
3. care; looking after; an introduction
4. a rice paddy
5. the New Year; January
6. to (make a) copy; to imitate
7. to have something to do; to have business
8. a winter holiday, vacation
9. a taxi fare
10. ballroom dancing

Review 4 (1–144)   p82

A.
1. いきどまり
2. ふそく
3. ゆうがた
4. しきり
5. ひろびろと
6. しゃせい
7. はなしかた
8. こくみん
9. せけんばなし
10. でんわだい

B.
1. 冬休み
2. 交じっている
3. 田んぼ
4. 回る
5. 主に
6. 用いる
7. 世の中
8. ナポレオン二世
9. 写す
10. 正しくない

C.
1. 住民
2. 以外
3. お正月
4. お兄さん
5. お代わり
6. 三回目
7. 主食
8. 大工
9. 八十円の切手
10. 南口

D.
1. g
2. a
3. f
4. q
5. k
6. i
7. m
8. l
9. r
10. t
11. h
12. b
13. s
14. c
15. d
16. e
17. j
18. p
19. n
20. o

E.
1. 兄 (と) 交代 (で) 犬 (の) 世話 (をすることにした)。
   My brother and I decided to take turns looking after the dog.
2. 市長 (の) 不正 (が) 公 (になった)。
   The mayor's wrongdoing was made public.
3. 内田 (さんはとても) 心 (の) 広 (い方です)。
   Mr. Uchida is a very tolerant person.
4. 今日中 (にそのデザインを) 仕上 (げなさい)。
   Have that design completed by the end of the day!
5. 去年 (の) 冬以来本田 (さんに) 会 (っていない)。
   I haven't seen Mr. Honda since last winter.
6. 駅 (の) 南口 (の) 前 (に) 車 (が) 二台止 (まっている)。
   There are two vehicles parked in front of the southern exit of the station.
7. 母 (は) 大切 (なものを) 引 (き) 出 (しにしまっている)。
   My mother keeps her valuable things in a drawer.
8. 主人 (は、) 今週 (ずっと) 元気 (がなかった)。
   My husband just hasn't been himself this last week.
9. 太田 (さん、この) 天文台 (へ) 来 (たのは) 何回目 (ですか)。
   Ms. Ōta, how many times have you been to this observatory, now?
10. 区民 (の) 力 (を) 合 (わせて、ポイすてをなくそう)。
   As residents of this ward, let's work together to rid the community of littering.

Exercise 13 (145–156)   p89

A.
1. いけださん
2. みょうじ
3. このむ
4. みずいろ
5. ひかっている
6. じもと
7. まにあう
8. しにました
9. かんがえかた

B.
1. f
2. d
3. e
4. i
5. g
6. c
7. h
8. a
9. b

C.
1. 足 (が) 早 (い)
2. (いい) 考 (えがある)
3. 色々 (な) 魚
4. 自分 (で) 行 (く)
5. 同 (じことを) 言 (う)
6. 大好 (きな) 人
7. (ローマ) 字 (で) 書 (く)
8. 手 (を) 合 (わせる)
9. 電池 (が) 切 (れた)
10. 同時 (に) 来 (る)

Exercise 14 (157–168) p95

A.

1. わたくし	6. いがく
2. ちかく	7. あかちゃん
3. きわめる	8. にくしょく
4. さくぶん	9. あいず
5. すまい	10. せきじゅうじ

B.

1. a moving car
2. to prepare (cook) dinner
3. to read a weather map
4. to take a short-cut
5. Please don't talk so loudly.
6. to eat meat every day
7. to buy some red socks
8. a not particularly well-known person
9. a private school
10. to live near a station

C.

1. 赤らめる	6. 手作りの
2. 間近	7. 私たちの
3. 走った	8. 有る
4. 地図	9. 赤くなる
5. 牛肉	10. 小さい声

Exercise 15 (169–180) p102

A.

1. おねえさん	6. むらびと
2. つかいかた	7. べつべつに
3. うりきれ	8. ペキン
4. わかれる	9. ちょうちょう
5. えいかいわ	10. ひくくない

B.

1. 英国	6. 日本大使
2. 前売り	7. 低下する
3. 東京	8. 使わないで下さい
4. 町外れ	9. 兄弟
5. 体中	10. 区別

C.

1. your (younger) brother
2. to use a telephone
3. to live in a town
4. to lower one's voice
5. a small village
6. to sell cheaply
7. a time for parting
8. the human body
9. to have two (older) sisters
10. to move up to the capital (Tokyo)

Review 5 (1–180) pp102–103

A.

1. ひくい	6. そんちょう
2. だいたい	7. わかれる
3. あね	8. したまち
4. きょうだい	9. うっている
5. つかわない	10. えいご

B.

1. 村人	6. 体力
2. 英会話	7. 上京
3. 区別	8. 市長
4. 弟さん	9. 早く
5. 大使	10. 前売り

C.

1. h	6. d
2. f	7. i
3. g	8. b
4. c	9. a
5. j	10. e

D.

1. various	6. a use
2. on sale	7. the outskirts of a town
3. a dead body	8. a literary style
4. a low (quiet) voice	9. a liking
5. cities, towns and villages	10. a different person

E.

1. q	11. c
2. k	12. d
3. m	13. h
4. n	14. b
5. o	15. t
6. j	16. f
7. r	17. e
8. p	18. i
9. s	19. a
10. g	20. l

F.

1. 姉(の)目(の)色(は)弟(と)同(じ)ではない。
2. 池田医院(が)私(の)家(に)一番近(い)。
3. 夕食(に)私(の)好(きな)肉(料理を)作(ろうと)考(えている)。
4. 有村(さんは)体(が)大(きくて)、声(が)低(い)。
5. (送)別会(に)間(に)合(うように)早目(に家を)出(た)。

6. 今、自分 (の) 住 (んでいる) 町 (を) 地図 (で探して みた)。
7. 広 (告の)「北京」(の) 文字 (が) 赤 (く) 光 (っていた)。
8. 英会話 (に遅れそうなので、必) 死 (に) 走 (った)。
9. (この) 花 (を) 作 (るのに) 多 (くの研) 究 (費が) 使 (われた)。
10. 有名 (な) 画 (家の絵が) 売 (りに) 出 (された)。

Exercise 16 (181–192)　　　　p109

A.

1. あおじろい	6. ただちに
2. こうぶつ	7. いもうとさん
3. ところどころ	8. にんきもの
4. しらない	9. ほこうしゃ
5. はじまる	10. ちゅうもん

B.

1. to have a smoke (a break)
2. where my brother is
3. to begin eating
4. to walk along the street
5. an old friend
6. something important
7. an honest way of doing something
8. to send for a doctor
9. to pour water
10. the blue sky overhead

C.

1. f	6. g
2. e.	7. d
3. j	8. a
4. i	9. h
5. b	10. c

Exercise 17 (193–204)　　　　p116

A.

1. うみ	6. あじわう
2. よる	7. いそぎなさい
3. こばやし	8. あした (あす、みょうにち)
4. さかなや	9. はかる
5. にほんかい	10. こうもん

B.

1. 世界中	6. 林道
2. 映画	7. 時計
3. 海外	8. 花屋
4. 味方	9. 計画
5. 急行	10. 子音

C.

1. 大 (きな) 音 (が) 聞 (こえる)。	
2. 夜中 (の) 二時 (ごろ)	
3. 町 (の) 明 (かりが) 見 (える)。	
4. 上映時間	
5. 明 (るい) 所 (に) 立 (つ)。	
6. (シェイクスピア) 文学 (の) 入門書	
7. 世界地図 (を) 見 (る)。	
8. 林 (の) 中 (を) 走 (る)。	
9. 電車 (が) 急 (に) 止 (まる)。	
10. 小学校 (の) 屋内 (プール)	

Exercise 18 (205–216)　　　　p122

A.

1. くび	6. けんきゅうしつ
2. おもわない	7. せいしゅんじだい
3. のりもの	8. あきたけん
4. きもち	9. もってくる
5. おもい	10. ビルがたった

B.

1. 秋の空、秋空	6. 金持ち
2. 建物	7. 春雨
3. 思い出	8. 県立の
4. 手首	9. 乗車する
5. 研究所	10. お手洗い

C.

1. 秋分の日	6. ナイフを研ぐ
2. 電車に乗る	7. 手をよく洗う
3. ホテルを建てる	8. 山口県に住む
4. 室内プール	9. 時々思い出す
5. 重大な	10. 去年の春休み

Review 6 (1–216)　　　　p123

A.

1. きもち	6. のせる
2. たてる	7. あき
3. あらいもの	8. かさねる
4. くび	9. やまぐちけん
5. おもわない	10. らいしゅん

B.

1. to catch a train
2. last spring
3. a prefectural senior high school
4. to remember one's father
5. to live in Kōchi Prefecture
6. a person with a long neck
7. to do research
8. to lift up a stone
9. a condominium is built
10. a heavy-looking object

C.

1. 水洗トイレ	6. 持ち味
2. 読書の秋	7. 手首
3. 石川県	8. 研究会
4. 持ち主	9. 青春時代
5. 重い物	10. 室外

D.

1. d	6. b
2. e	7. h
3. g	8. j
4. a	9. c
5. i	10. f

E.

1. j	11. c
2. o	12. k
3. g	13. r
4. t	14. q
5. a	15. d
6. i	16. l
7. f	17. p
8. b	18. m
9. n	19. e
10. s	20. h

F.

1. 来年(らいねん)の春(はる)には新(あたら)しい研究室(けんきゅうしつ)が建(た)つ。
   A new laboratory will be built next spring.

2. 妹(いもうと)の知(し)り合(あ)いが会社(かいしゃ)を首(くび)になった。
   An acquaintance of my sister's was let go by the company.

3. 今夜(こんや)は乗(の)り物(もの)に乗(の)らずに海(うみ)まで歩(ある)くことにしよう。
   I'm going to walk to the seaside tonight and not use any transport.

4. 秋(あき)になったら三重県(みえけん)に住(す)む姉(あね)の家(いえ)に行(い)こうと思(おも)う。
   I'm thinking of going to visit my sister in Mie Prefecture come autumn.

5. 林(はやし)さんは映画(えいが)の世界(せかい)には興味(きょうみ)を持(も)っていない。
   Mr. Hayashi shows no interest in the movies.

6. 見事(みごと)な時計台(とけいだい)が急(きゅう)に目(め)の前(まえ)に現(あらわ)れた。
   A wonderful clock tower suddenly appeared before us.

7. 直(す)ぐ服(ふく)を洗(あら)いなさい。
   Wash your clothes this minute!

8. 本屋(ほんや)で「青春(せいしゅん)の門(もん)」という本(ほん)を注文(ちゅうもん)した。
   I ordered the book *Seishun no Mon* at the bookstore.

9. 耳(みみ)に水(みず)が入(はい)ったので、近所(きんじょ)の医者(いしゃ)にみてもらった。
   I got some water in my ear and so I had the local doctor look at it.

10. 明(あき)らかに青木(あおき)さんは本音(ほんね)で語(かた)っていなかった。
    Clearly, Ms. Aoki wasn't speaking her mind.

Exercise 19 (217–228)   p130

A.

1. なんど	6. ひるやすみ
2. おちゃ	7. またない
3. しなもの	8. ようしょく
4. みおくる	9. ごじゅってん
5. ふべんな	10. はつばい

B.

1. 発見	6. 昼間
2. 春風	7. 上品な
3. 待合室	8. 送別会
4. 洋風	9. 大西洋
5. 駅員	10. 便り

C.

1. (店)員	6. (出)発
2. 昼(食)	7. 便(所)
3. (今)度	8. 茶(色)
4. (海)洋	9. (台)風
5. 送(金)	10. (作)品

Exercise 20 (229–240)   p136

A.

1. おこす	6. よわまっている
2. とくべっな	7. みんか
3. かえりみち	8. しゃっきん
4. まっしろな	9. だいがくいんせい
5. なつじかん	10. はくし

B.

1. 真夏の日	6. 学校に通う
2. 作家になる	7. 新聞の記事
3. 電車で帰る	8. 特に安い
4. 六時半に起きる	9. 乗り物に弱い
5. 夏休み中に	10. 早く帰ろう

C.
1. a one-way street
2. Please fill (this) in.
3. to read a letter
4. to be hospitalized
5. a brand new shirt
6. to write in one's diary every day
7. to stand up
8. to suffer from the summer heat
9. one's own house
10. to borrow a book

Exercise 21 (241–252)　　　　p143

A.
1. つよい
2. うまれる
3. しょくりょう
4. おそわる
5. すすむ
6. つとめる
7. ならっている
8. わるい
9. たび
10. くろい

B.
1. i
2. h
3. a
4. g
5. b
6. j
7. e
8. c
9. f
10. d

C.
1. (中国語を)教(える)
2. (世界一の)先進国
3. (日本語の)勉強
4. (目が)悪(い)
5. 黒字(である)
6. (心を)病(んでいる)
7. 青菜(を食べる)
8. (バスの)料金
9. 外国産(の車)
10. 強引(に飲ませる)

Review 7 (1–252)　　　　pp143-144

A.
1. りょうきん
2. わるい
3. ならっている
4. まっくろ
5. おわる
6. かりる
7. ひとりたび
8. うむ
9. つよめる
10. すすむ

B.
1. lessons
2. one's destination
3. powerful
4. an appetizer
5. a hospital
6. to go home
7. to get up early
8. to have poor eyesight
9. last summer
10. to teach English

C.
1. 大通り
2. ガリ勉
3. 進学する
4. 使用料
5. 真ん中
6. 気持悪い
7. 日帰り
8. 病
9. 見送り
10. 菜食

D.
1. 強(引に)
2. 旅(行する)
3. 悪(口を言う)
4. 病(気になる)
5. 黒(字)
6. 弱(点)
7. 勉(強する)
8. 進(歩する)
9. (入場)料
10. (りんごの)産(地)

E.
1. k
2. i
3. l
4. m
5. g
6. b
7. o
8. j
9. c
10. n
11. h
12. e
13. a
14. f
15. d

F.
1. 兄を病院に送っていった。
2. 真夏の勉強は暑くてつらい。
3. 旅先で特産品を買った。
4. 昼、家に帰ってお茶を飲んだ。
5. 次の便の出発を待たなければならない。

G.
1. (ようふくや)の(てんいん)が(くろい)コートを(う)った。
2. (しんがく)(きょうしつ)で(なら)った(じ)を(にっき)に(か)いた。
3. 「(わる)いけど、(つうこうりょう)を(か)りていいですか。」
4. (でんき)が(つ)く(たび)に(お)こされた。
5. (あおな)は(かみ)につつむと(なが)もちする。

Exercise 22 (253–264)　　　　p150

A.
1. やさい
2. ころがる
3. もちはこぶ
4. つごう
5. ぶんや
6. おわり
7. しんりがく
8. ことり
9. うごきだす
10. といあわせ

B.

1. 上野	6. 自転車
2. 運動	7. 大都会
3. 読み終わる	8. 白鳥
4. 五人家族	9. 組み立てる
5. 回転ドア	10. 一石二鳥

C.

1. 料理(が)上手
2. 電車(の)運転手
3. 東京都(に)住む
4. 運送会社
5. 学問(の)道(に)進(む)
6. 三人組(の)友人
7. 家族旅行
8. 食堂(で)食事(する)

Exercise 23 (265–276)   p157

A.

1. みじかくない	6. あける
2. かんき、さむけ	7. あつい
3. つく	8. さむくなる
4. あつめる	9. かしや
5. かいじょう	10. てがるな

B.

1. woods, a forest
2. to let someone use the telephone
3. a light vehicle
4. tomorrow morning
5. to assemble outside
6. Please answer.
7. the start of the swimming season
8. a short time
9. to concentrate
10. an occasion; a case

C.

1. 貸し切り	6. 運動場
2. 水着	7. 開発
3. 特集	8. 上着を着る
4. 青森	9. 売り場
5. 暑がり	10. 朝食

Exercise 24 (277–288)   p163

A.

1. いみ	6. とおくに
2. らくな	7. ししょく
3. かず	8. うたっている
4. くらい	9. ごはん
5. こころみる	10. たのしい

B.

1. 試してみる	6. 気楽な
2. 注意する	7. 遠回り
3. 働き者	8. 五番目
4. 朝飯前	9. 産業
5. 暗記する	10. 数週間

C.

1. j	6. i
2. f	7. b
3. h	8. c
4. g	9. e
5. a	10. d

Exercise 25 (289–300)   p170

A.

1. かお	6. ぎん
2. おや	7. せつめいする
3. どようび	8. あたま、かしら
4. くすり	9. とく
5. しちや	10. えいがかん

B.

1. 試験	6. 薬品
2. 点線	7. 月曜日
3. 顔色	8. 図書館
4. 題名	9. 父親
5. 質問する	10. 親しい

C.

1. an electric wire	6. Tuesday
2. a Japanese inn	7. a novel
3. an experience	8. a hostage; a prisoner
4. the Bank of Japan	9. a kind person
5. a deposit	10. a serious problem

Review 8 (1–300)   pp170-171

A.

1. だいめい	6. たいけん
2. たいしかん	7. くらい
3. らくな	8. くすり
4. したしい	9. うたわない
5. ひんしつ	10. にゅうし

B.

1. a herbal medicine
2. an assembly hall
3. a topic of conversation
4. a deposit
5. Tuesday
6. an electric wire
7. a number of people; many people

8. a test; an experiment
9. one's father
10. eye drops

C.
1. (注)意(する)
2. (知らん)顔(をする)
3. (今度の木)曜(日)
4. 説(明する)
5. 番(犬にいい犬)
6. (入)場(料)
7. (問)題(をとく)
8. (先)頭(に立つ)
9. (電話が)遠(い)
10. (洗)顔(クリーム)

D.
1. 親子
2. 金曜日
3. 質屋
4. 夕飯
5. 顔色
6. 頭文字
7. 気軽な

E.
1. 先週(の)日曜日 (last Sunday)
2. 質問(に)答(える) (to answer a question)
3. 親切(な)方(に)道(を)教(えてもらった)。
   (A kind person showed me the way.)
4. 点線(の)所(から)切(り)取(る) (to cut / tear off along a dotted line)
5. 頭(がいい)少年 (a bright boy)
6. 銀行(で、お)金(を)下(ろす) (to withdraw money from a bank)
7. 日本語(の)試験 (a Japanese test)
8. 小説(を)書く (to write a novel)
9. 毎週土曜日 (every Saturday)
10. 図書館(で)本(を)借(りる)(to borrow a book from a library)

F.
1. 朝、遠くの森で野鳥をたくさん見た。
   I saw many wild birds in a distant forest this morning.
2. 数学の問題集をやっとやり終えた。
   I finally finished the book of math drills.
3. 昨夜は家族で歌番組を楽しんだ。
   The whole family enjoyed watching a music program last night.
4. 親しい友達と食堂で軽くご飯を食べた。
   I had a light snack with a close friend in the cafeteria.
5. 今日は暑すぎて頭が働かない。
   It's so hot today I just can't concentrate!

6. 自転車なら図書館の帰りに銀行に行ける。
   If I ride my bicycle, I'll be able to go to the bank on the way back from the library.
7. 薬屋には、ここから一直線に行けば着きますよ。
   You'll reach the pharmacy if you continue straight ahead from here.
8. これは母の料理と同じ味だ。
   This tastes just like my mother's cooking.
9. この薬を毎食後に飲んで下さい。
   Please take this medication after every meal.
10. 今夜は仕寒くなるからセーターを着ていきなさい。
    It'll be cold tonight so wear a sweater.

Exercise 26 (301–312) p177

A.
1. かがく
2. そっている
3. かたな
4. ながい
5. ぶんか
6. ひきど
7. まるめる
8. くふう、こうふ
9. まゆみ
10. やさきに

B.
1. 石で出来た道
2. 日本刀の持ち主
3. 弓道を習う
4. 永遠に
5. 一戸建ての家に住む
6. 数学の記号
7. 丸一年になる
8. 夫と別れる

C.
1. 夫(人)
2. (雨)戸
3. 予(習)
4. (木)刀
5. 永(住)
6. (強)化
7. 丸(見え)

Exercise 27 (313–324) p184

A.
1. は、はね
2. うつ
3. むいていない
4. つきあう
5. たいらな
6. うしなう
7. むきあう
8. しつれいな
9. ひっし
10. すえっこ

B.

1. 電気代を払う	6. 未知の人
2. 羽目をはずす	7. 失言をする
3. 打ち合わせの時間	8. お礼を言う
4. 目の不自由な方	9. 気付かなかった
5. 必ず行く	10. 年末大売出し

C.

1. f	6. e
2. j	7. b
3. g	8. h
4. i	9. a
5. d	10. c

Exercise 28 (325–336)   p190

A.

1. つたえる	6. たけ
2. こめ	7. きゅうしゅう
3. まったく	8. なる
4. あたりまえの	9. いそがしい
5. おてら	10. つぎの

B.

1. 当日	6. 目次
2. 全国	7. 米屋
3. 正式な	8. 成長する
4. 伝言	9. 仕事で忙しい
5. 米国	10. 本の虫

C.

1. e	6. b
2. d	7. i
3. h	8. g
4. a	9. f
5. j	10. c

Review 9 (1–336)   p191

A.

1. むし	6. くふうする
2. まるめる	7. みらい
3. ばんごう	8. うつ
4. とうだいじ	9. つたわる
5. はんえいする	10. ほんしゅう

B.

1. 電話番号	6. 山寺
2. 南米	7. 強化
3. 正式な	8. 全体
4. 毛虫	9. 伝記
5. 本の虫	10. 弓道

C.

1. 当日 <ruby>とうじつ</ruby>	6. 自伝 <ruby>じでん</ruby>
2. 多忙な <ruby>たぼう</ruby>	7. テキサス州 <ruby>しゅう</ruby>
3. 安全な <ruby>あんぜん</ruby>	8. 丸見え <ruby>まるみ</ruby>
4. 新米 <ruby>しんまい</ruby>	9. 成長する <ruby>せいちょう</ruby>
5. 二次会 <ruby>にじかい</ruby>	10. 一平米 <ruby>いちへいべい</ruby>

D.

1. f	6. c
2. g	7. j
3. h	8. e
4. a	9. b
5. i	10. d

E.

1. 全(国)	11. (末)永(く)
2. (手)伝(う)	12. 平(日)
3. 忙(しい一日)	13. (見)当
4. (雨)戸	14. 失(礼)
5. (寺)院	15. (三)次(元)
6. (青)竹	16. (小)刀
7. (前)払い	17. 夫(人)
8. (作)成	18. 州(立)
9. (白)米	19. (気)付(く)
10. 予(言)	20. (記)号

F.

1. 「二羽の鳥がお寺の竹林に住み着いているらしい。」「あそこにはえさになる虫がたくさんいるからだ。」

   'Apparently two birds have moved into the bamboo grove in the temple grounds.' 'That's because there's lots of bugs for them to eat there.'

2. 「次の週末、空いていますか。」「ごめんなさい。成人式に行くことになっています。」

   'Are you free next weekend?' 'Sorry. I'm supposed to be going to a coming-of-age ceremony.'

3. 「九州のお寺で古くから伝わる弓矢と刀を見ることが出来た。」

   'I was able to see ancient bows and arrows and swords in a temple in Kyushu.'

4. 「必ずしも高いお米がおいしいとはかぎりません。」「本当ですね。料理の仕方によります。」

   'Just because rice is expensive doesn't mean that it tastes good.' 'That's right. It depends on how you cook it.'

5. 「平気でそんな失礼なことを言うなんて考えられない。」「全くだ。理由が分からない。」

'It's unthinkable that he would say something as rude as that so nonchalantly.' 'Honestly, I just can't understand it.'

6. 「忙しくて、化学の予習をする時間がなかった。」「今日、化学記号の少テストもあるよ。」

'I've been too busy to have time to prepare for our chemistry class.' 'We're having a quiz on chemical symbols today, too, you know!'

7. 未来に向けて、新しい意見が反映されている。

Looking to the future, it reflects a new way of thinking.

Exercise 29 (337–348)   p198

A.

1. かた、かたち	6. よつかど
2. たにがわ	7. きめていない
3. きしゃ	8. こまる
4. でんわきょく	9. はんたいご
5. はじめて	10. なかみ

B.

1. 初心者	6. 小麦
2. 身長をはかる	7. 両親
3. 三角の	8. 図形
4. 谷間	9. 困り者
5. 決心する	10. 人形

C.

1. to be from Kyushu
2. to use both hands
3. not, never saying
4. to like both (of them)
5. That's news to me.
6. to cut something at right angles
7. to talk things over person to person
8. a TV station
9. to wait at the corner
10. to drink barley tea

Exercise 30 (349–360)   p204

A.

1. じっか	6. ちあん
2. りし	7. つめたい
3. がんせき	8. すいえい
4. なきだす	9. ぼうねんかい
5. さとがえり	10. きょういく

B.

1. h	6. a
2. e	7. c
3. j	8. i
4. g	9. f
5. b	10. d

C.

1. 自由に取る	5. 人の名前を忘れる
2. 頭を冷やす	6. 若い社長
3. 泳ぐのによい所	7. 空き時間を利用する
4. 二三日で治る	8. まだ、実っていない

Exercise 31 (361–372)   p211

A.

1. さだめる	6. うかる
2. ぶんぽう	7. あらわす
3. しんそつ	8. こんじゃく
4. いちまい	9. せいふく
5. ひこう	10. もくてき

B.

1. 昔 (々)	6. 科 (学者)
2. (近代) 的	7. 受 (ける)
3. (三) 枚	8. 和 (食)
4. 制 (度)	9. 卒 (業生)
5. 表 (紙)	10. 方 (法)

C.

1. 和風 (わふう)	6. 枚数 (まいすう)
2. 作法 (さほう)	7. 的外れ (まとはず)
3. 昔話 (むかしばなし)	8. 強制的な (きょうせいてき)
4. 非行少年 (ひこうしょうねん)	9. 定員 (ていいん)
5. 卒業式 (そつぎょうしき)	10. 表向き (おもてむき)

Review 10 (1–372)   pp211-212

A.

1. きめて	6. やわらげる
2. そだてる	7. かたみ
3. さだまる	8. わすれもの
4. わすれっぽい	9. げか
5. うしなう	

B.

1. the breaststroke
2. a way of doing
3. loud crying
4. a (the) surface
5. exclusive, private
6. How many sheets?
7. education; schooling
8. Japanese clothes
9. modern(istic)

C.

1. 若々しい
2. 枚数
3. 昔々
4. 平和
5. 受験生
6. 定員
7. 対決
8. 制度
9. お冷

D.

1. 初(はじ)めての時(とき)
2. 教科書(きょうかしょ)を買(か)う
3. 受信(じゅしん)する
4. 四(よ)つ角(かど)
5. 科学的(かがくてき)
6. 制服(せいふく)を着(き)る
7. 卒業(そつぎょう)する
8. 人(ひと)を困(こま)らせる
9. 和風(わふう)

E.

1. s	11. d
2. f	12. i
3. g	13. a
4. p	14. c
5. q	15. k
6. m	16. j
7. e	17. b
8. r	18. h
9. n	19. o
10. l	20. t

F.

1. （むかし）、（たに）さんは、よく（よぎしゃ）に（の）って、（さとがえ）りをしていた。
   Ms. Tani often used to catch the night train back to her home town.
2. （そつぎょうしき）の（ひどり）が（けってい）した。
   The date of the graduation ceremony has been decided.
3. （つのだ）さんは、（わか）い（とき）、（ひこう）に（はし）って、（おや）を（こま）らせていたそうだ。
   When Tsunoda was a young man, I hear that he took to delinquency and caused his parents a good deal of trouble.

4. （じつ）は、（こんかい）（はじめ）て（わふく）を（き）ます。
   Actually, this will be the first time for me to try on Japanese clothing.
5. （やまがたけん）と（いわてけん）は、（りょうほう）とも（とうほく）（ちほう）にあります。
   Both Yamagata Prefecture and Iwate Prefecture are located in the Tōhoku region.
6. （たいいく）の（じかん）に、（およ）いだ（あと）（つめ）たい（むぎちゃ）を（の）んだ。
   In my physical education class, I drank some cold barley tea after having a swim.
7. （ほうか）（だいがく）の（あたら）しい（じゅけん）（せいど）が（はっぴょう）された。
   The law college announced a new examination system.
8. （やっきょく）で（か）った（くすり）を（の）んだら（いちじてき）に（なお）った。
   When I took the medicine I bought at the pharmacy, I had some temporary relief.
9. （しょうじょ）は（たいせつ）にしていた（いちまい）のカードを（でんしゃ）に（わす）れた。
   The little girl left one of her treasured cards behind on the train.

Exercise 32 (373–384)　　　　p218

A.

1. かっぱつな
2. あいかわらず
3. くさばな
4. さくじつ、きのう
5. こうべ
6. さす
7. もっぱら
8. みなさん
9. たんなる
10. しんじる

B.

1. 単(語)
2. 係(員)
3. 相(手)
4. (中)指
5. 活(力)
6. 神(社)
7. 星(空)
8. 昨(夜)
9. 専(有する)
10. (自)身

C.

1. 赤信号(あかしんごう)
2. 単行本(たんこうぼん)
3. 生活(せいかつ)する
4. 専門学校(せんもんがっこう)
5. 火星(かせい)
6. 昨年度(さくねんど)
7. 道草(みちくさ)を食(く)う
8. 指定(してい)された
9. 海草(かいそう)
10. 首相(しゅしょう)

Exercise 33 (385–396)   p225

A.
1. おりる
2. とばす
3. へんな
4. ほうめん
5. いんしゅうんてん
6. にもつ
7. せなか
8. ひこうじょう
9. のこりもの
10. はらっぱ

B.
1. an interesting story
2. one's face changes color
3. a tall lad
4. nothing remains
5. beautiful memories
6. cannot drink alcohol
7. to fly in the blue sky
8. to need money
9. changeable weather
10. to rain heavily

C.
1. f
2. g
3. h
4. i
5. j
6. e
7. d
8. c
9. b
10. a

Exercise 34 (397–408)   p231

A.
1. とまる、とどまる
2. うまごや
3. しまぐに
4. きいろい
5. なつまつり
6. はやい
7. へる
8. てはい
9. あらわれる
10. さいじつ

B.
1. registered mail
2. being too late
3. a horse-drawn carriage
4. the yolk of an egg
5. accounting
6. couldn't help but laugh
7. the actual spot, scene
8. to be worried
9. a home; a family
10. to inform someone immediately

C.
1. 気を配る
2. 留学生活
3. 速やかに帰る
4. 面白い経験
5. 広島に住んでいる
6. 馬に乗る
7. 笑顔になる
8. 新婚旅行に出かける
9. 庭仕事をする
10. 現金で払う

Review 11 (1–408)   p232

A.
1. めざしている
2. とまる、とどまる
3. すみやかに
4. あらわす
5. きいろ
6. くばる
7. しま
8. なかにわ
9. わらう
10. うまづら

B.
1. It is too late.
2. unnecessary things
3. There was a fire in the stable.
4. The paper has yellowed.
5. Please don't worry.
6. a plan is realized
7. to let someone know immediately
8. to go to the actual place
9. to ride a horse
10. newly married life

C.
1. 夏祭り
2. 市内局番
3. 新聞配達
4. 東京方面
5. 笑い話
6. 速く出来る料理
7. 経理部
8. 目立った変化
9. 火山島
10. 英語的な表現

D.
1. 専門家
2. 書留
3. 一昨年
4. 家庭
5. 体育祭
6. 半島
7. 現れる
8. 速達
9. 経験
10. 留学生

E.
1. 笑い声
2. 単語
3. 現金
4. 信号
5. 黄身
6. 前庭
7. 小降り
8. 手配
9. 正面
10. 祭日
11. 相手
12. 広島
13. 酒場
14. お経
15. 速度
16. 残業
17. 新婚
18. 馬車
19. 神話
20. 飛行

F.

1. 馬が草原を速く走るすがたが美しい。
   （うま　そうげん　はや　はし　　　　うつく）

   A horse galloping across a grassy plain is a beautiful sight.

2. 昨日、経験したことのないような大雨が降った。
   （きのう　けいけん　　　　　　　　　おおあめ　ふ）

   Yesterday I experienced the heaviest rainfall I've ever come across.

3. 姉は新婚旅行で南の島へ飛び立った。
   （あね　しんこんりょこう　みなみ　しま　と　た）

   My older sister flew off to an island down south on her honeymoon.

4. 「皆さんは、明日の祭日に何をしますか。」
   （みな　　　　　あした　さいじつ　なに）

   「私は、庭仕事をします。」
   （わたし　にわしごと）

   「私は、家で面白い本でも読みましょう。」
   （いえ　おもしろ　ほん　　よ）

   'What is everyone doing on tomorrow's holiday?'
   'I'm going to work in the garden.'
   'I'm going to read an interesting book, or something.'

5. 相変わらず、金曜日になるとあの人は酒屋に
   （あいか　　　　　きんようび　　　　　　ひと　さかや）
   現れる。
   （あらわ）

   As usual, when Friday comes around, he turns up at the liquor store.

6. 「専門医にみてもらう必要がありますが、あまり
   （せんもんい　　　　　　　ひつよう）
   心配しないで下さい。」
   （しんぱい　　　　くだ）

   'You need to see a specialist, but there is no real need to worry.'

7. 係員は、荷物一個一個に黄色いステッカーをはっ
   （かかりいん　にもついっこいっこ　きいろ　すてっかー）
   ていた。

   The official was applying yellow stickers to each piece of luggage.

8. 「残り少ない留学生活に何をする予定ですか。」
   （のこ　すく　りゅうがくせいかつ　なに　　　　よてい）

   'What are you planning to do in the remaining days of your time abroad as a student?'

9. 小さかった時、火星人は背が低いみどり色の生き
   （ちい　　　　とき　かせいじん　せ　ひく　　　　いろ　い）
   物だと信じていた。
   （もの　しん）

   When I was a child, I believed that Martians were little, green creatures.

10. 人を指して笑うのは失礼です。
    （ひと　ゆび　　わら　　しつれい）

    It's rude to point at people and laugh.

Exercise 35 (409–420)　　　p239

A.
1. しだいに
2. きょうじゅ
3. へや
4. しゅじゅつ
5. ふね
6. せっする
7. こまかい
8. しんせつ
9. やど
10. あきなう

B.
1. 左側通行
2. 面接試験を受ける
3. 宿泊料を払う
4. 文学部長
5. 細長い形
6. 商品の売り上げ
7. 台風の接近
8. 授業が始まる
9. 大雪が降る

C.
1. f
2. g
3. i
4. e
5. d
6. j
7. a
8. c
9. h
10. b

Exercise 36 (421–432)　　　p245

A.
1. むすぶ
2. おくれる
3. あたたかい
4. ぜんぜん
5. えほん
6. もっとも
7. みなと
8. うんかい
9. はれる
10. きたい

B.
1. 帰りが遅い
2. 地階
3. 結婚式
4. 晴れ着
5. 上達する
6. 気温が下がる
7. 空港使用料
8. 自然の美しさ
9. 二学期
10. 二時間遅れ

C.
1. g
2. d
3. j
4. e
5. i
6. h
7. a
8. f
9. b
10. c

Exercise 37 (433–444)   p252

A.

1. むりょう	6. からまっている
2. おとしもの	7. ばんざい
3. みょうばん	8. とうこう
4. どうぶつえん	9. せっすい
5. いたむ	10. あそんでいる

B.

1. i	6. a
2. f	7. c
3. g	8. b
4. h	9. d
5. j	10. e

C.

1. 電車で寝てしまう	6. 無事に帰る
2. 毎晩酒を飲む	7. 六十歳になる
3. 公園で遊ぶ	8. 山に登る
4. 会社を辞める	9. 遊園地でデートをする
5. 頭が痛い	10. 高い所から落ちる

Review 12 (1–444)   pp252-253

A.

1. ねる	6. あそびば
2. らっかする	7. やめる
3. おそい	8. いたいたしい
4. こんばんは	9. からまる
5. はたち	10. むせん

B.

1. to put a sick person in bed
2. That word isn't in the dictionary.
3. to appear in a scene in a novel
4. to enjoy oneself singing
5. to work from morning till night
6. one's eyes smart, hurt
7. to attempt the impossible
8. to climb a high mountain
9. a matter involving money
10. the pain eases a little

C.

1. f	6. j
2. h	7. i
3. g	8. d
4. b	9. c
5. a	10. e

D.

1. らっか	6. とうこうする
2. ばんねん	7. てんねんの
3. ぶじに	8. はなぞの
4. ひるね	9. ゆうえんち
5. にほんていえん	10. ばんざい

E.

1. 節（分）	6. 落（語）
2. 遊（び）	7. （毎）晩
3. （動物）園	8. （式）辞
4. 痛（い）	9. 無（料）
5. 寝（言）	10. （何）歳

F.

1. 明日の天気は、晴れ後曇り、所によって、夜遅く雪が降るでしょう。

   Tomorrow's weather will be fine, cloudy later in the day; later in the evening there will be scattered snowfalls.

2. 「安部さんは、二十三歳で結婚するために、会社を辞めるらしい。最近ではめずらしいですね。」

   'I hear that Ms. Abe is going to resign from the company at the age of twenty-three so that she can get married. These days it's not so common.'

3. 次第に関節の痛みがひどくなってきたので、手術を受ける決心をした。

   The pain in my joint gradually became unbearable, so I decided to have an operation.

4. 今晩、友達が乗った船が、八時半に出港した。

   This evening, the ship that a friend of mine was on, left port at 8:30.

5. 「お母さん、公園で遊んでいる時、たこの糸が絡んで、木の上に落ちちゃった。木に登って、取ってもいい？」

   'Mom, when I was playing in the park, the string on my kite became tangled and the kite fell into a tree. Can I climb up the tree to get it?'

6. 私の寝室は、二階の南側なので、いつも自然に暖まる。

   My bedroom is upstairs on the southern side, so it is always naturally warm.

7. 二学期の始めの英語の授業で、この宿題を発表するはずです。

   We're supposed to make a presentation of this homework assignment in our English class at the beginning of second term.

8. 近所の主婦が集まって、この商品を作っています。

   Local housewives are all getting together and making this product.

9. この上に、直接ふれないで下さい。
Don't touch this surface.
10. 「悪いけど、細かいお金が無い。」「じゃあ、明日で
いいよ。」
'I'm sorry, but I don't have any change.' 'Well, give
it to me tomorrow, then.'

Exercise 38 (445–456)   p259

A.
1. なく
2. ざつな
3. ひきざん
4. おく
5. しずかな
6. かんしん
7. はなごえ
8. つづける
9. さまざまな
10. じっさいに

B.
1. 練習 (れんしゅう)
2. 物置 (ものおき)
3. 耳鼻科 (じびか)
4. 関係 (かんけい)
5. 生活様式 (せいかつようしき)
6. 静まる (しず)
7. 手続き (てつづ)
8. 横顔 (よこがお)
9. 雑用 (ざつよう)
10. 耳鳴り (みみな)

C.
1. 横
2. 鳴き声
3. 国際
4. 続々
5. 予算
6. 鼻
7. 配置
8. 様
9. 関西
10. 安静

Exercise 39 (457–464)   p264

A.
1. よみにくい
2. しらべる
3. むずかしかった
4. ひこうき
5. おねがいします。
6. えらぶ
7. はし
8. ありがたい
9. あつい
10. おくる

B.
1. 強調
2. 歩道橋
3. 熱中する
4. 選手
5. 交通機関
6. 調節する
7. 橋本様/さん
8. 願書
9. 予選
10. 贈り物

C.
1. 結婚相手を選ぶ
2. 味を調える
3. この先、困難が待っている。
4. 母の日に花を贈る
5. ジェット機の時代
6. 行かないで！お願い。
7. 酒を熱くして、飲む
8. 仕事を見つけるのが難しい
9. 橋が落ちた
10. 熱々の料理があまり好きじゃない。

Review 13 (1–464)   p265

A.
1. うしなわれている
2. むずかしい
3. あつい
4. たんなる
5. はし
6. えらぶ
7. ばける
8. つづく
9. しらべる
10. おくる

B.
1. fair; just
2. addition; adding up
3. safe; acceptable
4. not necessary
5. emphasis; a prospect
6. calm; cool
7. organic vegetables
8. a number
9. the same; similar
10. an applicant

C.
1. こんんなん
2. まぎわ
3. とりしらべ
4. おきば
5. おくりもの
6. ねっちゅうする
7. よこがき
8. ひこうき
9. つかいにくい
10. ひきつづき

D.
1. 変化
2. 未成年
3. 熱心
4. 歩道橋
5. 選手
6. 贈答 (品)
7. 調 (っている)
8. 受付
9. 機関車
10. (お) 願 (いします)

E.
1. s
2. f
3. i
4. q
5. g
6. t
7. n
8. o
9. k
10. l
11. p
12. r
13. e
14. a
15. h
16. j
17. d
18. b
19. m
20. c

F.

1. (あした) までに (さんすう) の (れんしゅうもんだい) を (お) えなさい。
   Finish the calculation drills by tomorrow.

2. (ねつ) が (で) たので、(よこ) になってしばらく (やす) んだ。
   I was running a fever, so I lay down and rested for a while.

3. オリンピック (だいひょう) (せんしゅ) に、(はな) を (おく) ってはげました。
   I gave the Olympic athlete some flowers and encouraged him.

4. あの (くに) は (こくさい) (しゃかい) から (ひなん) されている。
   That country is being criticized internationally.

5. あの (ひと) は (こっか) (しけん) にごうかくして、とても (はな) が (たか) いでしょう。
   That person has passed the state examination and will be feeling proud of himself.

6. この (とし) の (こうつう) (きかん) は (はったつ) していて、(す) むのに (たいへん) (べんり) です。
   This city has a well-developed transportation system and is a convenient place to live.

7. (ゆび) を (な) らすのを (や) めて、(しず) かに (ま) っていなさい。
   Stop clicking your fingers and wait quietly.

8. それに (かん) しては、(はしもとさま) にお (ねが) いしてはいかがですか。
   With regards to that matter, why don't you ask Mr. Hashimoto to attend to it for you?

9. (ちょうみりょう) は (だいどころ) のキャビネットの (いちばん) (うえ) に (お) いてあります。
   The condiments are kept in the top of the kitchen cabinet.

10. そんな (ざつ) な (やりかた) を (つづ) けても むいみ) だ。
    It's meaningless to continue doing it in such a slipshod way.

ON-KUN Reading Index

ON-KUN YOMI INDEX	ROMANIZED INDEX	CHARACTER	CHARACTER NUMBER
あ			
あい	ai	相	382
あいだ	aida	間	99
あ・う	a(u)	会	57
あ・う	a(u)	合	148
あお	ao	青	185
あお・い	ao(i)	青	185
あか	aka	赤	167
あか・い	aka(i)	赤	167
あ・かす	a(kasu)	明	194
あか・らむ	aka(ramu)	明	194
あか・らめる	aka(rameru)	赤	167
あ・かり	a(kari)	明	194
あ・がる	a(garu)	上	16
あか・るい	aka(rui)	明	194
あか・るむ	aka(rumu)	明	194
あき	aki	秋	212
あきな・う	akina(u)	商	413
あき・らか	aki(raka)	明	194
あ・く	a(ku)	空	83
あ・く	a(ku)	明	194
あ・く	a(ku)	開	265
アク	AKU	悪	245
あ・くる	a(kuru)	明	194
あ・ける	a(keru)	空	83
あ・ける	a(keru)	明	194
あ・ける	a(keru)	開	265
あ・げる	a(geru)	上	16
あさ	asa	朝	275
あし	ashi	足	77
あじ	aji	味	193
あじ・わう	aji(wau)	味	193
あそ・ぶ	aso(bu)	遊	437
あたた・か	atata(ka)	温	422

ON-KUN YOMI INDEX	ROMANIZED INDEX	CHARACTER	CHARACTER NUMBER
あたた・かい	atata(kai)	温	422
あたた・まる	atata(maru)	温	422
あたた・める	atata(meru)	温	422
あたま	atama	頭	295
あたら・しい	atara(shii)	新	102
あ・たる	a(taru)	当	334
あつ・い	atsu(i)	暑	269
あつ・い	atsu(i)	熱	459
あつ・まる	atsu(maru)	集	268
あつ・める	atsu(meru)	集	268
あ・てる	a(teru)	当	334
あと	ato	後	88
あに	ani	兄	129
あね	ane	姉	179
あま	ama	天	33
あま	ama	雨	80
あめ	ame	天	33
あめ	ame	雨	80
あゆ・む	ayu(mu)	歩	191
あら・う	ara(u)	洗	216
あらかじ・め	arakaji(me)	予	309
あら・た	ara(ta)	新	102
あらわ・す	arawa(su)	表	368
あらわ・す	arawa(su)	現	405
あらわ・れる	arawa(reru)	表	368
あらわ・れる	arawa(reru)	現	405
あ・る	a(ru)	有	158
ある・く	aru(ku)	歩	191
あ・わす	a(wasu)	合	148
あ・わせる	a(waseru)	合	148
アン	AN	安	56
アン	AN	暗	279
い			
イ	I	以	127

ON-KUN YOMI INDEX	ROMANIZED INDEX	CHARACTER	CHARACTER NUMBER
イ	I	医	159
イ	I	意	280
い・う	i(u)	言	74
いえ	ie	家	231
い・かす	i(kasu)	生	47
いき	iki	活	374
い・きる	i(ikiru)	生	47
い・く	i(ku)	行	60
イク	IKU	育	353
いけ	ike	池	154
い・ける	i(keru)	生	47
いし	ishi	石	48
いそが・しい	isoga(shii)	忙	336
いそ・ぐ	iso(gu)	急	203
いた・い	ita(i)	痛	433
いた・む	ita(mu)	痛	433
いた・める	ita(meru)	痛	433
イチ	ICHI	一	1
いち	ichi	市	131
イツ	ITSU	一	1
いつ	itsu	五	26
いつ・つ	itsu(tsu)	五	26
いと	ito	糸	61
いぬ	inu	犬	116
いま	ima	今	28
いもうと	imōto	妹	192
い・る	i(ru)	入	7
い・る	i(ru)	要	390
いれ・る	ire(ru)	入	7
いろ	iro	色	152
いわ	iwa	岩	355
イン	IN	飲	98
イン	IN	引	113
イン	IN	音	200
イン	IN	員	228
イン	IN	院	229

ON-KUN YOMI INDEX	ROMANIZED INDEX	CHARACTER	CHARACTER NUMBER
う			
ウ	U	右	40
ウ	U	雨	80
ウ	U	有	158
ウ	U	羽	323
うい	ui	初	345
うえ	ue	上	16
うお	uo	魚	96
う・かる	u(karu)	受	361
う・ける	u(keru)	受	361
うご・かす	ugo(kasu)	動	260
うご・く	ugo(ku)	動	260
うし	ushi	牛	114
うしな・う	ushina(u)	失	313
うし・ろ	ushi(ro)	後	88
うた	uta	歌	288
うた・う	uta(u)	歌	288
うち	uchi	内	123
う・つ	u(tsu)	打	314
うつく・しい	utsuku(shii)	美	387
うつ・す	utsu(su)	写	133
うつ・す	utsu(su)	映	198
うつ・る	utsu(ru)	写	133
うつ・る	utsu(ru)	映	198
うぶ	ubu	産	250
うま	uma	馬	401
う・まれる	u(mareru)	生	47
う・まれる	u(mareru)	産	250
うみ	umi	海	201
う・む	u(mu)	生	47
う・む	u(mu)	産	250
う・る	u(ru)	売	174
うわ	uwa	上	16
ウン	UN	運	264
ウン	UN	雲	421

287

ON-KUN YOMI INDEX	ROMANIZED INDEX	CHARACTER	CHARACTER NUMBER
え			
エ	**E**	会	57
エ	**E**	回	143
え	**e**	重	213
エ	**E**	絵	423
エイ	**EI**	英	176
エイ	**EI**	映	198
エイ	**EI**	永	310
エイ	**EI**	泳	354
エキ	**EKI**	駅	105
え・む	**e(mu)**	笑	397
えら・ぶ	**era(bu)**	選	457
エン	**EN**	円	22
エン	**EN**	遠	281
エン	**EN**	園	440
お			
お	**o**	小	15
お	**o**	男	78
オ	**O**	悪	245
オ	**O**	和	371
オウ	**Ō**	王	23
お・う	**o(u)**	生	47
オウ	**Ō**	黄	406
オウ	**Ō**	横	456
お・える	**o(eru)**	終	253
おお	**ō**	大	19
おお・い	**ō(i)**	多	65
おお・いに	**ō(i ni)**	大	19
おお・きい	**ō(kii)**	大	19
おおやけ	**ōyake**	公	118
お・きる	**o(kiru)**	起	234
お・く	**o(ku)**	置	446
オク	**OKU**	屋	199
おく・らす	**oku(rasu)**	遅	432
おく・る	**oku(ru)**	送	217
おく・る	**oku(ru)**	贈	462

ON-KUN YOMI INDEX	ROMANIZED INDEX	CHARACTER	CHARACTER NUMBER
おく・れる	**oku(reru)**	後	88
おく・れる	**oku(reru)**	遅	432
お・こす	**o(kosu)**	起	234
おこな・う	**okona(u)**	行	60
お・こる	**o(koru)**	起	234
おさ・まる	**osa(maru)**	治	357
おさ・める	**osa(meru)**	治	357
おし・える	**oshi(eru)**	教	247
おそ・い	**oso(i)**	遅	432
おそ・わる	**oso(waru)**	教	247
お・ちる	**o(chiru)**	落	439
おっと	**otto**	夫	307
おと	**oto**	音	200
おとうと	**otōto**	弟	172
おとこ	**otoko**	男	78
お・とす	**o(tosu)**	落	439
おな・じ	**ona(ji)**	同	156
おも	**omo**	主	134
おも	**omo**	面	389
おも・い	**omo(i)**	重	213
おも・う	**omo(u)**	思	208
おもて	**omote**	表	368
おもて	**omote**	面	389
おや	**oya**	親	294
およ・ぐ	**oyo(gu)**	泳	354
お・りる	**o(riru)**	下	9
お・りる	**o(riru)**	降	394
お・ろす	**o(rosu)**	降	394
お・わる	**o(waru)**	終	253
オン	**ON**	音	200
オン	**ON**	遠	281
オン	**ON**	温	422
おんな	**onna**	女	14
か			
カ	**KA**	下	9
カ	**KA**	火	24

288

ON-KUN YOMI INDEX	ROMANIZED INDEX	CHARACTER	CHARACTER NUMBER	ON-KUN YOMI INDEX	ROMANIZED INDEX	CHARACTER	CHARACTER NUMBER
か	ka	日	34	かしら	kashira	頭	295
カ	KA	何	70	か・す	ka(su)	貸	272
カ	KA	花	71	かず	kazu	数	286
カ	KA	夏	230	かぜ	kaze	風	225
カ	KA	家	231	かぞ・える	kazo(eru)	数	286
カ	KA	歌	288	かた	kata	方	126
カ	KA	化	304	かた	kata	形	341
カ	KA	科	372	かた・い	kata(i)	難	463
カ	KA	荷	391	かたち	katachi	形	341
ガ	GA	画	177	かたな	katana	刀	301
カイ	KAI	会	57	かた・らう	kata(rau)	語	106
かい	KAI	貝	72	かた・る	kata(ru)	語	106
カイ	KAI	回	143	カツ	KATSU	活	374
カイ	KAI	海	201	ガッ	GA'	合	148
カイ	KAI	界	202	ガツ	GATSU	月	25
カイ	KAI	開	265	かど	kado	門	195
カイ	KAI	皆	373	かど	kado	角	338
カイ	KAI	絵	423	かな	kana	金	82
カイ	KAI	階	424	かなら・ず	kanara(zu)	必	315
ガイ	GAI	外	41	かね	kane	金	82
か・う	ka(u)	買	101	かみ	kami	上	16
か・う	ka(u)	交	144	かみ	kami	紙	235
かえ・す	kae(su)	帰	233	かみ	kami	神	379
か・える	ka(eru)	代	138	かよ・う	kayo(u)	通	239
か・える	ka(eru)	変	388	から	kara	空	83
かえ・る	kae(ru)	帰	233	からだ	karada	体	170
かお	kao	顔	297	から・まる	kara(maru)	絡	438
かかり	kakari	係	375	から・む	kara(mu)	絡	438
かか・る	kaka(ru)	係	375	か・りる	ka(riru)	借	236
か・く	ka(ku)	書	95	かる・い	karu(i)	軽	267
カク	KAKU	画	177	かろ・やか	karo(yaka)	軽	267
カク	KAKU	角	338	かわ	kawa	川	18
ガク	GAKU	学	81	かわ	kawa	側	417
ガク	GAKU	楽	282	か・わす	ka(wasu)	交	144
かさ・なる	kasa(naru)	重	213	か・わる	ka(waru)	代	138
かさ・ねる	kasa(neru)	重	213	か・わる	ka(waru)	変	388

ON-KUN YOMI INDEX	ROMANIZED INDEX	CHARACTER	CHARACTER NUMBER	ON-KUN YOMI INDEX	ROMANIZED INDEX	CHARACTER	CHARACTER NUMBER
カン	**KAN**	間	99	キュウ	**KYŪ**	弓	303
カン	**KAN**	寒	266	キュウ	**KYŪ**	泣	356
カン	**KAN**	漢	283	ギュウ	**GYŪ**	牛	114
カン	**KAN**	館	293	キョ	**KYO**	去	128
かん	**kan**	神	379	ギョ	**GYO**	魚	96
カン	**KAN**	関	447	キョウ	**KYŌ**	兄	129
ガン	**GAN**	元	117	キョウ	**KYŌ**	京	178
ガン	**GAN**	顔	297	キョウ	**KYŌ**	強	246
ガン	**GAN**	丸	302	キョウ	**KYŌ**	教	247
ガン	**GAN**	岩	355	キョウ	**KYŌ**	経	404
ガン	**GAN**	願	464	キョウ	**CHŌ**	橋	461
かんが・える	**kanga(eru)**	考	146	ギョウ	**GYŌ**	行	60
	き			ギョウ	**GYŌ**	業	284
き	**ki**	木	37	ギョウ	**GYŌ**	形	341
き	**ki**	生	47	キョク	**KYOKU**	局	340
キ	**KI**	気	58	ギョク	**GYOKU**	玉	42
キ	**KI**	記	232	き・る	**ki(ru)**	切	121
キ	**KI**	帰	233	き・る	**ki(ru)**	着	274
キ	**KI**	起	234	き・れる	**ki(reru)**	切	121
キ	**KI**	汽	339	きわ	**kiwa**	際	448
き	**ki**	黄	406	きわ・める	**kiwa(meru)**	究	160
キ	**KI**	期	425	キン	**KIN**	今	28
キ	**KI**	機	460	キン	**KIN**	金	82
き・く	**ki(ku)**	聞	108	キン	**KIN**	近	161
き・く	**ki(ku)**	利	350	ギン	**GIN**	銀	289
き・こえる	**ki(koeru)**	聞	108		**く**		
き・せる	**ki(seru)**	着	274	ク	**KU**	九	2
きた	**kita**	北	52	ク	**KU**	口	10
きた・す	**kita(su)**	来	79	ク	**KU**	工	110
きた・る	**kita(ru)**	来	79	ク	**KU**	区	115
き・まる	**ki(maru)**	決	342	く・う	**ku(u)**	食	89
き・める	**ki(meru)**	決	342	クウ	**KŪ**	空	83
キュウ	**KYŪ**	九	2	くさ	**kusa**	草	383
キュウ	**KYŪ**	休	59	くすり	**kusuri**	薬	296
キュウ	**KYŪ**	究	160	くだ・る	**kuda(ru)**	下	9
キュウ	**KYŪ**	急	203	くち	**kuchi**	口	10

ON-KUN YOMI INDEX	ROMANIZED INDEX	CHARACTER	CHARACTER NUMBER
くに	kuni	国	84
くば・る	kuba(ru)	配	402
くび	kubi	首	211
くみ	kumi	組	254
く・む	ku(mu)	組	254
くも	kumo	雲	421
くら・い	kura(i)	暗	279
く・る	ku(ru)	来	79
くるま	kuruma	車	75
くろ	kuro	黒	248
くろ・い	kuro(i)	黒	248
け			
ケ	KE	気	58
ケ	KE	家	231
ケ	KE	化	304
け	ke	毛	308
ゲ	GE	下	9
ゲ	GE	外	41
ゲ	GE	夏	230
ケイ	KEI	兄	129
ケイ	KEI	京	178
ケイ	KEI	計	204
ケイ	KEI	軽	267
ケイ	KEI	形	341
ケイ	KEI	係	375
ケイ	KEI	経	404
ケツ	KETSU	決	342
ケツ	KETSU	結	426
ゲツ	GETSU	月	25
ケン	KEN	見	73
ケン	KEN	間	99
ケン	KEN	犬	116
ケン	KEN	研	205
ケン	KEN	県	206
ケン	KEN	建	207
ケン	KEN	験	298

ON-KUN YOMI INDEX	ROMANIZED INDEX	CHARACTER	CHARACTER NUMBER
ゲン	GEN	言	74
ゲン	GEN	元	117
ゲン	GEN	験	298
ゲン	GEN	原	392
ゲン	GEN	現	405
こ			
こ	ko	子	13
こ	ko	小	15
こ	ko	木	37
コ	KO	古	43
コ	KO	去	128
コ	KO	戸	305
コ	KO	個	393
こ	ko	黄	406
ゴ	GO	五	26
ゴ	GO	午	27
ゴ	GO	後	88
ゴ	GO	語	106
ゴ	GO	期	425
コウ	KŌ	口	10
コウ	KŌ	行	60
コウ	KŌ	後	88
コウ	KŌ	高	92
コウ	KŌ	校	93
コウ	KŌ	工	110
コウ	KŌ	公	118
コウ	KŌ	広	130
コウ	KŌ	交	144
コウ	KŌ	好	145
コウ	KŌ	考	146
コウ	KŌ	光	147
コウ	KŌ	向	324
こう	kō	神	379
コウ	KŌ	降	394
コウ	KŌ	黄	406
コウ	KŌ	港	427

ON-KUN YOMI INDEX	ROMANIZED INDEX	CHARACTER	CHARACTER NUMBER
ゴウ	**GŌ**	合	148
ゴウ	**GŌ**	強	246
ゴウ	**GŌ**	業	284
ゴウ	**GŌ**	号	311
こえ	koe	声	166
コク	**KOKU**	石	48
コク	**KOKU**	国	84
コク	**KOKU**	黒	248
コク	**KOKU**	谷	343
ここの	kokono	九	2
ここの・つ	kokono(tsu)	九	2
こころ	kokoro	心	120
こころ・みる	kokoro(miru)	試	285
こた・え	kota(e)	答	276
こた・える	kota(eru)	答	276
こと	koto	言	74
こと	koto	事	182
この・む	kono(mu)	好	145
こま・か	koma(ka)	細	409
こま・かい	koma(kai)	細	409
こま・る	koma(ru)	困	344
こめ	kome	米	335
ころ・がす	koro(gasu)	転	257
ころ・がる	koro(garu)	転	257
ころ・げる	koro(geru)	転	257
ころ・ぶ	koro(bu)	転	257
こわ	kowa	声	166
コン	**KON**	今	28
コン	**KON**	金	82
コン	**KON**	困	344
コン	**KON**	婚	407
ゴン	**GON**	言	74
さ			
サ	**SA**	左	44
サ	**SA**	作	162
サ	**SA**	茶	219

ON-KUN YOMI INDEX	ROMANIZED INDEX	CHARACTER	CHARACTER NUMBER
サイ	**SAI**	西	63
サイ	**SAI**	才	111
サイ	**SAI**	切	121
サイ	**SAI**	菜	249
サイ	**SAI**	祭	408
サイ	**SAI**	細	409
サイ	**SAI**	最	428
サイ	**SAI**	歳	441
サイ	**SAI**	際	448
さか	saka	酒	396
さかな	sakana	魚	96
さ・がる	sa(garu)	下	9
さき	saki	先	64
サク	**SAKU**	作	162
サク	**SAKU**	昨	376
さけ	sake	酒	396
さ・す	sa(su)	注	187
さ・す	sa(su)	指	377
さず・かる	sazu(karu)	授	410
さず・ける	sazu(keru)	授	410
さだ・か	sada(ka)	定	365
さだ・まる	sada(maru)	定	365
さだ・める	sada(meru)	定	365
サッ	**SA'**	早	153
ザツ	**ZATSU**	雑	449
さと	sato	里	351
さま	sama	様	454
さ・ます	sa(masu)	冷	352
さむ・い	samu(i)	寒	266
さめ	same	雨	80
さ・める	sa(meru)	冷	352
さ・る	sa(ru)	去	128
サン	**SAN**	三	11
サン	**SAN**	山	12
サン	**SAN**	産	250
サン	**SAN**	算	450

ON-KUN YOMI INDEX	ROMANIZED INDEX	CHARACTER	CHARACTER NUMBER	ON-KUN YOMI INDEX	ROMANIZED INDEX	CHARACTER	CHARACTER NUMBER
ザン	**ZAN**	残	395	ジキ	**JIKI**	直	188
し				しず	shizu	静	451
シ	**SHI**	子	13	しず・か	shizu(ka)	静	451
シ	**SHI**	四	45	しず・まる	shizu(maru)	静	451
シ	**SHI**	糸	61	しず・める	shizu(meru)	静	451
シ	**SHI**	止	119	した	shita	下	9
シ	**SHI**	市	131	した・しい	shita(shii)	親	294
シ	**SHI**	仕	132	した・しむ	shita(shimu)	親	294
シ	**SHI**	死	149	シチ	**SHICHI**	七	3
シ	**SHI**	自	151	シチ	**SHICHI**	質	291
シ	**SHI**	私	163	シツ	**SHITSU**	室	210
シ	**SHI**	姉	179	シツ	**SHITSU**	質	291
シ	**SHI**	使	180	シツ	**SHITSU**	失	313
シ	**SHI**	始	181	ジッ	**JI'**	十	4
シ	**SHI**	思	208	ジツ	**JITSU**	日	34
シ	**SHI**	紙	235	ジツ	**JITSU**	実	358
シ	**SHI**	試	285	しな	shina	品	224
シ	**SHI**	矢	312	しな	shina	科	372
シ	**SHI**	次	326	し・ぬ	shi(nu)	死	149
シ	**SHI**	指	377	しま	shima	島	400
ジ	**JI**	耳	62	しも	shimo	下	9
ジ	**JI**	時	94	シャ	**SHA**	車	75
ジ	**JI**	仕	132	シャ	**SHA**	社	76
ジ	**JI**	字	150	シャ	**SHA**	写	133
ジ	**JI**	自	151	シャ	**SHA**	者	183
ジ	**JI**	地	155	シャク	**SHAKU**	石	48
ジ	**JI**	事	182	シャク	**SHAKU**	赤	167
ジ	**JI**	持	209	シャク	**SHAKU**	借	236
ジ	**JI**	寺	325	シャク	**SHAKU**	昔	363
ジ	**JI**	次	326	ジャク	**JAKU**	弱	237
ジ	**JI**	治	357	ジャク	**JAKU**	着	274
ジ	**JI**	辞	442	ジャク	**JAKU**	若	359
し・いる	shi(iru)	強	246	シュ	**SHU**	手	29
シキ	**SHIKI**	色	152	シュ	**SHU**	主	134
シキ	**SHIKI**	式	327	シュ	**SHU**	首	211
ジキ	**JIKI**	食	89	シュ	**SHU**	取	360

ON-KUN YOMI INDEX	ROMANIZED INDEX	CHARACTER	CHARACTER NUMBER
シュ	SHU	酒	396
ジュ	JU	受	361
ジュ	JU	授	410
シュウ	SHŪ	週	97
シュウ	SHŪ	秋	212
シュウ	SHŪ	習	252
シュウ	SHŪ	終	253
シュウ	SHŪ	集	268
シュウ	SHŪ	州	328
ジュウ	JŪ	十	4
ジュウ	JŪ	中	32
ジュウ	JŪ	住	164
ジュウ	JŪ	重	213
シュク	SHUKU	宿	411
シュツ	SHUTSU	出	46
ジュツ	JUTSU	術	412
シュン	SHUN	春	214
ショ	SHO	書	95
ショ	SHO	所	184
ショ	SHO	暑	269
ショ	SHO	初	345
ジョ	JO	女	14
ショウ	SHŌ	小	15
ショウ	SHŌ	上	16
ショウ	SHŌ	少	30
ショウ	SHŌ	生	47
ショウ	SHŌ	正	136
ショウ	SHŌ	声	166
ショウ	SHŌ	青	185
ショウ	SHŌ	星	380
ショウ	SHŌ	相	382
ショウ	SHŌ	笑	397
ショウ	SHŌ	商	413
ジョウ	JŌ	上	16
ジョウ	JŌ	乗	215
ジョウ	JŌ	場	270

ON-KUN YOMI INDEX	ROMANIZED INDEX	CHARACTER	CHARACTER NUMBER
ジョウ	JŌ	成	329
ジョウ	JŌ	定	365
ジョウ	JŌ	静	451
ショク	SHOKU	食	89
ショク	SHOKU	色	152
しら	shira	白	49
し・らせる	shi(raseru)	知	186
しら・べる	shira(beru)	調	458
し・る	shi(ru)	知	186
しる・す	shiru(su)	記	232
しろ	shiro	白	49
しろ	shiro	代	138
しろ・い	shiro(i)	白	49
シン	SHIN	新	102
シン	SHIN	心	120
シン	SHIN	真	238
シン	SHIN	進	251
シン	SHIN	森	271
シン	SHIN	親	294
シン	SHIN	身	346
シン	SHIN	信	378
シン	SHIN	神	379
シン	SHIN	寝	443
ジン	JIN	人	5
ジン	JIN	神	379
す			
ス	SU	子	13
ス	SU	数	286
す	su	州	328
ズ	ZU	図	165
ズ	ZU	頭	295
スイ	SUI	水	31
スイ	SUI	出	46
スウ	SŪ	数	286
すえ	sue	末	319
す・く	su(ku)	好	145

ON-KUN YOMI INDEX	ROMANIZED INDEX	CHARACTER	CHARACTER NUMBER
すく・ない	suku(nai)	少	30
すこ・し	suko(shi)	少	30
すす・む	susu(mu)	進	251
すす・める	susu(meru)	進	251
す・まう	su(mau)	住	164
すみ・やか	sumi(yaka)	速	398
す・む	su(mu)	住	164
せ			
セ	SE	世	135
せ	se	背	385
セイ	SEI	生	47
セイ	SEI	西	63
セイ	SEI	世	135
セイ	SEI	正	136
セイ	SEI	声	166
セイ	SEI	青	185
セイ	SEI	成	329
セイ	SEI	制	362
セイ	SEI	星	380
せい	sei	背	385
セイ	SEI	晴	429
セイ	SEI	歳	441
セイ	SEI	静	451
ゼイ	ZEI	説	290
セキ	SEKI	石	48
セキ	SEKI	夕	112
セキ	SEKI	赤	167
セキ	SEKI	昔	363
せき	seki	関	447
セチ	SECHI	節	444
セツ	SETSU	切	121
セツ	SETSU	説	290
セツ	SETSU	接	414
セツ	SETSU	雪	415
セツ	SETSU	節	444
せわ・しい	sewa(shii)	忙	336

ON-KUN YOMI INDEX	ROMANIZED INDEX	CHARACTER	CHARACTER NUMBER
セン	SEN	千	17
セン	SEN	川	18
セン	SEN	先	64
セン	SEN	洗	216
セン	SEN	線	292
セン	SEN	専	381
セン	SEN	船	416
セン	SEN	選	457
ゼン	ZEN	前	90
ゼン	ZEN	全	330
ゼン	ZEN	然	430
そ			
ソ	SO	組	254
ソウ	SŌ	早	153
ソウ	SŌ	走	168
ソウ	SŌ	送	217
ソウ	SŌ	相	382
ソウ	SŌ	草	383
ソウ	SŌ	贈	462
ゾウ	ZŌ	雑	449
ゾウ	ZŌ	贈	462
ソク	SOKU	足	77
ソク	SOKU	速	398
ソク	SOKU	側	417
ゾク	ZOKU	族	255
ゾク	ZOKU	続	445
そそ・ぐ	soso(gu)	注	187
そだ・つ	soda(tsu)	育	353
そだ・てる	soda(teru)	育	353
ソツ	SOTSU	卒	364
そと	soto	外	41
その	sono	園	440
そむ・く	somu(ku)	背	385
そむ・ける	somu(keru)	背	385
そ・める	so(meru)	初	345
そら	sora	空	83

ON-KUN YOMI INDEX	ROMANIZED INDEX	CHARACTER	CHARACTER NUMBER
チャ	CHA	茶	219
チャク	CHAKU	着	274
チュウ	CHŪ	中	32
チュウ	CHŪ	注	187
チュウ	CHŪ	昼	220
チュウ	CHŪ	虫	332
チョウ	CHŌ	長	85
チョウ	CHŌ	町	171
チョウ	CHŌ	重	213
チョウ	CHŌ	鳥	256
チョウ	CHŌ	朝	275
チョウ	CHŌ	調	458
チョク	CHOKU	直	188
つ			
ツ	TSU	都	258
ツイ	TSUI	対	347
ツウ	TSŪ	通	239
ツウ	TSŪ	痛	433
つか・う	tsuka(u)	使	180
つか・える	tsuka(eru)	仕	132
つき	tsuki	月	25
つぎ	tsugi	次	326
つ・く	tsu(ku)	着	274
つ・く	tsu(ku)	付	316
つ・ぐ	tsu(gu)	注	187
つ・ぐ	tsu(gu)	次	326
つ・ぐ	tsu(gu)	接	414
つく・る	tsuku(ru)	作	162
つ・ける	tsu(keru)	着	274
つ・ける	tsu(keru)	付	316
つた・う	tsuta(u)	伝	333
つた・える	tsuta(eru)	伝	333
つた・わる	tsuta(waru)	伝	333
つち	tsuchi	土	20
つづ・く	tsuzu(ku)	続	445
つづ・ける	tsuzu(keru)	続	445

ON-KUN YOMI INDEX	ROMANIZED INDEX	CHARACTER	CHARACTER NUMBER
つど・う	tsudo(u)	集	268
つと・める	tsuto(meru)	勉	242
つの	tsuno	角	338
つめ・たい	tsume(tai)	冷	352
つよ・い	tsuyo(i)	強	246
つよ・める	tsuyo(meru)	強	246
つら	tsura	面	389
て			
て	te	手	29
デ	DE	弟	172
テイ	TEI	体	170
テイ	TEI	弟	172
テイ	TEI	低	173
テイ	TEI	定	365
テイ	TEI	庭	399
テキ	TEKI	的	366
てら	tera	寺	325
で・る	de(ru)	出	46
テン	TEN	天	33
テン	TEN	店	86
テン	TEN	点	221
テン	TEN	転	257
デン	DEN	電	103
デン	DEN	田	139
デン	DEN	伝	333
と			
と	TO	十	4
ト	TO	土	20
ト	TO	図	165
ト	TO	度	222
ト	TO	都	258
ト	TO	頭	295
と	to	戸	305
ト	TO	登	434
ド	DO	土	20
ド	DO	度	222

ON-KUN YOMI INDEX	ROMANIZED INDEX	CHARACTER	CHARACTER NUMBER
と・い	to(i)	問	261
と・う	to(u)	問	261
トウ	TŌ	東	87
トウ	TŌ	読	107
トウ	TŌ	冬	140
トウ	TŌ	答	276
トウ	TŌ	頭	295
トウ	TŌ	刀	301
トウ	TŌ	当	334
トウ	TŌ	島	400
トウ	TŌ	登	434
ドウ	DŌ	道	100
ドウ	DŌ	同	156
ドウ	DŌ	堂	259
ドウ	DŌ	動	260
ドウ	DŌ	働	287
とお	tō	十	4
とお・い	tō(i)	遠	281
とお・る	tō(ru)	通	239
とき	toki	時	94
と・く	to(ku)	説	290
トク	TOKU	読	107
トク	TOKU	特	240
と・ぐ	to(gu)	研	205
ドク	DOKU	読	107
ところ	tokoro	所	184
とし	toshi	年	66
ととの・う	totono(u)	調	458
ととの・える	totono(eru)	調	458
と・ばす	to(basu)	飛	386
と・ぶ	to(bu)	飛	386
と・まる	to(maru)	止	119
と・まる	to(maru)	留	403
と・める	to(meru)	止	119
と・める	to(meru)	留	403
とも	tomo	友	38

ON-KUN YOMI INDEX	ROMANIZED INDEX	CHARACTER	CHARACTER NUMBER
とり	tori	鳥	256
と・る	to(ru)	取	360
とん	ton	問	261
な			
な	na	名	69
ナ	NA	南	91
な	na	菜	249
な・い	na(i)	無	436
ナイ	NAI	内	123
なお・す	nao(su)	直	188
なお・す	nao(su)	治	357
なお・る	nao(ru)	直	188
なお・る	nao(ru)	治	357
なか	naka	中	32
なが・い	naga(i)	長	85
なが・い	naga(i)	永	310
なか・ば	naka(ba)	半	50
な・く	na(ku)	泣	356
な・く	na(ku)	鳴	453
なご・む	nago(mu)	和	371
なご・やか	nago(yaka)	和	371
な・す	na(su)	成	329
なつ	natsu	夏	230
なな	nana	七	3
なな・つ	nana(tsu)	七	3
なに	nani	何	70
なの	nano	七	3
なま	nama	生	47
なら・う	nara(u)	習	252
な・らす	na(rasu)	鳴	453
な・る	na(ru)	成	329
な・る	na(ru)	鳴	453
なん	nan	何	70
ナン	NAN	男	78
ナン	NAN	南	91
ナン	NAN	難	463

ON-KUN YOMI INDEX	ROMANIZED INDEX	CHARACTER	CHARACTER NUMBER
に			
ニ	**NI**	二	6
に	**ni**	荷	391
にい	**nii**	新	102
ニク	**niku**	肉	157
にく・い	**niku(i)**	難	463
にし	**nishi**	西	63
ニチ	**NICHI**	日	34
ニャク	**NYAKU**	若	359
ニュウ	**NYŪ**	入	7
ニョ	**NYO**	女	14
ニョウ	**NYŌ**	女	14
にわ	**niwa**	庭	399
ニン	**NIN**	人	5
ぬ			
ぬし	**nushi**	主	134
ね			
ね	**ne**	音	200
ねが・う	**nega(u)**	願	464
ね・かす	**ne(kasu)**	寝	443
ネツ	**NETSU**	熱	459
ね・る	**ne(ru)**	寝	443
ね・る	**ne(ru)**	練	455
ネン	**NEN**	年	66
ネン	**NEN**	然	430
の			
の	**no**	野	262
のこ・る	**noko(ru)**	残	395
の・せる	**no(seru)**	乗	215
のち	**nochi**	後	88
のぼ・る	**nobo(ru)**	上	16
のぼ・る	**nobo(ru)**	登	434
の・む	**no(mu)**	飲	98
の・る	**no(ru)**	乗	215
は			
は	**ha**	羽	323

ON-KUN YOMI INDEX	ROMANIZED INDEX	CHARACTER	CHARACTER NUMBER
ば	**ba**	場	270
バ	**BA**	馬	401
ハイ	**HAI**	背	385
ハイ	**HAI**	配	402
バイ	**BAI**	買	101
バイ	**BAI**	売	174
はい・る	**hai(ru)**	入	7
は・える	**ha(eru)**	生	47
は・える	**ha(eru)**	映	198
ば・かす	**ba(kasu)**	化	304
はか・らう	**haka(rau)**	計	204
はか・る	**haka(ru)**	図	165
はか・る	**haka(ru)**	計	204
ハク	**HAKU**	白	49
バク	**BAKU**	麦	348
ば・ける	**ba(keru)**	化	304
はこ・ぶ	**hako(bu)**	運	264
はし	**hashi**	橋	461
はじ・まる	**haji(maru)**	始	181
はじ・め	**haji(me)**	初	345
はじ・めて	**haji(mete)**	初	345
はじ・める	**haji(meru)**	始	181
はし・る	**hashi(ru)**	走	168
はず・す	**hazu(su)**	外	41
はた	**hata**	機	460
はたら・く	**hatara(ku)**	働	287
ハチ	**HACHI**	八	8
ハッ	**HA'**	法	369
ハツ	**HATSU**	八	8
ハツ	**HATSU**	発	223
はつ	**hatsu**	初	345
バツ	**BATSU**	末	319
はな	**hana**	花	71
はな	**hana**	鼻	452
はなし	**hanashi**	話	104
はな・す	**hana(su)**	話	104

ON-KUN YOMI INDEX	ROMANIZED INDEX	CHARACTER	CHARACTER NUMBER
はね	**hane**	羽	323
はは	**haha**	母	51
はや・い	**haya(i)**	早	153
はや・い	**haya(i)**	速	398
はやし	**hayashi**	林	197
はや・まる	**haya(maru)**	早	153
はや・める	**haya(meru)**	早	153
はや・める	**haya(meru)**	速	398
ばら	**hara**	原	392
はら・う	**hara(u)**	払	317
は・らす	**ha(rasu)**	晴	429
はる	**haru**	春	214
は・れる	**ha(reru)**	晴	429
ハン	**HAN**	半	50
ハン	**HAN**	飯	277
ハン	**HAN**	反	306
バン	**BAN**	万	21
バン	**BAN**	番	278
バン	**BAN**	晩	435
ひ			
ひ	**hi**	火	24
ひ	**hi**	日	34
ヒ	**HI**	非	367
ヒ	**HI**	飛	386
ビ	**BI**	美	387
ビ	**BI**	鼻	452
ひ・える	**hi(eru)**	冷	352
ひがし	**higashi**	東	87
ひかり	**hikari**	光	147
ひか・る	**hika(ru)**	光	147
ひ・く	**hi(ku)**	引	113
ひく・い	**hiku(i)**	低	173
ひく・まる	**hiku(maru)**	低	173
ひく・める	**hiku(meru)**	低	173
ひ・ける	**hi(keru)**	引	113
ひだり	**hidari**	左	44

ON-KUN YOMI INDEX	ROMANIZED INDEX	CHARACTER	CHARACTER NUMBER
ヒツ	**HITSU**	必	315
ひと	**hito**	一	1
ひと	**hito**	人	5
ひと・つ	**hito(tsu)**	一	1
ひ・や	**hi(ya)**	冷	352
ひ・やかす	**hi(yakasu)**	冷	352
ヒャク	**HYAKU**	百	67
ビャク	**BYAKU**	白	49
ひ・やす	**hi(yasu)**	冷	352
ヒョウ	**HYŌ**	表	368
ビョウ	**BYŌ**	病	241
ビョウ	**BYŌ**	平	318
ひら	**hira**	平	318
ひら・く	**hira(ku)**	開	265
ひら・ける	**hira(keru)**	開	265
ひる	**hiru**	昼	220
ひろ・い	**hiro(i)**	広	130
ひろ・がる	**hiro(garu)**	広	130
ひろ・まる	**hiro(maru)**	広	130
ヒン	**HIN**	品	224
ビン	**BIN**	便	226
ふ			
フ	**FU**	父	35
フ	**FU**	不	124
フ	**FU**	歩	191
フ	**FU**	風	225
フ	**FU**	夫	307
フ	**FU**	付	316
フ	**FU**	婦	419
ブ	**BU**	分	36
ブ	**BU**	不	124
ブ	**BU**	歩	191
ブ	**BU**	部	420
ブ	**BU**	無	436
フウ	**FŪ**	風	225
フウ	**FŪ**	夫	307

ON-KUN YOMI INDEX	ROMANIZED INDEX	CHARACTER	CHARACTER NUMBER
フク	**FUKU**	服	189
ふし	fushi	節	444
ふた	futa	二	6
ふた・つ	futa(tsu)	二	6
フツ	**FUTSU**	払	317
ブツ	**BUTSU**	物	190
ふと・い	futo(i)	太	122
ふと・る	futo(ru)	太	122
ふな	funa	船	416
ふね	fune	船	416
ふみ	fumi	文	125
ふゆ	fuyu	冬	140
ふ・る	fu(ru)	降	394
ふる・い	furu(i)	古	43
ふる・す	furu(su)	古	43
フン	**FUN**	分	36
ブン	**BUN**	分	36
ブン	**BUN**	聞	108
ブン	**BUN**	文	125
へ			
べ	be	戸	305
ヘイ	**HEI**	病	241
ヘイ	**HEI**	平	318
ベイ	**BEI**	米	335
ベツ	**BETSU**	別	175
へ・る	he(ru)	経	404
ヘン	**HEN**	変	388
ベン	**BEN**	便	226
ベン	**BEN**	勉	242
ほ			
ほ	ho	火	24
ホ	**HO**	歩	191
ボ	**BO**	母	51
ホウ	**HŌ**	方	126
ホウ	**HŌ**	法	369
ボウ	**BŌ**	忙	336

ON-KUN YOMI INDEX	ROMANIZED INDEX	CHARACTER	CHARACTER NUMBER
ボウ	**BŌ**	忘	349
ほか	hoka	外	41
ホク	**HOKU**	北	52
ボク	**BOKU**	木	37
ボク	**BOKU**	目	54
ほし	hoshi	星	380
ほそ・い	hoso(i)	細	409
ほそ・る	hoso(ru)	細	409
ホッ	**HO'**	法	369
ホツ	**HOTSU**	発	223
ホン	**HON**	本	53
ホン	**HON**	反	306
ま			
ま	ma	目	54
ま	ma	間	99
ま	ma	真	238
ま	ma	馬	401
マイ	**MAI**	毎	68
マイ	**MAI**	妹	192
マイ	**MAI**	米	335
マイ	**MAI**	枚	370
まえ	mae	前	90
まさ・に	masa(ni)	正	136
ま・ざる	ma(zaru)	交	144
まじ・える	maji(eru)	交	144
ま・じる	ma(jiru)	交	144
まじ・わる	maji(waru)	交	144
ま・ぜる	ma(zeru)	交	144
まち	machi	町	171
ま・つ	ma(tsu)	待	218
マツ	**MATSU**	末	319
まった・く	matta(ku)	全	330
まつ・り	matsu(ri)	祭	408
まつ・る	matsu(ru)	祭	408
まと	mato	的	366
まな・ぶ	mana(bu)	学	81

ON-KUN YOMI INDEX	ROMANIZED INDEX	CHARACTER	CHARACTER NUMBER
まる	**maru**	円	22
まる	**maru**	丸	302
まる・い	**maru(i)**	円	22
まる・い	**maru(i)**	丸	302
まる・める	**maru(meru)**	丸	302
まわ・す	**mawa(su)**	回	143
まわ・る	**mawa(ru)**	回	143
マン	**MAN**	万	21
み			
み	**mi**	三	11
ミ	**MI**	味	193
ミ	**MI**	未	320
み	**mi**	身	346
み	**mi**	実	358
みぎ	**migi**	右	40
みじか・い	**mijika(i)**	短	273
みず	**mizu**	水	31
みずか・ら	**mizuka(ra)**	自	151
みせ	**mise**	店	86
み・せる	**mi(seru)**	見	73
みち	**michi**	道	100
み・つ	**mi(tsu)**	三	11
みっ・つ	**mit(tsu)**	三	11
みな	**mina**	皆	373
みなと	**minato**	港	427
みなみ	**minami**	南	91
みの・る	**mino(ru)**	実	358
みみ	**mimi**	耳	62
みやこ	**miyako**	都	258
ミョウ	**MYŌ**	名	69
ミョウ	**MYŌ**	明	194
み・る	**mi(ru)**	見	73
ミン	**MIN**	民	141
みんな	**minna**	皆	373
む			
む	**mu**	六	39

ON-KUN YOMI INDEX	ROMANIZED INDEX	CHARACTER	CHARACTER NUMBER
ム	**MU**	無	436
むい	**mui**	六	39
む・かう	**mu(kau)**	向	324
むかし	**mukashi**	昔	363
むぎ	**mugi**	麦	348
む・く	**mu(ku)**	向	324
む・ける	**mu(keru)**	向	324
む・こう	**mu(kō)**	向	324
むし	**mushi**	虫	332
むずか・しい	**muzuka(shii)**	難	463
むす・ぶ	**musu(bu)**	結	426
む・つ	**mu(tsu)**	六	39
むっ・つ	**mut(tsu)**	六	39
むら	**mura**	村	169
むろ	**muro**	室	210
め			
め	**me**	女	14
め	**me**	目	54
メイ	**MEI**	名	69
メイ	**MEI**	明	194
メイ	**MEI**	鳴	453
めし	**meshi**	飯	277
メン	**MEN**	面	389
も			
モ	**MO**	母	51
モウ	**MŌ**	毛	308
モク	**MOKU**	木	37
モク	**MOKU**	目	54
も・しくは	**mo(shiku wa)**	若	359
もち・いる	**mochi(iru)**	用	142
も・つ	**mo(tsu)**	持	209
モツ	**MOTSU**	物	190
もっと・も	**motto(mo)**	最	428
もっぱ・ら	**moppa(ra)**	専	381
もと	**moto**	本	53
もと	**moto**	元	117

ON-KUN YOMI INDEX	ROMANIZED INDEX	CHARACTER	CHARACTER NUMBER
もの	mono	者	183
もの	mono	物	190
もも	momo	百	67
もり	mori	森	271
モン	MON	聞	108
モン	MON	文	125
モン	MON	門	195
モン	MON	間	261
や			
や	ya	八	8
ヤ	YA	夜	196
や	ya	屋	199
や	ya	家	231
ヤ	YA	野	262
や	ya	矢	312
や	ya	谷	343
やかた	yakata	館	293
ヤク	YAKU	薬	296
やしろ	yashiro	社	76
やす・い	yasu(i)	安	56
やす・まる	yasu(maru)	休	59
やす・む	yasu(mu)	休	59
やす・める	yasu(meru)	休	59
や・つ	ya(tsu)	八	8
やっ・つ	yat(tsu)	八	8
やど	yado	宿	411
やど・す	yado(su)	宿	411
やど・る	yado(ru)	宿	411
やま	yama	山	12
やまい	yamai	病	241
や・む	ya(mu)	病	241
や・める	ya(meru)	辞	442
やわ・らぐ	yawa(ragu)	和	371
やわ・らげる	yawa(rageru)	和	371
ゆ			
ゆ	yu	雨	80

ON-KUN YOMI INDEX	ROMANIZED INDEX	CHARACTER	CHARACTER NUMBER
ユ	YU	由	321
ユ	YU	遊	437
ユイ	YUI	由	321
ゆ・う	yu(u)	結	426
ユウ	YŪ	友	38
ユウ	YŪ	右	40
ゆう	yū	夕	112
ユウ	YŪ	有	158
ユウ	YŪ	由	321
ユウ	YŪ	遊	437
ゆき	yuki	雪	415
ゆ・く	yu(ku)	行	60
ゆび	yubi	指	377
ゆみ	yumi	弓	303
ゆ・わえる	yu(waeru)	結	426
よ			
よ	yo	四	45
よ	yo	世	135
よ	yo	代	138
よ	yo	夜	196
ヨ	YO	予	309
よう	yō	八	8
ヨウ	YŌ	用	142
ヨウ	YŌ	洋	227
ヨウ	YŌ	曜	300
ヨウ	YŌ	要	390
ヨウ	YŌ	様	454
よこ	yoko	横	456
よし	yoshi	由	321
よ・つ	yo(tsu)	四	45
よっ・つ	yot(tsu)	四	45
よね	yone	米	335
よ・む	yo(mu)	読	107
よる	yoru	夜	196
よろず	yorozu	万	21
よわ・い	yowa(i)	弱	237

ON-KUN YOMI INDEX	ROMANIZED INDEX	CHARACTER	CHARACTER NUMBER
よわ・まる	**yowa(maru)**	弱	237
よわ・る	**yowa(ru)**	弱	237
よん	**yon**	四	45
ら			
ライ	**RAI**	来	79
ライ	**RAI**	礼	322
ラク	**RAKU**	楽	282
ラク	**RAKU**	絡	438
ラク	**RAKU**	落	439
り			
リ	**RI**	理	263
リ	**RI**	利	350
リ	**RI**	里	351
リキ	**RIKI**	力	109
リツ	**RITSU**	立	55
リュウ	**RYŪ**	留	403
リョ	**RYO**	旅	243
リョウ	**RYŌ**	料	244
リョウ	**RYŌ**	両	337
リョク	**RYOKU**	力	109
リン	**RIN**	林	197

ON-KUN YOMI INDEX	ROMANIZED INDEX	CHARACTER	CHARACTER NUMBER
る			
ル	**RU**	留	403
れ			
レイ	**REI**	礼	322
レイ	**REI**	冷	352
レン	**REN**	練	455
ろ			
ロク	**ROKU**	六	39
わ			
ワ	**WA**	話	104
ワ	**WA**	和	371
わか・い	**waka(i)**	若	359
わ・かる	**wa(karu)**	分	36
わか・れる	**waka(reru)**	別	175
わ・ける	**wa(keru)**	分	36
わ・ける	**wa(keru)**	別	175
わざ	**waza**	業	284
わす・れる	**wasu(reru)**	忘	349
わたくし	**watakushi**	私	163
わら・う	**wara(u)**	笑	397
わる・い	**waru(i)**	悪	245

Stroke Count Index

1 stroke	一 (p.1) [1]	**2** strokes	九 (p.1) [2]	七 (p.1) [3]	十 (p.2) [4]	人 (p.3) [5]	二 (p.3) [6]	入 (p.4) [7]	八 (p.4) [8]	力 (p.62) [109]	刀 (p.171) [301]	**3** strokes	下 (p.5) [9]	口 (p.5) [10]
三 (p.6) [11]	山 (p.6) [12]	子 (p.7) [13]	女 (p.8) [14]	小 (p.8) [15]	上 (p.9) [16]	千 (p.9) [17]	川 (p.10) [18]	大 (p.10) [19]	土 (p.11) [20]	万 (p.11) [21]	工 (p.63) [110]	才 (p.63) [111]	夕 (p.64) [112]	丸 (p.172) [302]
弓 (p.172) [303]	**4** strokes	円 (p.12) [22]	王 (p.12) [23]	火 (p.13) [24]	月 (p.14) [25]	五 (p.14) [26]	午 (p.15) [27]	今 (p.15) [28]	手 (p.16) [29]	少 (p.16) [30]	水 (p.17) [31]	中 (p.17) [32]	天 (p.18) [33]	日 (p.18) [34]
父 (p.19) [35]	分 (p.19) [36]	木 (p.21) [37]	友 (p.22) [38]	六 (p.22) [39]	引 (p.64) [113]	牛 (p.65) [114]	区 (p.65) [115]	犬 (p.66) [116]	元 (p.66) [117]	公 (p.67) [118]	止 (p.67) [119]	心 (p.68) [120]	切 (p.69) [121]	太 (p.69) [122]
内 (p.70) [123]	不 (p.70) [124]	文 (p.71) [125]	方 (p.71) [126]	化 (p.173) [304]	戸 (p.173) [305]	反 (p.174) [306]	夫 (p.174) [307]	毛 (p.175) [308]	予 (p.175) [309]	**5** strokes	右 (p.23) [40]	外 (p.23) [41]	玉 (p.24) [42]	古 (p.24) [43]
左 (p.25) [44]	四 (p.25) [45]	出 (p.26) [46]	生 (p.26) [47]	石 (p.27) [48]	白 (p.28) [49]	半 (p.28) [50]	母 (p.29) [51]	北 (p.29) [52]	本 (p.30) [53]	目 (p.30) [54]	立 (p.31) [55]	以 (p.72) [127]	去 (p.72) [128]	兄 (p.73) [129]
広 (p.73) [130]	市 (p.74) [131]	仕 (p.74) [132]	写 (p.75) [133]	主 (p.76) [134]	世 (p.76) [135]	正 (p.77) [136]	台 (p.77) [137]	代 (p.78) [138]	田 (p.78) [139]	冬 (p.79) [140]	民 (p.79) [141]	用 (p.80) [142]	永 (p.176) [310]	号 (p.176) [311]
矢 (p.177) [312]	失 (p.178) [313]	打 (p.178) [314]	必 (p.179) [315]	付 (p.179) [316]	払 (p.180) [317]	平 (p.180) [318]	末 (p.181) [319]	未 (p.181) [320]	由 (p.182) [321]	礼 (p.182) [322]	**6** strokes	安 (p.31) [56]	会 (p.32) [57]	気 (p.32) [58]
休 (p.33) [59]	行 (p.33) [60]	糸 (p.34) [61]	耳 (p.35) [62]	西 (p.35) [63]	先 (p.36) [64]	多 (p.36) [65]	年 (p.37) [66]	百 (p.37) [67]	毎 (p.38) [68]	名 (p.38) [69]	回 (p.80) [143]	交 (p.81) [144]	好 (p.83) [145]	考 (p.83) [146]
光 (p.84) [147]	合 (p.84) [148]	死 (p.85) [149]	字 (p.85) [150]	自 (p.86) [151]	色 (p.86) [152]	早 (p.87) [153]	池 (p.87) [154]	地 (p.88) [155]	同 (p.88) [156]	肉 (p.89) [157]	有 (p.90) [158]	羽 (p.183) [323]	向 (p.183) [324]	寺 (p.184) [325]
次 (p.185) [326]	式 (p.185) [327]	州 (p.186) [328]	成 (p.186) [329]	全 (p.187) [330]	竹 (p.187) [331]	虫 (p.188) [332]	伝 (p.188) [333]	当 (p.189) [334]	米 (p.189) [335]	忙 (p.190) [336]	両 (p.192) [337]	**7** strokes	何 (p.39) [70]	花 (p.39) [71]
貝 (p.40) [72]	見 (p.42) [73]	言 (p.42) [74]	車 (p.43) [75]	社 (p.43) [76]	足 (p.44) [77]	男 (p.44) [78]	来 (p.45) [79]	医 (p.90) [159]	究 (p.91) [160]	近 (p.91) [161]	作 (p.92) [162]	私 (p.92) [163]	住 (p.93) [164]	図 (p.93) [165]
声 (p.94) [166]	赤 (p.94) [167]	走 (p.95) [168]	村 (p.96) [169]	体 (p.96) [170]	町 (p.97) [171]	弟 (p.97) [172]	低 (p.98) [173]	売 (p.98) [174]	別 (p.99) [175]	角 (p.192) [338]	汽 (p.193) [339]	局 (p.193) [340]	形 (p.194) [341]	決 (p.194) [342]
谷 (p.195) [343]	困 (p.195) [344]	初 (p.196) [345]	身 (p.196) [346]	対 (p.197) [347]	麦 (p.197) [348]	忘 (p.198) [349]	利 (p.199) [350]	里 (p.199) [351]	冷 (p.200) [352]	**8** strokes	雨 (p.45) [80]	学 (p.46) [81]	金 (p.46) [82]	空 (p.47) [83]
国 (p.47) [84]	長 (p.48) [85]	店 (p.49) [86]	東 (p.49) [87]	英 (p.99) [176]	画 (p.100) [177]	京 (p.100) [178]	姉 (p.101) [179]	使 (p.101) [180]	始 (p.103) [181]	事 (p.104) [182]	者 (p.104) [183]	所 (p.105) [184]	青 (p.105) [185]	知 (p.106) [186]
注 (p.106) [187]	直 (p.107) [188]	服 (p.107) [189]	物 (p.108) [190]	歩 (p.108) [191]	妹 (p.109) [192]	味 (p.110) [193]	明 (p.110) [194]	門 (p.111) [195]	夜 (p.111) [196]	林 (p.112) [197]	育 (p.200) [353]	泳 (p.201) [354]	岩 (p.201) [355]	泣 (p.202) [356]
治 (p.202) [357]	実 (p.203) [358]	若 (p.203) [359]	取 (p.204) [360]	受 (p.205) [361]	制 (p.205) [362]	昔 (p.206) [363]	卒 (p.206) [364]	定 (p.207) [365]	的 (p.207) [366]	非 (p.208) [367]	表 (p.208) [368]	法 (p.209) [369]	枚 (p.209) [370]	和 (p.210) [371]

(continued next page)

Stroke Count Index (continued)

9 strokes	88 後 (p.50)	89 食 (p.50)	90 前 (p.51)	91 南 (p.51)	198 映 (p.112)	199 屋 (p.113)	200 音 (p.113)	201 海 (p.114)	202 界 (p.114)	203 急 (p.115)	204 計 (p.115)	205 研 (p.116)	206 県 (p.117)	207 建 (p.117)
208 思 (p.118)	209 持 (p.118)	210 室 (p.119)	211 首 (p.119)	212 秋 (p.120)	213 重 (p.120)	214 春 (p.121)	215 乗 (p.121)	216 洗 (p.122)	217 送 (p.124)	218 待 (p.124)	219 茶 (p.125)	220 昼 (p.125)	221 点 (p.126)	222 度 (p.126)
223 発 (p.127)	224 品 (p.127)	225 風 (p.128)	226 便 (p.128)	227 洋 (p.129)	372 科 (p.210)	373 皆 (p.212)	374 活 (p.213)	375 係 (p.213)	376 昨 (p.214)	377 指 (p.214)	378 信 (p.215)	379 神 (p.216)	380 星 (p.216)	381 専 (p.216)
382 相 (p.217)	383 草 (p.217)	384 単 (p.218)	385 背 (p.219)	386 飛 (p.219)	387 美 (p.220)	388 変 (p.220)	389 面 (p.221)	390 要 (p.221)	**10 strokes**	92 高 (p.52)	93 校 (p.52)	94 時 (p.53)	95 書 (p.53)	228 員 (p.129)
229 院 (p.130)	230 夏 (p.131)	231 家 (p.131)	232 記 (p.132)	233 帰 (p.132)	234 起 (p.133)	235 紙 (p.133)	236 借 (p.134)	237 弱 (p.134)	238 真 (p.135)	239 通 (p.135)	240 特 (p.136)	241 病 (p.137)	242 勉 (p.137)	243 旅 (p.138)
244 料 (p.138)	391 荷 (p.222)	392 原 (p.222)	393 個 (p.223)	394 降 (p.223)	395 残 (p.224)	396 酒 (p.224)	397 笑 (p.225)	398 速 (p.225)	399 庭 (p.226)	400 島 (p.227)	401 馬 (p.227)	402 配 (p.228)	403 留 (p.228)	**11 strokes**
96 魚 (p.54)	97 週 (p.55)	245 悪 (p.139)	246 強 (p.139)	247 教 (p.140)	248 黒 (p.140)	249 菜 (p.141)	250 産 (p.141)	251 進 (p.142)	252 習 (p.142)	253 終 (p.144)	254 組 (p.145)	255 族 (p.145)	256 鳥 (p.146)	257 転 (p.146)
258 都 (p.147)	259 堂 (p.147)	260 動 (p.148)	261 問 (p.148)	262 野 (p.149)	263 理 (p.149)	404 経 (p.229)	405 現 (p.229)	406 黄 (p.230)	407 婚 (p.230)	408 祭 (p.231)	409 細 (p.233)	410 授 (p.233)	411 宿 (p.234)	412 術 (p.234)
413 商 (p.235)	414 接 (p.235)	415 雪 (p.236)	416 船 (p.236)	417 側 (p.237)	418 第 (p.237)	419 婦 (p.238)	420 部 (p.238)	**12 strokes**	98 飲 (p.55)	99 間 (p.56)	100 道 (p.56)	101 買 (p.57)	264 運 (p.150)	265 開 (p.151)
266 寒 (p.151)	267 軽 (p.152)	268 集 (p.152)	269 暑 (p.153)	270 場 (p.153)	271 森 (p.154)	272 貸 (p.154)	273 短 (p.155)	274 着 (p.155)	275 朝 (p.156)	276 答 (p.156)	277 飯 (p.157)	278 番 (p.158)	421 雲 (p.239)	422 温 (p.240)
423 絵 (p.240)	424 階 (p.241)	425 期 (p.241)	426 結 (p.242)	427 港 (p.242)	428 最 (p.243)	429 晴 (p.243)	430 然 (p.244)	431 達 (p.244)	432 遅 (p.245)	433 痛 (p.246)	434 登 (p.246)	435 晩 (p.247)	436 無 (p.247)	437 遊 (p.248)
438 絡 (p.248)	439 落 (p.249)	**13 strokes**	102 新 (p.57)	103 電 (p.58)	104 話 (p.58)	279 暗 (p.158)	280 意 (p.159)	281 遠 (p.159)	282 楽 (p.160)	283 漢 (p.160)	284 業 (p.161)	285 試 (p.161)	286 数 (p.162)	287 働 (p.162)
440 園 (p.249)	441 歳 (p.250)	442 辞 (p.250)	443 寝 (p.251)	444 節 (p.251)	445 続 (p.253)	446 置 (p.254)	**14 strokes**	105 駅 (p.59)	106 語 (p.59)	107 読 (p.60)	108 聞 (p.60)	288 歌 (p.163)	289 銀 (p.164)	290 説 (p.164)
447 関 (p.254)	448 際 (p.255)	449 雑 (p.255)	450 算 (p.256)	451 静 (p.256)	452 鼻 (p.257)	453 鳴 (p.257)	454 様 (p.258)	455 練 (p.258)	**15 strokes**	291 質 (p.165)	292 線 (p.165)	456 横 (p.259)	457 選 (p.260)	458 調 (p.260)
459 熱 (p.261)	**16 strokes**	293 館 (p.166)	294 親 (p.166)	295 頭 (p.167)	296 薬 (p.167)	460 機 (p.261)	461 橋 (p.262)	**18 strokes**	297 顔 (p.168)	298 験 (p.168)	299 題 (p.169)	300 曜 (p.169)	462 贈 (p.262)	463 難 (p.263)
19 strokes	464 願 (p.263)													